Jacob
The Story of a Family

MAGGID

Michael Scharf Publication Trust
Yeshiva University Press

Jonathan Grossman

JACOB

The Story of a Family

The Noam Series

Translated by Sara Daniel

The Michael Scharf Publication Trust of
Yeshiva University Press

Maggid Books

Jacob
The Story of a Family

First English Edition, 2025

Maggid Books
An imprint of Koren Publishers Jerusalem Ltd.

POB 8531, New Milford, CT 06776-8531, USA
& POB 4044, Jerusalem 9104001, Israel
www.korenpub.com

The publication of this book was made possible
through the generous support of *The Jewish Book Trust.*

ISBN 978-1-59264-505-3, *hardcover*

Printed and bound in the United States

The Noam Series
is dedicated to the memory of

Dr. Noam Shudofsky *z"l*

by his family and friends

Noam loved the study of Tanakh
and enabled generations of students to
"Understand and discern, to listen, learn and teach, to observe, perform and fulfill all the teachings of the Torah with love."

Contents

Preface

This is the third volume of the Noam Series – a series of literary readings of the book of Genesis – that Hashem has granted me the privilege to write. The first volume explores Genesis 1–11, the second is dedicated to the Abraham cycle, and the present volume focuses on the Jacob cycle. The story of Isaac, Abraham's son and Jacob's father, is tucked away at the beginning of his son's narrative cycle, and we will discuss the significance of this below.

When Jacob reaches Egypt at the venerable age of one hundred and thirty, he summarizes his life to Pharaoh: "The years of my wandering are one hundred and thirty. Few and hard have been the years of my life, and I have not reached the age my fathers reached in their own wanderings" (Gen. 47:9). This is a rare glimpse into Jacob's perception of his own life with all its trials and tribulations. As the Roman dramatist Seneca expressed two thousand years ago:

> And so there is no reason for you to think that any man has lived long because he has grey hairs or wrinkles; he has not lived long – he has existed long. For what if you should think that that man had had a long voyage who had been caught by a fierce storm as soon as he left harbour, and, swept hither and thither by a succession of winds that raged from different quarters, had

> been driven in a circle around the same course? Not much voyaging did he have, but much tossing about. ("On the Shortness of Life," trans. John W. Basore)

Did Jacob spend his life being merely tossed about? Though this is Jacob's own summary, the reader of his story will see a far more complex journey: a journey accompanied by angels that teach him how to walk the fine line between heaven and earth; a journey where he meets the love of his life by the well as he flees for his life from his brother; and above all, a journey which sees the birth of twelve tribes, whose own struggles are recorded in the closing chapters of Genesis that overlap with the end of their father's journey. Jacob's story does not end where it begins. Rather than come full circle, his path will ultimately widen and fan out into the story of a nation named for his literal and figurative struggles.

The Noam Series is dedicated to the memory of Dr. Noam Shudofsky (1933–2005), an accomplished man whose entire life was devoted to the world of education, both formal and informal. Noam began his career as a Bible teacher, and advanced along the administrative path until he became the administrator of the Ramaz Yeshiva of Manhattan, for approximately forty dedicated years. He was extraordinarily devoted to his students and staff. His love for the Bible did not wane even after he was no longer actively teaching, and he was especially drawn to the literary approach of Bible study, an approach embraced by this work. Jewish identity was an inextricable part of his identity, and he maintained that every person must fulfill himself not only in an intellectual sense, but in life itself. Indeed, Noam was deeply involved in the international Jewish community. His intense efforts – both overt and covert – for the Jews of Russia, who were persecuted solely because of their Judaism, deserve special mention. His holy work and gifts for the land, state, and people of Israel continues to this day, his legacy perpetuated by his children, grandchildren, and great-grandchildren, many of whom live in Israel, as he and his wife Nechi dreamed. Nechi passed away on the seventh night of Hanukkah 5778 (2017), and I would like to dedicate this volume to her memory as well. Writing this book in their memory was a special privilege for me, and I was also privileged to become acquainted with his entire family, people whose lives are deeply rooted in love of Torah and love of humanity, and imbued with humility and devotion.

With great pleasure, I wish to thank everyone who helped bring this book to light, from its first conception to its final design. This journey began during a weekly course I taught to outstanding students of the Bible Department of Herzog College in the year 2016; the lively, sometimes fiery debates that took place during this course comprise much of the raw material for this book. Special thanks are due to my student Netanel Spiegel, whose wise, thorough notes were indispensable to me.

If Jacob's story is the story of a family, I wish to extend thanks to friends who are like family to me: Binny Shalev and R. Itamar Eldar, whose wisdom and insight are this book's engine and fuel. May they always be blessed with good health and joy to continue spreading their holy work and inspiration.

This book was originally published in Hebrew, and Sara Daniel undertook the challenge of translating each word – along with its nuances and connotations – into English. I am grateful for her literary sensitivity and keen knowledge of Bible study, and I thank her with all my heart.

My sincere thanks also go to publisher Matthew Miller and Maggid's dedicated publication team and the editors of the wonderful series this book now belongs to – Rabbi Reuven Ziegler, Caryn Meltz, Ita Olesker, Rina Ben Gal, Nechama Unterman, Debbie Ismailoff, Esther Shafier, and Doron Chitiz – whose generosity and professionalism guided this book's publication from start to finish. Special thanks go to Rabbi Dr. Stu Halpern, the Senior Advisor to the Provost of Yeshiva University, who oversaw this book's publication through Yeshiva University. His expertise and broad experience made every consultation a creative, original learning experience, and I thank him for his friendship and partnership.

Last but not least, of course, thanks are due to my own family – my wife, children, and grandchildren, who accompany me on every journey into the world of reading, writing, and study; who so patiently and so fruitfully hear out every thought and dilemma; who color every ordinary day with joy.

During the preparation of this volume in English, my father passed away – Prof. Avraham Grossman, of blessed memory. I discussed many of the narratives I analyze in this book with him, and I do not have words enough to express how profoundly he influenced my work, or the depth of the desire for learning and truth that he instilled in his children. May this book be for עילוי נשמתו as well.

Jonathan Grossman
Shevat 5785

Introduction

How many times is Jacob's name mentioned in the Bible? Biblical concordances disagree: according to Lisowsky's Hebrew concordance, it appears 349 times;[1] Mandelkorn notes only 345;[2] while Even Shoshan lists a full 350 instances of Jacob's name.[3] Such dissent about a mere technical issue certainly anticipates the extent of controversy and tension surrounding more fundamental questions about Jacob's character. Barely a scene of his life escapes exegetical debate about whether the Torah is praising or criticizing Jacob; about whether an action of his or his family is considered worthy or sinful. Though biblical narrative is usually characterized by its elusive, multifaceted nature, it is clear in exegesis as early as Midrash and as recent as contemporary scholarship that the deep, fundamental dissent inherent to Jacob's character far exceeds the usual range of dispute.

Jacob's character is indeed complex, and his inner world is largely hidden from the reader's eye. This complexity is an inherent, fundamental

1. Lisowsky, *Konkordanz*, 1623–24.
2. Mandelkorn, *Concordance*, 1441–42.
3. Even Shoshan, *Concordance*, 477–78.

part of the narrative objective and plot development.[4] Jacob himself summarizes his life in bleak, heartrending brevity before Pharaoh: "Few and hard have been the years of my life" (Gen. 47:9); and surprisingly, the text seems to sympathize with him, as emerges from a comparison between the biblical summary of Jacob's life and his fathers': "These are the days, the years of Abraham's life: he lived one hundred and seventy-five years. Abraham breathed his last and died in his ripe old age, aged and satisfied, and was gathered to his people" (Gen. 25:7–8). The summary of Isaac's life, though shorter, also mentions that he dies "aged and satisfied": "Then he breathed his last, and died, and was gathered to his people, aged, satisfied with his years" (Gen. 35:28–29).

"Aged and satisfied" is not a common phrase; elsewhere, it summarizes the lives of other patriarchal figures, Job (Job 42:17) and David (I Chr. 23:1), where the narrator presumably employs it to generate a connection with Abraham and Isaac. Yet it is absent in the account of Jacob's death: "Jacob lived in Egypt for seventeen years; the years of his life were one hundred and forty-seven.... There Jacob finished instructing his sons. And he drew his feet back onto the bed, breathed his last, and was gathered to his people" (Gen. 47:28; 49:33). The Sages already note the absence of the verb "and he died";[5] in the context of our discussion I wish to note, rather, the absence of Jacob's characterization

4. Right now, I am ignoring the general question relevant to the ancestral cycles: in which cases are Jacob's actions considered a symbol that represents the entire nation. This question especially concerns his interactions with Esau (Edom) and Laban (Aram). On the problem of reading Jacob and Laban's interactions as a foreshadowing of Israel's relationship with Aram, see below, in my discussion of chapter 31. The reader must be conscious of the disparity between Jacob the individual and Jacob the representative of a nation, and this awareness in itself can solve inconsistencies throughout the narrative cycle. Jacob, for example, is represented as a shepherd (25:27; ch. 30; 32:21; 33:18, and others), but he receives blessings that are more appropriate for a farmer (27:27–29). These blessings are justified not only because they were intended for Esau, but because in this scene, Jacob represents Israel, who will need blessings for fertile land (*Zobel*, "Jacob," 196). See further in Zobel for the significance of "Jacob" in prophetic and wisdom literature (202–8).
5. Typical of the Sages, they provide a midrashic explaination for this: "Our patriarch Jacob did not die.... I am interpreting a verse, as it is stated: 'Therefore do not fear, Jacob My servant, says the Lord, neither be dismayed, Israel, for I will save you from afar, and your seed from the land of their captivity' (Jer. 30:10). This verse juxtaposes

as "aged and satisfied." Thus both Jacob and the narrative itself present a complex portrait of his life, devoid of the overtones of joy that summarize the lives of Abraham and Isaac. To a great extent, Jacob's life is indeed tragic, and it is up to the reader to consider the meaning of this tragedy and its contribution to the Jacob narrative cycle.

Jacob's complex characterization is also related to a fundamental surprise that arises throughout the narrative cycle.

JACOB: CHOSEN ANEW

The story of Jacob and his election as part of the chosen line is surprising in itself. In the book of Genesis, Abraham is singled out to form a covenant with God, and God promises that his son Isaac and his descendants will perpetuate this covenant for all eternity: "God said: 'Nonetheless: Sarah your wife will bear you a son, and you shall name him Isaac. I will establish My covenant with him as an everlasting covenant for his descendants after him.... I will establish My covenant with Isaac, whom Sarah will bear to you this time next year'" (Gen. 17:19–21). The plain meaning of "establishing a covenant" with Isaac is that Abraham's covenant with God will be perpetuated through Isaac. In light of this, at the start of the Jacob cycle, the reader has no reason to suspect that there will be another process of election and rejection between Isaac's sons – ostensibly, both of Isaac's twin sons will be part of the nation founded by Abraham. This dynasty, fanning out into a nation through Isaac, will presumably be referred to as "the children of Isaac" (or, in the words of Amos, "the House of Isaac" – 7:16). Just as there is no "Zebulun cycle" or "Gad cycle," there ought not to be a "Jacob cycle." Essentially, Jacob should not only be compared to Zebulun or Gad, but to his father Isaac, as there is no Isaac cycle either. This is for the simple reason that Isaac is not characterized as an independent figure, but as Abraham's son, as the one through whom Abraham's blessing will begin to be fulfilled.[6]

Jacob to his seed: Just as his seed is alive [when redeemed], so too [Jacob himself] is alive" (Taanit 5b).

6. See further below, in the analysis of Genesis 26.

"These Are the *Toledot*"[7]

This issue is sharply underscored by exploring the book of Genesis' inner division into units beginning with the phrase "*Elleh toledot*" – "This is the story/These are the descendants":[8]

> 2:4: "This is the *story* of heaven and earth when they were created."
> 6:9: "This is the *story* of Noah."
> 10:1: "These are the *descendants* of Noah's sons."
> 11:10: "These are the *descendants* of Shem."
> 11:27: "These are the *descendants* of Terah."
> 25:12: "These are the *descendants* of Ishmael son of Abraham."
> 25:19: "This is the *family story* of Isaac son of Abraham: Abraham was Isaac's father."
> 36:1, 9: "These are the *descendants* of Esau – that is, Edom"/ "These are the *descendants* of Esau, ancestor of the Edomites, in the hill country of Seir."
> 37:2: "This is the *story* of Jacob's family."

The recurrence of the key phrase "*Elleh toledot*" invites a reading of the entire book of Genesis through the perspective of selection and rejection; through the underlying tension between universal and national: "Within the flow of human history, from the universal to the particular, the genealogies indicate God is separating out by selection a righteous lineage by whom He chooses to bless the world of nations."[9] This is indeed a fundamental reading of Genesis: how the Israelite nation gradually forms as parallel dynasties are rejected. This is presumably related to the selection of certain characters and their deeds, and it is also likely – corresponding with the worldview of R. Judah Halevi – that the *toledot* pattern in Genesis reflects the legacy of "divine influence"

7. Translator's note: For the sake of preserving the multivalence of the Hebrew word, I have retained the transliteration *toledot* in most of the text.
8. Besides Genesis, this formula appears twice elsewhere in the Bible: "These are the *toledot* of Aram and Moses" (Num. 3:1); "These are the *toledot* of Peretz" (Ruth 4:18).
9. Mathews, *Genesis I*, 34.

and "essence (*segula*)" that begins with Adam and is passed on through Seth to Enosh and Noah, from individual to individual, until "the sons of [Jacob] were all worthy of the divine influence, as well as of the country distinguished by divine spirit. This is the first instance of the divine influence descending on a number of people, whereas it had previously only been vouchsafed to isolated individuals."[10] In any case, the "*toledot*" pattern is marked by a surprising omission: If its purpose is indeed to highlight the chosen line, how can it be that Abraham is missing from this list? After the *toledot* of Shem and Terah, the next in the series are Ishmael and Isaac. Where is the *toledot* heading of Abraham, the ultimate founder of the covenant with God?

One fascinating solution is proposed by R. Yoel Bin-Nun: the text compensates for this omission with a double mention of Abraham in Isaac's *toledot* heading: "This is the family story of Isaac son of Abraham: Abraham was Isaac's father" (25:19). Instead of moving forward to Isaac's descendants, the text first looks back a generation to emphasize that "Abraham was Isaac's father." The emphasis on Isaac's father is echoed in the book of Chronicles: after reporting that "Abraham's sons were Isaac and Ishmael" (II Chr. 1:28), the rejected line is mentioned first: "Ishmael's firstborn was Nevayot, then Kedar, Adbeel, Mivsam... (v. 29)"; but when the focus shifts to Isaac, Abraham is mentioned once again: "Abraham had a son, Isaac. The sons of Isaac were Esau and Israel" (v. 34).

There are various explanations for this surprising formulation,[11] but R. Bin-Nun argues that it is linked to the omission of "These are the *toledot* of Abraham" in Genesis – that through Isaac, Abraham's story is echoed once again, the narratives of father and son fused and inseparable. The exegetical implication of his argument is that two narrative cycles are ensconced within this heading: the story of Isaac, but that of Abraham as well. Below I will discuss how each *toledot* heading tells the story of the father's children, and in this context the significance of

10. *The Book of Kuzari*, I:95, trans. Hartwig Hirschfeld.
11. I believe that the most convenient explanation is that the verse is a foil to Ishmael a few verses earlier: "These are the descendants of Abraham's son Ishmael, whom Sarah's maidservant, Hagar the Egyptian, bore to Abraham" (Gen. 2:12). Whereas Ishmael is the son born to the maidservant Hagar, Isaac is born to Abraham (Grossman, *Abraham*, 406).

R. Bin-Nun's theory will emerge in full: the narrative cycle devoted to Jacob and Esau (headed by "the *toledot* of Isaac") also relates the story of Isaac, who is the "*toleda*" of Abraham. In this sense, two *toledot* overlap.

Yet the basic question still stands: Why isn't there a separate narrative cycle for each patriarch? Why isn't there a *toledot* heading for Abraham, rather than a double mention of Abraham in Isaac's heading instead?

To solve this conundrum, I wish to clarify the meaning of the term "*toledot*" in its context within Genesis. Ibn Ezra interprets the word in the sense of "events": "These are the *toledot* – events, in the sense of '*ma yeled yom*,' which literally means 'What will the day bear.' Similarly, [this is the meaning of] 'This is the story of Jacob'" (Ibn Ezra on Gen. 6:8). By contrast, Ramban argues that the meaning of *toledot* is "descendants":

> "These are the *toledot* of Noah" – it has been explained as "events," in the sense of "what will the day bear," thus alluding to the entire section that follows. But this seems incorrect to me, for events that befall a person are not his "*toledot*." The literal meaning of the word is correct: "These are the *descendants* of Noah's sons"; "These are the *descendants* of Ishmael." This means "These are the *descendants* of Noah" – Shem, Ham, and Japhet. But it repeats "Noah had three sons" because the description was interrupted with "Noah was a righteous man, a person of integrity" to inform why he was the one chosen to build the ark. (Ramban on Gen. 6:8)

The debate is clear: assuming that these *toledot* headings introduce the unit that follows them,[12] there are headings that introduce genealogical lists (such as the *toledot* of Ishmael, 25:12), and headings that introduce long, winding narratives far richer than a genealogical list (such as the "*toledot*" of Terah, which introduces the story of Abram, or of Jacob,

12. Some propose that these headings are conclusion formulae (Wiseman, *New Discoveries*, or, more complex: De-Witt, "Generations"), but this is a problematic reading others have dismissed; see, for example, V. P. Hamilton, *Genesis I*, 9; Mathews, *Genesis I*, 32–33.

which opens the Joseph saga). This multivalence is aptly reflected in modern translations that translate the word "*toledot*" based on its context; it suffices to illustrate this with the two instances of the expression in chapter 25:

> 25:12: "These are *the descendants* of Ishmael" (New Jerusalem Bible), "This is *the line* of Ishmael" (JPS); 25:19: "This is *the story* of Isaac" (New Jerusalem Bible, JPS).

Rashbam, however, proposes a definition that can apply equally to both contexts:

> And now, intelligent people will perceive what the *Rishonim* explained. "These are the *toledot* of Jacob" – these are the history and events that befell Jacob. But this is nonsense, for every instance of "*elleh toledot*" in the Torah and Writings is either about the figure's children or, more often, his grandchildren, as I explained regarding "*elleh toledot* Noah"...his children's children, how he had three sons, and the Holy One, blessed be He, commanded him to bring them into the ark for twelve months, and after they left, "children were born to them after the flood" (10:1), until they increased to seventy, who became the seventy nations, as it is written, "from these the nations spread out"... (Rashbam on Gen. 37:2)

Rashbam points out that "*toledot*" refers not only to children, but also – more importantly, even – to grandchildren. Once a person has grandchildren, they have established their own household, their own clan.[13] Rashbam clarifies that the function of the *toledot* headings in Genesis is not merely to relate the names of children and grandchildren, but to explain how these ancestors managed to establish their household, their clan, their continuity – how their grandchildren came to be. According to this reading, *toledot* means both "events" and "descendants" – these headings describe the person's descendants, and

13. See further in: Wenham, *Genesis I*, 55–56.

sometimes, how these descendants came to be, despite the complications along the way.[14]

This insight has broad significance for deeper understanding of the themes and objectives of the entire book of Genesis. For our purposes, I wish to adopt Rashbam's reading in order to tackle our opening question. The omission of Abraham's *toledot* in no way detracts from the importance of the Abraham narrative, which indeed occupies a central place within Genesis, under the heading "These are the *toledot* of Terah" – that is, how Terah is granted grandchildren. Rather, the missing *toledot* heading of Abraham reflects upon the story of Abraham's *children* – upon the lack of Isaac's narrative cycle. Isaac is the sole protagonist in just one chapter (26), and even this chapter begins after the Jacob narrative has already begun. The absence of Abraham's *toledot* does not undermine the figure of Abraham, but of Isaac.

Yet we cannot stop here either – the question of why there is no Isaac narrative does not ring true. We began by asserting that if Isaac is the chosen one, then there is no real need for an Isaac narrative, for the birth of Isaac, the son of Abraham and Sarah, marks the end of the suspense regarding who will inherit Abraham's legacy and covenant with God. Ishmael is clearly rejected from the start, just as Isaac is clearly chosen, but at no point of the narrative is there any hint that the process of election and rejection will continue with Isaac's own children.

The real surprise, therefore, is not the absence of Abraham's *toledot*, but rather, the existence of Isaac's *toledot*. The fact that there is no Isaac narrative cycle can be taken for granted, for Isaac's birth is the culmination of all that leads up to it. Isaac is not a hero in his own

14. R. David Zvi Hoffmann disagrees; he sees the expression "*toledot* of Isaac" as the story of Isaac and not his sons', and thus claims that Jacob's story centers around his father. Jacob sets out to Padan Aram at Isaac's bidding, and eventually returns to his father. Similarly, he argues that Joseph's story also revolves around his father Jacob, and it is thus called the "*toledot* of Jacob" (37:2). This may be at least partially true of Joseph's story, but Jacob's story hardly revolves around his father. Sara Schwartz claims that the "*toledot*" formula in this case and in two other cases (2:4, 6:9) introduces the story of the *toledot* figure himself, and not his sons'. In this case, however, she concedes that the "*toledot* of Isaac" introduces both his story and his son's story (Schwartz, "*Toledot*").

right – he is Abraham's happily ever after. The great surprise is the existence of the Jacob narrative cycle. Isaac's *toledot* mark the beginning of a new saga; for whatever reason, new conflict arises and even though Isaac inherits his father's legacy, Jacob must be elected anew. God's election of Abraham must be reestablished, and it must be reestablished solely through Jacob.

This reading assumes that originally, Esau was supposed to be part of Abraham's chosen line and covenant.[15] But Esau is rejected, and it is up to Jacob to assert his position as an heir of Abraham's covenant. Elie Assis compares Ishmael's exclusion to Esau's rejection and reaches a similar conclusion:

> God intervenes and asserts that only Isaac is the chosen son, commanding Abraham to expel Ishmael. This is not the case in the next generation. God does not tell Isaac what to do; there is no divine interference in the struggle between the twins; nor is it declared that only Jacob will succeed their father. The difference between God's intervention in the two narratives is tremendous. This lack of divine intervention does not mean that Isaac must decide whom to select and whom to reject, as most commentators have understood; rather, it means that there is no question of selection at all – no issue of rejection clouds the story in the first place. God's passive stance supports the theory that Isaac assumes that both of his sons will continue his legacy, and neither of them will be excluded.[16]

Assis is correct that Isaac does not initially intend to reject one of his sons, but we can take a step further: God's passive stance reinforces the theory that God Himself intended that both of Isaac's sons would continue in his footsteps.

---

15. Nava Gutman proposes that Isaac assumes that both sons will inherit him, while Rebecca does not (Gutman, "Voice"). I disagree, and propose that this was the original plan and part of Abraham's chosen line – see especially below in my analysis of chapter 27.
16. Assis, *Identity in Conflict*, 58

This paradigm can be traced in several midrashim, notably in *Midrash Shir HaShirim Zutta*:

> Concerning Jacob and Esau: the name Jacob could have been bestowed upon Esau. Esau could have been called Jacob, and Jacob could have been called Esau; Esau could have produced kings, and Jacob priests; the first blessings would have befitted Esau, and the second Jacob; Leah and Zilpah could have married Esau, and Rachel and Bilhah Jacob; but all of these gifts were taken from him. (*Shir HaShirim Zutta*, ch. 1)

This unexpected crisis in Isaac's household is what leads to the Jacob cycle – to a story of a renewed covenant after one member of the covenant withdraws and departs to Edom. Contrary to initial expectations, the chosen people of Abraham's covenant with God are not "the children of Isaac," but rather, "the children of Israel."

JACOB AS ABRAHAM

> The spirit of my father grows strong in me… (Shakespeare, *As You Like It,* Act I, Scene I)

This reading is based on many assumptions and touches upon fundamental disagreements in analyses of the biblical narratives, especially concerning Rebecca's prophecy during her pregnancy (25:23) and the theft of the blessings (ch. 27), and I will discuss these in depth below. For now, I wish to support this reading based on the close analogy between Jacob and Abraham. Jacob essentially retraces his grandfather's footsteps and undertakes the same journey. Although this deserves further attention, for our purposes it will suffice to point out the main similarities.[17]

17. For further comparison between the two cycles, see Grossman, "Abraham and Jacob."

1. Jacob's Journey: Back and Forth

Leaving His Parents' Home

Jacob's abrupt flight from Canaan is one of the most unexpected reversals of the ancestral cycles. His father Isaac also plans to leave the land temporarily, but God forbids him to do so, so that the blessings of Abraham may begin to be fulfilled through him (see the discussion of ch. 26 below). God even promises Isaac that He will be with him and he will inherit the land "for the sake of My servant Abraham," and for this reason, he may not leave the land, even temporarily. Yet Jacob now flees the land and reaches Haran without any setbacks or prohibitions. God does not forbid him to leave the land promised to his father and grandfather; on the contrary, He encourages him and promises that He will accompany Jacob on his way until he returns to Canaan in order to fulfill Abraham's blessing. Through this promise, the reader learns that Jacob must return to the land of his father's birth and begin the journey anew.

Thus, like Abraham, the first revelation of Jacob's life concerns his departure from his land, his birthplace, and his father's house. Abraham hears the word of God when he sets out from Mesopotamia to the land of Canaan, while Jacob is about to journey in the opposite direction, but there is a profound connection between these two revelations. This is evident in a unique phrase that only appears in these two episodes: "Through you, all the families of the earth will be blessed" (12:3; 28:14). This expression is of special interest because it concerns the distant future and purpose of the nation and its role in history. Abraham and Jacob's journeys are inherently related to separation and segregation from the society around them, but God's initial revelation to them both hints that ultimately, their destiny is to channel blessing for all the nations, to be the connecting link for blessing between God and the whole world. It is no wonder that Isaac never hears this directly from God – he is the heir of his father's blessing and legacy, and it is taken for granted that all this applies to him as well. Yet it emerges that Jacob *does* need to hear of this destiny, of the divine purpose of the chosen nation, on the eve of his departure to Haran, the land his grandfather left when he was seventy-five years old.[18]

---

18. In my analysis of God's revelation to Jacob at Bethel, I will point out further connections between this revelation and the revelation to Abraham after he parts ways

Perhaps Rebecca and Isaac's instructions to Jacob also echo God's first command to Abraham. Rebecca urges her son, "Now, my son, listen to me. Flee at once to my brother Laban in Haran" (27:43), and Isaac adds, "Go at once to Padan Aram ... and there marry a daughter of your mother's brother Laban" (28:2). Abraham, too, departs for Haran after he is commanded to leave his father's house: "Go – from your land, your birthplace, and your father's house – to the land that I will show you. I will make you a great nation" (12:1–2). The possessive *lekha* appears in God's command – "*lekh lekha*," and in Rebecca and Isaac's words – "*beraḥ lekha, kaḥ lekha*," in both instances following a verb rather than a noun in an unusual grammatical form.[19]

If there is indeed a connection between the two sets of instructions, then the obvious difference between them is that Abraham is commanded to leave by God, whereas Jacob is bid by his parents. God will appear to Jacob soon after, but his initial departure is motivated by family reasons, unlike Abraham. We will yet see how this motif accompanies and shapes the entire Jacob cycle.[20]

The Journey Back to Canaan

Not only does Jacob's departure from his father's house recall Abraham's; his return to Canaan echoes his grandfather's path so closely that one wonders whether Jacob's departure to Haran is undertaken solely that he might reenact Abraham's journey to Canaan on his way back. Cassuto points this out and defines their journeys as "a journey of three parts," wherein each part concludes with the building of an altar. Abraham's journey unfolds thus:

1. From Haran to Shechem, where he builds an altar: "There he built an altar to the Lord who had appeared to him" (12:7).[21]

---

with Lot. See below.

19. Rashi, based on the Midrash, explains: "For you – for your pleasure and your benefit," while others such as Ramban and Radak do not see this as unusual.
20. The fact that Abraham sends his servant to find his son a wife, while Jacob travels himself, also supports this reading.
21. Based on the fact that Abraham's first stop is in Shechem, it appears that Abraham – like his grandson Jacob – also enters Canaan from the east.

2. From Shechem to the region of Bethel, where he is granted great revelation (13:14–17). There too he builds an altar: "And from there he moved on to the hills east of Bethel, and pitched his tent with Bethel to the west and Ai to the east. There he built an altar to the Lord and called on the name of the Lord" (12:8).
3. From Bethel to Hebron. This final stage completes the process of acquiring the land, and it is also concluded with the construction of an altar: "So Abraham took his tent and came to settle by the Oaks of Mamre, in Hebron. There he built an altar to the Lord" (13:18).

Jacob's return to the land recalls his grandfather's journey – he, too, comes back to Canaan in three stages, and he builds an altar after the first two:

1. From Haran to Shechem. Jacob enters from the east, and before he continues on to his father in Hebron, he builds an altar: "There he erected an altar and named it El Elohei Yisrael" (33:20).
2. From Shechem to Bethel. Like Abraham, Jacob is granted (double) revelation in Bethel, and he also erects an altar there: "There he built an altar and called the place El Bethel, because it was there that God had revealed Himself to him as he fled his brother" (35:7).
3. From Bethel to Hebron. Like Abraham's, Jacob's journey finally ends when he reaches Hebron, where his father is. Although Jacob does not build an altar, he joins his father, who lives in Hebron and presumably already has an altar for worship.

The similarity between these journeys invites a comprehensive comparison. Sometimes certain components feature in different stages – for example, the motif of sight is especially salient in God's revelation to Abraham during the first stage of his journey, with emphasis on how God "appears to him" (12:7), whereas a similar motif appears in the second stage of Jacob's journey: "Build an altar to God, who appeared to you"; "Because it was there that God had revealed Himself to him" (35:1, 7). It is important to note that in Bethel, Abraham also "called on the name of the Lord" (12:8), and he does not name the places he passes through.

Jacob, by contrast, does not call on the name of God, but he repeatedly gives names: "There he erected an altar and named it El Elohei Yisrael" (33:20) at the end of the first stage; "There he built an altar and called the place El Bethel" (35:7) at the end of the second stage.

What is relevant to our discussion, however, is the overall similarity between the two patriarchs' journeys to the land. Cassuto compares these journeys to Israel's entrance to the land, and thus reads the meaning of this connection as symbolic foreshadowing, "like father, like son." Even if he is correct, instead of merging Abraham and Jacob's journeys into a single symbolic process, I wish to emphasize how Jacob follows in Abraham's footsteps – rather than Isaac's. Unlike his father and son, Isaac builds an altar in Beersheba, and it is there that he "calls on the name of the Lord" (26:25). In this way, Isaac continues his father's legacy, but does not repeat it, and he extends the range and sphere of his altars and blessings. Jacob, by contrast, builds altars in precisely the same places that Abraham does. As Cassuto summarizes: "Jacob follows the exact same path that Abraham walked, camped in the exact same sites, and built altars in the exact same places."[22]

2. Two Spheres of Conflict: Parting Ways with His Brother, and Forming a Covenant with a Foreigner

The two main conflicts in the Jacob cycle (with Esau and Laban) are parallel to two conflicts in Abraham's life.

Conflict with a Foreigner

Jacob's relationship with Laban is parallel to Abraham and Isaac's relationships with Pharaoh and Abimelech – foreigners. Abraham (ch. 12) and Isaac's (ch. 26) interactions with the foreign leaders play out in three main scenes: (1) the patriarch deceives the foreign leader by presenting his wife as his sister; (2) the foreign leader bestows great wealth upon him; (3) they then form a pact, with the leader seeking to appease as well as reproach.

These elements are all present in Jacob's conflict with Laban. Laban is technically kin, but in the narrative he represents Aram; moreover,

22. Cassuto, *Genesis and Its Structure*, 247.

relatively to Esau, he represents conflict in a more distant sphere than the nuclear family. Their relationship begins with an act of deception in which a woman is mispresented as her sister, with similar language. When Jacob discovers that his wife is in fact her sister, he accuses, "What is this you have done to me? I served you for Rachel, did I not? Why did you deceive me?" (29:25); when Pharaoh discovers that Abraham presented his wife as his sister, he accuses, "What have you done to me? Why did you not tell me she was your wife?" (12:18), and Abimelech similarly accuses Isaac: "What is this you have done to us?" (26:10).

The comparison continues in the next scenes: Jacob acquires great wealth through Laban, leading to envy (just as the Philistines envy Isaac for the wealth he acquires through Abimelech), and their relationship concludes with a pact of reconciliation in Gal-Ed, with Jacob reproaching Laban. In both narratives, God appears to the foreign leader and warns them not to harm the patriarch: "God came to Abimelech in a dream one night and told him, 'You will die because of the woman you have taken. She is already married'" (20:3); "That night God came to Laban the Aramean in a dream and said to him, 'Take care not to say anything to Jacob for good or for bad'" (31:24).

I will discuss the connection between these conflicts below – especially in the context of Isaac's narrative being placed within the Jacob narrative – but for now, I wish to point out the most striking difference between these scenes. Abraham and Isaac are the ones who deceive the foreign king, whereas it is Jacob who is deceived by Laban. This difference contributes to Jacob's characterization as a tragic figure, as we will explore below.

Conflict with a Brother

Abraham and Jacob both part ways with a "brother." After leaving Ur of the Chaldeans and his brother Nahor, Abraham later parts ways with his nephew, Lot, who represents Terah's third son Haran (who died young). Lot accompanies Abraham on his journey, and their parting is described in more depth than Abraham's parting from his brother Nahor in Aram Naharaim. It is difficult to evaluate the Torah's representation of Lot. Should Lot have remained with Abraham until the end, or should Lot never have joined Abraham in the first place, because Abraham should have left his birthplace without anyone else from his father's house?[23] Either way, following the quarrel between their shepherds, Abraham and Lot part ways, and Lot settles in Sodom. Lot is repeatedly referred to as Abraham's "brother" (13:8; 14:14), which is unsurprising, given that Lot symbolizes Haran's branch of the family tree after his death. Abraham and Lot's parting is described thus: "The land could not support them living together; so many were their possessions that they were unable to live side by side.... So Lot chose for himself the entire plain of the Jordan. He traveled eastward, and the two men separated.... Lot settled in the cities of the plain, pitching his tent near Sodom" (13:6–12). Jacob and Esau's parting is described similarly. Even when the brothers are reconciled, they do not live together in Canaan (Esau actually leaves for Edom before Jacob's return, and I will discuss the dramatic implications of this fact in context), and the text's justification is the same: "[Esau] moved to another region, away from his brother Jacob, for their possessions were too great for them to remain together; because of all their livestock, the land where they were living could not support them both. So Esau settled in the hill country of Seir. Esau is Edom" (36:6–8). It is worth noting that this description – "their possessions were too great for them to remain together" – does not appear elsewhere in the Bible, and that following their parting, God appears to both Abraham and Jacob at Bethel and makes them similar promises. I will discuss the significance of this in more detail below, but for now, I wish to point out a further dimension of this complex comparison.

The connection between Abraham and Jacob's parting is revealed as even more profound when we note that both Lot and Esau turn to the east and settle among the people of the land. Lot settles in Sodom, and thereby parts ways with Abraham's blessing; Esau, born into the chosen line as Jacob is, forfeits Abraham's heritage when he moves to Edom and establishes an independent national entity.

There is an allusion to a meeting between these two spheres of fraternal conflict – with Esau and Lot – in the Jacob cycle. The Ammonites settle the territory from the Jordan to the Jabbok: "From the Jabbok to the

23. For a discussion of this question, see Cotter, *Genesis*, 91; Vaughn, "Disobedience," 117–23; Grossman, *Abraham*, 43–45, 68–69.

Ammonites, for the border of the Ammonites was strong" (Num. 21:24). This may be in dialogue with Jacob's struggle with the angel: when Jacob reaches the Jabbok, the angel stops him and hints that from that point on, the territory belongs to the descendants of Lot, and he may not pass. This, in turn, is echoed by Moses when he prevents the Israelites from passing through Ammonite territory and conquering it (Deut. 3:16).

3. Change of Name and Bodily Harm (*Gid HaNasheh* and Circumcision)

Abraham's name change in Genesis 17 is echoed in two separate episodes in the Jacob narrative: one at the Jabbok pass (Gen. 32), and the second at Bethel (Gen. 35). I will discuss the significance of this doubling below, but in the context of our comparison, Abraham's name change is parallel to both scenes in the Jacob narrative.

God names Isaac before his birth, but Abram's name is changed to Abraham, and Jacob's name is changed to Israel. A comparison of these changes shows that they are obvious analogies:

Abram to Abraham (Gen. 17)	**Jacob to Israel (Gen. 35)**
The Lord appeared to him and said, "I am El Shaddai."	God appeared to him ... "I am El Shaddai."
No longer shall you be called Abram. Your name will be Abraham.	Your name is Jacob; no longer shall you be called Jacob: Israel shall be your name.
I will make you exceptionally fertile, I will turn you into nations; kings will come from you.	Be fertile and multiply. A nation, a community of nations will come to be from you. Of your loins, kings shall come forth.
I will give you and your descendants after you the land where you now live as strangers.	The land I gave to Abraham and Isaac I surely give to you; to your descendants after you I will give the land.
When He finished speaking with him, God went up from Abraham.	God went up from him at the place where He had spoken with him.

This comparison leaves no room for doubt – Jacob's name change clearly echoes his grandfather's name change and the blessing that "El Shaddai" bestows upon him.

However, even before "El Shaddai" changes Jacob's name, the mysterious figure at the Jabbok tells Jacob that his name is now Israel. There, his name change is accompanied by bodily harm, by a physical injury, just as Abraham's name change is linked to the command of circumcision. Abraham must undergo circumcision, whereas Jacob is left "limping on his thigh" (31:32). In both scenes, this physical change has permanent religious implications. The children of Abraham are commanded to circumcise their sons forever, and to this day, Jews do not eat the *gid hanasheh* (sciatic nerve) in commemoration of Jacob's injury at the Jabbok.

Abraham's circumcision and Jacob's wound may even be similar: some read the vague terminology of Jacob's injury as a euphemism for a wound on his sexual organ, while others take the euphemistic language a stage further and argue that the wound itself is inflicted on his thigh as a euphemism for damage to his sexual organ. Ibn Ezra argues against this reading, but nonetheless, there is room to consider whether the *gid hanasheh* is symbolically linked to reproduction and fertility. In biblical language, the thigh is sometimes associated with progeny, as Jacob's own descendants are described: "Those who were descended of Jacob's thigh were seventy people in all" (Ex. 1:5; see also Gen. 46:26). The Sages already note this when Abraham's servant places his hand "under his master Abraham's thigh and swore this by an oath to him" (24:9) to bring a wife back for Isaac, as Rashi comments: "The one who swears must hold an object of a mitzva in his hand, such as a Torah scroll or tefillin, and circumcision was his first mitzva, which he achieved through pain, and it was the most dear to him."[24] The same may be true of the oath Jacob makes Joseph swear to him: "If I have found favor in your eyes, place your hand under my thigh and promise to deal kindly and truly with me: do not bury me in Egypt" (Gen. 47:29).[25] If so, it may

24. Rashi on Gen. 24:2 (based on Genesis Rabba 59:8). This may be the significance of Jacob's vow by "The Fear of his father Isaac" (31:53), as proposed by Koch, "*Pahad Jishaq*," 113–14; Ratzabi, "Fear"; Malul, *Society, Law, and Customs*, 207–13. Compare especially to Job 40:17.
25. See, for example, Malul, *Society, Law, and Customs*, 210–11; Sarna, *Understanding Genesis*, 170–71. For my position on the connection between these vows and birth, see Grossman, *Abraham*, 357–58.

well be that the wound Jacob sustains hints to the blessing of fertility. Ultimately, Jacob's name is changed in conjunction with an explicit blessing of fertility – "Be fertile and multiply. A nation, a community of nations will come to be from you. Of your loins, kings shall come forth" (35:11), so there is good reason to link the two.

The connection between circumcision and *gid hanasheh* is further reinforced given that both are acts of physical harm of an organ associated with reproduction that yet invoke divine blessing of fertility. Moreover, beside the mitzvot of circumcision and the prohibition of eating the *gid hanasheh*, there is only one additional command-blessing in the book of Genesis: "God blessed them, saying, 'Be fertile and multiply. Fill the earth and subdue it'" (1:28).[26] If *gid hanasheh* is, in one way or another, also associated with fertility, then all three mitzvot of Genesis are interconnected and linked to the blessing of fertility and birth.

This underscores a difference between Abraham and Jacob. I will first look at the prohibition of eating the *gid hanasheh*, which draws a chiastic parallel between the religious taboo and what befell Jacob (32:33):

> That is why, to this day, the Israelites do not eat the *gid hanasheh*
> by the *hip socket*:
> because he wrenched Jacob's *hip socket*
> at the *gid hanasheh*.

This structure reflects the connection between a prevalent custom in Israel and the personal life of Jacob. Note that the verse is not formulated as a command, but rather as an explanation of an existing custom; indeed, the Mishna claims that the prohibition of eating the *gid hanasheh* is not derived from this verse:

26. That God's words are considered a commandment is based on the double introduction "And God blessed them" / "And God said to them" Although some read the Ramban's commentary to mean that based on the repetition of the verb, this is an "actual blessing" and not just a bestowal of fertility, as it is in the context of animals (Gen. 1:22). According to this reading, the verse pronounced to humanity, "Be fruitful and multiply," is also not a commandment but a blessing.

> [*Gid hanasheh*] only applies to pure animals, but not to impure animals. R. Yehuda says: Even to impure animals. R. Yehuda says: Was the *gid hanasheh* not prohibited [from the time of] Jacob's sons, yet an impure animal was still permitted to them? They answered him: It was prohibited at Sinai, but it was mentioned in that context. (Mishna Ḥullin, 7:6).

The Sages hold that the prohibition of eating the *gid hanasheh* only applies to kosher animals, as a non-kosher animal is entirely prohibited anyway. R. Yehuda argues that the prohibition does apply to non-kosher animals, claiming that when Jacob struggled with the angel – before the Torah was given at Sinai – there was not yet any distinction between pure and impure animals, so the prohibition of *gid hanasheh* was a general prohibition. To this, the Sages reply that Jacob's struggle was not the source of the prohibition – it was only its origin story, "mentioned in that context."

The talmudic Sages' debate touches upon a further debate about the meaning of the phrase "*benei Yisrael*" – does it mean Israelites, or the literal sons of Israel? The Sages hold that it was the Israelite nation who refrained from eating the *gid hanasheh*, not Jacob's sons, as in the Tosefta: "They said to R. Yehuda: It does not say 'Therefore the sons of Jacob – Reuben and Simeon – do not eat the *gid hanasheh*,' but 'the Israelites' – those who stood at Mount Sinai" (Tosefta Ḥullin 7:4). R. Yehuda may have been of the opinion that Jacob's family did refrain from eating the *gid hanasheh* as a tribute to his struggle, as Radak writes: "Jacob's sons declared it forbidden in honor of their father, who was struck there, and they forbade their children" (Radak on Gen. 32:33).[27] The most straightforward reading, however, is that of the Sages – that "*benei Yisrael*" refers to the Israelite nation, as "to this day" applies to the Israelites who continue to uphold this custom.

This illuminates the most dramatic difference between these two commandments of Genesis. Circumcision originated as a divine

27. This is also implied by Bekhor Shor: "Therefore the Israelites do not eat – as a commemoration, for their father fought with the angel and it could not overcome him … it is a commemoration of honor and greatness."

command to Abraham, as part of a divine covenant, while the prohibition of eating the *gid hanasheh* began as a human response to Jacob's experience. Even the setting of each scene contributes to the different tones of the two commandments: Abraham fulfills God's commandment of circumcision "on that very day," whereas Jacob's mysterious struggle, the source of the prohibition of eating the *gid hanasheh,* takes place at night.

These differences form part of the complex comparison between the two narrative cycles, as we will discuss below.

4. Parting with the Son

Just as Jacob's departure from his father's house is parallel to Abraham's departure from his father's house; just as the conflicts he suffers throughout his life are comparable to the conflicts that accompany his grandfather's; so too is the final episode of the Jacob cycle – the sale of Joseph – parallel to the final episode of the Abraham cycle: the binding of Isaac.[28]

Firstly, the overall plots follow a similar pattern. Both Abraham and Jacob must part from the beloved son born to their wife after years of barren hope. At each story's end, Abraham and Jacob embrace the son who seemed lost to them forever.

But the similarities between them transcend the general narrative backbone; the two episodes share concrete details and even common language that proves that this parallel is intentional.

The story of Isaac's binding begins with God summoning Abraham and his iconic reply of "Here I am" (22:1). The sale of Joseph opens with Jacob addressing his son Joseph, who also replies, "Here I am" (37:13). This is followed by instructions to go to a certain place and perform a certain action. God orders Abraham to "take your son … and go" (22:2), while Jacob orders Joseph to "go" (37:14). Abraham does as he is told, and on the third day, "Abraham looked up and, in the distance,

28. The structure of the Abraham cycle shows that the cycle ends with the binding of Isaac, while from this point on the scenes involving Abraham should be considered a transition from the first generation to the fulfillment of Abraham's blessings in the second generation (see Coats, *Genesis,* 28; Grossman, *Abraham,* 18–23).

he saw the place" (22:4). Joseph, too, does as he is bid, and when he reaches his destination, "they saw him from a distance" (37:18).

A moment before he slaughters his son, an angel appears to Abraham and tells him: "Do not lift your hand against the boy; do nothing to him" (22:12). Similarly, just before the brothers kill Joseph, Reuben stops them: "'Do not lift a hand against the boy,' for his plan was to rescue him from their hands" (37:22). A ram is sacrificed in place of Isaac, and instead of killing Joseph, the brothers kill a goat and dip his coat in its blood in order to convince Jacob of Joseph's death. Even Reuben's return to his brothers after he finds that Joseph is no longer in the pit – "He went back to his brothers" (37:7) – echoes the end of the binding narrative: "Abraham went back to his young men" (22:19).[29]

Here, too, the similarity between the two episodes underscores their differences. The binding of Isaac is commanded by God, and Abraham becomes the archetype of the obedient believer. By contrast, Jacob does not part with his son because of divine command, but through a negative act of sibling rivalry. Joseph answers "Here I am" as the human son of a human father.

Jacob as Abraham

This comparison illuminates how Jacob clearly follows in the footsteps of his grandfather.[30] Not only does Jacob make the same journey as Abraham; the main complications that plague Jacob throughout his life also echo the issues that Abraham faces. Unlike Isaac, who succeeds his father, Jacob begins anew. His re-initiation into the covenant does not negate Abraham's initiation; rather, it serves to reaffirm their connection with God and His path.

---

29. I propose elsewhere that Joseph in Potiphar's house can be read as a continuation of the same plot, hence my comparison between the angel's words to Abraham, "Now I know that you fear God: for you have not withheld from Me your son, your only one" (22:12) and Joseph's words to Potiphar's wife, "No one in this house has greater authority than I. He has withheld nothing from me except you, because you are his wife. How could I do so great a wrong? It would be a sin against God!" (39:9). See further in Grossman, "Abraham and Jacob," 20.
30. Cassuto mentions additional connections, like giving the barren wife's maid to her husband. See Cassuto, *Genesis and Its Structure,* 263.

Certain verses that discuss God's choice of the patriarchs mention Abraham and Jacob, but overlook Isaac. As Isaiah describes in several prophecies: "And so, this is what the Lord has said – Abraham's Redeemer – to the house of Jacob: 'No more will Jacob be ashamed, his face no more grow pale'" (Is. 29:22); "And you, Israel, My servant, Jacob whom I chose, children of Abraham who loved Me" (41:8); "You are our Father though Abraham would not know us, though Israel would not recognize us. You, Lord, are our Father, named our Redeemer since time began" (63:16).

The Psalmist, too, sings: "Recall the wonders He has done, the marvels and judgments He has pronounced, O seed of Abraham His servant; O children of Jacob, His chosen ones" (Ps. 105:5–6); and Isaac's absence is especially salient when the book of Micah ends on this note: "You will show truth to Jacob, kindness to Abraham, as You swore to our fathers in the earliest days" (Mic. 7:22). The verse's parallel structure equates Abraham and Jacob with "our fathers," thus excluding Isaac from the patriarchy.[31]

In certain contexts, Abraham and Jacob indeed seem to share a status that differs from that of Isaac – both need to earn their way into the covenant. While the blessing is realized through Isaac, Abraham and Jacob both receive the blessings and pass them on to their children. In this, Joseph resembles Isaac: he is born blessed.

Jacob as Abraham?

Of course, Jacob is by no means identical to Abraham, and his narrative cycle presents a completely new perspective. While both travel from Haran to Canaan, they cover different geographical regions: Abraham is most active in Hebron and Judah; Isaac settles in Beersheba; while much of Jacob's drama takes place on the east side of the Jordan (Mahanaim, Sukkot, and Penuel), and in Bethel and Shechem.

Beyond their geographical spheres, a close comparison of grandfather and grandson in fact highlights the fundamental *differences* between

31. Ibn Ezra proposes that Isaac is absent in this verse because he is also the father of Esau-Edom (on Mic. 7:20). Radak, by contrast, proposes that the expression "our fathers" in the second stich alludes to the missing father – Isaac (ibid.).

their character and theological perception. This serves to illuminate a hidden thread woven throughout the book of Genesis.

The Hero and the Tragic Figure

The first obvious disparity between these two figures is their characterization. Both characters must leave their father's house to wander, both suffer conflict with their family and foreigners, and both believe they must part with their son. Yet throughout, Abraham is characterized as an active hero whose actions and choices propel the plot forward, while Jacob is a tragic figure who reacts to the circumstances that befall him. One salient example of this difference is how Abraham (and Isaac) intentionally deceive the foreign king and present their wives as their sisters, so that upon learning of their deception, the king indignantly cries: "What have you done to me/us?!" (Gen. 12:18; 20:9; 26:10). By contrast, Laban is the one who deceives Jacob by switching Leah and Rachel, so that it is Jacob who cries, "What have you done to me?!" (29:25).

Similarly, while Abraham initiates his parting from Lot following tension between them, Jacob is forced to run away to escape his brother's rage. When Esau – like Lot – later leaves Canaan for his own land, he does so for his own purposes, when Jacob is not even in the country.

Such differences are evident in every episode: Abraham willingly circumcises himself by divine command, while Jacob is unwittingly injured during an encounter with a divine figure – circumcision is a commandment that requires active participation, while refraining from eating the *gid hanasheh* prescribes passivity. Abraham willingly sets out to sacrifice his son, again by divine command, while Jacob's son is torn from him against his will, without his knowledge.

In every scene, Abraham is characterized as an active hero. He submits to God, but he *chooses* to submit to Him. He chooses to follow divine orders and leaves his father's house, offers up his son, parts ways from Lot, and deceives the foreign ruler. He forges his own path according to his moral and spiritual values.

By contrast, although Jacob suffers similar trials to Abraham, he submits to what befalls him, a tragic man of faith whose hands are bound. He is forced to leave his father's house to flee for his life, he is deceived by Laban, and he flees from Haran when he realizes that Laban's "manner toward him was not what it had been" (Gen. 31:2).

We will yet explore the deeper intricacies of Jacob's complex character, but for now this overview colors him as a tragic figure. He is driven from scene to scene against his will, yet all the while he maintains a deep, living connection with his God. Jacob is not tested with active tests of faith as Abraham is; rather, his test is to maintain his faith and his connection with God despite his difficult reality, and to maintain his belief in God's promise despite the long years he spends in Laban's household.

FROM DIVINE PRESENCE TO DIVINE ABSENCE

The Jacob narrative cycle is also unique in its theological context within Genesis, which gradually sees a shift from God's manifest shaping of reality to the world becoming the realm of human responsibility (while God peeks through the lattice). Abraham is granted revelation after revelation – God even visits him in his own tent, accompanied by a divine host. Joseph, by contrast, receives only hidden messages through dreams, and with the exception of a single revelation to Jacob (Gen. 46:2–4), God's providence of Joseph is entirely hidden. It is up to the characters to perceive God's hand in their lives.

The Jacob narrative cycle lies in between: between Abraham and Joseph; between open revelation and hidden providence. Jacob is also granted revelation, but not to the same extent as Abraham. Jacob's sublime dream of angels phases into revelation, a fusion of Abraham's revelations and Joseph's dreams. Both Sarah and Dinah are captured by foreign rulers, but while God strikes Pharaoh with terrible afflictions in retribution, and appears to Abimelech to reproach him, it is Jacob's sons who take vengeance on Hamor and Shechem for the assault of Dinah – nor is God's stance on this affair entirely clear.

In fact, God's stance remains unclear throughout most of the Jacob cycle. Only a meticulous literary analysis will yield the text's (complex) evaluation of Jacob's theft of the blessings; and even a rigorous literary analysis does not unequivocally reveal whether the text approves of Jacob's exploitation of his brother's ravenous hunger. This lack of obvious judgment led several scholars to assume that moral assessment is irrelevant in these narratives,[32] while others even surmise that the pursuit of moral values in these kinds of stories is downright anachronistic.[33] These views have fallen victim to the coy nature of the Jacob cycle. Indeed, there is no clear moral assessment in these narratives – not because it is absent or irrelevant, but because it is hidden.

The transition from open divine revelation to human initiative is especially salient through the narrative dichotomy. Jacob's eventual success in Haran is attributed to two factors: God watches over him, as promised when he sets out, but at the same time, Jacob uses his own wits. I will yet discuss how these two factors are intertwined, but for now, it suffices to point out how this dichotomy is immanent to these narratives; neither is sufficient in itself. The Abraham cycle glows with divine revelation; the Joseph cycle is propelled by human initiative and free will; in the Jacob cycle, the two threads are woven together. Let us now follow these two sets of footprints.

32. A salient proponent of this approach is Gunkel, *Genesis*, 319.
33. Niditch, *Biblical Folklore*, 49–50. See also the discussion (and justified reservations toward the approach in question) of Vrolijk, *Jacob's Wealth*, 147–48.

Pregnancy, Birth, and Childhood (Gen. 25:19–34)

> Be not afraid of greatness. Some are born great, some achieve greatness, and others have greatness thrust upon them.
>
> – Shakespeare, *Twelfth Night*, Act II, Scene V

Despite what many teenagers would like to believe, a person's story begins with their parents; and the same is true of the Jacob cycle, which begins with a description of his parents' marriage. In fact, the description of his parents' union foreshadows events that will later play out in the protagonist's life: "When Isaac was forty he married Rebecca, daughter of Bethuel *the Aramean of Padan Aram*, sister of Laban *the Aramean*" (25:20).

Given that Rebecca's origins are already known from the detailed story in Genesis 24, this repetition seems superfluous, especially to the description of Jacob and his twin's birth.[1] Rashi reads this emphasis as praise for Rebecca: "Daughter of Bethuel the Aramean, sister of Laban – had it not yet been mentioned that she was the daughter of Bethuel and the sister of Laban, and from Padan Aram? This serves

1. Rebecca's birthplace has several different names. In Genesis, she lives in "Aram Naharaim" (24:10); here, it is called "Padan Aram." Most assume that this is the same place with different names (see, for example, Hamilton, *Genesis II*, 175; Mathews, *Genesis II*, 385). For a different opinion, see, for example, Westermann, *Genesis II*, 412.

to praise her, for she was the daughter of a wicked man, the sister of a wicked man, and from a place of wicked men, but she did not emulate their deeds" (Rashi on Gen. 25:20).

Rebecca's praise in this verse can also be read in the opposite sense: she is worthy *because* she is from Padan Aram and not from Canaan. Abraham emphasizes to his servant that he is unwilling for Isaac to marry a Canaanite woman, and the text therefore emphasizes that Rebecca is indeed from Aram, from Abraham's own Aramean family.

Yet the language of this verse is not only in dialogue with the story of finding a wife for Isaac; it also anticipates Jacob's own experience.[2] Laban will prove to play a significant role in Jacob's life when he himself seeks a wife. This foreshadowing has great significance for the narrative cycle – it is already clear from the beginning that Jacob's journey to Haran is not the coincidental result of his theft of the blessing but rather a fundamental part of the plot, and the story of Jacob's birth opens with emphasis on the Aramean side of Jacob's family.

Jacob's narrative cycle takes place in three geographical spheres:

1. Introductory stories before Jacob's departure for Haran (how Jacob ends up in Padan Aram).
2. How Jacob establishes his family and fortune in Haran.
3. Jacob's return to his father in Hebron (and what happens on the way).

The first of these three sections opens with Isaac's marriage and emphasis of the bride's geographical origins. The second section describes Jacob's journey to Padan Aram to find a wife, given that, in the words of his mother Rebecca, "If Jacob marries a Hittite woman like them, one of the women of the land, why should I go on living?" (Gen. 27:46). Jacob's exile ends when he reaches Shechem (see the discussion in context), and the first concern upon his return is the question of Dinah's marriage to Shechem son of Hamor, the prince of the land.

Effectively, Jacob's narrative cycle opens with the title "These are the *toledot* of Isaac" (the eighth appearance of this heading in Genesis),

2. As proposed, for example, by Wenham, *Genesis II*, 174.

and consistent with the pattern throughout Genesis, the narrative focus is on the establishment of Jacob's family – Isaac's grandchildren. We will yet discuss the extent of influence the wives' origin has on the plot development. The most important part of the narrative cycle takes place where his family is established, in Padan Aram, and Jacob's narrative cycle ends when Jacob returns to his father and presents his family to him.

BARRENNESS, PREGNANCY, AND PROPHECY (25:21–23)

Isaac's "*toledot*" could have begun with more drama: Rebecca, like Sarah before her, is barren, and she and Isaac must pray to God to open her womb. After Abraham and Sarah's long, painful ordeal, the reader is prepared for narrative focus on this complication. Yet the news of Rebecca's barrenness is mentioned almost incidentally, and solved in a single breath with its mention: "And Isaac pleaded with the Lord on behalf of his wife, for she was childless. The Lord granted his plea and Rebecca became pregnant" (25:21). It is strange that Isaac's prayer for help is mentioned even before his plight, so that his actual plight – childlessness – seems secondary to his prayer. This may serve to reinforce his characterization as a man of prayer, as introduced in the previous chapter: "Isaac was just coming back from the direction of Beer-lahai-roi.... He had gone out in the field toward evening to meditate" (25:62).[3] Moreover, it creates the impression of a fast-paced story: Isaac prays, God answers his prayers, and Rebecca conceives. This sequence belies the fact that twenty years go by before Jacob and Esau are actually born! Some debate whether Isaac prays for twenty long years before his prayers are answered or whether he only prays after twenty years of infertility, whereupon God immediately responds.[4] I see no reason to assume that Isaac only begins praying after twenty years, but the very dilemma reflects the disparity between the actual unfolding of events and their representation in the text, where it seems that God answers Isaac as soon as he prays. The parallel structure of the two halves of the verse contributes to this reading:[5]

3. See Grossman, *Abraham*, 391.
4. Vrolijk, *Jacob's Wealth*, 46.
5. Fokkelman, *Genesis*, 88.

> Isaac *pleaded* with *the Lord* on behalf of *his wife*,
> He granted his *plea, the Lord,* and *Rebecca* became pregnant

Of course, in contrast to this impression, a quick calculation reveals that Isaac and Rebecca are married for twenty years before she becomes pregnant: Isaac marries Rebecca when he is forty years old (25:20), and the twins are born when he is sixty (25:26). The pace of verse 21 conceals the disparity between the fabula (the actual sequence of events) and the syuzhet (the way the story is told). Although technically both Abraham and Sarah *and* Isaac and Rebecca suffer decades of infertility, from a literary perspective, it is not accurate to state that "the barren condition of Rebecca parallels the Abraham-Sarah narratives."[6] The prolonged, detailed suffering of Sarah; the constant pleas and trials of Abraham, who eventually challenges God (15:2–3); the repeated divine promises – all this cannot possibly be compared to the brief sequence before Jacob's birth, which presents both crisis and solution within the same sentence.

The text seems more interested in emphasizing God's response to Isaac's prayer than the couple's plight, and showing that Isaac is blessed rather than distressed. On the one hand, there is archetypal importance that Isaac's sons are born to a barren mother – as was Isaac himself – thus emphasizing God's providence and intervention. On the other hand, the reader is not invited to share the couple's desperate anticipation for a child as they wait and grieve month after month for twenty long years. Jacob is indeed born following special divine intervention, but his parents' pain is downplayed. I will explore the full significance of this design in the context of chapter 26, the only chapter in Genesis devoted entirely to Isaac.

To Inquire of the Lord

Following Isaac's prayer, Rebecca also seeks God during her pregnancy:

> But the children clashed within her. She said, "If this is so, why am I living?" So she went to inquire of the Lord. The Lord said to her,
> "Two nations are inside your womb;

6. Mathews, *Genesis II*, 386.

two peoples are to part from you.
People will overpower people,
and the greater shall the younger serve." (25:22–23)

The juxtaposition of the couple's prayers, verse after verse, invites comparison between them.[7] Isaac prays to God about their painful barrenness and Rebecca prays to God about her painful pregnancy; just as God responds to Isaac's prayers, He responds to Rebecca; Isaac prays for Rebecca to become pregnant, and Rebecca prays because she is pregnant. The verses' structure makes it easier to compare the two parents: at first Isaac is the active subject in the text (vv. 19–21), but once Rebecca becomes pregnant, the narrative focus shifts to her (vv. 22–23).

This parallel also reveals the difference between Isaac and Rebecca, and we will yet explore how significant a difference it is: Isaac prays to God, but Rebecca "went to inquire" of God. What does "inquire" mean, and where does she go to do so? The theory that she goes to Isaac and asks him to pray on her behalf is not convincing;[8] Isaac does not seem to be aware of the prophecy, and if Rebecca had indeed asked Isaac to pray for her, it would likely have been explicit in the text.

A different exegetical direction perceives Abraham as Rebecca's advisor. Ibn Ezra, for example, writes: "The Lord told her through a prophet, or through Abraham himself, as he did not die until her sons were fifteen years old" (on Gen. 25:23). This reading is developed further in the book of Jubilees (19:15–30), where Abraham plays a decisive role in Rebecca's bond with Jacob – Abraham perceives Jacob as the chosen son, blesses him, and asks Rebecca to help fulfill this choice.[9] Yet this theory is clearly absent in the text itself. Could it be that Abraham plays so crucial a role without any such mention in the narrative? Would Abraham be aware of the prophecy without sharing it with Isaac?

---

7. See also Hamori, *Women's Divination*, 45–46.
8. Mathews, *Genesis II*, 387. Fleming claims that Rebecca receives the prophecy herself, directly (Fleming, "She Went to Inquire"), but this reading is problematic.
9. In this respect, Tal Ilan's rejection of the view that the book of Jubilees esteems women is correct (Ilan, "Review," 161–64). On the contrary: in the biblical narrative Rebecca is Isaac's equal or even superior regarding who is their chosen son, whereas in Jubilees, Abraham replaces Rebecca.

In any case, how Rebecca receives this prophecy[10] is only secondary to the content of the prophecy itself.[11] Yet the verb "inquire" – *lidrosh* – sets a certain tone for the prophecy and cannot be overlooked. In other places in the Bible, the verb "*lidrosh*" is associated with knowing the future (such as Ben-Hadad's inquiry of Elisha: "Will I recover from this illness?" – II Kings 8:8) or other hidden information (such as the whereabouts of Saul's donkeys). One of Moses' roles as prophet and leader is to answer the people's various questions: "The people come to me to inquire of God" (Ex. 18:15). Even if "the primary meaning of 'inquiring of God' was once consulting with an oracle about the future, as was prevalent throughout the middle east, but with time, this phrase also came to be associated with making pilgrimage to God's temple and keeping His commandments,"[12] the primary connotations still linger.

It is interesting to note that the disparity between Isaac, who prays, and Rebecca, who inquires, is expressed so subtly. Isaac's prayer is not represented with the more typical verb "*lehitpallel*," but rather, using the verb root A-T-R, which some associate with rite and ritual, especially sacrifice.[13] This is not evident in biblical Hebrew, but it is true of Arabic and Ugaritic, where the verb root A-T-R means slaughter or sacrifice. Some scholars posit that this means that Isaac makes sacrifices in his wife's presence.[14] I am not convinced that all biblical instances of prayer (with the verb root A-T-R) involve sacrifice,[15] but even if they

10. Sarna (*Understanding Genesis*, 182) claims that the text is vague as to where Rebecca "went" in order to disassociate her from any kind of cultic ritual.

11. Wenham, *Genesis II*, 175.

12. Saviv, "Seeking the Lord," 38.

13. This may be true of Ezekiel 8:11: "Each man had his censer in his hand, and a dense cloud of incense was ascending (*va'atar*)" (although in Ezekiel, the root A-T-R also means, simply, "prayer" – 35:13). If A-T-R is indeed related to sacrifice, then the names of three towns of Judah (or Simeon) are all related to the world of sacrifice: "Livnah (a play on *levona*, frankincense) and Eter (*atar*) and Ashan (a play on *ashan*, smoke)" – Josh. 15:42; see also Joshua 19:7.

14. Hamori, *Women's Divination*, 46. For further discussion, see Grossman, *Sacrificial Service*, 18.

15. See, for example, the plague of frogs, when the root A-T-R is simply pleading and crying out to God (Ex. 8:4–8).

do, then both Isaac and Rebecca receive what they seek. Isaac prays for pregnancy, and Rebecca indeed becomes pregnant; Rebecca seeks information and understanding about her future, and she indeed learns what is to come. In the words of Rashbam: "*To inquire of the Lord* – through the prophets of that time, as written 'to inquire of the Lord,' and as written: 'When the people come to me to inquire of the Lord'" (Rashbam on Gen. 25:22).

Describing Rebecca's action with this specific word takes on further significance in the broader theological context of Genesis. Rebecca receives God's word only after she attempts to seek it. This is a fundamental difference from the Abraham narrative cycle, where God appears to Abraham and Sarah time and again, even visiting them in their own home to announce the impending birth of their son, his name, and the future blessing that awaits him. The Jacob cycle opens with Isaac's prayer and with Rebecca's active search for the word of God, thus coloring the new narrative cycle in different theological tones than the first parts of Genesis.

Moreover, the fact that this prophecy is granted in response to Rebecca's "inquiry" also has specific implications. Rebecca asks to know what will become of her, and why her unborn child moves so frantically within her; the answer she receives is a glimpse into the future. This, I believe, settles an exegetical dilemma: Does the prophecy impart a moral message about the worthy path to follow, or is it merely an image of the future?[16] The use of the verb "*lidrosh*" shows that this not a commandment or moral directive, but an answer to Rebecca's question about herself and her children.[17]

Based on this narrative framework, we will now explore God's words to Rebecca and attempt to decipher what future awaits Rebecca

16. See, for example, Humphreys, *Character of God*, 163; Vrolijk, *Jacob's Wealth*, 42.

17. Assis argues that this prophecy does not refer to covenantal election or rejection, but rather to which son will be the head of the family (Assis, *Identity in Conflict*, 58–59). This reading is consistent with the plot, whereas Esau is only excluded much later. Yet the emphasis on "nations" and "peoples" implies that the two brothers will split off into two different nations.

and her sons. This prophecy lies at the heart of the scene's chiastic structure:[18]

A. **Isaac's marriage at the age of forty:** "When Isaac was forty he married Rebecca, daughter of Bethuel the Aramean of Padan Aram, sister of Laban the Aramean" (v. 20).
    B. **Isaac's prayer and Rebecca's pregnancy:** "Isaac pleaded with the Lord on behalf of his wife, for she was childless. The Lord granted his plea and Rebecca became pregnant" (v. 21).
        C. **Rebecca goes to inquire of the Lord:** "But the children clashed within her. She said, 'If this is so, why am I living?' So she went to inquire of the Lord" (v. 22).
        C'. **God's reply:** "Two nations are in your womb, two peoples are to part from you. People will overpower people, and the greater shall the younger serve" (v. 23).
    B'. **Rebecca gives birth:** "When the time came for her to give birth, there were twins in her womb" (v. 24).
A'. **Isaac becomes a father at the age of sixty:** "Isaac was sixty years old when they were born" (v. 26).

Isaac's age at his marriage and at the twins' birth reveals that twenty years pass during these brief lines. Even so, the verses of this scene do not focus on the plight of their barrenness, but rather on the difficulty of Rebecca's pregnancy.

The two inner components of the structure relate that Rebecca becomes pregnant (B) and gives birth (B'). Most biblical pregnancies are immediately followed by birth and the child's naming, such as: "The man knew his wife Eve / and she conceived / and gave birth to Cain, saying, 'With the Lord's help I have made a man'" (Gen. 4:1), or the birth of many of Jacob's own sons: "And Leah became pregnant and gave birth to a son / and named him Reuben" (29:32). Here, the formulaic biblical sequence is interrupted with rare focus on the pregnancy itself, setting this birth story apart from other birth stories.

18. For a similar concentric structure, see Mathews, *Genesis II*, 385.

The two central components (C–C') describe the suffering that moves Rebecca to inquire of the Lord. Aptly set in the scene's center, these verses transcend time and place and encapsulate the distant future of the two unborn children struggling within their mother's womb, "explaining the whole Jacob and Esau story in much the same way that 12:1–3 illuminates the Abraham story."[19]

Clashing Within Her

As stated, God's answer to Rebecca can only be fully understood if we understand her question. She is moved to inquire of the Lord when "the children clashed (*vayitrotzetzu*) within her" (25:22). Rashi cites two possible meanings of the word *vayitrotzetzu*:

> Our Sages interpreted it as an expression of "running," of "movement": when she would pass by the entrances of Shem and Eber [a place of Torah study], Jacob would move and struggle to get out, and when she would pass by the entrance of places of idolatry, Esau would struggle to get out. Another interpretation: they would clash with each other and fight about the inheritance of both worlds. (Rashi on Gen. 25:22)

The Septuagint seems to understand it in the sense of "running" or "movement" (ἐσκίρτων), but from a semantic perspective, it is more convenient to read the word in the sense of "crushing" or "smashing" (compare with Judges 9:53; Is. 36:6), as if the two brothers are crushing each other in prenatal sibling rivalry.[20] Some read their struggle as an actual physical struggle,[21] while others interpret it as the beginning of the struggle for primogeniture: the kicks and shoves that Rebecca feels are the two brothers shoving inside her, struggling to get the best position

19. Wenham, *Genesis II*, 180.
20. BDB, "R-TZ-TZ," 954: "The children *crushed* (thrust, struck) one another within her." By contrast, Zimran (*Conflicts*, 79), claimed that this verb has no connotations of a fight or tension.
21. Gunkel, *Genesis*, 288; Wenham, *Genesis II*, 175.

in order to be born first.[22] In either case, the reflexive form of the verb root reflects how *both* brothers are struggling, clashing with each other.

Thus, the rivalry between Jacob and Esau begins even before their birth, and grows along with them. Many years will pass before their struggle (*hitrotzetzut*) in the womb will conclude – at least openly – with reconciliation initiated when Esau runs (*vayarotz*) toward Jacob and embraces him (33:4), but their relationship will always be characterized with tension.

What does Rebecca learn from this response? Firstly, that she is carrying twins – which in itself explains her intense discomfort. Moreover, the fierce movement within her is in fact the beginning of a lasting struggle between the brothers: "Two nations are in your womb, / two peoples will part from you. / People will overpower people / and the greater shall the younger serve" (v. 23).

The first half of the verse announces that Rebecca's twins will grow into two nations. The second half describes their future rivalry: the text hints that throughout history, one will overpower the other, but ultimately, the younger brother will triumph over the elder brother.[23]

TWO BROTHERS (25:24–28)

> As thou sayest, charged my brother, on his
> blessing, to breed me well: and there begins my
> sadness… for my part,

22. Similarly: Y. Zakovitch, "Jacob, Deceit," 126; Fokkelman, *Genesis*, 88.
23. The Sages famously read this line as an ambiguous statement that can be read either way, and many adopt this position (see, for example, Shapira, "Jacob and Esau," 261–62), and grammatically, the line is indeed ambiguous. However, it seems more likely that the prophecy wishes to point out what is unusual about the pregnancy, and it is therefore more likely that the older brother will serve the younger brother, unlike convention, which dictates that the firstborn is the most powerful. As mentioned, Elie Assis notes that the prophecy that the greater will serve the younger does not entail the rejection of either brother (Assis, *Identity in Conflict*, 36–37) – it is only a comment about who the head of the family will be, but it does not actually exclude either brother from the covenant. However, given that the prophecy predicts that each brother will form his own separate nation, there is room to discuss whether the prophecy does in fact hint that one brother will be rejected.

> he keeps me rustically at home. (Shakespeare, *As You Like It*, Act I, Scene I)

R. Menachem Mendel of Kotzk once said: "If I am I because I am I, and you are you because you are you, then I am I and you are you. But if I am I because you are you, and you are you because I am I, then I am not I and you are not you."

Yet a person is clearly shaped by the people around them, especially their family. This applies sevenfold in the world of literature, where characterization is inherently forged through analogy to other characters in the text (or even other texts). Though comparison between siblings is ill-advised in the real world, it is a crucial, even necessary tool for reaching full understanding of a character in the world of literature[24] – especially in the case of twin brothers whose mother is warned of their rivalry before they are even born.[25] This prophecy invites comparison between them, and the brothers are defined and fully characterized in relation to each other.

It therefore comes as no surprise that Jacob and Esau's birth, childhood, and relationship with their parents are related entirely through comparisons between the two brothers:

Birth:
The first came out red. His whole body was like a hairy cloak, so they named him Esau. Then his brother emerged, his hand grasping Esau's heel (*akev*), so he named him Jacob (*Yaakov*).

Occupation:
Esau became a skilled hunter, a man of the field, while Jacob was an innocent man who stayed among the tents.

Parental Love:
Isaac loved Esau because he ate of his game, but Rebecca loved Jacob.

24. See further in Garsiel, *Literary Study*, 17–18.
25. See for example in Roubach, "Two."

These descriptions all mention Esau before Jacob (as opposed to the alternating descriptions of Cain and Abel in Genesis 4), true to their birth order, which creates a sense of order and clear comparison. Yet in each parallel, a certain element in the text challenges this order and apparent symmetry:

Birth (vv. 24–26)

> When the time came for her to give birth, there were twins in her womb.[26]
> The first came out red. / His whole body was like a hairy cloak, / so they named him Esau.
> Then his brother emerged, / his hand grasping Esau's heel, / so he named him Jacob.

The symmetry is clear: first, each baby is born / then characterized with a certain feature / then named. At the same time, subtle asymmetries hint at the tension that bubbles beneath the surface. When the first child born is referred to as "the first," we can assume that readers would expect him to be followed by "the second" – in fact, the term "the first" is meaningless unless it is followed by "the second." Yet Jacob is described not as "the second" but as "his brother." The text is already affected by the tension in the prophecy of Rebecca's pregnancy – the fact that Jacob is not relegated to "second" place despite their birth order foreshadows how the primogeniture will be challenged as the twins mature.

26. Some scholars claim that the "*vehinei*" in the birth scene cannot be an expression of surprise, because Rebecca already knows that she will have twins (see, for example, Zakovitch, "Jacob, Deceit," 133–34; Westermann, *Genesis II*, 413). Others argue that the word refers to surprise that the twins are born healthy, or that the prophecy is indeed true (see, for example, Gunkel, *Genesis*, 289).

Asymmetry is also evident in the brothers' naming: "they" name Esau,[27] while "he" names Jacob.[28]

These asymmetries frame the most significant difference of all: the newborn Esau is described by his appearance ("red, his whole body was like a hairy cloak"), but Jacob is described by his actions ("his hand grasping Esau's heel").[29] The reader, expecting a comparison that will emphasize the differences between the brothers, is confused, because the text describes the brothers using two disparate semantic fields. What does Jacob look like? Did Esau do anything unusual at his birth? One can compare a symphony by Mozart with a symphony by Beethoven, but how does one compare a symphony by Mozart with an apple?

The significance of this symmetry – and its repeated undermining – will only emerge after a close analysis of the sparse information provided about the two brothers. Esau is ruddy[30] and hairy. Theoretically, the description could be read thus: "His whole body was red – like a

---

27. The meaning of *Esav* is not entirely clear; perhaps the most logical reading is that it a partial anagram of *Se'ar*, hair (Westermann, *Genesis II*, 414); but we cannot rule out its association with the word *Me'useh*, "squeezed, pressed," as in "There were their breasts squeezed, there were their virgins' nipples fondled" (Ezek. 23:3). Perhaps the twins' vigorous wrestling meant that Esau emerged "squeezed" or "squished" (see further in Hamori, *Woman's Divination*, 56–58).
28. Several scholars assume that Jacob's original name was *Yaakov'el*, associated with God's protection (see, for example, Hamilton, *Genesis II*, 178). In the narrative, his name was shortened to *Yaakov* to link him to the heel he grasps during his birth. R. Yoel Bin-Nun claims that the omission of the theophoric element of Jacob's name is calculated to disassociate him from the pagan heroes who are named for their gods (Bin-Nun, *Chapters of the Fathers*, 119–23). It is worth recalling, however, that Jacob's name is later changed to a theophoric name – Israel.
29. Garsiel, *Midrashic Name Derivations*, 66.
30. Edom's association with "red" invites various opinions. Most assume that the word *Edom* is derived from *dam*, blood (Shalem, "Colors," 66), but other red entities are not associated with blood – such as the red heifer, the red horses in Zechariah, or the descriptions of Edom and David as "ruddy." Above, I adopt Snaith's view of the law of the red heifer (Snaith, *Numbers*, 271). Athaliah Brenner writes that the assumption that red means darkly tanned is inconsistent with the description of the now homeless leaders in Lamentations, whose skin is once "ruddy" but is now "blacker than pitch" (Lam. 4:7–8) – Brenner, "White and Red," 170–71. However, there is a difference between tanned skin and blackened skin, and the verse can also be understood if "red" means "tanned."

hairy cloak," so that the "hairy cloak" would in fact describe Esau's bold red coloring, rather than his hairiness. However, the important role that Esau's hairiness plays later on in the narrative rules out any such ambiguity in this line: Esau is clearly both ruddy and hairy – two components that will characterize his future descendants: his nation will be called "Edom," which literally means "red" (possibly based on the red soil of its hills) and they will live on Mount Seir, which literally means "hairy" (Gen. 36:9). Later on, Esau demands that Jacob give him "some of that *red* stuff" (25:30), so we will postpone further discussion of Esau's association with the color red to that context.

Esau's ruddiness and hairiness serve to characterize him as a bestial wild man, reminiscent of Enkidu from *The Epic of Gilgamesh*.[31] Enkidu's most striking feature is his hairiness (*šu'uram pagaršu*),[32] and he dwells in the wild, among the animals, who fear his shaggy visage.[33] Esau, too, is "a man of the field" (25:7), a shaggy wild man at home amongst the animals he hunts.[34]

Although it later emerges that Jacob is smooth-skinned compared to his hairy brother (27:11), there is no physical description of the newborn Jacob. Rather, the only information provided about him is the fact that he comes out of the womb with "his hand grasping Esau's heel." Symbolically, this can be read in two ways: as a manifestation of the conflict that begins in the womb, with Jacob grasping at Esau's heel in an attempt to stop him being born first;[35] or, alternatively, as a sign of Jacob's dependence on his twin brother – he must grasp Esau's heel to

31. Speiser, *Genesis*, 196; Hendel, *Jacob*, 116–21; Hamilton, *Genesis II*, 181; Hamori, "Gilgamesh."
32. Hamori, "Gilgamesh," 633.
33. Shifra and Klein, *Those Distant Days*, 193, lines 196–97.
34. See also: Galender, *Genesis II*, 236–37; Roland Hendel lists other pairs who represent a similar struggle between two cultures: Horus the Egyptian war god and his cousin Seth (Hendel, *Jacob*, 122–25); Hypsornius and Ozus – two brother gods who, according to Philon, also clashed (125–28).
35. See Rashi, Radak, and Ḥizkuni in context; Hamilton, *Genesis II*, 178; Wenham, *Genesis II*, 177.

be helped out of the womb.[36] In the wider context of the narrative, the first reading is more convincing – Jacob's tiny fist grasping Esau's heel is the first sign of the fraternal conflict Rebecca anticipates even before their birth, and this conflict will continue in the next scene, when Jacob attempts to wrestle the primogeniture away from the ravenous Esau.[37]

The brief account of the twins' birth is thus revealed as a complex structure indeed: the apparent symmetry of their descriptions is subtly undermined by the descriptions themselves. As I will yet argue, the characters' free choice is of utmost importance to the plot's development. The characters' capacity for choice is a meta-principle in biblical narrative in general, and it plays an especially crucial role in the Jacob cycle. For this very reason, the description of the twins' birth is of critical interest: Is their fate already sealed at their moment of birth? Does their first shrill cry already designate one as the heir of Abraham's legacy, and the other as the ruler of the Edomite hills on the eastern side of the Jordan? At first glance, the description of their birth seems to anticipate their later choices, but the image of the newborn Jacob grasping his brother's heel tilts the scale toward a different reading. The complex conclusion of their birth story is that the brothers indeed have different natures that set them along certain paths, but ultimately, their future will be determined by their own actions and choices.

At the same time, the verses' broken symmetry reveals a different aspect of the brothers: Esau's description is self-contained and independent, but Jacob is characterized in relation to his brother. This is evident in their names: Esau is named for his appearance, but Jacob is named for his attempt to control his brother.

This pseudo-symmetry is also evident in the next stage of the twins' life:

---

36. Galender comments that the fact that Jacob grasped Esau's heel implies that he did not emerge from the womb by himself, but that he needed his brother's help to be born (Galender, *Genesis II*, 233, n. 6).

37. R. Eliezer Hadad proposes that grasping the heel symbolizes a snake – who strikes its enemies on the heel (Gen. 3:15, 49:17). The snake is a slippery, smooth creature, and this generates further contrast between the smooth, slippery Jacob and the hairy Esau. See Hadad, "The Crooked."

Occupation (vv. 27–28)

> The boys grew up.
> Esau became a skilled hunter, a man of the field
> while Jacob was an innocent man who stayed among the tents.

Once again, while the structure initially appears symmetrical, a closer look at this description reveals subtle deviations. The difference in tense – "Esau became (*vayhi*)" and "Jacob was (*haya*)" underscores the contrast between them. The verse mentions Esau's occupation – "a skilled hunter," as well as his sphere of action – "a man of the field." Both of these descriptions can be paralleled with the description of Jacob, "who stayed among the tents." The latter seems to refer to shepherding (as in Gen. 4:21),[38] which can be contrasted with Esau as hunter. Moreover, given the biblical motif of conflict between farmers and shepherds,[39] there is room to debate whether this can also be contrasted with Esau being "a man of the field." Does this mean that Esau worked in the field, a man of the soil? In any case, the statement that Jacob "stayed among the tents" is a foil to Esau's sphere of action: Esau ventures out into the wild, into the open fields, while Jacob lingers by the tents, staying close to his home. Esau comes back, tired from his day in the field, while Jacob remains by the hearth.

But Jacob is also characterized with a more obscure description – "*ish tam*," which is generally translated as "an innocent man" (or "plain," "simple," "quiet"). Is this in parallel with "a skilled hunter (*ish yode'a tzayid*)"? A hunter is certainly a profession, but what about "*ish tam*"? Some read the word *tam* in a different sense than its common biblical meaning – based on the Arabic, *tim*, "*tam*" can be understood in the sense of "being conquered," "submissive," and in the context of the verse: a person who stays at home.[40] This certainly creates a striking

38. For example: Ibn Ezra and Bekhor Shor (unlike Rashi); Gunkel, *Genesis*, 290.
39. This is evident in the first biblical narrative about brothers: Cain and Abel (Gen. 4). Some, in fact, claim that this is the narrative's central objective; others do not. See my discussion of this in Grossman, *Beginnings*, 113–15.
40. Driver, "Vocabulary," 281.

contrast between Esau – the man of the field – and Jacob, who stays at home: "*tam* implies someone who finds satisfaction in a quiet life at home … in contrast to the wild life of the wild hunter."[41] This reading is already supported in the next scene, where Esau comes in after a day in the field to Jacob, who is cooking at home. Most exegetical attempts to draw a contrast between "an innocent man" and "a skilled hunter" load connotations onto the latter as an expression of cruelty and deception.[42] A more straightforward reading, however, simply admits that once again, these are different categories: Esau is characterized by two separate descriptions of an occupation, while the words "*ish tam*" describe Jacob's personality. An "*ish tam*" denotes a virtuous, moral person, upright and just, such as Job: "[Job] was innocent (*tam*), honest, God-fearing, and always turned away from evil" (Job 1:1).[43]

The childhood midrashim of Esau as a devious, evil hunter and Jacob as a righteous Torah scholar linger with many readers, but the literal text does not pass any moral judgments on Esau, and merely presents him as a hunter who works in the open field. Once again, while the text seems to invite comparison between the twins, the descriptions of each do not belong to the same semantic fields, thereby preventing full comparison between them.

This formulation seems intentionally misleading, and this may be the reason that the word "*ish*" is used twice to describe Esau ("*ish yode'a tzayid ish sadeh*"), but only once for Jacob ("*ish tam yoshev ohalim*") – this imbalance is calculated to upset the symmetry of the verse.

41. Keil and Delitzsch on this verse. See also Speiser, *Genesis*, 195; Hamilton, *Genesis II*, 181.

42. Rashi, based on the Midrash, writes about Esau: "He ate of his game – he knew how to lure and deceive his father with words." Ibn Ezra's commentary reflects a desire to maintain symmetry by showing how Esau's occupation reflects his character: "Hunting is a world full of deceit, for most animals are caught through deceit, while Jacob is Esau's opposite because he is an innocent man" (see also Ḥizkuni). See also: Garsiel, "Literary Structure," 71; Fokkelman, *Genesis*, 91.

43. Wenham proposes that Jacob's description hints that he was independent and cut off from the outside world (Wenham, *Genesis II*, 177). I prefer Von Rad's approach that this hints to Jacob's sense of morality (Von Rad, *Genesis*, 261). Frank notes that characterizing Jacob as "an innocent man" is antithetical to his name, which has the root A-K-V, deceit (Frank, "The Face of God," 8).

It is also interesting to note that within the sequence of the twins' birth and occupation, each brother is characterized as "whole" in a different sense: Jacob is "whole" in a moral sense, while Esau is "whole" in a physical sense, born with hair like a fully grown person.

The symbolic tension hinted through the brothers' characterization – the tension between raw, wild nature and the civilized culture of the tent – may move the reader to search for hints of which twin is the suitable heir for Abraham's legacy, but at this point, if the reader is able to overlook the story's end, the contrast between the brothers can be read as complementary personalities that will build God's nation together, combining the powers of nature and culture to serve God as one.

Parental Love (v. 28)

> Isaac loved (*vaye'ehav*) Esau because he ate of his game,
> and Rebecca loved (*ohevet*) Jacob.

The third description hints to troubling family dynamics. Differences in appearance, nature, and occupation can all bring welcome diversity to a family. Many, for example, describe the differences between Judah and Joseph as complementary forces that strengthen a budding nation. But each parent favoring a different child can result in unwanted tension within the family unit, and the seeds planted in this verse will later grow uncontrollably, tearing the family apart.

Like the two previous contrasts, the apparent symmetry of this verse is also undermined. The chiastic structure (Isaac loved – Rebecca loved) underscores how each parent favors a different son, but whereas Isaac's love for his son is explained – "because he ate of his game" – no explanation is given for Rebecca's love of Jacob. This difference can be ascribed to a technical reason: Isaac's love for Esau and his game will feature later on, when Isaac sends Esau out to hunt for his favorite game before he blesses him, so it is already mentioned here.[44] Rashbam writes similarly: "Esau's love for Isaac and Rebecca's love for Jacob is already

44. For example: Mathews, *Genesis II*, 392.

mentioned here to inform of what is to come: Isaac wanted to bless Esau, but Rebecca deceives him so that he blesses Jacob" (Rashbam on 25:28).[45]

Yet this difference can also be read in the same light as the other deviations in the text, which subtly portray Jacob in a more favorable light. Isaac's love for Esau is conditional – and conditional on food, no less – while Rebecca's love (conveyed in present tense!) for Jacob is unconditional, whole like Jacob himself.

What, then, is the meaning of this brief yet complex description? The apparent contrast between the brothers is challenged again and again, the comparison between them disqualified again and again. The apparent symmetry seems to characterize one brother in relation to the other, creating a sense of competition and rivalry, and Esau repeatedly seems to have an advantage over Jacob – he is the firstborn and favorite of Isaac, the heir of Abraham's legacy, while Jacob is loved by his mother, who comes from lowly Padan Aram.

Yet each time, a closer reading reveals that it is Jacob who has the advantage. Rebecca's favoritism seems to result from the prophecy she receives during her pregnancy, which dictates that the greater will ultimately serve the younger. Even though Esau is the "first," Jacob evades characterization as "the second," which perhaps anticipates the scene where Jacob will relieve his brother of his rights as the "first." As mentioned, Jacob's depiction as "*ish tam*" without any correlation to Esau's description, and the conditional aspect of Isaac's love for Esau, both subtly tilt the text in Jacob's favor.

Yet why aren't the brothers explicitly pitted against each other in a full-frontal comparison? If there is indeed underlying preference for Jacob, why isn't Esau vilified openly? Some exegetes do sketch out such a portrait of Esau, even based on these verses, such as Radak: "Rebecca only loved Jacob, because he followed the path of life while Esau followed the path of death – not only did he avoid wisdom and the ways of

45. I believe that Rashbam implies that Esau's occupation anticipates the theft of the blessings narrative, as he writes, "A skilled hunter – to hunt game to bring back," which is a direct quote from the latter scene (27:5), thus connecting the two scenes. On Rashbam's tendency to suggest foreshadowing, see Jacobs, "Foreshadowing."

God, but he chose an occupation that placed him in danger every day, and he was rash and reckless" (on Gen. 25:28).

But this reading is not explicit in the narrative; on the contrary, he is presented as a logical candidate for the heir of Abraham's covenant. In this way, the narrative manages to hold the stick at both ends: the apparently neutral portrait of the brothers allows the narrative to present Isaac's love without making him seem foolish, but beneath the surface, there are repeated hints of Jacob's potential.

At the end of the narrative's description of their birth and childhood, Esau and Jacob both seem to be suitable heirs of Abraham's covenant – complementary forces that will build a new nation together. To employ Claude Lévi-Strauss' discourse about mythology, Esau and Jacob respectively represent wild, unadulterated nature and civilized culture – the raw and the cooked. Virtuous, upright Jacob the shepherd will bring justice and morality to the children of Abraham's covenant, while wild Esau, grounded in reality, connected to nature, will channel God's blessing of earth and abundance, making the nation thrive.[46] The reader will not be sorry if the birthright is claimed by Jacob – it is best if virtuous Jacob sets the tone for the new nation, keeping wild, fierce, groundbreaking Esau in check. Together, Jacob and Esau will produce a powerful, blessed nation – at this point, there is no reason to suspect that the two will part ways. Yet Rebecca knows of a different future – and Rebecca loves Jacob.

SALE OF THE BIRTHRIGHT (25:29–34)

> Ay, better than him I am before knows me. I know
> you are my eldest brother; and, in the gentle

46. It is intriguing that the father loves wild Esau, and the mother loves cultured Jacob. Based on Claude Lévi-Strauss' structuralistic opposition between "nature" and "culture," William Hendricks shows that the father is associated with culture and the mother with nature (Hendricks, "Structural Study"). There is certain logic in ascribing culture to the father, who transmits tradition, and nature to the mother, who gives birth. Here, there is a reversal of these positions, and it is Isaac who goes out to the field and loves his wild son, while Rebecca is the one who lives in Sarah's tent (24:67) and loves her tent-dwelling son.

> condition of blood, you should so know me. The
> courtesy of nations allows you my better, in that
> you are the first-born; but the same tradition
> takes not away my blood, were there twenty brothers
> betwixt us: I have as much of my father in me as
> you; albeit, I confess, your coming before me is
> nearer to his reverence. (Shakespeare, *As You Like It,* Act I,
> Scene I)

After their prenatal struggle to be born first, this scene sees the brothers fighting like teenagers. There is no actual physical struggle, but every word that passes between them is rife with conflict. Moreover, the evaluation of the characters in this scene is particularly complex. On one hand, Jacob is portrayed as a manipulative opportunist who exploits his brother's hunger in order to attain the birthright. In the words of R. Abraham Saba, a fifteenth-century refugee of the Spanish Inquisition:

> It is difficult to defend the virtue and holiness of Jacob. Where is his sympathy; why does he treat his brother so cruelly? It is written, "If your foe is hungry, feed him bread" (Prov. 25:21); it is true all the more so of your own brother of your own flesh! (*Tzror HaMor* on Gen. 25:31)

Indeed, later on in the narrative, Esau will define this scene as a deception: "Is he not rightly named Jacob? Twice he has supplanted me. He took my birthright and now he has taken my blessing!" (27:36). Jacob does deceive Esau and Isaac in order to steal the blessing, but does Esau have the right to begrudge Jacob for their earlier transaction, when he explicitly agreed to forfeit the birthright in exchange for a bowl of stew? It emerges that Esau perceives this as an act of exploitation, a precursor to the theft of the blessing.[47]

47. The connection between the birthright and the blessing is mentioned in Ancient Near Eastern texts, where it seems that the firstborn is endowed with the power to bless and curse. This is implied (indirectly) by the curses appendixed to a vassal contract, threatening those who violate it: "May Marduk – the firstborn son – strike

On the other hand, Esau is portrayed as impulsive and irreverent of his birthright ("Esau disdained his birthright"!). In a moment of hunger, he is prepared to forgo his primogeniture. It is therefore no wonder that over the generations, while some exegetes side with Esau, many others side with Jacob, such as Radak:

> One day Jacob was cooking a stew, and Esau came in exhausted. Jacob's stew appealed to him, and he asked him for some. This story illustrates Jacob's virtue and Esau's rashness and impulsivity, for he was a glutton, while Jacob did not indulge in worldly pleasures, as is evident from the fact that he was cooking lentils, which is the least of dishes. The fact that he only agreed to give some to Esau at the price of his birthright, even though he was his brother, is also proof of his stature and wisdom – that he would not give up what he toiled to prepare for himself to an empty, reckless person who does not cherish the way of life, who in his gluttony was unable to wait until he prepared his own food, so that he craved the lentil stew that appealed to him – of this very situation it is said, "He who bestows gifts upon the rich will only lose" (Prov. 22:16). (Radak on 25:29)

In order to extol Jacob, Radak is forced to paint Esau in the least flattering of colors, as someone "empty and reckless." The midrash even surmises that Esau came home exhausted from all the murders he had committed that day.[48] On the other hand, Victor Hamilton points out that Esau's request contains a polite word of request ("*Let me* gulp down" – *hal'iteni na*), while no such word is found in Jacob's request ("First sell me your birthright"), and concludes that "Jacob is the aggressive one, dictating the terms of the transaction."[49]

---

with irrevocable sin and curse, as your fate" (ANET, 538). In this text, Marduk's primogeniture is linked to his ability to curse.

48. See also Nissan Ararat, who believes that this story reflects the brothers' qualities: Jacob is the naïve innocent man, who provides for guests, while Esau is the sly hunter who disdains the birthright (Ararat, *Truth and Grace*, 103–04).

49. Hamilton, *Genesis II*, 183. To be precise, it is not clear that the word "*na*" functions as a polite request word; it is more likely expresses urgency, "right now!" as Onkelos,

We will attempt to assess the characters' evaluation in the narrative through its analysis, but I first wish to point out a further complication related to the scene's purpose.

The apparent objective of this scene is to show how Jacob obtains Esau's birthright; even though Jacob cannot prevent Esau from being the first to leave their mother's womb, he manages to win the birthright later on. However, how is this transaction of any use to Jacob? Other scenes in the Bible show that the father has the power to choose his own successor, but nowhere else are the sons given the privilege of choosing the "firstborn" among them. Abraham, following divine command, banishes Ishmael from his household, but it is obviously not up to Ishmael and Isaac themselves. Jacob himself will one day choose Judah as the "firstborn" in Reuben's place, and select Ephraim over his brother Menashe, but do the sons themselves ever have any choice in the matter? If Isaac chooses Esau as his successor, then the twins' transaction will be meaningless.

A few scholars have noted a fifteenth-century BCE text discovered in Nuzi with an intriguing parallel to this scene, proposing that it illuminates the significance of Jacob and Esau's agreement as a business transaction. The Nuzi text describes how a man named Tupkitilla sells his birthright (the ownership of a grove) to his brother Kurpazah in exchange for three sheep,[50] illustrating that the financial aspect of a birthright can indeed be passed on from brother to brother.

Yet it is difficult to prove from one text that transferring a birthright was indeed prevalent in the ancient world. Some scholars rightly argue that the Nuzi transaction is no different from any other transaction, and there is little focus on the significance of the actual birthright.[51] While one might propose that Jacob and Esau are only arguing about the firstborn's financial advantages (as Ibn Ezra suggests), this reading is not convincing: there is no mention of any such assets in the scene. While the book of Deuteronomy dictates that the firstborn inherits a

for example, translates: "Let me taste it right now"; other modern translations have "Quick, let me have some of that red stew!" (NIB, NIV).

50. Gordon, "Biblical Customs," 5.

51. Van Seters, *Abraham*, 92–93.

double share, there is no reason to assume that this was the practice during Abraham's time, as Rabbenu Baḥya notes (and this custom was not the norm elsewhere in the Ancient Near East).[52]

It thus seems that the narrative focus is not on the outcome, but rather on Jacob and Esau's characterization in this scene, on the conflict between them, and how they manage this conflict.

The Scene's Structure

This brief episode is arranged in a concentric structure:[53]

A. Once when Jacob was cooking a stew,
- **B.** Esau came in, starving, from the field.
  - **C.** Esau said to Jacob, "Let me gulp down some of that red stuff. I am starved!"
    [That is how he came to be named Edom.]
    - **D.** Jacob said, "First sell me your birthright."
      - **E.** And Esau said, "Look, I am about to die. What use to me is a birthright?"
    - **D'.** But Jacob said, "Swear to me first." So he swore, and sold Jacob his birthright.
  - **C'.** Jacob then gave Esau bread and lentil stew.
- **B'.** He ate, drank, got up, and left.

A'. Thus – Esau disdained his birthright.

The structure itself often reveals much about the narrative process. Putting the structure aside, we will first explore the narrative components.

Esau "comes in, starving (*ayef*)" (B). Some read this as "exhausted,"[54] but the more logical interpretation is that he is "starving," hungry and thirsty. This meaning is clear in other verses, such as "He

52. "It was not the firstborn's privilege then to have twice the share of his father's possessions as later commanded in the Torah, but a privilege of leadership and honor, for he was to take his father's place and rule over the rest of his brothers, and they would honor him as their father" (Rabbenu Baḥya on Gen. 25:31).
53. Compare to Fokkelman, *Genesis*, 95.
54. For example: Wenham, *Genesis II*, 177; Westermann, *Genesis II*, 417; Kiel, *Genesis II*, 230.

said to the people of Sukkot, 'Please, provide loaves of bread for the men following me, for they are starving'" (Judges 8:5); "They served honey and curds from the flock and cheese from the herd for David and his troops to eat, for they thought, 'The troops must have grown hungry, weary, and thirsty in the wilderness'" (II Sam. 17:29).[55]

At the scene's end, Esau eats and drinks – that is, he is no longer "starving," and "he left." This constitutes a solid narrative framework: the scene begins when Esau enters Jacob's tent, starving, and ends when he leaves the tent, sated; that is, it all takes place on Jacob's turf. The story of Cain and Abel, by contrast, a different conflict between a farmer and a shepherd, takes place "in the field," and ends with the wild brother's gory victory. Here, the brothers meet in a more civilized domain – Jacob's tent – as he symbolically tends to his stew by the hearth.

The next two components (C–D) open with two requests: Esau asks to "gulp down some of that red stuff," while Jacob asks for Esau's birthright. The two corresponding components (C'–D') show that both brothers receive what they have asked for: Esau gets the food he craved, and in return, Jacob receives the birthright. Several issues catch the eye: first of all, Esau's use of the verb "let me gulp down" (*hal'iteni*) is unusual – it is, in fact, a *hapax legomenon,* a unique word in the Bible. The Akkadian verb *la'ātu* means "to swallow,"[56] and in rabbinic literature, the root is used to describe how animals are fattened, thereby connoting coarse, bestial "gulping." If this later use can be projected onto earlier texts, then it indeed characterizes Esau as a glutton; as Rashi explains, "I will open my mouth – pour a lot into it, as we learned: one may not force-feed a camel [on the Sabbath] but one may pour food into its mouth" (Rashi on 25:30). Even Esau's description of the stew as "red stuff" creates the impression that he is so ravenous that he doesn't even care what Jacob pours into his mouth.

Esau's plea for food, so desperate that he does not pause to see what Jacob is actually cooking, is followed by a surprising narrative anecdote: that his exclamation gives rise to the name of his future nation.

55. For *ayef* in the sense of "thirsty," see also Deut. 25:18; Jer. 31:24; Ps. 63:2; Prov. 25:25; Job 22:7.
56. CAD, l, p. 6

This is baffling: Why is Esau's rash description of the food so important that his descendants are named for it? Abarbanel proposes that this parenthetical statement does not refer to his future nation, but rather, it explains that Esau called the stew "red stuff" because of the stew's color (that is, it should be translated not "That is how he came to be named Edom" but "That is why he called it 'red stuff'").[57] This is a creative reading indeed, but it is an awkward syntactical fit, and the word אדום is vowelized as "Edom" with a *segol,* not as the color "red" with a *kamatz.*

The Torah may be mocking Esau with this description, intentionally ascribing the name of his future nation to something as trivial as the stew he craved. I have already noted that Edom may be named thus for the red color of its hills, and this scene adds another level of symbolism. Esau is born "red," which is one explanation for his future name, and this scene further reinforces his connection with this color.

What does the color red symbolize in the Bible? In some contexts – life. This is especially striking in the context of the laws of *tzaraat* – biblical skin-blight. The mark of the disease is white, and when the afflicted individual finally returns to life and society, his offering is bound in red – the red blood of the bird is further wrapped up with a scarlet thread. This requires more comprehensive analysis, of course, but in our context, the intensity of the color red reinforces Esau as a vivid, wild character – a ruddy, hairy creature who wolfs down his food like an animal.

The identity of this "red stuff" is only clarified when Jacob serves Esau "bread and lentil stew." Jacob supplements the red stew with bread, somewhat mitigating his initial miserly attitude toward his brother. Now it emerges that Jacob does not refuse out of stinginess, but out of his desire for the birthright, and once the transaction is complete, Jacob feeds his brother generously.

These two elements take on further significance if we adopt Ramban's reading that Esau had no idea what Jacob was cooking and thus

57. "This does not mean that for this reason, Esau is called Edom … but that Esau was so tired that he called the stew 'red stuff'.… Out of sheer exhaustion he did not recognize exactly what it was and he [was too hungry] to ask, but simply referred to it by its appearance: 'red stuff'" (Abarbanel on 25:30).

refers to it by its color: "That red stuff – it was red from the red lentils in it, or perhaps other red ingredients, but Esau did not know what it was and referred to it as 'red stuff'" (Ramban on Gen. 25:30). David Daube takes this a step further, and posits that when Esau ravenously asks for "that red stuff," he assumes that it contains meat. Jacob does not correct him, but uses his brother's desperation to secure his promise of the birthright, so that Esau only discovers that he has sold his birthright for a mess of lentils after he begins to eat.[58] Wenham also adopts this reading:

> And what was it [Jacob] gave? Not a rich meaty stew, that the word "red" back in v. 30 suggested, but only a dish of lentils. With this last-minute revelation we should be stunned. Fancy trading all those treasured rights of inheritance for a mere bowl of lentil soup. We are left to admire Jacob's sharpness and wonder at Esau's folly.[59]

This reading certainly sheds new light on Esau's later complaint: "Is he not rightly named Jacob? Twice he has supplanted me. He took my birthright and now he has taken my blessing!" (27:36). From the carnivorous Esau's perspective, he has certainly been deceived if the hearty meat stew he was expecting turns out to be a dish for vegans.

I am not convinced that this reading is supported within the plot. If Daube's reading was sound, we would expect to hear of Esau's disappointment with his first bite, but the swift sequence of verbs implies that he is satisfied: "He ate, drank, got up, and left." Perhaps the description that Jacob adds "bread" to the deal implies that he supplements the stew with bread and other dishes – "bread" is often a biblical synonym for food in general, or even a whole meal in the Bible (Gen. 18:5; Judges 19:5; and many more) – in which case Jacob does not deceive Esau, but ends up giving him the meat he expects and craves.

Nonetheless, the Ramban and Daube's reading reveals a literary technique employed in this scene: the reader does not know what food Jacob is preparing, so that he or she shares the perspective of Esau, who

58. Daube, *Biblical Law*, 193–95; and see also Von Rad, *Genesis*, 261.

59. Wenham, *Genesis II*, 178.

demands to eat without knowing what he will be served.[60] This is not a negative thing in itself – perhaps the stew's aroma appeals to him, or perhaps he is so hungry that he doesn't care what he eats – but under these specific circumstances, his disinterest becomes significant. How can it be that Esau sacrifices his birthright without even determining what food is bubbling inside Jacob's pot? Rabbenu Baḥya notes the careful order of the information presented in the narrative:

> Jacob then gave Esau bread and lentil stew – Here, the text reveals that what was mentioned earlier – "Jacob was cooking a stew" – is in fact a lentil stew.... This shows Esau's arrogance, pride, and inferiority. The text did not want to specify what kind of food it was before the sale, so that the reader would believe that it was a special, esteemed dish, given that he sold his birthright for it; for this reason, the text only mentions what kind of dish it was after the sale, as if to say: the stew mentioned before, the stew that Esau sold his very birthright for, was none but a measly lentil stew! This is a sign of his wicked qualities, and of his disdain for the birthright. (Rabbenu Baḥya on Gen. 25:34)

Kayyom – First

Before we discuss the central axis of the narrative, I wish to focus on an intriguing expression Jacob repeats to Esau. In both of Jacob's replies to Esau (D–D'), he requests that Esau will perform a certain action "*kayom*." He first asks that Esau sell him the birthright *kayom* and then attempts to ensure his agreement with an oath: "Swear to me *kayom*." How should this word be understood?

Many explain the word in the sense of "right now," such as Radak: "Finish a complete sale *today*"; Ramban: "This very moment"; Rashbam: "Immediately, right now sell me the birthright share of my

60. Gunkel proposes that Esau calls the stew by its color because he does not realize that it is lentil stew, and by "red stuff" he means a stew with bread (according to the Septuagint, it is a stew with a lot of vegetables). In any case, Gunkel also believes that the stew's contents were a surprise for Esau (Gunkel, *Genesis*, 291).

father's estate."[61] Others, however, propose that the biblical meaning can also be "first," before anything else is done.[62] This is generally how the sin of Eli's sons in Samuel is interpreted – they take off a portion of meat for themselves *before* the rest is offered as a sacrifice: "And if the man would say to him, 'Let them *first* (*kayom*) burn off the fat, then take as much as you want,' he would reply, 'No, hand it over at once – if not, I will take it by force'" (I Sam. 2:16). Similarly, before Saul returns home upon learning he is to be king, Samuel tells him to "*first* (*kayom*) stand here and I will let you hear the word of God" (I Sam. 9:27) – first, before he returns home.

If this is indeed the biblical sense of the word, then Jacob's emphasis to Esau is clear: he is seizing the moment and securing Esau's promise *first*, before Esau satisfies his hunger. Esau's agreement does not suffice for Jacob; he insists on Esau's oath *before* he eats.

The Narrative Climax

Surprisingly, it is not the transference of the birthright that forms the central axis of this scene, but rather, Esau's rejection of it: "And Esau said, 'Look, I am about to die. What use to me is a birthright?'" (v. 32). While Jacob and the text itself use a possessive suffix that ascribes the birthright to Esau – "*your* birthright" (v. 31); "*his* birthright" (v. 33) – Esau himself does not refer to it as "*my* birthright," but rather as "*a* birthright" (v. 32). This already hints to his indifference to this privilege.[63]

In light of the narrative design, I wish to return to our two opening questions – to the narrative objective, and the text's complex character evaluation. The scene's central axis implies that the narrative's objective is not to convey that the birthright is transferred from Esau to Jacob. God can choose Jacob even though he is the younger twin, and Isaac can still decide to bless Esau as the head of the family, regardless of what

61. Also: Speiser, *Genesis*, 195; Gunkel, *Genesis*, 292.
62. Rotenberg, "*Kayom*"; Westermann, *Genesis II*, 416. This reading is already suggested by Gesenius (in the later versions of his book – this comment is missing in earlier versions – *Hebräische Grammatik*, Leipzig 1889, 110). He differentiates between "*kehayom*" – right now, and "*Kayom*" – before anything else (Gesenius, *Hebräische Grammatik*, 112).
63. See also Vrolijk, *Jacob's Wealth*, 48.

the brothers decide between themselves. Rather, more than anything else, this scene illustrates Esau's attitude toward the birthright and its accompanying role as the head of the family. Not only is he willing to sacrifice it for mere food, he does not even bother clarifying *what* food Jacob will serve him, thus characterizing him as capricious, rash, and greedy. By contrast, whether the exchange has any practical implications or not, Jacob takes it seriously, and even has Esau swear on the transaction. This contrast subtly sways the reader in Jacob's favor.[64]

Esau's exclamation, "What use to me (*lamma ze li*) is a birthright?" echoes his mother's complaint during her pregnancy, "If this is so, why am I (*lamma ze anokhi*) living?" (25:22). This parallel hints that Esau is unknowingly validating this prophecy (with an oath!); before their birth, Rebecca hears that the elder shall serve the younger, and now the elder is indeed selling his birthright to his younger brother.[65]

The contrast between wild Esau and cultured Jacob has already been evident from birth, and now this characterization is reinforced through their actions. Esau is concerned about basic, short-term needs – food – while Jacob covets the birthright, which has long-reaching implications for his leadership and role in the family. This also follows from the scene's conclusion (A'). As already noted, the scene is framed by Esau's entrance and exit from Jacob's tent, but one last statement, outside the narrative framework, serves as its parting note: "Thus – Esau disdained the birthright" (v. 34). The scene could have ended otherwise: with focus on Jacob's selfish refusal to share his food with his starving brother, or with focus on the birthright exchanging hands – something in the vein of "and the birthright belonged to Jacob and his descendants to this day" (see, for example, I Chr. 5:1–2). Concluding with focus on Esau's attitude toward the birthright proves that the central axis's content

64. Gunkel adds that this disparity between the brothers is also reflected in their occupations. Esau is a hunter, living in the moment, while Jacob, a shepherd, must take the future into account in order to best care for his flock (Gunkel, *Genesis,* 291).

65. Zakovitch believes that the transaction presents Jacob as the rightful owner of the birthright, unlike their birth story (Zakovitch, "Jacob, Deceit," 130). See also Garsiel's reservations about Zakovitch's proposal that this refers to an alternate tradition (Garsiel, "Literary Structure," 67ff.).

is intentional – that the narrative objective is to highlight Esau's disdain toward the birthright.

Yet, as is often the case in biblical narrative, this evaluation is not black and white. Jacob is also subjected to subtle criticism that will be further developed as the cycle continues. Mirroring the final component (A') and its harsh criticism of Esau, the scene opens with an unusual verb: "Jacob was *stewing* a stew (*vayazed Yaakov nazid*)" (29). This verb does not feature elsewhere in the Bible in this sense, and it is semantically jarring – one does not "cake a cake" or "soup a soup."[66] The prophet Elisha, by contrast, "cooks (*uvashel*)" a stew (II Kings 4:38).[67] What is the significance of this unusual verb?

Some exegetes focus on this verb's connotations – the root Y-Z-D usually appears in the sense of "*zadon lev*," to act presumptuously or insolently.[68] The Midrash already notes the connection between the verb's two meanings:

> R. Ḥizkiya taught: [The use of the term *yazid* in this context teaches] that a man can get heated up (*mezid*) and produce sperm, but a minor cannot.... R. Mordekhai said to R. Ashi: From where may it be inferred that this word *mezid* means "heated up"? As it is written: "And Jacob cooked (*vayazed*) a stew." (Sanhedrin 69a)

Even without delving into the Talmud's actual question, for our purposes it suffices that the Sages connect "But if one schemes (*yazid*) against another and kills him by stealth" (Ex. 21:14) with "Jacob was cooking (*vayazed*) a stew."[69] Indeed, based on this verse, some exegetes believe

66. Translator's note: The word stew *is* used as a verb in English, but it is far more common to say "prepare a stew" or "cook a stew," whereas to "stew a stew" is not idiomatic, and sounds odd.
67. See also BDB, "*nazid*," 268.
68. See especially Shapira, "Jacob and Esau," 262–64. Westermann adds that the verb "*vayazed*" is at play with the sound "*tzayid*" which is characteristic of Esau. This connects the two brothers – one "*zad*" (makes stew) at home and one "*tzad*" (hunts) in the field.
69. R. Tzadok HaKohen of Lublin sees the connection between the verses as a lesson that the intentional murderer only does so when his evil inclination is particularly fierce: "When his urge is boiling over" (*Tzidkat HaTzaddik*, 250).

that Jacob intentionally timed his cooking to coincide with Esau's return home – that is, that he was cooking up a scheme, knowing how to exploit his brother's weakness. As the kabbalist R. Mordekhai HaKohen of sixteenth-century Safed writes:

> "Jacob was cooking a stew" – he was cooking up a scheme. Jacob thought: "Esau disdains and scorns everything – if so, for what would he sell me the birthright? Soon he will come in, starving and exhausted and ravenous, but he always brings game and prepares delicious food! I will prepare a different kind of food, something out of the ordinary, something nutritious ... something he will crave to eat, so that he will sell me the birthright for it." (*Siftei Kohen* on Gen. 25:29)

This may be too specific or too far-reaching an accusation to load onto a single verb, but the general direction is convincing: that the verb "ויזד" raises associations of intention, of deliberate manipulation.

This invites a second look at the narrative framework (A–A'). The very first and very last phrase both contain unusual verbs, and together they form a perfectly balanced microcosm of the entire scene:[70]

Jacob	cooked	a stew
Esau	disdained	the birthright

This framework hints to the scene's exchange: Jacob cooks a stew, Esau owns the birthright; Jacob gives Esau the stew in exchange for the birthright. "*Vayivez*," disdained, certainly casts criticism on Esau, but the connotations of "*vayazed*," cooked, suggest that Jacob, too, is not as innocent as the previous verses suggest – he acts with certain intent, scheming and showing no mercy for his starving brother.

70. The verb "*vayivez*" in this form appears once more in the Bible, describing Haman's attitude toward Mordecai and the Jews (Est. 3:6). Given that Haman represents Amalek, who is Esau's grandson, this supports the claim that Haman and Mordecai's relationship is in dialogue with Esau and Jacob's (as stated in Midrash Esther Rabba, 7:10). See further in Shapira, "Esther," 144–50; Grossman, "Dynamic Analogies," 399–403.

Of course, it is problematic to cast such harsh criticism based solely on a word's secondary connotations, but as we will see later on (especially in the story of the mandrakes), the text will refer back to this scene with more explicit criticism against Jacob.

In conclusion, this scene reinforces the narrative's descriptions of the brothers' birth and childhood. Esau's coarse wildness is reflected in his manner and his speech ("let me gulp down" / "that red stuff"). Even more striking, however, is the tension between the hunter roaming in the open field and the domestic figure stirring a pot upon the hearth. One of the fathers of structuralism, anthropologist Claude Lévi-Strauss, believes that certain binary oppositions form the basis of culture, and this is particularly expressed through myth. Universally, myths consist of underlying binary oppositions – of elements that oppose or contradict each other – and these tensions are resolved over the course of the myth. One of the most fundamental binary oppositions that constitute myth is nature-culture. Nature is wild, impulsive, visceral; culture is rational and calculating. Lévi-Strauss explores this tension, in part, through what he refers to as opposition between "the raw and the cooked."

The act of cooking inherently processes wild, unadulterated nature. Cooking unprocessed food is an act of mediation between nature and culture. Wild animals eat their food raw, so that the process of cooking essentially belongs to culture. Lévi-Strauss explores this theme through different kinds of cooking, processing, and preparation, but for our purposes, his initial distinction sufficiently illuminates our scene.

I have already pointed out that the narrative framework highlights Esau's movement from outside to inside and back outside again while Jacob remains inside, cooking.[71] Ever since his birth, Esau has represented wild nature, while Jacob is the quiet dweller of tents. It is inside the tent that culture, Jacob, is able to negotiate with and subdue nature, Esau. When Esau craves "that red stuff," nature is submitting to culture – he is

71. It is interesting that according to Strauss, the more food is processed, the lower its status in society. In his opinion, human society appreciates wildness, and roasted meat – which is only heated with fire – is prized more than stewed meat that is cooked in water (this claim is interesting given the cooking method of the Passover sacrifice). Wildness, too, is vital for the establishment of a nation, but it is better that the birthright is in Jacob's hands.

sacrificing his natural primogenital right in exchange for the products of culture, thus allowing Jacob to dominate. The concept of a birthright is in itself a cultural concept, a social construct that dictates the hierarchy within family and society. Though the reader may shift uncomfortably at Jacob's merciless exploitation of his brother's hunger, it is nonetheless reassuring that the birthright, the family reins, are now in the hands of cultured Jacob rather than wild Esau.

The Story of Isaac (Gen. 26)

> But just wait for their children and grandchildren, if you have time to wait – they bring to light the inner qualities of their grandfathers, the qualities that their grandfathers themselves did not know about. Often it is already the son that betrays his father: the father understands himself better once he has a son.
>
> – Friedrich Nietzsche, *The Gay Science*, Book One, 9

THE PLACEMENT OF CHAPTER 26

What happens after Jacob wins the birthright from Esau? How will this transaction affect Jacob and Esau's relationship and the general family dynamics? What happens next?

Despite the narrative suspense following the brothers' exchange, the natural protagonists – Jacob and Esau – suddenly step down from the stage, and they do not appear at all in the next scene, which focuses not on them but on their father Isaac.

The first step of deciphering the meaning of chapter 26 is to understand its placement. This is the only scene in Genesis in which Isaac is the true protagonist, and essentially, what could have been Isaac's narrative cycle is condensed into this single chapter. As I discuss in the introduction, Abraham's narrative cycle is introduced with the title "These are the *toledot* of Terah"; and then Jacob's narrative cycle is introduced with "These are the *toledot* of Isaac." But there is no narrative cycle for Isaac introduced with the *toledot* of his father Abraham, and the only scene in which Isaac stars appears only *after* Jacob's narrative cycle has already begun. The natural assumption that Isaac intermediates between Abraham and Jacob,[1] and that his story obviously appears between theirs, is not actually true.

Moreover, despite the fact that the twins' birth has already been mentioned, they are entirely absent from the chapter. Isaac presents Rebecca as his sister, and this ploy is not ruined by a pair of twin boys tugging at their hands and calling them Mommy and Daddy. Their absence creates the impression that this chapter (or at the very least, its first scene) is presented out of its chronological sequence: Isaac is not accompanied by his sons; he has not yet received God's blessing, and he has not yet amassed material wealth.[2]

On the other hand, despite the twins' absence, other details in the scene suggest that its placement *is* chronologically accurate: "Isaac reopened the wells that had been dug in the time of his father Abraham, which the Philistines had stopped up after Abraham died, and gave them the same names his father had given them" (26:18). Jacob and Esau are born when Isaac is sixty, which makes Abraham one hundred and sixty at their birth, and he dies fifteen years later. If so, then the story of the wells indeed takes place after Jacob and Esau's birth, and some commentators argue that the entire chapter is in its proper chronological place.[3]

If so, the confusion is great indeed: Jacob and Esau are entirely absent from the chapter, even though they have already been born. It is possible to differentiate between the scenes and propose that all of Isaac's encounters with the Philistines are compiled together – that Rebecca poses as Isaac's sister before the twins are born, while the conflict over the wells takes place many years later. But whether or not this is the case, chapter 26 seems to be the result of a conscious literary decision to focus

1. See, for example, in Boase, "Shadows," 319–20. Like many other modern scholars, she claims that Isaac, like Abraham and Jacob, has an independent narrative cycle (ibid., 334–35). This claim is baseless, and above all it reflects the surprise that Isaac's story is absent.
2. Nicol, *Genesis 26*, 15.
3. For example: Polzin, "Ancestress"; Ronning, "Naming of Isaac," 2; Hamilton, *Genesis II*, 192.

on Isaac and tell his story and his story alone, without his sons – as a narrative independent from what precedes or follows it. This reflects the chapter's fundamental ambivalence – on one hand, it is situated within the Jacob cycle, which undermines Isaac as a protagonist – but on the other, there is no mention whatsoever of Jacob and Esau, so they cannot overshadow him. This complexity has implications for the chapter's narrative objective, as we will clarify below.

Yet why isn't Isaac's story mentioned after the description of his father's death, before the Jacob cycle begins? This arrangement is significant within Genesis' overall structure, and it contributes to how the forefathers are perceived. As I discuss in the introduction, the crisis that takes place in Isaac's family means that Jacob must be chosen anew, while Esau is rejected, and the focus on what befalls Jacob is the result of his re-acceptance into the covenant. By contrast, Isaac is the chosen son of Abraham and Sarah, the undisputed heir of God's covenant. Isaac need not endure any trials and tribulations before he is accepted, before he receives God's blessing. This is underscored by his brief narrative's placement within his sons' narrative cycle – he has no narrative cycle of his own because the blessing granted in his father's narrative cycle is now fulfilled through him. His story is placed among his sons' because he still plays a crucial role as the bestower of his father's blessing, and as the one who sends Jacob to Padan Aram. After all, his own story is shaped by the story of Jacob.

At the same time, this placement makes a significant contribution in itself, and influences the narratives surrounding it. While Isaac's story initially seems out of place in the middle of a fierce fraternal struggle over birthright and blessing, its themes are in fact similar: competition with rivals and the fight to appropriate God's blessing.[4] As some rightly comment, chapter 26 shows how Isaac is indeed blessed by God, so that transmitting this blessing to the next generation becomes fully significant.[5] Moreover, the story of Gerar and how the blessing begins to be fulfilled through Isaac (see below) is certainly informed by the fact that Isaac has already begun to raise a family. In other places where blessings

---

4. Garsiel, "Literary Structure," 72.
5. See various formulations in Fokkelman, *Genesis*, 113–15; Mathews, *Genesis II*, 395–400.

of land and seed are integrated, the blessing of seed comes first. This is salient in Genesis 15, where many believe that the first blessing, the promise that Abraham's descendants will be as countless as the stars (15:1–6), is in fact later than the second blessing, the promise of the land (15:7–21); but that the scenes are reversed because inheriting the land is only possible after a heir has been born, for the sake of continuity.[6]

But beyond all this: the story of Isaac in Gerar, placed just before the story of Jacob's theft of the blessings and his flight to Haran, serves to foreshadow all the events that will soon befall Jacob.

AN "EXILE NARRATIVE"

This is related to understanding the genre of chapter 26 as an "exile narrative." Despite its opening with God's promise of inheritance, the narrative is riddled with conflict: Abimelech banishes Isaac from the land, in sharp contrast with Abimelech's invitation to Abraham: "Abimelech said, 'Here is my land. Live wherever you wish'" (20:15), and Abraham's stay following this invitation: "Abraham stayed on in the land of the Philistines for many days" (21:34). Moreover, the shepherds of Gerar quarrel with Isaac's shepherds over the wells he digs, and he is forced to wander from place to place. This gives the impression that far from God's blessing being fulfilled, the land belongs to the Philistines, and it is difficult to reconcile God's promise to Isaac with his easy concession of the wells his servants dig.

It is therefore no wonder that Ramban puzzles over the conflict over the wells, which he believes reflects badly on Isaac: "Much time is devoted to the incident of the wells, but the straightforward account has neither benefit nor honor for Isaac" (on Gen. 26:20). By contrast, Abarbanel argues that this incident reveals the great blessing bestowed upon Isaac, though he is forced to explain that the wells the shepherds of Gerar fought over ultimately remain in Isaac's hands:

> Isaac left the land – but he did not distance himself from the city… he dwelt there against their will. Moreover, he returned and

6. See a different formulation in Fidler, "Genesis XV." On the relationship between the two halves of Genesis 15 see Grossman, *Abraham*, 95–112.

> dug the wells that Abraham had dug and the Philistines had filled. And in order to maintain more control over them, he called them by the name his father had called them – to indicate that they were not new. Rather, he would open the wells that they had already filled with his own two hands and call them by their names. And they also dug and found a spring of living water...and even though the shepherds of Gerar fought about this well...behold, this well nevertheless stayed with the shepherds of Isaac.... And they also dug another well – and even though they also fought about it, it stayed with him; and he called it Sitnah, to [mark] their hatred (*sina*) toward him. Until, when they dug the third well, they did not fight about it; and he therefore called its name, Rehovot – as Isaac said, "The Lord has widened (*hirḥiv*) and made us fruitful in the land." That is, "Even though they sent me away from them, the Lord widened it for us in this land, against their will." And this is the reason for all of this story – about which Ramban did not find any benefit or honor to Isaac – being written here. Rather, [Ramban] explained it as a metaphor about our holy and glorious Temple. But in my opinion, it does Isaac a great honor, and that is why it is written here. And since Isaac did all of these things with a bold heart – as if he was the master of the land – when he came to Beersheba, the Lord appeared to him. (Abarbanel on Gen. 26)

I believe that the tension between these two opposite readings is already present in the text's *peshat*. God's blessing upon Isaac is clear throughout the chapter. On the one hand, the fact that Isaac's servants are able to find clear, fresh water wherever they dig reveals Isaac's deep, innate connection with the land. On the other hand, these wells are then appropriated by the Philistines (unlike Abarbanel's claim), which implies that the Philistines' power over the land is stronger than Isaac's blessing.

The solution to this ambivalence is related to Isaac's story as an "exile narrative" in which God's blessings are still dormant, hovering over the surface, but still unable to take root. Ramban discusses this in his commentary on God's revelation to Isaac at the beginning of the chapter, which forbids Isaac from traveling to Egypt:

> And in my opinion this is a further hint to the future. For Abraham's exile to Egypt because of famine hinted that his children would be exiled there, while his stay with Abimelech was not an exile because he settled there of his own will. However, Isaac's descent there due to famine hints at an exile, for he was exiled from his place against his will and he went to another land. His own exile was to the Philistine land, the land where his father lived. And it hints at the Babylonian exile, for this is the place of his ancestors, who were from Ur. (Ramban on Gen. 26:1)

Ramban claims that Isaac's journey to Gerar should be read as an exile narrative. While Isaac initially intended to go to Egypt, God commanded him to remain within Canaan's borders – to suffer exile within the land, under Philistine rule.

This illuminates the ambivalent nature of Isaac's sojourn in Gerar. Isaac remains within the boundaries of the land promised to his father, and he does not go down to Egypt. Yet it is no coincidence that in God's revelation to Isaac, the land is twice referred to in the plural: "For I am going to give all these lands to you and your descendants… and I will give them all these lands" (vv. 3–4). The land is always promised to Abraham in singular form; in the words of Wenham, "It is not merely the land of Canaan that is promised [to Isaac], but 'all these lands.'"[7] The use of the plural here creates the sense that the land promised to Isaac extends beyond the boundaries of the land promised until now. While these Philistine areas are technically part of the Promised Land, they are nonetheless on its borders, and Isaac's journey there can be considered, for literary purposes, an "exile narrative."

In other places, too, Gerar's status as part of Canaan is ambiguous. In the description of Canaan's borders in Genesis 10, it is unclear if it is in or out: "The Canaanite borders were from Sidon toward Gerar near Gaza" (10:19). The accepted reading is that Gerar is beyond Gaza, and the border extends toward Gerar but stops at Gaza.[8] While some

7. Wenham, *Genesis II*, 189.
8. Grintz, *Origins of the Generations*, 141–42; Alexander, "Geography," 985. This verse has various implications for understanding the relationship between Gerar and

propose the opposite – that the border extends beyond Gerar and stops at Gaza[9] – it is ultimately unanimous that in this verse, Gaza is defined as the western border. If so, why is Gerar mentioned at all in this verse? It seems that Gerar is inherently liminal in nature – though in some places it is considered part of Abraham's inheritance, it is situated on the border itself.

The narrative design contains elements that reinforce its reading as an "exile narrative," and this has implications for its objective, as I will discuss below. But moreover, in its broader context, this paradigm results in a striking analogy between Isaac in this chapter and Jacob's own exile, as we will explore in context.

With these working assumptions in mind, we will now delve into the chapter, which comprises four scenes:

1. "Isaac went to…Gerar": Isaac sets out for Gerar and God appears to him (vv. 1–5).
2. "Isaac settled in Gerar": Isaac presents Rebecca as his sister (vv. 6–11).
3. "Isaac left and camped in the valley of Gerar and settled there" (vv. 12–22).
4. "From there he went up to Beersheba": Isaac's covenant with Abimelech (vv. 23–33).

The chapter follows Isaac's geographical journey – his descent to Gerar and his eventual return to Beersheba – and it seems that a single thread weaves each stage of his journey together, revealing the chapter's objective.

ISAAC AND ABRAHAM

The description of famine that opens the chapter refers back to the famine of Abraham's time: "Another famine afflicted the land, apart from the earlier famine in Abraham's days" (26:1). As soon as Abraham reaches

---

Gaza. See a summary in Aharoni, "Gerar," 561–62.

9. Cassuto, *From Noah to Abraham*, 145–46.

the Promised Land, before he can even settle down, famine forces him to leave, and Isaac's story begins with the same pattern – a pattern that will continue to mirror his father's story. Isaac, like Abraham, will pretend that his wife is his sister; Isaac, like Abraham, acquires immense wealth; this wealth results in a quarrel between his own shepherds and rival shepherds, which leads him to part ways with his neighbors in Gerar, just as Abraham has to part ways with Lot.[10] This quarrel takes place between the "subjects" of one character and the "subjects" of another.[11] The comparison does not end there: After Isaac finally parts ways with the people of Gerar, God appears to him in Beersheba and he erects an altar after his revelation, just as God's revelation to Abraham in Bethel after he parts ways with Lot moves Abraham to erect an altar.[12]

Essentially, Abraham's spirit hovers over the entire chapter. Both of God's revelations to Isaac refer to him as the son who will fulfill the blessings granted to his father: "...fulfilling the oath I swore to Abraham your father...because Abraham listened to My voice and kept My charge: My commandments, My statutes, and My laws" (26:3–5); "I am the God of your father Abraham. Do not be afraid, for I am with you. I will bless you and multiply your descendants for the sake of Abraham My servant" (v. 24). The significance of this formulation cannot be overstated. The connection between Abraham and Isaac's blessings is not merely literary – the blessings literally state that they focus not on Isaac, but on his father Abraham. In a certain sense, God does not bestow the blessings on Isaac himself (as opposed to Ramban's reading, below) – Isaac only hears about the blessings that Abraham receives from God, blessings which are fulfilled through him as his son.

In one way or another, in fact, all four scenes of chapter 26 also happen to Abraham:

---

10. Compare to Mathews, *Genesis II*, 408. Cotter claims that based on this comparison, Isaac is parallel to Lot, who leaves due to his vast flock, but unlike Lot, who moves to Sodom, Isaac leaves the Philistines and turns to the "right direction" – to Beersheba (Cotter, *Genesis*, 195).
11. Dieckmann, *Segen für Isaak*, 284; Vrolijk, *Jacob's Wealth*, 69.
12. On the connections between this chapter and the entire Abraham cycle (and not just his first journey), see Bin-Nun, *Chapters of the Fathers*, 137–49.

1. Departure to a foreign place due to famine (Gen. 12).
2. The wife is presented to the foreign king as a sister (Gen. 12; 20).
3. The people of Gerar quarrel over wells (Gen. 21).
4. A treaty is formed with Abimelech in Beersheba (Gen. 21).

If so, Isaac does not seem to function as an independent character with his own story. Even in the only chapter where he is the sole protagonist, he is but an echo of his father, filling in the gaps his father left behind.

Yet before we write off Isaac (as he is presented in the text) as a pseudo-protagonist sandwiched between his father and his son, we will first analyze chapter 26 and its various components. This will reveal that although the close parallels with Abraham's story are significant, Isaac is far from a minor character. In a certain sense, one might even venture that Abraham's entire story is none but an introduction to this chapter, where God's promises to Abraham finally start to come true.

Beside the striking similarities between Isaac's journey and his father's, there is one dramatic difference between them: Abraham leaves Canaan and travels down to Egypt, whereas Isaac stops at the border, in Gerar. This difference holds the key to the unique aspects of our chapter and its objective, as we will soon explore.

ISAAC'S JOURNEY TO GERAR (VV. 1–6)

The order in which information is related in a narrative has a powerful influence over how the reader experiences the text and what aspects he or she focuses on. When the plot is presented in chronological order, the information seems "natural," but when certain details are out of sequence, they invite a closer look. This is salient in the opening scene of this chapter. We are first informed that "Isaac went to Abimelech, king of the Philistines, in Gerar" (v. 1), and only afterward do we learn that God forbids him to go down to Egypt: "The Lord had appeared to him: 'Do not go down to Egypt,' He had said. 'Stay in the land I tell you of. Bide in this land and I will be with you and bless you…' So Isaac now settled in Gerar" (vv. 2–6). Why do we learn that God forbids Isaac from traveling to Egypt only after he has settled in Gerar? Various answers have been proposed, but I believe that the simplest reading is one that appreciates the difference between the chronological sequence of events (fabula) and how they are presented in the narrative (syuzhet). Ramban writes similarly:

> It may be that "He had appeared to him" earlier – that before he left his home he was told "Do not go down to Egypt; stay in this land I tell You of" while he was still there, as you must live in this land, the land of Canaan, which includes many peoples and lands, for I now command you that you must never leave it. (Ramban on 26:2)

Ramban explains simply that God appears to Isaac *before* he travels to Gerar. God's command implies that Isaac intended to go to Egypt, but while he is still within the borders of the land, God decrees that he must not leave, and he therefore settles in Gerar.[13] If so, however, why doesn't the text mention Isaac's intentions? If we read the text in sequence, it seems that Isaac intended to go to Gerar in the first place, so that God's revelation to him is superfluous.

The advantage of this order is clear: the reader has no idea that Isaac ever considers leaving the land to go to Egypt. It is so obvious that Isaac must remain in the land that the narrative sequence prevents the reader from even contemplating this option. His intention to go to Egypt can only be inferred from God's revelation, but it is ruled out as soon as it is raised. This pattern will repeat itself in other scenes in this chapter: a certain possibility is simultaneously raised and ruled out, and it is through this that the blessing accompanying Isaac is evident.

The key to understanding why Isaac must not leave the land lies in God's promise, which is connected to God's promise to Abraham:

---

13. Although for the sake of adopting this formula, we must assume that Gerar is on the way to Egypt when coming from Beersheba, which is inconsistent with what we know about the roads leading from Canaan to Egypt. It may be that "Gerar" here refers to a region and not just to a city ("all these lands" – 26:3–4; Isaac plants in fields outside the city, and finds wells under Gerar's jurisdiction), and thus this revelation takes place on the eastern side of this region, and thus Isaac turns west to the city of Gerar itself.

"I am going to give all these lands to you ... fulfilling the oath I swore to Abraham your father" (v. 3). This language troubles Ramban – need God tell Isaac that He will keep His word? Would it ever occur to Isaac that God will fail to keep His word? Rather, Ramban argues that the promise God speaks of is a new promise for Isaac:

> There is no need for God to promise that He will not break the promise made to his father, for God is not a mere wavering human, and Abraham has no other descendant who is part of God's covenant, and the promise is unconditional ... it seems that the statement "I will fulfill the oath" is an oath in itself. And thus when it says in the Torah, "the land I promised to Abraham, Isaac, and Jacob," it refers to this, for there is no other promise to Isaac to be found, besides this one. (Ramban on 26:3)

Given Isaac's characterization, however, it would be more appropriate to argue that Isaac does not receive a new promise from God; instead, God is promising him that He is about to fulfill his father's covenant through him. There is no need for further promises; Abraham has received promise enough for both of them. This revelation is not a new promise in itself, but rather an announcement of its imminent fulfillment.

The blessing Isaac now hears is based on the promise Abraham received following the binding of Isaac. God did not explicitly "swear" to Abraham anywhere else, so when God tells Isaac that He is about to fulfill "the oath I swore to Abraham your father," we must turn to the oath sworn at the end of the binding of Isaac. The similar language that the two scenes share reinforces this connection:

God's Oath at the Binding of Isaac (22:16–18)	God's Revelation to Isaac (26:2–5)
	Bide in this land and I will be with you and bless you, for I am going to give all these lands to you and your descendants,
By My own Self I swear, says the Lord ...	fulfilling the oath I swore to Abraham your father.

God's Oath at the Binding of Isaac (22:16–18)	God's Revelation to Isaac (26:2–5)
I will bless you greatly and make your descendants as many as the stars of the heavens, as the sand on the seashore.	I will make your descendants as many as the stars of the heavens,
Your descendants will possess their enemies' gate	and I will give them all these lands.
and through your descendants will all nations of the earth be blessed,	All the nations of the earth will bless themselves by your descendants,
because you have listened to My voice.	because Abraham listened to My voice and kept My charge: My commandments, My statutes, and My laws.

The opening of Isaac's revelation, "Stay in the land *I tell you of*" (v. 2), also recalls God's instructions to Abraham at the beginning of the scene: "Go to the land of Moriah. There, offer him up as a burnt offering on one of the mountains, the one that *I tell you of*" (22:2). These are the only two appearances of this phrase in the Torah, which hints to an analogy between Isaac's stay in the land and Abraham's journey to Moriah.[14]

The striking similarity between the two revelations reveals that this is not merely a literary parallel – God is actually quoting the promise made to Abraham in His revelation to Isaac. In other words, after the phrase "fulfilling the oath I made to Abraham your father," the reader should insert a colon and read the blessing that follows as a quote of the blessing granted to Abraham.[15] The conclusion leaves no doubt that this is the same promise: "Because [Abraham] listened to My voice."

14. Wenham perceives certain duality in this similarity: on one hand, Isaac is requested to both be like and unlike his father Abraham (*Genesis II*, 189).

15. See also Weisman, *From Jacob to Israel*, 124. This similarity disturbs those selfsame scholars who believe that chapter 26 is an independent work unrelated to the Abraham and Jacob cycles, and they thus explain that this revelation is a later addition (Gunkel, *Genesis*, 294; Baden, "Pattern," 51–52. For a more complicated explanation that these verses contain two later additions, see Boase, "Genesis 26," 326; and compare to Von Rad, *Genesis*, 265–66). Yet instead of changing the data to fit the theory, it is preferable to build a theory that fits the data.

Why does God's oath to Abraham after Isaac's binding feature so prominently in God's revelation to Isaac? One explanation is that Isaac, as the one bound up on the altar as God swore this oath to Abraham, deserves to hear of its imminent fulfillment,[16] but there is a more trivial explanation. God bestows three promises on Abraham (in Haran, Shechem, and Bethel); two covenants (the Covenant Between the Pieces and circumcision); and one final revelation – the oath following Isaac's binding. This sequence implies that God's blessings to Abraham grow more and more binding, culminating in God's oath to Abraham that symbolically binds Him to His word as tightly as Isaac lies bound on the altar.[17] Therefore, the mention of any other promise to Isaac would set back the clock and lose the momentum that builds up over the course of the Abraham cycle. Now the time is ripe for God's final word to Abraham to be fulfilled through Isaac, Abraham's successor. (Moreover, following this logic, we will later deduce that if God makes promises to Jacob that recall His earlier promises to Abraham, this proves that Jacob, unlike Isaac, is rejoining the covenant anew.)

At the same time, comparing the oath made at Isaac's binding with the later revelation to Isaac also reveals differences between the two. The first part of the revelation, before God mentions the oath, has no parallel at Isaac's binding: "Do not go down to Egypt; stay in the land I tell you of. Bide in this land and I will be with you and bless you, for I am going to give all these lands to you and your descendants" (vv. 2–3). The focus of these verses is clearly the "land" and the prohibition to leave it, because Isaac is about to inherit "the land," which is mentioned three times in this brief opening: "Stay in the land I tell you of"; "Bide in this land"; "I am going to give all these lands to you and your descendants." Isaac's connection to the land is clearly different than his father's, for Abraham travels to Egypt, and Isaac must not leave Canaan's borders.

This prohibition, unique to Isaac, is explained in different ways. Rashi's approach is the most famous: "He said to him, 'Do not go down

16. Perhaps Isaac himself has already heard this vow when he was bound, as claimed by Wenham, *Genesis II*, 189. See also Vrolijk, *Jacob's Wealth*, 62–64.

17. See further Grossman, *Abraham*, 324–25; see a variation in Moberly, "Commentary," 320.

to Egypt, for you are considered a whole burnt offering, and it is not fitting for you to leave the land'" (on 26:2). Rashi seems to favor this reading as it emphasizes the sanctity of the land – an issue particularly dear to Rashi's heart.[18] A simpler reading, however, reasonably dictates that Isaac cannot leave the land because the promise is about to be fulfilled;[19] in order for the blessing to be realized, he must stay in the land and settle it. (This logic, too, has implications for the characterization of Jacob: if Jacob leaves the land with God's blessing, this is a sign of discontinuity, of recalibration – that he must begin the journey to covenant and blessing anew.)

At the same time, as mentioned, while Gerar is still considered within Canaan's borders, it is liminal and under foreign rule. Isaac's journey to Gerar prevents him from going down to Egypt, but it still ventures out of the ancestral sphere, allowing the narrative to function as an "exile narrative."

Abarbanel proposes that this opening revelation will accompany the entire chapter and be fulfilled in all three scenes:

1. "I will be with you" – protecting Rebecca from Abimelech.
2. "I will bless you" – Isaac acquires great wealth.
3. "I am going to give all these lands to you and your descendants" – the story of the wells and his departure from Gerar, and how Abimelech went to him to seek his alliance, as if he were the lord of the land.

This is an intriguing, unifying reading that lends the chapter cohesion,[20] although it is challenged by the meaning and significance of the second revelation in Beersheba, as I will discuss below.

The hypothetical possibility and immediate rejection of Isaac's departure from the land is raised once again in the next scene – not in relation to the land, but in relation to his wife Rebecca.

18. See further in Grossman, *Beliefs and Opinions*, 93–112.
19. For example: Mathews, *Genesis II*, 404.
20. Compare to the more complicated formulation of Gunkel, *Genesis*, 294.

"SHE IS MY SISTER" (7–11)

This episode is based on two parallel incidents with Abraham (Gen. 12/20),[21] and in a certain sense, it combines the two: Isaac and Rebecca travel due to famine, similar to chapter 12; and they travel to King Abimelech in Gerar, similar to chapter 20. The text seems to encourage this comparison from the outset: "Another famine afflicted the land, apart from the earlier famine in Abraham's days" (26:1). The reference to the famine in Abraham's time suggests that Isaac, too, intends to go down to Egypt as his father did; the report that Isaac goes to King Abimelech of Gerar recalls Abraham's second "She is my sister" deception.[22]

A comparative reading of the episodes reveals three features unique to our chapter, and all three share a single root:

1. In chapter 12, God strikes Pharaoh with "terrible afflictions," and in chapter 20, God appears to Abimelech and speaks to him, but there is no explicit divine intervention with Isaac and Rebecca.
2. Abraham acquires great wealth in both scenes. In chapter 12, Pharaoh bestows great riches upon Abraham while still under the impression that Sarah is his sister, while Abimelech showers gifts upon Abraham after his deception is revealed (this difference is related to the disparity between the double incidents in the Abraham narrative, which exceeds the scope of this discussion).[23] In this chapter, however, Abimelech does not give Isaac anything

---

21. Westermann proposes that this narrative is an imitation of Genesis 12 and also uses similar motifs to Genesis 20 (Westermann, *Genesis II*, 424); Hamilton writes that it explicitly refers to Genesis 12 and assumes Genesis 20 (Hamilton, *Genesis II*, 191); Aharoni claims that this is a kind of "corrective" of the two earlier chapters (Aharoni, "Three Narratives"). Alexander, by contrast, claims that Genesis 26 is not based on either of these even though they have common motifs (Alexander, "Wife/Sister," 149–51). I believe he is correct, as the stories are significantly different, although they are obviously in dialogue with each other.
22. Hoffmeier proposes that Abraham and Isaac claim that their wives are their sisters in order to effect diplomatic marriages, but this is preposterous as it explicitly contradicts the plot (Hoffmeier, "Wives' Tale").
23. This is explored further in Grossman, *Abraham*, 238–62.

at all – the foreign king is not the source of Isaac's wealth.[24] Isaac, like Abraham, does become wealthy in this scene, but from God's hand, not Abimelech's: "Isaac planted crops in that land, and that year he reaped a hundredfold because the Lord had blessed him" (v. 12).[25]

3. The main difference, and the basis for the first two differences, is that Rebecca is not taken into the palace – rather, she remains with Isaac. Sarah is taken into Pharaoh's palace, and later Abimelech's, and both kings nearly lie with her, but Rebecca is never in such danger. Rather, Isaac and Rebecca manage to live in Gerar without initially revealing their identity as a married couple, so that the plot never reaches the point where God must intervene; and because the king does not take the forefather's wife, he does not bestow gifts in exchange.

These differences color the familiar "She is my sister" trope in shades unique to Isaac and Rebecca's narrative, and with it, shape its own unique objective. Some suggest that Abimelech does not take Rebecca into his palace because the people of Gerar are still affected by the episode with Abraham. As Ramban writes:

> Abimelech, due to his treaty with Abraham, did not touch him or any member of his household, but the local people did make inquiries about his wife and he said, "She is my sister," and even so, neither the king nor any of his men dared touch her, for they recalled the incident with Abraham. (Ramban on 26:1)

---

24. Frolov claims that these wife/sister stories can be categorized as "the magic object is returned to its owner" folklore, wherein the wives are the magic objects returned to their rightful husbands and making their husbands wealthy, but this is preposterous; moreover, Isaac's wealth comes from God, not the king (Frolov, "Folkloric Background").
25. Similarly: Polzin, "Ancestress," 87–89.

Abarbanel writes similarly:

> The local people asked him about his wife, because the incident with Abraham had taught them not to touch a foreign married woman, and they therefore asked him if she was his wife. (Abarbanel on Gen. 26)

The disparity between the narratives, however, can also be inferred from their different literary objectives. When the foreign kings seize Sarah and take her into the palace, the reader is in tormented suspense, and God's promise of seed is under threat: Will Sarah ever be returned to Abraham? What will the foreign king do to her? There is no such suspense when Isaac and Rebecca travel to Gerar – she remains by his side throughout the chapter.[26] Moreover, regardless of actual chronological sequence, the reader has already been told that Jacob and Esau have been born to the couple, so there is no sense of threatened, unfulfilled promise looming over the scene. The question is not whether they will overcome the danger of famine and foreign rule in Gerar, but how.

Now the threads of the plot can be woven together: Isaac does not leave the land when famine comes, and neither is he parted from his wife. He remains in the land and remains with his wife, and the blessings of seed and land are granted without any threat. This is the episode's conceptual basis: Isaac is portrayed as the heir of Abraham, whose blessings are coming to fruition. The promises are not threatened – they have already begun to blossom. Isaac cannot leave the land because the land is blooming with blessing – God is fulfilling the promise made to Abraham, rather than making a new promise to Isaac.

Through the Window

Tentatively, I might suggest that this idea is also conveyed through how Abimelech discovers that Isaac and Rebecca are, in fact, man and wife: "When he had already been there for some time, Abimelech, king of the Philistines, looked down through the window and saw Isaac enjoying himself with his wife Rebecca" (v. 8). Abimelech peers through the

26. Compare to Von Rad, *Genesis*, 266.

window (his own? Isaac and Rebecca's?) and sees Isaac "enjoying himself" with his wife. Rashi believes that Abimelech "saw him lying with her" (as does Rashbam), while others read this as acts of marital affection rather than actual intercourse.[27] Either way, what Abimelech sees proves to him that Isaac and Rebecca are, in fact, a married couple.

The motif of looking through a window appears elsewhere in the Bible:[28] the mother of Sisera gazes through the window, anticipating her son's triumphant return: "Through the window she peered / Sisera's mother wailed through the lattice" (Judges 5:28); Michal, the daughter of Saul, looks down through the window as David dances before the ark: "Michal, Saul's daughter, was watching through the window; when she saw David – the king! – leaping and dancing before the Lord, she felt a rush of contempt for him ... and Michal, Saul's daughter, never had a child – to her dying day" (II Sam. 6:16–23); while Jezebel gazes out through the window in the moments leading up to her death: "When Jezebel heard, she lined her eyes with kohl and dressed her hair and looked out through the window" (II Kings 9:30). These three royal figures all gaze out at the imminent fall of their own royal line; they watch through the window as a new leader displays their triumph. Sisera's mother loses her son in battle, and the Canaanite king loses control of Israel; Michal shows contempt for David, and the narrator reveals that Saul's dynasty will never rise again, not even through Michal, who is married to David; Jezebel watches as a new king rides up to bring a gruesome end to Ahab's royal line.

Of course we should be wary of automatically copying a symbol's meaning to another context – gazing out through a window can have different meanings, especially shattered expectations. Yet there is room to entertain the notion that Abimelech, too, looks through the window to see a different power on the rise, an alternative to his own dynasty.[29] This motif hovers over the characters' heads as a hint to the distant future,

---

27. Abarbanel is firm on this point, as is Gunkel, *Genesis*, 295; Wenham, *Genesis II*, 190; Mathews, *Genesis II*, 406.
28. On this motif, see Abramsky, "Woman in the Window"; Ramon, *Window*.
29. Seeman claims that Abimelech watching through the window is not an indication of any danger or rivalry, given that the gender of the watcher affects the motif (Seeman, "Watcher," 3–7).

where God's promise to Isaac is fulfilled. It is not Abimelech who will rule over this land; God promises Abraham and Isaac that "I am going to give all these lands to you and your descendants" (v. 3).

THE QUARREL OVER THE WELLS

As mentioned, there are two different readings of this scene: Is Isaac portrayed as a blessed figure, in tune with the land, able to tap into its blessing; or a meek, submissive subject of the Philistines? I will argue below that there is merit in both readings.

In order to analyze the unit, we must first determine its beginning and end. Verse 12 marks the end of the previous unit: "Isaac planted crops in that land, and that year he reaped a hundredfold because the Lord had blessed him." The emphasis on "that land," "that year," indicates that the verse relies on the previous context: the same year that there was famine, the same year God instructed him to remain in the land – that same year saw an exceptionally abundant crop. The conclusion, of course, is that "the Lord had blessed him" because he fulfilled the Lord's will by remaining in the land.

As mentioned, this blessing completes the motif of becoming wealthy at the end of the "She is my sister" narrative. Rather than acquiring wealth through gifts from the foreign king, Isaac is blessed by the Lord. This further underscores the contrast between what the foreign kings do to Abraham and what they do to Isaac – or, to be more precise, what they do *not* do. Unlike Pharaoh, who sends Abram and Sarai away from his land, Abimelech allows Isaac and Rebecca to stay, and forbids his people from disturbing them; like the Abimelech of chapter 20, he invites Abraham's son to stay.[30] Although this invitation is temporary, as we will argue below, the reader is able to interpret this invitation within its wider context: God is the one who bids Isaac to "remain in that land," He is the one who blesses him, and this development hints to the beginning of Isaac's ownership of the land. This invites a closer look at how Isaac's departure from that area (26:16) fits in with the chapter's overall structure.

30. Hamilton, *Genesis II*, 200.

On the other hand, verse 12 describes Isaac's economic success, and in this sense serves as an appropriate opening for the next unit, which focuses on precisely that. Indeed, most exegetes consider this the opening verse of the well episode.[31] I believe that verse 12 serves as a bridge from one scene to the next; moreover, given that this scene also presents Isaac's relationship with the people of Gerar, there is no need to draw a stark line between the two units. Both reveal God's blessing on Isaac, with "and God blessed him" serving as a transition between them. Moreover, both scenes describe conflict that erupts between Isaac and the Philistines: in the first, between Isaac and Abimelech himself, and in the second, conflict breaks out between Isaac and "the shepherds of Gerar" – the local Philistines.

This scene has a chiastic structure:

A. God's blessing upon Isaac: "Isaac planted crops in *that land,* and that year he reaped a hundredfold because *the Lord had blessed him.*"

B. Isaac's success, and Philistine resentment: "The man became rich; he prospered more and more until he became very wealthy. He had flocks and herds and a large *retinue* of servants, and the Philistines envied him."

C. Abraham's blocked wells: "The Philistines had stopped up all the wells that his father's servants had dug in the time of his father Abraham, filling them with earth."

D. Order of expulsion: "Abimelech said to Isaac, 'Move away *from us.* You have become much too powerful *for us.*'"

D'. The order is executed: "So Isaac left *there* and camped in the valley of Gerar and settled *there.*

31. As Gunkel, *Genesis,* 295; Hamilton, *Genesis II,* 198; Mathews, *Genesis II,* 407; Vrolijk, *Jacob's Wealth,* 65.

C'. **Abraham's wells are reopened:** "And he reopened the wells that had been dug in the time of his father Abraham, which the Philistines had stopped up after Abraham died, and gave them the same names his father had given them."

B'. **Isaac's success, and Philistine resentment:** "Isaac's *servants* dug in the valley and discovered a well of fresh water, but the shepherds of Gerar quarreled with Isaac's shepherds, claiming that the water was theirs. So he called the well Esek, because they contended with him there. They dug another well, and there was a quarrel about that too; so he called it Sitnah."

A'. **God's blessing upon Isaac:** "He moved on from there and dug another well, and this time they did not quarrel over it; so he named this one Rehovot. 'Now *the Lord has given us space*,' he said, '*and we will flourish in the land*.'"

The scene's framework (A–A') underscores God's blessing upon Isaac, revealing the main objective of this episode. At first, this blessing is manifest in his abundant crop, and later, with his discovery of fresh water.

The image of Isaac's shepherds striking fresh water wherever they dig is a wonderful expression of Isaac's deep connection with the land – the earth yields its secrets to him; and the Philistines see, marvel, and resent this profound connection. In contrast to God's blessing, the envious Philistines twice display animosity toward Isaac (B–B'). In the first half, the text reveals that they "envied him"; in the second half, this envy stirs them to claim the wells as their own. Abraham is evoked in the context of these wells (C–C') – the text mentions the wells dug by Abraham, which were stopped up at one point by the Philistines. In the second half, Isaac digs up the wells that the Philistines filled with earth (according to Rashi; Ramban believes that these are different wells). The parallel between these two components is so striking that many wonder why the two descriptions are separated instead of forming a single sequence. In the heart of the scene, the Philistine king banishes Isaac: "You have become much too powerful for us."

In the second half of the scene, the characters are more active and more verbal. Abraham's blocked-up wells are only mentioned in the first half; in the second half, Isaac digs them up again and gives them the same names his father gave them (v. 18). In the first half, the narrator relates that the Philistines are envious,[32] but they only act upon this envy in the second half of the scene when their shepherds quarrel with Isaac's shepherds, claiming, "The water is ours!" (v. 20). This disparity is especially salient in the narrative framework: at first, the narrator mentions God's blessing in the text, while at the scene's end, it is Isaac himself who recognizes God's blessing and describes it: "Now the Lord has given us space and we will flourish in the land" (v. 22).

The scene's central axis (D–D') is especially striking – not only due to its central position but because of its content: Abimelech orders Isaac to leave his land. This expulsion is doubly surprising. Firstly, after Abimelech invites Abraham to stay, the reader might expect the king to extend the same invitation to his son. This is not only based on the close parallels between the episodes, but on the plot itself: Abimelech and Abraham swear that they will never harm each other's descendants, and Abraham himself accepts his invitation and stays in Gerar "for many days." This treaty, it turns out, does not endure for more than a generation, and his own son is already driven out from the land.

Beyond this political surprise, Isaac's expulsion is unexpected from a spiritual, thematic perspective. The scene's frame emphasizes God's blessing upon Isaac, yet it emerges that this blessing is of no use against the Philistine king: his newfound prosperity gets him thrown out of the very land God promised him! How can the scene's frame be reconciled with its center?

This tension reveals the process Isaac undergoes in this scene. The earthly king casts Isaac out, but the King of kings embraces him – Isaac leaves the shadow of the foreign king, and takes refuge in the shelter of God. The narrative's framework emphasizes that Isaac was never under Abimelech's protection at all – his blessing and success have always come

---

32. Westermann claims that the verse order should be reversed and verse 13 should be read after verse 14, because verse 13 summarizes Isaac's wealth. Thus he understands that it is Isaac's "greatness," mentioned three times in that short verse, that is the cause of the Philistines' envy (Westermann, *Genesis II*, 426). But it may be that the verse order shows that their envy stems not from God's blessing but from his wealth.

directly from God's hand. But the time is not yet ripe for Isaac to settle in Gerar. God accompanies him wherever he goes, and Abraham's blessing is coming to fruition, but Isaac must journey once more and return to Beersheba, the home of his father.

The question of Isaac's inheritance of the land is also related to the intriguing parallel between components C–C', which may illuminate the context of the conflict mentioned here. The mention that the Philistines stopped up Abraham's wells (v. 15) seems out of context – this information is preceded with a description of Isaac's growing wealth: "He had flocks and herds and a large retinue of servants, and the Philistines envied him" (v. 14); and followed by Abimelech's order of expulsion: "Abimelech said to Isaac, 'Move away from us. You have become much too powerful for us'" (v. 16). Verse 16 is apparently the direct continuation of verse 14 – when the Philistines become envious, Abimelech asks Isaac to leave. Why is mention of the stopped-up wells – which presumably happened a long time before – inserted between the description of the Philistines' envy and Isaac's expulsion?[33] It hardly seems likely that this verse features here for the sake of structural symmetry.

In order to understand this insertion, we must first ask why the Philistines blocked up the wells rather than take advantage of these water sources. The quarrel between Isaac and the shepherds of Gerar illustrates that water was a precious commodity in the area, so while it is possible that the Philistines destroyed Abraham's wells in an act of spiteful vandalism,[34] it would still be a reckless waste of resources. Another perspective, perhaps, is to read this scene as a political struggle for possession of territory in Gerar.

This reading is based on the Ramban's interpretation of the scene. Unlike other exegetes, Ramban does not present the Philistines as vandals acting out of spite, but as political players making calculated

33. It is not entirely clear when the Philistines stopped up these wells, but it seems that this happened before the present tension. A discussion of the various possibilities is found in Dieckmann, *Segen für Isaak*, 281–83.

34. As explained, for example, by Hamilton, *Genesis*, 200; this approach is supported by evidence of the way disputes were settled in the Ancient Near East (Shemesh, "Water Sources," 67–68).

decisions. As he writes about Isaac digging out his father's blocked wells (v. 18):

> [Rashi] implies that these are the aforementioned wells that "the Philistines stopped up and filled with earth" (26:15). This is not so, for how could it be that they gave him permission to do so, when they had argued, "They are a hazard for us because of invading armies"? Rather, these are other wells, in a different place, for the name of the place is "the valley of Gerar," or perhaps the wadi continued from Gerar to another area. When the Philistines grew envious – meaning, the officers in the royal city of Gerar – they stopped up the wells he had inherited from his father within the boundaries of the city of Gerar, but the king drove him out of the royal city and he went to another city, which was not necessarily part of his regime, although it was still in Philistine territory. There, there were other wells that Abraham had dug, for he lived there for a long time. Once Abraham had died, but Isaac had not gone to live there, the Philistines of that area stopped them up, but not out of hatred for him. (Ramban on 26:17–18)

Ramban gives voice to the Philistines, and even quotes Rashi, who presents a logical reason for their actions – "They are a hazard for us because of invading armies." He eventually explains that the Philistines of this story did not act out of spite against Isaac, but out of their own interests.

Even if we accept Ramban's general position, the Ḥizkuni's imagined justification for the Philistines is more straightforward: "The Philistines had stopped them up – so that Isaac would not retain control over them and gain power within the region." This is not merely a shepherd's quarrel over resources, but a strategic geopolitical struggle: Isaac digs within the Philistine region and finds water. Who really owns these wells? The area belongs to the people of Gerar, and Isaac finds water in their territory. Is their claim that "the water is ours" justified? Does this precious resource belong to the finder, or to those who control the region?[35] For this reason, perhaps, Isaac concedes so easily; the

35. This might also be a local law (Shemesh, "Water Sources," 103).

Philistines do not know that Isaac's agricultural success in that region is a harbinger of the near future, when he will have control over the entire land. They do not know that they are fighting a losing battle, and for now, they act – as Ramban writes – out of their own political interests.

This reading clarifies why they stopped up the wells that Abraham dug – they are a sign of Abraham's holding in the land. The wells Abraham dug symbolize his agreement with Abimelech (Gen. 21), which dictates that Abraham and his descendants have the legal right to occupy the land. After Abraham's death, the Philistines do not want to uphold this agreement, and they fill his wells with earth. While this act costs them water sources, it restores their political control over the land.

This of course explains why Isaac re-digs these wells and gives "them the same names his father gave them" (v. 18). They are not merely symbols of Abraham's continuity through Isaac; they also serve as actual historical evidence that Isaac is not a newcomer to the region, but heir to the land his father already settled.[36] The fact that Isaac knows exactly where to dig, and gives the wells the same names, shows that this is a continuous, known conflict.[37] Isaac repeats his father's actions, thus displaying his historical right to the land – which belongs to him not only because his father was there before him. In the same way, the people of Kfar Etzion who returned to the site after the Six-Day War did not dream of giving it a new name. The land was purchased by Shmuel Holtzman in the 1930s and named for him: the Yiddish-German word *holz* means "wood" – in Hebrew *etz* – "Etzion." The kibbutz was established in the early 40s, but most of the residents were massacred in the 1948 Independence War, and the entire region fell under Jordanian control. When Israel regained control of the West Bank in 1967, the kibbutz was the first settlement to be reestablished in a triumphant celebration of the people's historical connection with the land.

With this understanding, we can reconsider the context of verse 15. The reader of verse 14 assumes that the Philistines' envy is a local, recent development: "He had flocks and herds and a large retinue of

36. Westermann notes that renaming the wells revivifies them: when they were taken, they lost their names, and now Isaac "revives" them (Westermann, *Genesis II*, 426).
37. See also in Mathews, *Genesis II*, 123.

servants, and the Philistines envied him." Were Isaac's expulsion to have followed immediately after, it would be read as a direct result of their envy. But the reference to Abraham's wells sets this conflict within a wider historical conflict – now the reader can appreciate the Philistines' response not as petty envy at Isaac's prosperity, but as a broader struggle for power over the land. Isaac's motivation is also illuminated: he wants to regain control of these lands as part of his father's inheritance.

This broader historical context also echoes at the beginning of the book of Exodus. Surprising as it sounds, the story of Isaac in Gerar contains certain expressions that are also found in the Egyptian slavery narrative. This is especially salient in the central axis of the narrative: "Move away from us – you have become much too powerful for us" (v. 16). Pharaoh makes similar complaints about Israel: "The Israelite people are many and more powerful than we" (Ex. 1:9).[38]

The plot development is similar: Israel settles in Egypt with the king's blessing, grows and flourishes there, just as Isaac initially stays with the king's blessing and prospers. Just as Pharaoh then feels threatened by their prosperity, Abimelech, too, changes his attitude toward Isaac; and Israel are eventually sent away from Egypt ("After that, he will send you away from here, and when he does, he will drive you out completely" – Ex. 11:1) just as Abimelech expels Isaac ("You hate me; you sent me away from you" – Gen. 26:27).[39] There may even be room to compare Isaac's success: "The man became rich (*gadol*); he prospered more and more until he became very wealthy (*gadal me'od*)" (Gen. 26:13), with the description of Moses in Egypt: "And the man Moses was held in high regard (*gadal me'od*) in the land of Egypt" (Ex. 11:3). In a certain sense, the entire process of the descent to Egypt, as described in a nighttime revelation to Jacob, "And God spoke to Israel in a night vision.... 'I am God, the God of your father. Do not be afraid to go down to Egypt'" (Gen. 46:2–3), recalls Isaac's nighttime revelation in this chapter: "That

38. See also Wenham, *Genesis II*, 191; Hamilton, *Genesis II*, 200–201.
39. On the importance of the word "*shiluaḥ*" in the chapter's final scene, see below.

night the Lord appeared to him and said, 'I am the God of your father Abraham. Do not be afraid, for I am with you'" (26:24).[40]

This literary connection shows that the scene of Isaac in Gerar is loaded with national-historical importance. Though at first glance it seems to be a straightforward local squabble over resources, it is in fact a historical conflict over who controls Gerar, which is currently in Philistine hands, but Isaac and the reader know that it is promised to Abraham's descendants.

This comparison also lends a broader historical meaning to this episode from another angle. As mentioned, the "She is my sister" scene is a striking parallel with Abraham's own descent to Egypt. Many note that Abraham's journey to Egypt, as described in Genesis 12, foreshadows Israel's descent to and exodus from Egypt.[41] It now emerges that the scene of Isaac's conflict over his wells continues this analogy. Isaac, like Abraham, is harassed by the locals and driven away, and he, too, emerges with great wealth. Once again, the story of Isaac's sojourn in Gerar is – in a certain sense – an exile narrative.

If so, the difference between Abraham and Isaac once again rises to the surface: while Abraham's "exodus" takes place in Egypt, Isaac's "exodus" is from Gerar, within Canaan's borders. Now the full significance of God's words to Isaac emerges: "Do not go down to Egypt / Stay in the land I tell you of" (26:2) – the sequence associated with Egypt will befall you here, within the land. Isaac, too, is under God's – not Abimelech's – rule; Isaac, too, comes out with great wealth – but from God's blessing, not from Pharaoh's hand.

Following God's promise of inheritance, Isaac experiences exile and expulsion – as a *result* of God's blessing! This surprising model in

---

40. According to Radak (on Gen. 46:3), the main purpose of the revelation to Jacob when he goes down to Egypt is the reassurance that although Isaac was not allowed to go, Jacob *is* allowed; this is why Jacob makes sacrifices to "his father Isaac's God," and why God appears to him as the "God of your father" (46:1, 3).
41. The Midrash already notes this connection (Genesis Rabba 40:6: "You find that whatever is written with Abraham is also written about his sons"), and Ramban in its wake. See further: Cassuto, *From Noah to Abraham*, 228–30; Pratt, "Pictures"; Wenham, *Genesis II*, 291–92; Ronning, "Isaac's Name," 19: Reich, *Woman*, 36; Grossman, *Abraham*, 58–59.

fact anticipates the process that Israel will undergo: despite God's promise to the forefathers that their children will inherit the land, they must first go down to Egypt; the land will only be theirs several hundred years later. This complex historical process is clarified at the end of the Jacob cycle, and we will discuss it in that context.

Why, then, does God promise Isaac's imminent inheritance of "all these lands," as if the promise is about to be fulfilled, when this is not the case? With some hesitation, I wish to propose that the answer to this question can be found in the oath Abraham swears to Abimelech one generation earlier: "'Now swear to me here before God that you will not deal falsely with me or with my children or grandchildren. Show me and the land where you have lived as a stranger the same kindness I have shown to you.' Abraham said, 'I swear'" (Gen. 21:23–24).

Against his will, Abraham is forced to swear to Abimelech that he will show kindness to him and his people in exchange for the kindness that Abimelech has shown him.[42] At the same time, Abimelech swears that Abraham will forever keep the wells he has dug – a promise that is broken by Isaac's time (26:15), as is emphasized repeatedly when Isaac's wells are appropriated by the people of Gerar. Given that the people of Gerar break the covenant, it is surprising that Isaac is expected to respect it; on the other hand, does Gerar's betrayal justify Isaac's immediate inheritance of "all these lands"? If one side violates the covenant, they can hardly cast any accusations against the other side, but on the other hand, the weight of Abraham's oath still informs this scene, preventing Isaac from inheriting the land immediately.

A surprising echo of this complex issue resonates in Deuteronomy. Moses describes how Israel circumvents the lands of Edom, Moab, and Ammon because these territories were bequeathed to the descendants of Lot and Esau. After describing the history of these cousin-nations' land and whom they conquered it from, Moses suddenly mentions how "the Caftorites, emerging from Caftor, destroyed [the Avites] and settled in their place" (Deut. 2:23). "Caftorites" seems to be an ancient name for

42. On the atmosphere accompanying this vow – that Abraham is obliged to agree to Abimelech's terms – see Bin-Nun, *Chapters of the Fathers*, 100–113; Grossman, *Abraham*, 290–99.

the Philistines.[43] This anecdote seems anomalous within a description of Israel's journey along the eastern side of the Jordan and the nations they did not fight. What does the Philistines' settlement in Gaza have to do with the nations descended from Esau and Lot? Moses' speech seems to imply that the Philistines – who are originally from Caftor (Amos 9:7; Jer. 47:4) – conquered the region of Gerar from the ancient Avites (some of whom remain in the area – see Josh. 13:3), and have some kind of divine right to their land, similar to Esau, who conquered Mount Seir from the Horites; and the Ammonites, who conquered their land from the ancient Rephaim.

The surprising insertion of a southwest nation's conquest within a geographic description that focuses on the eastern side of the Jordan does not seem to be a random, coincidental example of a nation who conquered another nation.[44] History is a series of nations displacing other nations; Israel itself experiences conquest as both conqueror and conquered. Rather, there must be a deeper connection between Israel's prohibition against conquest of the descendants of Esau and Lot and mention of the Philistines' settlement in the territory "as far as Gaza."

Some propose that the Avites are mentioned because they were believed to be giants, like the Rephaim, who are mentioned in the same passage.[45] Yet even this connection seems somewhat technical, and does not justify Moses' mention of the Philistines' conquest of the Avites in his speech. Rather, the relevance of the Caftorim-Philistines can be understood from a different perspective: just as the descendants of Lot and Esau are entitled to their land because they are from Abraham's family,[46] the Philistines are entitled to Gerar because of their association with Abraham. Not because of their genealogy, but because of the

43. The relationship between the Caftorites and the Philistines is complex (see especially Gen. 10:14 on the one hand, and Amos 9:7 on the other). Some claim that the Caftorites reached the Gaza Strip before the Philistines, while others hold that they are a general name for seafaring folk, including the Philistines. See Mazar, "Caftor"; Prignaud, "Caftorim"; Drews, "Canaanites and Philistines."

44. Craigie, *Deuteronomy*, 113.

45. Merrill, *Deuteronomy*, 97.

46. See various formulations in Cassuto, *Genesis and Its Structure*, 312–13; Astour, "Symbolism," 69, 73; Bin-Nun, *Chapters of the Fathers*, 56–64; Grossman, *Abraham*, 76–78.

oath that Abraham swore to their ruler Abimelech. This does justify the Caftorim's mention in Moses' speech: Israel must not invade Seir, Moab, or Ammon because they are of Abraham's family, and Israel must not conquer the Philistines' land (at this stage) because Abraham swore that he would never harm Abimelech or his people in their land.

Isaac's itinerancy in Gerar reflects this ambivalence: God's blessing accompanies him, and he is promised that he will one day inherit these lands, but for now, the shepherds of Gerar have the upper hand, and Abimelech himself drives Isaac out of the land.

All's Well That Ends Well: A False Ending

The first well discovered by Isaac's shepherds – "Esek" – sparks a quarrel between them and the shepherds of Gerar (26:19–20); as does the second well, "Sitnah" (v. 21); but they allow him to use the third well, "Rehovot," without contesting him (v. 22). What causes them to suddenly desist? The reason for their sudden lack of animosity can be found in the description of its excavation: "He moved on from there and dug another well" (v. 22). Isaac's "moving on" is not merely a literary embellishment for variety's sake;[47] his place of residence is the very source of the quarrel. As mentioned, the Philistines believe that "the water is ours" because they rule over Gerar; Isaac's move to another place mollifies them, and Isaac can bless God for broadening his space.[48]

The language of Isaac's blessing is surprising: "Now the Lord has given us space, and we can flourish in the land" (v. 22). "Space" is the meaning of the well's name, "Rehovot," but why does he add "We can flourish (*ufarinu*) in the land"? The verb *parinu*, literally "and we can be fruitful," is usually associated with birth; here, it is associated with the new well. Rather than watering the soil, in this scene Isaac's focus is not farming but shepherding – the rivalry in this scene is between shepherds, not farmers.

47. It is interesting that the same verb appears in Abraham's first journey (12:8), and this verb root does not appear elsewhere in the Torah.
48. "They did not fight over it because he had moved away from their pastures, as is written, 'He moved away from there'" (Rashbam on 26:22. See also Radak there).

Some read this blessing as a reference to the flock: "There is no contention or quarrel, so we can breed and increase our livestock" (Radak on 26:22). While this reading is possible, I believe that Isaac has a specific intention in mind, even if it is less appropriate in context: through this blessing, Isaac alludes to God's promises of fruitfulness and fertility (Gen. 1:22, 28; 8:17; 9:1, 9; 17:20; 28:3). Although less relevant to the actual well, it fits in with the general theme of this scene (which culminates in the discovery of this third well): God's blessing being fulfilled through Isaac.

Isaac's third well and his blessing is a fitting end to the narrative: Isaac leaves the site of contention – all's well that ends well. Suddenly, to the reader's surprise, Isaac continues on his way and arrives in Beersheba; his servants dig a fourth well, and this sparks a whole new scene.[49] This unexpected deviation from the story brings a new revelation for Isaac. God's blessing at the start of the chapter is what set the narrative into motion; now a new revelation marks the end of the first trajectory, and the narrative is launched anew.

While the biblical pattern of three stages followed by a fourth is common, in most cases "the first three are repetitive and do not usually show any change or development from stage to stage, while the fourth sees a sharp turning point which is the climax of the entire literary unit."[50]

In Isaac's story, however, this "sharp turning point" already takes place during the third stage – the shepherds already leave him alone at this point – and thus it is the third well that can be counted as "the climax of the entire literary unit." Isaac digs a fourth well after the story's apparent resolution, so that in retrospect, the third well emerges as a false ending.[51]

The surprise at an unexpected revelation at the chapter's end, and the appearance of a fourth well, is evident in R. Ovadiah Sforno's commentary about the fourth well: "After he was stirred to invoke the Lord's name, Isaac's servants dug a successful well without any contention, and

49. On the literary technique of a "false ending," when a scene seems to end before it actually does, see Simon, *Prophets*, 115–17, and n. 4 there; Grossman, *Text and Subtext*, 210–18.

50. Zakovitch, *Three and Four*, i.

51. The hero's wanderings often follow a three-four pattern (Zakovitch, *Three and Four*, 391–419), and this could have easily been incorporated into this narrative, but as mentioned, the third well is a (false) ending of the quarrel at the well scene.

Abimelech went to him to form a covenant, and no longer sought to harm him" (on 26:26). According to Sforno, Isaac's conflict with the Philistines ceases when Isaac is stirred to invoke the Lord's name (which implies that Isaac is to be blamed for failing to do so until this point). This seems to concur with the reader's expectations that this third well marks the end of Isaac's conflict with Gerar. Yet the story does not actually come to an end: though the shepherds of Gerar do not contest Isaac's right to the third well, and though Isaac blesses God in a classic etymological conclusion,[52] Isaac journeys on to Beersheba and digs a fourth well. If the conflict has already ended, then what purpose does this fourth well serve? What is the relationship between the first three wells and Isaac's blessing, and the fourth well and the new revelation?

BEERSHEBA (24–33)

Isaac's ownership of the third well is not contested, yet he journeys on until he reaches Beersheba.[53] Beersheba seems to be presented as Isaac's home – he only travels to Gerar in order to survive the famine, but once it is over, he returns home.[54] Yet God's second revelation shows that Isaac is still concerned about the Philistines, even after his return to Beersheba. Unlike the first revelation, the second takes place at night: "That night the Lord appeared to him" (v. 24). A nighttime revelation offers reassurance in a time of fear, as God appears to Jacob after he flees from Esau (Gen. 28) and before he goes down to Egypt (Gen. 46). Indeed, God's opening statement to Isaac is: "I am the God of your father Abraham. Do not be afraid, for I am with you" (v. 24). As Rashbam rightly notes, God is obviously telling Isaac not to be afraid because he *is* afraid. Isaac

52. In his commentary on Sforno, R. Yehuda Kuperman comments that although the quarrel ends with the third well, it is not noted that they actually find water in the well that they dig – "It is unclear what the reaction will be when they find water in it" (Kuperman, *Sforno*, vol. 1, 159). But this is a problematic reading: Would Isaac bless God for granting space and fertility if the well did not have any water?
53. Westermann claims that the main role of the quarrels with the Philistines is to explain why Isaac wanders around Philistia (Westermann, *Genesis II*, 426–27).
54. Hamilton proposes that "Beer-lahai-roi" (25:11) is Isaac's permanent home, and it is in Beersheba or next to it (Hamilton, *Genesis II*, 204). He then proposes – correctly – that in this scene, the host and guest switch places; Isaac previously is a "guest" in Abimelech's land, and now Abimelech is a "guest" in Isaac's home (ibid., 205).

still feels threatened after his recent conflict with the Philistines, and God seeks to reassure him that He is with him, and he has no cause for fear.

But if so, then two surprising details of this nighttime revelation demand explanation. First, for some reason, God's words of reassurance to Isaac include a blessing of fertility: "Do not be afraid, for I am with you. I will bless you *and multiply your descendants*" (v. 24). How are the two connected? Second, why does Isaac build an altar and call on the name of the Lord here – "Isaac built an altar there and called on the name of the Lord" (v. 25) – rather than earlier? As mentioned, Sforno's reading contains implied criticism that Isaac should have called on the name of the Lord earlier, but is his criticism justified? It may be that this moment is more suitable a time to build an altar than the first revelation.

This detail, in fact, holds the key to the movement of the entire chapter. Isaac's stay in Gerar ends on a peaceful note, but under foreign rule, in an "exile narrative," Isaac can never truly find peace. Though these lands are promised to Isaac and his descendants, it is a promise for the distant future; for now, Isaac must wander from place to place in Gerar, digging well after well, head bowed, submitting to his antagonists.

God's first revelation to Isaac is directly related to his impending journey to Gerar, as is emphasized through the repetition of the expression "these lands": "I am going to give all *these lands* to you and your descendants … and I will give them all *these lands*" (26:3–4). The context implies that this expression most likely refers to the land of Gerar, which is an entire geographical region. One day these lands will be part of Isaac's inheritance, but for now, harassed by the Philistines, he cannot make his home there. Even Rehovot is not his home turf, and he journeys back to Beersheba, home of his father.

Now, finally, Isaac can build the first (and only) altar in the chapter. It is clear why he builds it in Beersheba, rather than near his previous wells, and why it is here, of all places, that he calls on the name of the Lord. Similarly, Abraham returns to his altar in Bethel after his brief exile in Egypt; and Jacob builds an altar in Shechem after his long stay in Haran. It is in the Promised Land that they call on the Lord's name, in the place where the Divine Spirit rests; only deep within Canaan's borders does Isaac emulate his father by calling on the name of the Lord. God's blessing burgeons within Isaac even in his exile in Gerar, but he builds his altar in the land.

As we will see below, Isaac's journey is parallel to Jacob's. Both are divided into two by two revelations; Isaac's stay in Gerar corresponds to Jacob's exile in Haran, and his return to Beersheba corresponds to Jacob's return and his construction of an altar in Shechem.

In this context, Isaac's pact with Abimelech takes on its full significance. The shepherds of Gerar already leave Isaac in peace when he digs the third well, Rehovot, but they do not form a pact there: Isaac will not have control over that land until the distant future. Beersheba, by contrast, is Isaac's own domain; there he receives Abimelech as a lord receives his subjects, and there he forms a pact with him.

This is clear from a comparison of God's two revelations to Isaac. As mentioned, some question God's complete disregard for His earlier promise that the land would become Isaac's, and His alternate focus on the proliferation of his descendants. Both revelations focus on Abraham's merit more than Isaac himself, but a comparison between them clarifies their differences:[55]

26:3–5	**26:24**
Do not go down to Egypt; stay in the land I tell you of. Bide in this land, fulfilling the oath I swore to Abraham your father.	I am the God of your father Abraham. Do not be afraid,
and I will be with you and bless you, for I am going to give all these lands to you and your descendants.	for I am with you. I will bless you
I will make your descendants as many as the stars of the heavens... because Abraham listened to My voice.	and multiply your descendants for the sake of Abraham My servant.

55. While the first revelation is clearly based on God's promise to Abraham at Isaac's binding, Westermann claims that this revelation is based on God's first revelation to Abraham (12:2; Westermann, *Genesis II*, 428). Dieckmann adds that Abraham's destiny promised in chapter 12 – "All families of the earth will be blessed through you" – is now fulfilled (Dieckmann, "Gen. 26"). If so, then this serves as a framework for the entire Abraham cycle – the first revelation is parallel to Isaac's first revelation, and the last is parallel to Isaac's second revelation. But I am skeptical that this revelation is indeed based specifically on Abraham's first revelation.

I have already noted the two revelations' different atmospheres: the second takes place at night, and God reassures Isaac that he need not fear. God's similar encouragement to Abraham and Jacob also takes place at night: "After these events the word of the Lord came to Abram in a *vision,* saying: '*Do not be afraid,* Abram. I am your Shield. Your reward shall be very great'" (Gen. 15:1);[56] "And God spoke to Israel in a *night vision*.... *Do not be afraid* to go down to Egypt, for there I will make of you a great nation..." (46:2–3).

Isaac's two revelations also differ in content. In the first, as mentioned, Isaac is blessed with the promise that he and his descendants will inherit the land. The second does not mention the land at all – rather, God's blessing will manifest through multiplication of his seed. The fact that the first revelation also mentions Isaac's seed (even though it is not the main focus) means that this pair of revelations cannot simply be perceived as a complementary pair of God's two most fundamental blessings, land and seed. Rather, the second revelation's focus on seed is directly related to the events of this scene: to the pact with Abimelech. This is not merely a symbolic connection that suggests that continuity depends on water and wells as much as it depends on having children;[57] rather, it colors this scene in historic tones that far transcend the narrative present.

ISAAC'S COVENANT WITH ABIMELECH

Isaac's covenant with Abimelech is framed by the discovery of the fourth well. After Isaac builds an altar, "there his servants dug a well" (v. 25), and following Abimelech's departure, Isaac's servants come and inform him about "the well they had dug; they said, 'We have found water'" (v. 32). This seems to refer to the same well mentioned before Abimelech's arrival:

56. On the connection between "vision" and night, see, for example, Gunkel, *Genesis,* 178; Miller, "Dreams."

57. As proposed by Schwantes, "Abrao."

> There his servants dug a well: Isaac did not name it until later, after Abimelech came to him from Gerar and they exchanged oaths – only then did his servants come to tell him about the well they had dug, and only then did he name it "*Sheva*" for the oath (*shevua*) that he and Abimelech exchanged. (Rashbam on 26:25).

The digging of the first three wells follow this sequence:

1. A well is dug (and water is found).
2. A quarrel with Gerar's shepherds ensues (or doesn't).
3. The well is named, based on whether Isaac experiences conflict or peace: Esek, Sitnah, Rehovot.

The same sequence occurs with the fourth well, but the quarrel is replaced with a covenant:

1. "There Isaac's servants dug a well" (v. 25).[58]
2. "Abimelech came to him .... 'Let us make a covenant with you.'" (vv. 26–28).
3. "Isaac's servants came and told him about the well that they had dug; they said, 'We have found water.' He named it Shiva" (vv. 32–33).

The covenant, coupled with the discovery of water, transforms the entire scene into a manifestation of God's blessing: "We have seen clearly that the Lord is with you .... And now – the Lord bless you" (vv. 28–29).

The combination of finding fresh water and a covenant with Abimelech recalls a similar episode one generation earlier, between Abraham and Abimelech. As mentioned, the shadow of their covenant looms over the entire chapter, and its contrast with Isaac's covenant with Abimelech illuminates Isaac's role in this narrative, and within

58. On the use of the unusual *vayikhru* instead of the more common *vayaḥperu* for "dug," see Grossman, *Text and Subtext*, 169–70, where I suggest that this hints to another meaning of this root – "to make a big feast," which hints to the feast Isaac prepares for his guests.

the ancestral narrative cycles in general. A comparison between the father and son's covenants with the foreign king reveals the differences between them:

Abraham and Abimelech (21:22–34)	**Isaac and Abimelech** (26:24–33)
	From there he went up to Beersheba. That night the Lord appeared to him and said, "I am the God of your father Abraham. Do not be afraid, for I am with you. I will bless you and multiply your descendants for the sake of Abraham My servant." Isaac built an altar there and called on the name of the Lord. There he pitched his tent, and there his servants dug a well.
At that time, Abimelech and Phicol, commander of his troops, said to Abraham,	Abimelech came to him from Gerar, with Ahuzat his advisor and Phicol the commander of his troops.
"God is with you in all you do. Now swear to me here before God that you will not deal falsely with me or with my children or grandchildren. Show me and the land where you have lived as a stranger the same kindness I have shown to you." Abraham said, "I swear."	Isaac said to them, "Why have you come to me? You hate me; you sent me away from you." They said, "We have seen clearly that the Lord is with you, so we say: Let there be a pact between you and us. Let us make a covenant with you that you will do us no harm, just as we did not touch you, just as we have done you nothing but good and we sent you on your way in peace. And now – the Lord bless you." Isaac made them a feast, and they ate and drank.
Then Abraham rebuked Abimelech for the well of water that Abimelech's servants had seized.... "Accept these seven lambs from me as testimony that I dug this well."	

Abraham and Abimelech (21:22–34)	**Isaac and Abimelech (26:24–33)**
That is why that place is called Beersheba, because there the two men swore an oath. Thus they made a pact at Beersheba. And then Abimelech and Phicol, commander of his troops, returned to the land of the Philistines.	Early in the morning they rose and exchanged oaths, and Isaac sent them on their way. They parted from him in peace. That day, Isaac's servants came and told him about the well that they had dug; they said, "We have found water." He named it Shiba, which is why the town is called Beersheba to this day.
Abraham planted a tamarisk tree in Beersheba, and there he called on the name of the Lord, the Everlasting God. Abraham stayed on in the land of the Philistines for many days.	

There is no doubt that both scenes are formed from the same components, yet the slight differences between them have acute significance, illuminating the nature of each forefather and their covenant with Abimelech (and the narrative's perception of Beersheba in each scene, accordingly).

The story of Isaac's covenant with Abimelech opens with a divine revelation of encouragement, the construction of an altar, and calling on the name of the Lord. A similar component is mentioned in the Abraham cycle, but only as a *consequence* of his covenant with Abimelech. This already draws a distinction between the characterization of Abraham and that of his son: Isaac only forms a covenant with Abimelech *after* God reassures him that He will be with him; *after* Isaac builds an altar and calls on the name of the Lord.

God's support of Isaac is consistent with another striking difference between the two covenants: the basis of Abimelech's request for a covenant. In both scenes, Abimelech states that God is clearly with the forefather ("God is with you in all you do"/"We have seen clearly that the Lord is with you"),[59] but then he must appeal to each one differ-

59. Rashi comments on the repetition of the root R-A-H "see," in this verse: "*ra'o ra'inu*" – We saw with your father, and we see with you" (on 26:28). As a side note, I will

ently. When he addresses Abraham, he is able to refer to the kindness he showed him, diplomatically mentioning how he allowed him to stay in his land: "Show me and the land where you have lived as a stranger the same kindness I have shown to you." After Abimelech's generous gesture to Abraham, Abraham cannot refuse him, and he immediately agrees: "I swear." When Abimelech appeals to Isaac, however, he has no such leverage – he himself drove Isaac out of his land! – and his only hope is to point out that Isaac left unharmed: "Let us make a covenant with you that you will do us no harm, just as we did not touch you, just as we have done you nothing but good and we sent you on your way in peace." Compared to his generosity to Abraham, Abimelech's insipid claim to Isaac, "We did not touch you," is laughable; moreover, it recalls the edict he issued to the people of Gerar after discovering that Rebecca was in fact Isaac's wife: "Whoever touches this man or his wife will be put to death" (v. 11) – though it promises protection, Gerar's ensuing treatment of Isaac is far from benevolent. Isaac owes nothing to Abimelech, and he does not hesitate to remind him: "Why have you come to me? You hate me; you sent me away from you."[60]

It is no wonder, then, that one generation earlier, Abimelech is the first to speak, and after achieving the desired covenant, he returns home of his own will: "Then Abimelech and Phicol, commander of his troops, returned to the land of the Philistines." By contrast, Isaac opens the dialogue with sharp reproach, and at the end of the scene, he is the one to dismiss Abimelech and company: "Early in the morning they rose and exchanged oaths, and Isaac sent them on their way." The verb "sent" (*vayshaleḥem*) should not be easily dismissed. Abimelech's entire claim for a covenant is based on the fact that he "sent [him] on [his] way in peace," and now it is up to Isaac to decide whether he wishes to reciprocate. Through this verb, Abimelech's arrival in Beersheba is weighed

comment that in the original manuscript, Rashi has "*ra'o ra'inu*" like in Genesis Rabba 64:10; Leviticus Rabba 27:5; Ecclesiastes Rabba 3:19.

60. Burton points out the absence of "*ḥesed*" in the Isaac narrative, which appears twice in the Abraham narrative (20:13; 21:23), as a reflection of the different tones of the narratives (Burton, *Jacob*, 86–93).

against Isaac's stay in Gerar. Abimelech *claims* that he sent Isaac "in peace"; now Isaac *actually* sends Abimelech away "in peace."[61]

The two covenants can also be contrasted through the different explanations each scene provides for the name "Beersheba." Although not strictly an actual border, Beersheba marks the southernmost edge of settlement in Canaan, as is evident from the biblical expression "from Dan to Beersheba,"[62] as well as from God's revelation to Jacob in Beersheba on his way down to Egypt (Gen. 46:1–4), and as such, serves as a fitting site for a covenant with the Gerarite king (just as Jacob's covenant with Laban is formed on Mount Gilead). Yet each scene presents a different explanation for the name "Beersheba."

Abraham's Beersheba is named for his oath (*shevua*) to Abimelech – whether the focus is on the seven (*sheva*) lambs that serve as testimony that the well belongs to Abraham, or the word "oath" itself, the place is named for Abraham's relationship with Abimelech. By contrast, Isaac's Beersheba is named for the well Isaac's servants dig there – the word "*sheva*" seems to be derived from the word "*shefa*," "abundance," or "*sova*," "sated" (as suggested by the translations of Aquila, Symmachus, Vulgate, and Peshitta).[63] In Abraham's story, Beersheba is named for a foreign king, but in Isaac's, the city is renamed for the blessing God bestows upon Isaac – a blessing that takes the form of a well of water. And thus the story of Isaac draws to a close.

Like Father, Like Son

Once again, Isaac's story is an "exile narrative," composed of narrative elements that befall his father, and others that befall his son. This intergenerational pattern illuminates the narrative's placement right before Jacob's flight to Haran, as certain elements in Jacob's narrative are also fulfilled – albeit differently – in Isaac's story in this chapter:

61. On "*shiluaḥ*" as a keyword in the chapter, see Vrolijk, *Jacob's Wealth*, 71–72.
62. See further in Heintz, "*be'er*," 465 (and the references there to Herbert Haag's study).
63. Loewenstamm, "*Be'er Sheva*," 7.

	Isaac's Story	**Jacob's Story**
Opening revelation: blessing of land and seed (Gerar/ the dream of the ladder)	The Lord had appeared to him: "Do not go down to Egypt," He had said. "Stay in the land I tell you of. Bide in this land and *I will be with you* and bless you, for I am going to give all these lands to you and your descendants, fulfilling the oath I swore to Abraham your father. I will make your descendants as many as the stars of the heavens, and I will give them all these lands. All the nations of the earth will bless themselves by your descendants." (26:1–6)	The Lord stood over him there and said, "I am the Lord, the God of Abraham your father, and the God of Isaac. The land on which you lie I will give to you and your descendants. Your descendants shall be like the dust of the earth, and you will spread out to the west, the east, the north, and the south. Through you and your descendants, all the families of the earth will be blessed. *I am with you.* I will protect you wherever you go. (28:10–22)
Exchanging a wife for a sister ("She is my sister" in Gerar/ Rachel is replaced by her sister)	The *local people* inquired after his wife; "She is my sister," he said. He was terrified to say "She is my wife." "*The local people* might kill me for Rebecca," he thought, "she is so beautiful." When he had already been there *for some time*, Abimelech, king of the Philistines, looked down from a window and saw Isaac enjoying himself with his wife Rebecca. Abimelech summoned Isaac. "She is your wife," he said. "Why did you say, 'She is my sister'?" Isaac replied, "I thought I might die because of her." "*What is this you have done to us?*" said Abimelech. "One of the people might have slept with your wife, and you would have brought guilt upon us." (vv. 7–11)	Then Jacob said to Laban, "Give me my wife – *my time is done,* let me come to her." So Laban brought together all *the local people* and made a feast… Then came morning – and it was Leah. Jacob said to Laban, "*What is this you have done to me?* I served you for Rachel, did I not? Why did you deceive me?" (29:1–30, 24)

	Isaac's Story	Jacob's Story
Financial success and foreign envy (The wells in Gerar/ Laban's envy of Jacob)	Isaac planted crops in that land, and that year he reaped a hundredfold because the Lord had blessed him. The man became rich; he prospered more and more until he became very wealthy. He had flocks and herds and a large retinue of servants, and the Philistines envied him. (vv. 12–23)	Thus the man's wealth swelled into a fortune. He had large flocks, female and male servants, camels and donkeys. Jacob heard that Laban's sons were saying, "Jacob has taken everything our father owned; of what belonged to our father, he has made all these riches." And Jacob saw that Laban's manner toward him was not what it had been. (30:25–43)
Revelation upon leaving "exile"	From there he went up to Beersheba. That night the Lord appeared to him and said, "I am the God of your father Abraham. Do not be afraid, for I am with you. I will bless you and multiply your descendants for the sake of Abraham My servant." (vv. 23–24)	The Lord said to Jacob, "Go back to the land of your fathers where you were born; I will be with you." "... And in the dream an angel of God said to me, 'Jacob.' I replied, 'Here I am.' '... I am the God of Bethel, where you anointed a pillar and made a vow to Me. Now – leave this land at once and return to the land where you were born.'" (31:3, 11–13)
Parting covenant with the foreigner (with Abimelech/ Laban)	Isaac built an altar there and called on the name of the Lord. *There he pitched his tent*, and there his servants dug a well. Abimelech came to him from Gerar.... They said, "We have seen clearly that the Lord is with you, so we say: Let there be a pact between you and us. Let us make a covenant with you that you will do us no harm, just as we did not touch you, just as we have done you nothing but good and we sent you on your way in peace. And now – the Lord bless you." (vv. 25–29)	When Laban overtook him, Jacob had *pitched his tent* in the hill country, and Laban and his kinsmen too encamped in the hill country of Gilead. "Come now, let us make a covenant, you and I, and let it be a witness between us." (31:25, 44)

	Isaac's Story	**Jacob's Story**
The parting meal	Isaac made them a feast, and they ate and drank. *Early in the morning* they rose and exchanged oaths, and Isaac sent them on their way. They parted from him in peace. (vv. 30–31)	Jacob offered a sacrifice on the hill and invited his kinsmen to break bread. And they ate and spent the night upon that hill. Laban *rose early the next morning.* He kissed his grandchildren and daughters goodbye and blessed them. Laban then left to return home. (31:30–31)
Naming the place	That day, Isaac's servants came and told him about the well that they had dug; they said, "We have found water." He named it Shiba, which is why the town is called Beersheba to this day. (vv. 32–33)	Jacob continued on his way – and angels of God encountered him. When he saw them, Jacob said, "This is God's own camp," and he named the place Mahanaim. (32:2–3)

These parallels, of course, are partial, not precise; each story follows its own course, with different settings, characters, and conflicts. Yet the fact that such different stories nonetheless share such striking parallels indicates that these parallels are no coincidence. Each narrative can be summarized in four central acts: leaving home and journeying to stay with a foreigner; deception involving the identity of wives and sisters; growing wealth results in threatening envy; a covenant with the foreigner and parting on peaceful terms. God's promise to Isaac, "I will be with you," is the first such promise in the book of Genesis; the second is to Jacob. Both forefathers receive God's promise of protection when a crisis forces them to leave home and begin wandering.

The linguistic connections between these scenes further reinforce the analogy between the plots. Certain expressions merit special attention, such as the phrase "the local people" (*anshei hamakom*) that describes the people of Gerar and Haran alike, and appears in only one other place in the Torah (in the story of Judah and Tamar – Gen. 38:22).

The similarities between the narratives also serve to underscore the differences between father and son. Isaac must not leave the land (for Egypt), while Jacob is encouraged to leave the land, and receives a special promise of protection while he is in Haran; Isaac deceives the local people by claiming that his wife is his sister, while Jacob is the one deceived when Laban replaces his intended wife with her sister; God's blessing upon Isaac is realized through farming, soil, and wells of water, while Jacob makes his fortune from breeding Laban's flock, albeit with God's help. There are further differences, of course, but these examples illustrate the central difference between them: Isaac's blessing is a given and he does not leave the land for its fulfillment, whereas Jacob must struggle to earn his place as Abraham's heir: he is forced to flee his home and suffers deceit at Laban's hand. He must leave the Promised Land to reenact his grandfather's journey, and journey from Haran back to Canaan.

Isaac's experience in Gerar is thus a valuable foil to the story of Jacob's flight to Haran. The comparison between father and son is an obvious tool for understanding biblical narrative,[64] but in this context, the comparison touches upon the very foundations of the narrative sequence and characterization of the three forefathers. Through this comparison, the reader of Jacob's story is invited to recall how similar conflicts are resolved in his father's story, and each time, the disparity results in surprise and disbelief at what Jacob must undergo. Shattered expectations are an inherent part of his narrative cycle: Jacob must write the story anew; he must struggle to earn a place in the covenant that his father effortlessly inherits from his grandfather.

64. Garsiel, *Literary Study*, 18.

Jacob Steals the Blessings (Gen. 27:1–28:9)

The robbed that smiles steals something from the thief.
– Shakespeare, *Othello*, Act I, Scene III

MORE THAN WORDS

The story of the blessings is a major narrative junction that dramatically shapes the entire Jacob cycle – and the ancestral line of the whole nation. For this reason, it is worth noting that the entire scene is completely driven by human initiative, and God plays no part in it. God does not tell Isaac to bless Esau, nor is it God who manipulates Isaac into bestowing the blessing upon Jacob in Esau's place. Rebecca is not acting on God's direct orders, even if her actions are informed by the prophecy she received during her pregnancy. Rather, Rebecca and Jacob are driven by their own understanding and their own decisions, and the significance of the implications their choices have cannot be overstated.

Kent Mathews notes the lack of divine intervention and reads the characters' actions as an extension of God's own hand: "As we often discover in the Old Testament, human responsibility is subsumed under the will of God's plan for the world."[1] Although this is often true of biblical narrative, whether Rebecca and Jacob's scheme is consistent with God's will is a far more complex issue in this scene; on the contrary, I will soon propose that God is not active in this scene because it is not

1. Mathews, *Genesis II*, 417.

clear whether Jacob's appropriation of the blessings is indeed consistent with divine will.

One premise of this narrative is that all the characters believe that Isaac's blessings have tangible significance, and they are considered an actual entity, not merely legal or psychological. The biblical perception of the nature of blessings is a complex issue, one that far exceeds the scope of this discussion. Abarbanel proposes that the term "blessing" is multivalent in itself,[2] which further complicates any discussion of the phenomenon and its meaning. I will note that the prevalent approach in modern scholarship perceives the blessing in this scene as some kind of wish, prayer, or expectation that will be fulfilled, but not more than that;[3] I highly doubt that this is how the blessing is grasped in the text. The narrative premise is that whoever stands before Isaac and receives his blessing will irrevocably become the blessed one, a status that Isaac himself is unable to revoke – no matter what, "he will be blessed" (27:33). A similar approach is found in the story of Balaam (whose blessing shares themes with Isaac's)[4] – words have power and cogency. Should Balaam pronounce a curse upon Israel, Israel will be cursed; should Jacob be the one to stand before Isaac as Isaac pronounces his blessing – even if he means to bless Esau – then Jacob will be blessed.

Ironic Semantics

The chapter is full of unexpected emphasis on family: "his son," "her son," "his father," in various inflections; repeatedly, rather than merely referring to the character by name, it adds the family connection between the speakers: "And Rebecca said to *her son* Jacob, 'I overheard your father

2. "*Berakha* is a common name, said by the blesser and the blessed. For there is blessing from the Creator, blessed be He, to His creations, and there is blessing from His creations to Him…" (Abarbanel on Gen. 27:1–10).
3. See especially two extensive studies devoted to the subject of blessing in Genesis: Westerman, *Genesis II*, 447–48; Mitchell, *BRK*, 99. Both say that the story of Isaac's blessing to Jacob ends in chapter 28. See further in Fretheim, "Blessing," Vrolijk, *Jacob's Wealth*, 97–98 (who sees the verb "*vayiten*" directed to God as a prayer).
4. Westermann, *Genesis II*, 440–41; Grüneberg, *Abraham*, 27–28. Walton comments that the food the sons bring recalls the sacrifices Balaam brought to stir divine inspiration (Walton, *Traveller*, 114).

say to *your brother* Esau'" (v. 6); or: "Jacob said to Rebecca *his mother*, '*My brother* Esau is hairy, but I have smooth skin'" (v. 11).

This key motif serves two functions in the narrative. The first is that this intense emphasis on family connection lends irony to a tale of deceit in which a mother sends her son to fool her husband into bestowing blessings that are intended for his brother. Even if the narrative's assessment of the characters is more complex than the latter description, the repeated emphasis on their family relationships creates disparity between how the characters are behaving and how a loving family should behave.[5]

Additionally, the repetition of "her son," "his son," "his father," and "his mother" makes it all too clear whose son is whose.[6] Isaac only calls Jacob "my son" in the final scene of the narrative, while Esau is largely referred to as "Isaac's son" (with a few exceptions I will discuss below). This division is salient when Rebecca overhears Isaac talking to Esau: "When Isaac was speaking to Esau *his son*, Rebecca was listening" (27:5). This reinforces the uncomfortable notion that Rebecca perceives Esau as Isaac's son more than her own.

FRAMING THE NARRATIVE, FRAMING THE CHARACTERS

More often than not, it is perfectly clear where a story begins and ends. When this is not the case, however, the challenge of delineation sometimes affects the meaning of the story itself, and our story is a a striking example of this.[7]

There is room to debate where the story ends, and whether to follow the Christian division into chapters, which dictates that Isaac sends Jacob to Haran at the beginning of a new scene, rather than at the end of the deception narrative. Far more problematic is the question of where the narrative begins: there are three possible starting points, each resulting in a different reading experience, and more importantly,

5. A similar phenomenon occurs with the repetition of the word "brother" in the story of Cain and Abel (Gen. 4) and the Joseph story (Gen. 37). Compare also to II Samuel 13:20. The repetition of father-son in Genesis 22 can also be understood in the same way (Polak, *Biblical Narrative*, 285–87).
6. Wenham, *Genesis II*, 206; Mathews, *Genesis II*, 428.
7. See further in Grossman, *Text and Subtext*, 201–02.

a different assessment of the characters. The complex circumstances of a son who, at his mother's command, deceives his father and steals a privilege intended for his brother, invite a comprehensive evaluation. On the one hand, the reader knows that Jacob is a more suitable head of the family, and he has already secured the birthright from his brother's grasp, but on the other, it is hard to justify his deception of his blind, elderly father, especially when the father in question has been blessed by God. Though he is following his mother's orders, the situation is still highly problematic: "The lamp of him who curses his father and mother will dim as darkness descends. An inheritance initially obtained in haste will not be blessed in the end" (Prov. 20:20–21). If one gains their inheritance through dishonesty, they will never enjoy it: What of Jacob, who deceives his father to steal his blessing from his brother?

Despite the gravity of this question, the narrative never clarifies who it sides with: "In so dramatic a story, the narrator successfully maintains objectivity and never reveals his stance: Does he condemn or approve of Rebecca and Jacob's deed?"[8] The answer is substantially affected by the seemingly trivial question of where the story begins.

THE ABRIDGED VERSION (27:1)

One's first impulse is to begin the story together with the Christian chapter division: when the elderly Isaac turns to Esau, the firstborn twin (27:1). The main justification for this division is the classic chronological description, "When (*vayhi*) Isaac had grown old" (27:1), which is an appropriate opening phrase for a new unit,[9] given that it creates the impression that some time has passed since the end of the previous scene.[10] Esau's marriage at the end of the previous chapter seems unrelated to the theft of the blessings, and can even be read as a literary

8. Avishur, *Genesis*, 171.
9. Compare, for example, "When (*vayhi*) humans began to multiply on earth, and daughters were born to them" (Gen. 6:1), or "Once (*vayhi*) the king had settled in his palace, and the Lord had granted him repose from all his surrounding enemies" (II Sam. 7:1).
10. See, for example, Schwartz, *Isaac*, 185. There might be an *inclusio* based on this delineation, as the narrative opens with Isaac's eyes (27:1), and ends with mention of Isaac's eyes (28:8), but I find this doubtful.

inclusio with the beginning of chapter 26 – two scenes that present a conflict related to marriage.[11] Moreover, the elderly father addressing his sons before blessing them is a common biblical opening motif (see Abraham's instructions to his servant [Gen. 24]; Jacob's instructions to Joseph [Gen. 47–48]; Joshua's will [Josh. 23]).

From the beginning of chapter 27, which is also a new section in the Masoretic text (*parasha setuma*),[12] the plot is cohesive, and scene follows scene in tight, gripping sequence.

According to this delineation, Esau (as well as Isaac) is portrayed as a tragic figure, cruelly deceived by his mother and brother. While he obediently follows his father's instructions, his brother steals the blessings that his father intends for him. When the story begins with 27:1, there is no hint to his mother's motives other than her special love for Jacob (25:28), and Rebecca and Jacob are thus cast in a harsh light. This negative portrait is reinforced by further narrative elements such as Rebecca and Isaac's lack of communication about who will receive the blessing, and Jacob's only inhibition about deceiving his father stemming from fear of being cursed for it (27:11–12). In contrast to this sly pair, (old!) Isaac and (the elder!) Esau are portrayed as victims of deceit.[13] Esau's classic virtuous reply, "Here I am" (27:1), and his marriage with Ishmael's daughter in an attempt to mollify his father, encourage the reader's sympathy for his pain. Sympathy is also generated by Isaac's reaction upon discovering Jacob's deceit: "Isaac was seized with a violent fit of trembling" (27:33), as well as by Esau's piteous response: "When Esau heard his father's words, he burst into a loud and bitter cry" (v. 34). Their wretched reactions seem to strengthen the bond between father and son, drawing further sympathy and indignation from the reader: while Esau is out hunting out of love and respect for his father, Jacob sneaks in, takes advantage of his father's weakness, and steals what his brother toils to earn. It is difficult to overlook the pain of father and

11. Mathews, *Genesis II*, 414.
12. See further in Emanueli, *Genesis*, 364; Speiser, *Genesis*, 205; Fokkelman, *Genesis*, 98.
13. Zakovitch rightly comments that the narrative takes special pains to preserve Jacob's honor by holding Rebecca accountable (Zakovitch, "Jacob, Deceit," 131). Although for our purposes, I will focus on the "two factions" at home: Isaac/Esau and Rebecca/Jacob.

son, who both openly criticize Jacob for his devious scheme: after Esau begs his father to bless him as well (implying that if this is possible, then the theft is not so severe an offense), Isaac apologetically explains that "your brother came *in deceit* and took your blessing" (27:35).[14] When the story begins with Isaac's instructions to his firstborn son, Isaac and Esau seem to be innocent victims duped by the wily Rebecca and the son she loves best.[15]

Yet though the beginning of chapter 27 is a convincing starting point, the narrative design nonetheless encourages a different reading – one that does not negate the first, but rather sets it within a broader context that invites a more complex assessment of the characters at play.

THE FULL VERSION (26:34)

Beginning the story just two verses earlier has an astonishing effect on the narrative dynamics. A single piece of information draws out a whole new set of coordinates that throw a dramatically different light on the scene and how it is read.[16]

This delineation is easily justified.[17] First of all, this episode also begins with the word "*vayhi*," which shows the passage of time: "When (*vayhi*) Esau was forty years old" (26:34).[18] This is the first reappearance of Isaac's son after the entire chapter has focused solely on Isaac, and it thus marks the beginning of a new chapter, one that moves on to the next generation. More importantly, the information related in this scene is explicitly mentioned later on, when Rebecca uses it as an excuse to send Jacob away: "Rebecca then said to Isaac, 'I loathe my life because

14. Isaac's words have special weight given the word "*mirma*" throughout the Jacob cycle (Frisch, "Moral Evaluation," 279–82).
15. Adar, Genesis, 77. Similarly: Fokkelman, *Genesis*, 100.
16. See especially Menahem Perry's classic article, "Dynamics."
17. Thus Dillmann, *Genesis II*, 210 (this is already salient in his subtitle for this unit: "He Is Blessed by Isaac"); Coats, *Genesis*, 197–206 (he considers Esau's marriages as the narrative framework); Wenham, *Genesis II*, 197–216.
18. Wenham, *Genesis II*, 202. This highlights the similarity between father and son: both Isaac and Esau marry at age forty.

of these Hittite women. If Jacob marries a Hittite woman like them, one of the women of the land, why should I go on living?'" (27:46).[19]

Esau's marriage is not only part of the plot, but it also plays a major role in shaping the narrative's structure. If the story begins in 26:34, then it opens with his marriage to the Hittite girls and concludes with his marriage to Ishmael's daughter, forming a striking *inclusio* that serves as the outer frame of a comprehensive chiastic structure.[20]

A common convention in ancient folklore is that each scene has only two characters at a time.[21] This is not always the case in biblical narrative, but when it does occur, the reader learns of the character's actions and intentions only through their interactions with the other character. This narrative style, "showing" rather than "telling," leaves much beneath the surface. We only learn that Isaac wishes to bless Esau through the instructions he gives him, and so much remains untold. Is Isaac aware of Rebecca's prophecy? Of Esau and Jacob's earlier transaction? We know Jacob's terse response to his mother's instructions, but what else is he feeling? Were the biblical narrator to elucidate as freely as, say, Homer, would we learn of Jacob's inner turmoil at the prospect of deceiving his father? That he is torn between disobeying the parent who loves him most, and showing such blatant disrespect for his own father, the heir of God's blessing?[22]

---

19. The repetition in this verse leads many to conclude that this is dittography, and the Septuagint emends to "If Jacob takes a wife from the daughters of the land, why should I live?"

20. Fokkelman and Fishbein note the narrative's chiastic structure, but their delineation is "abridged" (Fokkelman, *Genesis*, 98; Fishbane, *Text*, 49; see also Ska, *Introduction*, 33–34). Cotter and Samet adopt this structure, but add – I believe, correctly – Esau's marriages before and after (Cotter, *Genesis*, 197; Samet, *Studies III*, 113–33). Smith also adopts the full chiastic structure, and thus reaches the conclusion that Isaac, and not Jacob, is the protagonist (Smith, "Isaac"). This concurs with Sarah Schwartz's theory that this scene is part of the Isaac cycle (Schwartz, *Isaac*). For a different structure, see Sarna, *Genesis*, 190–97; Wenham, *Genesis II*, 202.

21. Olrik, "Folk Narrative," 135, 137.

22. See further in Walton, *Traveller*, 124–25. He claims that consistent with the hidden providence in the cycle, the characters' actions and knowledge are also shrouded in mystery.

Given that this story does follow the convention of just two actors per scene, it is easy to lay out its structure:

A. Esau marries Hittite women (26:34–35).
- **B.** Isaac and Esau: Isaac sends Esau to the field and states his intentions to bless him (27:1–4).
  - **C.** Rebecca and Jacob: Rebecca overhears her husband's intentions and tells Jacob what to do ("Now, my son, listen to me" – 27:5–17).
    - **D.** Isaac and Jacob: Jacob, dressed as Esau, comes to receive the blessing ("I am Esau your firstborn") and is blessed (27:18–29).
    - **D'.** Isaac and Esau: Esau comes to receive the blessing ("I am your son, your firstborn, Esau") and is blessed (27:30–41).
  - **C'.** Rebecca and Jacob: Rebecca overhears Esau's intention to kill Jacob, and tells Jacob what to do ("Now, my son, listen to me" – 27:42–46).
- **B'.** Isaac and Jacob: Isaac sends Jacob to Haran, and blesses him (28:1–5).

A'. Esau marries the daughter of Ishmael (28:6–9).

This chiastic structure underscores two aspects that illuminate the narrative objective. The central axis of such a structure usually highlights the climax (as opposed to modern literature, where the climax is usually postponed to the story's end). The central complication is not a moral question: whether Jacob is prepared to deceive his father and his brother. Rather, the narrative's suspense and its focus is strictly pragmatic: Will Jacob manage to deceive his father and steal the blessing intended for his brother?[23] This is not to say, however, that the moral question is overlooked entirely. Although it is downplayed within the

23. Ori Samet, "For Blessing." Elchanan Samet applies his method of division to this chapter and concludes that the turning point is after Jacob receives the blessing and leaves the tent just before Esau enters (Samet, *Studies III*, 114–15).

narrative structure, it is not dismissed, and we will yet see how the Jacob cycle engages with it.[24]

The second central aspect highlighted by the structure is how Esau's marriages frame Jacob's theft of the blessings. This has a dramatic effect on the reader's mindset, because Esau's marriage with the Hittite women is explicitly denounced in the text. Even if this initial criticism is focalized through Isaac and Rebecca, "These were a source of bitter sorrow (*morat ruaḥ*) to Isaac and Rebecca" (26:35), it nonetheless makes a grave impression on the reader – though the couple are divided in their preference for their sons, they both suffer bitterly from Esau's marriage. Whether the phrase "*morat ruaḥ*" indicates bitterness (Ibn Ezra and most modern scholars)[25] or rebellion and betrayal (Rashi, Rashbam, and Alter),[26] Esau's parents suffer terribly from their daughters-in-law, and this certainly calls Esau's worthiness as recipient of the blessings into question. Reading the story through this lens colors Esau in problematic colors from the outset.[27] Mathews rightly notes that the fact that Esau takes two wives at once (rather than a second wife after the first proves to be barren, for example) is subtly incriminating in itself; it connects him to Lamech, a figure associated with murder and sin.[28]

Portraying Esau in dubious tones does not in itself justify Rebecca and Jacob's actions, but it does suggest that the blessings are better off embraced by Jacob than by Esau and the Hittite women in his hairy embrace. We will now turn to analysis of the story through its scenes and structure.

---

24. Similarly: Walton, *Traveller*, 115–16; in contrast to Fretheim ("Blessing," 284), who claims that the moral question is not raised in the narrative at all.
25. When Naomi returns from Moab with her Moabite daughter-in-law, she urges the women of Bethlehem to refer to her not as Naomi but as "Mara" (Ruth 1:20). Is there any connection between the death of her sons after their marriage to Moabite women and Isaac and Rebecca's misery after Esau's marriage? The Sages explore this in the Midrash (Genesis Rabba 67:1) and even modern scholarship proposes that the threshold scene in Ruth 3 should be read in dialogue with Genesis 27–28 (Jones, "Who Are You, My Daughter?"). Perhaps this, too, can be added as a further link between the narratives.
26. See Alter, *Genesis*, 136. This also seems to be the reading of Pseudo-Jonathan.
27. For example: Sarna, *Genesis*, 397; and many others.
28. Mathews, *Genesis II*, 415.

A. Esau's Marriage with Hittite Women (26:34–35)

Esau marries at the age of forty, just as his father Isaac does (25:2). This hints to the bond between father and son, and that Esau is set to follow in his father's footsteps. Yet the continuation of the verse already challenges these expectations: though their age of marriage is the same, their wives differ in origin – forty-year-old Isaac marries "Rebecca daughter of Bethuel the *Aramean of Padan Aram,* sister of Laban *the Aramean*" (25:20), but forty-year-old Esau marries "Judith daughter of Beeri *the Hittite,* and Basemath daughter of Elon *the Hittite*" (26:34). The double emphasis on their Hittite origin demands attention. Some argue that Esau's marriage highlights the importance of marriage within the family (endogamy, like Isaac) as opposed to marriage with different clans (exogamy, like Esau).[29] I believe, however, that Esau's marriage is presented as problematic because he marries local Canaanite girls instead of daughters of Aram from outside Canaan's borders. Abraham strongly emphasizes this criterion when he sends his servant to find Isaac a wife in distant Aram.[30] Thus, the narrator's statement that these Hittite women are a source of bitter sorrow for Isaac and Rebecca is certainly in dialogue with Isaac's own marriage, hinting that Esau's new wives pose a threat to the family's continuity.

It is no coincidence that the narrative is framed with Esau's marriage. While it also plays a part in the plot itself – when Rebecca mentions the Hittite wives to Isaac as a pretext for sending Jacob out of harm's way (27:46) – the fact that it frames the entire narrative indicates that its contribution likely exceeds one specific purpose in the plot.

This opening detail has a dramatic effect on the text's character assessment. Perhaps Meyer's statement that these marriages cost Esau

---

29. Cotter, *Genesis,* 199.
30. This is a debate among *Rishonim,* but I believe that the above theory is the most straightforward. See Grossman, *Abraham,* 358–359. In any case, Esau's wives' names invite special attention, given that they are Jewish names – Judith, Beeri, Basmat, and Elon are Hebraic names: "Judith" (Yehudit) means the Hebrew language, spoken by the people of Judah; "Beeri" is the name of the prophet Hosea's father; "Basmat" is the name of Solomon's daughter (I Kings 4:15); "Elon" is a judge from the tribe of Zebulun (Judges 12:11) and a place in Israel (e.g., Josh. 10:12). Yet in this scene, they represent Hittite culture.

the privilege of continuing Abraham's line is an exaggeration,[31] but it certainly casts doubt on whether Esau is the appropriate recipient of the blessings. Yet even so, I believe that the main purpose of framing the narrative with Esau's marriage lies elsewhere. The narrative frame reveals that the issue of marriage is one of the central issues in the narrative. Following his deception, Jacob journeys to Padan Aram to find a wife from his mother's side, at his father's request. In contrast to Jacob, Esau's marriages are with local women: first with Hittite women who make his parents miserable, and finally with Ishmael's daughter, from his father's family. The narrative's framework establishes that marriage and continuity is one of its central themes.

B. Isaac and Esau (27:1–4)

The narrative exposition mentions that Isaac is blind, which hints that this detail will be relevant later on.[32] At this point in the story, the reader cannot imagine that Isaac's son will exploit his father's blindness and deceive him, but if it is noted at the beginning, it will certainly play a part later. The text explains that this blindness is the result of Isaac's old age: "When Isaac had grown old, when his eyes had grown so dim that he could not see" (v. 1).[33] Rashi is not satisfied with this explanation: "Grown dim – with their smoke.[34] Another explanation: to allow Jacob to take the blessings" (Rashi on 27:1, Leipzig manuscript).

Rashi is presumably disturbed by the fact that Isaac's body betrays him in his old age as if he were any old man, rather than an archetypal patriarch. After all, Abraham does not seem to suffer from any such afflictions: "Abraham breathed his last and died in his ripe old age, aged and

---

31. Meyer, *Die Israeliten*, 353. Note that Genesis 36 connects Esau's marriage with Hittites/Hivites and his move to Seir – see my discussion in context.
32. Compare to Gunkel, *Genesis*, 302.
33. Thus Rashbam's commentary seems superfluous at first glance: "from old age." But he is presumably challenging Rashi's reading. See also Wenham, *Genesis II*, 205.
34. Other editions of Rashi have "From their smoke, for they would offer incense and sacrifice to idols." A different edition presents a second option: "Another possibility: When he was upon the altar and his father was about to sacrifice him, at that moment the heavens opened and they saw angels weeping, and their tears fell down into his eyes and that is why they grew dim."

satisfied" (25:8); and as for Moses: "Moses was a hundred and twenty years old when he died; his eyes had not grown dim, nor his vitality fled" (Deut. 34:7). Why is Isaac denied the same divine protection? Why do his eyes grow dim?[35] Rashi's second answer is that the exposition sets the scene for the action about to unfold; were Isaac not blind, Jacob's deception would not have been possible (compare this to the description of David's old age: "Though they covered him with bedclothes, he never felt warm" – I Kings 1, which leads to Abishag's arrival at the palace).

It is interesting to consider Rashi's two different explanations in the context of the narrative boundaries. His first explanation looks at the previous verse: it perceives Isaac's blindness as the result of Esau's marriage and the noxious smoke of his wives' idolatry; while his second explanation presents his blindness as a detail that anticipates what is to come, looking forward rather than backward.

If Isaac's blindness is read in conjunction with Esau's wives, it takes on further meaning. Blindness plays an important technical role in the story – it allows Jacob to deceive him – but it also has symbolic meaning: the character is blind to what is happening around him.[36] Though Esau's wives make his life miserable, Isaac nonetheless decides to bless his son! As Abarbanel comments, "Love is blind ... perhaps this is the meaning of 'his eyes grew dim': that he is blind to anything to do with Esau, and he did not perceive the truth, nor properly his actions." His physical blindness can be read as symbolic obliviousness: "In many places in the Bible, blindness serves as a metaphor for lack of moral distinction. One of the most famous examples is 'bribes blind the sighted' (Ex. 23:8). No wonder, then, if a description of a father's actual blindness also hints, on a metaphorical level, to his faulty moral judgment."[37]

This is not the only example of a father's blindness to his son's faults. In the book of Samuel, the priest Eli also fails to deal with his

---

35. Commentators also attempt to explain Jacob's blindness in old age (and do not accept old age as a good enough reason). For example, R. Jacob son of Asher, Baal HaTurim, writes: "Just as Jacob deceived his father when his eyes grew dim, his sons did the same to him when he blessed them, and switched Ephraim and Menashe" (on 48:10).
36. See also Mathews, *Genesis II*, 417; Boase, "Shadows," 321.
37. Samet, *Studies I*, vol. 1, 64. This direction can be found in Genesis Rabba 65:5.

sons' depravity, and he, too, becomes blind in old age: "On that fateful day, Eli was lying in his usual place. His eyes had begun to grow dim, and he could no longer see. The lamp of God had not yet gone out, and Samuel was lying in the Lord's Sanctuary where the Ark of God was" (I Sam. 3:2–3).[38] God speaks not to Eli, who is lying in his "usual place," but to Samuel. At first, Samuel is blind to who is calling him, and it is none but blind Eli who opens Samuel's eyes to the speaker's identity. Eli's eyes have begun to "dim" (*kehot*), and this is clearly related to the fact that "his sons have been blasphemous, but he failed to rebuke (*khiha*) them" (I Sam. 3:13).[39] Eli's lack of vision serves little purpose in the plot, but it has acute symbolic significance.[40]

While Isaac is presented as blind, he is nonetheless characterized as the powerful agent of blessing. Though his world is dark and dim, he stretches out his hand to his beloved son and sends him out into the field so that he may establish their love forever.

The first dialogue in the story takes place between Isaac and Esau, and their mutual love and understanding is clear: Isaac asks Esau to bring him "delicious food, prepared in the way that I love" (27:4). Esau already knows what his father loves best; one of the first things the reader learns about their relationship is that Isaac "ate of his game" (25:28). Isaac's love for his favorite dish is mentioned twice more in the scene: by Rebecca (27:9) and in the narrator's description of its preparation (v. 14), and it is clear why Rebecca and Jacob are so careful to prepare the food just "the way he loves." The fact that Esau knows how to prepare his father's food just to his liking reveals much about their family dynamics. How a person likes their meat spiced, salted, smoked, seared, roasted – all these preferences are deeply personal, and Isaac's casual instructions to his son implies that he is the one who usually caters to his father's needs. I imagine that some readers might claim that a father-son bond based

38. On the common threads between the narratives, see Hepner, *Legal Friction*, 363–67.

39. See further on the wordplay in the story of Eli's sons in Garsiel, *Literary Study*, 61–65; Jacobs, *Measure*, 162–64.

40. Sylva claims that the blindness in the scene is symbolic – specifically, Isaac's blindness toward his sons' actions (Sylva, "Blessing," 282). I do not think such a harsh attitude toward Isaac is justified in the text.

on love for meat is superficial and nothing to be proud of,[41] but feeding and nurturing are acts of intimacy that offer a glimpse into their everyday lives and their filial affection. Food is obviously important to Isaac and his son, who, of course, sells his very birthright for a bowl of stew.

Isaac also seems to relish the very act of Esau's hunting: "So now, take your weapons, your quiver and bow, and go out into the field and hunt me some game" (27:2). Surely Esau knows that he needs to take his weapons along with him! Elchanan Meir proposes that Isaac elucidates each detail so that in his "obedience," Esau will be as worthy of the blessings as possible.[42] This reading is possible, but a more authentic perspective is that Isaac loves the field, and therefore describes it in loving detail out of sheer love and admiration for Esau's hunting. Isaac himself is a man of the field; now that he is old and sightless, he lives vicariously through his son. He savors the thought of Esau taking up bow and arrow and running through the fields he once traversed, and indulges himself by adding superfluous details in his instructions.[43]

Esau's reply also hints to their closeness, though it is but a single word: "My son," he said; he replied, "Here I am" (v. 1). Their brief, rapid exchange – "My son," "Here I am" – conveys instant, utter obedience. In the same way, Jacob responds to the angel who calls him in Haran (31:11), and to God Himself when He appears to him in Beersheba (46:2); as does Joseph to his father (37:13), and many other obedient others.

But above all, it is impossible to dismiss the most striking allusion of all: "He said to him, 'Abraham,' and he said, 'Here I am'" (Gen. 22:1). The similar opening between this scene and the binding of Isaac opens a series of analogies between the two narratives:

41. "The reader's heart becomes enraged at the father's intention to dictate the future – both of his sons and of the nations that will grow from them – all for the taste of game" (Zakovitch, *Jacob*, 35.)
42. Meir, *Genesis*, 52.
43. See a similar example in Naomi's words to her daughters-in-law when she talks of the futile non-hope of bearing any more sons for them (Ruth 1:12). See further in Grossman, *Ruth*, 95–101.

The Binding of Isaac (Gen. 22)	**The Theft of the Blessings (Gen. 27)**
(1) After these things, God tested Abraham. "Abraham!" He said. Abraham replied, "Here I am."	(1) When Isaac had grown old, when his eyes had grown so dim that he could not see, he summoned his elder son Esau. "My son," he said. Esau replied, "Here I am."
(2) Then God said, "Take your son, your only one, the one whom you love – Isaac – and go to the land of Moriah. There, offer him up as a burnt offering."	(3) "So now, take your weapons, your quiver and bow, and go out into the field and hunt me some game."
(3) He set out toward the place of which God had told him.	(5) Esau went out into the field to hunt game to bring back.
(7) Then Isaac said to his father, Abraham, "Father?" he said. He said, "Here I am, my son."	(18) He went in to his father; "Father?" he said. He said, "Here I am. Who are you, my son?"
He said, "Here is the fire and the wood, but where is the lamb for the burnt offering?" He replied, "God will see to a lamb for an offering, my son."	Isaac asked his son, "How did you find it so quickly, my son?" He replied, "The Lord your God brought it about for me."

My claim is not that the two stories are connected by a strong analogy; rather, that the subtle intertextuality generates a dialogue between them. When Esau answers "Here I am," he is likened to Abraham before his God at the binding, a faithful son who obeys his father without question. Isaac does not only love Esau because he hunts for him, but because of his deep, unwavering respect for his father. This parallel lingers throughout the story: just as Abraham answers "Here I am" later on, in our chapter Isaac also responds "Here I am" to Jacob dressed as Isaac. This similarity is especially striking, because in both cases, it is the father who responds thus to his son.

A comparison of the double "Here I am" in each narrative also exposes the unique tension in our chapter: "'Father?' he said. He said, 'Here I am, my son'" (22:7)/"'Father?' he said. He said, 'Here I am. *Who are you,* my son?'" (27:8). Isaac does not only respond, "Here I am," but adds, "Who are you, my son?" This slight difference shows that on one hand, the father is utterly devoted to his son ("Here I am"), but on the other, he is not certain of his identity ("Who are you?").

There is also certain similarity between the ensuing dialogue between father and son in each scene: one withholds the truth from the other, achieving deception through focus on God's providence. Abraham reassures his son that "God will see to a lamb for an offering," while Jacob claims that he has managed to return so quickly because "the Lord your God brought it about for me." In the earlier scene, the father deceives the son, hiding the fact that he is supposed to be the sacrifice; in the later scene, the son hides his identity from the father in order to obtain the blessings. From a different perspective, however, what is most striking is that as both father and son,[44] it is always Isaac who is the object of the other's deception, the one whose eyes are always blind to the truth.[45]

Reading the theft of the blessings in light of Isaac's binding first and foremost likens the love between Isaac and Esau to Abraham's love for Isaac.[46] God Himself testifies to Abraham's love for his son: "Take your son, your only one, the one whom you love – Isaac" (22:2), and the subtle link between the narratives shows that Isaac has a similar relationship with Esau.

But the significance of this parallel can be taken a step further: it implies that the theft of the blessings is also the story of a father's sacrifice of his son. Below, when the heartbroken Esau begs his father to bless him as well, I will discuss how this chapter is an irreparable tragedy for Isaac's relationship with his beloved Esau. Unwittingly, unseeingly, with his own two hands, Isaac severs the umbilical cord between him and

44. Sylva claims that the binding affected Isaac's personality, and that this is expressed in this scene (Sylva, "Blessing," 283–86).
45. Walton argues that at the beginning and end of his life, he does not control his own circumstances, and is controlled by others (Walton, *Traveller*, 116). It is interesting to note that in a sense, both scenes continue similarly: at the end of the binding scene, Abraham hears of the birth of Nahor's children and his granddaughter Rebecca, which leads to Isaac's marriage, and at the end of the blessings scene, Jacob is sent to Padan Aram to marry Nahor's great-granddaughter.
46. See also Westermann, *Genesis II*, 437.

the son he loves. At the last moment, Isaac is replaced with a ram – but Esau is replaced with Jacob.

Alongside Isaac's deep closeness with Esau, the narrator's language reflects the subtle yet complex ambivalence regarding Esau's status: "He summoned his *elder* son Esau" (v. 1). Throughout the chapter, the narrator refers to Esau not as the "firstborn" but as the "elder" son (vv. 1, 15, 42), although the characters themselves refer to Esau as the "firstborn" (Esau himself – v. 19 – and Jacob pretending to be Esau – v. 32). This implies that from an objective stance, Esau is no longer the firstborn – he sold his birthright to Jacob. Although he is the "elder son," he is no longer the "firstborn."[47]

The Nature of Isaac's Blessings

What is the nature of the blessings Isaac intends to bestow upon Esau? The answer to this critical question affects the meaning of the narrative. Isaac's vague statement to Esau, "So that my soul may bless you before I die" (27:4), can be read in different ways. Exegetes argue about the meaning of this phrase, and I will present the two main readings below.

Ramban believes that Isaac is clearly referring to Abraham's blessing of land and seed – the blessing of God's covenant:

> "That my soul may bless you" – he intended to bless him with Abraham's blessing that he will inherit the land, and that he would be the bearer of the covenant with God because he was the firstborn. (Ramban on Gen. 27:4)

According to this reading, much hangs in the balance. If Esau indeed receives Isaac's blessing then he will uphold Abraham's covenant with God, while Jacob – as the Ramban's reading implies – will be excluded. Isaac's intentions are the opposite of the prophecy Rebecca received

47. Compare to Shapira, "Jacob and Esau," 260–61. Fokkelman proposes that the word "firstborn" is downplayed in the story because its focus is on the blessings, not the birthright (Fokkelman, *Genesis*, 106–7).

during pregnancy,[48] and without Rebecca and Jacob's interference, Esau would have been the head of Abraham's line and the one to perpetuate his covenant.[49]

Radak offers a completely different reading. In his opinion, Isaac clearly believes that Jacob should be the heir of Abraham's covenant, and the blessing he plans to bestow upon Esau is of a material nature:

> Therefore Isaac asked his son Esau to bring him some game so that he would delight in him and bless him; he knew he needed to bless him, for he was not a moral, good man. But Jacob did not need a blessing, for Isaac knew that Abraham's blessing would be his, and the special covenant for Abraham's seed, and that his sons would inherit the earth; Abraham did not bless Isaac either. (Radak on 27:4)

Note Radak's reversal: Isaac does not wish to bless Esau out of his love for him, but rather because "he was not a moral, good man." Even if we do not adopt this premise, Radak's reading is still possible: Isaac favors Esau, but rather than Abraham's blessing, he intends to give him a blessing of wealth and power. Nechama Leibowitz also favors this direction: she claims that Abraham's blessing is waiting for Jacob, and at the end of the narrative, Isaac indeed bestows it upon him directly, without maneuver or masquerade. The blessing Isaac hopes to give Esau is one of material wealth and power, but Rebecca wants Jacob to receive this blessing as well:

> Plenty, abundance, a sound, thriving economy, a wealth of assets, dominion, and power – all this is intended for Esau. But the Abrahamite destiny, the blessing of seed and promise of land were never meant for Esau in the first place, for Abraham's

48. Hamilton proposes that Isaac's old age causes him to forget the prophecy, or to misinterpret it (Hamilton, *Genesis II*, 212). It may also be that Isaac is not aware of the prophecy at all.
49. Some modern scholars favor this reading as well, such as Boase, "Shadows"; Walton, *Traveller*, 111.

> blessing is not automatically passed on to the firstborn, but to the worthy alone.[50]

Leibowitz's observation is powerful: from a perspective of content, the blessing "Esau" receives from Isaac has little to do with the familiar blessing of Abraham, which Isaac intentionally bestows upon Jacob at the end of the story. The blessing meant for Esau focuses on material wealth and power. Kevin Walton claims that the blessings Jacob receives at the story's end are essentially an interpretation of the blessings Jacob obtains under disguise;[51] if so, then seeds of Abraham's blessing are already present in the blessings Isaac wishes to give to Esau. But the latter reading is not convincing: a comparison of the two blessings reveals no congruence between them; they are of two disparate spheres, neither of them an interpretation of the other.

Moreover, Leibowitz's reading is supported by Isaac's words to Esau at the beginning of the chapter: "I am old, and I do not know when I will die… so that my soul may bless you before I die" (27:2–4). Isaac opens and concludes his speech with the belief that his death is imminent, and he wishes to bless Esau before he passes. The fact that Isaac then lives on for many years is irrelevant here; Isaac believes – as do his family – that he is about to die, and he does not want to miss the chance to bless his beloved son. This lends his blessing the status of a deathbed blessing, a legacy, similarly to Jacob's mindset, "I am about to die" (Gen. 48:21), before he blesses his sons at the end of Genesis. There, Jacob's blessings touch upon the distant future, but there is no question of election and rejection, and Abraham's covenant will be perpetuated through all of them. A father's deathbed blessings to his sons are a well-known literary motif, and if the story is read thus, its implications can be narrowed down. If the blessing is purely material, and Jacob is assured a place in Abraham's covenant all along, then far less is at stake than if the

50. Leibowitz, *Genesis*, 193–95. Others also favor this direction: Jacob, *Genesis*, 574–77 [German]; Kiel, *Genesis II*, 293; Clifford, "Genesis 25," 401.
51. Walton, *Traveller*, 120–21. Among others, he writes that it does not make sense that the blessing of abundance will be granted to one brother and the blessing of inheritance to another (ibid., n. 89). I believe that he is correct, and I will solve this issue below.

story follows the Ramban's reading. Yet the thematic allusion to Jacob's blessings to his sons raises its own problems: Why doesn't Isaac summon both of his sons for a blessing? Even if only one will become the head of the family, why shouldn't the other be blessed as well?[52]

This exegetical debate serves another important purpose: as we will see below, it seems that Rebecca does not know what kind of blessing Isaac intends for Esau, and she may well be acting on the assumption – or at least the concern – that Isaac is about to choose Esau as Abraham's heir (Ramban's reading), while in fact Isaac is about to bless Esau with a less significant blessing of prosperity (Leibowitz's reading). This will emerge from an analysis of her words to Jacob, below. There is, however, a third possibility – one that is the most convincingly supported by the data in the text – and it is this reading that illuminates the narrative as one of the most significant turning points in Genesis, and even within Israelite history itself. This third possibility will gradually emerge with our analysis of the narrative.

C. Rebecca and Jacob (27:5–17)

The ancient convention of just two actors in each scene is especially salient as Isaac and Esau exit the stage and Rebecca and Jacob enter. It is not entirely clear where Rebecca is when she hears Isaac's instructions. When Sarah overhears the tidings of Isaac's birth, the text clarifies that "Sarah was listening at the opening of the tent behind him" (18:10) – because she stood behind him, Abraham did not see her,[53] but here, the only information provided is "When Isaac was speaking to his son Esau, Rebecca was listening" (v. 5). Although Rebecca's precise position – or hiding place? – is unclear, the sense is that she is eavesdropping, standing unseen offstage. This may contribute to one of the narrative's central questions: How can it be that Isaac fails to recognize that it is

52. Some modern scholars feel that the text harbors criticism of Isaac at this point (Jacob, *Genesis*, 577; Wenham, *Genesis II*, 205). But see Walton's reservations toward this reading (*Traveller*, 133, n. 40).
53. Zakovitch comments that the combination of "[woman's name]" + "listening" appears just once elsewhere in the Bible (I Kings 10:1; Zakovitch, *Texts in the Land of Mirrors*, 93). Though as mentioned, in our scene, the text does not explain how Rebecca technically hears.

Jacob, and not Esau, standing before him? While we will explore this in depth below, for now I wish to point out that if Isaac believes that Esau is the only one who hears his instructions, he is less likely to suspect that the son standing before him could be anyone but Esau. Isaac does not merely speak to Esau – he "summons" him for a private audience: "He summoned his elder son Esau. 'My son,' he said" (v. 1). R. Haim ben Attar notes this subtlety:

> "Rebecca was listening": the narrative is conveying that Rebecca was a prophet who always heard whatever Isaac said, even if he was not talking in her presence – contemplate this. For this reason it says "Rebecca was listening" and not "Rebecca listened" or "She would listen." It may be that Isaac spoke to him privately, and for this reason he believed that Jacob was Esau, because he had whispered in Esau's ear. Although Isaac was blind [and therefore could not see who was present when he spoke], he called him aside to speak with him privately, and perhaps this is hinted in the phrase "and he summoned Esau…" – meaning, they convened for secret matters. (*Or HaḤayim* on Gen. 27:5)

Isaac is less suspicious from the outset because he thinks that no one but Esau is aware of their plan; therefore, when Jacob appears with the food he requested, he has no reason to suspect that the son before him is anyone besides Esau.

Rebecca's instructions to Jacob ("*Now* [*na*] go to the flock and *bring me* two choice young goats") recall Isaac's instructions to Esau ("So *now* [*na*] take your weapons…and *hunt me* some game"). Esau is sent to the field to hunt some meat; Jacob is sent to the family's flock to bring in some meat; both will serve it to Isaac in exchange for his blessing. Both parents open their requests with the same expression, "*hineh*," and then instruct their sons to act at once, "*ve'ata*," due to the urgency of the situation. Isaac is afraid death is at hand, and he wishes to bless his son as soon as possible; Rebecca sees Esau setting out, and urges Jacob to act before his brother returns home. In biblical speech, "*ve'ata*" usually marks the beginning of the speaker's conclusion after they have conveyed the relevant information.

These similarly structured speeches map out the narrative's two factions: Isaac and Esau, men of the field, versus Rebecca and Jacob, the home team. Isaac is rooting for Esau to win the blessing; Rebecca is rooting for Jacob. Rebecca and Jacob may be playing against the rules, but the game is rigged to begin with: Isaac is the one with the power to bless and the power to determine the next head of the family. Thus, rather than upset the balance between the two sides, Jacob's deception restores a certain balance to the game.

Moreover, in her instructions to Jacob, Rebecca quotes Isaac's instructions to Esau, tells Jacob to fetch two kid goats from the flock, and then repeats some elements of Isaac's speech. In this way, Isaac's instructions are repeated three times in the narrative, in whole or partial form. Given that the narrative could have easily reported something along the lines of "Rebecca told Jacob what Isaac had said," this repetition invites comparison, which reveals different narrative perspectives. The contrast between them illuminates Rebecca's persuasive technique:

Isaac to Esau (vv. 1–4)	**Rebecca quotes Isaac (vv. 6–7)**	**Rebecca instructs Jacob (vv. 9–10)**
He summoned his elder son Esau. "My son," he said. Esau replied, "Here I am."	And Rebecca said to her son Jacob, "I overheard your father say to your brother Esau,	
"I am old, and I do not know when I will die.		
So now, take your weapons, your quiver and bow, and go out into the field and hunt me some game.	'Bring me some game	"Now, my son, listen carefully to my instructions. Go to the flock and bring me two choice young goats.
Then make me delicious food, prepared in the way that I love	and make me delicious food	I will make them into delicious food, in the way he loves.
and bring it to me to eat	so that I may eat	Then bring it to your father to eat
so that my soul may bless you before I die."	and give you my blessing before the Lord before I die.'"	so that he may give you his blessing before he dies."

The most striking difference is evident from the beginning of Rebecca's speech: she omits Isaac's detailed instructions for Esau to take his weapons, quiver and bow, and go out into the field. She even changes Isaac's verb, "hunt," to a more general "bring." Jacob will not necessarily assume that Esau has gone out to hunt for his father; perhaps he will prepare meat that he has already hunted. If so, then Jacob's time to act is limited, and the pressure is on.

Why does Rebecca omit this detail? If Jacob approaches Isaac without being fully informed, he is at risk of being caught. This change – and the other changes Rebecca makes – are calculated to persuade Jacob to agree to her scheme. If Jacob were to know that his father asks Esau to hunt fresh game, he might refuse to approach him – surely Isaac will realize Jacob's deception when he comes in so quickly from the field! We will see that Isaac is indeed suspicious of his son's prompt return, but at this stage, Rebecca's top priority is to persuade Jacob to commit, hoping that he will overcome any such obstacles along the way.

This mindset also explains another of Rebecca's manipulations – she tells Jacob that Isaac requests that Esau "make him delicious food," but omits the phrase "prepared in the way I love." Isaac's emphasis on his love for Esau's meat might deter Jacob, because it touches upon the heart of Esau's bond with his father. Isaac loves Esau because "he ate of his game"; only Esau knows how to prepare meat just the way his father likes it. All Isaac has to say is "the way I love," and Esau knows exactly what he means. How can Jacob possibly hope to meet his father's expectations? He can make a mean lentil stew, but the family rôtisseur is undoubtedly Esau. Rebecca knows that this detail might discourage Jacob, and she therefore leaves it out.

Rebecca also changes Isaac's instruction from "bring it to me to eat" to "so that I may eat." A good liar keeps their story as consistent as possible, and Rebecca is a good liar. She has already changed Isaac's verb "hunt me some game" to "bring me some game," so she omits it here to avoid suspicious repetition.

The last difference is perhaps the most fascinating of all. Why does Rebecca claim that Isaac tells Esau that he will bless him "before the Lord, before my death"? Why does she add the phrase "before the Lord," if Isaac never said it?

It could be that this change, like the others, is designed to spur Jacob into action. Mentioning "the Lord" gives the sense that Isaac's blessing will be momentous.[54] This reading is possible, but given its context, there is room to debate whether Rebecca's addition is an entirely conscious one. Perhaps this change is not part of her persuasive tactics, but rather a reflection of how she perceives the nature of Isaac's blessing. Rebecca is concerned that the blessing intended for Esau is a blessing that will be bestowed "before the Lord" – that is, a blessing of divine, eternal validity; possibly even the blessing of Abraham's covenant with God.[55]

If we follow Ramban's reading, this difference has no major implications; according to Ramban, Isaac indeed intends to bestow Abraham's blessing upon Esau:

> "Before the Lord" is only mentioned here because his mother explained to him that the blessing would be given before the Lord, with divine inspiration, and should Esau be blessed then the blessing would endure through his seed forever, and [Jacob] will not be able to withstand him. (Ramban on Gen. 27:7)

But if Isaac planned to bestow a different blessing upon Esau, one unrelated to Abraham's covenant with God (following Radak's reading), then this slight difference reveals that Rebecca ascribes far more importance to the blessing than Isaac intended.

Yet Rebecca's task is not over. On the one hand, she must persuade Jacob to implement her scheme, and she adjusts Isaac's instructions so as not to deter her son. But on the other hand, she must ensure that Jacob's act is as convincing as possible, and she must somehow familiarize Jacob with Isaac's actual language. Rebecca's solution is to incorporate the missing elements of Isaac's speech into her own instructions to Jacob, and this will prepare him for the task ahead. She therefore

---

54. As proposed, for example, by Wenham, *Genesis II*, 207; with different focus: Schwartz, *Isaac*, 197–98.
55. Some scholars claim that the phrase "before the Lord" is an addition that seeks to create balance between Isaac, who bestows the blessings, and the understanding that it is God's blessing he is bestowing (Westermann, *Genesis II*, 438). But this seems to be the result of various perspectives in the narrative, not of literary balance.

tells Jacob that she will prepare the kid goats "into delicious food, *in the way he loves*" (27:9), using the same phrase she omitted earlier; she also adds that Jacob should "*bring it* to your father to eat," once again echoing Isaac's original instructions; and omits her earlier description that Isaac will bless his son "before the Lord." This creates the proper semantic atmosphere without focusing upon the danger that threatens the son who is about to deceive his father.

Jacob indeed has reservations about his mother's proposal, but note the reason for his reluctance. The claim that Jacob is appalled and fiercely opposed to the idea of deceiving his father is unfounded;[56] he does not express any moral qualms about deceiving his elderly father, nor does he shrink at the injustice of stealing from his brother. Rather, he voices concern about being caught – and worries that if his father is not deceived, he will curse him rather than bless him. If so, the main tension in the narrative – as noted above, in our discussion of its chiastic structure – is not a moral conflict, but a pragmatic one... will Jacob manage to deceive his father? The nature of Jacob's concern is liable to spark indignation: How can it be that he is more concerned about getting caught than about the very notion of misleading his elderly, blind father?! Yet before judging Jacob too harshly, it is worth paying attention to certain aspects of Rebecca's speech.

In the exchange between mother and son, Rebecca is strikingly active, while Jacob is equally passive. Jacob's consent is presented as the response to his mother's adamant orders: "Now, my son, *listen carefully to my instructions*. Go to the flock and bring *me*.... *Do as I say. Go: fetch them for me*" (27:8–13). Rebecca opens and concludes her instructions with emphasis on his obedience. She even emphasizes that the kid goats he takes are *for her*.[57] The contrast between her insistence and his passivity is especially salient in the description of Jacob's disguise: "Then Rebecca took her elder son Esau's best clothes, which were with her in the house, and put them on Jacob, her younger son. She put the goatskins on his hands and the smooth part of his neck. She then handed her son Jacob the delicious food and bread that she had prepared"

56. Kautzsch, *Die Heilige Schrift*, 166.

57. Compare to Zakovitch, *Jacob*, 35.

(vv. 15–17). Rebecca takes the garments and dresses her son; she takes the food she has prepared, and places the dish in Jacob's hands. Jacob's passivity is underscored by the sudden mention that he is her "younger son" – this reinforces the sense that he is but a small child being dressed by his mommy, who then hands him a tray to serve his daddy. This image certainly distracts the reader from the fact that Jacob is at least forty years old.

This characterization serves to transfer responsibility from Jacob's shoulders to Rebecca's. If so, then the narrative's epicenter of conflict is not fraternal, but rather marital, which has far-reaching implications for any moral issues raised by this maneuver. It is hard to justify a son's deception of his elderly, blind father in order to usurp what that father intended for his brother. But the narrative intentionally frames this deception not as a son's conflict with his father, but as a dispute between husband and wife, each with their own favored son. Thus the epicenter of tension is not between brothers, but rather between parents.[58] This tilts the moral balance of the scene: it is not a case of the young and strong deceiving the old and weak, but rather of two sons acting on their parents' orders, with Rebecca seeking the fulfillment of a divine prophecy. I am not convinced that Rebecca's absence from the scene after she gives Jacob orders is evidence of criticism against her.[59] After all, she is acting on God's words to her during her pregnancy, and in the end, both the text and the reader favor the fact that Jacob is the one who receives the blessing. If Rebecca is but seeking to fulfill God's words, and if – as it later emerges – Isaac never intended to reject Jacob, then Rebecca's course of action is, in a certain sense, tragic. She sacrifices much for something that – it seems – she would have received anyway. But even if so, then she is a tragic figure, not an antagonist.

Rebecca spurs Jacob to action at two crucial narrative junctions: when she overhears Isaac's instructions to Esau she sends him to Isaac in Esau's place, and when she overhears Esau's murderous intentions against Jacob, she sends him to Haran. Once again, Rebecca's will eclipses Jacob's,

58. Wenham, *Genesis II*, 207.

59. Similarly Fokkelman, *Genesis*, 115–17. This is challenged fiercely by Allen, "On Me Be the Curse."

absorbing potential criticism against him. It is not Jacob's place to question the moral aspect of his mother's decision; if Rebecca determines that this is the necessary course of action, then Jacob does as he is told.

Even so, this is unquestionably the third scene of conflict between the brothers themselves. Esau triumphs at birth by being the first to emerge from the womb; Jacob manages to recoup the birthright when Esau sells it to him; and now, he manages to obtain the blessings as well.[60] The more the scene is in dialogue with its broader context, the less pronounced the criticism against Rebecca and Jacob. Jacob has purchased the birthright from Esau – perhaps he is also entitled to the blessings? Rebecca knows that the younger shall overcome the elder – perhaps she ought to contribute to the prophecy's fulfillment?

Our scene indeed recalls earlier acts; sometimes explicitly, sometimes implicitly. The first allusion to an earlier scene – in this case, the sale of the birthright – is in the description of the food Rebecca prepares: "She then handed her son Jacob the delicious food and bread that she had prepared" (27:17). Exegetes question this menu, given that it deviates from Isaac's requested meal. Radak, for example, writes:

> "Delicious food": no mention is made of the meat as it was included in what is described here as "delicious food." The latter is considered the main part of the meal as this is what he requested: "delicious food" – he wanted the meal to be well spiced. "And bread": she made him fresh bread. (Radak on 27:17)

Radak is initially troubled by the fact that meat is not mentioned, but there is no real issue – throughout the story, the "delicious food" Isaac requests includes meat (27:4, 7, 8, 14, 31), and Radak's answer is obvious. What is more interesting is that Rebecca adds "bread" ("fresh bread," as Radak explains) to the meal Jacob serves his father, even though it is not mentioned until now.[61] This is a surprising addition, given that the

60. Compare to Hamilton, *Genesis II*, 212.

61. Gunkel also comments that Isaac does not ask for "*leḥem*," but he adds this, along with wine (Gunkel, *Genesis*, 304). Hamilton sees these as additions that complete the meal (Hamilton, *Genesis II*, 221). Wenham proposes that alongside its ceremonial

meal is supposed to follow the menu that Isaac dictates to Esau. Would Esau have added bread? If Isaac did not explicitly request it, the bread might arouse suspicion.

Could the mention of bread be understood in the sense of "meat"? *Laḥam* (لحم) in Arabic means "meat,"[62] but this is an unlikely reading in our context, given that the bread is mentioned as an addition to the "delicious food," which presumably includes the spiced meat.

We cannot rule out the possibility that Rebecca includes the bread in order to protect Jacob from Isaac's potential curse. Isaac will presumably recognize the bread baked by his wife of at least sixty years. Esau might also include some of his mother's bread with the meal he serves, but if Jacob's real identity is discovered, then the inclusion of Rebecca's bread will signal to Isaac that this scheme was undertaken with her approval. With shrewd acumen she adds a loaf of her bread to the meal as a sign that Jacob was sent on her instructions, or, in her own words, so that "your curse will be on me, my son" (27:13).

Even if we adopt this reading, however, the bread serves yet a further purpose. Someone asks for a meal, promising a blessing in exchange, and the promised meal is served with a helping of bread. This, of course, recalls Jacob's transaction with Esau – there too, Jacob serves Esau bread in addition to the promised stew: "Jacob then gave Esau bread and lentil stew" (25:34).[63] If this allusion is intentional, then it too serves to mitigate potential criticism against Rebecca. Should the reader feel uneasy about her scheme, he or she is invited to recall Esau's attitude toward the birthright; it may be that Jacob is the rightful recipient of the blessings, given his transaction with his brother.

My goal is not to define the relationship between the birthright and the blessings; Isaac is apparently entitled to bless Esau despite his

---

suitability, Jacob brings the wine to quiet Isaac and his questions (Wenham, *Genesis II*, 209).

62. BDB, "*leḥem*," 536. This illuminates the wordplay of "He grants bread to all flesh" (Ps. 136:25).

63. Intriguingly, Radak claims that Jacob gives Esau wine with his stew and bread: "In exchange for his birthright, Jacob gave Esau bread and lentil stew. And he did not recall that he gave him wine, for he drank from the household wine" (on 25:34). This increases the connection between the two scenes even further.

rejection of his birthright,[64] although it may be that Isaac is unaware of his sons' transaction. If so, then the subtle allusion to the birthright episode once again mitigates Jacob's deception. We will soon see that the birthright is explicitly mentioned by Esau himself, casting the claim that Jacob has stolen his blessings in a complex light.

D. "Esau" Comes Before Isaac

This next scene marks the narrative climax. Will Isaac realize that the son standing before him is not his beloved Esau? His sight dimmed, the elderly Isaac uses his other senses to determine who is standing before him – but they fail him. For that moment, Jacob becomes his brother Esau. The innocent man who stayed among the tents becomes the wild man of the field, and thus he manages to secure his blessings.[65]

In this scene, Isaac calls Jacob "my son" again and again: "Here I am. Who are you, my son?"/"How did you find it so quickly, my son?"/"Come close and let me feel you, my son, to know – are you really my son Esau?"/"Are you really my son Esau?"/"Then serve me and let me eat some of my son's game so that my soul may bless you."/"Come close and kiss me, my son."/"The smell of my son is the smell of a field the Lord has blessed."

Isaac's obsessive repetition of "my son" reflects his strong love for his son; he loves to murmur it for the sheer pleasure of the very sound. Now Jacob stands before his father, hearing the love expressed so deeply for his brother – perhaps his heart skips a beat each time he calls him "my son." He is his son, but not the son Isaac means to address so fondly. Jacob can hardly bring himself to respond to this epithet with the corresponding "my father." This is salient through a comparison of Jacob's

---

64. This subject is explicitly raised in Jacob's blessing to Joseph's sons in Egypt. After Jacob places his right hand on the younger son's head, Joseph corrects his father, reflecting the belief that it is the eldest who is worthy of blessing and greatness. But Jacob insists on blessing Ephraim with his right hand, reflecting that it is the father's right to choose which son is worthy of his blessing, regardless of the birthright.

65. Hendel, *Jacob*, 129. See also R. Yoel Bin-Nun, *Chapters of the Fathers*, 154–64 ("For the first time since the birth of the two clashing sons, a completely new character appears before Isaac – its hands are Esau's hands and its voice is Jacob's voice – a most startling synthesis" – 159).

exchange with Isaac and Esau's words to his father when he comes in from the field: Jacob says "my father" but once (v. 18), while Esau ends every sentence with this phrase (vv. 31, 34, 38). Jacob seems to find it difficult to refer thus to his father while he is deceiving him, while Esau addresses him with true feeling, with a son's honest, unbridled love.[66]

Isaac's uncertainty about the identity of the son who stands before him is described in two stages:

vv. 18–23	vv. 24–27
He went in to his father; "My father," he said. His father replied, "Here I am. Who are you, my son?" Jacob said to his father, "I am Esau your firstborn. I have done as you asked. Please sit up and eat some of my game so that your soul may bless me"...	"Are you really my son Esau?" he asked. He replied, "I am." "Then serve me and let me eat some of my son's game so that my soul may bless you"...
Then Isaac said to Jacob,	Then Jacob's father Isaac said to him,
"Come close and let me feel you, my son, to know – are you really my son Esau?"	"Come close and kiss me, my son."
Jacob came close to Isaac his father, who felt him and said, "The voice is the voice of Jacob, but the hands are the hands of Esau." He did not recognize him, because his hands were hairy like those of his brother Esau and he blessed him.	So he came close and kissed him, and Isaac smelled the smell of his clothes and he blessed him.

The main components are each repeated twice, once in each stage: Isaac asks about the identity of Jacob, who replies that he is Esau; the request to eat so that the meal will be followed by a blessing (Jacob states this the first time, Isaac the second); Isaac's request that Jacob come close to

66. See further in Runge, "Paradigmatic Effects," 98–101.

him and Jacob's consent; and finally, "and he blessed him." This repetition invites closer analysis largely because of the first occurrence of "and he blessed him" at the end of the first half (v. 23), when the actual blessing is bestowed after Isaac eats, drinks, and asks about Jacob's identity once more (v. 27). As usual in such cases, some believe that the word is a corruption;[67] a different theory perceives the first "and he blessed him" as marking the start of the whole blessing rite, which includes eating, physical contact, and finally, the verbal blessing itself, so that the two instances are not strictly repetition.[68] Others propose reading the word as an explanation as to why Isaac then blessed Jacob rather than Esau – as the New American Bible translates, for example: "He failed to identify him because his hands were hairy, like those of his brother Esau; *so in the end he gave him his blessing*."[69]

I believe that the repetition of this verb charges the second half of the scene with further meaning.[70] In verse 23 Isaac decides to bless the one standing before him, and therefore the second stage of the scene describes his preparations for the actual blessing, but the parallel between the two stages reveals that Isaac continues to verify his son's identity. That is, the son approaching his father and their embrace is a typical part of a deathbed blessing rite (Gen. 48:10; 50:1),[71] but here, Isaac's kiss serves a further purpose: he is still attempting to ascertain that it is Esau who stands before him, just as he does when he asks Jacob to approach him during the first half. Isaac breathes in Jacob's scent before he blesses him, and while this serves as an introduction to the blessing that follows – "The smell of my son is the smell of a field the Lord has blessed" – when compared to its parallel component in the first half, when Isaac attempts to determine his son's identity by using his other senses, it seems that here, too, Isaac is making a last desperate attempt to identify his son using his sense of smell.

67. Volz, *Genesis*, 66.
68. Westermann, *Genesis II*, 440.
69. For example, Ska, "Sommaire proleptiques," and some modern translations (NAB, NEB).
70. On the technique of a multivalent reading emerging from a literary structure, see Grossman, "'Structural Ambiguity' in Ezekiel 33–48."
71. Wenham, *Genesis II*, 209.

In other words, Isaac determines that he will bestow his blessing at the end of the first stage: "*vayvarekhehu.*" But when he asks once again, "Are you really my son Esau?" and the whole scene essentially repeats itself, it emerges that Isaac is still plagued by doubt.[72]

I will discuss Isaac's blessing in depth in comparison to the blessing he eventually gives Esau. For now, I wish only to point out an intriguing parallel between Isaac's blessing and the prophecy Rebecca receives during her pregnancy. After a blessing for fertile soil (v. 28), Isaac then expresses (v. 29):

> May nations serve you; may peoples bow down to you.
> Be lord over your brothers, and may your mother's sons bow down to you.
> A curse on those who curse you; on those who bless you, blessing.

These three pronouncements are concerned with the blessed son's position of power. The first addresses national power; the second power within the family; and the third relates to his general position within society: those who seek the son's peace and blessing will also be blessed, while those who oppose him and undermine him will see their own downfall.

The opening verb "serve" recalls Rebecca's prophecy during her pregnancy: "The younger shall the elder serve"; and if we take into account that the word "peoples," *le'ummim*"" (in this context) only appears in this blessing and in Rebecca's prophecy: "Two peoples (*le'ummim*) are to part from you," then the connection between them is surely intentional. We will soon see that Isaac's consolation blessing to Esau also recalls this prophecy, which certainly serves as a background to our scene. Its significance is clear: the same way that the scene's dialogue with the sale of the birthright mitigates censure of Jacob and Rebecca, these allusions to the first incidence of sibling rivalry also set this deception within a broader context – one in which God Himself anticipates

72. Compare to Fokkelman, *Genesis*, 103. Ska proposes that the function of the first "he blessed him" is to relieve the suspense, for the reader now knows that Isaac will bless Jacob and not discover his deceit (Ska, "Limits," 112–13).

their struggle and the younger son's ultimate triumph. Perhaps this alone cannot justify Rebecca's scheme from a moral perspective, but each and every line in this scene is fraught with ambivalence.

How Can It Be That Isaac Fails to Recognize Jacob?

One of the most troubling questions of this scene is how does Isaac fail to recognize that Jacob, not his beloved Esau, is the son who stands before him? He indeed suspects him based on his voice (v. 22) and repeatedly asks who he is. Despite his lingering suspicions, Isaac does not ask his son any questions that would verify his true identity – questions that only Esau would know. How can it be that Isaac eventually bases his decision on the hairy arms he strokes, rather than the sound of Jacob's voice?

These troubling questions lead some exegetes to posit that Isaac *does* realize that the son before him is Jacob, but he chooses to bless him anyway. There are several variations of this theory, and given that this intriguing idea results in an entirely new reading of the story, I wish to devote a few lines to it.

A subtle variation of this reading is that Isaac recognizes Jacob as he stands before him, but he decides to complete the blessing rite anyway, even though this means that Jacob will now become the blessed son. Others have proposed more extreme formulations: Adrien Bledstein suggests that Rebecca and Isaac join forces behind the scenes and set up a trial of sorts to determine whether Jacob has the courage and daring to be worthy of Abraham's blessing.[73] Similarly, David Zucker posits that Isaac knows all along that Jacob will approach him – he and Rebecca plan this "deception" together in order to encourage Jacob's initiative and maturity.[74]

These readings have a certain allure, from both exegetical and psychological perspectives. The idea that Isaac does not recognize his son is disturbing, as is the evident tension between husband and wife, and this theory solves both issues. Unfortunately, however, it does not sit well with the text, which explicitly negates such a reading: "He did not recognize him, because his hands were hairy like those of his brother Esau"

73. Bledstein, "Rereading Genesis."
74. Zucker, "The Deceiver Deceived."

(v. 23). Had this statement been made from Jacob's perspective – "My father did not recognize me," for example – there would still be room for such a possibility; Jacob believes that he is deceiving his father, but that is not necessarily the case. But the narrator relates Isaac's blindness to the identity of the son before him as an objective fact, and there is no room to deny that Jacob's hairy arms successfully mislead his father. Isaac's shocked reaction when the real Esau appears before him does not seem to be staged either, and we have no choice but to assume that Isaac indeed fails to recognize that "Esau" is in fact Jacob.[75]

Perhaps Isaac's blindness symbolizes a far looser grasp of reality in general. Another possibility is that the "best clothes" that Esau keeps in his parents' home have certain significance.[76] The fact that he has a set of special clothing at his parents' home suggests that when he visits them, he changes out of his normal clothes and into these clothes, thus displaying a remarkable level of respect for his parents.[77] In a bold midrash, R. Shimon son of Gamliel – the head of the Sanhedrin in Usha, whose father ruled after the Bar Kokhba rebellion – expresses his own inferiority compared to Esau, whose respect for his father was unmatched:

> R. Shimon son of Gamliel said: I served my father my entire life, but I never showed him a hundredth of the respect that Esau showed his father; when I served my father, I wore dirty clothes, but in public I wore clean clothing. But when Esau served his father, he changed into clothing fit for royalty, saying, "It is

75. This question will also arise in regard to Laban's deceit, where it seems that Jacob does not recognize Leah and believes he is marrying Rachel. See below, in context.
76. Hamilton proposes that Esau's clothing in his parents' home suggests that he lives with them (Hamilton, *Genesis II*, 217). This is a strange conclusion.
77. Gershon Hepner proposes that these clothes symbolize the priestly garments, and Rebecca's dressing of Jacob is like Moses' dressing of Aaron and his sons when he sanctifies them as priests. Thus Jacob takes Esau's birthright-priesthood. He also believes that the phrase "that were in the house" hints to the Temple (Hepner, *Legal Friction*, 369–70). This is a creative, albeit homiletic reading; perhaps a more accurate formulation would be that garments in the Bible often represent certain status, and Jacob's donning of his brother's garments represents his usurping his status as the blessed firstborn.

> disrespectful to my father to wear anything but clothes fit for royalty." (Genesis Rabba 65:16)

Isaac, deprived of his sight, associates the feel of these special clothes so closely with Esau that it clouds his judgment.[78] As mentioned, Isaac's instructions to Esau are supposedly secret, so he is already disposed to perceive the son who offers him food in exchange for his blessing as Esau. When Isaac strokes the familiar sleeve, and tastes the familiar meat, and breathes in the familiar scent of the field, his sense of affection and familiarity overpowers any niggling doubt, and he is determined to bless his son.

D'. The Real Esau Comes Before Isaac

The second half of the narrative opens with a dramatic schism within Abraham's line. As soon as Jacob leaves, Esau comes in:

> Isaac had finished blessing Jacob,
> and Jacob had just left his father Isaac,
> when his brother Esau came back from the hunt.
> He too had prepared delicious food and brought it to his father. (27:30–31)

This description shows that the brothers do not meet at this point: neither in their father's tent, nor outside of it. Moreover, its language evokes two other biblical scenes that lend further depth to this scene. The phrase "He too had prepared delicious food and brought it to his father" (v. 31) recalls a different tale of two brothers who offered food, seeking their "father's" approval: "Abel too brought an offering: fat portions from the firstborn of his flock" (Gen. 4:4). This story is not only evoked by the phrase "he too," but by the comparable situation: two brothers compete for their "father's" blessing. The elder is a "man of

78. Yair Zakovitch proposes that Jacob's donning of Esau's special garments is reflected in Zechariah's prophecy against false prophets: "On that day the prophets will be ashamed of their vision, each one of them, when they prophesy. They will no longer wear a mantle of hair to deceive" (Zech. 13:4; Zakovitch, *Jacob*, 37).

the field," and the food he offers is rejected, while the meat offered by the younger son is accepted. Cain and Abel's feud does not end well, and at this stage, the reader indeed fears for Jacob's life – he may have won his father's blessing, but Abel's death has already shown that blessing alone does not offer protection from a brother's murderous wrath.[79] This precedent alone justifies Rebecca's fear for Jacob's life – Esau, like Cain before him, seeks vengeance against his younger rival.

Yet a different scene, much closer to home, is also alluded to through repetition of the verb "came out – *yatza*": "Jacob had just left (*yatzo yatza*) his father Isaac, when his brother Esau came back from the hunt" (v. 30). This repetition recalls Jacob and Esau's first appearance, when they first "came out" of their mother's womb: "The first came out red…then his brother came out" (25:25–26). This time, it is Jacob who "comes out" first,[80] while "his brother" is too late. Even though Esau emerges triumphant in his first scene, here Jacob manages to secure first place.

In order to understand the profound drama that takes place, I wish to address a fundamental question raised by this scene. After Isaac realizes that he has been deceived (and he immediately understands who has deceived him – "He said, 'Your brother came in deceit and took your blessing'" –27:35), he refuses to bless Esau as well. This is extremely strange. Even if Isaac cannot take back his blessing from Jacob, though it was unwittingly bestowed – "Who then was it that hunted game and brought it to me? I ate it all before you came, and I blessed him – *and he will be blessed*" (v. 33)[81] – why is he unable to bless Esau with a different blessing? Jacob will bless all twelve of his sons without any issue – there is

79. Compare to Westermann, *Genesis II*, 443.
80. Hamilton, *Genesis II*, 226; Vrolijk, *Jacob's Wealth*, 92.
81. Rashi and Radak understand that Isaac realizes that is it Jacob, and then decides that the blessings should go to him (similarly: Schwartz, *Isaac*, 230–31). A simpler reading is that of Ramban and Bekhor Shor, which is later supported in Isaac's own words to Esau: because the blessing was already given to Jacob, he becomes the blessed son: "And this is why Isaac trembled so: he realizes that his blessings were lost to his favorite son forever" (Ramban). If so, then words have power even when the speaker is not fully aware of who he speaks them to (see also Gunkel, *Genesis*, 305; Wenham, *Genesis II*, 211).

never any concern that Issachar will be deprived because Judah is blessed first. Yet a closer look at the text shows that Isaac is truly reluctant to bless Esau, even though he continues using the affectionate epithet "my son":

Stage 1 (27:34–35):
He said to his father, "Bless me, me too, my father!"
"Your brother came in deceit and took your blessing," he replied.

Stage 2 (vv. 36–37):
He said, "Is he not rightly named Jacob (*Yaakov*)? Twice he has supplanted me (*vayakeveni*). He took my birthright and now he has taken my blessing."
Then he said, "Do you not have any blessing left for me?"[82]
Isaac answered Esau, "I have made him lord over you and given him all his brothers as servants. I have endowed him with grain and wine. What then can I do for you, my son?"

Stage 3 (vv. 38–40):
Esau said to his father, "Have you only one blessing, father? Bless me, me too, my father!" And Esau wept aloud.
His father Isaac answered him and said: "Of the cream of the land your home shall be, of the dew of heaven above. By your sword you will live, and your brother you will serve; but when you move on, you will throw off his yoke from your neck."

Isaac's repeated evasion shows that truly, he does not want to bless him, while Esau, as expected, insists on a blessing from his father, however minimal. Yet surprisingly, Isaac initially stands his ground.[83] Why is Isaac so reluctant to bless his son?

---

82. Meir Shiloah reads the double "and he said" in this verse to mean that Esau speaks the first words to himself, and the next to Isaac (Shiloah, "And He Said," 263). This is possible, but it could be that after Isaac does not respond to Esau's first statement, the second "he said" indicates Isaac's silence.
83. This recalls Orpah.'s desire to return to Bethlehem with Naomi. Even after her first refusal, both Ruth and Orpah wish to remain with her. Even though she eventually returns to Moab, the three-stage dialogue expresses sincerity. Here, too, Isaac's

His reason is exposed when Isaac eventually capitulates and does bless Esau, but we can begin to understand his reluctance through a careful reading of his repeated refusal. Isaac summarizes Esau's would-be blessing to him, but the emphasis of this summary differs from the original blessing:

Isaac's blessing to Jacob (vv. 28–29)	**Isaac paraphrases this blessing to Esau (v. 37)**
God endow you with dew of heaven, the cream of the land, much *grain and wine.*	I have made him *lord* over you and given him all his brothers as servants.
May nations serve you; may peoples bow down to you. Be *lord* over your brothers, and may your mother's sons bow down to you.	I have endowed him with *grain and wine.*

Isaac reverses the order: when he blesses Jacob, he first mentions "grain and wine" before describing how he will be lord over his brothers; but when he describes that blessing to Esau, he begins with Jacob's lordship. In the latter description, Isaac even lowers Jacob's brothers to the level of "servants," which is far more degrading than merely "serving" him, as described in the original blessing. Moreover, whereas Isaac blesses Jacob with international power, not just power within his own family, in his description to Esau he focuses on Jacob's dominion within the family, which is especially painful to his brother Esau; he even redirects the verbs that originally refer to Jacob's power over the nations – "May nations *serve you*" – to Jacob's power over his own brother: "I have… given him all his brothers *as servants.*" Therein lies the rub; this emphasis explains Isaac's reluctance to bless Esau as well, as I will clarify below.

Isaac only capitulates after Esau repeatedly begs him for a blessing. His father, and the reader, are truly moved by the powerful figure

three-stage refusal before his acquiescence reflects that Isaac genuinely does not want to bless Esau.

of Esau breaking down and weeping bitterly for his lost blessing.[84] Esau, fierce hunter of beasts, is stirred to tears, and his father's compassion is stirred by the tender emotion beneath his hairy visage.

I will now turn to the blessing that Isaac eventually does grant his broken son, and explore why Isaac is so loath to bestow it in the first place through a comparison with his blessing to Jacob:

Isaac's blessing to Jacob (in disguise) (vv. 27–29)	**Isaac's blessing to Esau (vv. 39–40)**
God endow you with dew of heaven, the cream of the land, much grain and wine.	Of the cream of the land your home shall be, of the dew of heaven above.
May peoples serve you; may nations bow down to you. Be lord over your brothers, and may your mother's sons bow down to you. [85]	By your sword you will live, and your brother you will serve; but when you move on, you will throw off his yoke from your neck.
A curse on those who curse you; on those who bless you, blessing.	

Several differences demand explanation. First of all, God's name is entirely absent from Esau's blessing, even where it appears in Jacob's blessing in parallel. It is "God" who will endow Jacob with the dew of heaven and the cream of the land, but Esau will make his home with cream of land and dew of heaven without God's explicit bestowal – the verb "*latet*," accordingly, is missing too. Nor is Esau granted the abundance – "*much* grain and wine" – promised to Jacob.

84. I find it difficult to sympathize with the heartless claim that Esau's "pathetic begging and weeping do not make him an attractive character," as suggested by Vrolijk, *Jacob's Wealth*, 99.

85. From this Westermann learns that the blessings relate to Jacob's descendants and not to Jacob himself, for Jacob has only one brother (Westermann, *Genesis II*, 441; Wenham, *Genesis II*, 209). But Hamilton may be correct that this is a common literary expression and the plural does not mean that it cannot apply to the blessed son himself (Hamilton, *Genesis II*, 222). Nonetheless, it may be that these blessings refer to Jacob and Esau as archetypes of their future nations, as Ibn Ezra explains on 27:40.

These differences, and others, have led some to claim that Isaac's words to Esau are not a minimal blessing, but rather the opposite of a blessing. A leading proponent of this view is R. David Zvi Hoffmann, who argues that the *mem* of "*mishmanei*" implies distance and negation: instead of reading the verse "Of the cream of the land your home shall be," it should read: "*Far from* the cream of the land your home shall be, *far from* the dew of heaven above."[86] If so, then it is obvious why Isaac does not add "much grain and wine" – this is not a blessing of fertility or abundance.

R. Hoffmann supports his reading with several points:

1. Esau eventually settles in Edom (36:8), which is a barren wilderness.
2. When Isaac evades blessing Esau, he tells him: "I have endowed him with grain and wine. What then can I do for you, my son?" (v. 37). Isaac's premise is that because he has already promised the blessing of wine and grain to Jacob, he cannot give it to Esau as well.
3. His words to Esau lack the verb "to give," so it does not seem to be any kind of blessing of bestowal.

This also explains the chiastic contrast between his blessing to Jacob and his anti-blessing to Esau: the inversion of order reflects an inversion of content.

This is an intriguing reading, and R. Hoffmann's proof is compelling. Others adopt this direction, but claim that Isaac's speech is ambiguous: Esau interprets it as a blessing, but it can also be understood as a curse.[87] But even if we do favor this reading, there seems to be a deeper reason for Isaac's reservations. Why won't he grant him an explicit blessing of fertility? Why is he so reluctant to bless his beloved son?

---

86. As Gunkel, *Genesis*, 306; Hamilton, *Genesis II*, 228; Mathews, *Genesis II*, 436; Zakovitch, *Jacob*, 42–43. Westermann adds that Isaac's goal is to present the opposite of Jacob's blessings, so it is in fact a curse and not a blessing (Westermann, *Genesis II*, 443).
87. Zakovitch, *Jacob*, 42–43; Wenham, *Genesis II*, 212.

This dark secret bursts out in Isaac's next words to Esau:

> By your sword you will live, and your brother you will serve; but when you move on, you will throw off his yoke from your neck.

At first, Isaac tells Esau what he promised Jacob: Esau will "serve" his brother (similar to Noah's curse that his grandson Canaan will be a slave to his brothers).[88] Yet what Isaac now adds seems to limit Jacob's power over his brother: "When you move on, you will throw off his yoke from your neck." This will prove to be a key sentence to understanding the brothers' relationship. Suddenly, there is a way for Esau to break free of his brother's mastery over him.

What is the meaning of the word "*tarid*" – "move on" – which holds the key to Esau's freedom?

1. Ibn Ezra proposes reading it in the sense of "*tirdeh*" – oppress, dominate, rule over (or similarly, "break loose").[89] If so, the verse would read: "When you oppress and rule over your brother, you will throw off his yoke from his neck." The problem with this reading (besides the grammatical inaccuracy – "*tirdeh*" would have been more appropriate than "*tarid*") is its redundancy: if Esau is ruling over his brother, he has obviously thrown off his yoke. Moreover, how can this be reconciled with the fact that Jacob is supposed to rule over Esau? Radak favors this direction, explaining that "when the time comes for you to rule, you will throw off his yoke," but there is no indication in the verse itself that Jacob's dominion will end at a certain time.
2. Many medieval commentators understand "*tarid*" in the sense of "Restless, I wail (*arid*) and cry out" (Ps. 55:3) – that the verb is

---

88. See further Vrolijk, *Jacob's Wealth,* 94. The combination of "work" + "brother" supports this connection, but it is worth noting that this clearly refers to separate branches of Noah's sons. Here, the subject is more complex, and apparently depends on Esau's own decision, as I will explain below.

89. Gunkel, *Genesis,* 306. Similarly, some perceive the root R-O-D as "restless": when you are restless you will manage to shake off your brother's yoke (BDB, 923; Hamilton, *Genesis II,* 225; Mathews, *Genesis II,* 436).

association with weeping in grief or in speech. Rashi, for example, writes: "An expression of grief...that is, when Israel transgress the Torah, and you will have cause to grieve about the blessings he took, 'you will throw off his yoke'" (on 27:40). In the same vein, Ramban notes: "When you cry out from his provocation, you will throw off his yoke from your neck. This hints that Israel will not provoke them very much, or do them harm, as the text commands: 'Be very careful; do not provoke them'" (on 27:40).

3. There is, however, a third possibility; radical though it is, I believe that it illuminates the narrative best of all. Around thirty years ago, Lipa Ginat proposed reading the word *tarid* as a derivative of *lindod*, "to wander,"[90] which Yehuda Kiel adopted in his commentary in the *Daat Mikra* series.[91] This root takes on the same meaning in various verses: "Why has My nation said, 'We have strayed (*radnu*); we will never again approach You'?" (Jer. 2:31);[92] "Ephraim besieges Me with lies, the House of Israel with deception, but Judah still walks (*rad*) with God and remains faithful to the Holy One" (Hos. 12:1).[93] Ginat's theory is supported by a parallel verb in Akkadian, *redû,* which means "to travel," "to walk on," "to advance toward."[94] According to this reading, the verse reads thus: "When you move away, you will throw off his yoke from your neck."[95]

---

90. Ginat, "*tarid.*" The Ben Yehuda dictionary has "went, goes about." He brings Western etymology (Ben Yehuda, *Dictionary,* "R-O-D," 6469). Samet writes that Menahem Naor (in his book *The Bible and the Land*) holds thus (Samet, *Studies III,* vol. 1, 132).
91. Kiel, *Genesis II,* 283.
92. Holladay explains this in the sense of "We have moved on, and therefore we will not come to you." Holladay, *Jeremiah 1,* 108. Lundbom explains "break loose," like many other scholars, but has trouble with the verb's other appearances in Psalms and Hosea (Lundbom, *Jeremiah,* 292).
93. For example: Weisman and Levinstein, *Hosea,* 73.
94. CAD, r, 226.
95. Many explain the verse in Jeremiah 2 in the sense of "differentiation," such as Metzudot writes in context: "It means parting from the place of adherence" (Rashi writes similarly). This too can apply to our verse: "When you part ways – then you will cast off his yoke."

And thus the cat is let out of the bag. It is now clear why Esau's blessing pales in comparison to Jacob's; it is now clear why Isaac is so loath to give Esau his consolation prize. The only way Esau will manage to throw off his brother's yoke is to part ways with him; to leave the land Jacob will inherit, the land that will bless Jacob with much grain and wine. If Esau seeks freedom, he must settle in a different land and leave his family behind.[96] This means that Esau will leave his father's house and break away from the line of Abraham.

Needless to say, this is not what Isaac wants. Esau begs his father to bless him with whatever blessing remains, but Isaac cannot bear to reveal it because of his deep love for him. But after Esau pleads again and again, his tears break Isaac's heart, and he breaks down and tells him the terrible secret.

This reading also clarifies why Esau leaves Canaan and settles in Edom in Genesis 36. When Jacob returns from Haran he meets Esau, who has come from Seir. An interesting verse explains that Esau leaves for Edom because of the vast amount of property he has amassed: "Esau took his wives, sons and daughters, and all the members of his household, together with his livestock, his other animals, and all the possessions he had acquired in Canaan, and he moved to another region, away from his brother Jacob" (36:6). In my analysis of chapter 36, we will explore how this verse offers a different perspective of the brothers' separation, but for now, I wish to point out that Esau clearly *chooses* to leave Canaan. If Isaac's blessing to Esau implies that he will only be free of his brother's yoke if they part ways, it is obvious what motivates his migration. Esau indeed takes his family and moves elsewhere, where his sons can be princes and rulers instead of subjects to his brother Jacob.

What Were Isaac's Original Intentions?

The scene's end leads us to a fundamental question of the narrative: What did Isaac want in the first place? A straightforward reading implies

96. With some hesitance, I wish to point out Pseudo-Jonathan's unusual interpretation of Isaac's words to Esau: "Go now; what shall I do, my son" (27:37).

that Isaac never intended for the family to split up.[97] R. Samuel David Luzzatto (known as Shadal), believes that Isaac assumed his sons would remain together:

> As for Isaac's intentions ... he thought that Jacob would remain with Esau and both of them would inherit the land that God gave to Abraham, and that Abraham's blessing would be fulfilled through both of them, for both of them were the seed of Isaac and his wife.[98]

Shadal implies that Jacob and Esau are not comparable to Isaac and Ishmael; Ishmael is the son of a concubine, and even before Isaac's birth, Abraham is told that God will establish His covenant with him and not his older brother. But Esau is Jacob's twin, born to Isaac and Rebecca – and with their complementary strengths, together they could build a powerful nation ("the House of Isaac"?).

The content of Isaac's blessing to Jacob – intended for Esau – shows that this is not Abraham's blessing, but a blessing fit for the head of a family, a clan, a national or even international power. The combined blessing of fertile soil and leadership recalls Jacob's blessing to Judah as he hands him the family reins – as the leader of his brothers, but not to their exclusion. When Isaac exclaims, "May your mother's sons bow down to you" (27:29), his blessing is no different than Jacob's future words to Judah: "May your father's sons bow down to you" (Gen. 49:8). Jacob elects Judah as the head of the family without rejecting the others, and this is also Isaac's intention: to choose a son to lead the clan (a clan that includes his brother!) after his death.

---

97. Compare to Rackman, "Was Isaac Deceived," 41; Assis, *Identity in Conflict*, 45–59. Rackman believes (as do others) that Isaac wished to bless Esau with a material blessing and Jacob with a spiritual blessing = Abraham's blessing. But when he heard about the birthright transaction, he realized that the two could not cooperate, and he chose to bestow both blessings upon Jacob (Rackman, "Was Isaac Deceived?" 41–45). I do not believe that Abraham's blessing was originally supposed to be transferred to either of the sons at this point, as I will discuss below.
98. Shadal, *Commentary on the Torah*, 231.

In the end, however, when it is clear that Esau intends to move on and break away from the family in order to evade his brother's dominion, Isaac only leaves Abraham's blessing to one son – to the son who will return to the Promised Land.

Was Rebecca aware of the nature of Isaac's blessing? It is difficult to say. As mentioned, Rebecca reports that Isaac's blessing will be bestowed "before the Lord," which reveals her perception of its stature, nature, and scope. At the same time, however, Rebecca seeks the fulfillment of her prophecy, whether or not she is expected to do so.[99] Given that Rebecca is aware that her two sons will become two nations, from her perspective, Isaac's intention to promote Esau – even if it is "only" as head of the family – has far-reaching implications she must prevent at all costs.

Ancestral Fault Lines

Family continuity – of the family as a whole, a complete unit – is inherent to Abraham's covenant. In biblical thought, a nation is an extension of a single family, so when a certain family line is elected, every single son of that line is part of that covenant. This is reflected in the talmudic concept that "despite his sin – he is part of Israel" (Sanhedrin 44a, and elsewhere). Every one of Jacob's sons is considered part of the "children of Israel," even though Reuben lies with his father's concubine, and even though Jacob is critical of Simeon and Levi's violence against Shechem.

As discussed in the introduction, God's repeated promises to Abraham that the covenant will be fulfilled through Isaac are inherent to the nature of the family covenant: "Nonetheless, Sarah your wife will bear you a son, and you shall name him Isaac. I will establish My covenant with him as an everlasting covenant for his descendants after him" (17:19); "I will establish My covenant with Isaac" (17:21); "It is through Isaac that your descendants will be reckoned" (21:12). Ishmael

99. Fretheim comments that the fact that Rebecca seizes the reins shows that the prophecy may not have come true, and it is up to people to act to bring about its fulfillment (Fretheim, "Blessing," 285–86). This is consistent with Rebecca's character, but in any case, the definition of this prophecy as "an inquiry of God" condones human action.

is excluded because he is the son of Hagar; God's blessing will only be channeled through the seed of Abraham and Sarah.

But alas and alack – Esau now chooses to withdraw from the covenant, complicating Isaac's role as heir. Rashi attempts to smooth over this complication: "What I promised Abraham about his seed, I promised to you [Jacob], but not to Esau. For I did not say, 'Isaac will be reckoned as your descendants,' but '*Through* Isaac your descendants will be reckoned' – not all of Isaac's [descendants will be part of the covenant]" (on Gen. 28:15). This attempts to soften the sharp deviation from the covenant's projected path by postulating that only some of Isaac's descendants were supposed to be part of the covenant from the outset. Yet we must admit that the verses' plain meaning is that Isaac should have been the one to establish the covenant, yet its establishment was postponed by a generation. One of Isaac's sons is not part of Abraham's covenant, and therefore Isaac himself cannot found the nation.

The story of the theft of the blessings is a schism that leads to a new process of election. The new nation cannot be named for Isaac, because that would imply that all of his children are part of it. Now it is up to Jacob to take Abraham's blessings and begin the covenant anew. To this end, he leaves his father's house and journeys to retrace his grandfather's footsteps. God appears to him and bestows all the blessings once promised to Abraham, but unlike His blessings to Isaac, God's promise is not of continuity but of renewal, of a fresh start.[100] Jacob does not flee to Haran solely to escape his brother's wrath, or to find a wife from his mother's line, but to reenact Abraham's journey so that these blessings will be manifest through a family he establishes himself. This time, the process will unfold through more subtle divine help; while God walks Abraham through the process with revelation after revelation, God watches over Jacob from afar, peering through the cracks as he makes his own decisions along the way.

100. Assis claims that Jacob is given Abraham's blessing because he is about to leave Canaan. He claims that Isaac did not intend to only bless one of his sons, nor does Jacob understand that he alone is chosen (Assis, *Identity in Conflict*, 54–59).

***A Deadly Transition: Esau Plots His Brother's Murder* (27:41)**

Between Isaac's heartrending dialogue with Esau (D') and Rebecca's warning to Jacob that he must flee to Haran (C'), there is a transitional verse that is not a dialogue between two characters: "Esau resented Jacob because of the blessing his father had given him. He said to himself, 'The days of my father's mourning are close – I will kill my brother Jacob'" (41). This is not a scene in itself, nor is it a substantial structural component of the plot. The next scene is also followed by a similar transitional verse (27:41), and I will discuss the structural contribution of these two verses below. Though the narrator explicitly portrays Esau's malevolence, even so he is characterized in a complex light rather than as an irredeemable antagonist. "The days of my father's mourning" can be read in one of two ways. R. Joseph Bekhor Shor reads the verse as a parallelism: Isaac will soon mourn for his son/because Esau will kill him. It is quite surprising that Esau is prepared to cause his father such grief, but Bekhor Shor believes that Esau's love for his father has turned to anger: "He therefore said, 'My father blessed him, so I will soon make him mourn for him.'" This reading is certainly possible from a grammatical perspective, but it is unconvincing within the broader context of the plot. Esau is devoted to his father; this is clear not only from the beginning of the plot, but even after Jacob steals the blessings, when Esau marries Ishmael's daughter in an attempt to please his father. If so, it is unlikely that he would wish to cause him such grief, and the prevalent reading of the verse is far more convincing: Esau means to kill Jacob after Isaac's death, during or after the mourning period for Isaac himself.[101]

Esau thus controls his murderous anger for the time being. Ramban reads this as a practical consideration: "He was afraid that he would curse him by turning his blessing into a curse." But it can also be read as a sign of Esau's unwavering love for his father: despite his anger, he does not wish to cause him grief (as Rashi, Radak, and many others hold).

This redemption of Esau's character should not be dismissed. The text could have described how Rebecca sends Jacob away because of

---

101. For example, "*evel Moshe*" in Deuteronomy 34:8 is mourning for Moses, not Moses' mourning for others.

Esau's murderous anger without any mention of his self-control. Esau's ongoing sensitivity and respect for his father casts him in an ambivalent light; despite his (understandable) rage at his brother, he will not cause his father grief.

C'. Rebecca Sends Jacob to Haran (27:42–46)

Once again, Rebecca overhears something she is not supposed to hear, and once again, what she hears moves her to give her favorite son instructions: "Now my son, listen to me. Flee at once to my brother Laban in Haran" (v. 43). In this respect, this component (C') is parallel to (C), wherein Rebecca instructs Jacob to disguise himself as Esau and approach his father. Yet there is one important difference between them. Rebecca's instructions are followed not by Jacob's response, but by her ensuing words to Isaac. For the first and only time in the Bible, Rebecca speaks directly to her husband Isaac, preparing the ground for Jacob's imminent departure. To the reader's disappointment, perhaps, Isaac not does answer her; the reader is never to hear anything Isaac says to his wife. This verse, too, thus serves as a transition between Rebecca's instructions to Jacob, and Isaac's instructions to Jacob. Despite the brief moment of communication between mother and father, the house remains divided into two factions: Isaac and Esau, and Rebecca and Jacob. Until now, Isaac has only spoken to Jacob when he believes that he is Esau, but this dichotomy will be broken in the very next scene.

Rebecca's instructions to Jacob contain the "*shuv*" sound three times, from two different roots: Y-SH-B and SH-O-B: "Stay with him (*veyashavta*) a while, until your brother's rage subsides (*tashuv*). When your brother is no longer (*shuv*) angry with you" (vv. 44–45). Wordplay with these two similar roots is common in the Bible,[102] but their combination here generates a particularly astute effect. In Hebrew, her words read thus: "*Veyashavta imo yamim aḥadim ad asher tashuv*" – "Stay with him a while until *tashuv*" – the word *tashuv* means "return" in second person masculine singular, and this is a logical translation for her sentence

102. Ibn Ezra comments on this technique throughout his commentary (for example, Gen. 3:1; Ex. 22:5; Judges 15:4; 15:16; Hag. 1:11). On his sensitivity to wordplay, see Melamed, *Biblical Commentators*, vol. 2, 579.

so far: "Stay with him a while until you return." Indeed, the verb root SH-O-B features again and again in the story of Jacob's exile, emphasizing that his journey is only temporary, and he will return to his homeland as soon as possible: "I will bring you back (*vahashivotikha*) to this land" (28:15); "If I return (*veshavti*) to my father's house in peace" (v. 21). But the sentence goes on: "*ad asher tashuv ḥamat aḥikha*" – "until *your brother's rage* subsides." To the reader's surprise, the word *tashuv* here is not second person singular, but third person feminine singular, applying not to Jacob's return but to Esau's rage. Rebecca does not use the verb root SH-O-B about Jacob's return because his return is dependent not on his own free will, but upon Esau. Jacob will only be able to return home when Esau's rage subsides. This is the epitome of exile: not only is a person forced to leave his home, but he is powerless to determine when he can return.

Another Transition (27:46)

As mentioned, these are the only words Rebecca ever addresses to Isaac in the Bible, but even here, Isaac's verbal response is not recorded. Moreover, at first glance, it seems that this sentence is but a mere excuse to cover up her true motive for sending Jacob away: "I loathe my life because of these Hittite women. If Jacob marries a Hittite woman like them, one of the women of the land, why should I go on living?" (v. 46). Just a moment before, Rebecca informs Isaac that he must flee from Esau, but she does not mention this to her husband; does she wish to protect Isaac from knowledge of Esau's murderous thirst for vengeance, and pretend that she is merely sending Jacob away to find a wife?[103] If this is indeed an excuse, it explains her bumbling, awkward language: "If Jacob marries a Hittite woman like them, one of the women of the land" – her stuttering excuse reflects the prick of her conscience as she deceives her elderly husband.[104]

Yet this reading does not suffice. After all, marriage is an important motif in a narrative framed by a description of Esau's marriages. Although Rebecca's immediate motive is protecting Jacob from his

103. Hertz, *Pentateuch,* 238.

104. On this technique see, for example, Rendsburg, "Confused Language."

furious brother, within a broader context, sending Jacob to Haran to find a wife emerges as a major theme. Even if the reason she gives Isaac is an excuse, it is ultimately crucial in itself.

This verse, like the verse describing Esau's plan to murder Jacob, deviates from the narrative's otherwise tight chiastic structure. One might claim that these stray verses undermine the structure's integrity, but given that they are transitional verses between dialogues, they can be overlooked within the narrative's general sequence. At the same time, however, their contribution to the plot is far from negligible: in a certain sense, these two verses reveal the motivating factors of the entire narrative, as is evident from a comparison of the characters' shifting roles:

Isaac's Plan (27:1–40)	**Esau's Plan (27:41–28:9)**
Isaac wants to bless Esau	Esau wants to kill Jacob
Rebecca overhears Isaac's plan	Rebecca overhears Esau's plan
Rebecca spurs Jacob into action	Rebecca spurs Jacob and Isaac into action
Jacob carries out Rebecca's instructions	Jacob and Isaac carry out Rebecca's instructions
Esau acts "too late"	Esau acts "too late"

Neither Isaac nor Esau's plans come to fruition because Rebecca overhears them and intercedes. At the end of both halves, Esau ends up as a tragic figure; as someone who is trying to keep up with his brother, but who fails. At the end of the first half, he walks in with the special food his father requested, but he is too late, and desperately implores his father: "Have you only one blessing, father? Bless me too, my father!" (v. 38). Jacob has won the lion's share, but Esau still begs his father for a consolation prize. In the second half, when Esau realizes that his father cannot abide his wives, and that Jacob has left for Haran to marry, Esau takes Ishmael's daughter as a wife – once again emerging as a pale imitation of his brother.

This division emphasizes Rebecca's immense influence on the plot. She hears one character's intentions and manipulates another; at first she sends Jacob to execute her plan, and later influences both Jacob and her husband Isaac.

As I mentioned above, Rebecca's characterization absolves Jacob of any guilt. It is not his decision to deceive his father, nor does he choose to leave the Land. Indeed, the "curse is on her," rather than upon Jacob's head, and ultimately, both he and her husband capitulate to her will – which is all for the good of her son Jacob.

B'. Isaac and Jacob

Perhaps overshadowed by the narrative climax of Jacob's deception, this scene, too, sees one of the most dramatic moments of the entire story. Not only is it wrought with the historical significance of Isaac transmitting Abraham's blessing to Jacob, but it is also the only scene in which Isaac intentionally speaks to his son Jacob.

At the beginning of the narrative, Isaac summons Esau because he wishes to bless him: "He summoned his elder son Esau … so that my soul may bless you before I die" (27:1, 4); here, Isaac summons Jacob because he wishes to bless him: "Isaac summoned Jacob and he blessed him" (28:1). Reading these two scenes in parallel, Jacob's journey to Haran takes on its full significance. He is not merely running away from his brother's sword, following his mother's instructions; Isaac is sending him off in full ceremony, as a man on a mission – to marry an Aramean girl as he himself did before him. Just as Isaac sends Esau to the field, he now sends Jacob to the fields of Aram, and in this way Jacob will earn the blessing that awaits him.

The reader must admit that compared to Isaac's warm, intimate dialogue with Esau, his words to Jacob seem somewhat cold and stilted. His blessing to Jacob is just as exalted and sublime as his first blessing, but their interaction is devoid of any affection. After Isaac calls Esau, he fondly says to him, "My son," and Esau replies, "Here I am" (v. 1). Isaac exchanges no such pleasantries with Jacob; he cuts straight to the chase and bids him to go to Padan Aram.

Yet even so, Isaac's words still bring the reader a sense of relief. The story could have ended with violent expulsion of the son who stole the blessings away from the father's favorite; Isaac could have reprimanded him and banished him from his sight. Isaac's rapid conciliation with the new reality serves as strong proof for those who argue that Isaac was keeping Abraham's blessing for Jacob all along. Yet this scene is also consistent with the reading I proposed above. Firstly, it is worth noting Elie Assis' belief that Isaac's transmission of Abraham's blessing to Jacob does not exclude Esau from Abraham's covenant; Isaac is simply sharing the blessing with Jacob before he leaves his father's house. Jacob, instructed to leave Canaan, might fear that he is being rejected, so Isaac's blessing (and God's revelation to Jacob soon after) reassures him that despite his departure, he will still be part of the covenant.[105] If Assis' fresh, innovative reading is correct, then at this stage Isaac still hopes that the two brothers will build the nation of God's covenant together, despite the new hierarchy between them. I will add that for now, Esau has not been rejected, but when he leaves Canaan for Mount Seir, he effectively chooses to leave Abraham's covenant.

Yet even if we adopt the more prevalent reading that Isaac's bestowal of Abraham's blessing effectively elects Jacob and rejects Esau, we must be aware of where this blessing is integrated in the plot.

The blessing Isaac gives Jacob profoundly echoes the promises Abraham hears during the Covenant of Circumcision (Gen. 17). This is especially salient through the divine name "El Shaddai," which is the name God Himself uses during the Covenant of Circumcision (17:1); but other key phrases, such as "make you fertile and multiply you," "a community of peoples," "the land where of your wayfaring you live as a stranger," also strengthen the connection of this passage with Abraham's circumcision. Though the verb used in this blessing, "that you may possess," recalls the Covenant Between the Pieces (15:7–8), most of the blessing is in dialogue with the Covenant of Circumcision.[106]

Why is Isaac's blessing so evocative of circumcision? The answer is clear: the promise of circumcision is fundamentally related to fertility and establishing a family – which is relevant, of course, on the eve of Jacob's journey to find a wife. Fertility is at the forefront of the father's mind, and this is the blessing he gives his son. Two axes of blessing unfold over the course of the Abraham cycle; fertility is associated

105. Assis, *Identity in Conflict*, 54–59

106. It is thus not surprising that scholars look for "all families of the earth will be blessed through you." This blessing is related to Abraham with the Tetragrammaton, and Jacob will hear it in the next scene.

with the name Shaddai, while a different axis, associated with the Tetragrammaton, is promised in chapters 12–13.[107] These blessings, too, will soon be promised to Jacob – by God, in Jacob's vision of the ladder. Thus, on his journey back to his ancestors' homeland, he is promised two axes of blessing like his grandfather before him: one from his father, and the other from God.

Stephen Langton's division into chapters concludes the story of the theft of the blessings with Rebecca's complaint to Isaac, "I loathe my life because of these Hittite women" (27:46), while Isaac's instructions to Jacob to go to Padan Aram mark the beginning of a new chapter that ends with Jacob's vision of the ladder. This division seems logical: Isaac tells Jacob to travel to his uncle's house and Jacob immediately sets out; this forms a cohesive literary unit. Nonetheless, there are two reasons why it is more convenient to read Isaac's instructions to Jacob as part of the deception narrative. Firstly, as mentioned, the literary structure includes this scene, and even the scene after it – Esau's marriage – as part of the same narrative. The story opens with Esau's marriage to the Hittite women, and concludes with Esau's marriage to Ishmael's daughter. Within this framework, the components of the two halves are arranged in chiastic parallel order, and Isaac's instructions to Jacob are an organic part of the structure.

There is a further reason to reject Langton's division, despite the temptation to group Isaac's instructions together with their execution. In order to understand this reason, I will now present a central feature that has bearing on the entire Jacob cycle.

There is a dramatic difference between the instructions Jacob receives from his mother and father. Rebecca is terrified for her son's life – he must flee. Haran is a good option because her family will welcome the refugee, but the main point is that he must leave their home in Canaan where Esau lies in wait for him. By contrast, Isaac is more focused on Jacob's destination: he must travel to Laban in Padan Aram, and take one of his daughters for a wife. These two journeys are painted in completely different colors: Is Jacob a terrified refugee, snatching sleep

107. See both axes of this blessing in Grossman, *Abraham*, 164–70; 208–17; 281–89; 418–20.

in hidden places along the unbeaten path, always looking behind him to make sure he is not being followed; or is he a proud, shining-faced suitor, marching down the highway to his father's blessing? We will yet argue that the narrative alternates between these two portraits of Jacob along the way.

This dichotomy is also characterized by a subtle yet perceptible linguistic difference, here and throughout the narrative: Is Jacob fleeing for his life, or on a mission to find a wife? Rebecca tells her son to flee to "Haran" (27:43), while Isaac refers to his son's destination as "Padan Aram" (28:2, 5). The relationship between these place names is unclear. Some interpret "Padan" according to its Arabic and Aramaic meaning of "field" ("Padan Aram" = "the fields of Aram" [Hos. 12:13] = Aram Naharaim). Others argue that "Padan" should be understood based on the Akkadian word *padanu*, a synonym for *ḥarrânu*, meaning "way"; that is, Padan Aram is the ancient name for Haran, and the two have the same meaning.[108] Whether the city's two names share a meaning or not, in this narrative they refer to the same place – Laban's home. It is difficult to say why Jacob's flight from Esau is associated with "Haran" while his marriage is with "Padan Aram," but the distinction results in an intriguing *inclusio.* Abraham's journey begins with his departure from his father's home in *Haran* (11:31–31; 12:4), and now Jacob must also leave his father's home and flee to Haran.[109] At the same time, the Jacob cycle begins with a description of his father Isaac's marriage to Rebecca of *Padan Aram* (25:20), and now Jacob follows in his father's path and travels to find a wife from his mother's family in Padan Aram. For whatever reason, the two aspects of Jacob's journey are differentiated by the two names of Laban's hometown.

In light of this, I wish to point out the second disadvantage of Langston's chapter division: it is indeed convenient to group instructions together with their execution, rather than disrupt the two. But in this case, the beginning of *Parashat Vayetzeh* does not report the execution of Isaac's instructions, but of Rebecca's. Jacob leaves Beersheba

108. See this debate in Mathews, *Genesis II*, 386. It may be that Padam Aram refers to the region of the city Haran.
109. Compare to Vrolijk, *Jacob's Wealth*, 107.

and flees toward "Haran." This detail will have bearing on our analysis of the next *parasha*, the next unit. For now, I wish to point out that the execution of Isaac's instructions is included within the literary unit of Jacob's deception, even before the report of Esau's marriage to Ishmael's daughter: "Then Isaac sent Jacob on his way. He went toward *Padan Aram*, to Laban son of Bethuel the Aramean, brother of Rebecca, Jacob and Esau's mother" (28:5); and we even hear of Jacob's obedience to his father from Esau's perspective: "Esau learned that Isaac had blessed Jacob and sent him to *Padan Aram* to find a wife... and that Jacob had obeyed his father and mother and had gone to *Padan Aram*" (28:6–7). Jacob executes Isaac's instructions within the boundaries of this literary unit. The story of Jacob's ladder goes back again to Jacob's departure from Beersheba because it marks the execution of Rebecca's instructions that Jacob must flee to Haran.

Therefore Wenham is incorrect in claiming that Jacob fulfills his father's instructions, but not his mother's.[110] The next unit opens with focus on his departure from Beersheba, as his mother commands. True, the previous unit ends with his obedience to Isaac, but the fulfillment of his father's orders does not preclude his mother's; both are fulfilled through his exile to Laban's home.

Nonetheless, both aspects of Jacob's journey are present in Rebecca's complaint to Isaac: "I loathe my life because of these Hittite women. If Jacob marries a Hittite woman like them, one of the women of the land, why should I go on living?" (27:47). I have already noted that Rebecca's words seem to be a pretext for sending Jacob away because she fears for his life.

Yet this pretext is legitimate in itself: her words read as a continuation of the narrator's observation that Esau's wives are "a source of bitter sorrow to Isaac and Rebecca (26:35)... and Rebecca said to Isaac, 'I loathe my life because of *these* Hittite women'" (27:46). The word "these" gives the sense of something just mentioned – as if she is continuing the opening scene of our unit, referring to Esau's wives.

Thus the double objective of Jacob's journey to the house of Laban is already contained in Rebecca's complaint to Isaac. On the one hand,

110. Wenham, *Genesis II*, 214.

it is a diplomatic way of protecting Jacob from his brother's murderous wrath – that is, the beginning of his flight. On the other, it *is* an honest response to Esau's problematic marriage; one that initiates Jacob's journey to find a wife. Jacob's mother is thus responsible for his departure as well as his destination, and her words serve as a smooth transition between the two perspectives.

A'. Esau's Marriage with Ishmael's Daughter (28:6–9)

The end of the story is almost unbelievable. After poor Esau has been betrayed by his mother and brother, his beloved father deliberately bestows yet another blessing upon Jacob – the blessing of Abraham. One certainly expects Esau's fierce anger to turn to deep disappointment – at his brother, his mother, and above all, at the father he loves so deeply, who essentially condemns him to the role of servant unless he leaves his family forever. And suddenly, among all this heartbreak and disappointment, Esau learns that his parents disapprove of his wives, or to be precise: he seems less troubled by his mother's disapproval, but he realizes that "the Canaanite women displeased his father Isaac" (28:8). Hurt as he is, his father's displeasure agitates Esau, and instead of turning his back on the family that betrayed him, Esau marries another wife – all to please his father.

These verses are arranged in two beats, drawing a kind of parallel between Jacob and Esau's actions in response to their father's disapproval of Canaanite women:

> (6) *Esau saw* (*vayar*) that Isaac had blessed Jacob and sent him to Padan Aram to find a wife, and that when he blessed him, he commanded him not to marry a Canaanite woman,
>
> > (7) *and that Jacob had obeyed* his father and mother and *had gone* (*vayelekh*) to Padan Aram.
>
> (8) *Esau saw* (*vayar*) then that the Canaanite women displeased his father Isaac.
>
> > (9) *So Esau went* (*vayelekh*) to Ishmael and took Mahalat, daughter of Abraham's son Ishmael, a sister of Nevayot, to be his wife, with his other wives.

A marginal detail reinforces the aforementioned characterization. This scene is focalized through Esau, and it is fascinating to see how Esau has eyes for his father alone, while Jacob takes both his parents into consideration: "Esau saw that Isaac had blessed Jacob and … commanded him not to marry a Canaanite woman. Jacob had obeyed his father *and* mother…. Esau saw then that the Canaanite women displeased *his father Isaac*." Esau, like the reader, is presumably aware that his mother is equally appalled by his Canaanite wives – in fact, Rebecca is the one who orchestrates Jacob's journey – but his only concern is his father's displeasure.

These verses reflect Esau's observation and understanding of his parents' perception of his marriage. At first, Esau simply observes: Isaac blesses Jacob and forbids him to marry Canaanite women. Next, Esau draws conclusions from this observation: Isaac disapproves of Canaanite women.

In both parts, the first sentence describes the son's action as a result of his father's disapproval of Canaanite women: Jacob *goes* (*vayelekh*) to Padan Aram (v. 7), while Esau *goes* (*vayelekh*) to Ishmael "and took Mahalat, daughter of Abraham's son Ishmael, a sister of Nevayot, to be his wife." The status of verse 7 is not entirely clear: Is it a continuation of Esau's perception (as Rashi holds), or a parenthetical description by the narrator? Either way, it underscores Jacob's loyalty to his father *and* mother, compared to Esau's regard for his father alone. Jacob's obedience to his father in this scene creates a certain balance within the story, and perhaps even justifies his possession of the blessings.

The link between the two things Esau "sees" once again emphasizes the connection between the themes of blessing and marriage: "Esau saw that Isaac had blessed Jacob"/"Esau saw then that the Canaanite women displeased his father Isaac." This parallel hints to the reason why Jacob, and not Esau, receives their father's blessings; once again, the narrative framework justifies, to a certain extent, Jacob's act of deception.[111]

111. Rashbam writes similarly: Esau saw that Isaac blessed Jacob … he thought to himself: The blessings were taken from me because of my marriage to Canaanite women, and he married a daughter of Ishmael from Abraham's family. He thought to himself:

Does Esau's new marriage mollify his parents? Is he now worthy of their blessing? Esau's decision is problematic. On the one hand, he is marrying a woman who is not of Canaanite origin. While Rashi criticizes him for not divorcing his first wives, Esau's new marriage nonetheless conveys his desire to appease his father. On the other hand, do his parents' reservations stem from his wives' origin, or from their place of residence in Canaan? Each parent's emphasis is slightly different. Rebecca first refers to their nationality, but then complains about their geographical origin (27:46):

> I loathe my life because of these Hittite women.
> If Jacob marries a Hittite woman like them,
> one of the women of the land,
> why should I go on living?

Rebecca presumably adds "one of the women of the land" in order to persuade Isaac to send Jacob far away to her distant family, rather than look for a local woman of non-Canaanite origin. Isaac is indeed convinced and sends him to Padan Aram. From Isaac's perspective, the only issue seems to be a geographical one: "He sent him to Padan Aram to take a wife *from there*.... You are not to marry a *Canaanite woman*." Although "Canaanite woman" can be understood in the sense of nationality, it seems more likely that he is referring to location: women who live in the land of Canaan, regardless of their nationality.

If so, then Esau is imitating Jacob but missing the whole point: he takes a wife who is not of Canaanite origin, but is still local; one whose clan lives in the area, potentially seeking to mesh with the husband's clan. The ambivalent nature of Esau's marriage is a fitting closing act for a character as elusive as Esau.

A comparison of Jacob's journey to Laban's family and Esau's union with Ishmael's family creates a fascinating parallel: Jacob marries into his mother's family, while Esau marries into his father's family. This

---

Perhaps now I will be granted a share in Abraham's inheritance" (Rashbam on Gen. 28:6).

is salient through a comparison of the narrator's description of the events and Esau's perception of them:

The Story (28:1–5)	**Esau's Perspective (28:6–9)**
So Isaac called Jacob to him. He blessed him and charged him: "You are not to marry a Canaanite woman.	Esau saw that Isaac had blessed Jacob
Go at once to Padan Aram, to the house of your mother's father Bethuel, and there marry a daughter of your mother's brother Laban."	and sent him to Padan Aram to find a wife, and that when he blessed him, he commanded him not to marry a Canaanite woman,
Then Isaac sent Jacob on his way. He went toward Padan Aram, to Laban son of Bethuel the Aramean, brother of Rebecca, Jacob and Esau's mother.	and that Jacob had obeyed his father and mother and had gone to Padan Aram… So Esau went to Ishmael and took Mahalat, daughter of Abraham's son Ishmael, a sister of Nevayot, to be his wife, with his other wives.

Esau is not concerned with the content of Jacob's blessing itself; his focus is on the mission to marry a non-Canaanite girl. Yet in this context, where the text nearly repeats itself word for word, the slight differences between the versions clarify Esau's course of action. Each mention of Rebecca's family in the story is replaced with how Esau "sees" the events: Isaac sends Jacob to Padan Aram "to the house of your mother's father Bethuel," but all Esau "sees" is his father sending Jacob to Padan Aram; Jacob travels to Padan Aram "to the house of Laban…brother of Rebecca," but all Esau sees is that Jacob sets out to Padan Aram. He realizes that his father is sending Jacob to find a wife, but he is not aware that Jacob is sent to a specific family.

The omission of Rebecca's family from Esau's perspective is not mere abbreviation; rather, it shows that Esau focuses on his father's disapproval of Canaanite women, but overlooks his desire that Jacob marry into his mother's family. Thus Esau's marriage is a misguided attempt to please his father.

Thus each brother marries into the family of his favorite parent. Esau creates family ties with the paternal cousin that was rejected a generation before him. Fierce desert dwellers and chieftains and kings of the red rock of Seir are the alternative lines descended from Abraham, while Jacob, graced with his grandfather's blessing, heads to Padan Aram to establish the house of Israel.

EVALUATING THE CHARACTERS: DOES THE END JUSTIFY THE MEANS?

Assessing Rebecca and Jacob's actions in this story is complex. Does the Torah approve of Rebecca's initiative, or is there veiled criticism for their deception of blind old Isaac? Both approaches can be found in midrashic literature. Some side with Rebecca and criticize Isaac for wanting to bless Esau:

> "He who acquits the guilty, and he who condemns the innocent – both are anathema to the Lord" (Prov. 17:15). R. Yehoshua son of Levi said: Rebecca did not do this because she loved Jacob more than Esau, but rather, she said: I must prevent a mistake of "both are anathema to the Lord." Because he acquitted the guilty, his eyes went dim: "When Isaac grew old, his eyes became so dim he could not see." (Genesis Rabba 65:6).[112]

The author of the midrash begins by stating that Rebecca's motives were not personal but ideological; and furthermore, Isaac's blindness was a divine response to his "acquittal of the guilty" – that is, Esau. This midrash perceives Isaac's blindness as divine providence that would facilitate Jacob's deception: "Why did his eyes grow dim? The Holy One, blessed be He, knew that Isaac would want to bless Esau, so the Holy One made his eyes grow dim so that Jacob would be able to come and take the blessings and Isaac would not know whom he was blessing" (*Tanḥuma* on *Toledot* 8:8).

112. Later on, the midrash even states: "This moved them to say: Whoever has a wicked son or wicked student – his eyes will eventually grow dim" (Genesis Rabba 65:10).

On the other hand, other midrashim bring this story as an example of how God never lets a sin go unpunished, and always pays back a sinner (or his descendants) eventually:

> R. Ḥanina said: Whoever says that the Holy One, blessed be He, concedes – let his insides be cut to pieces! For He patiently waits to collect His due. Jacob made Esau cry out, as is written: "He burst into a loud and bitter cry," and where is this avenged? In the capital of Shushan, as it says: "And he burst into a loud and bitter cry" (Est. 4). (Genesis Rabba 67:4)

This midrash's premise is that Esau's bitter cry is justified, and must be avenged.

The complexity of the character assessment is already evident in the narrative itself. I identify with Assis' observation about the gaping voids in the narrative: "The author of the story intentionally crafted an ambiguous narrative…the narrative's message, I believe, is integral to its enigmatic form."[113] For our purposes, I wish to emphasize that there is no explicit assessment of any of the characters in the text, and we have no choice but to make the most of indirect appraisal. First and foremost is Isaac's explanation that "your brother came in deceit and took your blessing" (27:35). Defining Jacob's act as an act of "deceit" implies that it is illegitimate and dishonest. Moreover, Isaac's use of the phrase "your brother" is even more incriminating: it is Esau's own brother who deceives him – if Esau cannot trust his own brother, then who can he trust? The reader is reminded of Jeremiah's harsh criticism of the people:

> Let each man be on guard against his fellow, and let no one trust his own brother,
> for every brother acts deceitfully (*ki khol aḥ akov yakov*), and every friend spreads slander.
> Each man defrauds his fellow and speaks untruth; they have trained their tongues to speak lies.
> (Jer. 9:3–4)

113. Assis, *Identity in Conflict*, 43.

Jeremiah mentions the "deceit" that is spreading among the people: "Every *brother* acts *deceitfully – khol aḥ akov yakov*" – which plays, of course, on the literal meaning of Jacob's name, and recalls his deceit against his brother.[114]

Yet before we judge Jacob too severely, it is worth pointing out that although the reader is usually supposed to identify with Isaac, that may not be the case in this narrative. When Isaac is suffering among the Philistines, of course the reader takes his side against their hostile shepherds, but here, when Isaac's rival is his wife Rebecca, it is not at all clear that Isaac's perspective should be the reader's default perspective.

And indeed, despite the obvious criticism against a son who deceives his blind old father to steal his brother's blessing, it is clear that the text mitigates his guilt as much as possible. Firstly, the epicenter of tension is not between father and son but between husband and wife, while Jacob obeys his mother's explicit orders. Secondly, the subtle allusion to the story of Cain and Abel hints that the younger son is to receive the father's blessing, just as God accepts Abel's offering and rejects his older brother's; this analogy does not flatter Esau, who is painted in the murderous tones of Cain.

There are further contributing factors, but these suffice to show that the character assessment in this narrative is far from straightforward. It would be inaccurate to state that there is no assessment at all. Although it is not the narrative's central focus, there are still hints of its evaluation of the various characters' actions – but this evaluation is ambivalent at best.

The decision is further complicated in context of the brothers' history. After all, even before their birth, their mother is told that "the greater shall the younger serve," contrary to prevalent custom. And when Esau complains, "Is he not rightly named Jacob? Twice he has supplanted me. He took my birthright and now he has taken my blessing!" (27:36), he is essentially handing Jacob the best possible line of defense. Although Esau's intention is to portray Jacob as a serial deceiver, the mention of their transaction nonetheless works against the brother who rejected his

114. As proposed, for example, by Zobel, *Jacob*, 188. Rudolph even translates the verse thus: "Every brother is as deceitful as Jacob" (Rudolph, *Jeremiah*, 64).

birthright:[115] "By saying, 'I am your son, your firstborn, Esau' (v. 32), he is denying his total waiver, *by oath,* of his birthright (25:33), and he has not the slightest basis to accuse Jacob of seizing his birthright through deceit, for he sold it to him with full knowledge!"[116]

Effectively, Esau's mention of the birthright exposes the connection between the two scenes that has hitherto been bubbling below the surface. In both scenes, the birthright-blessing is linked to food (I have already noted that "bread" is added to the main dish in each scene),[117] and the character who requests food is concerned with his own imminent death. Esau relinquishes his birthright, claiming that he is starving to death: "Look, I am about to die – what use to me is a birthright?" (25:32), while Isaac wishes to bless Esau before his own death: "I am old, and I do not know when I will die" (27:2).[118] The Hebrew words for blessing, *berakha,* and birthright, *bekhora,* are anagrams, which highlights the connection between the two scenes.[119] In the words of Aharoni: "Many words and verses in this story only take on their full significance after a careful reading of all three acts, because each scene illuminates the others, clarifying and resolving their obscurities and ambiguities."[120]

Read within a broader narrative context, Rebecca and Jacob are cast in a dramatically different light, for the first two scenes provide each one with a hidden motive – one that the reader, too, is aware of.

115. For a detailed comparison between the birthright scene and the blessings scene, see Zakovitch, *Texts in the Land of Mirrors,* 91–92.
116. Zakovitch, "Jacob, Deceit," 132; Zakovitch, *Foreshadowing,* 98. For other opinions, see Ramban in context (the transaction was only for the primogenital share of the father's inheritance); Neufeld, *Marriage Laws,* 263 (Esau refers to himself as the "firstborn," which implies that he regrets the transaction); Brin, *Studies,* 60 (the transaction does not change Esau's title).
117. Albertz claims that food plays opposite roles in the two scenes: in the birthright scene, sharing their meal leads to tension; in the blessings scene, the meal moves Isaac to bless Jacob (Albertz, "Essen und Trinken").
118. Zakovitch, "Jacob, Deceit," 130–31; Zakovitch, "Foreshadowing," 97–98.
119. Given that it is Esau who interprets Jacob's name (27:36), it is likely that wordplay is intentionally used here. See also Brin, *Issues,* 60–61; Frisch, "Moral Evaluation." The idea Brin cites in Eisfeldt's name (ibid., n. 8) that Esau is referring not to the birthright but to the theft of the blessings in chapter 27 is problematic.
120. Aharoni, "Jacob and Esau," 327.

It is no coincidence that Christian exegesis and the scholars in its wake (such as Von Rad) tend to detach our scene from Rebecca's prophecy and Jacob's purchase of the birthright, thus increasing criticism against Jacob.[121] However, as I have already noted, Isaac's blessing is in subtle dialogue with Rebecca's prophecy, and thus Rebecca's maneuver is granted divine permission – at least from her perspective[122] – while Jacob's act is the next logical step of his transaction with Esau.[123]

As I initially noted, the narrative design itself invites various divisions, each one offering a different perspective of the characters. What does this shifting perspective contribute? The narrower the boundaries, the more accusing the portraits of Rebecca and Jacob; what is the point of this criticism, if it fades within a broader context?

Buber's observations illuminate this question:

> The primary role of the stories in Genesis is to explain how Israel's generations progress through its ancients' election, which must recur each generation anew; moreover, they must present how the elder is rejected through an act of divine providence; and one way or another, it cannot be condemned as an injustice... at the same time, he is not free to deny the essence of the theological-historical biblical secret, which dictates that divine providence allows room for human action and responsibility.[124]

In other words, Jacob's choice is presented in the narrative as the result of divine providence, but the way he obtains his blessing is not absolved of criticism. The inherent ambivalence of the text and its structure carries the divine message (which can also be found throughout the Bible) that "the end does not justify the means," and a person must act with

121. Unlike some midrashim that link all the scenes, and thus prevent potential criticism against Jacob. See Kellenberger, "Geburtsorakel und Betrugserzählung."
122. Zakovitch, "Jacob, Deceit," 133–34 (who even states that the scene's main objective is to vindicate Jacob); Fokkelman, *Genesis*, 86–94; Brin, *Studies*, 65, n. 16 (who sees the prophecy as an explanation that Jacob being the chosen one is part of the divine plan, but will not concede that Rebecca acts based on this knowledge).
123. For example: Sarna, *Understanding Genesis*, 183.
124. Buber, *Ways*, 291.

morality instead of assuming that his or her choices are justified because they fulfill divine will.

Famously, one of the most astonishing features of biblical narrative is its complex, multidimensional characters; the Bible does not shrink from telling of their flaws along with their virtues. The intricate ambivalence of this scene is part of a broader biblical theme: particular acts of deceit and injustice can be justified on a macro level, but on the micro level, the suffering these injustices cause cannot be overlooked. In the end, the individual frames that constitute the bigger picture also deserve attention, and even if the general principle is justified, the reader must not lose compassion for those who suffer along the way.

Thus it comes as no surprise that later on in the Jacob cycle, there are repeated hints that the blessings were unfairly taken, despite God's explicit election of Jacob in the very next scene:[125]

> The spiritual and sometimes physical destruction that God wreaks upon the heroes as part of His plan are utterly shocking. But, once again, God works in mysterious ways; His thoughts are not our thoughts, and His ways are not our ways.[126]

---

125. As already mentioned in some midrashim (such as *Old Tanḥuma, Vayetzeh,* 11), and, for example: Leibowitz, *Genesis,* 224–25; Rosenzweig, *Naharaim,* 12–13; Buber, *Ways,* 291–92; Fokkelman, *Genesis,* 128–29; Zakovitch, "Jacob, Deceit," 135 (who, as mentioned, blames Rebecca, although Jacob is the one who is punished); Frisch, "Moral Evaluation," 279–85.

126. Aharoni, "Jacob and Esau," 340.

Jacob's Ladder (Gen. 28:1–22)

But I, being poor, have only my dreams;
I have spread my dreams under your feet;
Tread softly because you tread on my dreams.
– William Butler Yeats

"One may not reach the dawn, save by the path of the night."[1] Kahlil Gibran's poignant words could have been written about Jacob, whose long journey begins with the fall of night in a cloud of fear, and ends with the gleam of dawn when he finally returns to Canaan's borders.

Two important encounters occur before Jacob reaches his destination. The first takes place on the first night of his departure, when he sees angels and God in a divine vision; and the second as soon as he reaches Haran, when he talks to the shepherds at the well, and – most important of all – meets Rachel. Both encounters have far-reaching implications for the rest of the Jacob cycle. We will first explore his famous dream and ensuing vow, seeking its hidden meaning as well as its obvious significance.

The first step of analysis is to note its context within the narrative sequence. The first verse is more telling than it seems: "Jacob left Beersheba and journeyed toward Haran" (28:10). Why is this information repeated when just a few verses earlier, the reader is told that Jacob carries out his father's instructions: "Then Isaac sent Jacob on his way.

1. Kahlil Gibran, *Sand and Foam*, 12.

He went toward Padan Aram, to Laban son of Bethuel the Aramean" (28:5)? His journey is even described from Esau's perspective: "Esau saw that Isaac had blessed Jacob and sent him to Padan Aram ... and that Jacob had obeyed his father and mother and had gone to Padan Aram" (28:6–7). Why, then, is this information repeated once again?

The most convenient explanation for this repetition is Rashi's: after the brief description of Esau's marriage, the text "returned to the previous topic." That is, this is a case of "connective repetition" – after a certain break in the narrative, the text returns to the main plot and reminds the reader of what was happening before its digression. In this case, after describing Esau's marriage, the text goes back to Jacob's journey. In the words of Abarbanel:

> At the end of the section of Isaac's *toledot*, it is written, "And Isaac sent Jacob on his way. He went toward Padan Aram etc.," and it then followed with what happened with Esau's wives, so when [the text] then wanted to tell of what happened to Jacob in Laban's house, and how he married there, had children, and became rich, it went back to the beginning and stated, "Jacob left Beersheba and went to Haran." (Abarbanel on Gen. 28)

Connective repetition, however, often introduces a new perspective or a slightly different nuance, rather than being merely technical; it also serves as an exposition to the new unit, anticipating the story about to unfold.[2] After briefly focusing on Esau's marriage, the text indeed reintroduces Jacob's journey – and presents a new angle of his departure. According to the earlier description, Jacob travels to Padan Aram following his father's order: "Isaac sent Jacob on his way. He went toward Padan Aram," while here, "Jacob left Beersheba and journeyed toward Haran." The name of Jacob's destination is of crucial importance within the context of the narrative cycle.

As mentioned, Jacob leaves Canaan for two reasons: his mother warns him to escape Esau's wrath, and his father bids him to find a wife

2. See further about this literary principle: Grossman, *Ruth*, 302–03, including footnotes.

from his mother's side of the family. Rebecca sends him to "Haran," while Isaac sends him to "Padan Aram." These alternating names reflect the nature of the scene in question: when Jacob journeys to "Haran," he is heeding his mother's warning; when his destination is referred to as "Padan Aram," his mission is to obey his father.

This distinction has dramatic implications for this scene and the significance of God's revelation to Jacob. Jacob's dream and God's revelation take place against a backdrop of desperation and fear for his life, and it is this fear that explains God's encouragement and promise that He will guard Jacob on his way. Jacob, fleeing his brother's murderous plot for revenge, is terrified for his very existence – he is concerned about food to eat and clothes to wear – and for this reason he needs a promise that God will watch over him and see that he returns home.

Moreover, this connective repetition introduces new content: "Jacob left Beersheba" (28:10). Jacob's place of origin is first mentioned in this description of his flight to Haran. This links his departure with the previous mention of Beersheba in Genesis – when Isaac flees Gerar: "From there he went up to Beersheba" (26:23). There, Isaac was also granted divine revelation offering him protection and providence wherever he went. I have already discussed how Isaac's "exile narrative" is closely linked to Jacob's "exile narrative," and this is also evident through a comparison between God's revelation to father and son:

Revelation to Isaac (26:24–33)	**Revelation to Jacob (28:11–19)**
That night the Lord appeared to him and said,	He decided to spend the night there, because the sun had set.... The Lord stood over him there and said,
"I am the God of your father Abraham.	"I am the Lord, the God of Abraham your father, and the God of Isaac.
Do not be afraid, for I am with you.	I am with you.
I will multiply your descendants..."	Your descendants shall be like the dust of the earth..."
He built an altar there.	He set it up as a pillar...
Therefore the city was called Beersheba to this day.	He named the place Bethel.

If so, perhaps "Beersheba" as the point of Jacob's departure is designed to generate continuity between these narratives. The story of Isaac's exile to the south-west ends in Beersheba, while Jacob's exile to the north-east begins with his departure from Beersheba. In both scenes, the forefathers are threatened by adversity, and in both, God promises that He will be with them wherever they go.[3]

This is the setting of Jacob's dream and God's revelation to him. We will now explore what takes place in this scene, and – of no less importance – what does not.

THE NARRATIVE OBJECTIVE

The narrative is not merely an etiological explanation of Jacob's sanctification, naming, and connection with Bethel. The overt objective of God's revelation to Jacob is to encourage the protagonist on his journey. God promises to watch over him wherever he goes, and indeed, after Jacob makes his vow the next morning, the narrator uses a unique expression to describe how Jacob continues on his way: "*vayisa Yaakov raglav,*" which literally means "and Jacob raised his legs" (29:1). This expression does not appear elsewhere in the Bible; eyes, voices (such as Esau's in chapter 27, and Jacob's in chapter 29), and even hands are frequently raised, but only Jacob "raised his legs." This suggests lightness of mood and movement; as Rashbam suggests, "Jacob raised his legs – after God's promise to him, he walked joyfully and swiftly."[4] This revelation gives Jacob strength for his long, difficult journey, for he knows that God is with him. In the words of Eliezer Schweid:

> From the reassuring knowledge that God is with him, Jacob draws the strength to embark on his mission, to "struggle" with

3. At the same time, it may be that the mention of Beersheba serves to link Jacob's flight to Haran with Israel's exile in Egypt, which also begins in Beersheba (Gen. 46:1–5). Jacob's revelation there is certainly in dialogue with Isaac's revelation in Beersheba, which links the three exiles: Isaac in Gerar; Jacob in Haran; Israel in Egypt.
4. As many other commentators, especially Radak: "Because God made him a promise and showed him this great vision, he rejoiced and moved his feet easily and went on his way happy and joyful, whereas until now he has walked with heavy steps as one who flees his father's house in sorrow."

> God and man, to hold on throughout all the ups and downs that await him, and to return as a person who has struggled with God and men and has prevailed.[5]

This may also be the role of the angels Jacob sees in his dream: guardian angels to watch over him on his way, similar to the angels Jacob will later encounter at Mahanaim on his way home from Haran,[6] who apparently also symbolize protection for Jacob. The angels at Mahanaim are of "God's own camp," that is, angels of war; perhaps they are connected to the angels of Bethel, as Rashi hints: "The angels who escorted him in the Land do not leave the Land, so they ascended to heaven, while the angels of outside the Land descended to escort him" (Rashi on 28:12).

It is therefore no wonder that the revelation at Bethel is alluded to throughout Jacob's exile, reflecting God's constant, if hidden, protection. When Jacob tells Laban, "For the twenty years *I was with you* (*anokhi imakh*)" (31:38), these words recall the only other place in the Bible where this phrase occurs – in God's promise of protection to Jacob at Bethel: "*I am with you* (*anokhi imakh*) and I will protect you wherever you go" (28:15). Similarly, Jacob tells Laban that "you had little before I came, but it has swelled into much. The Lord has blessed you wherever I have been" (30:30), and the rare verb "swell" (*vayifrotz*) occurs soon after about Jacob himself: "Thus the man's wealth swelled into a fortune" (30:43). This echoes God's blessing to Jacob at Bethel: "You will swell out (*ufaratzta*) to the west, the east, the north, and south" (28:14). Further examples are strewn throughout his journey, subtle reflections of God's promise that He will watch over Jacob until his return "to this land."

Yet if the narrative's sole purpose is to show God's encouragement to Jacob, then why is this scene so much more complex than, say, God's revelations to Abraham or Isaac? What is the point of the intricate sequence of dream, terror, promise, and vow?

---

5. Schweid, *Biblical Philosophy*, 157.
6. In some editions of the Bible, this is Genesis 32:2–3; in others, it is 33:1–2.

This emotional sequence, in fact, thinly veils a profound psychological drama. As a backdrop for my narrative analysis, I wish to quote an intriguing midrash:

> R. Naḥman began: "As for you, My servant Jacob, do not fear, declares the Lord, and Israel, do not be terrified" (Jer. 30:10), refers to Jacob, as is written: "And he dreamed: He saw a ladder..."
>
> R. Berakhya, R. Ḥelbo, R. Shemaya of R. Yossi, in the name of R. Meir: This teaches us that the Holy One, blessed be He, showed our father Jacob the ministering angel of Babylon ascending and descending, and of Media ascending and descending, and of Greece ascending and descending, and of Edom ascending and descending. The Holy One said to him: "Jacob, you too shall ascend," but at that moment our father Jacob was struck with fear and said: "You are saying that just as these descend, I too shall descend." The Holy One said to him, "Israel, do not be terrified – for if you ascend, you shall never ever descend." But he did not believe Him, and would not ascend.
>
> R. Berakhya, R. Ḥelbo, in the name of R. Shimon of R. Yossina, R. Meir interpreted: "Despite all this they went on sinning and did not believe in His wonders" (Ps. 78:32) – this refers to our father Jacob, who did not believe and would not ascend. The Holy One, blessed be He, said to him: "Had you only believed Me and ascended, you would never descend, forever, but because you did not believe and did not ascend, your children will be enslaved by these four empires." (*Pesikta DeRav Kahana* 23:2; see also Ramban's commentary on this section)

The author of this midrash complains that Jacob did not ascend the ladder in his dream, ascribes the lack of faith expressed in Psalm 78 to Jacob, and even argues that the enslavement of Jacob's descendants is the result of his failure to climb the ladder.

This is a strange, surprising midrash; why does it assume that Jacob should join the angels he dreams of and ascend the ladder as they do, and why is he incriminated for his fear? Psalm 78, which is the basis of this homiletical interpretation, states that children must be told of their ancestors' mistakes so as to avoid repeating them:

> He established a decree in Jacob and founded the teaching in Israel, charging our ancestors to teach it to their children so that the next generation would know it – the children yet unborn – and tell it, in turn, to their own children: to place their trust in God and not forget God's acts but keep His commandments instead of being like their ancestors, a wayward, rebellious generation, a generation not firm of heart, its spirit unfaithful to God. (Ps. 78:5–8)

This psalm explicitly refers to the generation that left Egypt, as is clarified a few verses later; on the level of *peshat*, the speaker did not have Jacob in mind. The midrash presumably cites this psalm for its historical paradigm in order to present Israel's enslavement to the four empires as the result of Jacob's sin, but once again, incriminating Jacob in this context is surprising.

Ultimately, as is often the case, the obscure, midrashic language reflects a deep reading that can be teased from the narrative structure. This scene is arranged in two parallel sections: Jacob's vision at night, and his vow in the morning:[7]

7. For similar proposals (with some fundamental differences), see Husser, "Métamorphoses," 372; Fokkelman, *Genesis*, 70–81; Bar Efrat, *Artistic Design*, 122–23; Peleg, "Jacob," 60–72. Rendtroff ("Jakob in Bethel"), and Terino ("Jacob") claim that the narrative has a chiastic structure framed by Jacob placing stones by his head (v. 11) and using these stones as a pillar (v. 18), but this leaves many relevant verses out of the structure. Nõmmik proposes a concentric structure from 28:10–29:1, with the central axis God's words to Jacob in verses 13–15 (Nõmmik, "Inclusio").

Jacob's Vision	**Jacob's Vow**
(10) Jacob left Beersheba and journeyed toward Haran	
(11) In time he chanced upon a certain **place** and decided to spend the night there, because the sun had set. *He took some stones* of the **place** and put them *under his head,* and in that place lay down to sleep. (12) And he dreamed: He saw a ladder set upon the ground, whose top (*rosho*) reached the heavens. On it, angels of God went up and came down.	(16) Then Jacob awoke from his sleep and said, "Truly, the Lord is in this **place** – and I did not know it!" (17) He was afraid and said, "How full of awe is this **place**! This is none other than the House of God, and this the gate of the heavens!" (18) Jacob rose early the next morning, took the *stone* he had placed *under his head,* set it up as a pillar, and poured oil on top of it. (19) He named the place Bethel; the town was *originally* (*larishona*) called Luz.
(13) The Lord stood over him there[8] and said, "I am the Lord, the God of Abraham your father, and the God of Isaac. The land on which you lie I will give to you and your descendants. (14) Your descendants shall be like the dust of the earth, and you will spread out to the west, the east, the north, and the south. Through you and your descendants, all the families of the earth will be blessed.	

8. Above, I state that the phrase "The Lord stood over him there" opens the second component of the first half. If the verse means that God stands over *him* – then this is presumably the introduction to God's words to Jacob. However, this can also be placed at the end of the first component: if this refers to the ladder, then this is still

Jacob's Vision	Jacob's Vow
	(20) Jacob then made a vow.
(15) I am with you.	"If God will be with me," he said,
I will protect you wherever you go	"protecting me on this journey I am taking, giving me bread to eat and clothes to wear,[9]
and **I will bring you back to this land,**	and **if I return in peace to my father's house,** then the Lord will be my God.
	(22) This stone I set up as a pillar will become a house of God, and of all that You give me I will dedicate a tenth to You."
for I will not leave you until I have done what I have spoken of to you."	

Both halves of the narrative end with the same word – the first time in God's promise to Jacob, and the second time in Jacob's vow to God.[10] This shows the mutual commitment that characterizes God and Jacob's bond in this scene; each half ends with one speaker making a promise to the other.

The first half of the scene describes Jacob arriving at a place that, as of yet, holds no significance for him – he merely stops there because the sun is setting, not because he means to spend the night in that particular spot.[11] The same is true of the stone(s) he places under his head – he merely grabs what is lying on the ground beside him.

part of the vision. The tension between the use of the Tetragrammaton and the mention of the angels of "God" leads Rendtroff to propose a concentric structure based on this difference.

9. Rashi sees "and give me" as parallel to God's promise "I will not leave you," but it is more common to see Jacob's request as parallel to God's "I will watch over you." (See, for example, Malbim; *Haamek Davar*.)
10. This may also be wordplay between God's word "*asiti*," and Jacob's vow, "*aser aaserenu*."
11. One of the meanings of the verb "*lifgoa*" is "to meet someone by coincidence." At the same time, this has several meanings, and each occurrence should be considered in context (see Rundgren, "Lexikon," 336–45; Grisanti, "P-G-E"). Sometimes the play on its ambiguity is intentional (see, for example, Grossman, *Text and Subtext*, 61–63).

And behold, in this most arbitrary of places, Jacob dreams of a "*sulam*" set upon the ground, whose top reaches the heavens. The meaning of the word "*sulam*" is not entirely clear, as it is a *hapax legomenon*, but it is presumably related to the word "*mesilla*," a raised path; the prevalent reading, the modern Hebrew word meaning "ladder," is also entirely logical, or it could refer to a climbing trail.[12] Either way, this "*sulam*" clearly serves to join the earthly and the divine: it is set upon the ground, but it reaches up to heaven.

The first half of the scene presents Jacob's vision: angels climb up and down a ladder, moving between heaven and earth. The word *vehineh* divides this first half into two separate stages: (1) behold! – Jacob sees a ladder, and behold! – angels are climbing up and down it; (2) behold! – God appears (to Jacob? upon the ladder?),[13] with a promise that is more than just a vision, and behold! God continues His promise. This last stage focuses on the immediate context of Jacob's journey, and it will soon emerge that there is profound significance in the division of God's promise into two distinct parts.

In contrast to the reassuring, sublime tone of the vision, Jacob's reaction is surprising: he awakens in startled fear.

In parallel to the three instances of the word "place" in the first half, the same word appears three times in Jacob's reaction to his vision: "Truly, the Lord is in this place"; "How full of awe is this place"; "He named the place Bethel." In the second half of the scene, the place undergoes a process of familiarization: from an unfamiliar, banal, arbitrary location to a place that Jacob recognizes, names, and sanctifies. There is God in this place! This is none other than the House of God, and this

12. See more on this debate in Griffiths, "Ladder"; Houtman, "Bethel." Oblath proposed that the ladder is the "gate of heaven," consistent with its depiction in Ancient Near Eastern literature (Oblath, "To Sleep"). He is correct that there is a symbolic connection between the Mesopotamian gateway to heaven – as I discuss below – but if this was so, then presumably the word "*shaar*" would have been used instead (Jacob uses this word later on).
13. For a summary of various proofs for both readings, see Vrolijk, *Jacob's Wealth*, 109–10. It is fascinating to follow the artwork that expresses this scene: in some, God is at the top of the ladder; in others, He is beside the dreaming Jacob.

the gate of the heavens! The most salient marker of this process is, of course, its new name – Bethel, *Beit El*, the House of God.

Note that the repetition of the word "place" in the first half anticipates the second stage. Jacob "chances upon a certain place" that will soon become an important holy site, but he is unaware of this. He is the one to expose its hidden sanctity. Careful attention to the process this place undergoes in the text can alleviate the confusion of certain modern scholars, who deliberate whether Jacob's night in Bethel should be considered an instance of "incubation" – the act of going to sleep in a holy site in order to induce divine revelation. On the one hand, Jacob stops for the night in Bethel, which is a holy site, so this is consistent with instances of incubation narratives; on the other hand, the language of the verse emphasizes that Jacob "chances upon" this place, and he only realizes its holy nature when he awakens. Some therefore define it as "unintentional incubation,"[14] but this definition is more confusing than helpful, given – as others point out – that the definition of incubation is intentionally going to sleep in a certain place in order to receive a divine revelation.[15] There is no indication that Jacob seeks revelation, and he has no idea that he is lying down on sacred ground. On the contrary: the place's holiness is only revealed after his inadvertent stay, and it is wondrous indeed that the sanctity of such sites is revealed to the travelers who stumble upon them (compare to the burning bush scene in Exodus 3).

A similar process occurs with Jacob's stone, which receives unusual attention in the narrative. Some surmise that the repetition of the word *even*, "stone," generates wordplay with the site's original name, which was "*Beit Aven*" or "*Beit Even*":

> The ancient name of the place was "*Beit Aven*" [house of stone] because of the enormous stone that stood there. The slight change in spelling (but not pronunciation) from "*Beit Aven*" (בית אבן)

14. Oppenheim, "Interpretation," 187.
15. Fidler, "Genesis XV," 148. Oppenheim believes that incubation dreams are not common in the Bible and the Ancient Near East, unlike Greek literature ("Interpretation, 187–88).

> to "*Beit Aven*" (בית און) [house of evil] is an intentional change that aims to present the temple and its site in a negative light.[16]

This is an interesting reading, but the narrative in Genesis 28 does not convey any criticism whatsoever against Bethel; such criticism can be found in the later prophets, but it is entirely absent in this episode. I believe, rather, that the stones serve a similar function to the emphasis on "the place." I have already mentioned that in the first part, there is no indication that the stones Jacob picks up have any significance; on the contrary, he merely takes "some stones of the place and put them under his head." And here too, the random stones Jacob happens to pick up are then charged with significance in the second half of the scene: "Jacob rose early the next morning, took the stone he had placed under his head, set it up as a pillar, and poured oil on top of it." Ibn Ezra and Radak suggest that Jacob pours oil over the stone so that he will recognize it when he returns: "For the oil stain will not be washed away by the rainwater" (Radak on 28:18),[17] but the simpler (and more accepted) reading is that pouring oil over the stone is an act of sanctification, of recognition of its significance, just as one anoints a king. This is supported by the fact that Jacob pours oil over the pillar once more when he returns from Padan Aram: "Jacob set up a stone pillar at the place where God had talked with him, and on it he offered a libation and poured oil" (35:14). If this is indeed a separate scene and not just another mention of this scene (see the discussion of chapter 35, below), then Jacob is pouring oil in order to sanctify stones and pillars. It is less likely that he would pour oil in order to mark the stone upon his return, and as he pours oil together with libations, the two acts are clearly related.

Thus the stone, like the place, undergoes a process of familiarization, from anonymity to significance – recognized, defined, sanctified.[18] Note that Jacob recognizes the "the place" as a holy site when he "awoke," and "the stone" is sanctified as a pillar when he "rose early the

16. Ne'eman, "Bethel," 16.
17. Radak writes that this shows how much the forefathers were revered in Canaan, as the Canaanites did not dare move the pillar after its erection (on Gen. 28:18).
18. Compare, especially, to Rendtroff, "Jakob in Bethel," Peleg, "Jacob," 67–72.

next morning." These two chronological markers help the reader trace the two parallel processes in the second half of the scene.

The word "*rosh*," "head," and its derivatives play a role in both sections of the narrative. In the first part, the "top" (*rosh*) of the ladder reaches the heavens, and in the second, Jacob pours oil "on top" of the pillar he erects. One does not usually refer to the "top" of a stone the same way one refers to a "hilltop" (Ex. 17:10) or "mountaintop" (Ex. 19:20), but this unusual mention of the "top/head" of the pillar seems to be related to the fact that Jacob pours oil on its "head" the way one anoints the heads of priests and kings. This personification is part of the process it undergoes in this chapter: a random stone, or pile of stones, becomes a sacred pillar, a thing of significance; the cornerstone of the house Jacob swears he will build in this place: "The stone the builders rejected has become the main cornerstone" (Ps. 118:22).

This emphasis on the stone's "head" is part of the more extensive wordplay in this chapter; Jacob's own head is mentioned twice: "*vayasem meraashotav*"/"*asher sam meraashotav*". This either means that he placed the stones *beneath* his head, or *by* his head, as in "He looked up and there, *by his head* (*meraashotav*), was a stone-baked cake and a flask of water" (I Kings 19:6); "And there was Saul, lying asleep within the circle, with his spear thrust into the ground *by his head* (*meraashotav*), and Abner and the men lying around him" (I Sam. 26:7); or, similarly: "At midnight the man started and turned over – there was a woman lying *at his feet* (*margelotav*)!" (Ruth 3:8). Either way, Jacob's head is mentioned in both sections. Will Jacob's head reach the heavens as the ladder does? Will his head be anointed with oil, like his stone? The answer will be revealed soon, in Jacob's vow.

The two parts of the narrative thus share parallel motifs, and they may even form a chiastic link. Oftentimes in the Bible, when an earlier verse is cited, it forms a chiastic sequence (this is generally referred to as "Seidel's Law").[19] Even within the same literary unit, repetition often

19. Seidel, "Parallels."

presents in chiastic order. Note the order of the motifs as they appear in the two parts of the story:[20]

A. In time he chanced upon a certain *place* and decided to spend the night there, because the sun had set.

  B. *He took some stones* of the *place* and put them *under his head,* and in that place lay down to sleep.

    C. *And he dreamed:* He saw a ladder set upon the ground, whose *top* (*rosho*) reached the heavens. On it, angels of God went up and came down.

    C'. *Then Jacob awoke* from his sleep and said, "Truly, the Lord is in this *place*... and this the gate of the heavens!

  B'. He took the *stone* he had placed *under his head,* set it up as a pillar, and poured oil on top of it.

A'. He named the *place* Bethel; the town was originally called Luz.

The components are arranged in chiastic order: in the framework (A–A') Jacob reaches "the place," and then names it; in B–B', he takes a stone, and then makes it into a pillar; the two central components (C–C') are Jacob's dream and his interpretation of it.

This structure justifies the claim that Jacob's initial response upon waking and erection of the pillar (vv. 16–19) are his reaction to his dream, while his vow (vv. 20–22) is his response to God's promise to him.[21] This claim places Jacob's vow in parallel to God's entire promise (vv. 13–15), but a careful comparison of the relevant verses reveals that Jacob responds to only some of God's words.

JACOB'S VOW

I will now go back to the overall structure of the scene and its two sections. There is a clear parallel between the two speeches – God's and Jacob's – at the end of each section. In the second section, Jacob responds

20. Rendtroff claims that the narrative has a concentric structure, centering on God's words to Jacob (Rendtroff, "Jakob in Bethel"). He divides the dream into sections, but I believe that it is one single component.

21. Spero, "Growing Understanding," 212.

to God's promise in the first by vowing to fulfill certain conditions when God's promise is fulfilled: "Jacob then made a vow: 'If God will be with me…'" (28:20). A biblical vow usually states a condition (Num. 21:2; Judges 11:30; I Sam. 1:11; II Sam. 15:8), and this expresses a close, living dialogue between the speaker and their God: the maker of the vow knows that their relief lies in God's hands, and through their vow, they create a private, intimate channel for a relationship with God. The person makes the vow through their own free will, not out of any preexisting obligation, and for this reason it brings them closer to God. The vow's fulfillment is marked by a sense of gratitude and praise, and in relevant psalms, the concept of a "vow" serves as a synonym for "thanksgiving," "praise," and "song" (Jonah 2:10; Ps. 22:26; 50:14; 56:13; 61:9; 65:2; 116:17–18).[22]

Therefore, Jacob's stipulations do not convey that he does not believe God's promise to him.[23] The biblical vow, even when conditional, does not express lack of trust; on the contrary, it creates a mutual, tangible relationship. Jacob's uncertainty that God's promise will be fulfilled is not due to his lack of trust, but rather because of life's instability: Will Jacob always be worthy of this protection? Will something happen that will render this promise invalid? Jacob's vow and conditions reflect an attempt to remain worthy of God's promise, to cultivate a deep, living dialogue with Him. In the eloquent words of Wenham: "But real experience of God must always result in heartfelt worship; here he gave all he had, the stone and the oil, and promised to give a tenth of all his future income when his affairs improved. To pray for a safe return showed faith, not disbelief."[24]

There is a striking connection between the protasis – the condition, which expresses fulfillment of God's promise – and the apodosis – what Jacob takes upon himself, underscoring the reciprocity:[25]

---

22. Haran, "*neder*," 786.
23. For criticism about Jacob's lack of trust in God's promise, see, for example, Humphreys, *Character of God*, 173; Weiss, "Jacob's Struggle," 21.
24. Wenham, *Genesis II*, 225.
25. This structure proves Ramban's claim that the expression "the Lord will be my God" marks the beginning of Jacob's commitment to God, rather than being part of the condition as the verse division would suggest. This debate continues in modern research. A convenient summary of those who believe that the end of verse 21 is

Protasis (vv. 20–21)	Apodosis (vv. 21–22)
If God will be with me	then the Lord will be my God
Protecting me on this journey I am taking, giving me food to eat and clothes to wear	This stone I set up as a pillar will become a house of God
And if I return in peace to my father's house	And of all that You give me, I will dedicate a tenth to You.

Jacob swears that if God will be with him, then Jacob will serve Him as his God; if God will provide all his needs, then Jacob will dedicate a tenth of all God gives him in return; if Jacob returns to his father's house in peace, he will ensure that God, too will have a House.

Jacob's apodosis recalls other biblical vows, such as Absalom's vow to serve God if he safely returns to Jerusalem: "For your servant pledged a vow when I was staying in Geshur of Aram, saying, 'If the Lord will bring me back to Jerusalem, then I will serve the Lord'" (II Sam. 15:8).[26] The promise of a tenth – essentially, a tithe – is also associated with vows and dedication in the Torah, especially Leviticus, which describes the various dedication possibilities. The relevant chapter opens with "When a person makes a spoken vow to the Lord to give the equivalent of the value of a person" (Lev. 27:2); then describes the laws of dedicating an animal, a house, a field, and eventually, the laws of tithing produce and animals: "All tithes from the land, whether seed from the ground or fruit of the tree, belong to the Lord; they are sacred to the Lord.... All tithes from the herd or flock – every tenth animal that passes under the shepherd's staff – shall be sacred to the Lord" (27:30–33). Some scholars even argue that "most sources in the Torah consider the tithe as a form of vow,"[27] and there is indeed room to debate whether the language of the text assumes that this is obligatory or, at least in Leviticus, a voluntary

part of the condition can be found in Vrolijk, *Jacob's Wealth*, 118. Assis also favors this view, and he also explains why there is no parallel component to "the Lord will be my God" in God's promise (Assis, *Identity in Conflict*, 63). Zakovitch leaves the question open (Zakovitch, *Jacob*, 56).

26. Parker also reads Jacob's words as similar to Absalom's vow, in the sense of "worshiping God" (Parker, "Vow," 699).

27. Haran, "*neder*," 789.

act – similar to the vow, dedication, and *ḥerem* in this section – wherein this formulation is an attempt to standardize the act of voluntary contribution to the Sanctuary. Either way, the integration of tithing in this section binds these commandments together, and this connection is also evident in Jacob's vow. At the beginning of his vow, Jacob refers to God in the third person, but by the end, Jacob appeals to God in the more intimate second person: "Of all that You give me, I will dedicate a tenth to You" (v. 22).[28]

Jacob's promise to build a house for God is also related to the biblical world of vows. This too is related to the act of tithing: the tithe must be brought to God's resting place, as is implied in the restrictions of what may be brought as a tithe: "Do not bring wages of prostitution or the payment for a dog *into the house of the Lord* your God in fulfillment of any vow, for both are abhorrent to the Lord your God" (Deut. 23:19); and in the list of items that must be brought to the Sanctuary (Deut. 12:17). For this reason, the fulfillment of vows (of tithes and offerings) is associated with the festivals of pilgrimage in certain texts and laws, given that people generally fulfilled their vows at these opportunities. Thus, in order for Jacob to offer tithe to God, he must also build Him a Sanctuary.

The language of Jacob's vow is parallel to the language of God's promise, thus expressing their living, mutual connection. Yet a careful comparison reveals slight differences between their words – differences which offer a glimpse into Jacob's psyche and convey that at that moment, Jacob is less interested in God's sublime, sweeping promises for the future, and more focused on his urgent, immediate needs: "Jacob's concerns are much more 'down-to-earth.'"[29]

The first difference is related to the extent of God's protection. God promises Jacob: "I will protect you wherever you go," while Jacob asks for more specific protection: "If God will be with me, protecting me on this journey I am taking, giving me food to eat and clothes to wear." Even though God promises protection "*wherever* you go," Jacob cites His words as if the promise specifically referred to "*this* journey." A similar discrepancy can be found in reference to Jacob's return. God promises

28. Assis, *Identity in Conflict*, 64.
29. Vrolijk, *Jacob's Wealth*, 115.

that "I will bring you back to this land," while Jacob specifies: "If I return in peace to my father's house." Jacob's father's house is indeed within the borders of the land, but Jacob seeks out a specific guarantee – his safe return to a specific place in a specific town.

How can these differences be understood? I will mention two exegetical directions, and then propose a third.

Rabbenu Baḥya: The Bare Necessities

Rabbenu Baḥya perceives these differences as a virtuous characterization of Jacob, who only seeks the bare minimum:

> "Giving me food to eat and clothes to wear": This is what the righteous ask of God: they do not seek luxury, only the bare necessities that a person cannot live without. It is known that a person's tendency to seek luxury causes them much trouble; therefore God-fearing people should be happy with their lot and make do with less and not crave luxury, and rejoice in their fear of God ... and for this reason the righteous Jacob asked for "food to eat and clothes to wear," which are necessities, showing the virtue of contentment, which is a righteous virtue, rather than seeking luxury, for the Torah despises this and restricts this even for kings, as it is written: "He must not accumulate wives and let his heart be led astray, nor should he amass large amounts of silver and gold" (Deut. 17:16).[30]

Indeed, Jacob's contraction of God's promise can be read as modesty or virtuous restraint, as if he is telling God: Your promises are vast and immense, but food to eat and clothes to wear will suffice for me; even this minimal provision is worthy of my grateful vow.

Rabbi Shlomo Ephraim Luntschitz (*Kli Yakar*): A New Angle

The *Kli Yakar* is disturbed by Jacob's conditional language, which implies that he is skeptical that God's promises will be fulfilled. He therefore suggests that Jacob's vow focuses on spiritual protection, which is an aspect

30. Rabbenu Baḥya on Gen. 28:20.

that God does not mention at all. He supports his argument using the aforementioned changes:

> God forbid that Jacob was skeptical of God's promise... the explanation is that Jacob was not at all seeking physical protection, as this was already promised to him, but rather spiritual protection from sin. The evidence for this is that God promises "I will protect you wherever you go," while Jacob says, "Protecting me on this journey I am taking," when he should have said "wherever," and the word "I" (*anokhi*) is also superfluous; God says, "I will bring you back to this land" – He takes responsibility for returning him, while Jacob says, "If I return in peace to my father's house" – Jacob takes responsibility for his own return; God says, "to this land," while Jacob says, "to my father's house."
>
> From all these changes we learn that Jacob was only seeking protection from sin, for this depends on a person's free will, and divine help is also needed, as David prayed, saying: "Divert my eyes from false visions; give me life through Your ways" (Ps. 119:37). Therefore for physical protection [God] mentions "*wherever* you go" – all ways, for all ways can be dangerous, and [Jacob] traveled many ways. But there is only one right path, so [Jacob] said, "protecting me on *this* way," as if pointing to a specific way: that is, the way of God, through Torah and commandments.[31]

The *Kli Yakar*'s central idea presents a challenge: Could it be that these slight changes indeed reveal a whole other facet that is not addressed in God's promise? I wish to adopt this direction, but with different semantics than the *Kli Yakar*'s notion of physical-spiritual protection.

Jacob Would Not Ascend the Ladder

In order to present a third approach to understanding Jacob's adaptation of God's promise, I wish to address the obvious disparity between the two halves of the structure. Literary structures highlight patterns within the plot and the meaning of these patterns; sometimes, the most meaning

31. *Kli Yakar* on Gen. 28:20.

lies not in the structure's symmetry, but in its asymmetry and imbalance, which highlights missing elements, deviation from the expected pattern, and so on.[32]

When Jacob stirs from his sleep, he reacts to the first part of the vision (he interprets the dream, pours oil on the stone, and names the place), and responds to God's promise of protection with a similar vow. But for some reason, Jacob does not respond to God's first promise. This absent component is not due to the narrative's redaction, as many scholars claim;[33] rather, it is an intentional literary technique that draws attention to its absence. Jacob's lack of response to God's first promise is most salient when he talks about what God will "give him." This verb appears in God's first promise to Jacob, which affirms that he will inherit the land: "The land on which you lie I will give to you and your descendants" (28:13), while Jacob uses it to refer to basic necessities, in parallel to God's second promise: "Giving me food to eat and clothes to wear... of all that You give me I will dedicate a tenth to You" (vv. 20–22).

Jacob's minimal request is not related to his humility or his desire for spiritual guidance. This is a dramatic reduction, because God's two promises are set in two completely different spheres. The first is a powerful historical and national promise: God bestows Abraham's blessing upon Jacob; the second is an individual promise of protection and personal safety. Jacob, it emerges, pays no attention to the historic part at all. Thus Bar-Efrat's reading of the symmetry between God's promise and Jacob's vow is only partially correct: "The parallel structure emphasizes that Jacob's actions respond to God's appearance, while Jacob's vow responds to God's promise. God is the initiator, while the human responds accordingly."[34] Jacob indeed responds to God's revelation to him, but not quite "accordingly."

In order to clarify this issue, we will analyze God's first promise:

32. Jerome Walsh devotes an entire chapter to what he calls "asymmetry." See Walsh, *Style and Structure*.

33. See the textual issues that lead Gunkel to this conclusion, *Genesis*, 308–09; Westermann, *Genesis II*, 452–53.

34. Bar-Efrat, *Artistic Design*, 123.

> I am the Lord, the God of Abraham your father, and the God of Isaac.
> The land on which you lie I will give to you and your descendants.
> Your descendants shall be like the dust of the earth, and you will spread out to the west, the east, the north, and the south.
> Through you and your descendants, all the families of the earth will be blessed.

These two verses contain all the elements of God's promise to Abraham: the promise of the land; the promise of seed; and their universal destiny. And indeed, the figure of Abraham hovers over this revelation in various ways.[35]

From the beginning, this revelation shows special focus on Abraham. God could have easily stated that He is the God of Jacob's fathers – Abraham and Isaac – but only Abraham is referred to as "your father." This emphasizes Jacob's particular connection with Abraham, and the blessings he receives indeed echo God's blessings to Abraham. This is especially salient in the blessing's conclusion: "Through you and your descendants, all the families of the earth will be blessed," which only appears in one other place in the Bible: in God's very first revelation to Abraham when he is bid to leave his father's house: "Through you, all families of the earth will be blessed" (12:3). Abraham is thus mentioned explicitly at the beginning and strongly alluded to at the end, and the revelation's content implies that it is here that God transfers Abraham's blessing to his grandson.

Or, to be more precise, the revelation to Jacob is in especial dialogue with God's revelation to Abraham at Bethel (13:14–17). First and foremost, of course, the two occur in the same place, but the two share a more profound connection: God appears to Abraham after he parts ways with his family, his nephew Lot, while God appears to Jacob after he parts ways with his family. Together, the two revelations mirror each other in a chiastic pattern:

35. Itzik Peleg even proposes that the angels ascending and descending the ladder represent the forefathers Abraham, Isaac, and Jacob (Peleg, "Jacob," 94–101). On the comparison to God's revelation to Abraham at Bethel, see ibid., 104–07.

God's Revelation to Abraham at Bethel (13:14–17)

A. "Raise your eyes and look around from where you are to the *north, south, east, and west.* All the land you see I will give to you and your descendants forever."

  B. "I will make your descendants *like the dust of the earth*: if anyone could count the dust of the earth, then could your descendants be counted."

    C. "Get up and walk through the length and breadth of the land, for *to you shall I give it.*"

God's Revelation to Jacob at Bethel (28:13–14)

    C'. "The land on which you lie *I will give to you* and your descendants."

  B'. "Your descendants shall be *like the dust of the earth.*"

A'. "And you will spread out to *the west, the east, the north, and the south.*"

Without going into too much depth, I wish to note a few interesting differences between the two revelations. Abraham's revelation repeats the promise of the land (in A and C), while God promises to "give" Jacob the land only once (C'); to Abraham, the four directions are mentioned in the context of receiving the land (A), but to Jacob, they are mentioned in the context of his descendants (A'). God emphasizes the promise of land to Abraham, and the promise of seed to Jacob.

This aside, I wish to focus on the striking chiasm.[36] The image of "dust of the earth" does not appear elsewhere in the Torah in the context of fertility aside from these two revelations; the phrase "to you I will give" features only here and in God's second revelation to Jacob at Bethel (35:12); and the four directions only appear in God's promise

36. This parallel proves that verse 14 is not a later addition, as some claim (see, for example, Gunkel, *Genesis*, 310–11), but an organic part of the revelation (though Gunkel believes that the part of Abraham's revelation that is parallel to this scene [13:14–16] is also a later addition).

in these two scenes.[37] I have argued elsewhere that Abraham's revelation in Bethel was supposed to be Abraham's first revelation in the land of Canaan, but that it was postponed until he parted ways with Lot.[38] Therefore God's promise to Jacob – which echoes God's promises to Abraham in His first revelation to him ("Through you, all families of the earth will be blessed") and in the central revelation in Bethel – is a revelation that expresses God's election of Jacob. Isaac has no need for any such blessings because he is Abraham's son, destined as the heir before his birth. But because Jacob and Esau part ways, one of them must be elected to begin the journey anew. The revelation at Bethel colors Jacob in Abraham's colors, and from now on, it is his responsibility to uphold the covenant with God.

Despite the exalted, celebratory tone of this promise, Jacob completely ignores it; his vow only relates to the second half and its promise of protection, not to the tremendous national-historical aspects he has just heard. While Abraham and Isaac do not respond to the promises about their nation's future either,[39] Jacob *does* react to a different part of God's promise, so his pointed lack of response to this aspect demands attention.

It seems that Jacob is caught up in his fear for his very existence – his brother wants to kill him, he is forced to flee his parents' home, and he has a long journey into the unknown before him. Jacob's lack of response implies that he is too distracted to accept God's sublime promises of land and descendants.

The disparity between God's promise and Jacob's vow is especially salient through one of the aforementioned differences, which can now be appreciated in full. God says to Jacob: "I will bring you back to this land" (v. 15), while Jacob expresses hope that he will "return in peace to my father's house" (v. 21). In light of Jacob's disregard for the national promise, the full significance of this disparity emerges: while it happens

37. To complete the chiastic mirroring, God's blessing to Abraham opens with a north-south axis and then moves to an east-west axis, whereas Jacob's blessing begins with west-east and then moves to north-south.

38. Grossman, *Abraham,* 48–49; 69–71.

39. In this way Grüneberg and Fokkelman excuse Jacob's lack of response to the historic promise (Grüneberg, *Abraham*, 86; Fokkelman, *Genesis*, 75).

to be "in this land," at this point in time Jacob has eyes only for "his father's house." Fleeing his broken home to escape his brother's wrath, he dreams of returning to his reunited family.[40] It is no coincidence that Jacob adds the word "in peace"; while its primary meaning is for Jacob to come home safely from his journey, it also hints that Jacob wants to come back to his childhood home unharmed (compare Gen. 26:19) by his own family; that he will be able to return (*lashuv*) once his brother's rage subsides (*tashuv* – 27:44). By contrast, God's vision for Jacob rises high above a specific family feud. For now, Jacob certainly needs reassurance and protection on his way to Laban, but the destiny that awaits him far transcends any fraternal quarrel. The promise that Jacob will return "to this land" follows closely after the promise that "the land on which you lie I will give to you and your descendants" (v. 12). One day, Jacob and his descendants will inherit the very land on which he now lies, hopeless and destitute. This presents a different perspective of Jacob's life and journey. While Jacob fears for his very survival, God speaks to him of his eternal destiny, of his power to change the world forever. For now, Jacob is at the beginning of his journey, engrossed in his distress, and he is not yet capable of grasping the glorious future that awaits him. But this, too, will come.

Jacob's tunnel vision recalls the theory of Maslow's hierarchy of needs.[41] According to the Jewish American psychologist Abraham Maslow, a person's different levels of need can be depicted in the form of a pyramid; the most basic needs are on the bottom of the pyramid, and each stage must be satisfied in order for the person to have motivation to fulfill higher forms of need. This hierarchy can be generalized thus:

1. The bottom level of the pyramid is basic physiological needs, such as air, food, water, sleep, etc.
2. The second level is safety – including shelter, a safe place to sleep, employment, health, and well-being.

40. Compare to Zakovitch, *Jacob*, 56.

41. I would like to thank my student and friend Yonatan Munitz for bringing this concept to my attention. Compare this to Aryeh Arzi's analysis of the Priestly Blessing in dialogue with Maslow's hierarchy: Arzi, "Priestly Blessing."

3. The third level is belonging – social needs such as being part of a society, a group, being loved and loving. This stage is a crucial part of a person's identity.
4. The fourth level is recognition and appreciation – the need to be esteemed, recognized, and appreciated within one's society.
5. The top of the pyramid is reserved for self-actualization – the need to express, achieve, and develop one's individual potential, creativity, and gifts.

Jacob's vow is concerned with the two lowest stages of this pyramid – physiological needs ("food to eat and clothes to wear") and personal safety and security ("protecting me on this journey"). At this point in time, Jacob cannot see that he is at the beginning of a personal, national, and historical odyssey, and his physiological needs are the very first step along a path that will reach the heavens.

"In dreams begins responsibility," wrote the poet William Butler Yeats. Perhaps the reader expects Jacob to embrace the great responsibility symbolized in his dream, but for the moment, things will have to wait.

DREAMING BIG

In light of this analysis, I now wish to return to the dream and its meaning. What does Jacob's ladder mean? Sometimes components in dreams are clear symbols of something else – three grapevines and the three baskets of bread represent three days; seven fat cows stand for seven years of plenty. Other dreams, however, are not symbolic, but rather dreams of revelation. God speaks to Abimelech and to Laban through their dreams, but there is no description of what they saw.[42] The status of Jacob's dream, however, is not so clear – is it a symbolic dream, or a dream of revelation? On the one hand, God speaks to him directly, and these promises are the main part of the dream. On the other hand, Jacob

42. In this context, Ibn Ezra's commentary on the dream is interesting: "It is surprising that R. Shmuel confused the dreams of common men with prophetic dreams" (on 28:11). R. Shmuel son of Ḥofni (Hai Ga'on's father-in-law) apparently wrote that such a dream was a common phenomenon, and this angered Ibn Ezra.

sees a divine ladder stretching to the heavens with angels ascending and descending, and this vision demands interpretation in itself.[43]

One exegetic extreme claims that the ladder itself is insignificant,[44] while others delve deeply into its symbolism,[45] but I believe that this vision is most significant in the context of the dream as a whole. The ladder forms a connection between heaven and earth, and its image precedes God's revelation. The dream is presented from Jacob's perspective, and it unfolds in three stages, of growing surprise:[46]

> And he dreamed:
> (*vehineh*) He saw a ladder set upon the ground, whose top reached the heavens(!)
> (*vehineh*) On it, angels of God went up and came down(!!)
> (*vehineh*) The Lord stood over him there(!!!)

The image of a ladder so tall that its top reaches the heavens already hints that this dream is about to transcend the mundane and the familiar. But look, there's more – this towering ladder is replete with angels of God! This further deviates from the earthly, and explicitly introduces the divine into Jacob's presence – Jacob is granted a glimpse into the heavenly host, into the movement of angels. Yet all this is mere prelude to the most heavenly of all – to the presence of God Himself. With this third *vehineh*, the dream transcends all earthly boundaries and touches eternity.

Once again, the ladder creates a bridge between heaven and earth, a path and gate for angels. The ladder is set firmly upon the ground, while its top reaches the very heavens. Even from the ground, the heavens can be reached; the sweeping panorama of history itself can be condensed

43. See further in Fidler, "Dreams," 146–48, and Peleg, "Jacob," 77–74.
44. Such as Ehrlich, *Der Traum*, 29; Richter, "Traum und Traumdeutung," 210.
45. See especially Itzik Peleg's interesting proposal that the ladder represents Jacob's journey to foreign lands – Haran; angels stand by to accompany him on his way, and God is standing there, overseeing it all (Peleg, "Jacob"). For an exaggerated over-reading of the dream through a Freudian psychoanalytical lens, see Couffignal, "Songe." He concludes that the sky symbolizes Isaac, the dreamer's father; the earth his mother Rebecca; and the ladder represents their relationship.
46. Compare to Fokkelman, *Genesis*, 51–52; Vrolijk, *Jacob's Wealth*, 108.

into human perspective and understanding through an encounter with the divine that watches over it all.

This is also expressed through the humble stone that Jacob places under his head. Though it is not part of the vision itself, it plays a similar role as a literary motif. Just as the ladder is set (*mutzav*) in the ground but reaches the heavens, Jacob's stone becomes a towering monument (*matzeva*) and tribute to the divine; just as the top (*rosho*) of the ladder stretches up to the divine, the top (*rosh*) of Jacob's stone is anointed with oil and thus sanctified. The stone, like the ladder, symbolizes the possible encounter between heaven and earth; the banal that becomes sanctified; the random stone that becomes the cornerstone of the house of God.

The ladder and the stone anticipate the process that Jacob himself will undergo in wake of his dream. As mentioned, Jacob's own head is emphasized at the beginning of the scene, as if he too is about to be anointed or crowned: "It is a story of initiation and transformation. A 'certain place' becomes Bethel; a stone becomes a pillar; and a man on the run becomes the holder of great promises."[47] I identify with this theme, but with one important reservation: this story marks the beginning of Jacob's journey, but his own head has yet to reach the heavens. Jacob has a long way to go before he is worthy of the great destiny that awaits him. For now he is more concerned with food, clothing, and his own safe return to his father's house than with inheritance of the land. The site of his dream and the stones beneath his head undergo transformation, but Jacob himself is not yet ready to touch the divine.

Jacob's tunnel vision may well be the reason for the midrash's criticism; for its accusation that Jacob failed to climb the ladder due to his lack of faith. If the midrash perceives the angels as symbols of future empires, then the dream is a reflection of the passage of world history. Jacob is invited to participate in history: he must climb the ladder before he can spread out to the west and east, to the north and south. But Jacob is still hesitant. He is not ready to embrace these promises; or, in the language of the midrash, he is not ready to climb the ladder; the lost, frightened man is not ready to take part in the march of history God reveals to him.

---

47. Vrolijk, *Jacob's Wealth*, 121.

The Sages read this as criticism of Jacob. Yet at the most basic level, it is not at all clear why this should be so. Jacob is about to undergo a process, and this dream marks the beginning of his journey. Upon his return from exile, Jacob will encounter angels once more, and there, his very name will change. There, we will consider whether Jacob is ready to embrace his place within history; whether Jacob will fulfill the vow to God on God's terms – upon his return "to this land," or on his own terms – upon his return in peace to his father's house.

In a certain sense, the tables can be turned: not only is the scene devoid of criticism against Jacob, but he is presented as a character who responds with modesty in the face of exalted promises, who is filled with reverence in the face of holiness. This characterization emerges when reading this scene in its broader context within Genesis.

THE LADDER OF BETHEL AND THE TOWER OF BABEL

The reading that Jacob's dream is an invitation to participate in the march of history can illuminate the fascinating dialogue between our story and the story of the Tower of Babel. The connection between the stories deserves special attention. The connection between them stems, first and foremost, from the fact that both constructions "reach the heavens." The builders of the tower plan: "Let us build ourselves a city and a tower whose top reaches the heavens" (Gen. 11:4), while Jacob's ladder is described similarly: "A ladder set upon the ground, whose top reached the heavens" (28:12). The tower narrative concludes with the naming of its setting: "That is why it was called Babel" (11:9); as does Jacob's dream: "He named the place Bethel" (28:19).

This brings the dialogue between the narratives to an intriguing boiling point. The Tower of Babel narrative's conclusion is generally read as a derisive etymology that mocks the Babylonian's self-perception. While the Babylonians themselves believe that their name is derived from the phrase Bāb-ilu = "the gate of god" (or, in a later form: Bāb-ilani, "the gate of the gods")[48] – that is, the place where divine beings descend from heaven and ascend from the underworld, the narrative in Genesis reveals that the name is actually derived from the word "confusion" – the

48. Landsberger, "Assyrische Königsliste," 68.

place where the nations were scattered and their languages confused. It is as if the Torah is saying to Israel's enemy Babylon, "Perhaps in your language [Babylon] is a name of honor and pride, but in our own language, it sounds like its meaning is 'confusion' – the confusion of languages that echoed there and caused the destruction and dispersion of its people in every direction."[49]

The etymology of the name Babylon is discussed in *Enuma Eliš*, the Babylonian creation epic, which also tells of the city of Babylon's founding. After Marduk's victory over Tiamat, he chooses a place for the gathering of the gods; where the gods will descend from heaven and ascend from the underworld: "I will call it 'Babel,' the house of the great gods" *("ābilim: bītāt ilānim rabiūtim")*.[50] Some claim that the name Babylon originated from a different, folk etymology,[51] but for our purposes, this is irrelevant; the story in *Enuma Eliš* is how the Babylonians perceived the birth of their city and the meaning of its name.[52]

The polemic in Genesis does not merely challenge the source of the city's name, but the very nature of its foundation: according to *Enuma Eliš*, the city was founded by the gods, whereas Genesis describes how the city was established by a group of humans who attempt to rebel against heaven's authority.[53] They intend that the tower will serve as a gate between heaven and earth, but God intervenes; whereas Jacob's dream presents an alternative structure that *does* allow divine beings (angels, not gods!) to climb up and down. The name "Bethel" is

49. Cassuto, *Noah to Abraham*, 158.
50. *Enuma Eliš*, 5:129.
51. Gunkel, *Genesis*, 97; Sarna, *Understanding Genesis*, 69; Ringgren, "*Bavel*," who writes that we do not know the original meaning of the name.
52. Elsewhere I propose that *Enuma Eliš* plays on the name "Babylon" to hint to movement of water and fertile earth (see the city's creation in 5:58: "*nambâ uptalliša ana babālim kuppu*"), while this tradition is mocked in the biblical story of Babel, where the builders are the ones who were scattered all over the earth, rather than life-giving water (see further in Grossman, "Double Etymology").
53. See further about the polemic between the narratives (especially concerning the term "its top reached the heavens" and the firing of bricks) in Speiser, "Word Plays"; Sarna, *Understanding Genesis*, 71; Grossman, "Double Etymology." Miller points out the uniqueness of the notion that people, not God, build the city, and compares our narrative to the founding of the Sumerian city Eridu (Miller, "Eridu," 243).

essentially a translation of the name "Babel"; and Jacob's exclamation, "This is none other than the House of God, and this the gate of the heavens!" (v. 17), echoes the Babylonian description of their own city. This is a striking example of a biblical response that intentionally undermines a contemporary cultural tradition.

The polemic in the Tower of Babel narrative serves a certain purpose within the postdiluvian narratives of Genesis,[54] but how is this polemic relevant on the cusp of Jacob's departure from Canaan? Yehuda Elitzur proposes that the Tower of Babel narrative should be considered the beginning of the Abraham cycle, and that Jacob's dream at Bethel continues this polemic. This scene shows that the gate of heaven is not in Babylon but Canaan; that God does not descend to watch over His world through elaborate, manmade skyscrapers, but in the open, natural field, with a mere stone representing the "house" of God.[55]

This reading is convincing, but in light of our analysis, I wish to propose a different angle. In the Tower of Babel narrative, the Babylonians attempt to build a name for themselves through a magnificent fortress city, protected by a skyscraping watchtower: "Let us build ourselves a city and a tower that reaches the heavens and make a name for ourselves, otherwise we will be scattered across the face of the earth" (11:4). The meaning of "making a name" is not merely achieving honor and recognition; it touches upon eternity itself. They wish to leave an impression that will endure beyond their death: to "make a name" is to achieve immortality.[56] In this narrative, Jacob is invited to achieve the Babylonians' desire – but in the right way. Jacob does not build the ladder connecting heaven and earth on his own initiative; rather, God shows it to him in a dream, inviting him to be like Abraham, to form a covenant with Him, and to leave his mark on history itself. It is God who shows Jacob the angels climbing the ladder, thus revealing his campsite as a holy place. In their arrogance, the Babylonians sought to overstep their boundaries and build an empire that would reach the skies. By

54. I develop this further in my first book in this series (Grossman, *Beginnings*, 265–90).
55. Elitzur, *Israel and the Bible*, 44–48.
56. See, for example, in Dvir, *Biblical Name*.

contrast, God invites Jacob to transcend his earthly boundaries and fix his gaze upon the heavens.

This is a fundamental principle in biblical thought. It is not humanity that determines whether a site is holy, but God. Moses stumbles upon God's mountain while he is out tending his father-in-law's flock, and there he sees the burning bush (Ex. 3). It is not Moses but God who deems the place holy, and Moses must obey God's decision: "Do not come close. Remove the shoes from your feet, for the place where you stand is holy ground" (Ex. 3:5). This is also expressed through the common phrase in Deuteronomy, "the place of the Lord's choosing," which shows that it is God who will choose the Temple site, and only at the right time; the identity of this site is not revealed throughout the Torah, even though this would have elevated Jerusalem's status.[57] Effectively, God's choice is already expressed in the binding of Isaac narrative (asserting the Mountain of Moriah's sanctity seems to be one of the narrative objectives). There, too, God initially conceals Abraham's destination from him, which serves to emphasize that God, not humanity, determines a place's sanctity: "Go to the land of Moriah. There, offer him up as a burnt offering on one of the mountains, the one that I will show you" (Gen. 22:2).[58]

The people in the Tower of Babel narrative, however, attempt to make a name for themselves: *they* select the building site (unlike the story in *Enuma Eliš*) for what they intend as the gateway for the gods, but no gods or even angels will ever pass through.

Our narrative is thus consistent with this biblical principle, and Jacob's initial perception of his campsite as arbitrary and banal reflects how a site's sanctity is a divine, not human, choice. Reading this scene against the Tower of Babel narrative underscores that Jacob is not seeking to make a name for himself – an aspiration that, we might argue, is the very apex of Maslow's pyramid of needs. Jacob's sights are nowhere near the top of the pyramid, nor does he attempt to climb that heavenly

---

57. See further: Cogan, "Jerusalem."
58. See further in Grossman, *Abraham*, 309–10. Although the Tabernacle was also erected in other places that were not chosen by God, these were only temporary places that were sanctified.

ladder – he is down below, grasping for bread and clothing, sorely lacking – for now – the motivation to relate to God's promise of eternity.

In this sense, we can adopt Rabbenu Baḥya's aforementioned reading: Jacob's disregard for God's exalted blessings shows the humility of someone who is not seeking to make a name for himself. Unlike the arrogant builders of Babel, Jacob shrinks from such aspirations and seeks only the bare necessities. In merit of this very humility, perhaps, God's blessings of eternity eventually come true; it is Jacob's descendants whose name endures among the nations.

Thus Jacob, having left his home and his homeland, continues on his way; God's promises in hand, his feet steady and sure. He lies down to sleep with a stone by his head, and wakes beside a pillar; curled up on the ground, lonely and frightened, he wakes at heaven's very gate.

Jacob and Rachel by the Well (Gen. 29:1–14)

I would kiss before I spoke.
– Shakespeare, *As You Like It,* Act IV, Scene I

After the revelation at Bethel, Jacob continues on his journey as a changed man. He flees his home, family, and land, but God promises him that He will always be with him, and that Jacob will yet return to the very land he now lies upon. As discussed above, in the context of God's encouragement, Jacob's new strength following the revelation is reflected in the unique expression "*vayissa raglav,*" which literally means, "he raised his legs." This verb root usually indicates strength and magnitude ("to raise one's voice" means to speak in a loud voice; "to raise one's eyes" is to gaze out to the distance; "to raise a hand" implies to strike something or to act with force).[1] Strengthened by God's promise of protection, he now continues on his way, his step lighter and swifter than the day before.

This sense of physical power also anticipates the ensuing scene, when Jacob rolls the enormous stone off the mouth of the well. A scene

1. Assis' conclusion is the opposite: that this expression conveys Jacob's loneliness and destitution, with nothing to lift but his own legs (*Identity in Conflict,* 61). He bases this reading on comparison with Gen. 42:46; Josh. 3:6, when *objects* are "lifted," but I believe that a more relevant comparison is to other combinations of this root + voice/part of the body.

that opens with a unique[2] expression of physical strength invites analysis of the character's actions throughout the scene.[3]

The continuation of the verse also invites special attention: "He went *artza venei kedem*." This is a very strange description: "*artza venei kedem*" isn't the name of an actual land. Where exactly did Jacob go, and who are these people? Some exegetes explain that this simply means that Jacob traveled in an eastern direction.[4] This may be true, but why is the reader told that Jacob journeyed in a certain direction, rather than his destination? This description is particularly intriguing given that it continues the story of Jacob's journey after his revelation, "Jacob left Beersheba and journeyed toward Haran" (28:10) – if this is connective repetition, then why has the name of the destination changed?

Perhaps this description alludes to two different names without having to choose between them. Rebecca sends Jacob to "Haran"; Isaac sends Jacob to "Padan Aram," and once again, both place names carry their own connotations. The expression "*artza venei kedem*" encompasses both descriptions. Yonatan Feintuch is correct to point out that "the expression '*artza venei kedem*' indicates that Jacob has reached the region of his destination, but not the destination itself; in any case, the events of the next few verses still take place on his way, before his journey comes to its definite end (as it does in verse 13, when he reaches Laban's house).[5]

Even if so, this does not sufficiently explain the charged word "*kedem*." In the book of Genesis, this word is not merely a direction, but a deeply loaded symbol. The rejected ones of Genesis are cast off to the east: Cain, who is doomed to wander, travels to Nod, "east of Eden" (4:16); Lot, who leaves Abraham, journeys to the east (13:11); as do his sons, Ammon and Moab. The sons of Abraham's concubine Keturah

2. On the possibility that this meaning is also fulfilled in Deut. 33:3, see Seeligmann, "Psalm."
3. It is difficult to determine whether this is intentional, but the motif of "*raglayim*," legs or feet, is prevalent throughout the Jacob cycle, used in both the literal and the figurative sense (see 30:30; 33:14; 49:33); see a discussion of how to understand the word *raglayim* in these chapters in Wolff, *Anthropology*, 67; Stendebach, "*regel*," 317.
4. Westermann, *Genesis II*, 464; Wenham, *Genesis II*, 230.
5. Feintuch, "Ladder and Well," 15.

are sent off to the east, far away from Abraham's chosen son: "While he was still living he gave gifts to the sons of his concubines and sent them eastward, away from his son Isaac, to the land of the East" (25:6). The word *kedem* thus reinforces subtle allusions that we have already pointed out: the sibling rivalry between Jacob and Esau that recalls Cain and Abel, with one brother then exiled to the east; Lot's separation from Abraham preceding the revelation at Bethel. The latter analogy can be further reinforced thus: Lot parts ways with his uncle and heads east; Jacob parts ways with his family and heads east toward his uncle. Note that Abraham explicitly sends his concubine's sons away "from his son Isaac"; Jacob's journey, too, hinges on the question of inheritance.[6]

The similarity between these three eastward journeys and Jacob's own flight, however, also underscores the keen difference between them. Cain, the disgraced brother whose offering was rejected, is the one who is banished to the east.[7] Lot – the nephew who prefers the delights of Sodom instead of Abraham's company – is the one who journeys eastward, his ill-gotten sons to inherit the eastern side of the Jordan. Abraham's sons are neatly dismissed to the east, out of the Bible. Yet in our story – at least for now – it is not Esau who makes his way to the east, but Jacob. This shatters the literary norms of Genesis, for it seems obvious that Esau will be the one to leave his home and wander eastward – so obvious, in fact, that this soon transpires (Gen. 36). But for now, it is Jacob who leaves the Promised Land, and the distinct description of his destination, "the land of the people of the East," stirs connotations of exile and rejection.

How can this be understood? Mere verses before, God appears to Jacob and invites him to join the covenant of Abraham, replete with blessings of land and seed; but now Jacob is making his way east, exiled as if he has been rejected.

6. Elsewhere I propose that although Keturah's sons are born before Genesis 25, the information is only related on the eve of Abraham's death to emphasize how his heir is chosen among his other rejected sons (Grossman, *Abraham*, 399).
7. See further on the inversion between these narratives about brothers in Fokkelman, *Genesis*, 53. He correctly emphasizes that this inversion prepares the ground for the brothers' reconciliation as opposed to murder.

This is a subtle reflection of Jacob's unique experience: on the one hand, he has just been blessed with Abraham's blessing, but on the other, he is exiled to the east as if he is unworthy of God's presence. As mentioned above, Jacob is indeed the chosen son, but the unexpected schism in Isaac's family, the unbridgeable chasm that now separates the brothers, means that Jacob must follow in his grandfather's footsteps and reenact his journey. Jacob is forced to travel eastward because he cannot simply inherit Abraham's covenant; he must start anew and earn his place as the chosen son. Just as Abraham's journey begins in the east, Jacob must begin his own journey from there: "Abraham's Journey: The Sequel."

A WELL AND THREE FLOCKS

Even before Jacob reaches the city, he sees a "well in a field" next to three flocks of sheep. For some reason, the narrative devotes considerable space to Jacob's conversation with the shepherds of these flocks; a surprising delay, given that the most significant encounter in this scene is Jacob's first meeting with Rachel. What purpose does this lengthy, even superfluous dialogue serve? How are these shepherds characterized? Ostensibly, Jacob's initial encounter with Rachel does not serve any purpose within the plot:

> This entire conversation [between the shepherds and Jacob], its simplicity and banality, is strange and demands explanation. It is not the Torah's way to go into lengthy details, to mention secondary characters who serve no purpose in the actual plot, to have its characters make banal conversation in order to set a certain tone or to describe the setting, as realistic and natural nineteenth-twentieth century literature does. Why, then, does the Torah see fit to tell of this small talk between Jacob and three shepherds that have never appeared before, and will never be mentioned again in the Torah?[8]

It is worth noting that Laban soon offers Jacob payment for his work, and Jacob asks for his younger daughter Rachel because of his love for

8. Leibowitz, *Genesis*, 219.

her: "And Jacob was in love with Rachel, so he said, 'I will work for you seven years for your younger daughter Rachel'" (29:18). This simple description would have been sufficient explanation as to why Jacob asks for Rachel's hand; the entire scene at the well could have been omitted without any harm to the plot.[9]

This preamble – and, most importantly, the shepherds' characterization – can be read in two different ways. Many read the shepherds of Haran as a collective character that serves as a foil to Jacob,[10] and, to a lesser degree, to Rachel. This reading claims that the shepherds are cast in a negative light; or to be more precise, the shepherds treat Jacob with reservation, so the Torah, in turn, treats them with reservation.[11]

This characterization is supported by their portrayal:

> Three flocks of sheep were lying beside it because this was the well from which the flocks were watered. The top of it was covered with a large stone. When all the flocks were gathered there, the stone would be rolled from the mouth of the well and the sheep watered. The stone would then be put back in place on top of the well. (29:2–3)

For some reason, there is no mention of "shepherds," just "flocks," as if it is the sheep themselves who gather by the well, uncover it, drink, and replace the stone.[12] There is no need to explain that it is the shepherds who see to it all, but this metonymy certainly implies that the shepherds are only secondary to their sheep. This is salient in their dialogue with Jacob, when their brief, terse replies to his questions create the sense that they are unwilling to welcome this stranger into their midst:

---

9. Ramban believes that this incident is described to show how strong Jacob is: that despite being weary from the long journey, he is able to lift a stone that can usually only be moved by all the local shepherds together (on 29:2).
10. See, for example, in Speiser, *Genesis*; Davidson, *Genesis II*, 151; Sherwood, "Jacob and Laban," 61; Alter, *Genesis*, 152; Vrolijk, *Jacob's Wealth*. 128.
11. See, for example, Speiser, *Genesis*, 223; Bazak, *Starting Point*, 71–72. Nechama Leibowitz hints to this reading in *Genesis*, 220.
12. It is no coincidence that several commentators emphasize that this refers to the shepherds, not to the herds themselves – such as Ibn Ezra and Radak (on 29:3).

> Jacob asked the shepherds, "Brothers, where are you from?"
>
> "We are from Haran," they replied.
>
> He asked them, "Do you know Laban son of Nahor?"
>
> "We know him," they said.
>
> He asked them, "Is he well?"
>
> "He is well," they said, "and look, here is his daughter Rachel coming with the sheep."
>
> "Look," he said, "it is still broad daylight. It is not yet time to gather in the animals. Water the flocks and take them back to pasture."
>
> But they said, "We cannot do that until all the flocks are gathered and the stone is rolled from the top of the well. Only then can we water the flocks." (29:4–8)

The difference between the speakers' attitudes is evident from the start: Jacob calls them "brothers," but they do not return his warmth. The difference between the lengths of their sentences also implies that Jacob attempts to make their acquaintance, while their brief responses show that they are not interested: "Do you know Laban son of Nahor?"[13] is answered with a single, unhelpful word: "*yadanu*" ("We know him"). Rather than start a conversation, asking him how he knows Laban and where he comes from, the shepherds of Haran do not wish to encourage the stranger who is asking nosey questions and disturbing their afternoon break.

This is further supported by the dialogue's grammatical structure: Jacob repeatedly "asks *them*," while they merely "said" – not "said to him," just "said." This, too, implies that Jacob is reaching out to them, trying to stir up a conversation, while they brush him off with minimal responses.

According to this reading, the shepherds are presented in the dialogue as a foil to Jacob's diligence, initiative, and work ethic. Their passivity may even serve as a contrast to Rachel herself: "While he was still talking with them, Rachel came with her father's sheep; she was a

13. Ramban wonders why Jacob mentions that Laban is the grandson of Nahor, rather than the son of Bethuel, and suggests that Nahor was far more esteemed than his son, perhaps given that he was Abraham's brother (on 29:3).

shepherdess" (29:9). The chronological description that links Rachel's arrival to Jacob's speech encourages comparison between them. Jacob's addressees are referred to as part of their flocks; Rachel is the first character who is actually described as a shepherd: "She was a shepherdess." The shepherds of Haran are loitering by the well, while Rachel is active, moving, tending to her father's flock.[14] Not only is the comparison between Rachel and the shepherds justified; so is a comparison between the unfriendly shepherds and Laban, who is, at least initially, warm and welcoming to his nephew. As Wenham summarizes Jacob's encounter with the shepherds of Haran: "This dialogue consists of four questions by Jacob and four rather surly replies by the shepherds, suggesting their suspicion of this young foreigner and his own brash self-confidence.... On the other hand, the shepherds' cold response to Jacob serves to accentuate the warmth of his reception by Laban."[15]

This scene recalls the scene of Moses at the well in Midian (Ex. 2), which also encourages this reading. There, the shepherds are explicitly problematic; after Reuel's daughters toil to fill the troughs for their father's flock, the shepherds come to drive them away and use the water in the troughs for their own flock. Were it not for Moses' intervention, they would have come home much later, as they usually did.

Reading the shepherds of Haran as problematic characters reinforces this analogy. Even if Haran's shepherds are not as violent as Midian's, their function in the narrative is clear. Why do Haran's shepherds place such a heavy stone upon the well? This is not a one-time event, but the usual custom: after the shepherds water their flocks, "the stone would be rolled from the mouth of the well and the sheep watered. The stone would then be put back in place on top of the well" (29:3). If the stone is so difficult to move, then why do they take pains to replace it each day, necessitating that all the local flocks must gather before they can be watered? The obvious answer is that this stone prevents any outsiders from using their well, guaranteeing that other shepherds or travelers that are not part of the usual "clique" are unable to water their

14. Unlike Eising, who claims that Rachel remains uncharacterized in this scene, like the shepherds (Eising, *Jakob*, 163).
15. Wenham, *Genesis II*, 230.

flock. Only when the local shepherds gather together are they able to remove this "lock."[16]

Similar to Moses' encounter with the shepherds of Midian, here too the locals have taken over the well. Yet Jacob, like Moses, waters the flock in defiance of those around him, who see his fierce strength and are afraid to confront him.[17] Like Moses, Jacob saves Rachel and waters her flock, and Laban, like Reuel, is delighted to meet such a brave, noble, potential son-in-law.

ARE THE SHEPHERDS OF HARAN INDEED LIKE THE SHEPHERDS OF MIDIAN?

There is, however, another way of reading the shepherds' characterization, and I am inclined to follow this alternative route. While comparisons between narratives highlight their similarities and may even help illuminate missing details in either scene, they also underscore differences between them; moreover, filling in gaps based on a parallel narrative may do injustice to the story, given that certain details are intentionally omitted, and should not be inferred from a different episode. Are Haran's shepherds indeed as problematic as Midian's shepherds? Haran's local shepherds, however cliquey, do not bully Rachel, and she is not really in need of Jacob's help. The Midrash[18] points out that one might expect Rachel to be treated even more badly than Reuel's daughters, given that there are seven of them while she is alone, but the local shepherds do not harm Rachel at all. Rather than giving the shepherds any credit, however, the Midrash perceives this difference as a sign of Rachel's divine providence. R. Haim ben Attar, who also notes this difference, does read this as positive characterization of the local shepherds:

> "He is well – and look, here is his daughter Rachel, coming with the sheep." Not only is all well with him, but he is able to send his

16. Thus "We cannot do that until all the flocks are gathered" might be a physical issue or political issue (see further in Sherwood, "Jacob and Laban," 42 incl. footnotes).
17. Vrolijk writes that not only does Jacob challenge the shepherds' usual order, he waters Rachel's flock first even though she arrives last (*Jacob's Wealth*, 130).
18. Genesis Rabba 70:11.

> young daughter out with the sheep, which is not true of Jethro, who sent his seven daughters out together, but even so the shepherds would drive them away. (*Or HaḤayim* on Gen. 29:6)

I believe that the Ben Attar's subtle praise of Haran's shepherds can be taken even further: that in contrast to the prevalent reading above, the differences between Jacob's and Moses' experiences at the well in fact illuminate Jacob's entire exchange with the local shepherds as a warm, positive interaction.

First and foremost, Jacob's greeting, "Brothers" (29:4), is certainly not uttered by Moses, who in fact does not speak to the bullying Midianites at all. By contrast, the shepherds of Haran answer Jacob's question directly, without any anger or reservation: "We are from Haran." Jacob asks them question after question, and they respond – that is, a conversation develops between them.

Most of their replies are briefer than Jacob's questions, and some, as mentioned, claim that this conveys reservation and hostility. Yet one response in fact volunteers more information than Jacob asks for: when Jacob asks how Laban fares, they reply, "He is well," and then add: "And look, here is his daughter Rachel coming with the sheep." Some argue that the latter addition is the narrator's description, not the shepherds' reply, but this results in an awkward cadence within the narrative sequence; it is more likely that this is a continuation of their reply, and that the previous brevity of their responses serves to highlight their most important comment of all: that Rachel, Laban's daughter, is approaching the well.[19] This may be her usual practice, or perhaps they see her coming from a distance. In the narrative context, however, there is an even simpler answer, related to Jacob's next question: "'Look,' he said, 'it is still broad daylight. It is not yet time to gather in the animals. Water the flocks and take them back to pasture'" (v. 7). Had the Torah wished to cast the shepherds in a negative light, their

19. The midrash that characterizes the shepherds in a negative light also interprets their longer reply as a reflection of their reservations toward Jacob: "They said if you want to chat, then here comes his daughter Rachel with the flock – it is women who like to talk" (Genesis Rabba 70:11).

answer might have been something along the lines of "This fellow came here as a migrant and now he is setting himself up as a judge!" (Gen. 19:9), or perhaps stony, indignant silence at the cheek of a passerby who dares pass judgment about their work ethic. Yet they respond patiently, without resentment: "We cannot do that until all the flocks are gathered and the stone is rolled from the top of the well. Only then can we water the flocks" (v. 8).

Above, I suggested that these shepherds are a possessive mob who keep the well to themselves and prevent outsiders from sharing their water. An alternative perspective, however, is that controlling the well is in fact a moral act that maintains social equality. This is their well, a precious local resource, and this way, they can ensure that the water is distributed equally. In fact, this is how they know that Rachel is coming: she, too, is part of the group, and the shepherds are sitting and waiting for her.

I tentatively wish to propose that the flocks are all waiting for Rachel, and that she is the last to arrive. Not only because of the biblical rule of three plus one (in our case: three flocks are waiting, and the fourth, Rachel, is the most important), but because as soon as she arrives, Jacob rolls the stone from the mouth of the well. It may be that Jacob rolls the enormous stone by himself, which is the prevalent view that reflects his great strength and enthusiasm, but it also may be – as Radak, for example, proposes – that he helps the other shepherds lift the stone. Either way, the shepherds do not seem to oppose his move, as they presumably would if he would undermine their local custom. It is more likely, rather, that the shepherds are waiting for Rachel, and as soon as she arrives, they lift the stone and begin watering the flocks.

If read thus, then the two stories are essentially opposite: the shepherds of Midian drive Reuel's daughters away and seize the water they drew from the well; the shepherds of Haran wait for Laban's daughter so she can water her father's flock together with them.

This reversal prepares the ground for another, more sinister reversal. Moses flees from his home, encounters hostile shepherds at the well, but finds calm and comfort in the home of his new father-in-law Reuel. Jacob, by contrast, flees from his home, encounters friendly shepherds at the well, helps them share the water equally… but then suffers conflict and hostility in the home of his new father-in-law. The devious shepherds of Midian in Exodus are replaced, in our story, by Laban.

THE SYMBOLIC WELL

This encounter at the well contributes to understanding of the narrative objective. Many modern scholars quote Robert Uri Alter's brilliant reading of the ancestral encounters at the well as a foreshadowing of the nature of their relationship. In a comprehensive study, Alter shows that their first meeting at the well is a microcosm of the nature of their relationship. Rebecca is the only woman of these well "type scenes" who shows initiative and helps the foreigner at the well, who is not the groom himself but his emissary. As for Jacob and Rachel, Alter proposes reading the well and the heavy stone upon its mouth as a foreshadowing of their relationship's main complication: Rachel's barrenness. The well is a common biblical symbol of fertility, and in this scene, the well – or womb – is blocked by an enormous stone. Only with great effort does Jacob manage to unblock the well and draw water; only with great effort is Rachel's womb unlocked.[20]

---

20. Alter refers to this as a "type scene," wherein courting scenes symbolically took place by the well, and all these courting scenes have certain elements in common. Michael Martin ("Betrothal Journey Narratives") expounds upon the elements that commonly feature in such narratives: (1) A future groom travels to a foreign land; (2) he meets a woman by the well; (3) someone draws water; (4) the suitor bestows gifts or shows some other form of courtship; (5) the suitor reveals his identity; (6) someone rushes to inform the woman's family; (7) the family responds with a blessing/invitation; (8) betrothal is arranged; (9) the suitor stays with the woman's family; (10) the suitor returns home; (11) he is greeted by his family upon his return; (12) the suitor lives with his family.

    Martin analyzes the scenes with Abraham's servant and Rebecca; Jacob and Rachel; Moses and Reuel's daughters; Boaz and Ruth; Saul and the girls; David; the story of Tobit, and others. He, too, like Alter, emphasizes that the individual features of each narrative are underscored by the common elements of the type scene. Both Alter and Martin read Saul's brief encounter with the girls as belonging to this type scene, even if it develops in a different direction. It is interesting that in this context, the Midrash precedes modern scholarship: "R. Akiva says: Whoever enters the city and encounters young girls is promised success. How do we know that this is so? Eliezer Abraham's servant entered the city, [met Rebecca] and the Lord granted him success.... Our teacher Moses entered the city and encountered young girls...

Centuries before Alter's analysis, Abarbanel proposed a similar reading, which is best conveyed in his own eloquent words:

> When Jacob saw the well in the field, he took it as a good omen for his marriage. For this was where Eliezer, Abraham's servant, conducted the test and trial for Isaac's marriage. And he believed that a well was a good omen for a woman, as Solomon pronounced about women: "Drink water from your own cistern, and running water from your own well" (Prov. 5:15). And "three flocks of sheep were lying beside it" – this hints to Abraham, Isaac, and Jacob himself, for all three took wives from the same well in Haran; that is, from the same prominent family. "Because this was the well from which all the flocks were watered" – and from those women their descendants came forth.
>
> As for the large stone he saw upon the well, he considered it an allusion to the barrenness suffered by all the matriarchs of that esteemed family: Sarah, Rebecca, and Rachel and Leah as well, as will be told. Their barrenness was the stone blocking the mouth of the well, so that water could not be drawn from it. But he was told that all the flocks gathered there to roll the stone off, and he took it as a sign that all the prayers and merits of the forefathers would remove and cancel that barrenness. But once the barrenness was removed from Sarah, it remained in Rebecca; and once it was removed from Rebecca in the merit of Abraham and Isaac, it would still remain in Leah and Rachel, for the stone was always rolled back in place. And for this reason, when the shepherds told Jacob of it, and he took it as a sign of things to come, when he saw Rachel he was resolved to marry her.
>
> "And he rolled the stone" – meaning, he was determined to remove her barrenness. "He watered the flock" – meaning, she would bear his children. This happened in the literal sense and

---

and the Lord granted him success.... Saul entered the city and encountered young girls... and he succeeded and rose to the throne. And from Jacob, who entered the city and encountered young girls, as it says: "Look, here is his daughter Rachel" (*Pirkei DeRabbi Eliezer*, ch. 35).

> Jacob took it as a sign – either regarding his devotion to God, or regarding his marriage.[21]

When is a narrative's symbolism considered *peshat* and not just *derash*? There are no clear criteria that determine this. It is intriguing that two leading scholars – one medieval and one modern – neither of whom usually charge narratives with symbolic meaning, both read Jacob and Rachel's encounter as a symbolic foreshadowing of the actual plot. Even without legitimizing the symbolic interpretation of certain scenes in general, I believe that one criterion is not easily disputable: when a particular motif is emphasized more than necessary, it demands interpretation. The obvious emphasis on the burning bush in Moses' first encounter with God – far more than is necessary for the actual plot – invites analysis of its symbolic meaning. Regarding our own scene, "The well is the most important feature, the center of all description and events, and it is clear that it is discussed for its own sake, not as a mere backdrop."[22] This justifies exploring the well as a symbol; not only do I agree with his justification, but I believe that the same applies to the stone, which is mentioned with striking frequency: "The top of it was covered with a large *stone*. When all the flocks were gathered there, the *stone* would be rolled from the mouth of the well and the sheep watered. The *stone* would then be put back in place on top of the well" (vv. 2–3). In this scene, the well and the stone form a compound symbol – that is, of course, until Rachel comes along, and Jacob removes the stone. Rolling the stone from the mouth of the well is mentioned three times,[23] a symbolic number that certainly draws attention to the act itself. This unusual focus justifies Abarbanel's reading and invites symbolic interpretations of these motifs in the text.

---

21. Abarbanel on 28:16ff.
22. Samet, *Studies II*, vol. 1, 129–30.
23. As defined by Fokkelman, *Genesis*, 128. There are various suggestions about the symbolic meaning of these "three flocks": some propose that they hint to the three women who will birth before the "stone" is removed from Rachel's womb (Janzen, *Abraham*, 113); others point out that Jacob must overcome three obstacles before he receives God's blessing (see various formulations in Walton, *Traveller*, 129; Vrolijk, *Jacob's Wealth*, 128; Samet, *Studies II*, vol. 1, 135–36).

WELL AND LADDER

If it is justified to load symbolic meaning onto the well, perhaps there is room to explore its meaning from a different angle. Abarbanel and Alter claim that the well and its stone foreshadow the nature of the couple's relationship, but this does not exclude the fact that the recurring motif of the stone takes us back to the previous scene: to God's revelation to Jacob at Bethel. There, too, the stone is a recurring motif – Jacob sets a random stone by his head, and then, upon waking, he anoints it and sanctifies it as a pillar.[24]

Moreover, the two scenes are in subtle dialogue through their structure. Jacob's dream in Bethel comprises of three stages, each marked with the opening word "*vehineh*," and as discussed, each stage introduces an element of increasing surprise, until God Himself appears to Jacob:

1. Jacob left Beersheba and journeyed toward Haran.
2. He chanced upon a certain place and decided to spend the night there ... and he dreamed:
3. (*vehineh*) He saw a ladder set upon the ground, whose top reached the heavens.
4. (*vehineh*) On it, angels of God went up and came down.
5. (*vehineh*) The Lord stood over him there.

This structure is identical to that of the next scene:

1. Jacob went on his way and came to the land of the people of the East.
2. And he saw:
3. (*vehineh*) there was a well in the field
4. (*vehineh*) three flocks were lying beside it ...
5. (*vehineh*) look, here is his daughter Rachel coming with the sheep.

---

24. See, for example, in Sarna, *Genesis*, 202. Fokkelman sees stones as a recurring motif in the Jacob cycle (Fokkelman, *Genesis*, 125).

This is not merely an external connection, but a common structure that expresses an identical narrative process. Jacob leaves one place and journeys to another; then, in his new location, he has a visual experience ("and he dreamed" in Bethel/"and he saw" in Haran).

The three stages of what Jacob sees progress in the same way. Jacob first perceives an inanimate object. Both the ladder and the well can be defined in similar terms: they both enable a vertical transition between two contrasting entities. The ladder allows angels to ascend from earth to heaven, while the well allows a person to stand on the ground and reach down in order to draw groundwater.[25]

Jacob then discerns animate figures by this inanimate object – not primary characters, but supporting characters that will mediate between Jacob and the protagonist he will soon meet. Only then does he encounter the central character, with whom he will enter into a covenant: God and Rachel.

What is the meaning of this surprising parallel between the ladder angels climb and the well from which the shepherds draw water? Perhaps this connection can affirm Ramban's symbolic reading of this scene, which he perceived as an allusion to the distant future, when Jacob's descendants will build a Temple:

> The authors of Genesis Rabba found in this a secret allusion to the future. For it so happened that he entered by the well, when only three of the flocks had gathered, at a time when the stone covered the mouth of the well and the flocks watched over it. All this serves to inform that he will be successful on this path and that he will have descendants worthy of this vision. For the well hints to the Temple, the three flocks to the three festivals of pilgrimage, "This was the well from which all the flocks were watered" – from there they will draw their holy spirit. Or, this could hint to "From Zion the Torah shall spring forth," for the Torah is likened to water, "and God's word from Jerusalem."

---

25. A ladder has rungs to reach the top; a well has a bucket with which to reach the bottom. Given the biblical belief that there is also *mayim bashamayim* (that the heavens also contain water), the comparison is reinforced.

> "There all the flocks would gather" – they will come from Hamath to the Wadi of Egypt. "The stone would be rolled and the flock watered" – from there they will draw their holy spirit; "The stone would then be put back in place" – a term for the next festival of pilgrimage. (Ramban on Gen. 29:2)

The connection between the ladder and the well validates Ramban's reading. Just as the ladder hints to the meeting of heaven and earth, so does the well; just as the ladder hints to the heavenly hosts, the well hints to future pilgrims; just as the ladder marks the site as "none other but the House of God," so does the well.

However, the meaning of the connection between the ladder and the well can also be read in the opposite sense of the Ramban's interpretation. Both episodes occur on Jacob's journey to Haran. In the first, God appears to him in a sublime revelation, replete with a promise of perpetual protection. In the second, it is Rachel who appears to him, and he rolls the stone off the well with all the strength he can muster. In this scene there are no dreams and no angels; no revelation and no mention of heaven. The encounter with Rachel is a scene that emphasizes how the plot is propelled by human action and initiation. It is not God but Jacob who stars in this scene. In Jacob's encounter with God he is fast asleep, entirely passive; he can only respond after it takes place, when he wakes up. A completely different Jacob appears in this second scene: he is the one who initiates conversation; he is the one who asks the shepherds why they are not working; and he is the one who rolls the enormous stone from the mouth of the well and waters the flock. This chapter opens with Jacob "rais[ing] his legs," and this expression anticipates the movement, physical strength, and initiative that will characterize the ensuing scene.

In other words, the two juxtaposed stones in each scene are charged with different meanings. The first stone becomes a pillar – a sanctified monument to God's name. The second stone remains a functional object, a stone that closes the shepherds' well. This pair generates a dichotomy that will characterize the entire Jacob cycle, and appear at every significant junction: God promises divine protection, but Jacob himself must show initiative and strength. Divine action must be coupled with human action.

This definition has dramatic implications for the figure of Rachel and her role in the Jacob cycle. In every scene, she represents the same fundamental theme: a person's actions can and should solve their own problems, and they must take action in order to shape reality. When she is unable to bear a child, she does not pray, or ask Jacob to pray; instead, she presents him with her handmaid in the hope that she will build a family through her; she then acquires the mandrakes Reuben brings to his mother, seeking to heal her infertility. She steals Laban's teraphim in order to help her family flee Haran, and there too – as we will see – alongside Rachel's action, Jacob and his family are also protected by divine intervention.

Jacob first meets Rachel by the well, not by the ladder, and this contributes to her characterization and role in the plot. Rachel is the one who delves into the depths of reality, seeking to draw water; like a well, she does not ascend to the sky, but plunges deep into the depths of the earth.

This characteristic is related to a fundamental question that touches upon understanding of her marriage to Jacob.

IS RACHEL JACOB'S INTENDED?

Perhaps this chapter heading sounds strange: When Jacob meets Rachel at the well and asks her father for her hand in marriage, Rachel becomes his intended. However, in the broader context of the Jacob cycle, this is a legitimate – even necessary – question. Given that Jacob travels to the land of the people of the East for two reasons, it is worth determining whether this scene is propelled by his flight from Esau, or by his search for a wife. On the surface, there is every reason to believe that the latter is the case – their betrothal is the result of their encounter at the well, where Jacob already kisses her and waters her flock. His love for her leads him to break etiquette and ask for her hand in marriage even though she is the younger daughter: "And Jacob was in love with Rachel, so he said, 'I will work for you seven years for your younger daughter Rachel'" (29:18).

Yonatan Feintuch indeed reads this scene as part of Isaac's mission, pointing out the repetition of the phrase "his mother's brother," which recalls Isaac's instructions when he sends Jacob to Padan Aram:[26] "When Jacob saw Rachel, daughter of Laban, his mother's brother, and the flock of Laban, his mother's brother... he watered the flock of Laban, his mother's brother" (29:10–11)/"Go at once to Padan Aram, to the house of your mother's father Bethuel, and there marry a daughter of your mother's brother Laban" (28:2).

According to this reading, Jacob's encounter with Rachel effectively fulfills his father's instructions, for the reader soon learns that Rachel will become his wife. Yet despite the sound logic of this claim, I believe that certain textual elements characterize this as another scene of his flight to Haran, escaping his brother's wrath on his mother's instructions.

This is evident in the language as well as the plot. Jacob asks the shepherds where they are from, and their answer sets the tone for the rest of the scene: they are from Rebecca's Haran, not Isaac's Padan Aram.

Moreover, the elements of the plot itself support this reading, as I will suggest through the following analysis: When Rebecca meets Abraham's servant at the well, she runs to her "mother's household" and tells her family "what had happened" (24:28). When Rachel meets Jacob at the well, she too runs to her father,[27] but it is Jacob who tells Laban "all that had happened" (29:13). What does Jacob tell Laban? If we assume that the scene is a courting narrative, fulfilling Isaac's instructions, then presumably Jacob tells Laban that he has come to marry his daughter. But if so, then the next verses are puzzling: After a month, Laban asks Jacob what he wants in exchange for his labor, and Jacob surprises him by asking for Rachel's hand in marriage. This exchange is nonsensical if Jacob has already told Laban why he has come, and it is not at all clear why it only happens a month after his arrival. If Jacob comes to Laban's house to find a wife, then this should have been mentioned immediately,

26. Feintcuh, "Ladder and Well," 13–14. Sarna also expresses that this formulation recalls the instructions that he received from his parents, but by referring to both parents, he does not seem to think that this refers specifically to his father's instructions (Sarna, *Genesis*, 202).
27. The Midrash concludes that Rachel runs to her father (and not to her mother, as Rebecca does) because her mother is dead (Genesis Rabba 70:29).

as it is when Abraham's servant comes to find a wife for Isaac. Moreover, if Jacob tells Laban of "Isaac's mission," then it is unclear why he arrives empty handed, instead of laden with gifts like his father's emissary a generation earlier.

It thus seems more likely that when Jacob tells Laban of "all that had happened," he is actually describing his conflict with his brother and his mother's instructions to flee his wrath.[28] This explains why Laban immediately offers to host him but only asks him about his salary a month later, and why Jacob's request for Rachel's hand in marriage is presented as a new idea – which it is, as it was not raised in their initial conversation.[29]

If Jacob is indeed portrayed in this scene as a fugitive rather than a suitor, there is significance to his weeping: "And Jacob kissed Rachel – and wept aloud" (29:11). Radak, for example, interprets his tears as tears of joy, but it seems more likely that these are the cathartic tears of a fugitive who has been forced to flee for his life, and has just reached the end of a journey fraught with fear. Upon meeting a family member who welcomes him and offers him haven and safety, he finally allows himself to break down.[30]

Feintuch correctly asserts that the text highlights that Rachel is the daughter of Laban, his "mother's brother," and that the flock Jacob waters belongs to Laban, his "mother's brother," which recalls Rebecca's instructions to "flee at once to my brother Laban" (27:43); this hints that the scene's emphasis is on the fulfillment of Rebecca's mission rather

28. As Fokkelman, *Genesis*, 588. Sarna finds it difficult to believe that he would tell him of his deception (Sarna, *Genesis*, 203; similarly Eising, *Jakob*, 166). However, given that Jacob acts on his mother's instructions, and he is now talking to his mother's brother, Laban will probably hear this story with less criticism than Sarna fears – what is important to Laban is that his sister favors Jacob and ensures that he receives his father's blessings.
29. As mentioned, it is likely that Jacob tells Laban about the blessings, and this gives his reply certain irony: "You are truly of my own bones, my own flesh" (29:14). Jacob has just proven that a family connection does not ensure protection against deceit; perhaps this anticipates that Jacob is about to be deceived by his own flesh and blood?
30. For further analysis of this scene as part of Rebecca and not Isaac's mission, see Grossman, "Jacob's Struggle," 22.

than Isaac's. Moreover, the epistrophic repetition of "mother" in these verses brings his "mother's" instructions to the forefront of the reader's consciousness – Jacob has fled to Haran to escape from his brother.

A comparison between this scene and Abraham's servant's encounter with Rebecca at the well suggests that Jacob's encounter with Rachel is coincidental, rather than a fulfillment of Isaac's instructions to go to Padan Aram to find a wife. For the sake of analysis, I will first mention a fundamental methodical issue inherent to narrative comparison. As discussed, some define such encounters at the well as "type scenes," or some other genre. The appropriate methodology for comparison is to read the relevant scenes in parallel and determine what makes each one unique in light of the regular pattern, because it is these deviations that lend each narrative its meaning.[31] For example, when Alter notes that Rebecca is the only prospective bride who is not in need of the man's help, and who waters the animals herself (Gen. 24), he reaches the conclusion that this anticipates the nature of the future couple's relationship: that Rebecca will be the one who moves Isaac to action – both with his knowledge (27:46) and without it (ch. 27).

There is, however, room to question this methodology, albeit cautiously. Alter's premise is that the reader is aware of the type scene, and will thus be able to note the relevant deviations in each instance, but it is important to note that each scene has its own narrative context that affects the specific details of each scene, even without any symbolic significance. In Abraham's servant's encounter with Rebecca, for example, the groom is not even present at the well, and it is the prospective bride, not the groom, who is under scrutiny; therefore she is the narrative focus. This set of circumstances is completely different in parallel type scenes – both Jacob and Moses are fleeing for their life when they reach the well, and their actions earn them their prospective father-in-law's respect. Can these first encounters at the well really be an accurate indication of the couple's future – as Alter claims – when the narrative contexts of each scene are so different?

31. See especially in Alter, *Biblical Narrative*, 66–77; Martin, "Betrothal Journey Narratives." For a comparison between well scenes that lead to marriage, see Gilead, "Encounters"; Culley, *Structure*, 4–43; Ararat, "Two Encounters."

I raise this deliberation – without presenting any conclusions – as a background for the following comparison. Whether or not this is indeed a broader literary convention, Jacob's encounter with Rachel at the well certainly reminds the reader of his mother's encounter with his father's emissary a generation earlier – if not as a type scene, then as an intentional analogy between the two episodes. Should we indeed apply elements of one scene to the other? This question is a dramatic one in our context, given that one of the most striking elements in the encounter with Rebecca is the interpretation of their meeting as the result of divine providence.

This element is clearly inherent to the plot, and it is explicitly mentioned by the servant after he discovers that the generous girl he meets is related to his master: "Blessed be the Lord, God of my master Abraham, who has not withheld His kindness and faithfulness from my master. As for me – the Lord has guided me on the way to the house of my master's close family" (24:26–27).

This component is entirely absent in Jacob's story. He neither bows to the Lord nor thanks Him; nor does he ask for any sign from God before he reaches the well. Is this difference significant? Are the similarities between the scenes calculated to underscore this difference? Abarbanel believes that this is the case; that the providence extended to Abraham's servant is similarly extended to Jacob when he meets Rachel, and he believes that Jacob, too, discerns this: "And now Jacob chooses Rachel for his wife; not only because of her beauty… but because God proved this to him while he was by the well, just as Rebecca was proved to be the one for Isaac in the same way, in the same place." Nahum Sarna writes similarly, if more cautiously: "The narrator gently exposes the hand of divine providence in the drama's development."[32]

This is a legitimate reading, but again, in such cases it may be that the key to the narrative objective lies in these very differences.

The contrast between these scenes is significant, and their differences have bearing on each plot – for example, because Jacob does not arrive with camels laden with gifts, he has nothing to offer but work.

32. Sarna, *Understanding Genesis*, 195. See also Hamilton, *Genesis II*, 253; Fokkelman, *Genesis*, 123–25; Humphreys, *Character of God*, 175.

In our context, however, I wish to draw special attention to a specific difference between the scenes. Rachel's arrival coincides with Jacob's exchange with the shepherds: "While he was still talking with them, Rachel came with her father's sheep; she was a shepherdess" (29:9). Rebecca's arrival also overlaps with the suitor's speech: "Before he had even finished speaking, Rebecca ... came out with her jar on her shoulder" (24:15). The difference is that Rachel arrives as Jacob is speaking to the *shepherds*, while Rebecca arrives as Abraham's servant is praying to *God*. It is thus no coincidence that the servant bows to God and thanks Him soon after, while this component is absent in Jacob's story. In the earlier scene, God's providence and response to the servant's prayer is clear, while one generation later, God is not present on the stage: there is no preceding prayer, no grateful conclusion, and no hint that the bride's arrival is linked to the suitor's appeal to God.[33]

Thus, unlike Abraham's servant's encounter with Rebecca – which marks the fulfillment of the servant's mission – Jacob meets Rachel by chance, by the well, on the outskirts of his destination city, and falls in love with her irrespective of his father's mission.

The interpretive implications of this cannot be overstated. Jacob does not take Rachel for a wife because his father told him to, or in order to perpetuate Abraham's blessing, but because he happens to fall in love with her. It is no coincidence that Jacob encounters her *before* he reaches Padan Aram (or that the shepherds respond that they are from "*Haran*"); once he reaches Laban's home, his request for his cousin's hand in marriage fulfills his father's instructions. But Jacob meets her before he reaches Padan Aram, before he enters her father's house; their connection is sparked outside the home sphere. This is an expression of spontaneous love – of the frightened, penniless refugee falling in love, with nothing to offer but the sweat of his brow – not of the formal marriage arrangement his father seeks for him.

This dichotomy hints to a niggling question: Is Rachel Jacob's intended, according to the original divine plan? I am not sure there is room for this question, but I wish to lay it out on the table here, at the

33. Various scholars comment on the lack of Jacob's prayer compared to Abraham's servant more subtly, such as Waltke, *Genesis*, 398.

very beginning of their relationship. We will yet argue that Jacob's marriage to two wives is complex, and it is not at all certain that Leah would be part of Abraham's line were it not for Laban's maneuver. The narrative's perception of Jacob's marriages is far from straightforward, and we will yet return to Jacob and Rachel's first encounter, to Jacob's love at first sight, and to his request for the younger daughter's hand in marriage.

According to this reading, the objective of the well scene is to characterize Jacob and Rachel's first meeting and relationship as one based on human initiative and emotions, not merely the result of Isaac's instructions to marry a daughter from the house of Laban.

WIVES AND SHEEP

I wish to briefly return to Jacob's first encounter with Rachel and the aforementioned epistrophe of "his mother's brother." This epistrophe is in fact part of a broader comparison between Rachel and her sheep (29:10–11):

> When Jacob saw
> *Rachel,* daughter   of Laban, his mother's brother,
> with the *sheep*   of Laban, his mother's brother,
>
> he stepped forward, rolled the stone from the top of the well,
> and watered (*vayashk*) the *sheep* of Laban, his mother's brother
> and kissed (*vayashk*) *Rachel*

Jacob sees two things that move him to action: he sees Rachel and he sees the sheep. The repetitive structure of this verse generates an analogy between them. Considering that the literal meaning of the name Rachel is "ewe," this wordplay creates an even more striking parallel.[34] There is further wordplay in the two actions Jacob performs in response to the

34. Garsiel (*Midrashic Name Derivations*, 118) proposes that there is intentional wordplay in Jeremiah about Rachel's name meaning sheep (Jer. 31:14–17).

two things he sees: he kisses (*vayashk*) Rachel and he waters (*vayashk*) the sheep.[35]

The link between Laban's daughters and his flock is also evident in a parallel scene where Jacob informs his wives that they are about to leave Haran: "Jacob sent word to Rachel and Leah to come out to the field where his flock was" (31:4). Laban himself reinforces this connection when Jacob leaves him: "Then Laban spoke up and said to Jacob, 'The daughters are my daughters. The children are my children. The flocks are my flock'" (31:43).

In summary, when Jacob arrives in Haran he sets his sights on two entities that belong to his mother's brother Laban: the flock and Rachel. By the time he leaves Haran, both entities will belong to Jacob, and he will bring them back to Canaan with him.[36]

35. Shemesh, "Rachel," 87–88. She adds: "This is the only case in the Bible of a man kissing a woman who is not his mother or daughter" (ibid., 88).

36. Compare to Sherwood, "Jacob and Laban," 49; Vrolijk, *Jacob's Wealth*, 130.

Marriage and Children (Gen. 29:15–30:24)

> They shall be married to-morrow, and I will bid the duke to the nuptial. But, O, how bitter a thing it is to look into happiness through another man's eyes! By so much the more shall I to-morrow be at the height of heart-heaviness, by how much I shall think my brother happy in having what he wishes for.
>
> – Shakespeare, *As You Like It,* Act V, Scene II

Jacob, having fled from his brother, finds haven in his uncle's home, and even falls in love with his cousin. Leaving the parents' home and settling in a new place is not a new motif in the book of Genesis; it is essentially the formula for every marital relationship: "That is why a man leaves his father and mother and cleaves to his wife and they become one flesh" (Gen. 2:24). Yet Jacob's journey is not colored with the usual festive tones of a courtship narrative – he does not arrive at Laban's home in the garb of a groom, and he is not laden with presents for his prospective bride. Jacob arrives as a frightened, penniless refugee, and his dependence on Laban will affect him until he leaves Haran.

It is not clear whether Jacob's encounter with Rachel at the well and his marriage with both of Laban's daughters can be divided into two separate units. There is no consensus in modern research,[1] and there are

1. Examples of scholars who analyze the narrative as a single unit: Westermann, *Genesis II*, 463–64; Sarna, *Genesis*, 194–96. Examples of those who read it as two distinct

indeed arguments for both approaches. When the two episodes are read together, Jacob's watering of Laban's flock already anticipates his role in Laban's house; moreover, the contrast between the shepherds of Haran and the scheming Laban is especially salient.

The well scene concludes with Jacob's arrival at Laban's home: "'You are truly of my own bones, my own flesh.' And Jacob stayed with him for a month" (29:14). What does Jacob do for a month? After Laban's heartwarming invitation, does Jacob rest from his harrowing journey and acclimatize himself to his new family and environment? The next verse suggests that this is not the case: "Then Laban said to him, 'If you are my brother, does that mean you should work for me for nothing? Tell me what your hire should be'" (29:15). How should Laban's question be understood?[2] Ramban raises two possibilities: that until now, Jacob has not been working, and Laban is diplomatically hinting to him that it is time for him to earn his board. Ramban's second suggestion has significant implications for the narrative's characterization:

> The text does not tell that Jacob was working for him, but it may well be that from the moment "he watered the sheep of Laban, his mother's brother," the flock remained in his charge, for when he saw that Rachel was a shepherdess, he felt sorry for her and did not want her to have to tend the flock any more, and he would tend to them out of his love for her. (Ramban on Gen. 29:15)

If so, then Jacob has been working for his uncle from the moment of his arrival. Ramban suggests that Jacob did so to spare Rachel, but it may well be that Laban cajoles him into working for him from day one, and

units: Gunkel, *Genesis*, 316–21; Von Rad, *Genesis*, 282–87; Speiser, *Genesis*, 221–27; Wenham, *Genesis II*, 229; Fokkelman, *Genesis*, 123–26.

2. I assume, together with most exegetes, that this phrase means, "Just because you are family, does that mean you should work for nothing?" Some read this to mean that Laban means that they are not kin – "Should even a family member work for nothing? And you are not even family" (Daube and Yaron, "Jacob's Reception," 61–62; see also Hamilton, *Genesis II*, 257; Sherwood, "Jacob and Laban," 86). Sherwood also claims that the connotations of "*vayeshev imo*" are of strangers who stay with someone, rather than of family (ibid., 76). If so, this is consistent with his claim that Laban relates to Jacob as if he is not family.

offers him payment for his labors after he realizes that it is worth his while for Jacob to remain with him.[3]

There is no way of determining which of Ramban's readings is correct, but the latter possibility is far more consistent with Laban's characterization as the narrative progresses. If so, then the description that Jacob "stayed (*vayeshev*) with him for a month" – *yashav* is a verb that suggests passivity – is somewhat misleading. While it implies that Jacob stayed and recovered from his journey, the next verse suggests that Laban's house is not the kind of place where someone can simply sit and rest when there is work to be done. The narrative sequence hints to Laban's firm hand: the description that the exhausted Jacob "stayed" for a month creates the impression that he indeed recuperates for a month, as one might expect after a harrowing journey, but the next verse shatters this illusion and thus portrays Laban as a miser.

Perhaps this reading vilifies Laban more than these verses explicitly do, but his characterization as the story goes on retroactively justifies this.

Before Jacob can reply to Laban, stating his payment, the narrator interjects with a description of Laban's two daughters:

> Laban had two daughters. The elder was called Leah and the younger Rachel.
> Leah had sensitive eyes; Rachel was beautiful and lovely.
> And Jacob loved Rachel.

This description is followed by Jacob's request for Rachel's hand: "So he said: 'I will work for you seven years for your younger daughter Rachel'" (v. 18).

This is a case of a "late introduction" – rather than being introduced at the beginning of the scene, Laban's daughters are mentioned just before they are relevant. This description is deeply significant in two contexts.

Firstly, their introduction completely overlooks the scene at the well. Jacob has already met Rachel and watered her flock in a classic

3. See also Alter, *Genesis*, 153; Hamilton, *Genesis II*, 258.

courting scene, and he has even kissed her – surely she will soon become his wife! Yet the tone of Leah and Rachel's introduction – "Laban had two daughters. The elder was called Leah and the younger Rachel" – is that of a new introduction, of characters the reader has never met before; as if the reader does not know that Laban's younger daughter is called Rachel.

Some scholars suggest that this is indeed an alternative tradition of Jacob and Rachel's meeting;[4] or perhaps a literary technique related to the dichotomy of Jacob's journey. Only at this point does Jacob begin to fulfill his father's instructions: Laban, Rebecca's brother has two daughters, and Jacob is to wed one of them, as his father has bid him. The reader could have skipped the encounter at the well entirely and gone straight to this description, which also explains why Jacob favors Rachel over her elder sister: Leah has delicate, pretty eyes (according to Rashbam, contrary to Radak),[5] but Rachel is beautiful from head to toe. Jacob's preference is clear; the well scene is redundant.

This has broader implications, of course: Isaac's instructions are fulfilled in the next scene, where despite Jacob's preferences for the younger sister, he marries Leah, the elder sister. Though he meets Rachel in an earlier scene, this is the dramatic infatuation of a refugee who finds comfort in a family member he happens to meet.[6]

Secondly, this introduction serves an additional purpose: it generates a subtle analogy between Laban's daughters and Rebecca's sons. Bethuel's two children each have two children: Rebecca, in Canaan, has two sons, and Laban, in Haran, has two daughters. The younger child of each is the family's designated shepherd, while the two older children do not tend to the flock. The Sages perceive this analogy as a basis for marital compatibility:

---

4. See, for example, Gunkel, *Genesis*, 319.
5. Speiser and Gail Yee also believe that the description of Leah's eyes is a positive one, suggesting "delicate eyes" (Speiser, *Genesis*, 25; Yee, "Leah"). They base this on Jacob's excuse to Esau that the children are "delicate" (33:13).
6. Sherwood proposes that there is intentional wordplay between the large ("*gedola*") stone over the well and Leah "*hagedola*" (Sherwood, "Jacob and Leah," 37). Beyond the fact that this is a common word, the well scene focuses on Rachel, with no mention of Leah there.

> Leah was in fact intended for Esau, and Rachel for Jacob. Leah would sit by the crossroads and ask about Esau's exploits. They would tell her: "He is an evil man who sheds blood, who robs passersby, ruddy and hairy like a cloak, a wicked man who has committed every possible abomination against God." When she heard this, she would weep, crying, "My sister Rachel and I emerged from the same womb – why should Rachel marry the righteous Jacob, and I the evil Esau?" She would weep and suffer until her eyes became tender. That is why "Leah's eyes were tender." (*Midrash Tanḥuma, Vayetzeh* ch. 4)[7]

The analogy between the two pairs of sibling persists in the next scene, of Jacob's marriage. In both families, one parent interferes in their relationship and irreversibly alters the course of their lives. Rebecca sends Jacob in Esau's place, depriving her elder son of the blessing he is about to receive; while Laban sends Leah in Rachel's place so that she is the first to marry Jacob.

The connection between these two scenes is hinted to in the text itself. Jacob's complaint to Laban, "What is this you have done to me?... Why did you deceive me?" (29:25), echoes Isaac's complaint to Esau: "Your brother came in deceit and took your blessing" (27:35). As the Midrash notes, Laban's reply to Jacob is slightly accusative: "This is not done in *our place* – to marry off the younger before the elder" (29:26), as if to say: perhaps in *your place* the younger usurps the elder's place, but not in *our place*. The Midrash draws a further juxtaposition between these scenes:

> All that night, he called her "Rachel" and she answered him. "Then came morning – and it was Leah!" He said to her: "Cheater, daughter of a cheater – when I called you 'Rachel' all night, did you not answer?" She said to him: "Is there a teacher without

7. Famously and vividly, the Midrash describes that Leah's eyes are "tender" from weeping – she wept ever since learning that she was intended for the wicked elder brother Esau (Genesis Rabba 70:16).

students? When your father called you 'Esau,' did you not answer him?" (Genesis Rabba 70:19)

The text itself hints to this reading through Laban's use of the words "younger" (*tze'ira*)/"firstborn" (*bekhira*). While Laban's daughters are introduced with the descriptions "*gedola – ketana*" (29:16), Laban himself uses the words "*bekhora – tze'ira*." Whatever the significance of this difference may be, the same balance is maintained in the blessing scene: the narrator refers to the brothers as "*gadol*" or "*katan*" but the characters themselves use the word "*bekhor*" instead of "*gadol*," "firstborn" instead of "elder": "When Isaac had grown old, when his eyes had grown so dim that he could not see, he summoned his *elder son* Esau" (27:1); "Then Rebecca took her *elder son* Esau's best clothes... and put them on Jacob, *her younger son*" (27:15); "Jacob said to his father, 'I am Esau your *firstborn*'" (27:19); "'I am your son, your *firstborn*, Esau,' [Esau] replied" (27:32).[8] If we consider that the sisters are exchanged during a feast – associated with food and drinking – then the parallel to Jacob's theft of the blessings is stronger still.

This connection seems intentional and significant, but it is difficult to define its contribution. Many see this as *midda keneged midda* – measure for measure: Jacob takes his brother's place in order to obtain his blessing, so providence sees to it that Laban puts Leah in Rachel's place. In the words of Nechama Leibowitz: "In order to emphasize how the punishment fits the crime, the words '*tzeira*' and '*bekhira*' are used instead of '*gedola*' and '*ketana*.'"[9] Martin Buber uses this episode as a striking example of how key words hint to divine retribution: "During his exile, where God is protecting him but not sparing him from hardship, Jacob experiences on his own flesh what it is like to be cheated by a member of his own family."[10] In this scene, Jacob is paral-

8. See further in Frisch, "Moral Evaluation," 282, and compare to Hamilton: "Just as Esau, an older brother, stands between Jacob and the blessing, here an older sister stands between Jacob and his true love" (Hamilton, *Genesis II*, 258).
9. Leibowitz, *Genesis*, 187.
10. Buber, *Ways*, 291.

leled to the two characters he deceives:[11] like Isaac, Laban deceives him during a feast, and places a different daughter before him than the one he requests; and like Esau, he works for a specific prize but fails to earn that prize despite his work. From this perspective, Laban's act of deceit is fitting punishment for Jacob, and this may certainly be the significance of the dialogue between these two scenes.

On the other hand, the clear connection between the scenes might allude to the "double causality" that accompanies Jacob's marriage.

What would have happened without Laban's act of deceit – would Jacob have married Rachel alone? Would she have been the mother of all twelve tribes? We are forced to admit that Laban's exchange has an unfathomable effect on Israel's history. This conclusion should not faze us; free choice is one of the most central themes in biblical narrative – including human actions that throw history sharply off course – and Jacob's theft of Esau's blessing is an apt example. Yet in this case, the narrative premise may be that Laban's act of deceit implies that Leah – and not Rachel – is fundamentally suited to Jacob. Jacob may favor the lovely Rachel, but against his will, providence dictates that he must marry Leah as well.[12] It makes sense that Jacob is drawn to his "twin" – to the younger sister, the shepherdess. But in the context of the complex relationship between Jacob and Esau, Jacob's marriage with Leah can also be justified. Jacob obtains Esau's birthright and even the blessings Isaac intended for his older son – through his own actions, he becomes the firstborn. If so, then perhaps the birthright Jacob acquires through human initiative – but predicted and guided by providence – implies that it is indeed Leah, the firstborn, rather than Rachel, the younger sister, who is a more fitting bride for him, especially given that their marriage transpires through a similar fusion of human action and covert providence.

---

11. Some claim that if a character can be paralleled to more than one character, this shows that the analogy is not intentional. But I believe that this fluidity is an inherent part of the analogy. See Grossman, *Text and Subtext*, 364–68.
12. As Sarna, *Genesis*, 205.

This reading can be detected in several midrashim: that the stable foundations of Jacob's house will be built through Leah and her children, and Laban's deceit is just part of the story. For example:

> "The elder (*gedola* [= 'greater']) was called Leah" – she was to receive greater gifts: eternal priesthood and eternal kingship. "The younger (*ketana* [= 'smaller']) was called Rachel" – she was to receive smaller gifts: Joseph for temporary leadership and Saul for temporary kingship [and Shiloh for temporary holiness: "He rejected the tent of Joseph and did not choose the tribe of Ephraim"]. (Genesis Rabba 70:15)

Given that the midrash favors Leah in the verse that introduces the two sisters, after which Jacob chooses Rachel and her "temporary" gifts, it seems that the author perceives Jacob's marriage with Leah as a positive incident that is not merely the result of Laban's maneuver. Once again, reading the marriage scene against Jacob and Esau's relationship in Canaan, it seems fitting that Jacob, the self-made "firstborn," should marry the firstborn Leah, even if he is drawn to Rachel.

Either way, although Jacob's encounter with Rachel at the well explains his preference for her, note how the text presents Jacob's request for Rachel's hand as a surprise:

> Laban had two daughters.
> The elder was called Leah / and the younger Rachel.
> Leah had sensitive eyes; / Rachel was beautiful and lovely.
> And Jacob was in love with Rachel, so he said, "I will work for you seven years for your younger daughter Rachel."

Leah is mentioned first, as the eldest daughter; Leah is described first; this structure leads the reader to anticipate that Jacob's request will follow this pattern: "And Jacob was in love with Leah." Instead, his reply breaks this pattern: he "skips over" Leah and asks for the "younger daughter Rachel."

R. Itamar Eldar suggested to me that this subtle surprise is intensified through a comparison between the two brothers of Canaan and the two sisters of Haran:

Jacob and Esau (25:25–28)	**Rachel and Leah (29:16–18)**
The first came out... they named him Esau. Then his brother emerged... he named him Jacob.	The elder was called Leah and the younger Rachel.
Esau became a skilled hunter, a man of the field, while Jacob was an innocent man who stayed among the tents.	Leah had sensitive eyes; Rachel was beautiful and lovely.
Isaac loved Esau because he ate of his game, but Rebecca loved Jacob.	And Jacob was in love with Rachel.
(Jacob takes the birthright, the *bekhora*)	(Jacob takes the firstborn, the *bekhora*, in marriage)

These descriptions and their sequence is similar, but there is one poignant deviation: while Jacob and Esau are each loved by a parent, only Rachel ever experiences her husband's love.

A MIND AT WORK

The key word of this unit is "*avad*," "work,"[13] and given that Jacob works for seven years for each wife, it is no surprise that the verb appears exactly seven times, beginning with Laban's question: "Though you are my brother, does that mean you should work for me for nothing?" (v. 15), and ending with how Jacob works for another seven years for his second wife: "He served him for another seven years" (v. 30).[14] The verb root A-B-D has several meanings, and it is sometimes difficult to discern

13. Frisch, "Moral Evaluation," 284.
14. Fokkelman, *Genesis*, 126, 130.

its meaning in a particular context: it can mean anything from the lowest form of slavery to an important political position.[15] Abraham, for example, has a "servant" whom he trusts so deeply that he sends him to find a wife for his son; this same servant is presented as the head of Abraham's household: "the senior servant of his household, who was in charge of all he had" (24:2).

How should the fourteen years that Jacob "serves" Laban be understood? Some read it as actual slavery,[16] given that Jacob has no money for a dowry – his only possible form of payment is to sell himself as a slave. Others claim that this reading is exaggerated, and Jacob's seven years for each wife are a form of contract of employment: Jacob works as a shepherd for Laban, tending to his flock.[17] The latter theory is more plausible, but it is no coincidence that the word "*avad*" is vague. The sense of work that pervades these verses, with its intense repetition, plays an important role in shaping the relationship between the uncle and his slave/servant/worker/nephew. For now, it is worth noting that there is certain irony in the fact that Jacob, whose father blesses him that "peoples will serve you" (27:29), and whose own brother is told, "Your brother you will serve" (27:40), is the one who must now serve his "brother" Laban.[18] Does this reflect upon the nature of these blessings and the process of their fulfillment? It is too early to say.

In any case, based on what we know of dowries in the ancient world, Jacob's offer seems more than generous.[19] Jacob, who loves Rachel, feels that he must work hard in order to rightly earn her hand, and this love makes the years "seem to him but a few days" (29:20). Jacob finds love during his exile in Haran, and perhaps this love will soothe his longing for his home and his mother, just as Rebecca's presence brings Isaac comfort "after his mother's death" (24:67). Similarly, in a clear nod to Jacob's seven years that fly by like days, Dostoevsky's Raskolnikov

---

15. Rüterswörden, "*eved*," 387–92.
16. Sherwood, "Jacob and Laban," 93; Fokkelman, *Genesis*, 130.
17. Morrison, "Jacob and Laban," 156. Compare also to Speiser, *Genesis*, 238–39; Finkelstein, "Herding Contract."
18. Similarly: Sarna, *Genesis*, 203; Sherwood, "Jacob and Laban," 87.
19. See Westermann, *Genesis II*, 466–67; Davidson, *Genesis II*, 153; Wenham, *Genesis II*, 235; Vrolijk, *Jacob's Wealth*, 142.

"resolve[s] to wait and be patient. They had another seven years to wait, and what terrible suffering and what infinite happiness before them!"[20] At the end of these years, however, Jacob finds himself at the center of an unexpected family drama, and here, too, Dostoevsky's words ring true: "Seven years, only seven years! At the beginning of their happiness at some moments they were both ready to look on those seven years as though they were seven days. He did not know that the new life would not be given him for nothing, that he would have to pay dearly for it, that it would cost him great striving, great suffering."[21]

THE SILENCE OF THE LAMBS

The Sages stage a famous drama in which Rachel tells Leah about the secret signs she has agreed upon with Jacob, while Leah, on her part, answers to the name "Rachel" all night long. Yet in the actual text, neither sister says a word. It goes without saying that no modern author would omit Rachel's response to Jacob when he kisses her at the well, or leave out the dialogue between Jacob and Leah when he discovers, to his shock, that he has married his love's sister instead. But even by biblical standards, this account is omissive. The daughters' silence is underscored by their father's verbosity, as is clear through the chiastic structure of this scene:[22]

A. (20) So Jacob worked for Rachel seven years.

> **B.** But so great was his love for her that they seemed to him but a few days.
>
> > **C.** (21) Then Jacob said to Laban, "Give me my wife – my time is done, let me come to her." (22) So Laban brought together all the local people and made a feast. (23) In the evening he took his daughter Leah and brought her in to him, and he came to her.

---

20. Dostoevsky, *Crime and Punishment*, trans. Michael R. Katz, 604.
21. Ibid.
22. Vrolijk begins his structure a verse earlier than mine, which results in a chiastic structure (Vrolijk, *Jacob's Wealth*, 136–37).

D. (24) Laban gave her his servant Zilpah – to his daughter Leah as her maid.

E. (25) Then came morning – and it was Leah. Jacob said to Laban, "What is this you have done to me? I served you for Rachel, did I not? Why did you deceive me?" (26) Laban said, "This is not done in our place – to marry off the younger before the firstborn. (27) *Wait until the bridal week of this one is over and then we will give you the other one also*, in return for your serving me another seven years."

E'. (28) Jacob did so. He completed that one's bridal week; then he gave him his daughter Rachel as a wife.

D'. (29) Laban gave his servant Bilhah to his daughter Rachel as her maid.

C'. (30) And Jacob came also to Rachel;

B'. and he loved Rachel more than Leah.

A'. And he served him for another seven years.

The division of Jacob's marriage scene into two halves is inherent to the plot – there are, after all, two weddings to two wives, and Jacob works for seven years for each. The sisters' names are also parallel: "Rachel" means "ewe,"[23] while the accepted meaning of the name "Leah" is "cow" (apparently related to the Akkadian word *lītu*, which is some kind of wild cow).[24] One day, when Pharaoh dreams of seven fat cows and seven scrawny cows, Joseph will recall the seven years his father worked for each wife, and realize that these animals represent years.[25]

23. "*Raḥel*" means "ewe," a mature female sheep. If so, there is subtle irony in Jacob's request for "Rachel, your *younger* daughter."
24. Von Soden, *Akkadisches*, 557–58; Yee, "Leah."
25. In a different context, R. David Fohrman proposes similar ideas: https://www.alephbeta.org/course/lecture/vayigash-understand-3.

But the scene's division into two halves also represents Jacob's sense of frustration. Everything is repeating itself; once again, Jacob is forced to work for his wife for seven years; once again, he celebrates a bridal week with a new wife; once again, Laban gives his daughter a maidservant. This repetition is an expression of his manipulation at Laban's hands. We can only presume that the second seven years do not fly by like days, despite his love for Rachel.

The chiastic parallel underscores the differences between his marriage to Rachel and to Leah. Jacob works for seven years *before* his first marriage, but he works for Rachel *after* he marries her – thus, with two weddings in the center, the scene unfolds in a perfectly symmetrical chiastic structure.[26] This is especially salient through the bestowal of the sisters' maidservants, where the text preserves this symmetry:

(24)	Laban gave *her*	his servant Zilpah
	to *his daughter Leah*	as a maid.
(29)	Laban gave *his daughter Rachel*	his servant Bilhah
	to *her*	as a maid.

Note that the bestowal of the daughters' maids interrupts the narrative sequence at a crucial point:

(23) In the evening he took his daughter Leah and brought her in to him, and he came to her.

(24) Laban gave her his servant Zilpah – to his daughter Leah as her maid.

(25) Then came morning – and it was Leah…

The text relates that Laban presents Leah with a maid on her wedding night, after Jacob has already taken her to his tent. Couldn't this have waited until the morning, after the bride and groom have risen after their first night together? Why is her handmaid mentioned at such a crucial

26. The order changes thus: Work-Love-Intimacy-Handmaid//Handmaid-Intimacy-Love-Work. A common misconception is that Jacob works for another seven years *before* marrying Rachel, but this is not the case. Thus there is no need to see the second "seven years" as a symbolic number (as Ravid, *Really Happened,* 131–37) or to adopt other complicated solutions.

moment? Zilpah is presumably mentioned here in anticipation of the role she will play later on – she too will bear sons to Jacob in Leah's name.

A similar pattern emerges in the second half of the narrative, albeit with less disruptive timing: "Jacob did so. He completed that one's bridal week; then he gave him his daughter Rachel as a wife. Laban gave his servant Bilhah to his daughter Rachel as her maid. And Jacob came also to Rachel; and he loved Rachel more than Leah. And he served him for another seven years" (29:28–30). Here, too, Laban presents Rachel with her new maid after he gives Rachel to Jacob but before Jacob consummates the marriage, thus "appending" Bilhah to Rachel's wedding night, just as Zilpah is appended to Leah and Jacob's first night.

I have already mentioned that there is a subtle chiasm in these verses:

(24)	Laban gave *her*	his servant Zilpah
	to his daughter Leah	as a maid.
(29)	Laban gave his daughter Rachel	his servant Bilhah
	to *her*	as a maid.

Zilpah is given to "her," and only then does Leah's name appear, while Bilhah is given to "Rachel," who is mentioned in pronoun form ("her") after Bilhah's name. The latter sentence is far more logical, given that a name usually appears before a pronoun so that it is clear whom the pronoun refers to. The unusual precedence of pronoun to name gives the sense that Leah's identity is eclipsed; this is further reinforced when Leah again appears as a pronoun while Rachel's name *is* mentioned: "He completed *that one*'s bridal week; then he gave him his daughter Rachel as a wife" (29:28). Laban discreetly marries Leah off to Jacob before he gives him his beloved Rachel, but the less Leah is mentioned by name, the better.

Lest we be impressed by Laban's generosity at the bestowal of a maid upon each daughter, note that this was an accepted custom, and perhaps even obligation;[27] by contrast, when Rebecca goes with

27. Speiser claims that this is reflected in ancient Horite customs documented on tablets found in Nuzi (Speiser, *Genesis*, 227). Given that there may be a connection between the name Bilhah and the Horite name Bilhan (Gen. 36:27), this is especially interest-

Abraham's servant, her family sends her with "her nurse" (24:59) as well as "maids" (v. 60), in the plural. Rather than generosity, the fact that Laban gives each daughter a single maid hints to his miserliness, an impression that may be reinforced by the maids' names. The name "Zilpah" may be related to smallness – the modern Hebrew verb root Z-L-P refers to the act of sprinkling, or piping a thin line, which certainly implies restraint; whereas the name "Bilhah" implies someone stunned or startled;[28] Bilhah's name may also be linked to the root B-L-H which means "faded," "old," "worn out,"[29] hinting that altogether, Laban's "gifts" are not very generous at all.[30] Is Laban's tight fist calculated to ensure that the family will remain within him in Haran? We cannot know for sure.[31] In any case, the fact that each daughter is given a single maid reinforces the parallel between them.

The repetition of Jacob's experience is further reinforced by the repetition of the word "*gam*," also, to describe his marriage to Rachel: "he *also* came to Rachel/he *also* loved Rachel more than Leah" (29:30). There is no escaping the fact that Jacob, deceived by Laban, is forced to repeat the entire process; he must even work for "another" seven years.[32]

At the central axis of this scene lies the reason why Jacob is forced to repeat this process: Laban's excuse for his deceit and proposal that Jacob marry Rachel as well. Laban's language reveals much about his attitude toward his daughters: "Wait until the bridal week of *this one*

---

ing, although others denied the specific association with Horites and showed that this was prevalent throughout Mesopotamia (Frankena, "Remarks"; Van Seters, "Jacob's Marriages").

28. Yeivin, "Conquest," 74. Bauer also proposes deriving "Zilpah" from the Arabic word that means "to be small" (Bauer, "Hebräischen Eigennamen," 78).
29. The root B-L-H does appear twice in the Bible in a positive sense of "pleasure," similar to the modern Hebrew word *billui*, leisure: see Is. 65:22; Job 21:13; see Gamberoni, "B-L-H," 131.
30. When Jacob's family goes down to Egypt (Gen. 46), the wives have double the descendants as the handmaids: Leah has 32; Zilpah 16; Rachel has 14; Bilhah 7.
31. See also Sherwood, "Jacob and Laban," 100; Vrolijk, *Jacob's Wealth*, 150.
32. The repetition of "*gam*" emphasizes Jacob's love for Rachel, but implies that Leah, too, is loved; thus the description that Leah is "hated" is relative to Jacob's love for Rachel, not that she is actually hated.

is over and then we will give you the *other one* also."[33] Laban does not mention his daughters by name; this is especially degrading in the context of a father who is giving his daughters away in marriage, when one might expect to find an attitude of special love and sensitivity before they are given to another man. He has little interest in his daughters' welfare, and sees them only in terms of the potential benefit they will bring him: seven years of work for each. One day soon, the daughters themselves will express this to their husband, offended and hurt: "He treats us like strangers, since he has sold us" (31:15). It is no wonder that in the next verse, focalized through Jacob, Rachel's name returns: "He completed that one's bridal week; then he gave him his daughter Rachel as a wife."[34] Beloved to her husband, Rachel is rescued from her father's disinterest and objectification, but Leah, unloved by father and husband, remains nameless.

If this is its central axis, what is the significance of this structure? As mentioned, it indeed emphasizes the symmetrical repetition and the fact that Jacob must go through the same process twice, but I believe it also serves to illuminate which characters are shaping the narrative – and which are not. Rachel and Leah do not speak at all in this scene; there is not a single word about Rachel's reaction to the mysterious kiss from a stranger at the well, not a single word about Rachel during the seven years Jacob works for her, and not a single word about Rachel's response to her father's deceit. Leah, too, is utterly silent, which allows for various readings about her involvement in this scheme (as I will discuss below). The central axis of this double marriage scene is not a dialogue between bride and groom, but between Laban and Jacob, while throughout the scene, Rachel and Leah are only mentioned as objects, never as subjects. This is a piercing portrait of a father who plays with his daughters like pawns while they remain silent. This is especially salient when Jacob discovers his bride's identity: "Then came morning – and it was Leah!

33. Perhaps the repetition of the pronoun "*zot*" even recalls Amnon's objectification of Tamar after he has violated her: "Send *this* (*zot*) away from me now, outside, and lock the door behind her" (II Sam. 13:17).
34. Vrolijk comments that every time Laban "gives" something to Jacob, he is disappointed (*Jacob's Wealth*, 143).

Jacob said to…" (v. 25). Surely Jacob's first response will be to his new wife who lies beside him in the morning light! Yet the reader is suddenly transported from the newlyweds' tent to that of Jacob's devious father-in-law: "Jacob said *to Laban* (!): 'What is this you have done to me? I served you for Rachel, did I not? Why did you deceive me?'"[35] Jacob addresses not Leah but Laban, whose daughters remain as silent as props. The only driving force of this scene is the relationship between Jacob and Laban.

This utter passivity leads to a further question: How complicit are Laban's daughters in his scheme?

Leah and Rachel's Involvement in the Act of Deceit

There is no question that Laban deliberately deceives Jacob. As some exegetes point out, his response to Jacob's request for Rachel's hand in marriage is already strangely suggestive: "Better that I give her to you than to some other man. Stay on with me" (29:19). He agrees that Jacob is a worthy suitor for his daughter, but – as Abarbanel notes – he does not explicitly say that he wants him as a husband for both his daughters, or that Jacob will have to marry the eldest first.[36] In this scene, Laban is portrayed as a manipulative swindler who cheats his nephew into working for him for another seven years.

But did Laban have accomplices to this scheme? Determining his daughters' level of compliance is critical to understanding the family dynamics – within Laban's nuclear family, but more importantly, within the family Jacob is about to build. The Sages perceive Rachel and Leah as fully complicit partners without whose consent Laban would not have been able to execute his plan. The Midrash describes how Rachel agrees upon secret signs with Jacob that will allow him to identify her as the bride, but then shares these signs with Leah; while Leah, on her

---

35. Nakarai proposes that the word "*lamma*" appears in the Bible when the question refers to the purpose of an action, whereas "*maddua*" refers to primary reason and motive (Nakarai, "LMH and MDU").

36. See Abarbanel, and similarly Von Rad, *Genesis*, 286; Sherwood, "Jacob and Laban," 95; Fokkelman, *Genesis*, 127; Hamilton, *Genesis II*, 259.

part, answers to the name "Rachel" all night long until Jacob discovers her true identity in the morning light.

Ramban explains that it is Leah's deceit that brings Jacob to hate her:

> Now Leah tricked her sister, and Jacob as well. For if we claim that she was complying out of respect to her father who grabbed her and brought her into him and she must not defy him, then she should have said or hinted that she was Leah. Rather, she disguised herself all night and therefore, he did not recognize her until he saw her in the morning. And therefore, Jacob hated her. (Ramban on 29:21).

At the other extreme, some argue that "at face value, Leah has no idea that there is any kind of deceit here, and she plays no part of it, and indeed, Jacob makes no claims against her" (R. David Zvi Hoffmann on 29:21).

Whether the sisters take part in this scheme is directly related to another question: How can it be that Jacob fails to recognize his bride? How can it be that he only realizes that "it was Leah" the next morning? From a realistic perspective, this is unconvincing, but thus the story goes. Similarly, the reader is forced to suspend his or her disbelief when Isaac is convinced that he is blessing Esau (although in this scene, at least, the narrative describes how Jacob takes measures to fool his father). In both scenes, the plot is unrealistic but still marches along to the immutable premise that Isaac is deceived by Jacob's costume and Jacob is deceived by Laban. Nonetheless, given that this question has implications for the sisters' level of involvement in their father's scheme, it is important to raise it.

There are several main approaches to how Jacob is deceived:

1. Jacob Was Drunk

Some pin utmost importance on the unassuming description of Laban's wedding feast: "Laban brought together all the local people and made a feast" (29:22). Note that Laban only brings Leah later on: "In the evening he took his daughter Leah and brought her in to him, and he came to her" (29:23) – the men have been drinking for a while before evening falls.[37] Laban presents Jacob with his bride, and the unsuspecting groom, his head swimming with wine, his senses dulled by drink and the ribald shouts of drunken revelers, leads her to his tent in the growing dim.[38]

> Laban was a cheat; for this is he called "Laban the Cheat," and he fully intended to get Jacob drunk in order to deceive him, so he would not distinguish between Rachel and Leah. Note that he does not make a feast for Rachel. (*Daat Zekenim* of Tosafot on 29:22).[39]

Indeed, there is no mention of a feast before Jacob weds Rachel a week later, and this supports the notion that the feast enables Laban's deceit. This is further reinforced through a comparison with Lot's daughters seducing their father in the cave. There, too, a man is manipulated into sleeping with two sisters. The word pair "*bekhira*" (elder) and "*tze'ira*" (younger) only appears in these two narratives, and in both cases, the elder sister lies with the man first: "The next day, the elder (*bekhira*) said to the younger (*tze'ira*), 'Last night I slept with my father. Let us get him to drink wine again tonight, then you go in and sleep with him'" (Gen. 19:34)/"This is not done in our country – to marry off the younger (*tze'ira*) before the elder (*bekhira*)" (29:26).

If reading Laban's ploy against Lot's daughters' ploy is justified, then this hints that wine is indeed the key to misleading the unsuspecting mate.[40]

---

37. Roland De Vaux's statement that marriage was followed by a feast might not be wholly accurate: in our story, the feast precedes the marriage (De Vaux, *Daily Life*, vol. 1, 42).
38. For example: Ravid, *Really Happened,* 126.
39. Thus R. Isaac Kara (uncle of R. Joseph Kara) adds that it is no coincidence that there is no description of any food at this "feast": "Unlike Abraham, who served food, and Lot… he served only wine to get him drunk, so that he would not know whether she was Rachel or Leah" (*Toledot Yitzḥak* on 29:22).
40. In the story of Lot's daughters the elder daughter is subtly criticized more than the younger daughter (see Grossman, "Lot's Daughters"); here, too, and definitely from Jacob's perspective, the younger daughter is favored over the elder.

2. Nightfall and Local Customs

Those who imagine Laban's feast as a modern wedding feast wonder how Jacob could possibly fail to realize that the bride sitting opposite him was Leah.[41] However, it is far more likely that this "feast" was a drinking fest for men only, before the bride was presented to the groom. There is no reason to assume that there was any kind of formal public ceremony involving the bride.[42] As mentioned, Laban only brings Leah to Jacob after the feast: "In the evening he took his daughter Leah and brought her in to him, and he came to her," and it seems that the combination of paternal assent and consummation effectively constitute marriage. There is repeated emphasis on the fact that Jacob actually lies with Leah: beginning with Jacob's request: "Give me my wife – my time is done, *let me come to her*" (29:21),[43] and continuing with the wedding night: "In the evening he took his daughter Leah and brought her in to him, *and he came to her*" (v. 23). This is a crucial detail because once the marriage has been consummated, there is no going back (presumably without official divorce); Jacob cannot simply reject Leah and marry Rachel instead, because she has already become his wife (compare Ex. 22:16; Deut. 22:28–29).

Laban's feast is a drinking fest for the local men, and Jacob is not granted a glimpse of the bride until the evening. If we combine this with the possibility that local customs dictated certain modesty, such as a veil that was only removed in the bridal chamber,[44] then it is feasible that Leah's identity was obscured by a veil and then the dark of night until the next morning.

---

41. On the contrary, the Jewish custom seems to be derived from the Haran custom: "To teach that it has always been a custom, and still is – for the groom or bride or parents to make a joyful feast to celebrate marriage. And the Sages based the seven days of joy after marriage on the verse 'Wait until the bridal week is over'" (Radak on 29:22).
42. De Vaux, *Daily Life*, 41. He notes that in Mesopotamia, it was acceptable to sign a contract (ibid., 42), presumably between the groom and the bride's parents. This is evident from the law of slander, where the two parties are the groom and the bride's parents (Deut. 22:13–19).
43. Zakovitch correctly notes that Jacob says, "Bring me my wife" without saying her name, thus leaving room for Laban's deceit (Zakovitch, *Jacob*, 67).
44. De Vaux, *Daily Life*, vol. 1, 42.

These first two possibilities may of course be combined, as Wenham writes: "The lateness of the hour, the veiling of the bride, and maybe a little too much drink allowed Laban to substitute the unloved Leah for the promised Rachel."[45]

3. A Long Period of Separation

R. Yaakov Medan claims that Jacob fails to recognize Leah because Jacob has not seen Rachel throughout the seven years he works for her: "Jacob meets Rachel when she is a young girl. During the years he works for her, Laban prevents any meetings between them, and Rachel thus matured and changed without Jacob seeing her. It could well be that Rachel and Leah looked similar, and on their wedding night, in the darkness, Jacob was unable to tell them apart."[46]

These first three explanations imply that Leah (and possibly Rachel as well) was complicit to the scheme; otherwise, she could have easily exposed her true identity. Yet the uneasiness lingers; even if wine, darkness, or unfamiliarity all played a part, didn't Jacob speak to his bride? How could Jacob fail to recognize his beloved during the most intimate act of all? There is another possible explanation, which is the least convincing from a semantic point of view – but from the perspective of plot, it has a clear advantage.

4. Jacob *Does* Realize That the Bride Is Leah

Jacob's failure to identify his wife until the light of day is so strange and so problematic that it forces us to read the text more closely – could it possibly be understood differently? Not without hesitation, I wish to propose that Jacob *does* realize that his bride is Leah during their wedding night, but rather than shame her and send her away, he only goes to complain to his father-in-law the next morning. From a chronological perspective, the verse should be read: "It was Leah! Then came morning, and Jacob said to Laban..." While the verse follows a different order, it could be that the chronological description, "Then came morning," introduces the main part of the verse – Jacob's accusation against Laban,

45. Wenham, *Genesis II*, 236.
46. Medan, *Close to You*, 238–39.

while his realization that his bride is Leah actually takes place before the morning.

The term "*vehineh*" usually shifts focus to the next stage, but there are exceptions in which it functions in the sense of "because" or "so far." For example, this is true of Moses' command to Pharaoh: "The Lord, God of the Hebrews, has sent me to tell you: Send My people forth, so that they may serve Me in the wilderness. *So far* (*vehineh*), you have not listened. This is what the Lord says…" (Ex. 7:16–17). Adele Berlin demonstrates a similar phenomenon in the story of Yael and Sisera: "Meanwhile (*vehineh*) Barak was chasing Sisera, and Yael went out to meet him. 'Come,' she said to him, 'I will show you the man you seek.' He came to her, and there was (*vehineh*) Sisera, sprawled out dead, with the tent peg through his temple" (Judges 4:22). The second *vehineh* describes what Barak sees, but the first functions differently: it brings the reader back to what has been happening while Yael is busy with Sisera in her tent.[47] The second *vehineh* is a classic "behold!"; the first is more accurately translated as "meanwhile."[48]

From a semantic and grammatical perspective, it is more convenient to read the "*vehineh*" in our verse as "suddenly, in the morning!" – but from a perspective of plot, and given that the phrase is not preceded by "and he saw,"[49] there is a clear advantage to the reading that Jacob already realizes his wife's identity at night, whereas in the morning he deals with the drama of facing Laban.

Another advantage of this reading is related to Jacob's silence against Leah. I have already mentioned that the word order suggests that he is about to speak to her ("Then came morning – and it was Leah. And he said to…"), but no dialogue is related between them. If

---

47. Berlin, *Poetics*, 63. She adds that alongside this role, the expression "*vehineh*" also serves to shift the narrative perspective to Yael's, who only sees that Barak is pursuing Sisera at that point.
48. Zebul's use of the word "*vehineh*" to Abimelech (Judges 9:32–33) can be understood in the same sense.
49. Adele Berlin is correct that even without the verb "*vayar*," the word "*vehineh*" hints to a focalization through the character in question and a new stage in the narrative (Berlin, *Poetics*, 62 – she proves this from I Sam. 19:16). But the lack of "*vayar*" in this verse allows for the alternative reading.

Jacob's confrontation only takes place the next morning, then it is clear why he addresses Laban, not Leah – in his sensitivity, Jacob does not express his shock and disappointment to Leah herself, but only to her cheating father.

This reading has several implications for understanding the twisted tale before us. First and foremost, Laban emerges as the only villain; Leah and Rachel are not his accomplices – they assume, perhaps, that their father made such an agreement with Jacob; perhaps the custom of marrying off the elder first is obvious to them, and we will yet see that Leah accuses Rachel of stealing "her" husband from her (30:15). This would be an odd accusation indeed if the two are part of Laban's deception – it would be more accurate to state that Leah is the one who takes Jacob away from Rachel. But if Laban in fact manipulates the three of them, then from Leah's perspective, she enjoys a single week of marriage before Rachel supplants her in Jacob's affections.

This also explains the lack of dialogue between Jacob and his wives: if they are not part of Laban's scheme, then he cannot accuse them; on the contrary, their father has cheated them as well.

We leave this scene with mixed feelings. On the one hand, Jacob marries both of Laban's daughters, and this is why he came to Haran in the first place. The lonely refugee becomes part of the family. On the other hand, Laban reveals his true colors. When she sends her son to her brother, Rebecca – one presumes – cannot imagine that Laban will betray her son in the most intimate of ways. He has left his father far behind, and the new father figure, it emerges, cares only for himself. It is at this point that Jacob becomes a father himself.

THE BIRTH OF JACOB'S SONS

The birth of Jacob's children could have been an uplifting climax within the Jacob cycle and in Genesis itself – twelve sons who will one day grow into the twelve tribes of Israel. Yet these verses are fraught with familial tension, rivalry, and pain. Four separate times, after Reuben, Levi, and Zebulun's birth, and after her son brings her mandrakes, Leah pronounces the phrase, "my husband," with poignant hope: "Now my husband will love me… now my husband will walk with me…" Rachel, by contrast, though deeply loved by her husband, never stops wishing for a child: "God has vindicated me. He has listened to my voice and given me a son" (30:6), and even when she finally gives birth to Joseph, pronounces, "May the Lord grant me another son also" (30:24). Thus both sisters are perpetually pining for what they do not have: Leah yearns for her husband to love her and be at her side, while Rachel longs for children to hold and raise.

This constant yearning is not merely directed to God and their husband; sadly, it also turns the two sisters against each other. The narrative explicitly conveys that Rachel is envious of her sister: "Aware that she had borne Jacob no children, Rachel became envious of her sister" (30:1). The Midrash questions this envy: "How could it be that Rachel is envious of Leah?" and answers, as Rashi cites: that Rachel is envious of her sister's good deeds, through which Leah merits to bear children. More simply, however, Rachel is desperate for children, and she envies how easily Leah bears one child after another. Bitter evidence of her resentment can be heard in her explanation for the name Naphtali: "Rachel said, 'I have struggled hard (*niftalti*) with my sister and I have won.' So she named him Naphtali (*Naftali*)" (30:8). More than joy, it seems, the birth of her maid's son brings her a sense of triumph. Rachel defines her rivalry with her sister as no less than "*naftulei Elohim*" – "an immense, mighty struggle."[50]

Jacob's children are born in four sets within the narrative, each set introduced by the verb root "saw," or, in one instance, "remembered," which marks the beginning of a new turn of events.[51] At first, it is God who sees Leah's plight: "When the Lord *saw* that Leah was unloved, He opened her womb, but Rachel was barren" (29:31). This is followed by

50. On "*Elohim*" in the sense of "immense" compare, for example, Jonah 3:2; I Chr. 12:23; and perhaps Gen. 1:2, 6:2–4 (on the last example, see Grossman, "Sons of God"). Onkelos translates "*Naftulei*" in the sense of prayer, from the root P-L-L, presumably based on the verb's proximity to the word "*Elohim*" (see further in Grossfeld, *Onkelos*, 109, n. 4), or perhaps on a more fundamental principle: "When the Bible describes the family dynamics harshly, the *Targum* softens this harshness out of respect for the forefathers. Sometimes this manifests through subtle sweetening of the language, but sometimes there is an actual change, as in our verse" (Posen, *Parshagan*, 560).

51. Compare to Mathews, *Genesis II*, 482.

the birth of Leah's first four sons. Rachel is the second one who "sees": "When Rachel *saw* that she had borne Jacob no children, Rachel became envious of her sister" (30:1). This marks the beginning of the second stage: the birth of Rachel's maid's two sons. This unit begins with human perception, not divine perception, and accordingly, these two births are the result of human initiation (Rachel gives her maid to Jacob), as opposed to God opening Leah's womb.

Rachel's perception is followed by a similar observation: "Leah *saw* that she was no longer having children, so she took her maid Zilpah and gave her to Jacob as a wife" (30:9). Leah, too, "sees" the situation and takes similar action, which results in the birth of two more sons, born to Zilpah.

After this, there is no more "seeing," but there are two instances of "listening," which both introduce another round of births. First God "listens" to Leah (30:17), who then gives birth to three more children. Finally, God "remembered Rachel and listened to her," and opens up her womb (30:22). Thus, in sequence: God sees, Rachel sees, Leah sees, and finally, God remembers Rachel. In order to understand the development of this birth sequence, we must consider the list in its entirety.

Jacob's children are born one after another in an almost continuous list, but two incidents interrupt this list, and both of them affect the family structure, given that the birth mother changes after each incident.

"I Had Maidservants, and Others Were Born in My House"

The first story that interrupts the list of births opens with Rachel's frustration, which moves her to give her maidservant to Jacob as a surrogate of sorts:

> When Rachel saw that she had borne Jacob no children, she became envious of her sister. To Jacob she said, "Give me children! If not, let me die!" Jacob grew angry with Rachel, and said, "Am I in place of God, who has kept you from having children?" "Here is Bilha my handmaid," she said. "Come to her. Let her give birth on my knees so that I too can build a family through her." (30:1–3)

This episode is necessary to explain why Bilhah, and then Zilpah, are given to Jacob as wives. Through this act, four sons are born to Jacob in clear symmetry: two to Bilhah, Rachel's maid, and two to Zilpah, Leah's maid. Note that surprisingly, the legal status of the two maids' marriage to Jacob seems no different from that of Rachel and Leah – they, too, become Jacob's "wives": "So she gave him her maid Bilhah as a wife"/"She took her maid Zilpah and gave her to Jacob as a wife" (30:4, 9); while similarly, "Laban gave him his daughter Rachel as a wife" (29:28). Aside from the word maid/daughter, the verses are otherwise identical. This definition is presumably important for the sons' status: these four sons will become fully fledged tribes of Israel, so their mothers are described as proper wives of Jacob.

"The Mandrakes Impart Their Scent"

The second incident during these years of birth is the story of the mandrakes, and understanding this incident and its narrative objective poses a far greater challenge.

Initially, the reader might feel uncomfortable with Leah's actions in the story: her barren sister begs her for "some of [her] son's mandrakes" – just some of them – but she refuses and accuses her poor sister of stealing her husband away from her: "Is it not enough that you have taken away my husband? Now you want to take my son's mandrakes too!" (30:15). Rachel is then forced to "buy" some of the mandrakes. The Sages, however, read this completely differently, and surprisingly enough, their bitter criticism is directed against Rachel:

> R. Eliezer said: This one lost and this one lost; this one won and this one won. Leah lost the mandrakes and won (two) tribes and the birthright; Rachel won the mandrakes but lost tribes and the birthright.
>
> R. Shmuel son of Naḥman said: Leah lost the mandrakes but was rewarded with tribes and burial [with her husband], Rachel won the mandrakes but lost tribes and burial [with her husband]. (Genesis Rabba 72:3)[52]

52. There are different versions of this midrash; some explain that Leah gained tribes but lost the birthright to her sister Rachel. See the discussion in the footnotes of

Both opinions in this midrash present a cynical view of the sisters' negotiations: each one pays a certain price for certain gain. Leah indeed loses the mandrakes when she gives them to Rachel, but she gains the birth of two tribes and either the birthright or burial with her husband; Rachel, on the other hand, acquires the mandrakes, but pays a heavy price: precisely what Leah gains. This ostensibly "equal" presentation of each sister's loss and gain exposes the irony of this midrash and casts Rachel as impulsive and foolish. Does the text itself encourage such a harsh reading of Rachel? Is the question of birthright – which is indeed a central theme in the Jacob cycle – actually raised in this episode? And is the midrashic claim that Rachel "lost" two tribes justified?

It sometimes happens that an initially absurd-sounding midrash touches upon a deep vein of truth within the narrative; though they may sound harsh or far-fetched, the vivid images of the midrash in fact illuminate a certain reading in the text.

I will turn to the narrative itself, and explore whether its design is consistent with the objective hinted through this midrash. In order to understand the significance of this brief episode and its implications for Jacob's family, I first wish to present three textual conundrums within the list of births.

The first anomaly is related to the language of these descriptions of birth: each birth is described in one of two styles. The first is a simple, straightforward style which is used in (almost all of) the matriarchs' births, and the second is used for the handmaids' births:

Leah
Reuben: Leah became *pregnant and bore* a son.
Simeon: She became *pregnant again and bore* a son.
Levi: She became *pregnant again and bore* a son.
Judah: She became *pregnant again and bore* a son.

Bilhah (Rachel's handmaid)
Dan: She became pregnant and bore *Jacob* a son.

Genesis Rabba, Theodor Albeck edition, 838–839.

Naphtali: Bilhah, Rachel's maid, became pregnant again and bore *Jacob* a second son.

Zilpah (Leah's handmaid)
Gad: And Leah's maid Zilpah bore *Jacob* a son.
Asher: Then Zilpah, Leah's maid, bore *Jacob* a second son.

Leah
Issachar: And she became pregnant and bore *Jacob* a fifth son.
Zebulun: Leah became pregnant again and bore *Jacob* a sixth son.

Rachel
Yosef: She became *pregnant and bore* a son. She said, "God has taken away my shame..."

Leaving the births of Issachar and Zebulun aside for the moment, this pattern is coherent and logical. The matriarchs Leah and Rachel give birth without any need of further explanation, while the text emphasizes, in an accepted alternative biblical formula, that the handmaids bear sons "for Jacob." The father's identity is clear, but it is less clear who is considered the baby's mother.

The exception to this rule is the language used to describe the births of Issachar and Zebulun. Why are their births described in the formula used for the handmaids' births?

The second anomaly is related to God's intervention throughout these years: divine intervention is mentioned three times in this chapter. The first two are clear, but the third is surprising. The first instance marks the beginning of the birth years, starting with Leah's fertility as divine compensation for Jacob's lack of love: "When the Lord saw that Leah was unloved, He opened her womb" (29:31).

The third instance is similarly clear: "Then God remembered Rachel and listened to her and enabled her to conceive" (30:22). Rachel's barrenness can only be healed by God. There is a clear connection between the fertility God bestows upon Leah and the long-awaited birth of Joseph: in both cases, God "opened her womb." At the same time, there is a special sense of festivity when Rachel finally conceives: God does not merely "see" or "listen" to her; He also "remembers" her.

But God's second intervention is surprising. After Leah buys the privilege of a night with Jacob from her sister, "God listened to Leah," and she conceives. After four births, why is this necessary? The verse does not state that God "opened her womb" – her womb is already open. Why is this so?

The third anomaly, which is particularly disconcerting when reading the full story in sequence, is that after the birth of Judah, her fourth son, Leah "ceased having children" (29:35). This is apparently clear to the characters as well, given that Leah then gives Zilpah to Jacob in order to produce more "sons" through her, but it is difficult to justify this when the chapter is read in full. Soon after, Leah gives birth to three more children: Issachar, Zebulun, and Dinah. What, then, is the meaning of "she ceased having children"? Theoretically, this phrase can be read as temporary infertility: Radak, for example, writes, "She ceased having children at that time, and this was from God, in order that the handmaids may also have children with Jacob" (on 29:35); Ḥizkuni explains that the word "ceased" (*vataamod*) implies a temporary rather than permanent phase.[53]

Considered within the narrative timeline, however, this reading is problematic. The narrative chronology runs thus:

- Jacob works for seven years for Rachel.
- Jacob marries Leah, and then marries Rachel a week later.
- He then works for Laban for another seven years, during which all his sons are born.
- After Joseph is born, Jacob tells Laban he wishes to return home, but he then acquiesces to Laban's request that he stay longer, and over the next six years, he makes his fortune.

53. There is room to consider whether "*laamod*" is indeed synonymous with "stop." See, for example, Radak's *Sefer HaShorashim* ("*amad*"). Although Leah does go on to have more children, he simply writes that she "*stopped* having children."

Given that Jacob only explicitly requests to return to Canaan after Joseph is born, there are no children born to him during his last six years in Haran, and given that Joseph is the youngest son (until the birth of Benjamin in Canaan), it seems that Jacob's children are all born during the seven years he works for Rachel. That is, in seven years, Leah bears seven children – six sons and a daughter. If so, then when, exactly, does Leah "cease to have children" after her fourth son? R. Bekhor Shor, who favors this direction, explains that Dinah and Zebulun are twins:

> "She ceased to have children" – for in the first year, Leah bore Reuben; in the second – Simeon; in the third – Levi; in the fourth – Judah; in the fifth year, she "ceased to have children," and gave her maid to Jacob. In the sixth year – Issachar; in the seventh, Zebulun and Dinah at the same time – it does not say that she "conceived" Dinah. Zebulun, Dinah, and Joseph were born at the same time, in the seventh year. (R. Bekhor Shor on 29:35)

The assumption that the lack of the phrase "she conceived" implies that Zebulun and Dinah are twins is unconvincing, given that the description of Dinah's birth is unique within this chapter in several respects: she is the only girl; there is no explanation given for Dinah's name; and she does not become a tribe in Israel, which may explain any discrepancies in itself.

Ibn Ezra proposes a completely different reading: he interprets the description "she ceased having children" as a decision Leah makes: "'This time, I will thank the Lord' implies that after four sons, she thanks the Lord, and she does not wish for any more. That is, I will thank the Lord, who gave me all these, and it is enough for me. For this reason, she ceased to have children" (Ibn Ezra on 29:35). This reading has several implications for understanding the dynamics within Jacob's nuclear family. It could also be that the decision is not Leah's but Jacob's – perhaps after having four sons with the wife he does not love, he moves into Rachel's tent permanently, and does not visit Leah any more.[54] I will yet return to this idea, but it is worth noting already now that when

54. As proposed also by Mathews, *Genesis II*, 481.

Leah gives Zilpah to Jacob, the impression is that she wants more children but cannot conceive ("Leah saw that she was no longer having children" – 30:9), and to this end Jacob agrees to marry Zilpah. Thus a straightforward reading of the text implies that Leah does not stop having children out of choice, so she follows Rachel's lead and gives her maid to Jacob as well.

The Mandrakes as a Turning Point

I believe that the three aforementioned anomalies in the text are essentially one and the same. Leah indeed needs divine intervention in order to bear her last three children, because she already "ceased to have children." Originally, it seems, Leah was supposed to bear just four children, but Issachar, Zebulun, and Dinah were born to her as the result of special providence, contrary to the original divine plan.

To clarify: as the Sages mention in several places, the fact that Jacob's sons total a neat dozen is no accident. Jacob's sons will ultimately be twelve in number; the only question is how to reach it (compare Gen. 17:20; 25:16; 35:22; 49:28).[55] Moreover, the number of sons born to each wife is also predetermined, with a 2:1 ratio between the matriarchs' sons and the maids' sons. This is evident in this birth narrative (eight sons are born to Leah and Rachel, and four to Bilhah and Zilpah), but even more so in the description of the number of Jacob's descendants who go down to Egypt (Gen. 46). The figures provided in the latter description maintain this ratio: those descended from Leah number thirty-two;[56] from Zilpah sixteen; Rachel fourteen; and Bilhah seven. It is no coincidence that Leah's descendants are twice the number of Zilpah's, nor that Bilhah has half the number of descendants as Rachel – the same ratio as that of the birth narrative.

It is interesting to note that Nahor's family also follows this pattern. Nahor, too, has twelve sons: eight born to his wife, and four to his

55. See the discussion of Esau's genealogy, below. There, too, the text manipulates the numbers to reach a total of twelve descendants.

56. Famously, although Leah has thirty-two descendants, the text summarizes: "These were the sons whom Leah bore to Jacob in Padan Aram, besides his daughter Dinah. In all, male and female, they numbered thirty-three" (46:15), and various explanations are provided for this disparity.

concubine (Gen. 22:20–24), and as Rashi comments: "His concubine Reumah also had children: her family was equal [in number] to the families[57] of Abraham: just as in Abraham's family, twelve tribes descended from Jacob – eight from the wives and four from the maidservants – here, too, eight descended from the wives, and four from the concubines."[58]

As it unfolds, the list of births gives the impression that the division of sons will be symmetrical. Leah gives birth to four sons, and "ceased to have children." Bilhah, Rachel's maid, has two sons; Zilpah, Leah's maid, has two sons; now, presumably, Rachel will give birth to the remaining four. Indeed, God sees that Leah is unloved, and for this reason He opens up her womb first: to create closeness between Leah and Jacob; so that Jacob will spend time with Leah and their children in her tent. Yet ultimately, a husband's love is not an adequate substitute for children, and it does not make sense that Rachel will have just two sons – like the handmaids – while Leah has six, just to balance out the situation. When the text states "She ceased having children," this is its intention: Leah has had her four sons, and she is not meant to have any more. Judah's name reflects this: as opposed to the names of her first three children, which all express some kind of wish, Judah's name reflects gratitude and closure: "This time I will praise the Lord" (29:35).[59] Similarly, when Abraham makes his final statement in a dialogue with God, he uses the phrase "*hapaam*": "Please, may the Lord not be angry, but let me speak just one more time (*akh hapaam*)" (Gen. 18:32).[60] Leah has had her four sons, and now the reader anticipates the birth of Rachel's four sons.

---

57. The *Mikra'ot Gedolot HaKeter* version has "*lemishpaḥat*" (family) (*Genesis*, vol. 1, 194), but the Leipzig manuscript has "*lemishpeḥot* (families)."
58. See also Genesis Rabba 57:3, and the discussion in Grossman, *Abraham*, 334–35.
59. Leah also uses the phrase "This time" after Levi's birth (29:34), for this marks closure of the process of closeness between her and her husband. At the birth of her next son, for the first time, instead of naming him based on her relationship with her husband, Leah thanks God.
60. Leah also uses the phrase "This time" at the birth of her sixth son (30:20). Perhaps the first man's statement of his newly created wife, "This time, at last (*zot hapaam*), is bones of my bones and flesh of my flesh" (Gen. 2:23), also forms a contrast between "this time" and the previous attempts (see Grossman, *Creation*, 113–16). For a different reading, see Shaviv, "*zot hapaam*".

But this is not to be. For some reason, Rachel's womb remains closed, and for some reason, Leah goes on to have more children. This is so unexpected that there is need for special divine intervention: "God listened to Leah, and she became pregnant and bore Jacob a fifth son" (30:17). There is no such statement before the births of her second, third, or fourth son; once God opens her womb, it remains open. But after "she ceased having children," God must intervene in order to bring about the births of two more sons and a daughter.

Why does Leah's womb open anew? Why is Leah granted six out of twelve tribes while Rachel gives birth to just two, like Bilhah and Zilpah? The only hint to this imbalance is found in the story of the mandrakes. After the handmaid's four sons are born, the reader anticipates the birth of Rachel's sons, but the incident of the mandrakes follows instead. In the words of R. Levi in Genesis Rabba: "Come and see how pleasing this transaction of mandrakes was to Him who spoke and the world came to be, for through the mandrakes came two of the greatest tribes of Israel: Issachar and Zebulun. Issachar sat and studied the Torah, while Zebulun would travel the seas and provide food for Issachar, and thus the Torah grew in Israel" (Genesis Rabba 72:5). Let us now turn to the story of the mandrakes and explore its meaning.

> During the wheat harvest, Reuben went for a walk and found mandrakes in the field. He brought them to his mother Leah.
> Rachel said to Leah, "Please give me some of *your son's* mandrakes."
> She replied, "Is it not enough that you have taken away my husband?
> Now you want to take *my son's* mandrakes too!"
> "Very well," said Rachel. "Let him sleep with you tonight in exchange for *your son's* mandrakes."
> When Jacob came back from the field that evening, Leah went out to meet him and said,
> "You are to come to me, for I have hired you with *my son's* mandrakes." (30:14–16)

The mandrake incident opens with a description of Reuben's action: "During the wheat harvest, Reuben went for a walk and found mandrakes in the field" (v. 14). The phrase "Reuben went" recalls another episode in Genesis: "Reuben went and lay with Bilhah, his father's concubine" (35:22).[61] The connection between these two episodes is striking: in both, Reuben has a significant effect on his father's relationship with his wives. In the mandrake incident, he is but a secondary character, but there is significance in the fact that the episode opens with him, that Leah receives her mandrakes from her son, and we will yet see that there is a more profound connection between these two actions of Reuben.

What of the seemingly insignificant detail that this took place "during the wheat harvest"? This is one of the Talmud's examples of the "superfluous" details in the Torah that Menashe son of Hezekiah would mock (Sanhedrin 99b), and its purpose is indeed obscure. The talmudic Sages attempt to justify its inclusion by explaining that this detail illuminates Reuben's character: "Rava, son of R. Yitzḥak, says that Rav says: From here it can be seen that the righteous do not extend their hands to robbery" (see also Rashi on this verse). According to this reading, the context generates surprise: given that it was the time of the wheat harvest, the reader might expect Reuben to present his mother with a sack of wheat, but rather, to his credit, he brings her a bunch of mandrakes, an ownerless plant that grows wild.

This chronological detail indeed draws a connection between "wheat" and "mandrakes." The fact that Reuben goes out during the wheat harvest, yet returns with mandrakes, hints at the similarity between the two plants. Wheat – bread – is the most basic, the most essential, of foods, while the characters relate to these mandrakes as if they, too, are vital to their existence. This is related to the properties of this plant, which are associated with love and fertility. One craves love and the other craves children, and both sisters covet the plants fiercely, as desperately as a starving person craves wheat.

---

61. This is immediately followed by "And Israel heard," similarly to the end of the mandrakes scene: "And God heard Leah."

As soon as Reuben finds the mandrakes, "he brought them to his mother Leah" (v. 14). Note that the narrator does not use the word "give," which implies a transferal of ownership, but rather the verb "brought": Reuben does not perceive himself as the mandrakes' owner. He is still a little boy who brings all the treasures he finds home to show his mother.[62] Leah's closeness with her young firstborn is also shown through the repetitive pronouns that emphasize their relationship: "his mother... my son... your son... my son." This emphasis hints to Reuben's motives in the narrative.

Though Reuben's part in the scene may seem trivial, the fact that he is mentioned at all (when it would suffice to state that Leah had some mandrakes) suggests that his role is more crucial than it seems. The fact that he brings the mandrakes straight to his mother reflects his emotional state. He is the eldest of Leah's sons, the most keenly aware of his father's absence from his mother's tent night after night, the most painfully aware of his mother's loneliness. Perhaps Leah confides in her son, telling him of her tense relationship with her sister, of her pain, of Jacob's attitude toward her. Perhaps Reuben's gift of mandrakes expresses a deep desire to comfort his mother, to bring her a little joy, to remind her that he is more precious to her than the love of ten husbands.

Thus the repeated emphasis that these mandrakes were brought to her by "her son" expresses what they mean to her – far beyond their value as an aphrodisiac or remedy for infertility. These are "her son's mandrakes," a sign of her child's love for his mother – perhaps the only love she has ever known. She will even describe thus to Jacob, who is surely confused by her instructions: "I have hired you with my son's mandrakes!"

We cannot know what Reuben thinks when he realizes that his mother has given his gift, or part of it, to his aunt Rachel. Perhaps Leah attempts to explain what she has gained by passing them on to her sister, but I am not sure that a young child is able to appreciate why his mother has relinquished the special present he brought to her so lovingly. This

---

62. Mathews proposes that the verb "*vayavei*" is used here to raise connotations of another meaning of this verb in the Bible – in its sexual sense (Mathews, *Genesis II*, 487).

brings us back to the second time that "Reuben went" – both times, as I will discuss below, Reuben believes that he is acting for the sake of his mother's honor, in the hope of bringing his father back to Leah's tent. It may also be that the transferal of his mandrakes to his mother's rival foreshadows the transferal of Reuben's birthright to his rival brothers.[63]

Either way, Reuben's loving relationship with his mother serves to reflect more than Leah's feelings; it is also a mirror of Rachel's deep longing. She, too, repeats that Leah has received the mandrakes from her son: "Please give me some of *your son's* mandrakes"/"in exchange for *your son's* mandrakes." Rachel sees the mother and son's love for each other, and she wants a part in it. Such a request from the wife who has her husband's love can be read as impertinent, but it also offers a glimpse into her deep despair: as if what she is truly asking is not "Please, give me some of your mandrakes," but "Please, give me some of your son's love."

Rachel's sorrow is too much to bear. Not only has God closed her womb, but her family are turning their backs on her as well. First, Jacob responds angrily to her frustration: "Jacob grew angry with Rachel, and said, 'Am I in place of God, who has kept you from having children?'" (30:2), and now, her sister Leah spurns her request with a furious accusation: "Is it not enough that you have taken away my husband? Now you want to take my son's mandrakes too!" (v. 15).

Leah refers to Jacob as "my husband," rather than "our husband." Technically, Leah indeed marries Jacob first, and only then Rachel marries Jacob, joining the family as the favorite wife. Yet her words portray the series of events in an ironic light – the reader, of course, knows that Jacob planned to marry Rachel and worked for seven years for her, while Leah is the one who has "taken away" Rachel's husband.

This statement, which can indeed be completely reversed, testifies to the irreconcilable perspectives within Jacob's nuclear family. Rachel, who sees things differently from Leah, proposes a quick fix ("Let him sleep with you tonight") for Leah's fundamental complaint ("You have taken away my husband"). Just one night with Jacob? Leah's sense of loneliness and rejection is constant, part of her everyday life. By entering into such negotiations with her sister, Rachel illuminates two central

63. Sasson, "Love's Roots."

aspects of the family's shaky dynamics: firstly, Rachel, immersed in her own sorrow, is not aware of her sister's – in fact, the rivalry between them only exacerbates their distress, and creates a wider chasm between them. Secondly, the fact that Leah relinquishes her precious mandrakes for just one night with her husband testifies to her desperation – even a single night with her husband is not to be taken for granted. The next verses will see how excitedly Leah welcomes Jacob to her tent, which, of course, reflects the extent of her usual loneliness.

The sisters' agreement is immediately followed by Jacob's return home. The fact that the text relates Leah's announcement to Jacob, "You are to come to me, for I have hired you with my son's mandrakes" (v. 16), rather than merely describing how Jacob slept with Leah that night, contributes to the couple's characterization, and vividly portrays how deeply Leah misses her husband. The fact that she goes out to meet him as he comes in from the field, and brings him into her tent right away, "teaches that she did not even let him wash his feet" (Genesis Rabba 72:5). How did Leah know that Jacob was approaching? We can imagine how breathlessly and impatiently she waited inside for him, peeking outside every so often, sending little Reuben out to see if his father was on his way. In the words of the poet Rachel, "Perhaps she waits in the darkness / in one room or another / perhaps she sits in the light / taut as a string" (from the poem "A Tear").

As soon as Jacob approaches, she "went out to meet him," exclaiming, "You are to come to me." She then adds the reason: "For I have hired you (*sakhor sekhartikha*) with my son's mandrakes." The repetition of the verb – "*sakhor sekhartikha*" – underscores the elation of her tone.[64]

This closes a circle: the episode opens with Reuben's discovery of mandrakes "in the field": "Reuben went for a walk and found mandrakes *in the field.* He *brought them* (*vayavei otam*) to his mother *Leah*"; and now: "When Jacob came back *from the field* that evening, *Leah* went out to meet him and said, 'You are *to come to me* (*elai tavo*).'"

64. A completely different reading emerges from the midrash that criticizes Leah and her daughter Dinah for "going out" – an unnecessarily harsh midrash, in my opinion, and see my discussion of Dinah and Shechem below.

While some exegetes are critical of Leah in this scene (for refusing to share her mandrakes with her sister), most readers feel sympathy for a wife who is forced to "hire" her husband in order to spend the night with him. Further sympathy comes from a different direction: from Jacob's characterization in this scene.

The phrase "When Jacob came back from the field that evening" (30:16) is in dialogue with two parallel scenes in his narrative cycle. The first figure to come in from the field is Esau, just before he sells his birthright: "Once when Jacob was cooking a stew, Esau came in exhausted from the field" (25:29). The second is Jacob, here, who comes home to Leah. Later, Jacob's sons will come back from the field to hear the news of their sister's rape: "Meanwhile, Jacob's sons, having heard what had happened, came back from the field. They were shocked and furious" (34:7).

For now, I will compare the first two scenes: the two brothers, Esau and Jacob, who both come in from the field. This similar opening suggests that Jacob's actions will have something to do with Esau's: how each brother acts after they come in from the field. But in fact, within the broad analogy between the two scenes, it is not Jacob but Rachel who is parallel to Esau.

In both scenes, one sibling has something that the other one desires. Jacob is cooking a red lentil stew, and Leah has a bouquet of mandrakes (which were also apparently some shade of red).[65] In exchange for the lentil stew, Esau gives Jacob his birthright, while in exchange for the mandrakes, Rachel "gives" Jacob to Leah.[66]

What is the significance of this comparison? Zakovitch suggests that this is some kind of retribution for Jacob's coercion of Esau:

> It is thus evident that the incident of the mandrakes is in dialogue with the incident of the stew, and that it suggests covert criticism of Jacob through the principle of measure for measure: just as Jacob acquires the birthright in exchange for a trivial thing

65. *Dudaim* are identified as mandrakes, "whose grapelike fruit is juicy, yellow and red, and whose scent is sweet like pineapple" (Patai and Zohary, "*dudaim*," 646).
66. Not all fully adopt this analogy; see further in Ben Reuven, "Mandrakes" (the author's surname is really Ben Reuven!); Zakovitch, *Texts*, 16–17.

> such as lentil stew by exploiting a weakness – his brother's hunger – thus Jacob's hated wife acquires the right to sleep with him in exchange for a trivial thing – the mandrakes.[67]

Zakovitch bases his theory on Jacob's utter passivity in the later scene. Not only does he remain silent when his wives determine where he will sleep that night, "Jacob, the seasoned salesperson in the first story, becomes, in the second story, the entity that is purchased" (ibid.).

If we adopt this direction, the aforementioned midrash is justified: according to several versions of the midrash, Leah forfeits her mandrakes, but thus obtains "the birthright."[68] The Sages presumably integrated this motif – which is otherwise entirely absent in the mandrakes story – solely based on this parallel. By introducing the "birthright" into this midrash, the Sages establish the birthright story as the backdrop to this story.[69]

If so, it becomes clear why the Sages criticize Rachel for "selling" a night with Jacob. As Rashi writes (based on Genesis Rabba): "Because she belittled sleeping with her righteous husband, she did not merit to be buried with him." Both Esau and Rachel forfeit their invaluable privilege for a plant that they can presumably obtain for themselves, free of cost: lentil stew, as mentioned, is a humble, cheap food, easily prepared, and mandrakes grow wild. Esau gives away the birthright for mere stew, and the midrash suggests that Rachel, too, similarly forfeits "the birthright." Just as the birthright scene ends with a negative appraisal of Esau: "Thus Esau disdained his birthright" (25:34), the Sages project this same view onto Rachel: thus Rachel disdained a night with her husband, or, in Rashi's words, "belittled sleeping with her righteous husband."[70]

The comparison between the two stories, however, is also related to the portrayal of the character who is present in both: Jacob. Fokkelman

---

67. Zakovitch, *Texts*, 17.
68. As mentioned, there are different versions of this midrash, and in some, it is Rachel who "gains the birthright" (hinting to Joseph).
69. On this midrashic method, which is based on a literary analogy but only writes the results, see Sasson, "Analogies."
70. For an alternative reading, which compares Rachel's desire for fertility and Esau's desire for lentil stew, see Shemesh, "Rachel," 100–01.

believes that it is Jacob in the birthright scene who should be paralleled to Rachel: in both cases, the younger sibling implements a transaction in order to obtain what they desire.[71] I do believe, however, that Yael Shemesh is correct in her assertion that "the analogy between Rachel and Esau is far more salient in this narrative."[72] And if so, intriguingly enough, then the entity parallel to Jacob in our story is none but the lentil stew: he is the object passed from hand to hand. It is his wives who decide where he will spend the night, and it is obvious from their exchange that Jacob's own opinion is entirely irrelevant. In fact, Jacob's passivity in this respect is already evident: his exchange with Rachel ends with her suggestion that he take Bilhah as his wife: "She said: 'Here is Bilhah my handmaid. Come to her'" (30:3). Jacob's only response is his acquiescence: "Jacob came to her" (v. 4). Moreover, when Leah copies Rachel's idea and gives Jacob her own maid, her request is not even mentioned in the narrative. Its absence, along with Jacob's general passivity about his bedmate ever since Laban nonchalantly responds to his accusations, serves to characterize Jacob in a certain way.

Jacob's passivity is also salient in his response – or to be precise, his lack of response – to Leah's announcement that she has "hired him" for the night. Here, too, Jacob's reaction to this strange transaction is withheld from the reader. Does he attempt to appeal to Rachel? Is he angry with his wives? Does he, perhaps, look into Leah's eyes and follow her tenderly back to her tent? We can only guess, but the silence of the text speaks more loudly than any such theory. Once again, the scene's parallel to the birthright scene acts as a mirror for Jacob's character: once, Jacob was the one who initiated a transaction with his brother; now he is the object passed from hand to hand.

Jacob's passivity is also highlighted through the scene's allusion to another biblical scene. I have already noted that those who suggest that Jacob does not recognize his bride because he is drunk can rely on the scene's covert parallel with the story of Lot and his daughters. The mandrake incident continues this analogy; not only because the scene depicts two sisters deciding which of them will sleep with a certain man,

71. Fokkelman, *Genesis*, 140.

72. Shemesh, "Rachel," 100, n. 68.

but also through its similar language. The mandrake scene ends thus: "So that night he slept with her" (30:16). The phrase "that night" echoes the story of Lot's daughters: "That night they gave their father wine to drink. Then the elder daughter went in and slept with him..." (19:33). I am not aware of another biblical story that depicts a man's sexual passivity, especially not to the extent that "he was unaware when she lay down and when she arose" (19:33). Jacob is not drunk when he enters Leah's tent, but the subtle allusion to Lot underscores Jacob's passivity: his wives decide whom he will sleep with, at least "that night." We can even argue that the parallel to Lot's daughters is maintained when this interaction also results in the birth of two sons.

In light of this analysis, I will reiterate our opening question: What is the story's significance within the birth sequence of Jacob's children? I began with quoting the midrash that Leah only gave birth to Issachar and Zebulun as a result of this scene: "Through the mandrakes, two great tribes in Israel came to be: Issachar and Zebulun" (Genesis Rabba 72:5).

This approach is consistent with the aforementioned surprising midrash that Rachel "loses" two tribes to Leah because of the mandrakes incident. The premise of this midrash is that Rachel was supposed to give birth to four sons – like her sister Leah – but by relinquishing a night with Jacob, she (unknowingly) gives up two tribes; while by relinquishing the mandrakes, Leah gains the two tribes that Rachel loses.

As bold as this midrash is, it emerges that the text itself supports this reading. Rachel is searching desperately for a cure for her fertility, but by doing so, she loses "two tribes"; Leah has already given birth four times and "ceased to have children," but by favoring a night with her husband over a bunch of mandrakes, God listens to her and her womb is opened anew. Rachel is left with an armful of flowers and an empty womb; "The text mentions this to teach you that there is no knowledge, wisdom, or advice stronger than God, and even though mandrakes are useful for encouraging pregnancy, they do not help Rachel, for Leah gives birth to three more children, while Rachel remains barren until God remembers her."[73]

73. Ehrlich, *Bible*, 86.

Some claimed that in light of our story, it is incorrect to assume that mandrakes were considered a remedy for infertility in the biblical period, given that "Leah, who gave up her mandrakes, gave birth to a son, while Rachel, who received the mandrakes, did not give birth."[74] Yet the precise opposite is true, and one narrative objective is to challenge the tradition that mandrakes hold the key to pregnancy. Not because there was no such tradition, but rather because it was so prevalent that Jacob's own family held by it.

It is theoretically possible to claim that after Judah's birth, Jacob moves in permanently to Rachel's tent, and ceases to visit Leah altogether – until the mandrakes incident, when he rekindles his relationship with Leah. Based on this reading, too, this scene dramatically affects the structure of Jacob's family – but not due to divine providence. While this story does show that Jacob's default bed is Rachel's, I have already noted that the fact that Jacob accepts Zilpah without comment shows that he fully supports Leah's continued attempts to bear more children, if need be through her maid. Moreover, the birth story of Issachar, who is born as a result of Leah's night with Jacob: "*God listened* to Leah, and she became pregnant and bore Jacob a fifth son" (30:17), shows that her renewed fertility is the result of divine grace more than human intervention.

For this reason, the births of Issachar and Zebulun are phrased in the same formula as the handmaids' births. Unlike Leah's first four births, these two are "hired" from Rachel; Issachar and Zebulun should have been Rachel's sons.

Thus the two narratives that interrupt the sequence of births – Jacob's marriage to the handmaids and the mandrakes episode – are both directly related to the shaping of Jacob's family and the distribution of the tribes among the mothers. A direct comparison highlights the similarity between these scenes:

74. Patai and Zohary, "*dudaim*," 645.

	Jacob's Marriage to the Handmaids (30:1–3)	**The Mandrakes (30:14–16)**
Background: Leah has something Rachel does not have:	Rachel saw that she had borne no children to Jacob, and she became envious of her sister.	During the wheat harvest, Reuben went for a walk and found mandrakes in the field. He brought them to his mother Leah.
Rachel asks for what she lacks:	To Jacob she said, "Give me children! If not, let me die!"	Rachel said to Leah, "Please give me some of your son's mandrakes."
Refusal (through a rhetorical question):	Jacob grew angry with Rachel, and said, "Am I in place of God, who has kept you from having children?"	She replied, "Is it not enough that you have taken away my husband? Now you want to take my son's mandrakes too!"
Rachel takes initiative to obtain what she wants by having Jacob sleep with another woman:	"Here is Bilhah my handmaid," she said. "Come to her. Let her give birth on my knees so that I too can build a family through her."	"Very well," said Rachel. "Let him sleep with you tonight in exchange for your son's mandrakes."
Jacob sleeps with a woman other than Rachel:	So she gave him her maid Bilhah as a wife. Jacob came to her.	When Jacob came back from the field that evening, Leah went out to meet him and said, "You are to come to me, for I have hired you with my son's mandrakes." So that night he slept with her.

In both scenes, Rachel is desperate for children, and to this end she gives Jacob to another woman's embrace: "Here is Bilhah my handmaid. Come to her"/"Very well. Let him sleep with you tonight." Through these actions, she hopes to have a child of her own (the handmaid's children will be considered her own, and the mandrakes will help her conceive).

This comparison presents many facets worthy of discussion, especially regarding how Rachel's initiative shapes the plot: her longing for children moves her to sacrifice her closeness with her husband. This pattern is an apt reflection of the tension between the sisters: one has children, and the other a husband. In a certain sense, Leah and Rachel's roles are a direct continuation of their respective marriages to Jacob. Rachel is the girl he falls in love with, while Leah is given to him because of his birthright; thus Rachel is his lover and Leah is the mother of his children, foundress of the nation of Israel (the Midrash proposes that Lamech's wives, Adah and Zillah, have similar roles).[75] This dichotomy, however, is elegant in literature and messy in real life: both Rachel and Leah want to be beloved wives and happy mothers of children. Rachel feels that without children, she would rather be dead (30:1), and Leah feels that her husband has been stolen from her (30:15). Jacob's love for Rachel is not enough for her, and Leah is miserable because the father of her children does not love her.

For the sake of our discussion, I wish to highlight the similar results of each scene: after Rachel "gives" Jacob to her handmaid, Bilhah gives birth to two sons; after Rachel "gives" Jacob to Leah, Leah gives birth to two more sons.

Intriguingly enough, after Issachar is born as a result of the mandrakes incident, he is named not for the mandrakes but for Leah's bestowal of her handmaid upon Jacob: "'God has rewarded me (*sekhari*) for giving my maid to my husband,' so she named him Issachar (*yissakhar*)" (30:18). This is fascinating in two respects: firstly, given that the root S-KH-R is also used in the mandrakes scene ("You are to come to me, for I have hired you [*sakhor sekhartikha*] with my son's mandrakes" – 30:16), Issachar's name also resonates with this scene, thus serving as another point of comparison between the two scenes. The birth that results from the mandrake scene is linked to Jacob's marriage with Leah's handmaid, which in turn links the birth of sons through handmaids with Rachel's attempt to conceive with the help of mandrakes.

75. In Rashi's words: "So was the custom of the generation of the Flood, one [wife] for propagation and one for marital relations … Adah: She was the one for propagation, called so because she was despicable to him and removed from him. *Ada* is the Aramaic translation of *sura*, turn away. Zillah: She was the one for marital relations, [so named] because she would always sit in his shadow (*betzillo*)" (on Gen. 4:19).

Secondly, the reason given for Issachar's name hints to the price that Leah pays for sharing her husband with yet another woman. Who ever dreamed of her husband taking her handmaid as a second wife, with its complicated implications for their relationship and the handmaid's new status within their family (the case of Abraham, Sarah, and Hagar certainly suffices as an example!)? Leah believes that God sees her self-sacrifice for the sake of bearing more children to Jacob and rewards her with more children in return. We can only imagine Rachel's response: after all, she is the first to present Jacob with her handmaid, and it certainly pains her to bring another wife into the family when she is already forced to share her husband with her sister. Now, when Leah expresses her belief that she is being rewarded for her sacrifice, how does Rachel feel, when her sister's arms are full once more but her own womb remains closed?

In summary, Issachar and Zebulun's status differs from that of Leah's first four sons. They are still her sons, of course, but the narrative hints that they should have been born to Rachel. Issachar and Zebulun are born to Leah as a result of Rachel's initiative to obtain the mandrakes, just as the handmaids' sons are born as a result of her initiative to give their mothers to Jacob.

This division illuminates the different appearances of God's name throughout the sequence of births. Leah's first four sons are associated with the Tetragrammaton, the "Lord": first "*the Lord* saw that Leah was unloved and opened her womb" (29:31); then her sons are named with "the Lord" in mind: "*The Lord* has seen my affliction.... *The Lord* has heard that I am unloved.... This time I will praise *the Lord*" (29:32–35).

The next scene sees the harsh exchange between Rachel and Jacob, followed by Jacob's marriage with the handmaids. In this scene, only the name "God" is used: "Jacob grew angry with Rachel, and said, 'Am I in place of *God*, who has kept you from having children?'... Then Rachel said, '*God* has vindicated me. He has listened to my voice and given me a son'...'With hard struggles (*naftulei elohim*)[76] I have struggled

76. As mentioned, the accepted reading is that the phrase "*naftulei elohim*" does not refer to God but is rather an expression of immensity – an enormous quarrel. So this verse is irrelevant to our discussion.

with my sister and I have won.' So she named him Naphtali" (30:2–8). But we cannot neatly differentiate between the sisters' sons, who are associated with "the Lord," and the handmaids' sons, who are linked to "God," because Issachar and Zebulun – Leah's two youngest sons – are also associated with the name "God": "*God* listened to Leah, and she became pregnant and bore Jacob a fifth son. Leah said, '*God* has rewarded me for giving my maid to my husband'...'*God* has given me a precious gift,' said Leah" (30:17–20).

If so, then births that follow the "original divine plan" are associated with the Tetragrammaton, while births that result from human initiative are associated with the name "God." It is no wonder that Joseph's long-awaited birth is also associated with "the Lord": "And she named him Joseph, saying, 'May *the Lord* grant me another son also'" (30:17–20).

Yet this division is challenged by Joseph's birth, which is also associated with the name "God": "Then *God* remembered Rachel and listened to her and enabled her to conceive. She became pregnant and gave birth to a son. She said, '*God* has taken away my shame'" (30:22–23). This verse is redolent with redemption, echoing another famous verse: "And God heard their groaning, and God remembered His covenant" (Ex. 2:24). Joseph's birth, it seems, sees the fusion of two axes in the plot: Rachel was supposed to be the mother of tribes in Israel all along, but Joseph is also the result of her unwavering determination to redeem herself from her own dire straits.

This convergence is an inherent part of Rachel's characterization, which will also have significant bearing on her son Joseph. I have already pointed out that Rachel introduces a new twist of human initiative each time she steps onto the stage. She offers her handmaid to Jacob; she covets the mandrakes, and later, she will steal the teraphim. Rachel is Jacob's first love, the girl a lonely refugee encounters just before he reaches Haran, and she maintains this thread of human initiative through the narrative cycle. When she finally gives birth, therefore, her birth is associated with both divine names: "the Lord" implies that this birth was anticipated all along, but the name "God" hints that this birth, although part of the divine plan, is also the result of her tireless efforts to solve her own problems.

Rachel's characterization and the birth of her son Joseph are also unique among other biblical narratives of barrenness.

RACHEL AND OTHER BARREN WOMEN IN THE BIBLE

Scholars have pointed out that there are many common motifs in narratives depicting barren women in the Bible, and that they constitute a certain genre we might refer to as "barrenness" narratives (or "the birth of the savior" narratives).[77] The main features of these narratives include:

- A description of the barren woman's plight
- Other characters' attitude toward her barrenness
- Her worthiness of a miracle (due to a good deed or prayer)
- Annunciation (through prophecy, angel, or prophet)
- A description of the son's destiny
- The parents' reaction to these tidings
- A description of the miracle itself – the barren woman conceives[78]
- The son's naming, the explanation for the name, and the parents' gratitude

Of course, not all components feature in every story, but these are the main building blocks of narratives of this genre, such as the birth of Isaac, Sarah's son (Gen. 17–18); the birth of Rebecca's twins (Gen. 25); our own story – the birth of Rachel's son (Gen. 30); the birth of Samson, born to Manoah's wife (Judges 13); the birth of Samuel, born to Hannah (I Sam. 1); and the birth of the Shunamite woman's son (II Kings 4). The

77. See, for example, Zakovitch, *Life of Samson*, 74–83; Simon, "Birth of Samuel," 93–110; Ackerman, "Moses Birth Story"; Tzohar, *Barrenness in the Bible*. Compare to components Jarrell lists in what he calls "birth narratives" (Jarrell, "Birth Narrative," esp. 5 and the tables at the end of his article).
78. I do not mean a "miracle" based on its strict definition. Fokkelman rightly claims that in the story of Hannah, for example, there is no description of any supernatural miracle (Fokkelman, *Samuel*, 53). Nonetheless, because this is a barrenness narrative, God's special intervention is clear (as Fokkelman himself emphasizes).

similar plot of these narratives helps define the unique features of each individual story, and which motifs are absent or central.

In this context, of course, I wish to focus on the story of Rachel and how these elements manifest in her story:

- A description of the barren woman's plight is salient throughout the births of Jacob's children, but Rachel's pain is described explicitly in the description "When she saw that she had not borne children to Jacob, she was envious of her sister" (30:1).
- Other characters' attitude toward her barrenness: Jacob's reaction to Rachel's frustration is anger: "Jacob grew angry with Rachel and said, 'Am I in place of God, who has kept you from having children?'" (30:2).
- Worthiness of a miracle (due to a good deed or prayer): *This element is not explicitly mentioned* (but may be hinted through the description that God listened to Rachel).
- The bearer of tidings *is absent in this story.*
- A description of the son's destiny *is absent in this story* (though Joseph has a unique role later on, there is no mention of it here).
- The parents' reaction to these tidings *is obviously absent in Rachel's story, as there are no tidings.*
- A description of the miracle itself – the barren woman conceives: "Then God remembered Rachel and listened to her and enabled her to conceive. She became pregnant and gave birth to a son" (30:22–23).
- The son's naming, explanation for the name, and the parents' gratitude: "She said, 'God has taken away my shame,' and she named him Joseph, saying, 'May the Lord grant me another son also'" (30:23–24).

Before Rachel finally conceives, there is a striking absence of communication with God. There is no prophecy, angel, or any bearer of tidings announcing that Joseph's birth is imminent (as is the case with Sarah, Manoah's wife, and the Shunamite woman), nor is there any explicit description of Rachel's prayer or any other form of request (unlike Isaac, who prays, or Hannah, who prays and makes a vow).[79] The absence of this element is particularly salient compared to other stories of this genre,[80] but even on its own, the utter absence of any kind of prayer from Rachel or Jacob is surprising.

The lack of dialogue between the characters and God is underscored through Jacob's reference to God in his angry response to her: "Am I in place of God, who has kept you from having children?" (30:2).[81] "Jacob's rebuke, then... is virtually an explicit reference by one of the characters to the traditional requirements of the type-scene."[82] But his words do not fulfill this requirement; on the contrary, they emphasize precisely what is lacking in the narrative: Jacob is not God, and he cannot open a sealed womb. Why, then, do Rachel and her husband fail to turn to the One who *can* open a sealed womb? And just to make sure that no reader misses this surprising omission, these verses contain an ironic link between what God sees and what Rachel sees: "*And the Lord saw* that Leah was unloved, and He opened her womb, but Rachel was barren" (29:31)/"*And Rachel saw* that she had not borne children to Jacob, and she became envious of her sister" (30:1).[83] One might claim that she definitely prayed (as Radak does, for example), but this only exacerbates the question: Why isn't Rachel's prayer mentioned in the text, as convention dictates? What literary purpose does this pointed absence of prayer serve?

---

79. Compare to Alter, *Biblical Narrative*, 211; Simon, "Birth of Samuel," 54; Shemesh, "Rachel," 92. Jarrell claims that biblical "birth narratives" are a kind of covenant between God and the mother (Jarrell, "Birth Narrative"). In Genesis, he explores the story of Hagar (ch. 16), of Sarah (ch. 18), and of Rebecca (ch. 25). It is no coincidence that he overlooks the story of Rachel, which has no annunciation or revelation.
80. Fuchs points out a similar omission in the stories of Ruth and Tamar, which are also part of this genre (even if their barrenness is circumstantial). She correctly emphasizes that divine intervention is salient in Ruth's pregnancy (4:13), but there is no prayer or annunciation in these narratives (Fuchs, *Sexual Politics*, 83–85). Still, it is not clear whether these are strictly considered narratives of barrenness that raise expectations for all the aforementioned components.
81. Wenham, *Genesis II*, 244.
82. Alter, *Biblical Narrative*, 234.
83. Compare to Westermann, *Genesis II*, 474; Wenham, *Genesis II*, 244.

Some might claim that this glaring omission serves as covert criticism against Rachel, but I believe that it serves a completely different purpose. Eventually, the son born to Rachel will save his whole family and an entire nation from starvation; Joseph will become the head of the family and its provider. Yet he will do so without direct communication with God. While God appears to the three patriarchs, Joseph never experiences a divine revelation. Joseph is granted understanding through his ability to interpret dreams, and effectively, reality itself. He is the one who reassures his brothers: "And now, do not be distressed or angry with yourselves that you sold me here, for God sent me ahead of you to save lives" (Gen. 45:5). He perceives even his brothers' sin as part of divine providence over the family. In this sense, Joseph paves the way for times of exile and their hidden providence, when God's hand shapes reality without any transcendental clarification that this is so. This concept is conveyed through the absence of direct communication between Joseph's parents and God before his birth. Joseph's long-awaited birth is ostensibly natural; yet, as Joseph himself will convey, God's hand in fact shapes even the most natural of events.[84] Based on this paradigm, the absence of this convention does not reflect badly on Rachel and her actions; rather, it anticipates the nature of her son and his relationship with God.[85]

I wish to conclude this discussion with a different midrash, one that presents a similar view of Rachel.[86] Lamentations Rabba describes how Israel's ancestors attempt to plead with God as Israel are sent to exile:

> Abraham spoke up to the Holy One blessed be He and said: "Master of the World, at the age of one hundred you gave me a son, and when he matured and became a young man of thirty-seven You said to me, 'Offer him up as a burnt offering before Me,' and I treated him cruelly, without mercy, and I myself forced

84. Divine intervention is stated explicitly (30:22), but no angel comes to Joseph's parents bringing tidings of her imminent pregnancy or the birth of a son.
85. This reading may be consistent with the claim that Genesis draws an analogy between Rachel and Joseph (Shemesh, "Rachel," 105–06).
86. I am grateful to my dear friend R. Itamar Eldar for illuminating for me Rachel's characterization in this midrash.

him – will You not remember this for me, and have mercy on my children?"

Isaac spoke up and said:
"Master of the World, when my father said to me, 'God will show us the lamb for the offering, my son,' I did not hinder Your words, and I was willingly bound upon the altar, and I stretched out my neck toward the blade – will You not remember this for me, and have mercy on my children?"

Jacob spoke up and said:
"Master of the World, did I not stay at Laban's house for twenty years, and when I left his house, the wicked Esau attacked me and tried to kill my sons, and I gave myself up for death instead of them? And now they are in their enemies' hands like sheep to the slaughter, after You raised them like chicks, and I suffered the pains of raising children for most of my life – will You not remember this for me, and have mercy on my children?"

Moses spoke up and said:
"Master of the World, was I not a faithful shepherd for Israel for forty years..."

A Divine Voice issued forth and said, "It has been decreed before Me..."

At that moment, Mother Rachel jumped forward before the Holy One blessed be He and said:

"Master of the World! It is known before You that Your servant Jacob's love for me knew no bounds, and he worked for my father for seven years for me.... I contained my desire and had compassion for my sister that she not suffer disgrace, and I gave her all the signs that I had given to my husband, so that he would think that she was Rachel...

> I acted kindly with her, I was not jealous of her, and I did not cause her to be shamed and disgraced..."
>
> God's mercy was stirred at once, and He said: "For your sake, Rachel, I shall return Israel to their place – for there is a reward for your labor.... And there is hope for your future – declares the Lord: Your children shall return to their country."[87]

Unlike the forefathers who appeal to God, Rachel does not merely "speak up"; with great passion and fervor, she "jumped forward" before God, even though He has already decreed that Israel's fate is sealed. After the previous speakers fail to stir God's mercy, Rachel comes forward and manages to revoke the evil decree. She does not behave with the same reserved etiquette as the men before her – she "jumps forward" when it is not her place to do so. Yet it is this very breach of convention, this very show of passion, that moves God to show mercy to His people. This midrash shows that a mother's deep compassion for her children – *raḥamim*, "mercy," after all, essentially comes from the word *reḥem*, "womb" – can be far more potent than a father's compassion for his children, but in the context of our discussion, it is no less important to point out her attitude toward a divine decree. God's will silences Israel's forefathers, but Rachel persists until this decree is revoked.

Talia Horovitz adds that Abraham and Isaac base their pleas on the binding of Isaac – that is, on the merit of their obedience (or upon their faith despite the harsh circumstances of reality, similar to the pleas of Jacob and Moses), while Rachel bases her plea on her initiative and free will:

> Unlike the forefathers, who comply with God's will, Rachel took initiative on her own. No one obliged her to do anything – on the contrary. First, she made up signs with Jacob to defy her cheating father. Later, she shared these signs with her sister in order to prevent her shame. The midrashic language ("At that

87. Lamentations Rabba 24.

> moment Mother Rachel jumped forward before the Holy One") hints to her assertiveness as much as it hints to the forefathers' passivity ("Abraham spoke up...Isaac spoke up"). "Jumping forward" is far more forceful than "speaking up".... In this midrash, Rachel emerges as a bold, determined, and powerful character who revokes the decree "at once": "God's mercy was stirred at once, and He said: 'For your sake, Rachel, I shall return Israel to their place.'"[88]

Rachel, who never loses hope, is the one who will accompany Israel in their darkest hour, in a time of exile, when God's face is hidden. The way she lives her life – that a person must take action to bring about their own redemption – has the power to give Israel hope even in exile, when there is no clear sign of divine revelation, when God's hand and face are hidden.

88. Horowitz, "Rachel."

The Property Agreement (Gen. 30:25–43)

> This is it, Adam, that grieves me,
> and the spirit of my father, which I think is within me,
> begins to mutiny against this servitude.
> I will no longer endure it,
> though yet I know no wise remedy how to avoid it.
>
> – Shakespeare, *As You Like It,* Act I, Scene I

Before us lies a rare example of a text that invites two opposite readings. How should we evaluate Jacob's request to make his own fortune? Jacob remains in Haran for six more years in order to increase his wealth, and exegetes debate whether the text condones or condemns the extra years he spends there after his children are born.

The question is raised in the plot itself when Jacob asks Laban's permission to return to his homeland after Joseph is born: "After Rachel had given birth to Joseph, Jacob said to Laban, '*Send me on my way* to my own land. Give me my wives and my children for whom I have worked for you, and let me go. You know very well how much work I have done for you'" (30:25–26). Jacob does not mention "his father's house" for obvious diplomatic reasons – he does not wish to draw attention to the fact that he sorely misses his "real" family. Jacob's homeland, however, remains Canaan, and he focuses on this more objective fact when raising the subject of his departure with the "family" he has lived with for fourteen years.

Laban understands that his fortune has come to him through Jacob, and he therefore asks Jacob to stay on: "'If you will allow me to say so, I have learned by divination that it is because of you that the Lord has blessed me.' He added, 'Name your hire and I will pay it'" (30:27–28).[1] Laban's request should come as no surprise to the reader, after Laban (and his mother) respond similarly to Abraham's servant a generation earlier. There, too, Abraham's servant requests, "*Send me on my way* to my master" (24:54), and there, too, Laban attempts to keep his sister in Haran for the time being: "Let the young woman stay with us a year or ten months. Then she may go" (24:55).

Though Laban's response is predictable, Jacob's reaction is not. Although Abraham's servant stands firm and insists upon returning to Canaan immediately: "*Send me on my way that I may go back* to my master" (24:56 – compare this to Jacob's request, "*Send me on my way that I may go back*"), Jacob does not hold his ground, but suggests that he stay until he makes his own fortune.

Does this subtle allusion to Abraham's servant cast any criticism upon Jacob for lingering in Haran? To be fair, there are significant differences between the narratives. Abraham's servant must bring Rebecca back to Canaan so she can marry Isaac, and any delay necessarily delays their marriage; Jacob, by contrast, is already married, and he has already begun to raise his family. Moreover, Jacob has nothing of his own. If he returns to Canaan now, he will return with many mouths to feed, but nothing of his own to feed them with – until now, all his work has been for Laban. This is not the case with Abraham's servant: Isaac, the heir to all of Abraham's wealth, is waiting for his bride back in Canaan, ready to raise his family.

R. Ovadiah Sforno attempts to understand Jacob's initial request to return to Canaan even though he has nothing of his own:

1. It may be that "*niḥashti*" can be understood in light of the Akkadian verb *naḥāšu*, meaning "to prosper, flourish" (Finkelstein, "Herding Contract," 34, n. 19). If so, it is strange that he would use divination to understand how he became rich; usually divination is used to determine the future (see also Hamilton, *Genesis II*, 282).

> Send me on my way and I will go: Even though he had nothing but his own staff in hand, he still had enough to live on with his wives and children – at least enough to buy food, clothing, and provisions for the way. For otherwise, such a righteous, wise man would not have wanted to leave if that would have meant death by starvation; moreover, it cannot be that Laban, who was a rich, important person in his city would have agreed to send him off with his daughters and grandchildren if they would all die of hunger, thirst, or lack what to wear on such a long journey. (Sforno on Gen. 30:25)

If this is the case, what should we make of Jacob's decision to remain in Haran? The argument still rages to this day. Some denounce Jacob's decision to remain in Haran for economic reasons:

> The second half of Jacob's stay – for economic purposes – is not justified: Jacob did not travel to Haran to make his fortune, and this purpose does not justify delaying his return to his homeland, his fulfillment of his vow, or honoring his father and mother. It is especially grave that Jacob does not set a limit for this delay; only external events and God's word to him limits his stay there to six years.[2]

On the other hand, others believe that the events that take place during this extended stay are a clear indication of God's providence. Mathews, for example, argues that Jacob's burgeoning family and burgeoning flock signify the fulfillment of God's blessing.[3]

Can this central question be resolved based on the hints scattered throughout the narrative? This is an example of one of the most challenging conundrums in biblical narrative analysis: a certain scene contains clear textual markers, but these markers can be interpreted in different ways. One concrete anchor for the analysis of this scene is the reverberating echo of God's revelation to Jacob at Bethel, but what does

2. Samet, *Studies I*, vol. 1, 81.
3. Mathews, *Genesis II*, 491.

this analogy contribute? Two opposite directions can be mapped out using the same textual data.

Several key phrases in this chapter recall God's revelation to Jacob at Bethel. This is especially salient in Jacob's proposal that he will continue to tend Laban's flock:

> He said to him, "You know well how I have worked for you and how your livestock have fared under my care. You had little before I came, but it has swelled into much. The Lord has blessed you wherever I have been. Now, when can I do likewise for my own household?"
> Laban asked, "What shall I give you?"
> Jacob replied, "Do not give me anything. If you do this one thing for me, I will continue to shepherd and guard your flocks." (30:29–31)

The verb "swelled" (*vayifrotz*), which is repeated once more in the chapter's conclusion: "Thus the man's wealth swelled into a fortune" (30:43), echoes God's blessing to Jacob in his vision of the ladder: "You will spread out (*ufaratzta*) to the west, to the east, to the north, to the south" (28:14). Jacob's next words, "The Lord has blessed you wherever I have been," are essentially the fulfillment of God's promise at Bethel that "through you and your descendants, all the families of the earth will be blessed." The continuation of Jacob's exchange with Laban also contains several motifs that have accompanied the narrative since the vision of the ladder. Jacob asks Laban, "When can I do likewise for my own household?" and this recalls the two houses Jacob mentions in his vow: "If I return in peace to my father's house" (28:21) and "This stone I set up as a pillar will become a house of God" (28:22).

These verses also mention "giving," which may also deepen the parallel between the two scenes: Laban asks Jacob, "What shall I *give* you?" and Jacob responds, "Do not *give* me anything," which may be in dialogue with Jacob's earlier vow that "of all that You *give* me, I will dedicate a tenth to You" (28:22).

With some hesitation, I wish to draw attention to the end of the verse. Jacob promises Laban that he will guard his flock on the condition that he pays him what is due: "*If* (*im*) you do this one thing for me, I will continue (*ashuva*) to shepherd and *guard* (*eshmor*) your flocks." Perhaps it is not too farfetched to claim that this follows the pattern of Jacob's vow to God: "*If* (*im*) God will be with me, *protecting me* (*ushmarani*) on this journey... and if I return (*veshavti*) in peace" (28:20–21). There too, God's promise concerns property and livelihood: "Giving me food to eat and clothes to wear."

There are other cues throughout the rest of the chapter, but these certainly suffice to posit that this intertextuality is intentional. For whatever reason, Jacob's agreement with Laban is in dialogue with the vision of the ladder and Jacob's vow. But the exegetical question remains: What is the purpose of this dialogue, and how does it illuminate the text's attitude toward the extra years Jacob spends in Laban's house?

On the one hand, it is possible to argue that these allusions suggest criticism of Jacob's extra time in Haran, taking on an ironic, bitter note: Jacob's dream promises that he will grow and "spread out" in every direction in the land of Canaan, but instead, all that grows and "spreads" is Laban and Jacob's wealth, in Haran. In his dream at Bethel, Jacob longs for his father's house and even vows to build a house for God, but now, the only house that interests him is Laban's, where he seeks to make his fortune. Right now, Jacob is concerned with dividing up Laban's property, with no thought for the "tithing" he promises God at Bethel. It is no wonder that according to this reading, God is not involved in this scene at all; that this scene deals with strictly earthly matters, in contrast to the first fourteen years in Haran, when God opens the mothers' wombs and hears their prayers.[4]

On the other hand – to be precise, on the opposite hand – these allusions can also be read as proof that Jacob's success in Haran marks the beginning of the fulfillment of God's promise at Bethel. His second agreement with Laban is a further example of God's providence, which

---

4. Samet writes that because Jacob is criticized for staying to increase his fortune, this wealth brings him trouble and he is eventually forced to flee Laban's house (ibid.). But this proof is problematic (as Samet himself acknowledges) given that his first agreement with Laban was problematic as well, and Jacob can hardly be criticized for marrying his cousins.

goes far beyond Jacob's original concern for "food to eat and clothes to wear." This is how the Creator rewards His devoted ones, showering them with blessing.

Despite its importance, this is not an easy question to resolve. I am inclined to favor the approach that the text does not disapprove of Jacob's extended contract with Laban – on the contrary, it is a striking expression of God's munificence and protection over Jacob in exile, even though Laban seeks his destruction. Moreover, as I will soon clarify, Jacob's wealth is not merely an economic advantage; it should be considered within a much broader context.

Without dismissing the legitimacy of the first reading, I am doubtful that the multiple allusions to the revelation at Bethel are all ironic. Nor is it accurate to present the events of this chapter as devoid of divine intervention, given that at its end, Jacob is granted another revelation that explicitly states that God increases his wealth despite Laban's efforts to thwart him. We will soon explore how information is divided between two separate scenes and the contribution of this literary technique, but in the end, when both scenes are read in sequence, there is no doubt that it is God who helps Jacob's wealth swell into a fortune.

Above all, an additional parallel between this scene and a description of Abraham's wealth tilts the scale toward the reading that Jacob's prolonged stay brings God's blessing. The summary that "thus the man's wealth swelled into a fortune. He had large flocks, female and male servants, camels and donkeys" (30:43) recalls the description of Abraham's wealth in a parallel scene featuring Abraham's servant and Laban: "The Lord has blessed my master greatly, and he has prospered. He has given him sheep and cattle, silver and gold, male and female servants, camels and donkeys" (24:35). Had the text wished to criticize Jacob, it would have used language that does not recall the wealth of his grandfather, who is certainly portrayed in a positive light in that context.[5]

5. It is worth noting that those who claim that the text criticizes Jacob for staying to increase his wealth can further claim that while it is mentioned that Abraham is blessed and made wealthy by God, this aspect is absent in regard to Jacob, and not by chance. As I have mentioned, it is difficult to determine Jacob's evaluation in the text.

Were Jacob to remain in Haran for the sole purpose of making his fortune, there would be more room to debate whether his decision meets the text's approval. Jacob's financial situation, however, is not merely a reflection of his bank statement; it also has implications for his social and spiritual standing, because it reveals whether he is independent or dependent on Laban. This issue will be resolved in his exchange with his wives (ch. 31), but it is already worth pointing out that the root E-B-D features over and over again in this chapter. Although Isaac blesses Jacob (disguised as Esau) "May peoples serve you; may nations bow down to you" (27:29), for the first fourteen years thereafter, it is Jacob who must serve others. This begins with his first agreement with Laban: "'If you are my brother, does that mean you should *work* for me for nothing? Tell me what your hire should be'... he said, 'I will *work* for you seven years for your younger daughter Rachel'.... So Jacob *worked* for Rachel seven years.... 'What is this you have done to me? I *served* you for Rachel, did I not? Why did you deceive me?'... 'Wait until the bridal week of this one is over and then we will give you the other one also, in return for *your serving me* another seven years'.... And he *served* him for another seven years" (29:15–27). Jacob mentions this at the beginning of his second agreement with Laban: "Release me to go home to my own land. Give me my wives and my children for whom I have *worked* for you, and let me go. You know very well how much *work I have done for you*" (30:26).

Yet from the moment Jacob asks Laban, "Now, when can I do likewise for my own household?" this root is not used to describe his cultivation of his own flock. In a certain sense, Jacob's wealth is far more than a description of economic wealth: "Thus the man's wealth swelled into a fortune. He had large flocks, female and male servants, camels and donkeys" (30:43). Some scholars find the use of the word "man" surprising, to the extent that some argue that the chapter originally ended differently;[6] why is Jacob suddenly referred to as a "man"? The word seems to express that Jacob has become a man in his own right, a citizen with legal and financial rights, as the Baalei Tosafot point out: "What is a 'man'? An important person" (on Gen. 30:43). Jacob is finally a "man" of proper standing, with "female and male servants" of his own.

6. Westermann, *Genesis II*, 484.

Thus Jacob should not be criticized for staying in Haran for purely financial reasons. Jacob's accumulation of wealth represents the process of becoming a free, independent man with property of his own. Note the linguistic similarities between Jacob's accusation against Laban and Deuteronomy's law of freeing slaves: "Had the God of my father – the God of Abraham, the Fear of Isaac – not been with me, *you would have sent me away empty-handed.* But God saw my plight and the toil of my hands, and He rebuked you last night" (31:42)/"If a fellow Hebrew, man or woman, is sold to you, he or she shall work for you for six years; in the seventh year you shall send him or her forth free. And when you send one forth free, *do not send him empty-handed.* Provide for him liberally from your flock, your threshing floor, and your winepress, giving him a share in the things with which the Lord your God has blessed you" (Deut. 15:12–14).[7] There is a profound connection between the narrative and the law, and not only through the phrase "send away empty-handed." Laban, like the slave owner, enjoys God's blessing ("The Lord has blessed you wherever I have been"), and Jacob flees from Laban's house after six years of work. Jacob eventually leaves with a large "flock," just as the slave owner is instructed to provide his freed slave with animals from the "flock." However, without Jacob's acumen and God's providence, Laban would have surely sent him away "empty-handed" instead of with a large fortune.

This suggests that the narrative favors Jacob's decision: his extra years in Haran depict his transition from Laban's servant to a free man with legal and financial independence, one who is entitled to leave his father-in-law's house freely, with his own fortune in tow.

We will yet return to this topic in our analysis of Jacob's conversation with Rachel and Leah (ch. 31), but with this background in mind, I wish to explore how Jacob's flock actually increases so dramatically.

How Does Jacob Become Rich? (The Relationship Between Chapter 30 and Chapter 31)

As I have already hinted above, there are two parallel theories about how Jacob makes his fortune and how he deals with Laban. In

7. Cassuto, *Genesis and Its Structure*, 203–04.

chapter 30 (vv. 25–43), Jacob is depicted as a shrewd shepherd with a secret method of breeding spotted sheep. By contrast, in chapter 31 (vv. 1–16), Jacob tells his wives a completely different tale: it is God who guides his hand, and each time Laban changes the terms of their agreement, the ewes miraculously give birth to whatever pattern Jacob has been promised. What is the relationship between the two descriptions?

There are three main approaches proposed in research;[8] I will describe them all briefly before proposing a theory of my own.

1. **A chronological division:** The first approach, the most prevalent among medieval exegetes, draws a distinction between Jacob's initial tactic and what happens next. For the first year of their agreement, Jacob uses a shepherd's trick to make the flock bear speckled young (the speckled young will become his, according to his agreement with Laban). The second account in chapter 31 describes what happened after the first year – that is, the reader hears about it for the first time from Jacob's perspective, together with Rachel and Leah. It emerges that Laban keeps changing their agreement, but God appears to Jacob in a dream and reassures him that no matter what, God will watch over Jacob and increase his wealth.
2. **The second story explains the first:** Various theories explain that Jacob's dream in chapter 31 fills in the narrative gaps in chapter 30. Ralbag, for example, writes about the dream Jacob tells his wives: "I believe that God revealed this secret in the prophecy – that is, that he should use the sticks as he did, and use them to reach this result, so that the 'rams that mount the flock' will sire young that are streaked, speckled, or spotted" (on Gen. 31:11–12). As mentioned, there are various versions of this approach, and I will soon elaborate on Yehuda Felix's theory that the dream

8. It is interesting to note that scholars who usually argue that two similar passages are from two separate traditions or sources agree that in this case, the textual evidence does not support two different sources, and they believe that they form a single sequence (see, for example, Gunkel, *Genesis*, 331–32; for another position, see Von Rad, *Genesis*, 307; Brenner, "Genesis 30").

hints to understanding of genetic inheritance, which Jacob uses for selective breeding. Cassuto's explanation is more general: according to the revelation in the second chapter, Jacob knew that whatever agreement he would make with Laban, God would bring him success.[9] According to this approach, the two narratives should be read as two parallel perspectives of the same period: one as the plot told by the narrator, and the other Jacob's own experience of the events.[10]

3. **Jacob invents the revelation to convince his wives:** Given that this dream is only mentioned by Jacob but not by the narrator, some posit that Jacob in fact invents this revelation in order to convince his wives to leave. The prevalent opinion is that this revelation indeed took place, but for various reasons the reader only hears about it from Jacob himself. Gad Dishi, however, argues that it is actually invented by Jacob in order to persuade his wives to leave Haran (I will address this further in my discussion of the next chapter, below).[11]

I wish to transfer this question from the realistic-historical playing field to the literary playing field. Even if the two explanations for Jacob's wealth are essentially one, it is no coincidence that the reader first learns that Jacob grows rich thanks to his "stick trick," and only then hears that God was helping him all along. The sequence in which information is given, especially in such cases, should be perceived as an intentional literary tactic. In this way, Jacob is characterized as a person who can provide for himself, achieve financial independence, and thus escape the devious clutches of his father-in-law. If the reader would first hear that God tells Jacob what kind of agreement to form with Laban, this would negate Jacob's own agency and his resourceful means of making his fortune. It is no coincidence that the Israelites, who only leave Egypt when Pharaoh

9. Cassuto believes that the revelation is not mentioned in the first half in order to allow criticism against Jacob for deceiving Laban; I will reject this reading below (Cassuto, *Genesis and Its Structure*, 202).
10. I will return to this in my discussion of chapter 31.
11. Dishi, *Jacob*, 109–15.

forces them out of his land, and who receive all their worldly possessions from the Egyptian spoil, must undergo a long process in the wilderness in order to become a free, independent nation. Jacob, on the other hand, does not need any such process because he engineers his own fortune; he is no longer Laban's servant and dependent; Albert Camus would perceive him as a rebel.

THE FINE PRINT

> Laban asked, "What shall I give you?"
> Jacob replied, "Do not give me anything. If you do this one thing for me, I will continue to shepherd
> and guard your flocks.
> Let me go through all your flocks today and remove every speckled or spotted sheep, every dark-colored lamb, and every spotted or speckled goat. They shall be my hire.
> Let my honesty testify for me in the future, whenever you come to check the wages you have paid me. Any goat
> not speckled or spotted or any lamb not dark colored in my possession shall be considered stolen." (30:31–33)

The prevalent reading is that Jacob tells Laban to remove all the speckled, spotted, and dark-colored animals from his flock, and from then on, all the new dark-colored young will become Jacob's, and any light-colored young will become Laban's. This proposal delights Laban, of course – as a seasoned shepherd, he knows that it is much more common for a light-colored animal to bear light-colored young, and if he has the chance to remove all the dark animals first, then the chances of dark young from a light flock are even more remote.

Why does Jacob propose such a bizarre agreement? Some claim that he intends to use his "trick" from the outset, so while Laban eagerly agrees to such terms, laughing at his fool of a son-in-law, Jacob is inwardly rubbing his hands with glee at his imminent scheme.[12]

12. This is the prevalent approach among both medieval and modern scholars. See, for example, Wenham, *Genesis II*, 255–56.

Though this reading is possible, it is strange indeed. The devious Laban would certainly be suspicious when Jacob seems to be setting himself up for failure; moreover, Jacob cannot be certain that his "stick trick" will succeed, and it is unlikely that he would gamble his future on such a stunt. I also remain unconvinced that Jacob should be portrayed as someone who intentionally sets up Laban for failure. Rather, I believe, the story unfolds completely differently.

As mentioned, the exegetical consensus is that the spotted and dark animals are removed from Laban's herd in order to prevent the birth of such young later on – this will presumably increase Laban's share and keep Jacob's to a minimum. Yet a careful but straightforward reading of the verse reveals a different understanding: "Let me go through all your flocks today and remove every speckled or spotted sheep, every dark-colored lamb, and every spotted or speckled goat. They shall be my hire" (30:32). Jacob asks to divide up the flock right then and there to prevent any disagreements between him and his father-in-law: he will take the dark animals and Laban will receive the light-colored animals, so that the division will be self-evident: "Let my honesty testify for me in the future, whenever you come to check the wages you have paid me. Any goat not speckled or spotted or any lamb not dark-colored in my possession shall be considered stolen" (30:33).

Jacob is not referring only to the flock's future young; he asks for the dark animals that are currently in Laban's flock. The scholars who propose this reading argue that even though this is the most straightforward reading of the text, it is incongruous with the rest of the story, where it seems that Jacob must resort to unusual tactics to breed "streaked, speckled, and spotted young."[13] I believe, however, that the narrative itself explains this inconsistency.

---

13. For a striking example of such an analysis, see Gunkel, *Genesis*, 327–28. He claims that this is a fusion of two sources, and that the narrative that presents Jacob's deal with Laban (E) that he will receive all the speckled sheep is much shorter:

> (26) "Give me my wives and my children for whom I have worked for you, and let me go. You know very well how much work I have done for you." (28) He said, "Name your hire and I will pay it." (32) "Let me go through all your flocks today and remove every speckled or spotted sheep, every dark-colored lamb, and every spotted or speckled goat. They shall be my hire. (33) Let my

After their agreement, but before Jacob begins his curious tactics, Laban himself removes the animals that Jacob requests as his hire: "That day Laban removed the streaked or spotted goats, all the speckled or spotted female goats – every one that had a trace of white – and every dark-colored lamb. These he placed in the care of his sons" (30:35). This action should not be dismissed – a careful comparison between their agreement and what Laban actually does reveals a small but significant disparity:

Jacob's Proposal (v. 32)	**Laban's Action (v. 35)**
Let me go through all your flocks today and remove every speckled or spotted *sheep,*	That day Laban removed the streaked or spotted *male goats,*
every dark-colored lamb,	all the speckled or spotted female goats – every one that had a trace of white –
and every spotted or speckled goat.	and every dark-colored lamb.

While Jacob and Laban agree to remove every spotted lamb and kid, Laban also makes sure to remove the mature billy goats (*hateyashim*) – as Rashi emphasizes: "the male goats."[14] It seems that Laban himself removes all the relevant animals from the flock, despite their agreement that Jacob will do this (as he suggests: "Let *me* go through all your flocks today"). Laban removes these spotted male goats together with the rest of the animals for Jacob, and "placed them in the care of his sons," who tend Jacob's flock, while Laban's flock remains in Jacob's care. At first glance, perhaps it seems petty to focus on the age of the animals Laban removes from the flock, but this subtle discrepancy poses a serious

honesty testify for me in the future, whenever you come to check the wages you have paid me. Any goat not speckled or spotted or any lamb not dark colored in my possession shall be considered stolen." (34) Laban said, "Agreed. Let it be as you have said."

14. Based on Jacob's gift to Esau, it is clear that *ez* is the female goat and the *tayish* is the male. The accepted terms for various kinds of flock animals (see, for example, "*tzon*" in the *Encyclopedia Biblica*):

problem to Jacob – if all the mature males are gone, there are no spotted or colored males to sire spotted young!

Though this direction has not been developed in research, some exegetes have proposed similar theories. Ramban writes: "The reason that the text relates 'On that day, he removed the male goats' is because Jacob merely said, 'Remove the speckled and spotted from the goats,' but Laban was concerned about the male sires, so he removed both male and females" (Gen. 30:35). Sforno writes similarly: "On that day, he removed the male goats – after he said, 'Let it be as you have said,' *he changed his mind* and on that day, removed both young and mature animals" (on Gen. 30:35).

It thus emerges that once again, Laban breaks their agreement, and now Jacob must deal with an unforeseen problem: there are no more spotted male goats in the flock who will pass this characteristic on – from now on, Laban's flock will produce only white young.

WHITE STRIPS

Once Laban removes the colored animals from the flock, it is unlikely that the white animals will produce any colored young. Jacob attempts to compensate by peeling patches off of branches and placing the branches by the flocks' watering troughs. How does this "trick" work? Scholars have proposed several theories:

1. The most prevalent explanation is that Jacob believes that this will affect the color of the flock's young, and even if we now know that this is scientifically ineffective, it is no different from his wives' belief in the healing properties of mandrakes in the previous chapter. People may harbor such beliefs, but the text teaches us that ultimately, it is only God who has the power to

	Sheep:	**Goats:**
Newborn	*taleh* (lamb)	*gedi* (kid)
Young	*seh* (lamb)	*se'irat izzim/sa'ir* (kid)
Mature Male	*ayil* (ram)	*tayish* (billy)
Mature Female	*reḥela/raḥel* (ewe)	*ez* (nanny)

See further in Lincoln, "Sheep and Goats."

heal infertility (30:22) or to protect His believers against their enemies (31:12).[15]

2. Yehuda Felix claims that Jacob knows that his actions will have no bearing on the outcome of the flock, but he does not wish to reveal the genetic secrets that God teaches him in his dream, so he uses the same useless tricks as the other shepherds in order to hide his knowledge.
3. Dov Eshbal proposed over fifty years ago that Jacob does not place the sticks in the water troughs for their appearance, but for their chemical properties: these shoots contain substances that will cause the ewes to go into heat earlier than Laban anticipates.[16]

The problem with the first two approaches is that the text does not support them: rather, according to the narrative, this action actually does cause the flock to produce speckled young. Felix's theory is even more problematic: there is no proof at all that Jacob is acting for the sake of appearance. Eshbal's suggestion is creative, but again, it is not supported by the text; the verb *vayatzeg*, "He *set* the peeled shoots in all the water troughs so that they would be in front of the flocks when they came to drink" (30:38), implies that the main purpose of these shoots is for the flocks to *see* them.

Eshbal is correct, however, that Jacob uses the shoots to affect the flock's mating preferences. The verse concludes with the description "They would mate when they came to drink, and since they mated by the shoots, they bore streaked, speckled, and spotted young" (v. 39). One possible reading is that these shoots influenced the flock's mating preferences, swaying them toward spotted or speckled mates.[17] As mentioned, there are barely any spotted animals in Laban's herd, and he must ensure that the ewes will favor the few spotted rams as mates; according to the text, these speckled shoots draw the females to the few speckled males. Proof of this reading lies in the next part of the narrative, when Jacob uses these "streaked, speckled, and spotted young" to further affect

15. See especially in Hamilton, *Genesis II*, 284.
16. Eshbal, "*Akkudim, Nekuddim U'Veruddim*," 49.
17. As suggested by my father and teacher.

the flocks' mating preferences: "Jacob set apart the young of the flock, and he made the others belonging to Laban face the streaked and dark-colored animals" (30:40).

Alongside this theory, I wish to tentatively propose a further reading. How can it be that white sheep produce spotted sheep, when both mother and father are white? Jacob later describes the following dream to his wives: "Once, during the breeding season, I had a dream: I saw that the rams mounting the flock were streaked, speckled, or spotted" (31:10). Rashi explains that angels take spotted sheep from Laban's sons' flock, bring them to Jacob's flock by night, and return them before morning. Thanks to modern genetics, however, we are able to explain this phenomenon without having to resort to theories of supernatural nocturnal sheep heists.

Thanks to the experiments of Gregor Mendel, a nineteenth-century Augustinian monk and scientist, we now know that certain genetic characteristics are dominant or recessive. Each gene contains two alleles for a certain trait, and the dominant allele dictates the organism's phenotype (appearance), even though the recessive trait also forms part of that organism's genotype (genetic material that is passed on to offspring). For example, it is not uncommon for dark-eyed parents to have children with light eyes: dark eyes are a dominant trait, but if both parents carry a recessive gene for light eyes, there is a 1:4 chance that their child will be born with light eyes. In the case of sheep, dark-colored wool is a recessive trait, while light coats are dominant (and therefore more common – were this not the case, the conniving Laban would never have agreed to Jacob's proposal). Many white sheep, however, carry the gene for dark or patterned coats (these are said to be heterozygous for the relevant gene), but these sheep will only produce colored young if the young inherit a recessive gene from both parents.

The probability of two heterozygous parents producing light or dark young is classically expressed in the following table, wherein the dominant gene (which results in a white coat) is marked with the letter A, and the recessive gene (for a colored coat) is represented by the letter a:

	A	a
A	AA (white)	Aa (white)
a	Aa (white)	aa (colored)

Approximately 25 percent of the couple's offspring will be homozygous for the dominant gene; half will be heterozygous – that is, carriers of the recessive gene, but dominant in phenotype; and 25 percent will be heterozygous for the recessive gene, and therefore recessive in phenotype – in the case of sheep, with a speckled, spotted, or striped coat. As biologists and geneticists emphasize in their studies, it is not the case that precisely 25 percent of a couple's offspring will be speckled – rather, this is an estimation; for every birth, there is a 25 percent chance that a speckled lamb will be born.

It may well be that this is where Jacob's "trick" comes into play. Felix's theory that an angel reveals the secret of Mendelian inheritance to Jacob is not convincing; it is more likely that Jacob, a veteran shepherd, realizes that he has some influence over the color of his flock, even if he is unable to articulate precisely how this influence works.

After all, this theory eludes even modern geneticists: how are recessive genes selected? Are these 25 percent, these individuals with recessive phenotypes, born merely by chance? Perhaps this outcome is influenced by the environment? Perhaps there is significance to awareness, thought, and intention? Recent studies have shown that certain environmental factors – primarily nutrition – may influence phenotype. Of particular interest is Dan Hurley's study (based on an earlier study by Randy Jirtle of Duke University) that shows that maternal nutrition during pregnancy has bearing on phenotype: pregnant mice who ate diets rich in certain methyl groups produced young of a certain fur color in numbers that deviated significantly from the classic Mendelian 3:1 ratio.[18]

The mysteries of the genome have hardly been exhausted, and a recent groundbreaking study claims that phenotype may even be subject to change after birth, influenced by a person's experiences throughout life.[19] But intuition and common sense have long preceded science (albeit inconsistently), and it is not absurd to posit that Jacob, an experienced

---

18. Hurley, "Trait vs. Fate."
19. It suffices to mention the title of Sharon Moalem's book (co-written with Matthew LaPlante) to understand that these questions are a hot topic in current research: *Inheritance: How Our Genes Change Our Lives – And Our Lives Change Our Genes* (Grand Central Publishing, 2014).

shepherd, knows how to manipulate certain aspects of the mating process and thus affect phenotypic distribution. In other words, though the peeled shoots cannot change the flock's genetic material, it could be that Jacob's action has a bearing on the element of randomness that otherwise governs each birth – on which alleles pair up, and on which genetic traits manifest in the phenotype.

If so, then unlike Felix's theory, chapter 30 is not the result of divine intervention. On the contrary, the narrative describes Jacob's ingenuity and creative efforts based on his experience and intuition. For this very reason we must clarify the relationship between chapter 30 and Jacob's description to his wives that God intervenes on his behalf, and that the angel reveals that his flock will bear speckled young. I will address this in my analysis of Jacob's discussion with his wives below.

STRONG AND WEAK?

Jacob takes care to set up the peeled shoots by the troughs when certain animals are mating: "Whenever *hamekusharot* animals were mating, Jacob would place the shoots in the troughs facing them so that they mated facing the shoots. But *uvhaatif* animals he did not put there, so *haatufim* went to Laban and *hakkeshurim* to Jacob" (30:41–42).

According to the prevalent reading, the word "*hamekusharot*" means "stronger, faster" – that is, Jacob strategically places the peeled shoots by the troughs when the stronger animals are mating, so the best of the young will come out speckled and belong to him. Jacob is not interested in receiving the weaker – "*atufim*" (compare Is. 57:16; Lam. 2:11–19; Jonah 2:8; and many verses in Psalms) – members of the flock, so he does not set up the shoots when they are mating. To Laban's chagrin, not only is Jacob's share growing much faster than Laban anticipated, but his flock is far stronger than Laban's.

Yet this reading poses a linguistic challenge. One meaning of the word "*atufim*" is indeed "weaker," but how can we justify reading the word "*mekusharot*" as "stronger" or "faster" when the root K-SH-R has nothing to do with this meaning?[20] Athalya Brenner offers an alternative

20. On the possible connections between these words, see Hamilton, *Genesis II*, 281, n. 24 (the strongest of the flock are as if "tied together" as a strong group), or, alternately,

explanation of these words,[21] which in turn reveals that Jacob increases his flock using a different strategy.

After Jacob manages to breed a substantial group of speckled animals, he effectively creates two separate groups within Laban's flock: "Jacob set apart the young of the flock, and he made the others belonging to Laban face the streaked and dark-colored animals. Thus he bred separate flocks for himself, and he did not let them breed with Laban's flocks" (30:40). Now, when his own colored animals only breed amongst themselves, they bear only colored young (a recessive phenotype, as mentioned, is necessarily homozygous, and thus only produces young with the relevant recessive trait). Laban's white animals bear mostly white young, with the occasional colored exception.

The next verse then describes how Jacob deals with these two flocks. The word "*mekushar*" is semantically linked to the word "*akuddim*" – "tied" is obviously related to "binding," as in *akedat Yitzḥak*. Brenner proposes that the colored sheep have stripes on their legs that resemble ropes, as if they are bound, and that the word *keshurim* is in fact a synonym for *akuddim* – that is, "streaked" or "striped." This is a more linguistically sound interpretation of the word: that the first flock Jacob tends are his own streaked, speckled, and spotted animals; indeed, in the next chapter, he tells his wives: "Once, during the breeding season, I had a dream: I saw that the rams mounting the flock were streaked (*akuddim*), speckled, or spotted" (31:10). The second flock are Laban's: "*atufim*" can be read in the sense of "enveloped" or "entirely covered" – these animals are enveloped in coats of pure white (compare: "The meadows are clothed with sheep / the valleys are *covered* [*yaatfu*] in grain"– Ps. 65:14).[22] Initially, Jacob sets up the peeled shoots while all the animals are drinking; now, after he has divided up the flock according to the color of their wool, he only places the shoots by his own flock, and does not take the trouble to do this while Laban's white flock are drinking.

Conrad, "*kashar*," 197 (based on an Arabic verb and not the Hebrew root K-SH-R).

21. Brenner, "Genesis 30."

22. See also Ps. 73:6; Job 23:9. On the meaning of A-T-F as "covering," as the modern Hebrew meaning, see Alden, "A-T-F."

What is the purpose of this differentiation? The answer is obvious for those who believe that these shoots stimulate the sheep to mate. Jacob is interested in cultivating his own flock, and has no reason to encourage the white animals to reproduce more rapidly than usual. But even according to my aforementioned theory – that Jacob believes this action has a certain influence over the color of the flock's young – Jacob's actions are logical. Jacob cannot be certain that his colored flock will continue to produce only colored young; no angel has whispered the principles of Mendelian inheritance in his ear. His years of experience have shown him that a flock of colored ewes bear colored lambs, but to be sure, he continues doing his part. With an ever-growing flock of his own, he concentrates his efforts on his own colored sheep; it is not worth his time to deal with Laban's flock, which only occasionally produces a colored lamb or kid.

This scene's conclusion is: "Thus the man's wealth swelled into a fortune. He had large flocks, female and male servants, camels and donkeys" (30:43). As I have already noted, the tone of this verse is positive, encouraging: the unusual verb "*vayifrotz*" echoes God's promise to Jacob when he departs for Haran, and even recalls Abraham's blessing. This scene, then, ends on this triumphant note, but the atmosphere is about to change.

Jacob Leaves Laban's House (Gen. 31)

Jacob's wealth grows during his extra years in Laban's house, and he becomes an independent, autonomous individual. Chapter 31 begins with the tension that Jacob's new status stirs in Laban's household; tension that moves him to leave Laban's house and return to his homeland. The unit begins with a description of Laban's sons' growing resentment at Jacob (31:1) and concludes with another mention of "Laban's sons": "Laban rose early the next morning. He kissed his sons and daughters goodbye and blessed them. Laban then left to return home" (32:1). This framework already hints to the process that unfolds over the course of this chapter, which opens with tension between Laban's sons and Jacob's family, while at the unit's end, the "sons and daughters" Laban kisses are in fact Jacob's family.[1]

The narrative is divided into four main acts: the decision to leave Haran (vv. 1–16); the family's escape and the theft of the teraphim (vv. 17–21); Laban's pursuit of the family and their argument (vv. 22–44); and the peace treaty between the clans (vv. 45–55). The four acts of this long unit are deeply interconnected, and throughout my analysis, I will flit back and forth between them.

1. Compare to Mathews, *Genesis II*, 507.

THE DECISION TO LEAVE HARAN

Two forces compel Jacob to leave Haran. Firstly, Laban's family's attitude toward him changes: "Jacob heard that Laban's sons were saying, 'Jacob has taken everything our father owned; of what belonged to our father, he has made all these riches.' And Jacob saw that Laban's manner toward him was not what it had been" (31:1–2). Secondly, God appears to him and informs him that it is time for Jacob to come home: "The Lord said to Jacob, 'Go back to the land of your fathers where you were born; I will be with you'" (v. 3).

Jacob mentions both these aspects to his wives:

> So Jacob sent word to Rachel and Leah to come out to the field where his flock was. He said to them, "I see that your father's manner toward me is not what it used to be. But the God of my father has been with me…
> And in the dream an angel of God said to me…'I am the God of Bethel, where you anointed a pillar and made a vow to Me. Now – leave this land at once and return to the land where you were born.'" (31:4–13)

This dichotomy is central to the narrative design and objective, as I will discuss below. For now, I wish to draw attention to Laban's changed attitude toward Jacob, which is described from two perspectives: Laban's sons, and Laban himself:

> Jacob heard that *Laban's sons were saying*, "Jacob has taken everything our father owned; of what belonged to our father, he has made all these riches."
> And Jacob saw that *Laban's manner* toward him was not what it had been. (31:1–2)

Laban's sons are only mentioned twice in the entire story – the first mention is after Jacob has been in Haran for fourteen years and Laban places Jacob's share of his flock in their care, and the second instance is here. Why is their appearance significant? When Jacob tells his wives of their family's resentment toward him, he mentions their father's attitude, but not their brothers', even though their animosity is mentioned in the narrative.

Yehuda Kiel suggests that Jacob does not tell his wives of their brothers' resentment because he wishes to spare their feelings and prevent "strife among brothers" (Prov. 6:19).[2] This is a sensitive but unlikely reading; there is no reason to assume that the women feel closer to their brothers than to their father.

I believe that this description reflects the rising tension in Laban's household. Jacob firsts hears how his brothers-in-law are muttering about him behind his back, but Laban initially manages to hide his resentment of his son-in-law's growing wealth. Eventually, however, Laban too breaks down, which of course poses a much greater threat to Jacob's position in Laban's household: the brothers are not necessarily any higher within the family hierarchy than Jacob, who is married to two of Laban's daughters, but as the head of the household, Jacob's standing with Laban is crucial. When Jacob tells his wives of their father's resentment, it effectively includes that of the entire clan. Yet the narrator's mention of Laban's sons shows that this is a gradual process. Like most cases of Jews settling in foreign lands throughout history, society initially welcomed the Jews and benefited from the prosperity they brought, but with time, their (mostly financial) success led to resentment, envy, and hatred. The growing hostility of an environment that is no longer willing to tolerate the foreigner is the main trigger for Jacob's return home.

Jacob thus tells his wives of their father's growing animosity, all the while drawing a contrast between Laban, who is not treating him as he should, and God, who protects him (vv. 5–9):

> I see that your father's manner toward me is not what it used to be / But the God of my father has been with *me* (*imadi*).
> You well know how I have worked for your father with all my strength. Your father cheated me, changing my wages ten times / but God has not let him harm *me* (*imadi*).
> If he said, "The speckled animals shall be your hire," then all the flock would give birth to speckled young. If he said, "The streaked

2. Kiel, *Genesis II*, 366 (in the name of R. Isaac Samuel Reggio).

> animals shall be your hire," then all the flock would give birth to streaked young. / God has taken your father's livestock and given it to me.

The subtle refrain of "*imadi*" that describes God's help serves two purposes. Firstly, "*imadi*" creates a contrast between Laban's attitude toward Jacob – he is no longer "with him (*vehineh einenu imo*)" (31:2) as before, while God *is* "with him." Secondly, this repetition echoes the vow Jacob makes on the eve of his departure to Haran: "If God will be *with me* (*imadi*), protecting me on this journey I am taking, giving me bread to eat and clothes to wear…" (28:20). Jacob is expressing that God has kept His part of their agreement: He does not allow Laban to mistreat him, and He has even "taken [Laban's] livestock and given it to" him.[3] Jacob's flock, in particular, represents the fulfillment of his need for "food to eat and clothes to wear" – the flock provides Jacob and his family with both food and clothing.

This, of course, evokes the final part of Jacob's vow: "If I return in peace to my father's house" (28:21). The time has come for Jacob to bring his family back to his father's house, trusting that God will accompany them and prevent Laban from harming them in any way.

After this introduction, Jacob describes his dream, which has two main parts: an explanation that his wealth is a gift from God, and God's request that Jacob return to Canaan. The latter, of course, is Jacob's most important conclusion:

> Once, during the breeding season, I had a dream: I saw that the rams mounting the flock were streaked, speckled, or spotted. And in the dream an angel of God said to me, "Jacob." I replied, "Here I am." He said, "Raise your eyes and look around at all the rams mounting the flock – they are streaked, speckled, or spotted, for I have seen all that Laban is doing to you. I am the God of Bethel, where you anointed a pillar and made a vow to Me. Now – leave this land at once and return to the land where you were born." (31:10–13)

3. See further: Assis, *Identity in Conflict*, 74–76.

What is the relationship between the two parts of the dream – between the secret of the flocks and the order to return to Canaan? Ramban suggests that these are two separate dreams that take place on two different nights: one night, Jacob dreams that his flock will bear speckled young, and recently, he has dreamt that God orders him to return home.[4] This is not impossible, but either way, Jacob juxtaposes the two parts, which creates a certain poetic effect: it is their juxtaposition that clarifies that Jacob's wealth is a blessing from God, and for this very reason, he must fulfill God's request to leave Haran and return to Canaan. Just as the first part of the dream is realized, Jacob must realize the second part of the dream.

The semantics that color the first part of the dream are surprising. At first glance, it seems to be a symbolic dream, followed by an interpretation (similar to the vision of the ladder – after Jacob sees a vision, he also hears a verbal revelation). Yet the elevated tone of the passage seems at odds with its content. The angel calls Jacob by name and he answers with a classic "Here I am (*hineni*)" like the story of Isaac's binding, or Moses' first revelation at the burning bush. The angel's opening words, "Raise your eyes and look around," also recall God's exalted promise to Abraham that he will inherit the earth. But instead of gazing out at the rolling hills of the Promised Land, Jacob is told to look upon the humblest of sights – upon the rams mounting the ewes, and the color of their coats! This invites a closer comparison between God's revelation to Abraham at Bethel and the night vision Jacob describes to his wives:

4. Ramban writes:

   The statement "Lift up now your eyes, and see, all the he-goats" was made to him when he served Laban for his flock, during mating time in one of the first years, and the statement "I am the God of Bethel" was made to him after that, at the time of the journey, for after He said to him, "Leave this land at once," he no longer remained in Haran to further tend Laban's flocks so that the he-goats would mount the flocks and the flocks would give birth to speckled and spotted. But on the morrow of the dream, he sent for Rachel and Leah and told them his dream, and they left Haran. (on 33:13) See also Kiel, *Genesis II*, 369.

Abraham in Bethel (Gen. 13:14–17)	**Jacob in Haran (31:11–13)**
After Lot had separated from him, the Lord said to Abraham, "*Raise your eyes and look around* from where you are to the north, south, east, and west. *All the land you see I will give to you* and your descendants forever.	"And in the dream an angel of God said to me, 'Jacob.' I replied, 'Here I am.' He said, '*Raise your eyes and look around* at all the rams mounting the flock – they are streaked, speckled, or spotted, *for I have seen all that Laban is doing to you.*
[God will increase your descendants:] I will make your descendants like the dust of the earth.	[God will increase your flock!]
Get up and walk (***kum** hit'halekh **baaretz***) through the length and breadth of *the land*, for to you shall I give it."	I am the God of Bethel, where you anointed a pillar and made a vow to Me. Now – *leave this land at once* (***kum** tzei min **haaretz***) and return to the land where you were born.'"

The connection between the two revelations is fascinating. Though their contexts are completely different, the two share similar language, and even certain similarities in plot. The phrase "Raise your eyes and look around" appears only twice in the Torah – in these two revelations, directing the forefather's attention to a particular sight. Abraham will inherit the entire land, and God tells him to fix his gaze upon it; God sees what Laban is doing to Jacob, and thus directs his attention to the flock he will soon inherit. Even the conclusion is similar: both are directed to rise and walk about the land.

These linguistic similarities are further reinforced by the plot of each scene. Firstly, Abraham's revelation takes place in Bethel, and the angel speaking to Jacob introduces itself as "the God of Bethel, where you anointed a pillar and made a vow to Me" (31:13). Moreover, both revelations are associated with the forefather's parting with a family member because their flock has grown too large, causing tension between them: God appears to Abraham after he parts ways with Lot because their flocks have grown so large that "the land could not support them living together" (13:6), and Jacob must move on when Laban begins to resent the size of his son-in-law's flock.

What purpose does this comparison serve? Once again, there are two possible directions. Those who believe that Jacob is criticized for remaining in Haran will argue that this parallel underscores the gap between Jacob and his grandfather: Abraham lifts up his eyes and gazes upon the Promised Land, while Jacob has eyes only for his sheep. In Abraham's story, it is his covetous nephew who chooses the plain of the Jordan for its water and pastureland, while here it is Jacob himself who dreams of wealth through his growing flock.

But here, too, I am drawn to the alternative: the comparison does not create a contrast between grandfather and grandson, but rather a parallel. Jacob, like Abraham, raises his eyes and sees the promise of God's blessing. After all, God justifies Jacob's wealth from a moral perspective: "I have seen all that Laban is doing to you" (see the comparison between Jacob's departure from Haran and the Exodus from Egypt, below). The parallel between the revelations justifies the ostensible disparity between the high register of Jacob's dream and its content: it is not merely a promise of material wealth, but a reassurance of God's providence: God sees Laban's treatment of Jacob, and He will protect him and care for him wherever he goes.

In other words, Jacob's wealth is an expression of God's blessing and protection that fulfills the conditions of Jacob's vow in Bethel. Rather than inviting criticism against Jacob for his decisions and dreams, the comparison with God's revelation to Abraham hints that God's protection of Jacob is an extension of the covenant. God's protection is not limited to Canaan's borders; rather, God will protect His devoted ones wherever they are and save them from whoever is oppressing them.

Thus Jacob describes his wealth as an expression of God's grace, but not in vague, general terms: his dream specifies precisely how Jacob accumulates his wealth. Jacob knows what sheep to ask Laban for because God reveals what kind of young the flock will bear. This paints a very different picture from the one presented in the previous scene and invites an obvious question: What is the relationship between the two descriptions? According to chapter 30, Jacob manages to increase his wealth with wit and grit, painstakingly monitoring the flock's selective breeding until, eventually, "the man's wealth swelled into a fortune; he had large flocks" (30:43). By contrast, chapter 31 describes how it is God who ensures that the flock will bear whatever favors Jacob's terms with Laban: "God has taken your father's livestock and given it to me" (31:9).

How, then, does Jacob become rich? Is it through his own efforts, or the result of God's providence? As I have already noted, there are several different approaches to the relationship between the chapters, but there is first need to answer a preliminary question: Do the dreams Jacob describes to his wives actually take place? After all, the text itself does not mention these dreams, and we only learn of them when Jacob tells of them. Could it be that Jacob invents them in order to persuade his wives to leave Haran? As mentioned, some argue that this is the case;[5] Dishi adds that not only does Jacob fabricate these dreams, but his entire speech is full of hyperbole and fabrication calculated to persuade them to come back with him to Canaan. For example, Dishi perceives the claim that "your father cheated me, changing my wages ten times" (31:7) as a gross exaggeration; there is no mention of any changes to their initial agreement in the text itself. Laban obviously deceives Jacob in their first agreement when he gives him Leah in Rachel's place, and Jacob takes advantage of this precedence to incriminate Laban to his daughters. To this end, Dishi argues, it is obvious why Jacob does not mention his maneuvers with the peeled sticks; Jacob wants to emphasize God's hand in his wealth, and downplay any human intervention.[6]

According to this reading, Jacob's attempt to persuade his wives to leave their father's house recalls a parallel scene one generation earlier: when Abraham's servant attempts to persuade Rebecca's family to send their daughter with him to Canaan. There, too, the servant manipulates certain details in order to emphasize God's hand and God's will in the matter.[7] Rebecca's family is indeed convinced: "This is surely from the Lord: there is nothing for us to say to you, bad or good. Here is Rebecca in front of you. Take her; go. Let her be the wife of your master's son, as the Lord has spoken" (24:50–51).[8] The servant's story has made the right

5. Salman and Wénin, "Rhétorique."
6. Dishi, *Jacob,* 109–14.
7. See further in Eldar, "The Servant and Rebecca"; Grossman, *Abraham,* 376–384.
8. Remember the phrase "There is nothing for us to say to you, bad or good" – we will make use of it later on.

impression, and the family is convinced that events have indeed unfolded according to God's will. Laban's daughters are similarly impressed by Jacob's story that it is God who has bestowed their father's wealth upon its rightful owner, their husband: "All the wealth that God has taken from our father belongs to us and our children. So do whatever God has told you" (31:16). Just as Abraham's servant's exaggeration convinces Rebecca's family, Jacob's story achieves similar success.

Needless to say, according to this reading, the relationship between chapters 30 and 31 is self-evident: only one of them actually takes place, while the second is merely rhetoric. Jacob makes his own fortune, unaided by angels or dreams, and soon after, he makes his own cover story as well.

This theory is not without allure; it explains why these dreams are never mentioned by the narrator, and why the reader only hears of them together with Jacob's wives. But it is riddled with problems. First and foremost, Jacob soon makes these accusations against Laban himself: "Twenty years I spent working in your household – fourteen for your two daughters and six for your flock – *and ten times you changed my wages*" (31:41). Jacob would not challenge Laban about something that did not take place.[9]

Moreover, we know that Jacob's words are framed with truth: "I see that your father's manner toward me is not what it used to be" (v. 5); "Now – leave this land at once and return to the land where you were born" (v. 13). While there are biblical characters who augment their lies with truth for the sake of persuasion – as Abraham's servant does, for example – Jacob's speech has a sense of authenticity. While Jacob's dreams are not mentioned by the narrator, their connection to Jacob's dream at Bethel and even God's revelation to Abraham lends them validation. All this, of course, is besides the fact that to claim that Jacob tells an outright lie to his wives – a lie about a divine revelation, no less! – is a radical assertion with drastic implications for Jacob's character.

Of course, this brings us back to the relationship between the two descriptions of how Jacob makes his fortune. As mentioned, some

9. Gad Dishi proposes that "ten times" in fact hints to a change of quantity, and to Laban's exchange of Rachel and Leah (Dishi, *Jacob*, 110–11).

read chapter 31 as a clarification of chapter 30 – that Jacob explains to his wives how God was helping him all along. This theory has several variations, such as Felix's bold claim that God reveals the secret of genetic selection to Jacob in his dream, which enables him to increase his flock; in a more cautious formulation, Hamilton explains that Jacob's creative attempts to manipulate the flock's color using peeled shoots are futile and it is God who helps him increase his flock.

Yet an unbiased reading of chapter 30 implies that Jacob becomes wealthy through his own actions. According to the narrative, the peeled shoots work; they cause the flock to produce speckled young. There is no hint in the text that Jacob goes through these motions for show (as Felix argues), or that the shoots have no effect (as Hamilton argues). The narrative premise is that Jacob's actions result in the birth of speckled young – as mentioned above, it seems that they have actual bearing on genetic distribution.

If so, then the conclusion must be that the narrative intentionally presents alternate explanations for Jacob's success – explanations that should be read as two parallel contributing factors.[10] According to chapter 30, it is Jacob's initiative, creativity, and diligence that allow him to best Laban even after he removes the speckled males. According to chapter 31, it God who helps him by causing the flock to bear whatever young favors Jacob's agreement with Laban: God sees how Laban's treachery and manipulation oppresses Jacob, and recompenses Jacob for his suffering. The only way to reconcile these two axes is to read them in parallel. I will soon show how the contradictions between the chapters is mitigated in the text, because the narrative's main objective is to present how Jacob grows wealthy from both perspectives. This model is found elsewhere in the Bible; one striking example is the story of how the nations spread out across the earth. Chapter 10 portrays this as a natural process as Noah's family increases generation by generation, while chapter 11 presents a different story: when all of humanity gathers together to build a tower, God scatters them and separates them with

10. Fokkelman comments that the identical length of the two descriptions (sixteen verses each) gives the impression that these are parallel descriptions of the same event (Fokkelman, *Genesis*, 159).

language in order to limit their power. This dichotomy also invites a wide range of theories about the relationship between the two chapters, and there, too, I favor a similar model: a description of natural events is intentionally presented together with a story about divine intervention in human history.[11]

Perhaps it is for the sake of this dichotomy that Jacob's dreams are only presented to the reader in his own words. In this way, the reader experiences God's intervention as the motivation for Jacob's actions; the natural inclination is to perceive Jacob's description to his wives as the reason behind his actions. This is further reinforced by the fact that throughout chapter 30, Jacob remains silent. In this way, the two sections complete each other: chapter 30 depicts his actions, while in chapter 31, he explains the motivation behind them.[12] This congruence would be less feasible if the dreams were presented by the narrator. In their present form, the reader is able to experience the two chapters as parallel descriptions: "During the breeding season" – that is, when Jacob is busy with his peeled shoots – God informs him that his plan will succeed: the human initiative is sealed with divine approval.

If so, then these two descriptions function as a two-faceted story of double causality. Why is it so crucial to present the reason for Jacob's wealth in two separate passages?

This doubleness is inherent to the relationship between human and God portrayed in the Jacob cycle. Each significant narrative junction is illuminated from both these perspectives: as the result of human action, and of divine will and intervention.[13] Jacob's departure from Haran is motivated by this fundamental duality. Both growing tension in Laban's house and divine command force Jacob to leave Haran, and

11. For further reading of the two accounts of the nations' dispersion, see Grossman, *Beginnings*, 287–88. For a similar analysis of the description of the conquest of Jericho and Ai, see Assis, *Joshua*, 123–59.

12. Anderson, *Jacob*, 144. Scott Noegel claims that Jacob's silence in chapter 30 is calculated to increase ambiguity and a sense of concealment (Noegel, "Deceptive," 16–17).

13. See further in Lipton, *Dreams*, 143–44; Samet, *Studies I*, vol. 1, 143–53; Breuer, *Chapters of Genesis*, vol. 2, 503–09. For various possibilities of how to read the two chapters, see also Anderson, *Jacob*, 142–54.

though their consequence is one and the same, the narrative maintains their distinct threads. The story of Jacob's wealth also follows this pattern: he makes his own fortune, but he makes it with God's help.[14]

Once again, the Jacob cycle lies in the intersection between the clear, straightforward revelation of the Abraham cycle and the hidden providence of the Joseph cycle. God appears in a revelation to Jacob by night, in a dream, but the reader only hears about this dream in Jacob's own words; Jacob achieves independence and wealth by the sweat of his own brow, but his hands are guided by God.

THE FAMILY'S ESCAPE FROM HARAN

This leads us to the family's flight from Haran and its narrative objective. Why does Jacob flee without informing Laban of his decision to return to Canaan? Could Laban have forced him to stay? It is worth recalling that at the end of the (second) seven years he spends working for Rachel, he does ask Laban for permission to return home: "After Rachel had given birth to Joseph, Jacob said to Laban, 'Release me to go home to my own land. Give me my wives and my children for whom I have worked for you, and let me go. You know very well how much work I have done for you'" (30:25–26). Laban convinces him to stay on with his flock, but presumably Jacob has the option of leaving. Why does he now choose to flee?

The first to ask this question is Laban himself. After he catches up with Jacob, he berates him: Laban said to Jacob, "What have you done? You have deceived me, and carried off my daughters like captives of the sword. Why did you leave secretly? Why did you deceive me by not telling me? I would have sent you off with celebration and song, with tambourines and harps. You did not even let me kiss my grandchildren and daughters goodbye. You have behaved foolishly" (31:26–28).

14. Johan Taschner's proposal is intriguing: there are three reports of how Jacob grows wealthy, from three perspectives (not just two): from Jacob's (30:37–42); then Jacob's report to his wives (31:5–13); and finally, the divine perspective, in his dream. He holds that the dream explains his actions, and makes God the true hero of these events (Taschner, *Verheissung und Erfüllung*, 111–13).

Jacob's reply reveals the fear that serves as his main motive for his escape: "I was afraid; I thought you would take your daughters away from me by force" (31:31). This is a most surprising answer. Why should a husband fear that his father-in-law will steal his daughters away from him? After all, Jacob has married them; he worked a full seven years for each one, and they are raising a large family together.

It emerges that despite Jacob's financial independence, Laban still perceives him as his indentured servant, rather than as his son-in-law. In fact, Laban's own words justify Jacob's concern: a moment before they form a covenant between them, Laban remarks to Jacob: "The daughters are my daughters. The children are my children. The flocks are my flocks. All that you see is mine" (31:43). Laban's possessiveness is a response to Jacob's complaint: "You have rummaged through all my possessions. What have you found that belongs to your house? Put it here in front of my kinsmen and yours and let them decide between the two of us!" (31:37). While Jacob claims that Laban is wrongfully accusing him, for he has found nothing of his own in Jacob's tents, Laban indignantly replies: I didn't find anything of mine? It is all mine! Your whole family is mine, and your whole flock is mine! You, Jacob, speak of "my possessions," but they are all truly mine, not yours!

Laban's mindset is also reflected in the covenant he eventually forms with Jacob. There, he warns Jacob: "If you mistreat my daughters or take other wives besides my daughters, even though no one else is present, remember that God is the witness between me and you" (31:50). Exegetes discuss the meaning of the word "mistreat." The Talmud in Tractate Yoma 37b links Laban's warning to marital rights (Ex. 21:10), and R. Saadia Gaon and Rashi favor this direction: Laban warns Jacob against withholding marital rights from his daughters. Ibn Ezra challenges this reading by arguing that even if Jacob acts thus, it is not a serious offense, or in any case not a sufficiently serious basis for a covenant, and he prefers a different interpretation: "The meaning is that he should not cause them any harm by forcing them to do anything they do not want to do" (on Gen. 31:50). This explanation is accepted by most *Rishonim*,[15] and is prevalent in modern research as well. Nonetheless,

15. See, for example, Radak and Bekhor Shor.

this reading is also strange. Jacob has been living with Laban for the past twenty years – does he really suspect that he will mistreat his daughters? Neglect his children? A more convincing proposal is made by Paradise: that Laban's warning should be read in dialogue with Exodus 21 (and with Akkadian marriage contracts); not in the specific context of marital rights, but as a general marriage contract. That is, Laban is incorporating accepted marriage terms into their agreement: "He shall not reduce her food, her clothing, or marital rights" (Ex. 21:10).[16]

If this is the case, then it seems that Laban is somewhat slow to grasp that his little girls are growing up and getting married – marriage agreements are generally made at the time of betrothal, not many years later, when the couple are already raising a large family together. Perhaps the fact that the son-in-law remained with his wives' family has made such an agreement unnecessary until this point, but the literary effect remains: Laban's insistence on the kind of contract that is usually made at the time of marriage implies that until now, he believed that he had authority over his daughters. Only after Jacob and his family escape does Laban relinquish his grasp and hand them over to their "new" husband.

This mindset reveals much about his perception of Jacob's status: as mentioned, Laban sees Jacob as a kind of servant, perhaps one whose status is similar to the Hebrew slave in Exodus: "If his master gave him a wife and she bore him sons or daughters, the woman and her children shall remain her master's, while he shall leave alone" (Ex. 21:4). If the Hebrew slave wishes to remain with his family, he must stay with his master: "But if the slave declares, 'I love my master, my wife, and my children; I do not want to go free,' then his master shall bring him before the judges. He shall take him to the door or to the doorpost and pierce his ear with an awl; after that he shall then remain his slave forever" (ibid. 5–6). It may well be that this is what Laban has in mind from the outset, when Jacob asks to leave after Joseph's birth. Jacob realizes that even now, Laban may attempt to prevent his departure with his family.[17]

16. Paradise, "What Did Laban Demand?"
17. Yehuda Kiel sees Laban's demand as a reflection of his self-perception as an omnipotent ruler, and he even compares him to the "sons of God" who desire all that

Jacob therefore decides to escape; if he asks Laban's permission, it is not unlikely that Laban will hinder him once again. Laban cannot stop Jacob from leaving, but he might prevent him from taking his wives and children with him.

This reading is supported by the extensive analogy between this chapter and the Exodus from Egypt; the central motifs of each plot illuminate the surprising similarity between them.[18]

	Jacob in Laban's House (Genesis)	**The Exodus from Egypt (Exodus)**
	Jacob is initially welcomed.	Jacob's family is initially welcomed.
Israel become slaves	Give me my wives and my children for whom I have worked for you, and let me go. You know very well how much work I have done for you (30:26).	The Egyptians imposed backbreaking labor on the Israelites... all the work they forced upon them was intended to break them (Ex. 1:14–15).
The family grows	Thus the man's wealth swelled into a fortune (30:43).	But the Israelites were fruitful and burgeoned; they multiplied and became exceptionally strong.... But the more they were oppressed, the more they increased and spread (1:7, 12).
The host resents their increasing flock/ population	And Jacob saw that Laban's manner toward him was not what it had been (31:2).	Come, let us deal wisely with them in case they increase (1:10).

they see: "Laban does not budge from his fundamental mindset of an ancient ruler, that 'all is mine'" (Kiel, *Genesis II*, 385). Rather, I believe that Laban still perceives Jacob as his slave, given their shared past.

18. See Cotter, *Genesis*, 236–37; Ahitov, *Jacob*. Further allusions are the Israelites' departure from Egypt with great wealth; in this light, we might entertain reading crossing the Jabbok in parallel to crossing the Reed Sea.

	Jacob in Laban's House (Genesis)	**The Exodus from Egypt (Exodus)**
God "sees" and saves	For I have seen all that Laban is doing to you (31:12).	I have seen My people's suffering in Egypt; I have heard them cry out amid their oppressors (3:7–8).
	Jacob in Laban's House (Genesis)	**The Exodus from Egypt (Exodus)**
The slave requests release	Release me to go home to my own land. Give me my wives and my children for whom I have worked for you, and let me go. You know very well how much work I have done for you (30:25–26).	Send My people forth, so that they may serve Me in the wilderness (7:16, and many more). With our youths and our elderly folk we will go, with our sons and our daughters, our sheep and our cattle, we all must go, for it will be our festival of the Lord (10:9).
The slave leaves with the master's possessions	God has taken your father's livestock and given it to me (31:9).	Thus they despoiled Egypt (12:36; see also 3:22).
The master hears of his slave's escape	On the third day, Laban was told that Jacob had fled (31:22).	The king of Egypt was told that the Israelites had escaped (14:5).
The master pursues his slaves and catches up with them	Taking his kinsmen with him, he pursued him for seven days, catching up with him in the hill country of Gilead (31:23–25).	So the king harnessed his chariot and brought out his army… and he pursued the Israelites… and chased and caught up with them (14:7–9).
God protects Israel before their actual encounter	That night God came to Laban the Aramean in a dream and said to him, "Take care not to say anything to Jacob for good or for bad" (31:24).	Then the angel of God who had been traveling ahead of the Israelite camp moved and went behind them, and the column of cloud moved from in front of them to their rear (14:19–20).

	Jacob in Laban's House (Genesis)	**The Exodus from Egypt (Exodus)**
The master is blessed through his slave	I have learned by divination that it is because of you that the Lord has blessed me (30:27).	But bless me too (12:32).
Get out!	Now – leave this land at once and return to the land where you were born (31:13).	Get up, get out from among my people, you and the Israelites. Go (12:31).

This analogy is already implied in the Passover Haggada, which, in a comparison that seems strange at first glance, contrasts Laban – who seeks to destroy everyone – and Pharaoh – who seeks only the death of the Israelite males. An analysis of the midrashic components listed there shows how they are common to Jacob's journey to Haran and his descent to Egypt:

> Go forth and learn what Laban the Aramean sought to do to our father Jacob. Pharaoh only made a decree against the males, but Laban sought to uproot everyone. As it is said: "The Aramean wished to destroy my father, and he went down to Egypt and lived there as a stranger, few in number, and there he became a nation – large, mighty, and great."

1. He went down to Egypt – forced by divine decree.
2. And lived there as a stranger – this teaches us that our father Jacob did not intend to settle in Egypt, but only stay there temporarily.
3. Few in number – as it is said: "Your ancestors went down to Egypt with seventy people…"
4. And there became a nation – this teaches that Israel were distinguished there.
5. Large, mighty – as it is said: "The Israelites were fruitful and burgeoned; they multiplied and became exceptionally strong…"
6. And great – as it is said: "I made you flourish like the shoots of the field… I said to you, 'In your blood, live!'"

7. And the Egyptians dealt cruelly with us – as it is said: "Let us deal wisely with them."
8. And oppressed us – as it is said: "They placed slave masters over them to oppress them with forced labor."
9. Subjecting us to harsh labor – as it is said: "The Egyptians imposed back-breaking labor on the Israelites."
10. We cried out to the Lord, God of our ancestors – as it is said: "From their servitude their plea rose up to God."
11. And the Lord heard our voice – as it is said: "And God heard their groaning."
12. And He saw our oppression...

Jacob's descent to Haran is also (1) forced by divine decree. (2) He never intends to settle there, but only to stay "until your brother's wrath subsides." (3–6) Jacob travels to Haran on his own, but leaves with a large family and household. (7–9) In Haran, as in Egypt, Jacob's host treats him poorly: first he switches his daughters, and then attempts to cheat him out of his due. Jacob's speech below sounds more like the bitter complaint of a mistreated slave who must please his difficult master than that of a son-in-law who joins the family business. (10–12) God sees Jacob's distress and protects him from harm and deception.[19]

Given that this list is introduced with an explicit comparison ("Pharaoh only made a decree against the males, but Laban sought to uproot everyone"), it may be that the author of the Haggada was also alluding to this extended comparison between the exiles of the father and his children. The claim that Laban is in fact worse than Pharaoh may be counterintuitive, but Laban effectively seeks to "uproot everyone" by forcing Jacob to return to Canaan without his wives and children, thus condemning the tribes of Israel to a future in Haran and excluding them from Abraham's eternal covenant.

How does this comparison contribute to our understanding of Jacob's flight from Haran? Aside from the general tone this analogy sets

19. According to Jeffrey Geoghegan, Passover is associated with ancient sheep-shearing festivals (Geoghegan, "Passover"). If so, then Jacob escaping while Laban goes to shear his sheep is a further, subtle, allusion between the narratives.

for this scene, I first wish to point out two aspects that it illuminates, both of which are worthy of a deeper analysis in themselves:

Firstly, this extensive analogy might move the reader to anticipate a similar ending, but the two plots have different, almost opposite endings. God hardens Pharaoh's heart to pursue Israel and the Egyptians drown in the sea, but appears to Laban in a dream and warns him against harming Jacob. Given that Pharaoh's final pursuit of Israel plays a central part in the retribution against Egypt ("I will harden Pharaoh's heart, and he will pursue them. I will be glorified over Pharaoh and all his force, and the Egyptians will know that I am the Lord" – Ex. 14:4), it is surprising that this motif is entirely absent from Jacob's "exodus." Instead of warning Laban against harming his son-in-law, God could have punished him as the Egyptians were punished. This disparity is related to the significance of Jacob and Laban's covenant, as I will discuss below.

Secondly, Pharaoh's final pursuit of Israel has two objectives. As mentioned above, this serves to punish Pharaoh and the Egyptians, but it is also intended for the sake of Israel's education, as Moses tells Israel: "Fear not. Stand firm and see the deliverance the Lord will bring you today. The Egyptians you see today, you shall never see again. The Lord will fight for you. You stay silent" (14:13–14). This goal is indeed fulfilled, when after their enemies drown, "the Israelites saw the Egyptians dead on the seashore, and witnessed the wondrous power the Lord had unleashed against the Egyptians. The people were in awe of the Lord, and they believed in Him and in Moses His servant" (14:31). That is, Israel must break free of their mental enslavement to Egypt. They must see with their own eyes how their oppressors' bodies lie dead on the seashore, and they must see with their own eyes God's powerful mastery over them all. Does Jacob undergo a similar process when he escapes from Laban's clutches? Perhaps Jacob's harsh accusations against Laban should be perceived thus. Jacob does not utter a word of complaint to Laban's face during his twenty years in Haran, but in Mount Gilead, he finally opens his mouth and speaks his mind to Laban. This show of strength asserts his independence.

These comments suffice for the sake of our discussion, and I will now address the main issue highlighted by this analogy: in Haran, it emerges, Jacob is a slave. The Israelites are slaves to Pharaoh, and

Jacob is a slave to Laban. There is room for comparison between Laban and Pharaoh, and Jacob must flee Haran just as Israel flees from Egypt because it is not at all clear that Laban will let Jacob go.

This retroactively clarifies the importance of Jacob's earlier conversation with his wives. From a perspective of plot, perhaps this scene initially seems superfluous – we do not hear about Abraham's exchange with Sarah before they travel to Egypt, or of Jacob's exchange with his wives before he goes down to Egypt to meet Joseph. Why is their conversation so important in this context?[20]

It does not occur to Laban that his daughters are complicit in the family's escape. He accuses Jacob: "You carried off my daughters like captives of the sword"; this reveals his assumption that Rachel and Leah went with Jacob against their will. Note that Laban refers to them as "my daughters" rather than "your wives" – he still believes that they belong to him. For this reason, it is important that the reader knows whose side they are on. Not only do Rachel and Leah consent to this move, they too wish to cut ties with their father:

> Rachel and Leah answered him,
> "Do we still have a share in the inheritance of our father's estate?
> He treats us like strangers.
> He has sold us and spent the money.
> All the wealth that God has taken from our father belongs to us and our children.
> So now do whatever God has told you." (31:14–16)

Their speech has two parts: justification of their father's wealth being transferred to Jacob, and their conclusion (marked with the common phrase, "and now"), wherein they agree to leave Haran and travel to Canaan.

The main part of their speech justifies Jacob's wealth. Their perception that "God has taken" Laban's wealth confirms where their

20. This disturbs Gunkel, who holds that "Jacob's discussion with his wives is not necessary in the narrative context," and thus claims that in the J source, there is no parallel evidence of this dialogue (Gunkel, *Genesis*, 331).

loyalties lie, but moreover, they address their father's attitude toward them, complaining that he has alienated them and treated them like outsiders: "He treats us like strangers." The term "stranger," "*nokhri*," is important in this context. Usually, it refers to someone who is not an Israelite, but it is sometimes used to denote an outsider, someone who is not a member of the family, like the temptresses warned against in Proverbs (Prov. 2:16; 7:5); or "My family never comes; my friends are gone. I am a stranger, now, an outsider (*nokhri*) to my maidservants, my household" (Job 19:14–15).[21]

Here, of course, it does not refer to a non-Israelite, but to an outsider, someone who is not part of the family. Laban may accuse Jacob of mistreating his wives, but he is the one who makes his daughters feel like outsiders. From a rhetorical perspective, their mention of their children is powerful – they are alienated from their father, but they will cling to their children. Their father does not deserve his wealth anymore – it belongs to "us and our children." Rachel and Leah have changed sides: they are no longer "Laban's daughters," but "Jacob's wives." It is no wonder that the phrase they coin, "Do we still have share or portion in our father's estate," becomes a catchphrase that expresses shifting political loyalties, as when Sheba son of Bichri rebels against David: "We have no portion in David and no share in the son of Jesse!" (II Sam. 20:1); or when Judah and Israel split into two separate kingdoms: "We have no part in David nor any share in the son of Jesse! To your tents, O Israel! Now look to your own house, O David!" (I Kings 12:16).[22]

Thus, "if Jacob thinks he needs to convince his wives, he is wrong. They already believe him and are prepared to support him, not because

21. As well as: "There will be a man to whom God gives wealth and possessions and honor so that he lacks nothing his heart desires. And then God will not grant him the power to partake of it, and a stranger will consume it all; this is empty breath and an evil sickness" (Eccl. 6:2). In some cases, the multivalence of the word results in exegetical debate, such as Exodus 21:8 – is the prohibition against selling one's daughter to non-Jewish "foreigners" (as Ibn Ezra holds) or to someone outside the family (as Rashi)? See also Ramban's debate on this verse.
22. Compare to Wenham, *Genesis II*, 492. Frisch (based on Malamat) rightly claims that this does not necessarily reflect rebellion so much as the violation of the covenant (Frisch, *Kings*, 118).

of what Laban has done to Jacob, but because of what Laban has done to them."[23] The first generation, Abraham and Sarah, leave the land of their birth and travel to Canaan at God's command; in the second generation, Rebecca journeys to join them after her family ask her, "Will you go with this man?" and she replies, "I will go" (24:58). Now, this third generation, it is Jacob's wives who must decide whether to leave Haran and reestablish their lives in Canaan.

Once again, the shifting level of divine intervention reflects the general trend in Genesis. God's command to Abraham is direct, open revelation, and it is the sole reason for Abraham's journey – there is no evidence of any family tension driving Abraham away from his father's house (on the contrary – Abraham's father joins his son on his journey from Ur of the Chaldeans, but he ends up remaining in Haran, while Abraham continues to Canaan alone). Rebecca's journey to Canaan is also characterized by a certain level of providence: Abraham's servant encounters her at the well following his prayer-divination. But at the same time, Rebecca's exchange with her family suggests underlying tension that also motivates her to leave them behind: her readiness to leave with a perfect stranger when her family prefers that she stays home for a year or so hints that as Laban's sister, she might be able to identify with Laban's daughters. One generation later, this tension has fully erupted: although God appears to Jacob and commands him to return to Canaan, what motivates Laban's daughters' departure is their deep resentment toward their father. This gradually shifting balance between divine and human factors motivating the journey from Haran to Canaan is consistent with the Jacob cycle's placement within the broader pattern of Genesis.

Some accuse Jacob's wives that their complaints are too materialistic, and that they focus entirely on their financial entitlement, but this is not, in fact, the epicenter of their speech. As mentioned above, wealth in this chapter serves as a gauge of Jacob's autonomy. Jacob and his wives' possessions are a reflection of their independence. Given that the alternative is that Jacob will be portrayed as Laban's slave, his possessions are in fact the clearest indication of his status. "What a slave

23. Hamilton, *Genesis II*, 289.

acquires, his master acquires," but if Jacob's growing flock is his salary, then he is no slave; he is the independent head of his own family rather than a subordinate branch of his father-in-law's.

THE THEFT OF THE TERAPHIM

> Thou art thy father's daughter; there's enough. (Shakespeare, *As You Like It,* Act I, Scene II)

Rachel and Leah's loyalty to their husband and rejection of their father is confirmed through Rachel's theft of the teraphim, especially in her exchange with Laban in her tent. This act proves beyond all doubt that Laban's daughters are on Jacob's side.

Yet this theft makes an even more important contribution to the tense atmosphere that pervades the entire scene: it is not certain that Jacob will manage to return home with his family. For the sake of clarification, I will explore this episode in depth and analyze its possible consequences.

The precise nature of these teraphim and why Rachel steals them remains a mystery. It is unlikely that they are actual idols, considering that there are also teraphim in David's house, as Ramban notes; this challenges Rashi's interpretation (which is based on Genesis Rabba) that Rachel attempts to prevent her father from idolatry.[24] On the other hand, the fact that Laban seeks them so desperately, and that Rachel steals them and is prepared to lie in order to keep them, indicates that these are not common trinkets available in the local marketplace. These teraphim are obviously meaningful to Laban and his family.

One fascinating modern theory is the subject of fierce controversy regarding the interpretation of inscriptions found in Iraq, in the ancient city of Nuzi. Based on inscriptions discovered in the 1930–40s, some

24. Moreover, it hardly makes sense that Laban will cease idolatry if these specific teraphim are stolen. As Ibn Ezra already notes, if Rachel's goal was to prevent her father from idolatry, then why doesn't she bury the teraphim as soon as they leave Haran? Why does she keep them and hide them instead of destroying them? Still, R. Samson Raphael Hirsch adheres to this reading.

argue that these teraphim are "household gods" that determine inheritance. Rowley claims that this inscription indicates that if a person only has daughters, but no sons, then their sons-in-law (who are adopted by their father-in-law) will inherit them, but if a son is born to him after his daughter's marriage, then they must split the inheritance between them. However, if the son-in-law is in possession of these "household gods," then he alone will inherit the father. According to Rowley, when Jacob married Leah, Laban did not yet have any sons,[25] and this inscription is therefore relevant to this case: by obtaining these "household gods," Jacob will prove that he alone is considered Laban's heir.[26]

Greenberg attacks this idea from two directions. Firstly, he challenges the interpretation of the Nuzi inscription: he reads that it dictates that the father commits to bequeathing his estate to his son-in-law in any case, and the teraphim have no bearing on his inheritance. Moreover, Greenberg argues that Jacob does not seem to have any interest in inheriting Laban – the two clans form a pact and part ways in peace. I believe that Greenberg's second claim is problematic – after all, Jacob's exchange with his wives is entirely concerned with his acquisition of Laban's property, and this scene is closely followed with Rachel's theft of the teraphim. It is difficult to predict how the economic relationship between the clans would have played out without the pact that Laban forced upon Jacob. But Greenberg is correct in asserting that the Nuzi inscriptions are irrelevant to this chapter in Genesis, despite Rowley and Speiser's enthusiasm.[27]

Greenberg himself proposes reading Rachel's theft according to Flavius Josephus' story about a widow who secretly brought her first

25. See a similar idea in C. Gordon, "The Story of Jacob and Laban in the Light of the Nuzi Texts," *BASOR* 66 (1937), 26.
26. Rowley, "Servant of the Lord," 302. See also Burrows, "Complaint"; Flynn, "Teraphim."
27. See also Gvaryahu, "Teraphim." Yet there is no clear conclusion to this day; in 1985, Johan Huehnergard published five Akkadian texts that were discovered in the ancient Amorite city Emar (in the modern day Tell Meskene in Aleppo, Syria); one of them showed that possession of the household gods was proof of ownership of family property. Huehnergard compared this to our narrative (Huehnergard, "Biblical Notes").

husband's household gods to her second husband's home "because it is local custom to keep objects of cultic ritual at home and then take them along to a new destination" (*Antiquities of the Jews* 18:9:5). Greenberg assumes that this kind of custom was also prevalent in biblical times, and for this reason Rachel steals the teraphim – because they were dear to her.[28]

However, I believe that the most feasible reading, favored by most exegetes and scholars, is that these teraphim are some kind of divination device used for telling the future. This is evident from various biblical scenes (see Judges 17:5; 18:17–18, 20; Hos. 3:4; [II Kings 23:24]), especially the king of Babylon's attempt to devise the best way of attacking Jerusalem: "For the king of Babylon stands at the fork in the road, at the beginning of the two roads, to perform a divination: shaking arrows, inquiring of teraphim, scrutinizing the liver" (Ezek. 21:26).[29] The idea that these teraphim have mystical properties move some to propose that Rachel takes the teraphim for the same reason she covets the mandrakes: in the hope that they will bring her blessing and fertility.[30] Yet the fact that this scene is not concerned with childbearing or fertility seems to bring us back to Ezekiel, which *is* relevant to the narrative's themes: the king of Babylon stands by a fork in the road, uncertain of the best path to take. Here, too, Rachel and her family are setting out on a journey, so she takes the teraphim to help guide them on their way – or, moreover, to prevent Laban from using them in his pursuit. Either way, of course, her theft does not seem to help: Laban catches up with them anyway, and it is God who protects them, not Mesopotamian figures of divination.

In any case, the narrative's concern with these teraphim is not merely pragmatic; it also serves a literary objective, in two respects. Firstly, it calls attention to the fear that Jacob's family will be forced back to Laban's household; this is particularly validated through the literary connection with the "theft" of Joseph's chalice. Although the

28. Greenberg, "Teraphim."
29. Some propose that Michal uses the teraphim to help David escape through sorcery, but the biblical text downplays this (Rouillard and Tropper, "Trpym").
30. Macchi, "La Dernière Rencontre."

chalice is not actually stolen, the accusation of a family member serves as the basis for comparison between the two narratives, especially given that the two missing objects are both associated with divination in the ancient world. Joseph instructs his steward to tell the brothers of the chalice's importance: "Is it not from this that my master drinks and that he uses for divination?" (Gen. 44:5). In fact, the two plots are strikingly similar:[31]

	The Teraphim (Gen. 31)	**The Chalice (Gen. 44)**
Departure: The object is in the possession of a family member, but the head of the party is unaware of this	(17) So Jacob put his children and wives on camels… (19) Meanwhile, when Laban had gone to shear his sheep, Rachel had stolen her father's teraphim.	(2) Then put my chalice – the silver chalice – in the mouth of the youngest one's bag… (3) As morning showed its first light, the men were sent on their way with their donkeys.
Pursuit of the thief	(23) Taking his kinsmen with him, he pursued him for seven days, catching up with him in the hill country of Gilead… (25) And Laban overtook Jacob.	(4) Go after the men at once… (6) And he caught up with them.
Accusation of theft	(26) Laban said to Jacob, "What have you done? You have deceived me… and carried off my daughters like captives of the sword… (30) Why did you steal my gods?"	And he repeated those words to them.

31. The Midrash already hints to this analogy (Genesis Rabba 92:8). See further in Daube, *Biblical Law,* 101; Hamilton, *Genesis II,* 562–63; Zakovitch, *Texts,* 18–19. He mentions further connections I have not mentioned.

	The Teraphim (Gen. 31)	**The Chalice (Gen. 44)**
The accused responds, unaware that the object is in their possession	(31) Jacob answered Laban, saying, "I was afraid; I thought you would take your daughters away from me by force. (32) But if you find your gods with anyone here, *they shall not live.*"	(8) Why would we steal silver or gold from your master's house? (9) If any of your servants is found with it, *he shall die,* and the rest of us will become my lord's slaves.
The search	(33) So Laban went into Jacob's tent, Leah's tent, and the tents of the two female slaves, but found nothing. Leaving Leah's tent, he entered Rachel's.	(11) Each of them quickly lowered his bag to the ground, and each opened his bag. He searched, beginning with the oldest and ending with the youngest.
The result of the search	(35) So he searched but did not find his teraphim.	The chalice was found in Benjamin's bag.
Accusation of ingratitude	Jacob accuses the accuser.	Joseph accuses the accused.

These two scenes unfold similarly, step after step, with one dramatic difference between them: Rachel does steal the teraphim, but is not caught, while Benjamin does not steal the chalice, but is caught. It is worth noting that Benjamin is Rachel's son, as is Joseph, who frames him, which only adds to the intriguing dialogue between these scenes.

This analogy, naturally, invites a reading of the later story – the "theft" of the chalice – against the background of the theft that takes place a generation earlier.[32] For our purposes, however, I wish to point out how the tone of our narrative shifts when read against the later episode. Even if this is not the analogy's main objective, the chalice episode presents a possible alternate ending to our scene. What would have happened, had Laban discovered Rachel's theft? This comparison helps the reader understand what is at stake in Jacob's heated exchange with Laban. Although Jacob tells Laban, "But if you find your gods with anyone here,

32. Yair Zakovitch holds that this comparison expresses criticism at Rachel's actions; Benjamin's incrimination is a punishment for Rachel's theft (Zakovitch, *Texts,* 19).

they shall not live" (31:32), just as Joseph's brothers unknowingly propose, "If any of your servants is found with it, he shall die" (44:9), this is presumably hyperbole.[33] A more likely fate is what Joseph's steward tells the brothers: "Let it be as you say, but only the one with whom it is found shall be my slave. The rest of you can go free" (44:10). And indeed, after the chalice is discovered in Benjamin's sack, the brothers beg to serve Joseph in Benjamin's place: "Judah replied, 'What can we say to my lord? What can we speak? How can we prove our innocence? God has uncovered your servants' guilt! We are now my lord's slaves – we and the one in whose possession the chalice was found.' 'Heaven forbid that I should do such a thing,' he said. 'The man in whose possession the chalice was found will become my slave. As for the rest of you, go back to your father in peace'" (44:16–17).

This same threat looms over Jacob's family: if Laban finds the teraphim, there is a very real threat that they will be forced to return to Haran as Laban's slaves;[34] if not as slaves, given that Rachel is Laban's own daughter, they will at least be dragged back to Haran against their will. The theft of Laban's precious teraphim exacerbates the suspense that already pervades the scene – even after they have been traveling for seven days, they may be forced to turn back to a life of servitude to Laban. If Laban finds the teraphim, Jacob is doomed; moreover, the reader knows what Jacob does not – that for once, justice is on Laban's side, and Rachel's secret might be her husband's undoing.

The Search for the Teraphim

The three verses describing Laban's search for the teraphim are fascinating in themselves (31:33–35):

> So Laban went into Jacob's tent, Leah's tent, and the tents of the two female slaves, *but found nothing.*
>
> Leaving Leah's tent, he entered Rachel's. But Rachel had taken the teraphim and put them inside a camel cushion, and

33. See Jackson, *Theft*, 63, 110; Phillips, *Criminal Law*, 141.
34. Similarly: Gvaryahu, "Teraphim."

> was sitting on them; and Laban rummaged through the tent *but found nothing.*
>
> She said to her father, "Do not be angry, my lord, but I cannot get up for you, for the way of women is with me now." So he searched *but did not find his teraphim.*

Laban's search for the teraphim is described in three stages, each ending with the reassuring phrase: "but found nothing."[35] These "stages," however, are calculated to serve the syuzhet (the way the story is told), not the fabula (the actual sequence of events): the narrator briefly mentions that Laban searches in Jacob's, Leah's, and the handmaids' tents; then slows down to describe his search in Rachel's tent, the true center of the drama. Only after Rachel successfully deceives her father is the narrator able to conclude that "Laban did not find his teraphim"; though he has not searched anywhere else since he "found nothing," his exchange with his perfidious daughter brings his search to an end.[36]

This exchange is thus the narrative climax. The apple does not fall far from the tree; not only does she lie to his face, she does so while respectfully referring to him as "my lord." For our purposes, it is especially important to note how she begins her little speech: she asks that her father not be "angry" (*al yiḥar*) because she is unable to rise. This paves the way for Jacob's "anger" (*vayiḥar*) in the next verse: Rachel successfully manipulates the two men in her life to withhold or express their anger to suit her needs, without either of them knowing that it is she that stole the teraphim. What is the meaning of this design?

In this way, it seems the narrative is able to hold the stick at both ends: Jacob is able to blast Laban for his harsh treatment and ingratitude, thus parting ways with Laban on a triumphant, independent note. Yet the text undermines Jacob's indignation by hiding the truth from him: Laban, despicable though he is, is not falsely accusing Jacob. Thus, Jacob's diatribe is inherently ambivalent: on one hand, Laban deserves Jacob's

---

35. In the parallel narrative, the root M-TZ-A is also a keyword.
36. Unlike Rashi, who writes that Laban knows that "she is one who touches everything" (on 31:33) – Rashi says that he specifically goes back to her tent because she is his prime suspect.

wrath for his years of abuse, but the specific trigger for his rant is misguided. This is a crucial point: though the reader is sympathetic toward Jacob, his household is nonetheless guilty of the theft Laban accuses him of. This ambivalence reflects not only upon the text's attitude toward Rachel's theft, but also upon its complex assessment of Jacob's escape.

Until now, we have justified the family's flight; there is real concern that Laban will not allow them to leave Haran. Yet the specific verb used to describe their escape, "*vayignov Yaakov et lev Lavan haarammi*," that literally means, "Jacob *stole* Laban's heart," hints to certain criticism at this move. As R. Abraham Saba expresses:

> It says "Jacob stole Laban's heart" to show that Jacob acted unfairly by leaving without Laban's permission. For after God, blessed be He, promised protection, and God, blessed be He, was able to tell Laban "Take care not to say anything to Jacob, for good or for bad," as He told him on the way...for this reason, it says "Jacob stole Laban's heart." For the Torah called him a thief "by not telling him he was running away." For Jacob should have told Laban that he was leaving – he should have trusted in his God.[37]

Although we can certainly understand and sympathize with Jacob's motives, the text repeatedly hints that his maneuver is unnecessary. God Himself appears to Laban and warns him against harming Jacob; moreover, Laban easily catches up with Jacob even though he has a three-day head start, which implies that his escape is futile anyway. God's warning to Laban, "Take care (*hishamer*) not to say anything to Jacob for good or for bad" (31:29), leaves such a strong impression on him that he repeats it to Jacob; the root of "*hishamer*" perhaps hints to God's promise to Jacob that "I will protect you (*ushmartikha*) wherever you go" (28:15).[38] God indeed protects Jacob in this scene, and it seems that the text disapproves of Jacob family's unnecessary theft of both heart and teraphim: "Rachel had *stolen* her father's teraphim. Jacob *stole* the heart of Laban the Aramean by not telling him that he was running away" (31:19–20).

37. *Tzror HaMor* on Gen. 31:20.
38. Rofé, *Angels*, 188.

This ambivalence recalls how Jacob steals the heart of his father Isaac and his brother's blessings. There, too, it is not clear as to whether the end justifies the means; the dishonesty that Jacob repeatedly employs remains a complex, problematic part of his character throughout his narrative cycle.

Laban's entrance to Rachel's tent subtly echoes Jacob's manipulation of his father Isaac. It is difficult to determine whether this allusion is intentional, [39] but deception and theft go hand in hand, and the fact that both scenes depict a child misleading their father certainly invites this comparison. In both scenes, the child lies in order to obtain something that is not theirs: Jacob desires the blessings, and Rachel desires the teraphim.

Moreover, these scenes share common motifs and language: Jacob takes advantage of Esau's expedition to the field, just as Rachel exploits the fact that her father has gone to shear his sheep. Isaac does not recognize Jacob (*lo hikkiro* – 27:23), and similarly, Jacob tells Laban: "In the presence of our kinsmen, see (*hakker*) if there is anything of yours here, and take it" (31:32). Both scenes share a sense of shifting movement, of swift entrance and exit: "Jacob had just left his father Isaac, when his brother Esau came back from the hunt" (27:30)/"Leaving Leah's tent, he entered Rachel's" (31:34).

Above all, note the language used to describe the child's deception of their father. In both scenes, the father attempts to feel his way to the truth: "Come close and let me feel you (*vaamushekha*), my son…. Jacob came close to Isaac his father, who felt him (*vayemushehu*)" (27:21–22); "Laban rummaged (*vayemashesh*) through the tent but found nothing…. You have rummaged (*mishashta*) through all my possessions" (31:34–37); both scenes make use of the verb pair rise/sit ("*lakum*"–"*lashevet*"): "Please sit up (*kum na sheva*) and eat some of my game" (27:19)/"But Rachel had taken the household gods…and was sitting (*vateshev*) on them…. She said to her father, 'Do not be angry, my lord, but I cannot get up for you (*lo ukhal lakum*)'" (31:34–35). It is no wonder that the fathers show similar resignation; these are the only two instances in Genesis that a character gives up and says, "What can

39. See, for example, Cohen, "Patriarchal History."

I do."[40] This is what Isaac says to Esau after they realize that Jacob has taken the blessings: "What then can I do for you (*ma e'eseh*), my son (27:37)"; and what Laban says to Jacob after his search is unsuccessful: "But what can I do now (*ma e'eseh*) about these?" (31:43).[41]

This analogy hints to the circles of lies and deceit that envelop Jacob and his family. Jacob, who exploits his father's blindness in order to win his blessing, is now blind to his wife's (and his mother's niece, after all!) similar deception against her father. Once again, in both scenes the reader sympathizes with the schemer's end, but not with his or her means.

We have already mentioned that Jacob's exile in Haran is framed with two deceptions, these two thefts, and it is worth noting an additional circle that emerges from this comparison – which characters are parallel to which in the two narratives? Until now, we have focused on the child's deception of his or her father, so that Laban is paralleled to Isaac. However, the younger Jacob steals the blessings from Esau, so in a certain sense, Laban is paralleled to Esau: both lose something that is precious to them that then becomes Jacob's. Esau loses the blessings his father intended for him, while Laban loses the teraphim, which he considers a symbol of divine blessing and protection.

And indeed, some of the aforementioned connections link Laban to Esau. Laban is cheated when he goes out to shear his sheep; Esau is cheated when he goes out to the field to hunt; Laban's movement in and out as he goes rummaging through the tents recalls Jacob and Esau's movement in and out of Isaac's tent. Thus there is certainly basis for the parallel between Laban and Esau, and this is no trivial matter: Rachel is obviously parallel to Jacob, as both deceive their fathers to take something that is not theirs, but if Laban is parallel to the figure of Isaac, then this comparison is cast in a very different light than if Laban

40. This phrase appears twice more in the Torah: Exodus 17:4; 33:5.

41. Speiser believes that this theft has further significance (Speiser, "Teraphim"). Rachel steals them to have the upper hand in her father's inheritance, just as Jacob outwits his father to steal his brother's blessings. Both scenes have similar themes of deception and concealment – as does Jacob's attempt to outwit his father-in-law regarding the flock. All this, of course, is true assuming that Rachel's theft is related to her sibling rivalry, which I find doubtful.

is parallel to the figure of Esau. To deceive an Isaac figure is certainly more problematic than to deceive an Esau figure. Esau sold his birthright for a mess of lentils, and he is married to Hittite women who make his parents miserable – that is, he is a problematic figure in himself. If Laban is parallel to Esau, then Rachel's deception is not nearly as harsh as the deception of a benevolent father-figure like Isaac.

The full significance of the comparison between Laban and Esau transcends the boundaries of this scene. We will soon see that Jacob's encounter with the angels at Mahanaim (32:2–3) links Jacob's confrontation with Laban at Mount Gilead with his encounter with Esau. I will yet discuss the meaning of the concatenation of these scenes into one continuous act, which shows that there is a connection between the two most difficult confrontations of Jacob's life: his confrontation with Laban and his confrontation with Esau. Both of them are deceived and cheated of something precious by Jacob and his household, but in the end, both of them part ways with Jacob in peace.

JACOB'S CONFRONTATION WITH LABAN

Before we discuss the broader significance of Jacob's parting with Laban, I wish to explore Jacob's tirade against Laban (31:36–42). Some read these verses as a narrative climax,[42] and in many senses they are correct. This is the first time since the morning after his first wedding that Jacob "confront[s] Laban," and in a certain sense, his speech marks a turning point in Jacob's characterization. Finely wrought with rhetoric and poetic devices, it forms a chiastic structure:[43]

A. Jacob became indignant and confronted Laban, saying: "What is my crime? What wrong did I do that you come chasing after me? You have rummaged through all my possessions. What have you found that belongs to your house? Put it here in front of my kinsmen and yours and let them decide between the two of us!

42. Wenham, *Genesis II*, 496.

43. See further in Grossman, *Ambiguity*, 117–19.

B. For the twenty years I was with you, your sheep and goats did not miscarry. Not once did I take a ram from your flock as food.

C. I never brought you an animal torn by wild beasts. I bore the loss myself. Whether it was stolen by day or by night you demanded payment from me.

C'. By day I was ravaged by the heat; at night by the freezing cold. Sleep fled from my eyes.

B'. Twenty years I spent working in your household – fourteen for your two daughters and six for your flock – and ten times you changed my wages.

A'. Had the God of my father – the God of Abraham, the Fear of Isaac – not been with me, you would have sent me away empty-handed. But God saw my plight and the toil of my hands, and He rebuked you last night."

The artistic, formal structure of this speech is already justified by the impact it has on the understanding of Jacob and Laban's relationship, and even more meaning can be yielded through an analysis of its symmetry.

The frame of Jacob's speech (A–A') directly addresses Laban's accusation that Jacob has stolen his teraphim.[44] In his opening, Jacob mentions "all my possessions," and that there is nothing among them that "belongs to [Laban's] house." In his conclusion, Jacob reiterates that had it been up to Laban, Jacob would have left empty-handed – even without the possessions Laban has just rummaged through. Moreover, Jacob's speech is framed with the root Y-C-Ḥ, which can mean "decide" or "criticize": "Let them *decide* (*veyokhiḥu*) between us"; "And He rebuked (*vayokhaḥ*) you last night."[45] This expression, along with the description that Jacob "confronted" Laban, colors his speech with legal tones.[46] But

44. Jacob is moved to speak out of anger, but the fact that Laban is actually right for once makes his speech somewhat ironic.

45. As sensed by Fidler, "Dreams," 101. On the meaning of *tokheḥa* and its legal significance (in the *hitpael* form) see BDB, 406–407.

46. Wenham (*Genesis II*, 277) disagrees with the accepted approach in research that this is a formal legal encounter. He is correct that this is not the main framework of Jacob's speech, but it is no coincidence that Jacob's language has legal connota-

as is sometimes the case, it is the disparity between similar components in the structure's frame that illuminate the process that unfolds over the course of the unit. While Jacob opens his speech by inviting his men and Laban's men to judge between them, by its end, he reveals who the true Judge is: "God saw and rebuked you last night."[47] Note that Jacob has only just learned that God appeared to Laban to warn him against harming him; Jacob is surely elated to learn that God is watching over him even without his knowledge (and I will discuss the further significance of the verb root Y-C-Ḥ below).[48]

Jacob then lays out his case against his treatment during the long years he worked for his father-in-law. He twice mentions that he has worked for him for twenty years, which gives his claim that "your sheep and goats did not miscarry" far more weight: it is no great achievement to successfully tend the flock for a few weeks, but to maintain such care for twenty years is a whole different story. Note the slight difference between these statements, which expresses growing alienation between the characters: "For twenty years I was with you," is then followed by "Twenty years I spent working *in your household.*" This implies that Jacob is initially closer to Laban, but over the years he distances himself from him.[49]

The comparison between these two components (B–B') reveals a play on the names of Jacob's wives, *Raḥel* and *Lea,* and the animals

---

tions, which creates a sense of injustice and corruption. On Jacob's legal language, see Finkelstein, "Herding Contract."

47. This is a classic case of meaning getting lost in translation; these two instances of the root Y-C-Ḥ are almost universally translated as entirely different words, so the *inclusio* is lost. One modern translation whose objective is to preserve wordplay as much as possible is that of Buber and Rosenzweig (see more about this undertaking in Niehoff, Buber-Rosenzweig), who translate here: "daß sie *entscheiden* zwischen uns zweien" – "und gestern abend hat er *entschieden.*" Both instances are translated in the sense of "decide between."

48. The Midrash connects God's revelation to Laban at night to protect Jacob to God's nightly revelation to Balaam (Genesis Rabba 52:2). In the story of Balaam, too, Israel are unaware of God's protection. For a comparison of these narratives from a different angle, see Kahn, "Balaam is Laban."

49. Fokkelman, *Genesis,* 117–76. Perhaps this is why Jacob uses the word "*anokhi*" in the first half but not the second. Fokkelman adds that the verb "*avadtikha*" in the second half might have negative connotations.

he tends: "*reḥelekha*" and "*eilei tzonekha*," ewes and rams. Some have shown that throughout Jacob's time in Laban's household, the text is full of wordplay based on their names, which, as mentioned, literally mean "ewe" and "cow,"[50] and in his speech, Jacob employs similar wordplay.

"*Raḥel*" in the sense of "ewe" is very rare in the Bible. Except for here, it appears once more in the Jacob cycle (32:15), in Isaiah (53:7), and in the Song of Songs (6:6). Jacob's use of this rare word alludes to its connotation, as Yehuda Kiel hesitantly suggests: "Although I have my doubts, I would say that Jacob uses this word to hint to Rachel, [Laban's] 'younger daughter.'"[51]

I believe that he is correct, and his theory is supported by the parallel component in the chiastic structure: in the first half, Jacob says that throughout his time as Laban's shepherd, "your sheep and goats did not miscarry." In the second half, he mentions what he has worked for: "Fourteen for your two daughters and six for your flock." Thus "your two daughters" are parallel to "your sheep and goats," which shows that Laban's daughters are already alluded to in the first half of his speech.[52]

At the heart of his speech, Jacob focuses on the harsh reality of the days and nights that slowly add up to twenty years of work. Alone, the description "twenty years" may depreciate the grueling hours and days of daily life, so Jacob balances out "twenty years" by emphasizing the higher resolution unit of "day-night."

The heart of his speech demands special attention. Jacob first mentions that Laban charges him for any lost or stolen sheep: "Not once did I take a ram from your flock as food. I never brought you an animal torn by wild beasts. I bore the loss myself. Whether it was stolen by day or by night you demanded payment from me." Jacob's diatribe is prompted by Laban's accusation of theft, and now he turns the

---

50. Noegel, "Deceptive."

51. Kiel, *Genesis II*, 382, and Shemesh, "Rachel," 83.

52. Perhaps Rachel is alluded to in another verse. The lover describes his love thus: "Your hair is like a flock of goats streaming down from Gilead. Your teeth are like a flock of ewes (*hareḥelim*) rising up from washing; each mother ewe bore twins, not one among them lost" (Song. 6:5–6). Jacob's encounter with Laban is in Gilead, and Jacob mentions "your ewes and goats," and thanks to his careful protection, "not one of them was lost."

tables on him: studies exploring the laws of shepherding in the ancient world show that a shepherd was exempt from compensating his master for losses of up to 15 percent of his flock,[53] the assumption being that a certain number of thefts or losses are inevitable. The shepherd is even able to bring the remains of the animal's torn carcass in order to avoid having to compensate the owner: "If it was torn by a wild animal and the second man brings the remains as evidence, he need not make good the loss" (Ex. 22:12; cf. Amos 3:12).[54] Jacob is pointing out that not only did he not steal Laban's teraphim; but contrary to the accepted custom, he never took advantage of his right to bring Laban the carcasses of animals devoured by predators, and he even paid for stolen animals. This recalls the brothers' logical defense against Joseph's accusation that they have stolen his chalice: "Heaven forbid that we should do such a thing! Look, we brought back to you from Canaan the money we found in the mouths of our bags. Why would we steal silver or gold from your master's house?" (Gen. 44:8).

Jacob then describes the physical suffering he experienced day by day: "By day I was ravaged by the heat; at night by the freezing cold. Sleep fled from my eyes." It is as if the last time he knows a solid night's rest is in Bethel, while the years he spends in Haran are one long, restless night; he will not rest easy again until he parts ways with Laban and returns home.

Once again, unusual words invite a closer look: it may be that the rare, lyrical word for heat – *ḥorev* – is calculated to chastise Laban for his complaint "You have deceived me and carried off my daughters like captives of the sword (*ḥarev*)" (31:26). In response to Laban's accusation of theft and mistreatment of his daughters, Jacob retorts that he even repaid Laban for any "stolen" sheep, and was severely mistreated by Laban himself.

53. Morrison, "Jacob and Laban."
54. The laws of Hammurabi also relate to this issue (section 244, 246), and well as Hittite law (section 75).

JACOB PARTS WAYS WITH LABAN WITH A COVENANT: THREE CIRCLES

A Personal-Familial Parting

Until now, we have discussed Jacob's escape from Laban's household in the personal, familial context; Jacob and his family must leave Laban to return to his birthplace. This parting is especially based on their familial connection, which is emphasized throughout Jacob's time in Haran through use of the word "brother/kinsmen (*aḥ*)." Laban already refers to Jacob as his "brother" upon his arrival ("Then Laban said to Jacob, 'If you are *my brother*, does that mean you should work for me for nothing?'" – 29:15), but here, this word becomes one of the scene's keywords, appearing with such vehement frequency that it sometimes seems to come at the price of textual clarity.

Firstly, "Laban's kin" are mentioned twice: "Taking his kinsmen (*eḥav*) with him, he pursued him for seven days, catching up with him in.... Laban and his kinsmen (*eḥav*) too encamped in the hill country of Gilead" (31:23–25).

At this stage, there is no mention of Jacob's "kinsmen," so the anticipated symmetry is broken: instead of "Jacob had encamped with his *kinsmen* in the hill country/Laban and his *kinsmen* too encamped in the hill country of Gilead," it says: "Jacob had encamped with his *tent* in the hill country/Laban and his *kinsmen* too encamped in the hill country of Gilead."

Next, Laban's "kinsmen" are mentioned together with Jacob's "kinsmen," twice: "In the presence of our *kinsmen*, see if there is anything of yours here, and take it.... Put it here in front of my *kinsmen* and yours and let them decide between the two of us!"

This repetition is logical if these people serve as "kinsmen" in the legal sense:[55] following an accusation of theft in the ancient world, it was accepted that the accuser would search through the accused's possessions (as in the aforementioned case of Joseph's brothers – Gen. 44:12). The accused would allow the accuser to search in the presence of witnesses, and if they did not find the item, the accused would be

55. See, for example, Gunkel, *Genesis*, 338.

declared innocent. Thus the repeated mention of these kinsmen in this scene expresses that this process is an accepted legal act. If Jacob is found guilty, these kinsmen will testify to his guilt, but if not, then they will testify to his innocence. Laban only accuses him of stealing the teraphim, but Jacob is so certain of his innocence that he urges Laban to search for any of his possessions at all: "You have rummaged through all my possessions. What have you found that belongs to your house? Put it here in front of my kinsmen and yours and let them decide between the two of us!" (31:36).

I have already noted that this scene is colored with legal terms and motifs, starting with the suggestively legal verb describing Jacob's confrontation: "Jacob became indignant and *confronted* (*vayarev*) Laban. 'What is my crime?' he asked Laban. 'What wrong did I do that you come chasing after me?'" (31:36). The root R-Y-B often connotes contention or argument (with or without physical violence), such as: "If two people *fight* (*yerivun*) and one strikes another with a stone or with his fist" (Ex. 21:18), but another prevalent meaning of the verb is "to accuse" or "to reproach," sometimes in an explicitly legal context, such as: "When two people have a *dispute* (*riv*) they shall go to the court of justice and the judges shall decide between them, acquitting the innocent and condemning the guilty" (Deut. 25:1); or "May the Lord be Judge, and judge between me and you. May He witness and *contend on my behalf* (*veyarev et rivi*) and defend me from you!" (I Sam. 24:15); or "the Lord has a *dispute* (*riv*) with the nations. He enters into judgment with all flesh" (Jer. 25:31), among many others.[56] Even if our scene does not take place in an official legal setting, the "*riv*" at hand is a claim of injustice: the oppressed speaks up against his oppressor, and in this sense, the scene takes on a legal nuance.

Additional words encourage this theme, especially these two verses: "In the presence of our kinsmen, see if there is anything of yours here, and take it" (v. 32); "What have you found that belongs to your house? Put it here in front of my kinsmen and yours and let

---

56. See further: Ringgren, "R-Y-B," 474. Limburg believes that the root R-Y-B comes from the legal world (Limburg, "R-Y-B").

them decide (*veyokhiḥu*) between the two of us!" (v. 37).[57] The verb "*lehokhiaḥ*" is part of an intriguing dialogue between this scene and Abraham's covenant with Abimelech:[58]

	Abraham and Abimelech	**Jacob and Laban**
God appears in a dream to protect the forefather:	But God came to Abimelech in a dream one night and told him, "You will die because of the woman you have taken" (20:3).	That night God came to Laban the Aramean in a dream and said to him, "Take care not to say anything to Jacob for good or for bad" (31:24).
The forefather's reproach:	Then Abraham *rebuked* (*vehokhiaḥ*) Abimelech for the well of water that Abimelech's servants had seized (21:25).	"You have rummaged through all my possessions. What have you found that belongs to your house? Put it here in front of my kinsmen and yours and *let them decide* (*veyokhiḥu*) between the two of us!" (31:37).
The foreigner's justification:	But Abimelech said, "I do not know who has done this. You did not tell me; I had not heard about it until today" (21:26).	Then Laban spoke up and said to Jacob, "The daughters are my daughters. The children are my children. The flocks are my flocks. All that you see is mine. But what can I do now about my daughters or the children they have borne? (31:43).
The covenant:	and the two of them forged a covenant (21:27).	Come now, let us make a covenant, you and I,
Testimony:	... as testimony (*le'eda*) (21:30).	and let it be a witness (*le'ed*) between us" (31:44).
The forefather swears:	Abraham said, "I swear" (21:24).	Jacob swore by the Fear of his father Isaac (31:53).

57. On the legal background of the verb "*lehokhiaḥ*" see, for example, Wilson, "Ezekiel's Dumbness," 99–100.
58. See also Fabry, "Y-KH-Ḥ," 65.

	Abraham and Abimelech	**Jacob and Laban**
The place is named:	That is why that place is called Beersheba, because there the two men swore an oath (21:31).	Laban called it Yegar Sahaduta, while Jacob called it Galed (31:47).
The characters part:	And then Abimelech and Phicol, commander of his troops, returned to the land of the Philistines (21:32).	Laban then left to return home. And Jacob continued on his way (32:1–2).

This connection is part of the broader comparison between Abraham and Jacob discussed in the introduction. In the context of our discussion, it is worth noting that while Abraham and Abimelech forge a covenant without any "kinsmen" for witnesses, Jacob and Laban's covenant does require human witnesses. This illustrates the nature of their relationship: though Jacob and Laban are kin, their relationship is more strained than that of Abraham and Abimelech!

The verb "to recognize (*lehakir*)" is also recognized as a verb of legal significance (as in, for example, Deut. 21:17). Daube demonstrates how this verb functions in several biblical narratives (with especial focus on Jacob's recognition of Joseph's robe – 37:33). He points out several examples where this verb is intentionally employed for its legal connotations.[59]

The same seems to be true in this scene, and the term "kinsmen" should also be read in this sense. At the same time, however, these kinsmen serve a different literary purpose that shapes both characterization and plot, which I will soon clarify.[60]

Finally, Jacob addresses his "kinsmen" twice: "Jacob said to his *kinsmen*, 'Gather stones'.... He offered a sacrifice on the hill and invited his *kinsmen* to break bread (31:46, 54).

Who are the kinsmen Jacob addresses? The *Rishonim* are divided: Rashi believes that they are Jacob's sons: "They were his sons, who were

59. Deut. 33:9; Is. 63:15; Jer. 24:5; Ps. 142:5–6; Ruth 2:10, 19. Daube, *Studies in Biblical Law*, 3–8.

60. The use of legal terms for literary purposes is common in the Bible, and there are other instances of such use for the verb "*lehakir*." See Grossman, *Ruth*, 39–45.

like brothers to him, drawing close to him in times of trouble or war" (on 31:46, based on Genesis Rabba). Ramban argues that this refers to Laban's men: "And Jacob said to his kinsmen: to Laban's kinsmen who came with him, because he did not want to address his father-in-law directly, out of respect. Thus 'he called his kinsmen to break bread' – to Laban's kinsmen, and he did not address Laban out of respect, as if he owned everything and all was his."[61]

The source of deliberation is clear: from a perspective of plot, it makes sense that all the participants, from both parties, will together build the pile of stones that will serve as testimony to their covenant; it certainly makes sense that they will all break bread together. On the other hand, the grammar of the verse implies that Jacob only instructs his own kin to "gather stones."

In order to hold the stick at both ends, Radak's reading (the first solution he proposes) is best: "His kinsmen – his own men, and even though Jacob tells his own men, Laban and his men also gathered stones and everyone made a mound of stones together and broke bread together; Jacob with his men and Laban with his men ate together upon the mound" (on 31:46). That is, while the narrator only relates Jacob's words to his kinsmen – his family and the rest of the people who join him on his journey to Canaan – it makes sense that Laban's kinsmen also participate in the construction of the testimonial pillar and the meal that binds their covenant.

If we do adopt this reading, however, there is need to justify the text's focus on Jacob's kin; I believe that the omission of Laban's kin's contribution to the covenant expresses that it is a parting of "good riddance" rather than a treaty based on peace and love. Instead of responding to Laban's short speech, instead of prolonging their conversation, Jacob merely turns to his own kinsmen: "Gather stones." *This is what Laban wants; let's just get this over with.* Once the mound is formed, it is

61. Kiel writes similarly: "Jacob called = he invited Laban's 'kinsmen' to the meal" (*Genesis II*, 393). Most modern scholars adopt Rashi's view – see Hamilton, *Genesis II*, 314; Mathews, *Genesis II*, 532. Scholars who agree with Ramban that Laban's "kinsmen" are his actual kin have generally adopted the ancient Latin translation *Vetus Latina*, which replaces "Jacob" with "Laban" in this verse: "And Laban said to his brothers…"

Laban who makes a formal speech about the nature of their covenant, while once again, Jacob remains silent. *Let the old man say whatever he wants; anything it takes to get this over with.* For this reason, perhaps, the text focuses on Jacob's side: Jacob is ready to part ways and move on; he has nothing more to say to Laban, and he focuses on his own family.

Thus the narrative opens with a double mention of Laban's kinsmen (while intentionally omitting Jacob's), concludes with a double mention of Jacob's kinsmen (while intentionally omitting Laban's), and mentions both of their kinsmen twice in between. This pattern reflects how Jacob breaks away from Laban's family. Each side's "kinsmen" remain at their own end of the narrative, while in between, the "*eḥav*" of both sides are mentioned together with the aggressive "*riv*" that comes between them. Each side has its own kinsmen, its own clan, and its own head of the household. Laban and Jacob are no longer "brothers," no longer kin. Some scholars even read Jacob's words to Laban, "Put it here in front of my kinsmen and yours and let them decide between the two of us!" as an invitation to their kinsmen to "choose between the two of us" – to choose sides (as in "the one You have *chosen* [*hokhaḥta*] for Your servant Isaac" – Gen. 24:14).[62] This bold reading calls up the powerful image of a son-in-law (and nephew) who has grown distant from his father-in-law (and uncle), who now bids their common kin to choose sides, forcing them to decide where their loyalties lie.

Jacob's parting from Laban is thick with familial tension, but this is only one dimension of this complex narrative. Beyond Jacob's personal parting from his family member, their paths also diverge in a religious sense and a national sense.

A Religious Parting

Our scene contains hints that Jacob's parting from Laban also reflects a religious parting. This is hinted throughout the narrative, and I wish to focus here on two central elements. Until this chapter, the story of Jacob's stay in Haran assumes that the two men share a spiritual, religious discourse; this is especially salient when Laban speaks about God as the governing force: "I have learned by divination that it is because of you

62. Hamilton, *Genesis II*, 306.

that the Lord has blessed me" (30:27). It is also obvious to Jacob that Laban's blessing comes from God: "The Lord has blessed you wherever I have been" (30:30). When Laban's daughters name their sons, they use the more intimate Tetragrammaton as opposed to the more universal "God"; in general, throughout the narrative, the sense is that the two clans – the son of Abraham and the son of Nahor – do not have different faiths. Yet Jacob's departure from Laban's house, and especially the covenant between them, suddenly reveals a religious disparity. For the first time, we hear that Laban serves gods other than the Lord, God of Israel. Laban accuses Jacob of stealing his household gods: "But why did you steal my gods?" (31:30), thus exposing that he has gods that are not supposed to be in Jacob's possession. In this context, it is especially intriguing how Laban refers to God: "I have the power to harm you, but last night *your father's God* spoke to me" (31:29). In Laban's dream, God does not introduce Himself as such, but Laban still refers to Him in this way, which draws a clear distinction between Jacob, who serves his father's God, and Laban, who apparently does not. For the first time, Laban differentiates between Jacob's "father's God" and "my gods," which is surprising, given that until now, Laban has referred to God as "the Lord," giving no indication of any religious difference between him and his nephew. Jacob's response reinforces this distinction: "Had the God of my father – the God of Abraham, the Fear of Isaac – not been with me, you would have sent me away empty-handed" (31:42). The God who controls their relationship is the God of Jacob's father and not the god of Laban, who is not part of Abraham's covenant.

This distinction reaches a climax in Laban's covenant speech, where he mentions the deities of each clan: "May the God of Abraham, the god of Nahor, and the god of their father be our judge" (31:53). Throughout his time in Haran, Jacob has been praying to his own God while Laban prays to his father's Mesopotamian deities, but this only becomes apparent to the reader when Jacob leaves. It is here that the need for witnesses from both religions are required, for Laban and Jacob serve different gods, and speak different languages.[63] Thus the Torah deviates from its usual discourse and mentions Nahor's gods in

63. Assis, *Identity in Conflict*, 78.

parallel to the God of Jacob's father. This parallel is albeit spoken by Laban, but even so, it is surprising that these words are included rather than downplayed. The mention of Laban's gods contributes to the sense of the divergence of two distinct religions. The distinction between the two clans is not merely social or technical; it is also religious and cultural. Laban's unusual statement is immediately followed by "Jacob swore by the Fear of his father Isaac," reinforcing the sense that his clan has its own unique culture, one that is distinct from the culture of Padan Aram.

This seems to be the significance of the Aramaic language that features in the text: "Laban called it Yegar Sahaduta, while Jacob called it Galed" (31:47). This is the only narrative in the Torah where a foreign character is quoted in their own language. Pharaoh does not speak to the Egyptians in Hebrew; nor, one presumes, does Balaam's donkey address Balaam in Hebrew. Yet their speech is translated for the sake of the biblical audience. Why is it so important to mention Laban's Aramaic name for Galed? This is a unique, momentous expression of the fact that the two characters who are now forming a covenant speak two different languages.[64] This brings us to the third circle – the national parting.

A National Parting

It is generally true that Jacob represents the Israelite nation throughout his narrative cycle, while Esau represents Edom, and Laban Aram.[65] Laban gradually becomes a synecdochic representative of the Aramean nation. When Jacob escapes with his family, Laban is referred to as "Laban the Aramean" for the first time since Jacob's arrival in Haran: "And Jacob deceived Laban the Aramean" (31:20). This designation forms an

---

64. Bompiani adds that throughout the narrative, the characters use Aramaic terminology (Bompiani, "Style Switching").

65. This reading is certainly consistent with Gunkel's general approach to the Genesis narratives (Gunkel, *Genesis*, esp. xviii–xix). But many others adopt this in regard to the Jacob cycle in particular. See especially Noth, *Pentateuchal Traditions*, 92; Mariottini, "Laban"; Loza Vera, "La berît." Compare also to Assis, *Identity in Conflict*, esp. 38–39 (regarding Esau-Edom), and for a wide survey of the Sages' approach to Laban's characterization, see Zetterholm, *Laban*.

inclusio with his escape from his father's house: "Then Isaac sent Jacob on his way. He went toward Padan Aram, to Laban son of Bethuel the Aramean" (28:5), but were this its sole purpose, it would have been more appropriately placed after he parts ways with Laban for good, at Galed. Rather, the mention of Laban's nationality at the beginning of this scene adds another layer of meaning that transcends Jacob's personal parting from his uncle and father-in-law.

In this context, Laban's simile takes on further meaning: "You have carried off my daughters like captives of the sword" (31:26). Scholars have already noted that the broad semantic fields introduced by a metaphor or simile have bearing on the text itself.[66] Here, the use of a simile that evokes war and capture connotes nations fighting each other and taking captives. In fact, the verse preceding Jacob and Laban's confrontation is rife with military overtones: "When Laban overtook him, Jacob had pitched his tent in the hill country, and Laban and his kinsmen too encamped in the hill country of Gilead" (31:25). The two camps pitch their tents opposite each other like two enemy camps preparing for war, as seen, for example, in Israel's war against the Philistines: "The Philistines were stationed on a hill on this side, Israel were stationed on a hill on that side, and the valley lay between them" (I Sam. 17:3). This is further reinforced by the aforementioned similarity to Pharaoh's pursuit of the Israelites. Two camps are ready for battle; this is no mere family feud, but a confrontation between two nations.

Moreover, beyond these hints in the text, this national dimension bursts out in the covenant itself.

Jacob and Laban's Covenant (vv. 45–55): Family Pact or International Treaty?

A brief reading of these verses already reveals that this covenant is characterized by certain doubleness; it suffices to note the two monuments which serve as testimony to the covenant. Jacob agrees to Laban's proposal to forge a covenant: "Jacob took a stone and set it up as a pillar" (31:45), but in the next verse, he also instructs "his kinsmen" to erect an additional monument, which then receives two names in two different

66. See especially Greenstein, "Metaphors."

languages: "Jacob said to his kinsmen, 'Gather stones.' They took stones and made a mound, and there by the mound they ate. Laban called it Yegar Sahaduta, while Jacob called it Galed" (vv. 46–47).

What is the relationship between the pillar Jacob sets up and the mound of stones he commands his kinsmen to erect? A brief comparison clarifies the following:

1. Jacob is responsible for the pillar, while the "kinsmen" are responsible for building the mound.
2. Jacob "sets up" a pillar using one stone, while the "kinsmen" make a "mound' out of many stones.
3. The sides eat together by the mound, but not by the pillar.
4. The mound has two names in two languages. It seems that the pillar, too, receives a name, Mizpah,[67] but even though Laban is the speaker, it is not given an Aramaic name in addition to its Hebrew one: "It is also called Mizpah (*VehaMitzpa*) because he said, 'May the Lord keep watch (*yitzef*) between me and you when we are out of each other's sight'" (31:49).

These differences all lead to the same conclusion: it is the mound Galed that serves as testimony to the covenant, while the pillar is unrelated. Mizpah serves a different purpose, as I will discuss below.

While this is not a warm, friendly alliance so much as a concession to part ways in peace, defining their separation as a "covenant" necessarily implies reconciliation: "Come now, let us make a covenant, you and I" (31:44). Because this covenant has significance beyond Jacob the individual, there is value in all his "kinsmen" participating in the making of Galed (especially according to Rashi's reading that these "kinsmen" are Jacob's sons, with him "in trouble or war"). The kinsmen's participation in the erection of the pillar is apparently less relevant. The second difference also fits in with this concept: many stones forming a single mound is an apt expression of the covenant that joins different groups together. A similar symbol is used in the covenant at Sinai (Ex. 24:4) as well as the covenant on the plains of Moab facing Mount Ebal (Deut. 27:2–4;

67. Unlike Ibn Ezra, who believes that Mizpah is another name for "*Gal*" (on 31:46).

Josh. 8). Needless to say, the same is true of the ritual meal eaten at the mound while there is no mention of the pillar. The sense of different entities converging is also evoked by the double naming of the mound: it is given two names to express its relevance for two peoples, serving as a border-stone of peace between them. The pillar, on the other hand, has one name in one language; it is not an expression of a mutual bond but a one-sided commitment.

Thus Galed's purpose is clear, but what purpose does the pillar Mizpah serve? Laban's speech reveals two roles for the two monuments and specifies which one is intended for which party (vv. 48–53):

> Laban said, "This mound is a witness between me and you this day." That is why it is called Galed.
>
> As for Mizpah, it is called thus because he said, "May the Lord keep watch between me and you when we are out of each other's sight. If you mistreat my daughters or take other wives besides my daughters, even though no one else is present, remember that God is the witness between me and you."
>
> Laban then said to Jacob, "Here is the mound and here is the pillar I have set up between us. This mound is a witness, and the pillar is a witness, that I will not go past this mound on your side and that you will not go past this mound and pillar on my side with intent to do harm. May the God of Abraham, the god of Nahor, and the god of their father be our judge."

Laban opens by defining the mound (v. 48), then defines the pillar (vv. 49–50), and finally combines the two. The mound, as mentioned, testifies to the eternal covenant between Jacob-Israel and Laban-Aram. Mizpah, however, is not mentioned in the broader national context; it remains associated with Laban's personal, familial demands from Jacob. Laban's warning against Jacob taking additional wives or mistreating his daughters is a private demand from Jacob the individual, not Jacob the budding nation – it is a marital contract the groom must sign before the father transfers the bride to his care. This exposes a further difference between the monuments: Galed expresses a mutual agreement and commitment between the speakers, whereas the pillar reflects Laban's one-sided demands from Jacob.[68]

Thus, before us are two separate focal points: Galed serves as a national covenant and boundary-stone, anticipating the future and the nations these figures represent. The pillar Mizpah, by contrast, represents Jacob's personal obligations toward his father-in-law's daughters. And indeed, Laban's final words emphasize that the mound signifies mutual commitment, while the pillar is only relevant for Jacob:

> This mound is a witness, and the pillar is a witness,
> that I will not go past *this mound* on your side
> and that you will not go past *this mound and this pillar* on my side
> with intent to do harm.

Both sides are bound by the pillar, but Jacob must look to both mound and pillar. Essentially, this is inherent in the pillar's name: "It is called Mizpah because he said, 'May the Lord keep watch between me and you when we are out of each other's sight. If you mistreat my daughters or take other wives besides my daughters, even though no one else is present, remember that God is the witness between me and you'" (vv. 49–50). Galed is a boundary marker, a warning sign to those who seek to conquer the other side, but Mizpah is a watchtower: "May the Lord keep watch between me and you." The two characters will no longer be in each other's sight, and this pillar will supervise Jacob's deeds and treatment of Laban's daughters.[69] Thus in addition to the mutual covenant, Jacob also makes a personal vow: "Jacob swore by the Fear of his father Isaac" (v. 53).

We can thus summarize that Jacob and Laban's covenant has two distinct facets: Jacob's personal commitment alongside a national covenant. Jacob and Laban are the heads of two clans; there is tension

68. Similar to Westermann, *Genesis II*, 499.

69. This verse may reflect the belief that the pillar signifies God's presence, like the pillar Jacob erects in Bethel because it is God's house; God will watch over the Canaanite border from His vantage point at Mizpah (compare to Gunkel, *Genesis*, 342).

(but cold peace) between them now, and there will be tension between their nations in the future. For now, though, the two complex decades they have spent together end with an optimistic covenant that they will never cross the other's border with intention of conquest. For now, they part ways in peace, and Laban has the chance to kiss his daughters and grandchildren goodbye (though he does not kiss Jacob himself): "He kissed his grandchildren and daughters goodbye and blessed them. Laban then left to return home" (32:1).

Given that the hill country of Gilead becomes the border of the two nations, this "hill" thus serves as the backdrop throughout the scene, mentioned six times: "He headed for the *hill* country of Gilead...he caught up with him in the *hill* country of Gilead.... Jacob pitched his tent in the *hill* country, and Laban and his kinsmen too encamped in the *hill* country of Gilead.... Jacob offered a sacrifice on the *hill*.... And they ate and spent the night upon that *hill*." The national dimension of the narrative reveals the significance of this "hill" as the site of Jacob's covenant with Laban.

This brings us back to the analogy with the Exodus from Egypt. Not only does it draw attention to Jacob's state of servitude to Laban and the need for divine help in order to break free from Haran, it also amplifies the scene's national overtones. The Exodus from Egypt marks the nascence of the Israelite nation; the "Exodus from Haran" is also a formative event in which Jacob is transformed from an individual to the father of the Israelite nation, a nation distinct from its surroundings both geographically and culturally. It is the story of Jacob and his family, but for the first time, Jacob also symbolizes the nation of Israel, just as Laban symbolizes Aram.

Intriguingly enough, it is difficult to point out a time in history that reflects this cold peace between Israel and Aram. There is harsh war between Israel and Aram throughout the Bible, despite Jacob's covenant with Laban. Yehezkel Kaufmann even mentions this as proof of the Torah's precedence: had Jacob and Laban's story been written during the time of the Prophets (as many scholars hold), then the relationship between them would certainly have been portrayed differently.[70] It

70. Kaufmann, *Religion of Israel,* vol.1, 195.

seems that the national aspect in the narrative is intended to present a "possible" relationship as opposed to an actual historical reality. Jacob and Laban's parting hints to the complicated nature of Israel's relationship with Aram: until now, the forefathers have taken wives from Aram Naharaim, but now there is an established border between them, a mound meant to symbolize a truce that in fact serves as a barrier. The future wars between the nations thus reinforce the threads of tension woven throughout this narrative, even if the covenant depicts a more ideal relationship of mutual understanding.

Angels in Mahanaim (Gen. 32:1–3)

One of the most cryptic episodes in the Jacob cycle – second only to Jacob's struggle with the angel – is Jacob's encounter with the angels at Mahanaim:

> Laban rose early the next morning. He kissed his grandchildren and daughters goodbye and blessed them. Laban then left to return home. Jacob continued on his way – and angels of God encountered him. When he saw them, Jacob said, "This is God's own camp," and he named the place Mahanaim.

For whatever reason, angels encounter Jacob, but they do nothing and say nothing to him; he only notices them and names the site of this brief encounter. What is the meaning of this sighting, and what is its purpose? Would the narrative cycle somehow be lacking if these two short verses were not included? This incident is as short as it is surprising.[1]

---

1. Modern scholarship has two central approaches: that the original scene was longer and the current text omits the actual plot (such as Sarna, *Understanding Genesis*, 203), and that this is an etymological anecdote explaining the name "Mahanaim." See this debate in Gunkel, *Genesis*, 342–343.

R. Joseph Bekhor Shor explains that the angels remain silent because they only appear in order to honor Jacob: "It seems that these angels – who say nothing that is recorded – only came to honor him, as people go out to meet those who have journeyed from afar" (on 32:2). The main advantage of this interpretation is that it is sensitive to what is missing and gives this omission meaning: rather than filling the angels' silence with unwritten content, it explains that their appearance is meaningful in itself. But even before this reading, there is room to ask why Jacob is granted such honor at this point in the plot.

Houtman raises an intriguing direction: that the episode should be read in parallel to Jacob's vision of the angels at Bethel (a connection I will discuss further below), and that Mahanaim should be interpreted similarly: "It is the place where the messengers of God, the servants of the King of the world, have their home; from there they go out to fulfil orders everywhere on earth, thither they return after finishing their tasks."[2] Read thus, Jacob's exile in Haran is framed with his exposure to the holy sites of angels. The connection between his encounter with angels at Mahanaim and his vision of angels in Bethel is solid and convincing, but the nuance of the language challenges this theory: "Mahanaim" – the *camp* of God (in contrast to "Bethel" – the *house* of God) indicates a temporary site as opposed to a permanent home. Thus rather than a story about a holy site, it seems that Jacob's encounter at Mahanaim is a brief, dramatic encounter that happens along the way.[3] Moreover, the fact that Mahanaim does not appear again in the Bible as a holy site (its only other mention in biblical narrative is as the royal residence of Ishboshet, who is a temporary, doomed ruler) makes it difficult to read this incident as a story that celebrates a place of divine worship.

We will yet return to Houtman's theory, but I believe that the best way to interpret this verse is through Jacob's own reaction: "This is God's own camp." Is the significance of Jacob's statement the fact that he

2. Houtman, "Mahanaim." Based on its parallel to Bethel, Houtman believes that it makes sense to read Mahanaim as another prophetic dream.
3. Houtman is aware of this issue and explains that the inherently temporary nature of a camp expresses the flexible nature of God's connection with humanity ("Mahanaim," 39).

identifies these angels? Some exegetes believe so, such as Bekhor Shor, who emphasizes that Jacob recognizes these figures as angels "because he was familiar with them and knew them" (on 32:3). Others argue that the verse's focus is the fact that only Jacob can see these angels: "He alone saw the camp of angels around his own camp, and that is why he named the place Mahanaim – for these two camps: his own and the angels'" (Ibn Ezra on 32:2). According to this reading, it is no coincidence that the verse is phrased "When he saw them" – he alone sees them and identifies them as angels. According to these readings, the focus of this episode is Jacob's reaction to his identification of these beings.

Yet perhaps the most significant aspect of these verses is Jacob's definition that these angels are God's "camp." The biblical term "*maḥane*," "camp," is not only "an area of ground temporarily occupied by a group of people who set up tents or booths or the like for shelter and lodging" (*Even Shoshan Dictionary*, "*maḥane*"); it frequently denotes a military camp, with soldiers. For example: "When you are *encamped* (*Ki tetzei maḥane*) against your enemies, guard against any impropriety" (Deut. 23:10); "Barak chased the chariots and camp to Haroshet Hagoyim, and all of Sisera's *camp* fell by the sword; not a single man survived" (Judges 4:16); "Get up," he announced, "for the Lord has delivered the Midianite *camp* into your hands!" (Judges 7:15). In this context, we can also understand the description of Israel's "camp" in the wilderness: "The Israelites shall encamp in their respective camps, each by his own banner, in his division" (Num. 1:52); these are just a few of many examples.[4] One particularly fascinating instance in this context is the description of David's camp, which uses the phrase "God's own camp": "They helped David against the raiders, for they were all valiant warriors, and they became officers of the army. Day by day, men kept coming to David to support him until his camp was as great as God's own camp (*kemaḥane Elohim*)" (I Chr. 12:22–23).[5]

4. See Helfmeyer, "*Ḥana*," 8–9.
5. Perhaps the word *Elohim* expresses the size of the camp (as in Naphtali's name, above, and other examples; see my discussion of "*Benei Elohim*" in Grossman, "Sons of God"). But though the meaning is different in both places, it may be that the text in Chronicles is based on these verses in Genesis, if only as wordplay.

Jacob does not merely identify these beings as angels – as the narrator has just done – but as a military camp.[6] There are other biblical narratives with heavenly hosts that fight, such as the king of Aram's search for Elisha:

> "Do not be afraid," he said, "for there are many more with us than with them."
> And Elisha prayed. "O Lord," he said, "open his eyes now, so he may see."
> The Lord opened the boy's eyes, and suddenly, the hill was full of horses and fiery chariots all around Elisha. (II Kings 6:16–17).

Jacob's sighting of this heavenly camp on the eve of his entrance to the land recalls Joshua's encounter with a commander angel on the eve of his entrance to the land:

> When Joshua was near Jericho, he looked up and suddenly saw a man standing opposite him, drawn sword in hand. Joshua approached him and asked, "Are you for us or for our enemies?" He said, "No, for I am the commander of the Lord's hosts. Now I have come!" (Josh. 5:13–14).

The fact that Jacob sees these angels during a crucial narrative transition only amplifies the mystery. Joshua's encounter with the angel is also difficult to read, and its specific role within the narrative is not entirely clear either. For the sake of our discussion, I wish to apply Joshua's question to Jacob's angels: Are they for him or his enemies? I assume that most readers take this episode as a brief shout of encouragement to Jacob – the angels appear to cheer him and guide him on his way (as

6. As proposed by Helfmeyer, "*Ḥana*," 16, and many others. Sforno wonders about the redundancy of this explanation, as this information was just related, and thus explains that through this encounter, Jacob defines his own camp as "God's camp" (on 32:3); As R. Yehuda Kuperman explains Sforno's reading: that based on this encounter, Jacob feels that his own camp reaches the rank of "God's camp" (Kuperman, *Sforno*, vol. 1, 195). I believe that Jacob's explanation expresses that he identifies them not merely as angels, but as angels of war.

suggested by Ibn Ezra, Rashbam, Ramban, Radak, among others) – but given that soon after, another encounter with an angel results in a desperate combat, there is certainly room for this question. Some indeed read Mahanaim as a foreshadow of his imminent divine struggle (especially through the verb "*vayifge'u*," which means "harmed" as well as "met").[7]

Nonetheless, Joshua's angel is not "for his enemies," nor does it seem that these angels intend Jacob any harm. God's camp arrives to accompany Jacob on his way, as promised: "Go back to the land of your fathers where you were born; I will be with you" (31:3). Unlike Joshua, Jacob does not engage with these divine escorts; this implies that their role is obvious to him: now that he is on his way, and especially now that he has parted from Laban for good, his guardian angels have arrived. The expression "*vayifge'u*" sometimes expresses coincidence, but it can also signify intentional meeting, such as "They met Moses and Aaron, who stood awaiting them as they left Pharaoh" (Ex. 5:20). Moreover, this particular verb is in dialogue with Jacob's arrival at Bethel on his way to Haran, as we will see below.

BEGINNING OR END?

In order to fully understand this scene we must first determine the unit's boundaries, which in this case is a complex task. This debate is already evident in the difference between the ancient Jewish division into *parashot* and Langton's division into chapters: the former places the Mahanaim episode at the end of the previous scene so that it concludes his parting from Laban; while the latter begins a new chapter (32) with this incident so that it introduces a new unit – his meeting with Esau.[8]

7. Zakovitch, "Jabok, Penuel, Mahanim, Bethel: Biblical Name Explanations as a Mirror of Ideological Struggles," *Ariel* 100–101 (1994), 193 [Hebrew]; see also Houtman, "Mahanaim," 38, where he claims that this reading is highly hypothetical.
8. In some editions, chapter 32 opens with Jacob's parting from Laban, while others (mainly English translations) begin with our verse 2: Jacob's encounter with angels. This reflects a further debate: Even if the encounter with Esau begins with an encounter with angels, does the story begin with parting from Laban, or with the description of Jacob's next experience?

This episode could also be considered an independent unit, unrelated to what happens before and after it.[9]

A careful analysis leads to a far more complex conclusion than any of the above. This brief incident is both end and beginning; its design and placement encourage its reading as the conclusion of his exile as well as the introduction to his reunion with Esau.

On the one hand, it seems that Jacob's sighting of the angels continues the description of Laban's departure:

> Laban rose early the next morning. He kissed his grandchildren and daughters goodbye and blessed them.
> *Laban went* (*Vayelekh... Lavan*) to return home.
> *Jacob went* (*VeYaakov halakh*) on his way – and angels of God encountered him. (32:1–2)

Vayelekh Lavan / VeYaakov halakh – the reversal of the classic predicate/subject order in the second verse characterizes it as a contrast to the first verse: Laban goes on his way, and so does Jacob. The dispersion of characters is a classic ending in biblical narrative,[10] and this is definitely constructed as the scene's end: Laban "rose early the next morning" after he has spent the night on the hill where they made their covenant; he kisses his grandchildren and daughters goodbye (after complaining that he did not get a chance to do so because of their escape – "You did not even let me kiss my grandchildren and daughters goodbye" – 31:28). He also blesses them; their escape has become a formal parting. Just as Jacob flees to Haran because of his brother's wrath but still leaves with his father's blessing, his wives flee from their father's house but ultimately leave him with his blessing.[11] Laban then "left to return home," and Jacob, too, "continued on his way." On his way, "angels of God encountered him." This encounter is the direct continuation of his parting from

9. As claimed by Gunkel, *Genesis*, 342–43 (following Meyer), and similarly Skinner, *Genesis*, 405.

10. On the characters' parting as the closing of a circle, see especially Seeligmann, "Hebräische Erzählung."

11. Sforno is aware of this analogy, and appreciates Laban's blessing, but still differentiates between the force of Laban's blessing and Isaac's blessing (on 32:1).

Laban: Laban goes on his way, to be met by his shepherds and flock, and Jacob goes on his way, to be met by angels.

Further proof that this incident serves to conclude his time in Haran is the *inclusio* it forms with his vision on the eve of his departure for Haran. As I have already hinted, the textual connection between the two scenes is striking:

Jacob's Departure to Haran (28:11–19)	His Return from Haran (32:1–2)
He happened (*vayifga*) upon a certain place	They encountered (*vayifge'u*) him,
And there were angels of God.	angels of God.
He said, "... this is none other than the house of God!"	When he saw them, Jacob said, "This is God's own camp!"
And he named that place Bethel.	And he named that place Mahanaim.

Rashi already notes this connection and reads this scene as the end of his exile in Haran. He comments that the angels on the ladder are "ascending and descending: the angels who escorted him in the Land do not leave the Land, so they ascended to heaven, while the angels of outside the Land descended to escort him" (on Gen. 28:12), while at Mahanaim "the angels of the Land of Israel come toward him to escort him to the Land" (on Gen. 32:1).[12] As mentioned, Houtman takes this a step further and proposes that both places are holy sites. In other words, the incident at Mahanaim offers further understanding of the nature of angels: Bethel is a permanent gateway where angels ascend and descend, but the story of Mahanaim shows that angels are not bound to one particular place; they are able to set up camp wherever there is need.

Thus the scene at Mahanaim is a fitting conclusion to Jacob's exile in Haran – as expressed through the Jewish division into *parashot*.[13] On the other hand, the brief episode's design hints that it also marks

12. On the connection between the two encounters with angels, see also Westermann, *Genesis II*, 452.
13. This direction is favored by Dillmann, *Genesis II*, 270–71; Sarna, *Genesis*, 223; Wenham, *Genesis II*, 266; Assis, *Identity in Conflict*, 69.

the beginning of the next unit: of Jacob's meeting with Esau, following Langton's division.[14] This is evident through the scene's language and the semantic fields it evokes. The word "camp," especially in plural form, links this scene to the next chapter, in which "camp" features as a keyword (and which ends with Jacob setting up camp in Shechem – 33:18).[15] Another keyword introduced in the Mahanaim episode is *malakhim*: "angels," which also means "messengers"; immediately after Jacob meets "angels" (*malakhim*), he sends "messengers" (*malakhim*) to Esau (32:4). The Midrash explores this wordplay:

> How many messengers passed before our father Jacob as he entered the Land? R. Huna said in the name of R. Aibu: sixty myriads.... R. Yudan said: He took some of them and sent them as messengers before him.[16]

Even if the word appears in two different senses (see Ibn Ezra in particular),[17] the juxtaposition of the same word demands attention. This invites a different interpretation of the relationship between Mahanaim and Jacob's dream in Bethel. Perhaps the two do not only form an *inclusio*; perhaps they can be read as parallel openings: the dream in Bethel encourages Jacob before his exile and time with Laban; the encounter with angels in Mahanaim encourages Jacob before his meeting with Esau.

The inner structure of Jacob's meeting with Esau also frames Mahanaim as part of the unit. The first half of the unit opens with the angels at Mahanaim, while the second half of the unit opens with Jacob's struggle with the angel (see below).

---

14. For example: Fokkelman, *Genesis*, 197; Mathews, *Genesis II*, 545–49.
15. Speiser, *Genesis*, 254; Wenham, *Genesis II*, 296; Fokkelman, "Secrets of the Night." I believe that Fokkelman exaggerates by stating that opening the scene of the brothers' reconciliation with Jacob's encounter with angels is fundamental to the narrative objective because one ought to address a brother as if addressing God.
16. Genesis Rabba 74:17.
17. R. Medan tends to see this midrash as the plain meaning of the text: "The messengers that Jacob sends to Esau are the angels he encounters in Mahanaim" (Medan, *Close to You*, 255).

Thus this brief episode is both ending and beginning; both the Jewish division into *parshiyot* and the Langton division into chapters are justified. Jacob's encounter with the angels in Mahanaim is a "narrative nexus" that concludes his exile in Haran and anticipates his imminent meeting with Esau.[18] Though the story of the brothers' reunion is an independent narrative, it should also be read as the continuation of Jacob's time with Laban.[19]

This brings us to the narrative objective. Between the two greatest conflicts of Jacob's life, between his two most difficult confrontations – his relationship with his uncle Laban and with his brother Esau – Jacob encounters guardian angels. The fact that Mahanaim serves as a nexus unit hints that angels accompany Jacob wherever he goes, and the potentially violent nature of these confrontations necessitates that these guardian angels be angels of war. They are with Jacob as he leaves Laban and as he makes his way toward Esau; they represent God's perpetual providence over him.

This nexus also encourages a comparison between the units, and it is no coincidence that the scene is an encounter with angels. It is an angel that appears to Jacob in Haran, protecting him from Laban's manipulation: "In the dream an angel of God said to me, 'Jacob... I have seen all the Laban is doing to you'" (31:11–12); and soon, before his reunion with Esau, he meets yet another angel. For whatever reason, this divine figure attacks Jacob and even injures him instead of protecting him (as we will explore further below), but the repeated appearance of angels framing each confrontation creates a pattern that is only reinforced by the nexus unit of Mahanaim.

---

18. On these verses as a nexus unit, see Westermann, *Genesis II*, 504 (he mainly sees the scene as the introduction to Jacob and Esau's encounter, but writes that this unit also concludes Jacob and Laban). On this phenomenon in general, see Grossman, *Text and Subtext*, 193–96 (this unit is discussed there). This term is synonymous with the term "Janus Parallelism," where one word has two parallel meanings, one based on the preceding text, and one based on the following text. While Janus Parallelism refers to individual words or phrases, a "nexus unit" is a small narrative unit.
19. Compare to Zakovitch, "Jacob, Deceit."

As mentioned above, Jacob's deception of Laban is superfluous from both a pragmatic and theological perspective: Laban catches up with him, *and* God protects him from harm. If we read the Mahanaim incident as part of this paradigm, then the angels Jacob sees are supposed to encourage him before his reunion with his brother. Jacob should know that God will continue watching over him as promised. Yet to the reader's surprise, Jacob is filled with trepidation, which I will explore below.

A moment before we delve into the story of Jacob's reunion with his brother, I wish to make a prefatory comment based on the Mahanaim nexus. As mentioned, Jacob's encounter with angels forms an *inclusio* with his flight to Haran;[20] his exile is framed with guardian angels and the promise of protection. Beyond the artistic contribution of this *inclusio*, it also has implications for the plot: if his encounter in Mahanaim marks the end of his exile, then it is time for him to fulfill the vow he made in Bethel. This chapter of his life has come to a close, and God has indeed watched over him; now there is expectation that he will go and pay his vow. This expectation is beautifully expressed by R. Joseph Hertz: "Jacob continued on his way – to Bethel, the place where God sent him to pay his vow. This vision confirmed that God was aware of his promises."[21] Even if it is not stated explicitly, the angel's command implies that God now anticipates the fulfillment of his vow. Hertz asserts that the angel's revelation to Jacob in Haran – "I am the God of Bethel, where you anointed a pillar and made a vow to Me. Now – leave this land at once and return to the land where you were born" (31:13) – constitutes proof that God has indeed heard his prayer and vow. Until now, Jacob cannot have been sure whether his dream in Bethel was truly a divine revelation or a vivid reflection of his own inner turmoil. The angel's revelation in Haran lends validity to the revelation in Bethel: validity to the dream, and new validity, of course, to his own vow.

---

20. See Ramban's discussion of Rashi's explanation that the angels of Mahanaim are angels of the Land of Israel. Ramban finds this problematic because Jacob has not yet entered the land; he is correct that this does not mark Jacob's actual entrance to the land, but only the end of his exile. See below, in my analysis of Sukkot and Shechem.

21. Hertz, *Pentateuch*, 117.

Thus the delineation of the exile narrative is not merely an aesthetic issue; it has bearing on the actual plot. Now that Jacob has come full circle, the reader expects that he will pay his vow. We will soon attempt to understand why Jacob seeks reconciliation with Esau before fulfilling his vow.

The Meeting of Jacob and Esau (Gen. 32:4–33:15)

> Thus must I from the smoke into the smother;
> From tyrant duke unto a tyrant brother.
>
> – Shakespeare, *As You Like It,* Act I, Scene II

Jacob was just in Mahanaim, but now he is already sending messengers to his brother Esau – who, it suddenly emerges, lives in Mount Seir, in Edom. This surprises many scholars: Why doesn't Jacob cross the Jordan and enter Canaan? Why does he send messengers all the way to Edom, and why does Esau travel so far just to meet his brother? Gunkel, clearly exasperated, draws the conclusion that if Esau indeed lives in Edom, then it cannot be that Jacob encounters angels in Mahanaim; and if Jacob does see the angels in Mahanaim, then according to the original story, Esau must have lived somewhere closer than Edom.[1]

I believe that this is one of those cases where the question becomes the answer. If Jacob indeed sends messengers all the way to Edom, even though he is on the brink of Canaan's borders, then the brothers are clearly going to great pains to meet each other despite the distance. This contributes to their characterization: Jacob is so terrified of Esau that he sends messengers to him the moment he reaches the borders of his homeland; he hopes for reconciliation before he reaches

1. Gunkel, *Genesis*, 344. Gunkel cites Meyer that ancient Edom was much farther north than it was later on, and it may be that Esau is not actually that far from Jacob.

his father's house. These fears grow even more when he hears that Esau is coming with four hundred men, despite the great distance between them. To Jacob's mind, this only proves that Esau's bitter hatred toward him has not dissipated even after twenty years. Esau is not making a casual gesture; it is clear to Jacob – and to the reader – that he has specific intentions, which terrifies his brother.

Jacob sends messengers assuming that his brother's rage still burns and he must appease him: "Time heals some wounds, reasons Jacob, but exacerbates others."[2] Unlike the Joseph narrative, where it is the victim who proposes reconciliation with the brothers who sold him, here it is Jacob – the offender – who initiates reconciliation.[3] Will Esau accept his apology?

This episode is characterized by what we might dub the "broken telephone effect." Jacob sends messengers with a specific message for Esau: "Say the following to my lord Esau: Your servant Jacob says, 'I have been staying with Laban; until now I have remained there. And I have acquired cattle, donkeys, sheep, and male and female servants. I am sending this message to my lord to find favor in your eyes'" (32:5–6). Yet there is no mention of these messengers' meeting with Esau, what they report, and how he responds; the plot simply skips this stage and goes straight to the messengers' report. Here, too, instead of quoting Esau's reply, they merely describe his actions: "We came to your brother Esau. He is on his way to meet you, and with him, four hundred men" (32:7). This omission is just as irritating: Does Jacob interrogate them about Esau's response? Is Esau silent in response to his brother's message?

Once again, this is a case of "broken telephone" – Jacob does not see Esau's response to his message with his own eyes; he only hears the messengers' description, which is emphatically neutral. The lacunae in this scene are so salient that they cannot be coincidental; the reader – like

2. Hamilton, *Genesis II*, 320.
3. Nechama Leibowitz debates whether Jacob reaches out as a gesture of peace or to display his power and intimidate his brother (*Genesis*, 241). Since Jacob addresses his brother as "My lord," the first is more likely, and R. D. Z. Hoffmann concurs (*Genesis II*, 485).

Jacob himself – is intentionally kept in the dark about Esau's intentions.[4] Does he approach Jacob in order to fight him or make amends? Two possible interpretations of Esau's actions are both supported by the text: one thread is that Esau sets out to confront Jacob, but following Jacob's generous gifts and submissive attitude, he changes his mind and embraces him in conciliation; a second possibility is that Esau never means any harm in the first place, and Jacob's concerns are groundless.

It is no coincidence that commentators have always been divided in this respect. Rashi believes that Esau intends to harm Jacob: "We came to your brother Esau – you would say 'He is my brother' but he acts like the wicked Esau, still gripped with hatred" (on Gen. 32:7, based on Genesis Rabba 80:71). Note how Rashi reads the text to Esau's detriment: the messengers refer to Esau as "your brother," which suggests closeness – though the narrator also describes Esau as "Jacob's brother" when Jacob sends messengers to Esau: "Jacob sent messengers ahead of him to his brother Esau in the land of Seir, the country of Edom" (32:4). However, Jacob instructs his messengers to refer to Esau not as "his brother" but as his "lord": "Say the following to *my lord* Esau: *Your servant* Jacob says, 'I have been staying with Laban … I am sending this message to *my lord* to find favor in your eyes'" (32:5–6).[5] The messengers' description of Esau as "your brother" thus implies that Esau's attitude toward Jacob is forgiving and brotherly, consistent with the narrator's usage, and unlike Jacob's fears. Yet Rashi argues that it means precisely the opposite: Jacob sends messengers to "his brother Esau," but Esau will not treat him as a "brother."[6]

---

4. The general sense is that Jacob fears that Esau will fight him, as Leah Frankel, for example, writes: "Whatever Esau's intentions, one thing is clear: Jacob believes that Esau is intent on war" (Frankel, *Chapters*, 112). Nonetheless, Shapira proposes that Jacob prepares for both possibilities (Shapira, "Jacob and Esau," 272).
5. Speiser claims that Jacob's words "to my lord, to Esau" are part of the message (*Genesis*, 254). I am not convinced that this is the case, but either way, the messengers saying "your brother" changes the title Jacob uses.
6. This reading is favored by R. D. Z. Hoffmann, *Genesis II*, 489. He also favors Ramban's aforementioned approach that Esau did not receive Jacob's messengers at all, but rather "informed them through his men that he was coming toward him," and even proposes to read Amos' prophecy about Edom (Amos 1:11) as an allusion to this scene (ibid., 490).

Rashi favors this reading throughout the narrative, and detects similar tension in Jacob's prayer: "Rescue me, I pray, from my brother's hand, from the hand of Esau – from the hand of my 'brother' who does not act like my brother but as the wicked 'Esau'" (on 32:12). According to Rashi, Jacob's fear is justified; Esau intends to harm him, but "he was overcome with mercy when he saw [Jacob] bowing down before him again and again" (on 33:4). Ramban also favors this direction, and takes Esau's silence in the face of Jacob's messengers as a sign of his wrath:

> It seems to me that Esau did not receive the messengers properly and paid them no heed. Perhaps they did not even come before him because he did not at all give permission for them to come before him and speak to him, for otherwise, the text would have related that Esau questioned them concerning his brother's welfare, his circumstances, and those of his household and children, [and that he asked] that they convey greetings to Jacob and tell him that he is proceeding toward him to see him, and they would have told it thus to Jacob. The text, however, does not narrate that the messengers transmitted a word in Esau's name – instead, he kept his wrath in his heart, and he came with his army with evil intention. (Ramban on 32:8)

Rashbam, however, proposes a different reading. He disagrees with Rashi's earlier interpretation of the messengers' words, and writes: "We have come to your brother, to Esau, and you have found favor in his eyes, as you said. And now, out of joy for your arrival, and out of his love for you, he comes toward you with four hundred men in your honor" (on 32:7). According to Rashbam, the messengers do not share their master's concern; not only do they interpret Esau's actions as reconciliatory, it does not even occur to them (at this stage) that Jacob experiences their reply differently. Unlike their interpretation, "Jacob was acutely afraid – in his heart. Even though he showed the messengers that [Esau] meant to honor him, he believed that Esau's intentions were not good but evil" (on 32:8). Jacob acts as if Esau indeed means to honor him, as his messengers believe, but inside, he is terrified. Eventually, the messengers prove correct and Esau indeed runs to embrace his brother.

Modern scholars, too, are torn between these two readings, both of which have basis in the text. Let us first consider the messengers' words; do they connote conciliation or enmity? It may be, of course, that their words are entirely – in fact, inherently – neutral. This is R. Joseph Bekhor Shor's reading: "We do not know whether his intentions are good or bad, for his only reply to us was: 'I will go and speak with him face to face, and since I will speak to him, what need I say to you?'" (on 32:7). Others, however, argue that the messengers' reply does hint to the nature of Esau's intentions.

ESAU COMES TO FIGHT

The most convincing argument for those who claim that the messengers' report bodes ill is his considerable entourage: "He is on his way to meet you, *and with him, four hundred men*" (32:7). Why does Esau approach with such an enormous group? If he means to reconcile with Jacob, then the purpose of all those men is not clear; if he means to fight his brother, of course, then it is obvious. It is worth pointing out that in the Bible, a unit of "four hundred men" is a respectable fighting force; "four hundred men" gather to David when he flees Saul, and "he became their leader" (I Sam. 22:2). These four hundred men (and another two hundred who stay behind) comprise David's attack force (I Sam. 25:13; 30:10).[7]

Further support for this reading is Jacob's reaction to the messengers' report: "Jacob was acutely afraid and distressed" (32:8). While it may be that Jacob is misinterpreting their words, or that the messengers themselves have misinterpreted Esau's response, the reader's only access to events is through the speaker's interpretation, and his or her natural tendency is to identify with the protagonist. If Jacob – who receives the messengers in person – understands them a certain way, the reader is hard-pressed to understand them differently.

This approach is reinforced through the analogy between Jacob's recent confrontation with Laban in Gilead and his impending meeting with Esau. Just like Laban, Esau approaches with "his kinsmen" with malicious intent, but instead of harming Jacob, they ultimately part

7. For example: Sarna, *Genesis*, 224; Weinfeld, *Genesis*, 189–90; Shapira, "Jacob and Esau," 271–73; Alter, *Five Books*, 177.

ways peacefully. Ramban's explanation of Esau's change of heart, "And with this he was comforted, for the hearts belong to God, who sways them however He wills" (on 32:8), could also apply to Laban's change of heart in the previous scene. Laban's intentions change after explicit divine revelation; Ramban argues that Esau's intentions are also shaped, covertly, by God's will.

ESAU COMES IN PEACE

While the story can be read assuming that Esau means to fight Jacob but eventually changes his mind, the messengers' words can be interpreted differently. I have already pointed out that they refer to Esau as "your brother" while Jacob calls him "his lord"; while it makes sense that the messengers favor "brother" over calling Esau Jacob's "lord," the word "brother" is superfluous: "We came to Esau" would have been sufficient. Thus use of the word "brother" suggests friendship and amity, and that Jacob's fears are baseless; Esau will treat him as a brother.[8] Abarbanel, for example, writes:

> They believed that he was coming to honor him, and for this they came back to Jacob and told him, "We came to your brother, to Esau," that is, why should you call him "my lord" when he is your loving, faithful brother, and "He is on his way to meet you" means that it is not enough for him to receive your message – he himself is coming to receive you.[9]

The phrase "*holekh likrat*" – "on his way to meet you" – also implies reconciliation, as Amnon Shapira writes:

> Besides our verse, the phrase "*holekh likrat*" appears fourteen times, out of which three have military connotations; but eleven times – that is, 78 percent of occurrences – have peaceful connotations, and this is the main resonance that an ancient Hebrew

8. Sarna, *Genesis*, 224.
9. Abarbanel on Genesis. Later on, he explains that Esau's four hundred men are there to honor Jacob.

> attuned to linguistic nuance would associate with the phrase "*halikha likrat*."[10]

I am not convinced that statistics are the best way to determine the connotations of a certain phrase, when so much depends on context. Careful analysis of the isolated phrase does not result in a *necessary* connotation – as Sarna puts it, it is a "phrase that can convey either enmity or amity."[11] Shapira is correct, however, that the 78 percent of occurrences associated with peace may influence the reading of "your brother." The word "*gam*" – "also" – used by the messengers also has certain bearing: we came to *your brother*, and he, too, is coming to you, gladly, in peace.

Thus we can also add what Rashbam already alludes to: an analogy between this scene and the scene of Moses' return to Egypt after his exile in Midian. There, too, his brother comes out to meet him: "Have you not a brother, Aaron the Levite? He, I know, is able to speak. Even now he is setting out to meet you, and when he sees you his heart will rejoice" (Ex. 4:14). Beyond the similar language, there is a broader analogy between Jacob and Moses. A comprehensive comparison exceeds the scope of this discussion, but for now I will point out the main similarities between the figures:[12]

- Moses, like Jacob, is forced to flee his birthplace and family.
- Moses, like Jacob, meets his future wife at the well, among the local shepherds.
- Both heroes marry this girl and move in with their father-in-law.
- Both heroes work as shepherds for their father-in-law, and sons are born to them there.
- God appears to both and orders them to return to their birthplace.

10. Shapira, "Jacob and Esau," 271.
11. Sarna, *Genesis*, 224; similarly: Hamilton, *Genesis II*, 322.
12. Coats, "Moses in Midian." Martin sees this as part of the "courting narrative" genre, and includes Saul, Ruth, and other examples (Martin, "Betrothal Journey"). But within this wider definition, one loses the specific unique parallels between Jacob and Moses.

- Though they fulfill this command, both are attacked by a divine figure on their way.[13]
- Upon their return, their brother comes out to meet them, embracing or kissing them.

For the sake of our discussion, Rashbam's analogy is convincing; reading Esau's "meeting" with Jacob against Aaron's "meeting" with Moses seems to imply that Esau, like Aaron, will rejoice in his heart upon his brother's return.

The confusion surrounding analysis of the messengers' words is great indeed. Both parts of their message can be read to suit either interpretation. A reader who is convinced that the first half of their message implies that Esau seeks conciliation can read the four hundred men accompanying him as a glorious entourage; as Ḥizkuni, for example, writes: "'He is on his way to meet you' – to greet you with joy. 'And with him, four hundred men' – to show you honor" (on 32:6).

On the other hand, a reader who sees the four hundred men as an ominous sign can detect tension and fraternal strife in the messengers' use of "your brother," as R. Shlomo Ephraim Luntschitz expresses in his earlier commentary: "Not only is he dissatisfied with you, he also approaches you for no other reason than to fight with you, and proof of this is the four hundred men with him, who must be coming to fight" (*Kli Yakar* on 32:7).

In fact, the very report of the messengers' return amplifies the ambiguity of Esau's intentions. If he means to fight, then why would he allow Jacob's messengers to return and warn him? On the other hand, perhaps he is so convinced of his own strength that he wishes to strike fear into Jacob's heart prior to their meeting (as Nahash the Ammonite does before attacking Jabesh Gilead – I Sam. 11:1–3).[14]

---

13. See especially Adar, *Genesis*, 88–89; Benor, "Blood Groom." Benor also compares the angel touching Jacob on the thigh and the foreskin touching Moses' feet (Ex. 4:25).
14. Fokkelman, *Genesis*, 201; Wenham, *Genesis II*, 290.

How, then, should their message be understood? This is a striking example of narrative ambiguity – of intentional ambiguity.[15] The messengers' reply is formulated in a way that allows two opposite readings. R. Shlomo Ephraim Luntschitz detects this ambiguity and reaches the conclusion that the messengers themselves are uncertain: "We came to your brother who seems to show brotherhood and love, but we also see the opposite of this because he is coming to meet you, and therefore we are confused" (*Kli Yakar*, ibid.).

This complex design contributes to the narrative objective. First and foremost, it builds suspense before the brothers' meeting. In the words of Emanueli:

> This vague formulation, which can be understood either way, is intentional. It does not disclose the well-known ending. In this way it increases suspense, and leaves the question open as to whether Jacob was correct in his assessment, or if Esau did mean to attack but was swayed by the impressive gift.[16]

But beyond building suspense, this ambiguity makes a contribution in itself, touching upon the narrative's characterization. I wish to present R. Mordechai Sabato's fascinating reading, with some slight modifications.

JACOB'S DOUBLE PREPARATION

R. Sabato points out that Jacob prepares himself for both possibilities – for both war and conciliation – and these preparations are presented in two separate, parallel sections. To illustrate, here are the two sections in which Jacob prepares to meet Esau:[17]

---

15. Fokkelman senses that Jacob's encounter at Mahanaim already raises conflicting expectations – does it express God's protection, as when he encountered the angels at Bethel, or does the fact that these seem to be angels of war suggest that war with Esau is imminent? (Fokkelman, *Genesis*, 198).
16. Emanueli, *Genesis*, 426.
17. According to this division, the prayer and dividing the camp into two are part of the same preparation, that which anticipates Esau's violence; it is logical that fear of an impending war stirs Jacob to prayer. The Sages differentiate between "war" and "prayer" and explain that Jacob prepared for his meeting in three ways: with gifts,

	Preparations for War (32:8–10)	An Attempt at Appeasement (32:14–22)
Jacob's Response: Camp (*Maḥane*) and Gift (*Minḥa*)	Jacob was acutely afraid and distressed. He divided the people with him into two camps, along with the flocks, the cattle, and the camels.	Then, from what he had at hand, he selected a gift for his brother Esau: two hundred female goats, twenty male goats, two hundred ewes, twenty rams, thirty milk camels and their young, forty cows, ten bulls, twenty female donkeys, and ten male donkeys. He put them in the care of his servants, each herd by itself, and he told the servants, "Go on ahead of me. Keep a space between the herds."
Explanation of Jacob's Action	"If Esau comes and attacks one camp," he thought, "the other camp may still survive."	He instructed the first, "When my brother Esau meets you and asks, 'To whom do you belong? Where are you going? Who owns all these animals ahead of you?' you must say, 'They belong to your servant Jacob; they are a gift sent to my lord Esau – and he is coming behind us.'" He likewise instructed the second and third and all the others who followed the herds, "You shall say the same thing to Esau when you meet him. Also say, 'Your servant Jacob is coming behind us.'" He thought, "I will pacify him with these gifts I am sending on ahead. Then I will face him. Perhaps he will accept me."

prayer, and preparation for war. R. Breuer proposes that this is based on the text's threefold division (as opposed to my proposed division into two): first Jacob prays; then he sends a gift; then he struggles with the angel, whom the Sages identify as Esau's ministering angel – it is this struggle that R. Breuer defines as "war" (Breuer, *Chapters of Genesis*, vol. 2, 551–54).

	Preparations for War (32:8–10)	**An Attempt at Appeasement (32:14–22)**
Prayer	Then Jacob prayed, "God of my father Abraham and God of my father Isaac, Lord, You who said to me, 'Go back to the land where you were born and I will deal well with you,' I am unworthy of all the kindnesses and the faithfulness that You have bestowed upon Your servant. When I crossed the Jordan I had only my staff, and now I have become two camps. Rescue me, I pray, from my brother's hand, from the hand of Esau. I am afraid he will come and kill us all, mothers and children alike. Yet You said, 'I will deal well with you and make your descendants countless, like the sand of the sea.'"	
Spending the Night	He spent the night there.	So the gifts went on ahead of him, while he remained in the camp that night.[18]

18. The last verse combines *minḥa* and *maḥane,* thus revealing the wordplay of the entire scene. This marks the end of Jacob's preparations, and he goes to sleep for the night – the fact that he then wakes up in the middle of the night is surprising, as I will soon discuss.

Both parts conclude with the description of Jacob "spending the night" there, which hints that his two kinds of preparation took place at the same time and ended with nightfall (as opposed to one long sequence that took place over two days). Jacob, anticipating Esau's violence, divides his camp into two, but at the same time, he sends a generous gift in the hope of appeasing him. As R. Breuer notes, there is certain similarity between these two actions – in both, Jacob divides his camp into two in the hope that at least one group will survive: he divides his family into two in the hope that if Esau attacks one camp, the other will have the chance to escape; he divides his livestock into two in the hope that one group will appease Esau and thus ensure that he keeps the remaining animals.[19]

The anagrammatic words *minḥa-maḥane* ("gift" and "camp") function as a pair of keywords in this scene, each appearing in one of the two sections. "*Maḥane*" (camp) is mentioned throughout his preparations for a violent encounter, and appropriately enough, it carries military connotations. "*Minḥa*" (gift) is mentioned throughout the second half, in the hope that his gifts will move Esau to "accept" Jacob.

Note that Jacob's prayer is included within the first stage – the fear Jacob mentions in his prayer is that Esau will attack his family: "I am afraid he will come and kill us all, mothers and children alike." The central motifs that appear when he divides up his camp are also mentioned in his prayer: his "fear" of Esau (32:8, 12); his concern of "attack" (vv. 9, 12); and his "two camps" (vv. 8, 11).[20] It is thus clear that Jacob's prayer relates to his fear of Esau's violence; he prays as if on the eve of battle.

Thus Jacob's twofold preparations end with the fall of darkness, when he sets up camp to "spend the night." Yet no sweet dreams or restful sleep await him. Following the double emphasis on his retirement for the night, the reader might expect to hear that "Jacob rose early the next morning" (or some other variation) to meet his brother – and the next verse indeed begins "Jacob rose." Yet to the reader's great surprise, Jacob does not rise "the next morning," but rather, "that night" – that same night, which will prove to be the longest night of his life.

19. Breuer, *Chapters of Genesis*, 556.
20. Gunkel, *Genesis*, 345.

Certain linguistic parallels mark Jacob's wrestle with the angel as the epicenter of Jacob's meeting with Esau, indicating that Jacob's struggle has bearing on the story of the brothers' reunion:[21]

> The episode of Jacob's struggle with the divine is emphasized as the center of Jacob's meeting with Esau; not only in its form, but from a thematic perspective. Without a description of the divine struggle, the meeting between Jacob and Esau will lose its true theological significance.[22]

This reading is not unanimously accepted,[23] and the significance of Jacob's name change to Israel certainly transcends the immediate context of his meeting with his brother. Yet its placement between Jacob's preparations for his meeting with Esau and their actual meeting does draw attention to its context. At the point of highest narrative suspense, the reader is suddenly transported to a wondrous battleground between the human and the divine, and it cannot be that this struggle is unrelated to Esau's imminent arrival.

R. Sabato proposes that this scene is indeed directly related to the ambiguity of Esau's intentions, and to Jacob's preparations for both war and conciliation. He believes that when he sets out to meet his brother, Esau himself is yet undecided as to how he will receive him, and what tips the scales is Jacob's struggle with the divine figure, whom R. Sabato identifies as Esau's ministering angel. Jacob's struggle with the angel is the hidden key that determines the nature of Esau and Jacob's reunion. If Jacob loses to his angel, then Esau, too, will attack and perhaps even defeat his brother; but if Jacob manages to overcome the figure, then

---

21. This is widely accepted among scholars today; see Von Rad, *Genesis*, 315; Kodell, "Jacob Wrestles"; Coats, *Genesis*, 229–31; Curtis, "Structure"; Blum, "Gen. 32"; Köckert, "Jakobs Gegner"; Sabato, "Jacob and Esau"; Breuer, *Chapters of Genesis*, vol. 2, 557; Samet, *Studies I*, vol. 1, 89–104.
22. Weimar, "Analyse," 63.
23. For a leading example, see Sarna, *Understanding Genesis*, 202–06. Modern research generally assumes that the struggle is an independent narrative (see the references in Westermann, *Genesis II*, 515).

he will also be able to overcome Esau, who will thus greet him with a loving rather than deadly embrace.[24]

WHY DOES JACOB RISE AT NIGHT?

I wish to veer slightly from R. Sabato's path and place the narrative climax at a different point in the scene. I have already mentioned that despite the emphasis on Jacob setting up camp for the night, he is forced into a wrestling match until the dawn, whereupon his name is changed. Yet his sleep is already disturbed before he encounters his mysterious opponent.

As mentioned, both of Jacob's preparations conclude with the narrator's report that Jacob settles down for the night. Following this information, the reader expects to hear of what takes place the following morning – when Jacob wakes and meets his brother – but instead, the next verse relates that Jacob stirs while it is still nighttime: "The same night he got up and took his two wives, his two maids, and his eleven children, and crossed the ford of the Jabbok. He took them and sent them across the stream, and likewise everything that he had. And Jacob was left alone" (32:23–25). Why does Jacob suddenly rise in the middle of the night and move his family across the Jabbok? Surely crossing through a wadi in the light of day is safer; it seems unlikely that the site of his meeting with Esau is so important to him that he suffers the hassle of crossing with his wives, children, and animals in the middle of the night. Moreover, given that the Jabbok flows from east to west (the lower Jabbok bisects the width of Mount Gilead and flows into the Jordan), the accepted reading is that Jacob comes from the north and crosses the wadi as he travels south with his family.[25] If so, then this move brings him closer to his brother, not further. Given his fear of attack, it seems illogical to cross over a wadi that could serve as a natural defense line between Jacob and Esau and raise the chances of at least one "camp" evading Esau's attack. R. David Zvi Hoffmann's argument that "there is no reason to be found in the text for Jacob's crossing of the Jabbok by night. It seems that the Mover of all causes moved Jacob to be left alone,

24. Sabato, "Jacob and Esau." Similarly: Breuer, *Chapters of Genesis*, vol. 2, 558; Samet, *Studies I*, vol. 1, 89–104.
25. For example: Weinfeld, *Genesis*, 190–91.

struggle with the angel, and overcome it" is not convincing.[26] Even if this nocturnal crossing serves a certain divine purpose, Jacob must have his own motives for this strange move.

Rashbam illuminates these verses with a bold theory:

> He meant to flee a different way, and thus crossed the wadi at night. Just as David flees from Absalom over the Jordan and through Mahanaim, as Jacob does, at night: "They said to David, 'Set out and cross the waters at once'.... David set out at once along with all the troops who were with him, and they crossed the Jordan; by the light of morning, every last one of them had crossed the Jordan.... Meanwhile, David had reached Mahanaim, while Absalom crossed the Jordan"...
>
> "And Jacob was left alone" – that is, he helped all that was his across, until he was the only one who had yet to cross, and he wished to follow them in order to flee in a different direction, to deliberately avoid Esau. (Rashbam on Gen. 32:23–25)

Rashbam's theory casts the scene in an entirely new light: Jacob attempts to placate his brother, but that night, tossing and turning, he understands that too much is at stake. If Esau is marching toward him with four hundred men, perhaps his anger is too fierce to be assuaged by mere gifts, and right there and then, Jacob attempts to flee before it is too late. Rather than crossing the Jabbok toward Esau, in the dark of night he attempts to flee in the opposite direction.[27] Jacob presumably hopes to enter Canaan from a different place, or perhaps he plans to flee to a different region; in either case, he seeks to avoid the confrontation he so dreads.

Rashbam bases this on an analogy with David's flight from Absalom, which also takes place at night in the vicinity of Mahanaim (II Sam. 17:22–24). There, too, the protagonist flees from a family member who threatens to kill him. The fact that David manages to escape supports this reading: the dead of night is, indeed, a suitable time to run away.

---

26. Hoffmann, *Genesis II*, 495.
27. R. Medan assumes that Jacob moves his family northward that night, but believes that Jacob means to turn back and confront Esau (Medan, *Close to You*, 260).

Thus Rashbam understands the role of the divine figure: "The angel wrestled with him so that he could not escape, so that he would see the fulfillment of God's promise that Esau would not harm him."

If so, then the reason for the struggle becomes clear: God wishes to prevent Jacob from fleeing Esau. The figure holds fast to him all night so that he will not be able to journey on before Esau arrives. As they grapple, Jacob is encouraged to meet Esau and reassured that he will be able to overcome him: his new name is Israel (*Yisrael*), for "you have struggled (*sarita*) with God and with humans, and have prevailed" (32:29). The statement that Jacob has striven "with humans" presumably refers to Esau, whom Jacob fears.[28] His adversary, therefore, is not Esau's ministering angel, but rather a messenger of God, who wants Jacob to confront his brother (see further below).

Rashbam's theory is reinforced by the narrative's artistic structure, which arranges the story into two parallel halves, each opening with Jacob's encounter with angels and concluding with the naming of the site:

	Jacob's preparations for his meeting with Esau: Mahanaim	**The meeting with Esau: Penuel**
Encounter with the divine	32:2–3: Jacob also went on his way, and the angels of God met him ... he named that place Mahanaim.	32:24–30: So Jacob was left alone, and a man wrestled with him till daybreak .... So Jacob called the place Peniel.
Esau and his four hundred men	32:7: When the messengers returned to Jacob, they said, "We went to your brother Esau, and now he is coming to meet you, and four hundred men are with him."	33:1: Jacob looked up and there was Esau, coming with his four hundred men;

28. Von Rad may be correct that the etymology can be understood in a broader sense: "Perhaps, 'God and men' is only a superlative, stirring idiom which may not be pressed" (Von Rad, *Genesis*, 317; also: Westermann, *Genesis* 12–36, 518), but even if so, this meaning may still serve to encourage Jacob about his impending meeting with Esau. See also Waxman, "Jacob Was Left Alone."

	Jacob's preparations for his meeting with Esau: Mahanaim	**The meeting with Esau: Penuel**
Dividing his family into two	32:8: Jacob *divided* the people who were with him into two groups, and the flocks and herds and camels as well.	33:1: So *he divided* the children among Leah, Rachel, and the two female servants.
Jacob's gifts to Esau	32:14–20: From what he had with him he selected a gift for his brother Esau.... He instructed the one in the lead: "*When my brother Esau meets you* and asks, 'Who do you belong to, and where are you going, and who owns all these animals in front of you?' then you are to say, 'They belong to your servant Jacob. They are a gift sent to my lord Esau, and he is coming behind us.'"	33:8–9: *Esau said, "What do you mean by all this camp that I met?"* Jacob answered, "To find favor with my lord." But Esau said, "I have enough, my brother; keep what you have for yourself."
Explaining these gifts as appeasement of Esau	32:21: "And be sure to say, 'Your servant Jacob is coming behind us.'" For he thought, "*I will pacify him with these gifts I am sending on ahead; later, when I see his face, perhaps he will receive me.*"	33:10: Jacob said, "No, please; if I find favor with you, then accept my present from my hand; *for truly to see your face is like seeing the face of God – since you have received me with such favor.*
Jacob and his family's movement	32:23–24: That night Jacob got up and took his two wives, his two female servants, and his eleven sons and crossed the ford of the Jabbok. After he had sent them across the stream, he sent over all his possessions.	33:14–17: Let my lord pass on ahead of his servant, and I will lead on slowly"... So Esau returned that day on his way to Seir. But Jacob journeyed to Sukkot.

Both halves of the narrative open with an encounter with the divine: Jacob is first visited by angels of war, of "God's camp" – whose role is presumably to accompany Jacob and watch over him as he journeys (similarly to Joshua's encounter with God's angel before his conquest of

Jericho). The second half also begins with a divine encounter, but this time Jacob is attacked, hindered, and prevented from crossing back to the family that awaits him.[29] In both scenes, Jacob then names the site of his revelation: Mahanaim and Peniel.

Each encounter with angels is followed by the news that Esau approaches with four hundred men, which leads Jacob to divide his camp into two halves. Both sections then describe Jacob's gifts to Esau in surprising detail; these gifts are clearly a crucial aspect of the narrative. The first gift comprises an extensive list (32:14–16):

> He spent the night there. Then, from what he had at hand, he selected a gift for his brother Esau:
> two hundred female goats, twenty male goats,
> two hundred ewes, twenty rams,
> thirty milk camels and their young,
> forty cows, ten bulls,
> twenty female donkeys, and ten male donkeys.

This level of detail is surprising. What difference does it make if Jacob sends Esau two hundred goats or one hundred and fifty? One purpose of the list is to illustrate the magnitude of Jacob's gift, but there is still a sense that the extent of its detail serves a further purpose. Before any further discussion of possible objectives, it is worth pointing out that the list is organized in "families" – female and male goats; ewes and rams; even mother camels and their young. I sense that this reflects Jacob's biggest fear: he is prepared to sacrifice so much in the hope of protecting his family, his wives and children. This is possibly hinted through use of the word "*reḥelim*," ewes, which as I pointed out in the context of Jacob's rant against Laban at Mount Gilead, is a rare word indeed. "*Reḥelim*," of course, evokes the name of Jacob's most beloved wife, Rachel; he will give up all his *reḥelim* to protect his dear Rachel. Is the list's conclusion

29. Ramban already notes the connection between these scenes: first he meets (*vayifge'u*) the angels at Mahanaim, then he meets another angel who actually "*paga*" – in the sense of "harming him" (*Guide for the Perplexed*, part 2, ch. 42). See also R. Medan, *Close to You*, 263–64.

with ten "*ayarim*" (rather than the more common "*ḥamorim*") an allusion to Jacob's young sons? We can neither prove nor disprove this.

In any case, the extensive detail of this list draws attention to Jacob's gift, and this focus is also mirrored in the second half of the narrative. There, a lively debate ensues about whether Esau will accept this gift or refuse it:

> Esau asked, "What did you mean by all the camp (*maḥane*) that I met before?"
>
> He said, "To find favor in your eyes, my lord."
>
> But Esau said, "I have plenty, my brother. Let what is yours remain yours."
>
> "No, please," said Jacob. "If I have found favor in your eyes, accept this gift from me, for seeing your face is like seeing the face of God, and you have shown me favor. Please accept my blessing that was brought to you, for God has been gracious to me, and I have everything."
>
> Jacob pressed him, and he accepted. (33:8–11)

The length of this exchange and Jacob's need to "press" Esau to accept his gift shows that this is a real argument, not mere etiquette ("Oh, you shouldn't have!"). Why is it so important to Jacob that Esau accept his gift?

As mentioned, in both halves of the narrative, an extensive description of Jacob's gift is juxtaposed with the mention of Esau's imminent arrival. In order to understand why this gift is so important, and why it is inherently linked to Esau's arrival at Jacob's camp, I will first turn to the conclusion of Jacob's speech: "Please accept my blessing that was brought to you, for God has been gracious to me, and I have everything" (33:11). Use of the loaded word "blessing" in the context of their relationship speaks volumes. The "*minḥa*" that Esau refers to as a "*maḥane*" is, Jacob claims, a "*berakha*," a blessing. It was the theft of his brother's blessing that caused Jacob's exile, and now, upon his return home, he attempts to repay him for this blessing.

As many have noted, this is evident in his repeated bowing to Esau. Seven bows is not mere etiquette; Jacob is clearly drawing Esau's (and the reader's) attention to this act. Isaac's blessing was "May peoples serve you; may nations bow down to you. Be lord over your brothers, and may your mother's sons bow down to you," and Jacob is deliberately demonstrating the opposite of this blessing, by bowing and referring to Esau as "my lord."[30]

But if so, what is the purpose of Jacob's struggle with the mysterious figure, and his name change? Jacob begins the process of restoring the stolen blessings before that fateful night, and continues the next morning. Those who argue that Jacob's struggle endows him with new strength and power are mistaken;[31] afterwards he remains just as servile, bowing and groveling to his brother. The exegetical challenge is to understand why this struggle occurs if Jacob maintains the exact same stance throughout. According to Rashbam, this is easily resolved: the very purpose of this struggle is to ensure that Jacob follows through with his plans instead of running away and avoiding his brother. This will be clarified further through analysis of Jacob's struggle with the divine figure, but for now I wish to draw attention to an aspect of the structure that supports Rashbam's reading.

Both halves of the narrative conclude with Jacob's movement, but Rashbam's theory suggests that there is an inherent link between them. At the end of the second half, Esau proposes that they travel together in the direction of Seir, Esau's new home: "Let us be on our way. I will go beside you" (33:12). Jacob refuses, expressing that he will follow along at a much slower pace: "Let my lord go on ahead of his servant, and I will go slowly at the pace of the livestock before me and the pace of the children until I come to my lord in Seir" (vv. 13–14). Yet despite this promise, he turns west, toward Sukkot: "So that day Esau started back on his way to Seir, and Jacob journeyed on to Sukkot" (vv. 16–17). If we adopt Rashbam's approach, this movement away from Esau mirrors the end of the first half, where Jacob suddenly rises in the middle of the night to travel away from Esau.

---

30. The Amarna letters and texts found in Mari also contain "lord-servant" as expressions of submission, as is bowing seven times (see Meitlis, *Crossroads*, 87–89). The connection between *gevir* and *adon* results in keen wordplay in Ps. 12:5.
31. See, for example, Kodell, "Jacob Wrestles," 68; Günther Plaut, *Genesis*, 222.

In light of this, I believe that the purpose of the divine figure's struggle against Jacob is to keep him in Mahanaim until the break of day so that he cannot avoid confronting his brother. Let us now turn to this famous scene.

JACOB'S STRUGGLE WITH THE "MAN"

> Sir, you have wrestled well and overthrown
> More than your enemies. (Shakespeare, *As You Like It,* Act I, Scene II)

A notorious obstacle to biblical exegesis is over-familiarization. We hear the stories of the Bible as tiny children; they are told to us in a certain way, and the stories are so familiar to us that it often proves difficult to take a step back and consider the text objectively. Michel de Montaigne devotes an essay to the topic entitled "On Custom, and That We Should Not Easily Change a Law Received," which neatly begins thus:

> He seems to me to have had a right and true apprehension of the power of custom, who first invented the story of a country-woman who, having accustomed herself to play with and carry a young calf in her arms, and daily continuing to do so as it grew up, obtained this by custom, that, when grown to be a great ox, she was still able to bear it. For, in truth, custom is a violent and treacherous schoolmistress. She, by little and little, slyly and unperceived, slips in the foot of her authority, but having by this gentle and humble beginning, with the benefit of time, fixed and established it, she then unmasks a furious and tyrannic countenance, against which we have no more the courage or the power so much as to lift up our eyes.[32]

These words should be repeated before every new reading of an old story, and they apply sevenfold to the following analysis. Not without

32. De Montaigne, *Essays.*

hesitation, I seek Montaigne's "courage [and] power" to read the scene of Jacob's struggle with fresh, unprejudiced eyes.

This disclaimer notwithstanding, our premise is that Jacob's adversary is not a normal "man," although it is referred to as such. The view that this is an angel is ancient, and already found in the Bible itself; in the book of Hosea: "He *struggled with* (*vayasar el*) *the angel* and overcame him" (Hos. 12:4–5), the Hebrew letters of "struggled with" spelling out the name Israel. This reading is also evident from analysis of the text itself. First and foremost, Jacob himself names the site "Peniel, for I have seen God face to face, and yet my life has been spared" (v. 31). Were Jacob alone to have made this identification, one could claim that the narrator does not identify with it, but the "man" also tells Jacob that "you have struggled with *God* and with humans, and have prevailed" (v. 29). If so, then Jacob's opponent is either "God" or a representative. Moreover, asking for a name is the symbolic act of seeking the elusive identity of a divine figure. Samson's parents, like Jacob, try and determine the identity of their divine visitor, who also refuses to provide an answer: "'Why should you ask my name?' the Lord's angel replied to him, 'for it is wondrous'" (Judges 13:17–21). "Why should you ask my name," then, seems to be a classic angelic reply to inquisitive mortals.

Nonetheless, there is room to deliberate whether his opponent is an angel or God Himself in the form of a man.[33] After all, in these chapters angels are generally referred to as "angels of God," but the word "angel" does not even appear once, whereas Jacob (and the narrator) state that Jacob has wrestled with "God." The etymology of "Peniel" ("the face of God") can be derived from Jacob's emotional state (cf. especially Judges 6:22), but the explanation "for I have seen God face to face and yet my life has been spared" (32:31) is more fitting after an encounter with God Himself, such as "The Lord spoke to Moses face to face" (Ex. 33:11). God tells Moses "Nor can you see My face, for no one can see Me and live" (Ex. 33:20), so it is clear why Jacob feels such miraculous relief after seeing God's face; God will not reveal His name, but Jacob survives His presence.

---

33. A similar debate accompanies the story of the angels who visit Abraham. See Grossman, *Abraham*, 160–61 (and 506, n. 20).

Whether Jacob wrestles with an angel or with God, the most important detail for our purposes is that the reader, like Jacob, does not initially know the attacker's identity, which will result in a narrative climax.

The story of Jacob's struggle is generally told as follows: God/an angel comes to wrestle with *Jacob*, who wants to cross the *Jabbok* (the wordplay here is clear). The angel, realizing Jacob is winning, strikes him in a certain place in the leg. When dawn breaks, the angel begs Jacob to let him go, but Jacob demands its blessing in exchange. The angel then changes his name to Israel and blesses him. Jacob asks the angel to reveal its own name, but the angel refuses. The end of the episode contains two etiological conclusions: Jacob names the place "Peniel" because "I have seen God face to face, and yet my life has been spared" (v. 31), and "Israelites do not eat the sciatic nerve by the hip socket" (v. 33) because of Jacob's injury.

Few question this particular portrayal of events, but it in fact presents several difficulties. I wish to focus on three central issues (although my alternative reading will solve other issues as well):

(1) This sequence contains a logical flaw. The divine being attacks Jacob and prevents him from crossing the Jabbok. When the angel sees that Jacob is about to shake off his grasp ("When he saw that he could not prevail against him"), it strikes Jacob on the thigh and thus manages to keep hold of him. Yet when dawn is about to break, why is it that the angel suddenly begs Jacob to let him go?! The angel is the one who attacks Jacob and bars his way; Jacob is no doubt desperate to escape from his assailant and cross over to his family. If so, then it makes more sense that Jacob will run back (or limp back) to his family as soon as he is able – how can it be that the angel is the one who begs Jacob to let him go, and why would Jacob, rushing back to his family, refuse? It is also unclear why the divine being is so desperate to leave at daybreak. Angels are not confined to the dark of night elsewhere in the Bible;[34]

34. The Sages explain that the angel had to return to heaven to sing (Genesis Rabba 78:2). And if you might wonder whether there aren't angels enough to replace it that morning, the Midrash already explains that Jacob asks the same question, whereupon the angel explains that if it misses one day, it will not be allowed to come back the

and there is no indication in the narrative that the angel is rushing off to somewhere else.[35] Rather, the speaker's justification that he must leave because dawn has come implies that it is obvious to the reader why the struggle must end at daybreak.

(2) If the angel is the one who makes two statement-blessings, the relationship between them is not entirely clear. Jacob is only willing to release the angel in exchange for a blessing: "I will not let you go, unless you bless me," so the angel responds by changing Jacob's name: "You shall no longer be called Jacob, but Israel, for you have struggled with God and with humans, and have prevailed" (v. 29). The narrative sequence implies that this name change functions as the requested blessing, but the narrative continues: "And there he blessed him" (v. 30). While this can be read as a summary of the previous verses – "It is left to the narrator to present the outcome"[36] – such a summary seems superfluous just two verses later. The simpler reading is that of Radak: "He blessed him there – aside from naming him Israel for having 'struggled with God and prevailed,' he blessed him with another blessing" (on 32:30). What is this other blessing? It may be, as Ramban and others explain, that "the text did not cite the blessing," or "when he left him, he thanked him and blessed him" (*Haamek Davar* on 32:2), or, as R. Joseph Bekhor Shor and some modern scholars claim, "He then parted ways in peace,"[37] meaning that the actual name change is the blessing Jacob demands, and this second blessing is but a polite farewell.

---

next day. Some modern scholars perceive the angel as a kind of harmful demon that loses its powers at daybreak (see, for example, Weinfeld, *Genesis*, 189). But this is inconsistent with biblical theology (as pointed out by Westermann, *Genesis II*, 515). Some argue that Moses is attacked by a similar entity on his way to Egypt (Ex. 4:24–26 – see Westermann, *Genesis II*, 517), but this does not seem to have any basis in the text either. The same problem applies to the theory that the angel is "Esau's ministering angel" – the only example of a similar theological approach can be found in the book of Daniel (see further in Grossman, "Jacob's Struggle," 11, n. 7). Nonetheless, there are various explanations of this "ministering angel" – see below.

35. R. Breuer feels that we have no choice but to agree that two divine events take place here: "Jacob is able to hold his own even against an angel; and he is even able to triumph over an angel" (Breuer, *Chapters of Genesis*, vol. 2, 563).

36. Mathews, *Genesis II*, 559.

37. Speiser, *Genesis*, 255; Hamilton, *Genesis II*, 327, 336.

Even after this proposal, however, this reading remains awkward. Jacob demands a "blessing," and as the angel departs, "he blessed him there." It seems unlikely that the two instances of the word "blessing" are not connected. What is the relation between Jacob's name change and the blessing that follows?

(3) The outcome of this struggle is obscure, as the Midrash tells: "R. Berakhya says: We do not know who won; whether it was the angel or Jacob."[38] The most common interpretation is that Jacob overcomes the angel and refuses to let it go without a blessing. If this is so, however, then how can the angel refuse to reveal its name? Why doesn't Jacob refuse to let the angel go until it reveals its name, considering that there is special power in knowledge of divine names: "If one knows the name of a spirit, one can call it."[39]

It seems that the angel manages to evade this question too easily; if it has been overpowered by Jacob, how can it refuse? Moreover, Jacob's etymology for the name "Peniel" gives the impression that Jacob did not have the upper hand in this struggle, but rather, that he merely survived it: "Peniel, for I have seen God face to face, *and yet my life was spared*" (v. 31). Other instances of the verb root "preserved" (N-TZ-L) clearly describe a situation in which the survivor barely managed to escape with his life (such as Josh. 9:26–27; Ezek. 14:12–20), so this etymology is inconsistent with the idea that Jacob triumphs over his assailant and only releases the angel after it capitulates and blesses him.

The question of Jacob's victory is relevant to my earlier question. Many claim that Jacob's struggle with the angel gives him new strength – as reflected in his new name – and he is now able to confront Esau with confidence and power.[40] Yet even a cursory reading reveals

38. Genesis Rabba 77:25.

39. Westermann, *Genesis* 12–36, 518.

40. Leon Kass, for example, writes that after Jacob's struggle with the angel, he is no longer afraid of Esau; that there is no mention of his fear after this scene (Kass, *Beginning of Wisdom* [Free Press, 2003], 470). This observation is accurate, but when Jacob actually meets Esau, his behavior suggests that he is still afraid, and Kass admits: "We observe that his terror of Esau causes him to humiliate himself in the presence of his children, resulting in poetic justice for Jacob, who humiliated his old blind father" (ibid.).

that Jacob himself has not read his struggle in this light: he continues to prostrate himself before Esau, expressing servitude that borders on worship ("If I have found favor in your eyes, accept this gift from me, for seeing your face is like seeing the face of God, and you have shown me favor" – 33:10). If the point of Jacob's struggle is that he emerges victorious, it seems to have no bearing whatsoever on his actual confrontation with Esau.

Based on these three observations, I wish to propose a different paradigm of this famous episode. To this end, I will first note that this narrative employs the literary device of basic ambiguity; the narrator does not specify which character performs each action in the story. This ambiguity begins as soon as Jacob is attacked: "When *he* saw that *he* could not prevail against *him, he* touched *him* on the hip socket" (v. 26). Who could not prevail against whom, and touched whom on the hip socket? The previous verse mentions two wrestlers: "So Jacob was left alone, and a man wrestled with him till daybreak" (v. 25), making it difficult to determine the subject of verse 26. The ambiguity of this sequence is so acute that Gunkel proposes that in one narrative tradition, it is Jacob who touches God on the hip:

> When Jacob sees that he is not superior in bodily strength to the other, he employs – as is extremely fitting to his character in general – a wrestler's trick (similar to Odysseus) and smites the opponent on the hip socket, that is, the joint of the thighbone.[41]

Gunkel goes on to explain that after Jacob strikes his opponent there, the tables turn and he manages to overcome him. Yet this is a problematic reading, given that it is Jacob who is injured there: "And Jacob's hip was put out of joint as he wrestled with him." Jacob, it emerges, is injured by his opponent; at the narrative's end, it is reported that Jacob limps as a result of the assault. The beginning of the verse, however, is indeed ambiguous and allows either reading.

While this first ambiguity is resolved immediately, the second instance of syntactical ambiguity is not explicitly clarified in the text:

41. Gunkel, *Genesis,* 349; similarly, Breuer, *Chapters of Genesis,* vol. 2, 565.

"Then he said, 'Let me go, for the day is breaking.' But he said, 'I will not let you go, unless you bless me'" (v. 27). Who asks whom to be released because of the dawn? The prevalent reading is that the angel begs to be released and Jacob insists that it bless him first, as in Charles Baudelaire's classic poem, "*Réversibilité*": "*Mais de toi je n'implore, ange, que tes prières / Ange plein de bonheur, de joie et de lumières!*"[42] Yet from a syntactical perspective, it is equally possible to read that Jacob is the one asking for release.[43] Jacob is the subject at the end of the previous verse – "Jacob's hip was put out of joint as he wrestled with him" – so the pronoun at the beginning of the next verse can certainly apply to him; "he" begs for release.[44]

Despite the prevalent reading of this story, not only the verse's syntax allows for Jacob to be read as the one who asks for release; from a perspective of plot, it is the more feasible option. As I have noted, the "man" is the one who attacks Jacob, the one who hinders him; Jacob's only interest is to return to his family across the Jabbok. The exposition illuminates the entire episode: a man launches an attack on Jacob and manages to detain him until the dawn (32:25).

Intriguingly, in the book of Hosea, the identity of the one who pleads "let me go" retains its ambiguity:

> In the womb he grasped his brother's heel;[45]
> as a man he struggled with God.

42. Baudelaire, *Fleurs du Mal,* 25.
43. Some translations add the word "the man" as the one who asks for release: "The man then said: Let me go" (NAB; NIB; NIV) in order to solve this ambiguity for its readers, but this eliminates the other possible reading of this verse.
44. See further: Grossman, "Jacob's Struggle." Weisman lists this possibility, but he claims that this is inherently ambiguous and cannot be determined absolutely: "Both meanings are legitimate from a perspective of biblical syntax. According to one reading, Jacob overcomes the 'man,' who 'could not overcome him'... in the other Jacob is hurt and asks him to let him go" (Weisman, *Jacob to Israel,* 80).
45. The term "*ono*" is interpreted in the sense of power (as Hosea mentions a few verses later in 12:9), but the other meaning of this word is hinted here – it is also associated with falsehood and evil (and Hosea uses this sense in 12:12). See also Andersen and Freedman, *Hosea,* 607). It is interesting that after Jacob's name is changed a second time, his son Benjamin is born and named "Son of my sorrow (*oni*)" by his mother.

> He struggled with the angel; he overcame him;
> he wept and begged for his favor. (Hos. 12:4–5)

Assuming that the phrase "wept and begged for his favor" refers to Jacob's struggle with the angel, it is unclear whether Jacob or the angel begs and weeps. Many interpret that the angel is the subject of this clause, but Hosea's language is crafted with ambiguity. The Midrash echoes this: "He wept and begged for his favor – I do not know who wept to whom. When it says 'Let me go, for the dawn is breaking,' that is, the angel wept to Jacob" (*Yalkut Shimoni* Genesis 133). The accepted exegetic reading is that the angel is the one who begs for release, but the verses in Genesis retain their ambiguity, and the more logical reading in Hosea – from a stylistic and contextual perspective – is that it is Jacob who begged and wept. Some modern scholars believe that this description is calculated to present Jacob in an unflattering light,[46] considering that this prophecy reproaches the Kingdom of Israel for following in the deceitful ways of its ancestor.[47]

Back to Genesis. So far, I would present our story as follows: God, or one of His angels, launches an attack on Jacob to prevent him from avoiding confrontation with Esau. When the attacker realizes that Jacob is about to elude his grasp and flee, he strikes him on the hip and thus manages to maintain his hold on Jacob so that he cannot rejoin his family across the Jabbok. When Jacob realizes that dawn is breaking, he is seized with dread – Esau is on his way to meet him and his family, who remain stranded without their father and protector – and he begs the attacker to let him continue on his way. The attacker only agrees to release Jacob if he gives him a blessing. I will discuss the meaning of this demand below, but for now, let us continue the story.

Jacob hesitates and does not rush to bless his assailant; at this point, of course, he is not yet aware of the man's identity, and it does not

46. Although some claim that the name Jacob is brought here in a positive sense, as the archetype as someone whom God blesses in closeness (see, for example, Ackroyd, *Hosea and Jacob*; Emmerson, *Hosea*, 129).
47. For example: Wolf, *Hosea*, 206; Hubbard, *Hosea*, 204. On the debate and the difficulty of deciding which is correct, see Andersen and Freedman, *Hosea*, 607–608.

occur to him that he has been attacked by a divine being. It is no coincidence that the narrator employs the banal word "man" – angels (and even God Himself) are elsewhere referred to as "men" before their identity is revealed, and in such cases the particular moment of revelation is crucial to the plot (such as the angels' visit to Abraham and then Lot in Genesis 18–19). The same is true here – revealing the assailant's identity is part of the narrative process. There is no criticism against poor Jacob for his reluctance to bless his mysterious attacker – from his perspective, this highwayman deserves to be imprisoned, not blessed. On the other hand, as the sky begins to grow light, Jacob grows more desperate to return to his family before Esau arrives with his four hundred men.

In response to Jacob's silence and hesitation, the "man" opens his mouth once more to change Jacob's name to Israel, thus revealing his identity for the first time – "You have struggled with God." Jacob suddenly realizes that he has been wrestling all night with none but God Himself (had he realized this earlier, he no doubt would have surrendered at once). In his shock, Jacob asks the figure his name – seeking to discover whether he has a name, like people of flesh and blood, or whether his name is concealed: "What is his name or the name of his child? Surely you know!" (Prov. 30:4; perhaps Jacob seeks to change the name of the figure he has just grappled with?).[48]

As mentioned, Samson's parents also try and determine the identity of their divine visitor, who is similarly evasive: "'Why should you ask my name?' the Lord's angel replied to him, 'for it is wondrous'" (Judges 13:17–21). Manoah's question reveals his skepticism of the visitor's identity – in the words of the Midrash, "He did not realize that it was an angel, and that is why he asked its name"[49] – but only after the angel refuses to answer his question, and only after it soars to heaven on the altar's flame, is Manoah convinced that "he had been an angel of the Lord." This seems to be the case in our narrative as well. The attacker

48. *Meshekh Ḥokhma* understood the question of the name as related to the blessing: "For the blesser must know the name, so as to know whom the blessing will apply to… and if so the angel that blessed Jacob is already blessed and thus you do not need to bless or know the name" (on Gen. 32:30).

49. Numbers Rabba 10:5. See further in Zakovitch, *Life of Samson*, 64–66.

only reveals his identity when he gives Jacob his new name, and Jacob's first reaction is to ask his own name in return as an act of clarification. When the man refuses to answer, Jacob is convinced that his opponent is indeed a divine being, and he finally capitulates and "blesses him there."[50]

This marks the end of the story and the narrative climax. The "man" has managed to detain Jacob until the new day (when it is too late for Jacob to avoid Esau) and they part with words of blessing. The final two verses are, as noted, an etiological conclusion that expresses the miracle of Jacob's survival.

Within this paradigm, the textual difficulties listed are no longer difficulties. Were Jacob able to return to his family, he would, but he cannot; the "man" retains his hold on him. The relationship between Jacob's name change and the blessing emerges: the divine figure changes Jacob's name to Israel in order to reveal the nature of the attack and the attacker's identity. This name change is also calculated to encourage Jacob before the confrontation with his brother: if he is able to struggle against God, he has nothing to fear from Esau. As for the blessing, Jacob is not the receiver but the bestower; his assailant demands a blessing from Jacob as condition for his release. Dawn has broken, and it is too late for Jacob to avoid Esau, but he is desperate to return to his family before his brother arrives. The pervading atmosphere at the story's end, with the naming of Peniel and the defeated image of Jacob limping back toward his family, is far more coherent: Jacob is not victor of his struggle, but rather mere survivor.

Before I discuss the meaning of Jacob's blessing and the narrative objective, I wish to address an apparent issue that results from this reading: the "man's" double speech in verses 27–28. He first says to Jacob, "I will not let you go unless you bless me." Instead of a response, the man opens his mouth once more to announce Jacob's new name (vv. 28–29). This sequence in fact poses no problem; it is a prevalent biblical narrative technique: when a character is instructed to perform a certain action he is reluctant to carry out, the instructor then speaks a second time. Meir

50. Unlike this reading, most exegetes hold that it is the angel who blesses Jacob at the end of the scene, although Targum Pseudo-Jonathan writes: "And Jacob blessed him there." Compare to Onkelos, who omits the name Jacob there.

Shiloah devotes an entire study to this phenomenon, bringing many examples of what he designates "waiting for a response or action."[51] One fitting example of this phenomenon is the angel's blessing to Hagar after she flees from her mistress:

> The angel of the Lord to her, "Return to your mistress, and submit to her."
> The angel of the Lord said to her, "I will so greatly multiply your offspring that they cannot be counted for multitude."
> The angel of the Lord said to her, "Now you have conceived and shall bear a son; you shall call him Ishmael, for the Lord has given heed to your affliction. (Gen. 16:9–11)

Here, too, the repetition of "the angel of the Lord said" creates the impression that Hagar does not immediately respond to the angel's order to return to her mistress (it may also be that Hagar initially refuses because she is not aware of the speaker's true identity). The angel therefore continues speaking, promising certain blessings in order to persuade her to return. Here, too, the angel announces a name for the child who will be born to Hagar (this name, like "Israel," is also based on the character's connection with God).[52]

In the context of the Jacob cycle, it is especially appropriate to compare the double "*vayomer*" (and he said) to the previous episode in which Jacob beseeches his adversary to "release" him: "Jacob said to Laban, 'Release me to go home to my own land'" (30:25). Note the similar development between the two scenes, including the double "*vayomer*" that expresses how the character continues speaking:

51. Shiloah, "And He Said…and He Said," 252–53. One such example is the people of Sodom's threat to Lot (Gen. 19:9) – when Lot does not act as they expect, they threaten him again.
52. See further in Grossman, *Abram to Abraham*, 199–200.

	Jacob and Laban (30:25–30)	**Jacob and the Angel**
Background	After Rachel had given birth to Joseph,	And Jacob was left alone…
Jacob's request	Jacob said to Laban, "Let me go home to my own land."	And he said, "Let me go, for dawn is breaking."
Refusal (because of Jacob's "blessing")	But Laban said to him, "If you will allow me to say so, I have learned by divination that it is because of you that the Lord has blessed me."	But he replied, "I will not let you go unless you bless me."
The refuser continues speaking	He said, "Name your hire and I will pay it."	And he said to him, "What is your name?"… "No longer will your name be Jacob, but Israel."
Jacob agrees	He said, "You know well how I have worked for you and how your livestock have fared under my care. You had little before I came, but it has swelled into much. The Lord has blessed you wherever I have been. Now, when can I do likewise for my own household?"	Jacob asked, "Please tell me your name"… and he blessed him there.

Both scenes progress similarly: Jacob asks, "Let me go," but both antagonists refuse to release him, seeking the blessing that accompanies him wherever he goes. Jacob is silent at their refusal, and therefore both characters continue speaking in order to persuade him. Laban's speech is also marked with a double "And he said," which indicates that Jacob does not reply to the first part of his speech. Only after the second part, Jacob is somewhat mollified.

Jacob's name change can be understood in the same way. Jacob does not initially respond to the angel's request for a blessing. The angel therefore continues speaking and pronounces Jacob's new name, which expresses his ability to wrestle with the divine. Jacob is appeased by this momentous announcement and blesses the angel. In this light we will explore the significance of Jacob's name change and the importance of the blessing the angel demands from Jacob.

THE MEANING OF THE BLESSING

What, then, is the blessing the angel asks for? Why is it so important for a divine figure to receive a blessing from a mortal? I believe that this should be discussed on two levels. Firstly, given that the blessing itself is not provided – only "He blessed him there" – the simplest way to understand this phrase is not as a title but as the entire content of this "blessing." This verb is often used as an expression of parting or a sign of friendship, as in the following verses, for example:

- Laban rose early the next morning. He kissed his grandchildren and daughters goodbye and blessed them. Laban then left to return home (Gen. 32:1).
- Jacob blessed Pharaoh and left Pharaoh's presence (Gen. 47:7).
- Moses saw that all the work had been done just as the Lord had commanded – and Moses blessed them (Ex. 39:43).
- When David had finished offering the burnt offering and the peace offerings, he blessed the people in the name of the Lord of Hosts (II Sam. 6:18).

All these verses – and many others – do not describe the actual verbal content of the blessing; rather, the phrase "bless" expresses fondness and approval. Laban parts ways with his family with blessings of peace; Jacob leaves Pharaoh's presence with an expression of friendship and alliance.

This is how the angel's request for a blessing should be understood. The angel, still grasping Jacob, asserts that it will release Jacob as soon as he "blesses him" – that is, as soon as Jacob internalizes that this struggle is for his own good, and is willing to part peacefully. At first, of course, Jacob only stares back in silent indignation: What kind of an attacker wrestles with his victim all night, only to insist on parting ways in peace? Only after Jacob realizes that he has been wrestling with an angel – or, in its own words, with "God" – is he willing to "bless him," to express forgiveness and appeasement. Jacob's "blessing" is an acknowledgment of his new identity. God does not wish to leave His servant Jacob in a state of conflict and tension, but rather in peace; similarly, every *Amida* prayer ends with a blessing of peace.

This explanation, however, is not sufficient. In this case, the plot expresses deeper, broader symbolic significance. The motif of "blessing" is woven throughout the Jacob cycle; some perceive it as a general keyword. This word even accompanies the reader in chapter 26, Isaac's exile in Gerar. There, God explicitly blesses Isaac whatever he does and wherever he goes, and there we proposed that this is the main theme and objective of this chapter. The motif of blessing also accompanies his son, but unlike his father Isaac, Jacob's path of blessing twists and turns, beset with obstacles and conflicts. Jacob steals his brother's blessings in an act of deceit, yet his father supplements this with a blessing of fertility on the eve of his departure to Haran; immediately after, in a vision, God promises Jacob that "through you and your descendants, all families of the earth will be blessed" (28:14). At this point, the reader is exposed to Jacob's two kinds of blessing: the blessing he steals from his brother and father, and the blessing bestowed upon him by God.

"Blessing" remains with Jacob throughout his exile in Haran. Laban reveals that God's promise is coming true, and he is indeed blessed through him: "I have learned by divination that it is because of you that the Lord has blessed me" (30:27), and Jacob reiterates: "The Lord has blessed you wherever I have been" (30:30). There are further mentions, but these suffice to illustrate that the motif of blessing that is so central in Isaac's story also accompanies his son; Jacob acquires Esau's blessing through theft, while Laban's blessing through him is granted by God.

Now Jacob prepares for a reunion with his brother. The blessings intended for Esau are in Jacob's possession – what will become of them? Surely his exile in Haran has shown him that he has no need of the stolen blessings, for God has showered him with blessing of his own. The scene of his struggle with the angel should be read in this context. As mentioned, the narrative structure hints that this struggle should be read in parallel to his brief encounter with angels in Mahanaim. Just as the angels of Mahanaim guide him and guard him on his way, so too does the angel – even if, at first glance, the opposite seems to hold true. This is not a struggle Jacob is meant to win; it is a struggle that seeks to show Jacob that he holds the key to blessing. Even the angel itself seeks Jacob's blessing! To this end, Jacob's name is changed (or, as I will discuss below, he learns that his name will soon be changed) in order to allow him to progress through the anticipated process. Rather than grasp at Esau's heel, he grapples with God Himself. Rather than snatch his brother's blessings, he receives his own blessing directly from God.

Thus, Jacob's speech to Esau can be fully understood: "'No, please,' said Jacob, 'if I have found favor in your eyes, accept this gift from me, for seeing your face is like seeing the face of God, and you have shown me favor. Please accept my blessing that was brought to you, for God has been gracious to me, and I have everything.' He pressed him, and he accepted" (33:10). Jacob refers to his gift to Esau as a "blessing," hinting that he now repays him for the blessings he stole. In response to Isaac's incrimination, "Your brother came in deceit and took your blessing (*vayikkaḥ birkhatekha*)" (27:35), Jacob now tells his brother, "Please accept my blessing (*kaḥ na et birkhati*)."[53] Given that the word "blessing" with a first person possessive suffix appears only three times in the Torah, it is likely that Jacob's words hint directly to Esau's bitter lament that "now he has taken *my blessing*" (27:36). Yet note the complete sentence: Jacob returns Esau's stolen blessings to him because he is now in possession of God-given blessings of his own: "For God has been gracious to me, and I have everything." Jacob compares seeing Esau's face to seeing the face of God – the reader is certainly reminded of the night's struggle in Peniel; the purpose of this comparison is not to equate the two meetings, but to show that one has replaced the other. Through his struggle with the angel, Jacob has learned that he is blessed directly by God, and he has no need for the blessing he seized from Esau. Now, after his encounter with the angel, he can meet Esau, bow before him, and restore the blessings he once stole from him – not because he is

53. See further: Waxman, "Jacob Alone"; Angel, "Heeling." Vivian Hidary proposes that the emphasis of the mothers and children "*niggashim*" (approaching) Esau echoes the intense repetition of the verb root N-G-SH in the theft of the blessings (27:21–27); moreover, the two hundred goats Jacob sends to Esau alludes to the goat Jacob served his father to obtain the blessings (Hidary, "Succoth," 186–87).

no longer blessed, but because he understands that he is blessed from a higher source.

In this sense we can return to the Sages' reading that the angel Jacob wrestles with is "Esau's ministering angel" and cast it in a new light: the angel is not sent by Esau but by God, and its purpose is to represent the cheated Esau and ensure that Jacob meets him and returns his stolen blessing. Thus the angel serves as an advocate for Esau, yet ultimately acts in the best interests of both brothers.

In fact, we can even take this a step further:[54] in the Jacob cycle, "blessing" is presented as a tangible entity that can be passed from hand to hand: "Your brother came in deceit and *took* your blessing" (27:35); "He *took* my birthright, and now he has *taken* my blessing" (27:36); "*Accept* my blessing" (33:11). For this reason, the word "blessing" often appears with a possessive suffix: "my blessing," "your blessing." Thus when the "man" asks Jacob to bless him, we can read this as a request for Jacob to physically hand over Esau's blessings; to give them up. Jacob hopes to avoid meeting Esau, but the angel physically restrains him and forces him to hand over the stolen blessings. Blessing will reach Jacob directly, honestly, not through deception – and to this end the angel bids Jacob, "Bless me." Jacob transmits blessing to the "man" in an act that anticipates its rightful return to his brother Esau.

JACOB'S NAME CHANGE

In light of all this, what is the meaning of Jacob's name change to Israel? Given that later on in the cycle God will give him this name again (35:9–13), what is the significance of its mention here? This is further complicated by the fact that the name change at Bethel makes no mention whatsoever of Jacob's name change at the Jabbok; it is as if Jacob's name is changed to Israel for the first time.[55] One solution is to consider this earlier name change a mere annunciation of what is to come: that

54. I am indebted to my student Sagiv Zehavi for pointing this out to me.
55. Many modern scholars hold that these are two separate sources; nonetheless, some of them do point out connections between the two scenes, and between the name change in Bethel and the vision of the ladder (28:10–22), and thus ascribe these similarities to later redaction (see especially Westermann, *Genesis II*, 553).

the angel at Jabbok whispers that Jacob's true name is Israel, but God will only implement this change in Bethel. This idea is supported by the simple fact that the text continues to refer to him as "Jacob" over the next few chapters, until he reaches Bethel. The three instances of the word "Israel" that appear before chapter 35 refer only to the nation Israel, and not to the individual: "That is why, to this day, the Israelites do not eat the sciatic nerve by the hip socket" (32:33); "There he erected an altar and named it 'God, God of Israel'" (33:20);[56] "They were shocked and furious, for Shechem had committed an outrage in Israel by sleeping with Jacob's daughter. Such a thing cannot be done!" (34:7). Jacob is often referred to as "Jacob" even after chapter 35, but he is also referred to as Israel, and the two names are used intermittently, while he is not called "Israel" even once before he reaches Bethel.[57]

But even if we adopt this solution, it does not clarify why there is a need for two naming narratives, or why Jacob is told in advance that his name will be changed later. In fact, this "annunciation" only exacerbates the anomaly: If Jacob is told that his name will be changed in order to convince him to confront Esau, then why doesn't the naming itself take place then and there at the Jabbok? And if it is so crucial that the actual name change occurs in Bethel, then why is it even mentioned by the Jabbok? I will address this in my analysis of Jacob's return to Bethel, but for now, I will note that there are two vital components: on the one hand, the name change must take place at Bethel after Jacob has fulfilled his vow; on the other hand, it is crucial to expose Jacob and the reader to this impending change already here, while he is still trying to avoid confrontation with his brother.

The language of this scene deviates from the usual language of similar episodes in Genesis. First of all, the "man" asks Jacob for his name: "'What is your name?' he asked. 'Jacob,' he replied" (32:28). The last time someone in the narrative asked his name, his answer was "I am

56. There is room to debate regarding this verse; some claim that "Israel" here should be understood as Jacob's name (for example: Cross, *Canaanite Myth*, 49. But I believe that Westermann is correct that the phrase "God of Israel" refers to the nation, and the same is true in this context (Westermann, *Genesis II*, 529). Perhaps this is intentionally ambiguous (as Mathews, *Genesis II*, 576).

57. Segal, "Jacob and Israel."

Esau, your firstborn" (27:19)[58] – this, of course, is when Jacob attempts to steal his brother's blessings. Now, replying to his mysterious attacker, Jacob reveals his real name, and the angel informs him that his name will soon change. Unusually, Jacob's new name is announced with the verb root A-M-R, *said*: "Jacob will no longer be *said* as your name, but Israel" (32:29), rather than the usual K-R-A, *called*: "Your name will no longer be called Abram; your name will be Abraham" (Gen. 17:5); "Your wife Sarai will no longer be called Sarai, for Sarah is her name" (17:5); "Your name will no longer be *called* Jacob, for Israel will be your name" (35:10). While the two are synonyms, each verb root has different connotations. The verb "say" in this context does not refer to how people will address Jacob himself, but to the people who will *talk* about Israel; what people will say *about* Israel. When Isaiah says, "No more will fools be called noble, nor will it *be said of* villains, 'generous'"[59] (Is. 32:5), he is not referring to the names of these fools or villains, of course, but to what people will no longer say *about* them. "Well, you know what they say" – what *they* say about someone often reflects a social or spiritual change,[60] as evident, for example, in the prophecy of Jeremiah: "It will come to pass that you will multiply and be fruitful in the land. Then, declares the Lord, *they will no longer talk* of the Ark of the Lord's Covenant. It will neither enter anyone's mind nor be remembered nor be missed; nor will it be replaced by another" (Jer. 3:16–17; see also 31:28).[61] This is similar to the prophecy of Ezekiel: "As I live, declares the Lord God, you will no longer use this proverb in Israel" (Ezek. 18:3; see also 12:23).

This has profound significance in relation to Jacob's name change to Israel; by employing the verb A-M-R, the "man" hints that Israel is not merely a new name, but that it has the power to eclipse Jacob's old name and all its negative associations. People will no longer speak of him as the

---

58. Compare to Holmgren, "Genesis 32," 9.
59. On a tangent, I wish to point out although *nadiv* in the biblical sense means "noble" or "elite" (e.g., Num. 21:18), here *nadiv* seems to function in the modern sense, of "generous," for this verse contrasts avarice with generosity (*shoa* is also "noble," but *kilai* is a miser – see Radak in context). Nonetheless, Amos Hakham argues that even in this context, *nadiv* simply means "elite" (Hakham, *Isaiah I*, 335).
60. Hamilton, *Genesis II*, 333.
61. See further about Jeremiah's prophecy in Weinfeld, "Spiritual Metamorphosis," 19.

old deceitful "Jacob," but as "Israel." This is especially relevant within the Jacob-Esau narrative dynamics; when Esau learns that Jacob has stolen his blessing, he exclaims, "Is he not rightly named Jacob (*Yaakov*)? For he has *supplanted* me (*vaya'keveni*) these two times. He took away my birthright; and look, now he has taken away my blessing" (Gen. 27:36). This is the meaning of the statement: "You shall no longer be called Jacob" – he will no longer be associated with the negative implications of his name. From now on, another name will cancel out the implications that have plagued him since birth.

This paradigm also encourages the idea that the etymology of the name Israel is not only related to the root S-R-H, struggle,[62] but also to the root Y-SH-R, meaning straight – which is, of course, the opposite of A-K-B, crooked, as in the famous prophecy "And the crooked ground (*akov*) shall be made straight (*mishor*)" (Is. 40:4).

By changing his name from Jacob to Israel, the "man" who has not allowed Jacob to dodge the expected meeting with his brother is hinting that Jacob must relinquish the blessings that he obtained through crooked, indirect ways. God has promised that Jacob is entitled to the blessings outright, straightforwardly, directly from God; now he must shed his evasive, deceitful history, and meet his brother directly. Rashi's commentary leads to a similar reading: "No longer will your name be Jacob – No longer will it be said that the blessings came to you through trickery and deceit, but through authority and openness, and soon the Holy One will appear to you in Bethel and change your name" (on 32:29). This invites a careful reading of the episode's conclusion.

---

62. By this I do not mean that this is the etymological origin of the name Israel, but that this explanation hints to the contrast with the name Jacob. Albright takes this a step further by claiming that the name comes from the root Y-SH-R (Albright, "Israel"). I have already noted that Eliezer Hadad sees Jacob grasping the heel as a symbol of his triumph through deceit – as a serpent and he thus perceives the name Israel as a hint to *yashrut*, the quality of uprightness, despite the narrative's explicit etymology: "One name has several meanings, some of which are covert" (Hadad, "The Crooked," 14, esp. n. 14).

"The Sun Was Rising on Him as He Moved on from Penuel, Limping on His Thigh" (32:32)

This conclusion adds a further twist to this tale. The narrative focuses on Jacob as he limps away from the scene, "limping on his thigh." Ironically, as the shrewd, crooked Jacob, he walks perfectly straight, but as Israel – *Yisra-El* – he can no longer walk straight, and he limps.[63] In context, this reversal makes perfect sense. The angel forces Jacob to confront his brother, but this confrontation will not be a physical attack. On the contrary, Jacob now approaches Esau with clear physical inferiority; his superiority over Esau manifests itself through the fact that he does not need his stolen blessings anymore, for it is God Himself who blesses Jacob directly.

The new sun shines down on Jacob as he limps back to his family, coming full circle with the sun that sets as he leaves his father's home and journeys toward Haran (28:10). This marks the end of his exile and the birth of a new nation, Israel.

EATING THE *GID HANASHEH*

The etiological explanation that the Israelites do not eat a certain part of the animal because of the injury Jacob sustained in his fight serves as an appendix after the episode's conclusion. The previous verse – Jacob limping away in the pink light of dawn – mirrors the opening verse of the struggle: "And a man wrestled with him until dawn" (32:25). Thus this etiological description serves as an appendix after the narrative conclusion, rather than as a conclusion itself.

This verse is arranged in a concentric structure:

That is why the Israelites do not eat the *sciatic nerve*
    by the *hip socket*
        to this day,
    because he wrenched Jacob's *hip socket*
at the *sciatic nerve*. (32:33)

63. Similarly: Benor, "Blood Groom," 6.

Aside from the naming of Penuel, which links this scene to the distant future, the description of the Israelite custom also bridges the gap between past and future, its concentricity drawing an apt connection between the legendary struggle and the enduring custom. According to the prevalent reading that Jacob overcomes his attacker and refuses to release him until he blesses him, however, it is strange that this struggle is commemorated through the injury Jacob sustained. Rather than celebrating his victory, why is the only aspect of his defeat immortalized through legal tradition?

Commemorating the injury of a human ancestor through the prohibition of eating this part in animals is also strange: "The prohibition is concerned with a part of an animal's body whereas the event that gave rise to it was concerned with a person."[64] A more fitting commemoration, perhaps, would have been to make a physical mark on the thigh, or even some kind of custom that involves walking on a specific date as a tribute to Jacob's limp.

And indeed, some commentators explain the prohibition of eating *gid hanasheh* differently. Sforno proposes a fascinating psychological explanation that this custom is meant to downplay the importance of the sciatic nerve in general: "So that the harm inflicted on [Jacob's] hip socket will seem negligible" (on 32:33).

R. Asher son of Yehiel (the Rosh) makes an even bolder suggestion: "That is why the Israelites do not eat the sciatic nerve – meaning, that because they left him to walk alone and he was harmed by this, they missed out on a delicacy for all generations as a reminder of their sin."[65] This custom is not a reminder of victory but of Jacob's sons' negligence – because they left their father alone, he was attacked and barely survived, and as punishment, the *gid hanasheh* is off-limits to them.

Another theory is that the fact that the injury is commemorated through the bodies of animals, rather than through a different sign or action on the human body, shows that with this custom Israel represents the angel and not Jacob himself. When Israel slaughter and eat animals,

---

64. Westermann, Genesis 12–50, 520.
65. Rosh on 32:33; his commentary is included in the book *Hadar Zekenim* ("Glory of the Elders"), printed in Livorno in 1840.

they do not eat the *gid hanasheh*; unlike the angel, who strikes below the belt, Israel do not touch this part of the animal. In this way, they express that Israelites do not fight unfairly.[66]

I believe, however, that this prohibition is not incorporated into the narrative as a tribute to Jacob's victory, nor, as my proposed reading might imply, to Jacob's defeat, but as commemoration of this divine touch. The meaning of the verb N-G-A in this verse is not entirely clear – does it mean that Jacob's thigh was *struck*, with force (as in: "But if You would cast forth Your hand and *strike* all that he has" – Job 1:11), or merely *touched* by God's hand (such as: "The angel of the Lord came back a second time and *touched him*. 'Get up; eat,' it said, 'or the long journey will prove too much for you'" – II Kings 19:7)?[67] In either case, the use of force can be perceived as a semantic extension of the more neutral sense,[68] and regardless, there is no real difference in plot – God either strikes his thigh or touches his thigh, and leaves Jacob with a limp. This word generally appears in a neutral sense in the Bible,[69] although there may be certain exceptions.[70]

While again, there are no significant implications for the plot either way, understanding the word in a certain sense casts the scene in different colors. God touches Jacob's thigh, and his thigh cannot bear this divine touch; it shudders like the mountains that tremble at God's touch: "He looks down to earth and it trembles; He *touches* the mountains and they smoke" (Ps. 104:32). This divine touch, in a sense, sanctifies the designated limb; it becomes off-limits for mere mortal consumption. From the moment God touches Jacob's thigh, it is consecrated for his descendants.

---

66. As suggested by my daughter Talia.
67. This debate is expressed in various translations: "He *struck* Jacob's hip at its socket" (NAB); "He *touched* the socket of his thigh" (NAS).
68. L. Scheinhorst, ,"N-G-A," 203–9.
69. Westermann, Genesis 12–50, 513; Scheinhorst, "N-G-A," 204; Alter, *Genesis*, 181.
70. One exception to this may be an extremely difficult verse in II Samuel 5:8: "*Kol makke Yevusi veyigga batzinnor*." This verse is given to extensive debate in scholarship, and I discuss its meaning – including that of the word *veyigga* in this context – in Grossman, "Did David Actually Conquer Jerusalem?"

This is how the prohibition can be understood: it is a tribute to the contrast between human frailty and divine strength. The narrator does not say that Israelites do not eat the thigh socket because of Jacob's limp, but rather because God "struck Jacob on the hip socket at the thigh muscle." The focus is not upon the result of this touch, but on the touch itself. This scene is charged with the atmosphere of Jacob's rebirth. After struggling with Esau in the womb, Jacob emerges clutching at his brother's heel and receives his first name, Jacob (25:26); now, after struggling with God all night, God touches his thigh and he receives his second name – Israel.[71]

This illuminates why Israel choose to refrain from eating the *gid hanasheh*. Humans, mortals, "limp" by definition – they suffer from physical pain and emotional pain, fears and limitations. Pitted against an angel – not to speak of God Himself – they are limping, powerless, insufficient. Yet the prohibition of *gid hanasheh* immortalizes the possibility of an encounter between the limping human and the divine; of God's touch upon mere mortals. Israel's power lies in their relationship with God, a bond that is not measured by physical strength, but by how they seek His presence.

As described in the introduction, there is a profound connection between the two commandments based on the ancestral cycles in Genesis: circumcision, which God commands Abraham (Gen. 17) and the prohibition of eating the *gid hanasheh,* which Israel take upon themselves following Jacob's struggle with the divine figure. Surely Sigmund Freud, who perceives even Medusa's beheading as an expression of castration,[72] would detect similar symbolism in Jacob's injury. After all, to look into Medusa's eyes causes certain death, while Jacob marvels that he has seen God face to face and lived. In this case, however, we do not need to resort to Freudian theory in order to recognize the connection between Jacob's injury and circumcision. I have already

71. Holmgren sees this as covert cooperation between Jacob and the angel – both hold their opponent's leg, which leads him to conclude that there is no criticism in the text when Jacob acts out of deceit – not at his birth, when he grasps his brother's heel, nor later, when he steals the blessings (Holmgren, "Genesis 32").

72. Freud, *Culture,* 129–31.

contrasted and compared the two in the introduction; but I believe that this comparison has further significance. These laws – which both touch upon flesh itself – reflect the potential connection between flesh-and-blood humans and God. They commemorate the God of Israel's bond with the nation's forefathers by governing life, the eating that sustains it, and the sexuality that engenders it.[73] As Abraham Joshua Heschel expresses: "Man is not an innocent bystander of the cosmic drama. His closeness to the divine is greater than we can possibly believe."[74]

JACOB AND ESAU'S BRIEF REUNION (33:1–15)

Jacob's struggle with the angel opens the second half of this scene, which then describes the brothers' reunion. At this point, the reader is still in suspense – what are Esau's intentions, and how will he act when he sees Jacob? The narrative maintains its ambiguities for as long as possible, and ultimately only discovers them along with Jacob himself. As he limps back to his family, "Jacob looked up – and saw Esau coming with his four hundred men" (33:1). At this point, as mentioned, Jacob divides up his camp – this time, his family – placing each child with its mother.

The messengers have reported that Esau is "on his way to meet you," without clarifying his intentions; now is the moment of truth, and "Esau *ran to meet him* – and embraced him. He threw his arms around his neck and kissed him, and they wept" (33:4). After twenty years apart, Esau does not merely "walk" toward his brother; he *runs* toward him. Yet the scene unfolds before the reader in slow motion, slowed down by five verbs (ran, embraced, threw his arms around his neck, kissed, wept) – the first four describe Esau's actions, whereas only the fifth describes the two brothers crying together.[75] This is consistent with the spirit of the plot: it is up to Esau to set the tone of their reunion, and Jacob only allows himself to cry along with his brother after Esau has made his feelings clear.

---

73. R. Medan adds that it is appropriate that Jacob receives a new name after his injury, just like newborn boys are named at their circumcision (Medan, *Close to You*, 262).
74. Heschel, *God and Man*, 136.
75. Wenham, *Genesis II*, 298.

Even at this stage, after their warm reconciliation, it is difficult to determine whether Esau initially means to fight Jacob but then changes his mind, "which brings us to the dramatic turning point of the narrative,"[76] or whether Jacob's fears have been unfounded all long, and Esau's mighty entourage was always intended as a welcoming committee.[77] Astonishingly, both possibilities are encouraged even after the brothers' ostensibly warm embrace, focalized through Jacob and through Esau. Esau asks in amazement, "What did you mean by all the camp (*maḥane*) that I met before?" (33:8), and his use of a word charged with military connotations rouses the reader's suspicions: Did Esau originally plan an attack, or is it Jacob whose suspicions move him to divide his family and possessions into two "camps"?

It may be that Esau feigns surprise with the diplomacy of someone who is eager to accept a gift, but initially refuses out of politeness. Yet even after Jacob informs him that this procession is his gift to him, he refuses: "I have plenty, my brother. Let what is yours remain yours" (33:9), and he only gives in and accepts the gift after Jacob "pressed him" (33:11). The verb "pressed," *vayiftzar*, often occurs in the Bible in situations of two conflicting interests, and in all other instances, both parties' stances are authentic.[78] Thus the combination of Esau's repeated refusal and the narrator's use of the verb "*vayiftzar*" imply that Esau's reluctance to accept the gift is genuine.

This, of course, supports the theory that Esau never had violent intentions, so from his perspective, Jacob's gifts are superfluous. The formulation of his refusal characterizes him as someone who has come a long way in the twenty years since his blessings were snatched away from him: "I have plenty" is the sentiment of someone satisfied with his lot; someone who feels that God has dealt him a good hand. Given that the narrative focuses on Jacob after he leaves Isaac's home, the reader can only imagine how Esau's relationship with his parents changes over the years, when he is left alone with them. At one point he obviously leaves Canaan and moves to Seir, but this seems to have been a peaceful, loving

76. Adar, *Genesis*, 87; Wenham, *Genesis II*, 304.
77. Speiser, *Genesis*, 260.
78. See Gen. 19:3–9; Judges 19:7; II Kings 2:17; II Kings 5:16.

parting; one preceded, perhaps, by many meals of game, after many days in the field in his special hunting clothes.[79] Now Esau is able to approach his brother with genuine warmth and acceptance, to the extent that he "embraced him, threw his arms around his neck, and kissed him." So much hangs on the simple phrase "and they wept"; it is the narrowest of windows into the intense emotional world of twins who have been apart for twenty years.

The claim that Esau has sought reconciliation all along is reinforced by his offer to travel together: "Let us be on our way. I will go beside you.... Let me leave some of my people with you" (33:12, 15). Presumably, Esau would not make such an offer if the "people" in question were armed fighters who were initially prepared to fight Jacob; if he had originally planned to attack, it is more likely that Esau would disregard their presence, embarrassed. Rather, his proposal that these men accompany Jacob suggests that they are indeed part of an entourage meant to honor his brother, not fight against him.

At the same time, however, other details – focalized through Jacob – hint that Esau's original intentions were not as loving, but Jacob's tactics changed his mind. This is especially true of Jacob's comparison between his meeting with Esau and his meeting with God: "For seeing your face is like seeing the face of God, and you have shown me favor" (33:10).[80]

This sentence is packed with hidden meaning – perhaps overlooked by Esau – that the reader is invited to consider nonetheless. At first glance, this comparison seems to continue Jacob's line of self-effacement before his brother – comparing his firstborn brother to God, just as he addresses him as "my lord" and himself as "your servant." Esau presumably takes this to mean that Jacob is renouncing the birthright he took in their youth. Yet the reader rightly suspects that this is no innocent comparison; Jacob has recently struggled with God, and the phrase "For seeing your face is like seeing the face of God, and you have shown

---

79. Compare to Assis, who makes the opposite claim that Esau was living with Isaac all this time (*Identity in Conflict*, 90). Either reading may be correct; there is no way to decide between them.

80. Fokkelman notes the chiastic structure of Jacob's speech (*Genesis*, 226) and holds that this verse is its center and thus invites special attention.

me favor" certainly echoes Jacob's exclamation after wrestling with the "man" at Peniel: "For I have seen God face to face and yet my life has been spared" (32:31).[81]

The comparison between Jacob's meeting with Esau and his encounter with the angel the night before is even more salient given the chiastic structure of these verses (33:9–11):[82]

A. "I have plenty, my brother. Let what is yours remain yours."
  B. "No, please – If I have found favor (*ḥen*) in your eyes,
    C. accept this gift from me,
      D. for seeing your face
      D'. is like seeing the face of God, and you have shown me favor."
    C'. "Please accept my blessing that was brought to you,
  B'. for God has shown me favor (*ḥanan*),
A'. and I have everything."

Jacob's long speech is a response to Esau's refusal to accept his gift because "I have plenty" (A): he urges him to accept because he has even more than "plenty" – he has "everything" (A').

The next two components (B–B') hint to a comparison between Esau and God: Jacob hopes that he has found "favor" (*ḥen*) in Esau's eyes (B), and in parallel, states that God has "shown me favor" (*ḥanan*) (B'). This bold flattery is explicit at the heart of his speech (D–D'), where he repeats the keyword "face": "For seeing your face is like seeing the face of God."

This comparison thus implies that Jacob feels toward Esau the same way he feels toward the angel – forced conciliation following a fierce struggle. From Jacob's perspective, as he wrestles with the angel all night long, he believes that Esau, too, intends to harm him, but just as he survives seeing God's face, he also survives the encounter with his brother.

---

81. See, for example, Radak on 33:10; Rosenzweig, "Naharaim," 14; Bar Efrat, *Artistic Design*, 24; Sarna, *Genesis*, 230; Kiel, *Genesis II*, 443; Alter, *Five Books*, 185, who also points out the alliteration between "*vatirtzeni*" and "*vatinatzel nafshi*".
82. Fokkelman, *Genesis*, 226.

This is reinforced through Jacob's refusal to join Esau's journey. Jacob's fear persists despite their apparent reconciliation; after all, Esau's warriors remain by his side. He even refuses to accept Esau's offering that some of his warriors escort him ("Let me leave some of my people with you"), which shows that Jacob harbors reservations until the very end of the scene.[83]

Some feel uncomfortable with Jacob's lie to Esau at the end of the scene. After promising that he will join him in Seir, Jacob continues to Canaan.[84] While this reflects his lingering fear, he should not be castigated too harshly, especially given the fact that the brothers' relationship echoes the relationship between the two nations they represent. As Holmgren correctly asserts:

> Let us look at this conversation again and consider it as a conversation between two figures who represent two nations. Esau (i.e., Edom) invites Jacob (i.e., Israel) to accompany him to Seir (i.e., to Edom!). If Jacob (Israel) had accepted this invitation, he would have been under the power of Esau (Edom). Jacob's future is not in Edom but in Canaan which later is to become Israel (God's chosen people). It was absolutely necessary for Jacob (Israel) to go to Canaan if he were to become the father of the nation Israel.... For Israelites, Jacob is an example of the wise person who knows how to act wisely in the presence of threatening power. He told a lie to outwit an enemy who would have prevented the birth of Israel.... Jacob is admired because he was not so naïve as to be lured to Edom.[85]

The scene cannot end with a new conflict between the brothers, because its main objective is to show their conciliation, but nor can it end with Jacob journeying to Edom and staying with his brother. Rather, Jacob's

83. Compare to Sternberg, *Poetics*, 244.

84. Von Rad, *Genesis*, 328, who believes that Jacob's mistrust is that of a trickster. See also Alter, *Five Books*, 186. Wenham explains that Jacob cannot leave Canaan for Seir, because God has commanded him to go to Canaan (Wenham, *Genesis II*, 299).

85. Holmgren, "Genesis 32," 12–13.

agreement to dwell with his brother, but his ensuing entrance to the Promised Land, thus holds the stick at both ends.[86]

The Assessment of Jacob

How is Jacob evaluated in this scene? Midrashic literature already presents two conflicting views. Some criticize Jacob harshly for initiating a meeting with Esau in the first place:

> R. Huna quotes: "Like someone who grasps a dog's ears is someone who intercedes in a dispute not his" (Prov. 26:17). Naḥman son of Shmuel said: Once there was a vicious bandit, fast asleep by the road. Someone passed by and began to rouse him, saying, "Get up, it is not good to sleep here." He woke up and began to beat him.... Thus the Holy One blessed be He said: He was going his own way, but you sent him a message, saying "So says your servant Jacob"...[87]

These arguments lead to further midrashim that criticize Jacob – overtly and covertly – for not letting sleeping dogs lie. Some disapprove of Jacob's submissive attitude toward Esau:

> When Jacob called Esau "my lord," the Holy One blessed be he said to him: You humbled yourself and called Esau "my lord" eight times, and for that I will make eight of his sons king before your sons become king, as it says, "And these are the kings who reigned in the land of Edom..."[88]

A different midrashic approach, however, praises Jacob for his actions:

> And Jacob sent. Of this Solomon spoke, through the divine spirit: "Blessings upon the righteous head" (Prov. 10:6); this verse refers to Jacob and Esau. "Blessings upon the righteous head" refers to

---

86. This open ending leaves room for the complex, ambivalent relationship between Israel and Edom in the rest of the Bible. See Assis, *Identity in Conflict*.
87. Genesis Rabba 75:3.
88. Ibid., 75:11.

> Jacob, and "Violence covers the mouth of the wicked" refers to the wicked Esau. Happy are the righteous, who are blessed in heaven and earth...[89]

Both midrashic approaches are upheld by the medieval commentators: Ramban criticizes Jacob, while Rashi and others make no such accusations;[90] and the debate continues throughout later exegesis and even contemporary scholarship. Some show how the brothers' reunion is loaded with irony that casts Jacob in a problematic light;[91] others feel that Jacob's submission elevates him: "The parable of the wise person can be said of Jacob: 'When the Lord approves of a man's ways, He will cause his enemies to make peace with him' (Prov. 16:7)... this reconciliation serves to confirm Jacob's authority over all the land on both sides of the Jordan."[92]

The question of Jacob's characterization in this scene is also affected by the fundamental ambiguity surrounding Esau's original intentions toward his brother. If Esau indeed harbors animosity toward Jacob but his actions manage to sway him, then Jacob should be commended for preventing violence and bloodshed. If, however, Esau never intends any harm in the first place, and travels all the way from Seir to embrace and forgive his brother, then Jacob emerges as overly suspicious and mistrustful.

Yet in light of Rashbam's reading that the angel forces Jacob to confront Esau and restore his blessings to him, it seems that God favors Jacob's submission before his brother. This does not mean that the narrative elevates Esau above Jacob; on the contrary, it characterizes Jacob as the chosen one, the one blessed directly by God. From this privileged stance, Jacob can and must make amends with the brother he once deceived.

---

89. Ibid., 75:8.
90. See further in Leibowitz, *Genesis*, 241–44; Frankel, *Chapters*, 112.
91. Wenham, *Genesis II*, 288, 298 (eventually, he praises both brothers – 304); Good, *Irony*, 98; Garsiel, "Literary Structure," 78–79; Medan, *Close to You*, 252–58. Compare also to Buber, *Ways*, 292.
92. Kiel, *Genesis II*, 408; Emanueli, *Genesis*, 446; Skinner, *Genesis*, 415.

"He Made Huts for His Livestock" (Gen. 33:16–17)

The woods are lovely, dark and deep,
But I have promises to keep,
And miles to go before I sleep,
And miles to go before I sleep.
– Robert Frost, "Stopping by Woods on a Snowy Evening"

Jacob and Esau's reunion ends with the brothers' parting:

So that day Esau started back on his way to Seir,
and Jacob journeyed on to Sukkot.
There he built himself a house
and made huts (*sukkot*) for his livestock;
that is why he named the place Sukkot. (33:16–17)

At the end of Jacob's parting with Laban at Galed, Laban returns home and Jacob journeys on; here, too, Esau returns home, while Jacob continues to Sukkot.[1] And just as we debated whether the episode in Mahanaim marks the end of Jacob's time with Laban or the beginning of his meeting with Esau, a similar debate arises about his stay in Sukkot. Is this the conclusion of his reunion with Esau, a brief independent unit, or an introduction to the violation of Dinah?

1. See especially in Weimar, "Analyse," 58–59.

This time, however, the decision is easier; it seems that Jacob's journey to Sukkot serves as the conclusion of his reunion with Esau, as is evident in the narrator's contrast between Esau's return home and Jacob's journey: "So that day Esau started back on his way to Seir/and Jacob journeyed on to Sukkot" (33:16–17). Placing the subject before the predicate ("*veYaakov nasa*" as opposed to the typical "*vayissa Yaakov*") is a classic biblical means of creating contrast – Esau returns home/Jacob journeys on, and forms a chiastic parallelism. Esau "returns," but Jacob "journeys on" because he is still on his way home, and Sukkot is merely a stop on the way. Yet the narrator does not report that Esau actually reaches Seir, but rather that he "started back on his way to Seir." Our protagonist is Jacob, and once Esau has parted ways with him, he is no longer of any interest; his journey to Seir is only mentioned to serve as a contrast with Jacob's journey. The contrast between the brothers' journeys is even more striking if we accept Nahum Sarna's claim that Jacob travels northward to Sukkot, while Esau turns south to Seir.[2] This is not entirely accurate, given that Sukkot is to the west of Penuel (perhaps slightly northwest),[3] but Sarna is correct in noting that the text draws a clear contrast between the brothers – one turns back to Seir, and the other travels on toward Canaan.

Although Esau is not the narrator's focus here, I wish to draw attention to the chronological detail, "On that day (*bayom hahu*)." Elsewhere in the Bible, the phrase "On that day" expresses certain celebration or historical significance. A few examples should suffice: "On that day the Lord made a covenant with Abram: To your descendants I will give this land, from the River of Egypt to the great river Euphrates" (Gen. 15:18); "On that day, he blessed them: By you shall Israel bless, saying: 'May God make you like Ephraim and Menashe'" (Gen. 48:20); "On that day, the Lord saved the Israelites from the Egyptians" (Ex. 14:30). Even when the tone is not festive, it usually expresses certain anomaly, such as: "On that day the Lord's rage burned, and He swore: None of the

2. Sarna, *Genesis*, 231; similarly: Alter, *Genesis*, 187.
3. Mathews, perhaps, is more cautious: "If Deir Alla is the correct site, then Jacob moved north and west, the opposite trek of Esau, who returned south to Mount Seir" (*Genesis II*, 572).

men twenty years of age or above who left Egypt will see the land that I swore to give Abraham, Isaac, and Jacob" (Num. 32:10–11). The punishment that the Israelites must wander in the desert for forty years before entering the land is, of course, one that changed the course of history.[4]

If so, then why is this dramatic phrase used to describe an ostensibly banal description of Esau's return home? Perhaps its purpose is just that – to add drama and historical significance to Jacob's parting from Esau. "On that day," relates the text, "two nations go their separate ways": this farewell does not merely depict the parting of two brothers, but the formation of two distinct nations. The implications of Esau's move to Edom far transcend the narrative present – they shape history itself.[5]

What, then, is the meaning of Jacob's brief, uneventful stay in Sukkot, and why is it even reported to the reader? Jacob presumably makes several stops on his journey to Canaan; it makes sense that he sets up camp and shelter for his livestock in other places as well. The fact that Sukkot is mentioned at all demands explanation.[6]

While we ponder the scene's inclusion in the first place, it is worth noting that its content is somewhat surprising. Not only is emphasis placed on Jacob's livestock and the "huts" he builds for it, but the place is actually named for these huts! Jacob builds a "house" for his family there, but the narrative focuses on the "huts" he builds for his animals and repeats the name "Sukkot" three times: "Jacob journeyed on to Sukkot (*Sukkota*)/There he built himself a house and made huts (*sukkot*) for his livestock; that is why he named the place Sukkot."

I believe that the intense focus on "Sukkot" is calculated to divert the reader's attention from a different detail in this brief scene. Were the text not focused on the inherently temporary "huts," the reader might

4. Some places initially seem meaningless, but in context, emerge as significant, e.g.: "On that day Isaac's servants came to tell him about the well they dug, and they said to him, 'We have found water'" (Gen. 26:32). Because this well is discovered in parallel to Isaac and Abimelech's covenant (Beersheba!), it then becomes a symbol of Isaac's covenant with Gerar.
5. Similarly, after Lot parts ways with Abraham, God appears to him.
6. Mathews learns from this that Jacob's excuse to Esau, that they travel slowly, is in fact true, because they need to make a temporary stop soon after (Mathews, *Genesis II*, 573).

think that the "house" Jacob builds symbolizes his return "home." Now that Jacob has made peace with Esau, he is able to "return home" in safety, mission accomplished. His exile in Haran is over (as mentioned in the incident at Mahanaim), for he is no longer afraid of his brother, and he is finally able to build a home of his own. Indeed, some suggest that this is what this episode symbolizes: "The mention of building a house and booths suggests permanent settlement. The reader might wonder whether this means that Jacob does not plan to return to Bethel."[7] On the contrary; the narrative design encourages the opposite reading: the focus on "Sukkot" hints that Jacob has yet to settle down for good. It is worth recalling that Sukkot is to the east of the Jordan (Judges 8:4–5), in the valley to the west of Penuel (Judges 8:8; the "Valley of Sukkot" is also mentioned in Ps. 60:8; 108:8). Jacob has yet to cross the Jordan and enter the land of Canaan proper.[8] Thus his stay in Sukkot is inherently ambivalent: it is his first stop after parting ways with Esau, but his journey is not quite over.

Ramban notes this in his commentary on Jacob's next stop, Shechem: "Thus Jacob, having come from Padan Aram, arrived safely at the town of Shechem in Canaan" (33:18). This verse emphasizes that Shechem is actually in Canaan, which, as Ramban points out, shows that the same cannot be said of Sukkot:

> "Jacob arrived safely" – I believe that the text speaks thus because in Sukkot, he was still afraid of Esau, for it was east of the Jordan, in the kingdom of Sihon, and… it was closer to Seir. Thus, until he entered the land of Canaan Jacob did not feel safe, for only then did he know that Esau would not touch him for his father was nearby, or because the people of the land would help him as his father was a prince of God among them, or because the merit of having entered the land would save him. Therefore, it now says that he "arrived safely" in the land where his father lived, for God protected him on his way against all of his enemies.… It says in

7. Vrolijk, *Jacob's Wealth*, 255.
8. It is interesting that the narrative does not mention how Jacob and his family cross the Jordan, as one might expect for its symbolic importance.

> Genesis Rabba that "throughout all those months in Sukkot, he would honor Esau with the aforementioned gift" because he was still afraid of him, and therefore sent him a monthly or perhaps annual gift. (Ramban on Gen. 33:18)

The midrash Ramban cites – that Jacob continued sending gifts to Esau throughout his time in Sukkot – is a poignant expression of the ambivalent nature of this scene. Jacob, still beyond the Jordan, is still plagued by fear and insecurity. Only once he enters Canaan is Jacob able to breathe a sigh of relief and begin a new chapter in his life.[9]

Yet if this is the case, then why is this stop in Sukkot mentioned at all? Why is it a relevant part of Jacob's journey? As mentioned, Jacob presumably makes other stops along the way, considering the fact that he travels with a large flock and little children (33:13–14). Why does this particular stop deserve a place in the text?

There are two possible exegetical directions here: one extends outwards, beyond the bounds of the narrative; the other turns inwards, perceiving the pattern of Jacob's journey as the main objective of this scene.

Jacob's delay in this particular place may be related to its proximity to Canaan's borders and its future significance in Israelite history. In a certain sense, Sukkot is perceived as a parallel city to Shechem, the two mirroring each other on the two sides of the Jordan, together marking Canaan's eastern boundary.[10] This is (twice) reflected in Psalms: "I will divide up Shechem and measure out the Valley of Sukkot" (60:8; 108:8); as Rashi comments (in some manuscripts): "Shechem and Sukkot – they

9. Assis proposes that Jacob briefly stops in Sukkot out of fear that Esau will not approve of his move to Canaan (*Identity in Conflict*, 80–81), and this is consistent with our theory, but not with the structure Gunkel proposes in *Genesis*, 356: that this is part of "Jacob in Canaan" (33:17–35:22). According to Ramban, this stop marks the end of Esau and Jacob's reunion, whereas "Jacob in Canaan" only begins with his arrival in Shechem (33:18–20).
10. On Sukkot's identification as Tel Deir Allah (which already begins in the Yerushalmi, Shevi'it, 9b), see Seely, "Succoth."

were on the edge of Canaan, as we saw when Jacob arrives in the land through Sukkot and Shechem" (on Ps. 60:8).[11]

In the story of Gideon, the people of Sukkot play a significant part; Sukkot seems to have been a well-known city for a considerable time. Our scene offers an etiological explanation for the name of this city: it was Jacob himself who named it upon return from exile in Haran, and this, too, seems to be part of the narrative objective. Given that there is a cultic pagan site in Samaria also named "Sukkot" ("Sukkot Benot" in II Kings 17:30),[12] it may be that this narrative attempts to disassociate Sukkot on the eastern bank of the Jordan from ancient idolatry. One day, King Solomon will cast the bronze vessels for the Temple near this very spot: "The king had them cast in clay molds on the Jordan plain between Sukkot and Tzartan" (I Kings 7:46). Dutch excavations of this site revealed that the city once served as a center for metalwork, and was even the site of a temple. Thus the origin story of Sukkot as Jacob's campsite and temporary shelter for his livestock may serve as a subtle polemic: Sukkot is not named for Assyrian or Canaanite deities, but for the huts Jacob built for his sheep, goats, and cattle.

Yet this scene can also be read as a vital albeit brief part of Jacob's journey home. Without his stop in Sukkot, the text would presumably have run thus: "So that day Esau started back on his way to Seir, while Jacob, having come from Padan Aram, arrived safely at the town of Shechem in Canaan, and he set up camp within sight of the town." If so, then Jacob's parting from Esau would have concluded with Jacob's arrival in Shechem. By comparison, Jacob parts ways with Laban and reaches Mahanaim – and this model may be precisely what the text is trying to avoid. As we already discussed, Mahanaim serves as a nexus between Jacob's parting from Laban and his reunion with Esau, linking the two greatest conflicts in Jacob's life: Laban and Esau. Were Jacob to leave Esau and immediately arrive in Shechem, then Shechem, too, would be

11. The same verse appears in two different psalms, but in Psalm 60 Rashi reads "Shechem" as the name of the city, whereas in 108, he reads it as "portion": I shall divide the land of my enemies to Israel, like "one *portion* (*shekhem*) more than your brothers."
12. For attempts to identify "Sukkot" with local deities, see Herion, "Succoth-Benoth."

perceived as part of the same chain: as the conclusion of Jacob's parting from Esau and the beginning of his new life in Canaan. Rather, Jacob's stop in Sukkot serves as a hiatus in the narrative cycle; as an interval that allows for true closure after his parting from Esau before he enters the land of Canaan and starts life anew.

To this end, Jacob stops for a while in Sukkot; his stay is uneventful, but that is the point – to pause before entering Canaan. As befits its name, Jacob's stop in Sukkot is temporary by definition, a temporary lull between two momentous units.

The Altar at Shechem and the Story of Dinah (Gen. 33:18–34:31)

This brings us to one of the most complex, haunting episodes in the Jacob cycle. Beyond the usual complications in the text, the plot itself is marred by rape, massacre, and a bitter quarrel between Jacob and his sons. One of the most complicated questions throughout this chapter is how the characters are evaluated in the story: on the one hand, how the text perceives the deed of Simeon and Levi, and on the other, how Jacob himself is characterized. This, of course, is subject to various specific exegetical difficulties – especially concerning Dinah herself. Is this indeed a tale of rape and abduction, or perhaps one of courting and seduction? It is no coincidence that Adele Berlin uses this episode to demonstrate how some biblical narratives are wrought with such fundamental ambiguity that the best way to tackle them is to shift focus from the text itself to its exegesis.[1]

WHERE DOES THE STORY BEGIN?

Before we dive into the narrative's deep murky waters, a more technical question must be decided – where does the story begin?

1. Berlin, "Literary Approaches."

As is evident from this chapter's title, I believe that Jacob's purchase of the field in Shechem serves as the beginning of the story of Dinah (as opposed to Langton's division into chapters). This is by no means unequivocal, but two factors tip the scales in favor of this division.

Firstly, simple geography connects the two events: Jacob purchases the field in Shechem, and this is where the drama takes place. Location is an especially decisive factor in an odyssey, where each stop on the way naturally divides the narrative into units.[2] In Mahanaim, Jacob leaves Laban forever; in Sukkot, he parts ways with Esau; and his arrival in Shechem marks the beginning of his new life in Canaan. His purchase of a field, erection of an altar, and the story of Dinah all occur in one place, so it makes sense that the three events form a single unit – especially since Jacob leaves for Bethel at the beginning of the next chapter (35:1).

Secondly, the narrator reports that "thus Jacob arrived safely (*shalem*) in Shechem" (33:18). This phrase is read in various ways, and many adopt Rashi's interpretation that "*shalem*" refers to Jacob: "*shalem* – [literally] 'whole' physically – his limp had healed; 'whole' in his wealth – he lacked nothing despite all the gifts he had given to Esau; 'whole' in his Torah – he did not forget his learning in Laban's house."[3] Based on this reading, Jacob's flight to Haran comes full circle here, echoing his vow at Bethel: "If God will be with me, protecting me on this journey… and if I return *safely* to my father's house…" (28:20–21). God's promise of protection is fulfilled; Jacob has safely returned home.[4]

Moreover, the altar can also be perceived as part of Jacob's fulfillment of his vow: "There he erected an altar and named it El Elohei Yisrael" (v. 20). The altar's (surprising) name shows that Jacob has

---

2. Sometimes a narrative's setting connects units that initially seem unrelated. One such example is the two events that take place in Rephidim: their complaint about the lack of water (Ex. 17:1–7) and the battle against Amalek (17:8–16).
3. Based on the Talmud, Shabbat 33b; Genesis Rabba 79:5. See a discussion of "*Shalem*"/"*BeShalom*" in Emerton, *Studies*, 64–69.
4. Skinner and Gunkel believe that describing Jacob as "*shalem*" is a sign of his successful departure from his brother, and believe that the description is related the meeting with Esau (Skinner, *Genesis*, 416; Gunkel, *Genesis*, 356). However, given that this is his first stop in Canaan, this can be perceived as the end of the entire exile unit.

accepted God as *his* God, as he said he would if he comes home safely (28:21). This reading is supported by the verb *vayatzev* – "he erected," which is an unusual verb given that altars are usually "built" (*vayiven*) or "set up" (*vayakem*). Some scholars are so troubled by this verb that they propose emending "altar" to "pillar," and the masculine pronoun "*vayikra lo*" to "*vayikra lah*."[5] Rather, I believe that this unusual verb is intentionally employed to echo Jacob's pillar and vow in Bethel[6] – "the ladder set (*mutzav*) upon the ground"; God, who "stood (*nitzav*) over him there," and the "pillar (*matzeva*)" he erects. Now Jacob "erects" an altar, and even if he has yet to fulfill all the terms of his vow (he has not yet reached Bethel), it seems he has begun.[7]

These readings suggest that Jacob's purchase of a field and erection of an altar are an independent unit marking the end of his exile:[8] after all this time, he finally has land of his own.

But even if this altar and Jacob's safe arrival hint to literary closure, it is surprising that the word used is "*shalem*" instead of the more typical "*beshalom*" (as in: Gen. 26:29–31; Ex. 18:23). Thus Rashbam's explanation of this word is more convincing than Rashi's reading:

> Jacob arrived in *Shalem* – in the city named Shalem…"the city of Shechem" means the city belonging to Shechem, like "Heshbon is the city of Sihon, king of the Emorites" (Num. 21:26), as it is

5. Wellhausen, *Die composition*, 48, n. 1; Skinner, *Genesis*, 416; Gunkel, *Genesis*, 356; Westermann, *Genesis II*, 529; Walton, *Traveller*, 195. They believe that the change to "altar" is calculated to wipe out any traces of the forbidden "pillars" (Deut. 16:25). See also Rofé, *Faith*, 67–74.
6. Berman, "Jacob's Pillars," 15. Mathews also writes that the altar is mentioned to link him to his grandfather, who also built an altar in Shechem (Mathews, *Genesis II*, 576, n. 488), and see more about this comparison in my introduction.
7. On the spiritual difference between "altar" and "pillar," see Leibowitz, *Genesis*, 270–74; she also discusses the unusual verse "*lehatziv*" in this context.
8. See further in Mathews, *Genesis II*, 573–74. This delineation is also adopted by Assis, *Identity in Conflict*, 81, n. 61. Wenham, *Genesis II*, 287 also claims that these verses mark the closure of the Esau unit *and* the beginning of the Dinah narrative.

> written: "Shechem son of Hamor the Hivite, prince of the land, saw her." (Rashbam on Gen. 33:18).[9]

According to this reading, *shalem* is not an adjective pertaining to Jacob, but the name of a city: Shalem. Rashbam argues that the continuation of the verse, "the city of Shechem," should be read as "the city that belongs to Shechem," as in, "He went to Aram Naharaim, the city of Nahor" (Gen. 24:10). Rashbam is correct that mentioning the city's name after the definition "city" deviates from the usual biblical style; not to mention that there is a village next to Shechem named "Salem" – perhaps this preserves the place's original name?[10]

If we indeed adopt the position (as many modern scholars do)[11] that Shalem is the town where Shechem lives, the question arises: If the "prince of the land" is Hamor, father of Shechem, then why is the city described as "the city of Shechem" rather than "the city of Hamor"? This presumably prepares the ground for Shechem's centrality in the ensuing story.

This is even more salient in Jacob's purchase of the field: "He bought the plot of ground where he pitched his tent from the sons of Hamor, father of Shechem, for one hundred *kesita* of silver" (v. 19). Jacob buys the field from "the sons of Hamor, father of Shechem."[12] The verse needs to be read twice to understand its strange formulation: Jacob buys the field from Shechem and his brothers, but the verse is phrased so that Shechem is cast in the spotlight. This emphasis on Shechem anticipates the role he is soon to play, and indicates that these verses serve as an

9. Bekhor Shor explains that this refers to the place name, but that "the city of Shechem" refers to the city name and not just to the ruler's son.
10. Reading "*Shalem*" as the place name is also reflected in some ancient commentaries, such as the Septuagint, the Vulgate, and the Peshitta. "Shalem" is a place in Gen. 14:18, so this comes as no surprise. See further in Cohen, "Shalem." Moshe Zipor comments that the book of Jubilees combines the two meanings: "He arrived in Shalem, which is east of Shechem, in peace" (Zipor, *Septuagint*, 429).
11. As Westermann, *Genesis II*, 528; though others disagree, such as Gunkel, *Genesis*, 356.
12. For the sake of easier reading, the Septuagint ignores "*benei*" and has: "And bought the field plot where he pitched his tent, from Hamor the father of Shechem" (Zipor, *Septuagint*, 419).

exposition to the story of Dinah. In the words of Ibn Ezra (on 33:18): "For now the story of Dinah is about to begin."

The Field as Exposition

How does this exposition contribute to the story of Dinah? Just as Abraham's purchase of the cave of Machpelah – a separate burial site for his family – serves to differentiate him from the people of the land,[13] Jacob's purchase of the field is an expression of his segregation. He has just entered the land of Canaan; he is able to integrate into the local culture and become one with his neighbors. But Jacob does not enter the city; rather, he sets up camp "within sight of the town" – on its outskirts, not inside. His grandfather Abraham reaches Canaan and roams "*until* the region of Shechem, up to the Oak of Moreh" (12:6), stopping before he enters the town, and Jacob does the same.[14] He buys a "field" – a term that in biblical narrative often serves as a foil to "town" – and there he erects an altar.

The Talmud paints a quaint portrait of Jacob's attempt to begin a "normal" life among the locals, interpreting the phrase "*vayiḥan et penei ha'ir*" in the sense of "*ḥen*," grace – that is, Jacob graced the city with his innovative improvements:

> "*Vayiḥan et penei ha'ir*" – Rav said he established currency for them; Shmuel said he established markets for them; R. Yoḥanan said he established bathhouses for them. (Shabbat 33b)

Whether Jacob "improved the city" with currency, markets, or bathhouses, the Talmud implies that Jacob seeks the reassuring rhythm of daily life. But he does not adopt their currency or buy membership for their bathhouses; he does not shop in their marketplaces. Rather, he

13. This emerges from the analysis of the dialogue between Abraham and the Hittites (see Grossman, *Abraham*, 338–54).
14. See especially Cassuto, *From Noah to Abraham*, 221–22.

establishes a Hebrew currency of his own; one that celebrates the culture of the God of Israel.[15]

As mentioned, his purchase of the field demonstrates his segregation from the local people; he does not become one of them, but remains in his own sphere and erects his own altar.

The scene's conclusion confirms that his intention is to keep to himself: "There he erected an altar and named it El Elohei Yisrael" (v. 20). The altar's name testifies to the God of Israel's special attitude toward His own people. In this context, it is worth mentioning a peculiar midrash whose meaning is illuminated by this reading: "*Vayiḥan et penei ha'ir* – he arrived on Sabbath eve as the sun was setting, and established boundaries before the Sabbath" (Genesis Rabba 79:6).[16] Arriving just before the Sabbath, Jacob marks the boundaries of his territory, defining inside and out, "us" and "them."

Thus begins the story of Dinah; with Jacob's family setting itself apart from the local culture, from the people of the land. On the one hand, he does interact with them for business's sake, and settles on the outskirts of their city. It soon emerges that these locals are happy to do business with this wealthy family: "These people are friendly toward us. Let them live in the land and trade in it" (34:21). On the other hand, he keeps his distance, and does not set up camp in their midst; rather, he buys land outside their town and there erects an altar for his own God.

Jacob wished to dwell in peace, but the tragedy of Dinah was sprung upon him.

The narrative's exposition is crucial to the understanding of its objective. Jacob attempts to establish his own separate clan and keep his distance from the locals, but his daughter Dinah wants to meet them: "Dinah, the daughter whom Leah had borne to Jacob, went out to see the daughters of the land" (34:1). If her outing is read in dialogue with Jacob's altar, built outside the bounds of the city, her venture outside

---

15. According to the midrash, the opposite holds true: "*Vayiḥan et penei ha'ir* – he charmed the important figures in the city by sending them gifts" (79:6).
16. Ibid.

her father's sphere expresses the breach of the walls Jacob attempts to build, if only symbolically.[17]

The Midrash castigates Dinah for her "outing":

> "And subdue it" (Gen. 1:28) – The man must subdue his wife so that she will not go out to market. For a sorry end awaits every woman who goes out to market, as we learn from Dinah, as is written: "And Dinah went out."[18]

The Sages also refer to Dinah as a "*yatzanit*" – literally, "one who goes out," based on the phrase "*vatetzei Dina*"; perhaps translated best as "a loose woman" or "slut," the word is used as a euphemism for "prostitute." These midrashim treat Dinah far too harshly; rather, I believe, she is characterized as a curious girl who wishes to explore the new city for herself. Moreover, the text emphasizes that she wishes to see "the *daughters* of the land" – perhaps, as a lone girl growing up with ten brothers, she longs for some feminine company for a change.

Nonetheless, despite her harmless intentions, Dinah's "outing" does break down the boundaries Jacob attempts to build between him and the local people. This is alluded to, perhaps, in the phrase "the daughters of the land." While it shows that Dinah's motives for leaving the house are not sexual or romantic – she merely seeks feminine companionship – this phrase does recall the beginning of Jacob's journey. Rebecca's excuse for sending Jacob away uses this same phrase: "Rebecca then said to Isaac, 'I loathe my life because of these Hittite women. If Jacob marries a Hittite woman like them, one of the *daughters of the land*, why should I go on living?'" (27:46). Jacob, like his mother Rebecca, seeks to keep his family away from Canaanite culture, from the "daughters of the land" that Dinah now goes out to see.

To clarify: I do not believe that this verse criticizes Dinah, but various hints in the text do anticipate the possible hazards of such an

17. Genesis Rabba explains that the connection between the altar and the story of Dinah is that of crime and punishment: Jacob acted with unjustifiable pride in calling the altar "El, God of Israel," and Dinah is taken as his punishment (79:8).
18. Genesis Rabba 8:12.

outing. Though Dinah acts out of innocent curiosity, her venture into a different sphere breaks down the boundaries Jacob attempts to build, with devastating results.

DINAH AND SARAI

Before our analysis of the story itself, I wish to point out a thematic connection between the story of Dinah and the scene where her great-grandmother Sarai is captured by Pharaoh (Gen. 12). Beyond the obvious similarities – a woman is seized by a foreign ruler against the husband or father's will – further connections suggest that the story of Dinah should be read in dialogue with the capture of Sarai.

The most obvious connection is that both foreign rulers suffer physical harm as a result of their lust for these women: God strikes Pharaoh "with afflictions," while the entire city of Shechem suffers for their leader's actions. Following this harm, the woman is returned to her family, and Jacob's sons, like Abraham, grow wealthy from the woman's captors.

Another aspect of this analogy is related to the characters' geographical context: Abram arrives in Canaan following God's command, and he builds an altar at Shechem. From there he moves on to Bethel, where he builds another altar, but before God's revelation to him in Bethel he first goes down to Egypt, where Sarai is captured. After his return to Canaan, he goes back to Bethel, where a proper revelation awaits him (13:14–17). Jacob, too, follows a similar path: he reaches Canaan (at God's word), buys a field in Shechem and builds an altar, and before he continues to Bethel, his daughter Dinah is captured. After she is returned to her family, he travels on to Bethel, where he builds another altar and God appears to him.[19]

This analogy, as mentioned in the introduction, is part of a broader analogy between Abraham and Jacob. The difference between

19. For this reason, I believe that the analogy of Sarai and Pharaoh is more appropriate than Sarah and Abimelech (Gen. 20), which Galender argues is also in dialogue with our scene (Galender, *Genesis II*, 281). Nonetheless, the aforementioned central claim also applies to the latter scene.

them, and the nature of the Jacob cycle, can be demonstrated through three different focal points.

Divine Intervention

One of the most striking differences between the two episodes is how the woman is returned to her family. God strikes Pharaoh and his household with "terrible afflictions" to punish him, but in Shechem, God is not mentioned at all. Where is God while Dinah languishes for three days in Shechem's house? It is Simeon and Levi who finally free her, replacing God's terrible afflictions with a terrible human sword.

This difference touches upon the broader theological pattern of Genesis, which sees God's hand gradually giving way to human action. Without passing judgment on Simeon and Levi (for now), the fact that they are the ones to free Dinah is consistent with Genesis' theological trajectory.

Married Woman or Marriageable Girl?

The second difference touches upon the woman's status. Sarai is Abraham's *wife,* while Dinah is Jacob's *daughter*. This difference is not marginal, because it leads to a fundamental disparity between the narratives: as a married woman, Sarai cannot remain in Pharaoh's household – it would be an irremediable tragedy for Abraham to lose his wife. By contrast, Dinah can theoretically remain in Shechem's house. There are certainly more fitting grooms out there than Shechem, who captures Dinah and violates her, but if she remains with him, for whatever reason, their union will ultimately be a legal, official marriage. Fleishman shows that "marriage by abduction" was common practice in the ancient world – a man who desired a certain woman but could not pay her bride price might capture her, sleep with her, and only then marry her with the family's consent.[20] We will soon argue that Jacob indeed considers appeasing Shechem and his father (albeit only in retrospect). The central theme is already present in the exposition: Jacob purchases a field on

20. Fleischman, "Social Aspects." A striking example of this is the Benjaminites' abduction of the girls after Israel swear that they will no longer marry with their tribe (Judges 21:19–24).

the outskirts of Shechem: Will he keep his distance from its people or interact with them? This theme is not part of Sarai's capture by Pharaoh, but it serves as a key question in this scene.

Fathers and Sons

The third difference I wish to note between these scenes is related to each story's characters. Abraham's wife is seized from him, and he is the one who faces Pharaoh's wrath: "What have you done to me?... Now take her. Go" (12:18–19). By contrast, it is Dinah's brothers who become involved. Moreover, the younger generation is active on both sides: it is not Hamor who takes Dinah but his son, and it is not Jacob who responds but his sons: "We cannot do this ... we will take our daughter and go" (34:14–17).

This disparity aptly reflects the context of each scene within its narrative cycle. For Abraham, Sarai's abduction is but another trial Abraham must suffer before God's promise to him is fulfilled. He must leave the land due to famine and his wife due to Pharaoh's lust, but he will return to both. In the Jacob cycle, Dinah's abduction reflects the imminent generational transition; focus shifts to Jacob's sons while Jacob remains passive, and he will soon take a backseat role when his beloved Joseph steps onto the stage. Given that Joseph's story takes place in Jacob's own lifetime, it emerges that Jacob's sons do not develop into twelve distinct heroes, but together they evolve into the promised nation. This story already raises the question of who will inherit their father as the family leader – and who will not, and why.[21]

With these differences and themes in mind, we will now turn to the analysis of the story itself, and see how they are manifested.

RAPE OR LOVE STORY?

One of the most fascinating aspects of this episode is how each character is evaluated. The story ends with an argument between Jacob and his sons, and their dramatic accusation: "Should our sister be treated like a whore?" (34:31). There is no clear answer, and given that biblical

21. In this respect, note that it is not the firstborn Reuben but Simeon and Levi who take action here.

narrative is by nature ideological, the fact that this scene ends without a clear moral statement is surprising;[22] perhaps the narrative itself explores this question.[23] Nonetheless, certain clues throughout the narrative suggest that one side is favored more strongly. This scene's complexity begins with a crucial question – that of Shechem's characterization. The more repugnant his character, the easier it will be to sympathize with Simeon and Levi. Yet the text does not make the reader's job that easy.

The scene opens with Shechem's encounter with Dinah, and there is inherent tension in his characterization:

> Dinah, the daughter whom Leah had borne to Jacob, went out to see the daughters of the land. When Shechem son of Hamor the Hivite, prince of the land, saw her, he took her, lay with her, and violated her. He became deeply drawn to Dinah, Jacob's daughter, and, in love with the young woman, he spoke to her heart.

When Sarai is captured by Pharaoh, the text clearly emphasizes her utter passivity; only Pharaoh and his officials are culpable: "When Abram came to Egypt, the Egyptians saw the woman, saw that she was very beautiful indeed. And when Pharaoh's officials saw her, they praised her to Pharaoh, and the woman was taken into Pharaoh's palace" (12:14–15). The repetition of "Pharaoh," along with the passive verb – "the woman was taken" – leaves no doubt that the men are wholly responsible, while Sarai is blameless; note that the text states that "*Abram* came to Egypt" without mentioning Sarai at all before the Egyptians notice her beside her husband.

By contrast, Dinah's story begins with *her* "outing": she "went out to see the daughters of the land." While this by no means justifies

---

22. This is of course more complex; see Simon, "Biblical Narrative"; Grossman, *Text and Subtext*, 31–33.
23. There are few biblical narratives which spark such extreme controversy. Some claim that the narrative objective is to explain why Simeon and Levi lose their inheritance (e.g., Galender, *Genesis II*, 281–82); others argue that it praises Simeon and Levi for protecting their sister; still others claim that its objective is to discourage intermarriage with foreigners, with disapproval of Jacob's approach and justification of Simeon and Levi's (e.g., Amit, *Hidden and Revealed*, 194–210).

Shechem's actions, she is not entirely absolved of responsibility as Sarai is. Shechem, like Pharaoh's officials, sees her, but it is Dinah who "sees" first: "Dinah, the daughter whom Leah had borne to Jacob, *went out to see* the daughters of the land." To go out to see is to be seen by others; in the words of the Midrash: "R. Berakhya said in the name of R. Levi: When one who had a piece of meat held it in the open, a bird swooped down and snatched it away from him; in this way, when 'Dinah went out,' immediately 'Shechem son of Hamor saw her.'"[24]

Evaluating the characters becomes even more complicated given the description of Shechem's actions. The two verses devoted to Shechem's treatment of her paint an (almost) contradictory portrait.[25] On one hand, he seizes Dinah against her will: "he took her / lay with her / and violated her (*vaye'anneha*)" (v. 2). The verb "*vaye'anneha*" implies that Dinah suffers, and presents Shechem as violent and aggressive.

On the other hand, the next verse describes him as a romantic, besotted, sensitive lover: "He became deeply drawn to Dinah, Jacob's daughter / and, in love with the young woman / he spoke to her heart" (v. 3). These three descriptions are almost antithetical to the previous three descriptions, yet in a certain sense, they can be read as an alternative perspective of the same act:

> He took her (v. 2) / He became deeply drawn to Dinah (v. 3)
> He lay with her (v. 2) / he loved the young woman (v. 3)
> He violated her (v. 2) / he spoke to her heart (v. 3)

The verb "*vayikkaḥ*" (took) in verse 2 is an expression of drawing two entities together, but it does not necessarily express physical contact (such as "He took two lads with him and Isaac his son" – Gen. 22:3). The first verb in verse 3, "*vayadbek*" (cleaved/clung/deeply drawn) expresses closeness even more deeply – touch and actual merging (such as "He struck the king of Israel through the *joints* [*hadevekim*] of his armor" –

24. Genesis Rabba 80:5.

25. These verses are a classic example of how word choice can affect narrative tone and character evaluation. See Polak, *Biblical Narrative*, 22; Grossman, *Text and Subtext*, 45–47.

II Kings 22:34; "Do you know how dust solidifies, how clods of earth *amass* (*yedubaku*)" – Job 38:38).[26] Though the expression "he became deeply drawn to her" is metaphorical, the raw physical connotations of the root "D-B-K" linger in this description.[27]

There is a similar relationship between the second pair of stiches. "He lay with her" can express physical intimacy, but the pronoun "*otah*" rather than "*immah*" usually indicates a one-sided rather than mutual sexual experience. This is evident in the parallel narrative – Amnon's rape of Tamar: "'Come, lie *with me* (*shikhvi immi*), my sister.' 'No, my brother,' she said to him, 'do not violate me'.... But he would not heed her voice, and he overpowered her and violated her and lay *with her* (*vayishkav otah*)" (II Sam. 13:11–14). When Amnon attempts to seduce her, he uses "*immi*," but after she refuses, her rape is described with the phrase "he lay with her (*otah*)."[28] Here, too, this particular pronoun, combined with her "violation," gives the impression of violent rape (although see below). The next verse, however, presents a different perspective of Shechem's feelings toward Dinah and their sexual relationship: "He loved the young woman."

Finally, in parallel to her "violation" (v. 2), Shechem "speaks to her heart" (v. 3). Both descriptions are an indirect description of Dinah herself. She never utters a single word – which makes it difficult to get an accurate sense of their relationship – but the word "he violated her" expresses pain and suffering. Yet the parallel phrase, "he spoke to her heart," hints to reassurance and consolation. Other instances of the phrase "speak to [their] heart" are associated with "*neḥama*," and they assume that the listener is truly comforted, as when Joseph reassures his brothers: "'So, do not be afraid. I myself will provide for you and your children.' And he comforted them and spoke to their hearts" (Gen. 50:21); or when Ruth tells Boaz, "I hope to find favor in your eyes, for you

26. See further in Wallis, "D-B-K."
27. Brook, "D-B-K."
28. Not all accept this division (see, for example, Feinstein, *Sexual Pollution*, 68). The situation is more complicated due to the laws of rape and seduction in Deuteronomy, which do not reflect this division. See further about this and the biblical connotations of "*lishkav et*" in Grossman, "Lot's Daughters."

give me solace, for you have spoken to your servant's heart" (Ruth 2:13).[29] Here, too, the phrase lends a genuine sense of comfort and reassurance.[30]

It is thus no wonder that verse 2 only refers to Dinah using pronouns – "her," while her name and identity are suddenly mentioned in verse 3: "He became deeply drawn to Dinah, Jacob's daughter." Reading this against the story of Amnon and Tamar reveals the disparity between the two violators: Amnon has no love for Tamar. On the contrary; after he violates her, "Amnon hated her with a fierce hatred; his hatred for her was fiercer than the love he had felt toward her" (II Sam. 13:15). By contrast, after Shechem lies with Dinah, he is drawn to her even more deeply; he loves and comforts her.

A bold midrash compares Shechem's love for Dinah in verse 3 to God's love for His people(!):

> R. Shimon son of Lakish said: God expresses love for Israel with three expressions: cleaving (*devika*), longing (*ḥashika*), and desire (*ḥafitza*).... We learn this from the story of that wicked man. "He was drawn to her" (*vatidbak*); "He longed for her (*ḥasheka nafsho*)"; and "He desired Jacob's daughter (*ki ḥafetz bevat Yaakov*)." R. Abba son of Elyashiv adds two more: [God expresses love for Israel] through love and through speech.... We learn this from the story of that wicked man: "He loved the young woman"; "He spoke to her heart."[31]

Thus this inconsistent, ambiguous character cannot be written off as a classic antagonist. Based on this ambivalence, I wish to address one

29. The example from Ruth is of special interest because it concerns a Judean man comforting a non-Israelite woman, and there too there are hints that Ruth is harassed by the young men in Boaz's field until he intervenes. Boaz even uses the root D-B-K. Ultimately, this is another example of marriage with a foreigner.

30. Joüon claims that this phrase originally meant physical stroking and touch of the heart and chest area, and then became a figure of speech, and thus concludes that "speaking to her heart" is not only emotional, but involves physical touch as well (Joüon, "Heart," 53).

31. Genesis Rabba 80:7.

of the most dramatic, crucial questions of this narrative: Did Shechem actually rape Dinah?

"VAYIKAḤ OTAH… VAYE'ANNEHA"

Ostensibly, the verb "*vaye'anneha*" describes sexual violation, which is a fitting term for rape. This is the verb used in the story of Amnon and Tamar: "'No, my brother,' she said to him, 'do not *violate me* (*te'anneni*) – such things are not done in Israel…but he overpowered her and *violated her* (*vaye'anneha*) and lay with her" (II Sam. 13:12–4). This is the most prevalent reading, as Ramban explains:

> All forced sexual relations are referred to as "*innui*," such as "You may not sell her for money or treat her as a slave, since you have violated her (*innitah*)" (Deut. 21:14); or "As for my concubine, they violated her and she died" (Judges 20:5). The text is expressing that she was forced and she would not submit to the prince of the land, to her credit. (Ramban on Gen. 34:2)

The first source Ramban mentions is a problematic example, for the law of the beautiful captive woman seeks to *prevent* Israelite soldiers from the accepted practice of raping enemies' wives in wartime: rather, the Torah demands that the soldier bring her back home and take her as a formal wife.[32] Though even if this example is problematic, the principle still stands: the word "*vaye'anneha*" means that something is done to the woman against her will.

Nonetheless, some commentators reject this reading and claim that this is a story of seduction, with no indication that Shechem acts against Dinah's will. The first to present this view is R. Saadia Gaon: "He lay with her *vaye'anneha* – he lay with her and had intercourse with her."[33] That is, the meaning of "*vaye'anneha*" is simply "intercourse."[34]

---

32. Although Yael Shemesh argues that in the context of the captive wife, the verb A-N-H also refers to forced sexual relations (Shemesh, "Rape," 5, n. 15).
33. *Torah Hayim, Genesis*, vol. 2, 113.
34. Though as my friend Jesse Salem pointed out to me, it could be that R. Saadia Gaon wishes to emphasize that the "*innui*" is related to "he lay with her" and not to any other physical abuse; that is, that he indeed holds that it is rape.

There are several variations of the reading that "*vaye'anneha*" does not mean rape. Ibn Ezra claims that the suffering associated with the root refers to the technical discomfort associated with loss of virginity.[35] Another possibility is that the verb is not necessarily associated with suffering at all, but is merely a synonym for intercourse: "If he marries another woman alongside her, he shall not reduce her food, her clothing, or her *marital rights* (*onatah*)" (Ex. 21:10).

Yet we cannot overlook the fact that this is not the usual term for intercourse, and it could be that this root is particularly associated with problematic, immoral relations.[36] At least two biblical examples support this reading. The prohibition against sleeping with a married woman in Deuteronomy branches out into two separate cases. If the woman is raped, then only the rapist is executed: "He came upon her in open country. The betrothed woman may have cried out for help, but no one was there to rescue her" (Deut. 22:27); but if the woman complied then she, too, must be killed: "Because she did not cry out for help in the town" (22:24). In this context, the Torah uses the root "*innui*": "And the man because he *violated* (*inna*) the wife of his fellow" (ibid.): this is not a case of rape (as is evident from the fact that the woman, too, is held accountable), but even so, the Torah uses the term "*innui*."[37]

---

35. When Ibn Ezra states that it is "*kedarkah*" ("in the usual way") he is disagreeing with Rashi, who based on some midrashim, comments that this verb implies that he lay with her "not in the usual way" (and because in the case of Amnon and Tamar, it first says "*vaye'anneha*" and only then "*vayishkav otah*," Malbim explains, "He first raped her in an unusual way, so that she would not lose her virginity, but this did not satisfy him, so he lay with her in the usual way" (on II Sam. 13:14).
36. See especially Bechtel, "Not Raped," and Van Wolde, "Does *innâ* Denote Rape?" who argue that עינוי hints to shame and humiliation, but not necessarily through rape, but through forbidden or inappropriate sexuality. The definition of rape is subjective in different cultures and periods of history, as correctly pointed out by Feinstein ("Sexual Pollution," 69), so this narrative must be read within its biblical paradigm.
37. Yael Shemesh claims that this law, usually referred to as the "law of the seducer," refers to rape, but the woman is incriminated if she did not cry out. If this incident takes place in a populated area, she is accused because she could have cried out for help; crying out is an indication of whether or not there was consent (Shemesh, "Rape," 5–6).

Another example of this root in the context of forbidden relations is in Ezekiel's description of Jerusalem's sins: "Their father's nakedness they have uncovered within you / the impure, menstrual woman they have bedded (*innu*) within you. One man committed abominations with another's wife / another has defiled his daughter-in-law with depravity / another in you has bedded (*inna*) his sister, the daughter of his father – within you!" (Ezek. 22:10–11). In context, these forbidden relations do not seem to be accusations of *forced* relations as much as *forbidden* relations – that is, *innui*.[38]

Some take this approach a step further and propose that the verb "*vayikkaḥ*" is an expression of formal marriage.[39] After all, "taking" is the usual biblical term for taking a woman in marriage. The description of Judah's marriage to the daughter of Shua, for example, follows an almost identical sequence: "There, Judah *saw* the daughter of a Canaanite man whose name was Shua, and he *married her* (*vayikkaḥeha*) and *came to* her" (Gen. 38:2). Judah (1) sees her, (2) "takes" her in marriage, and (3) comes to her; according to this reading, Shechem does the same by taking Dinah and only formalizing the marriage with her family afterwards.[40] This reading is reinforced through the expression "He became deeply drawn (*vatidbak*) to Dinah, Jacob's daughter" (34:3), as the verb "D-B-K," of course, echoes the very genesis of marriage: "That is why a man leaves his father and mother and *cleaves* (*vedavak*) to his wife and they become one flesh" (Gen. 2:24).

This further step, however, is problematic. The root "L-K-Ḥ" is the most common term for biblical marriage, but it is often used in a general sense; not every case where a man "takes" a woman necessarily refers to marriage. One infamous example should suffice: "David sent messengers

38. Nonetheless, Rimon Kasher believes that the word *innui* does mean without consent: that the menstruating woman does not want sexual relations and it is thus considered rape, as is incest (Kasher, *Yeḥezkel 1–24*, 442). It is worth pointing out that the verb A-N-H is mentioned *after* Shechem "lies with" Dinah, so our goal is to analyze what this addition contributes to the more straightforward "*vayishkav otah*." If the root hints to inappropriate sexuality (even with consent), then its purpose is clear.
39. See especially Gruber, "Shechem Son of Hamor."
40. I have already mentioned Fleischman's proposal that Shechem and his father are now completing the terms of an "abduction marriage."

and *took her* (*vayikkaḥeha*); she came to him and he lay with her" (II Sam. 11:4). In fact, in most cases in which the root "L-K-Ḥ" expresses formal marriage, the word "wife" appears as well,[41] as in Jacob's own parents' marriage: "Isaac brought her into the tent of his mother Sarah. He *took* Rebecca *as his wife*, and he loved her" (Gen. 24:67); "When Isaac was forty he *took* Rebecca, daughter of Bethuel the Aramean of Padan Aram, sister of Laban the Aramean, as his *wife*" (25:20).

An even closer example of the verb L-K-Ḥ + "wife" = formal marriage can be found in this story; it is so close, in fact, that it challenges the reading that "*vayikkaḥ*" in verse 2 possibly refers to marriage. If Shechem asks his father to arrange formal marriage between himself and Dinah in verse 4: "Shechem said to his father Hamor: 'Take this girl as a wife for me,'" then it cannot be that he has already married her. He does not say, "I have married this girl; now go negotiate with her father"; his request implies that they are not yet married.

Even if we reject the theory that Shechem takes Dinah in marriage, the fundamental question remains: Does Shechem rape Dinah or seduce her? This longstanding dilemma exposes the adroit literary technique of the opening scene. Even if the reader reaches the conclusion that Shechem rapes Dinah, it is no coincidence that her abduction is described with the gentlest verb that can possibly be used in this context – the downright nuptial "*vayikkaḥ*." A more appropriate verb for a rape scene would be "*vayaḥazek*" – "he *grasped hold* of her" – as Amnon "grasped hold" of Tamar before he rapes her (II Sam. 13:11).[42] To "grasp hold" expresses physical force, unlike the gentle "took," which, as noted, is often metaphorical or even associated with marriage. It is no coincidence that the aforementioned laws in Deuteronomy use the verb "*vayaḥazek*" to describe a case of rape: "But if the man encounters the betrothed woman in the open country, *forces her* (*veheḥezik bah*) and

41. Shapira, "Response."
42. See also the additional use of the verb later on in this scene: "But he would not heed her voice, and *he overpowered her* (*vayeḥezak mimena*) and violated her and lay with her" (II Sam. 13:14).

lies with her" (Deut. 22:25).[43] The text refrains from using such strong language to describe Shechem's actions, and even employs verbs with connotations of formal marriage – that is, at this stage, Shechem is not unequivocally condemned for his actions. Though the verb "*vaye'anneha*" certainly suggests problematic sexuality, the scene is intentionally shaped with ambiguity.

Why is Shechem presented in such an ambivalent light? Why isn't he charged with outright rape, as Amnon is? Perhaps this justifies Jacob's anger toward Simeon and Levi later on; if Shechem is not portrayed as the classic antagonist, then Simeon and Levi's reaction is more problematic.

Yet as we will soon see, the text clearly makes an effort to defend Simeon and Levi's position, while harboring reservations toward Jacob's.

What, then, does this characterization serve? I believe that Shechem's gentility and love allows for the possibility of marriage negotiations. As we will see below, the notion of marriage between Shechem and Jacob's daughter causes fierce dispute within the family; some are adamantly opposed, while others agree that while Shechem is not the ideal groom, circumstances ought to allow for a compromise. This would not be realistic if Shechem were simply a rapist; if so, the narrative conflict would be "How do we overcome him?" rather than "Should we overcome him?"

This theme is related to what has already been introduced in the exposition: the question of Jacob's relationship with the people of Shechem. There is no discussion as to whether Abram should form ties with Pharaoh and Egypt through Sarai, but the question does arise here, and it is facilitated by Shechem's ambiguous characterization: whatever the meaning of "*vaye'anneha*," he "takes" Jacob's daughter and lies with her before taking her for a wife, but he speaks to her heart and falls deeply, hopelessly in love with her.

---

43. In contrast with the much shorter description of relations with consent: "If a virgin is betrothed to be married, and a man encounters her within a town and lies with her" (Deut. 22:23).

SHECHEM'S REQUEST OF HIS FATHER

This ambiguity is maintained when Shechem asks his father to obtain Dinah's hand in marriage for him. In the ancient world, a woman who was no longer a virgin was not in high demand as a wife. Though this may offend the modern ear, the law in Exodus dictates that a man who seduces a virgin must take responsibility for her future by marrying her: "If a man seduces a virgin who is not betrothed, and lies with her, he must pay her bride price and marry her" (Ex. 22:15). The girl's family has a right to refuse, but the decision is up to them, and not her seducer.[44] Moreover, this same law applies to rapists and their victims: "If a man encounters a virgin who is not betrothed and rapes her, and they are caught in the act, the man who lay with her shall pay the girl's father fifty shekel of silver, and she shall become his wife. Because he violated her he does not have the choice to divorce her as long as he lives" (Deut. 22:28–29).[45]

And indeed, after Amnon rapes her, Tamar's plea that he keep her as a wife is just as desperate as her protests against her violation: "Amnon said to her, 'Get up! Be gone!' 'Don't!' she said to him. 'This great wrong – to send me away – would be even worse than what you did to me before'" (II Sam. 13:15–16). As surprising as it sounds, Tamar perceives Amnon's dismissal as even crueler than her rape.

Unlike Amnon, Shechem takes responsibility for the woman he has violated. His request to arrange a formal marriage with Dinah fulfills the spirit of the law in Exodus and Deuteronomy, even more generously than the law dictates, for he does not limit himself to the regular bride price: "Let me but find favor in your eyes and I will give whatever you ask. Set the bridal price and gifts as high as you like. I will give whatever you ask of me; only give me the young woman as my wife" (34:11–12). In addition to the bride price, he also offers "gifts" that will presumably be given to Dinah herself.[46] Even if this should not be considered compensation

44. "If her father refuses to let him marry her, he must still pay out the full bride price for virgins" (Ex. 22:16).

45. A similar custom is found in ancient Assyrian law (sections 55–56, ANET, 185).

46. In Gen. 24:53, there is a clear distinction between what the bride receives and what her family receives. It is not entirely clear if the family keeps the dowry (Gunkel, *Genesis*, 364; Westermann, *Genesis II*, 540); from Laban's daughters' complaint, it seems that the bride eventually kept her dowry (Lipiński, "M-H-R," 145).

for her violation, as some claim,[47] Shechem is certainly taking full responsibility. Once again, Shechem is not being portrayed as a paragon of virtue – he did, after all, seduce a young girl who was exploring the local town – but had the text wished to vilify him, he could easily have been cast in a far more sinister light.

As mentioned, Shechem's complex characterization allows the reader to take Hamor's proposal seriously. Dinah's family is able to consider an economic relationship – and even marriage – between the two clans. Shechem and Hamor's generous offer cannot be dismissed so easily, although it is not necessarily the right decision.

THE HOUSE OF JACOB'S RESPONSE

How, then, does Jacob's family respond to their offer? Here lies one of the greatest mysteries in this episode; two entirely different plots can be sketched out based on our understanding of their reply. It is difficult to decide between the two readings, but I do believe that one of them ultimately solves more textual issues.

This is Jacob's sons' response to Hamor and Shechem's offer:

> Jacob's sons responded to Shechem and his father Hamor, and they spoke deceptively: he had, after all, defiled their sister Dina. They told them,
> "We cannot do this. To give our sister to an uncircumcised man would be a disgrace to us.
> Only on one condition will we agree with you: If you become like us, circumcising all your males,
> then we will give you our daughters and take your daughters for ourselves.
> We will live with you and become one people.
> If you do not agree to be circumcised, we will take our daughter and go." (34:13–17)

47. Westermann, *Genesis II*, 540.

The Weakening of Shechem

The accepted reading is that Jacob's sons already give this response with revenge and massacre in mind – they plan to attack the town and rescue Dinah when every male is weak and hurting. In ancient times, a "city" is not a bustling settlement of tens of thousands of people as it is today; smaller towns may have consisted of just one large clan. But even if the local clan is just forty men strong, Jacob's sons will have a hard time rescuing their sister against their hosts' will. Thus Jacob's sons come up with a plan to weaken the men of that town so that they will easily be able to overpower them and set Dinah free. The Netziv's commentary is a fine example of this reading:

> They were wise to say, "to an uncircumcised man" rather than "to an uncircumcised people" in case the town would not agree to circumcision, and then they would be able to fight them, and in any case, they wanted Shechem himself to get circumcised. So that it would not be too difficult to take Dinah with force, if not everyone would make the same sacrifice as Shechem did. And so it was: Shechem circumcised himself first. (*Haamek Davar* on 34:17).

The Netziv points out that Jacob's sons are careful to give Shechem the initial impression that they are concerned with him personally, rather than first demanding that the entire town must be circumcised. This is to ensure that Shechem will definitely get circumcised even if the rest of the town refuses, because as Dinah's captor, it is the most important to cripple him so that they can rescue her.

According to this reading, the brothers assume that Shechem and his father will agree, and perhaps even manage to convince the rest of the city to get circumcised as well, which will put them at a disadvantage for a few days. It is worth pointing out that circumcision was a prevalent custom in the ancient world even outside of Israel; there is evidence that ancient Egyptian priests and even much of the population followed this practice.[48] Thus this stipulation might not seem so

48. Quack, "Beschneidung." He shows that the custom of circumcision was accepted in Egypt as early as 4000 BCE. It is intriguing that he says that the instrument of choice

unreasonable to Shechem and his town – as is evident in the fact that they accept their terms.

One of the problems with this reading is justifying Jacob's anger at the story's end. If this was the plan all along – and it seems that Jacob is present during their negotiations – then why is he so surprised at Simeon and Levi's actions? (Ramban, for one, asks this question.)

There are various possible excuses, but the most convincing, perhaps, is that Jacob did not hear their response. Indeed, at first, it seems like Hamor only addresses the brothers: "Meanwhile, Jacob's sons, having heard what had happened, came back from the field.... Hamor spoke with *them* and said, 'My son Shechem has his heart set upon your daughter'" (34:8). Although Shechem does join in the conversation and address both the brothers *and* Jacob: "Shechem said to her father and brothers, 'Let me but find favor in your eyes...'" (v. 11), only the brothers seem to respond, with no mention of Jacob: "Jacob's sons responded to Shechem and his father Hamor, and they spoke deceptively: he had, after all, defiled their sister Dinah" (v. 13). The verse is clearly phrased from their perspective: "*their* sister Dinah," and their response also gives the impression that Jacob is not present: "We cannot do this. To give *our sister* to an uncircumcised man would be a disgrace to us" (v. 14). In the ancient world, brothers had certain influence over their sisters' marriage ("We have a little sister; her breasts are not yet grown. What shall we do for our sister when a suitor comes for her?" – Song. 8:8);[49] it is not surprising that they are the ones in charge of negotiations. When they speak on behalf of the entire clan, it is appropriate for them to refer to Dinah as "our daughter" (v. 17), but it is less likely that Jacob would refer to her as "our sister."

---

was a flint (compare to Ex. 4:25; Josh. 5:2). Nonetheless, he claims that in ancient Egypt they would not entirely remove the foreskin, but only cut it. See further in Galpaz-Feller, "Stela." It is worth noting that after the Israelites perform circumcision when they enter Canaan, they remove "the shame of Egypt" from themselves; if the Egyptians would scorn those who were uncircumcised, then this description becomes clear.

49. This verse (and the next) are inherently ambiguous regarding whether the brothers intend to protect their sister for her good or to harass her – as they do at the beginning of the Song. See especially in Segal, "Double Meanings."

While Jacob's absence and later anger can be justified, it is more difficult to explain why only Simeon and Levi act as they do. Where are all of "Jacob's sons," who together respond "deceptively"? While they indeed loot the town, they do not participate in the fighting; nor do they rescue Dinah. Ibn Ezra attempts to solve this by suggesting that the brothers know their plans, based on the word "deceptively," but if the brothers are all aware of their intentions, why do Simeon and Levi fight alone? The fact that Jacob only rebukes Simeon and Levi reinforces the assumption that the two acted alone, while it is not relevant to blame the rest of the brothers. If the "sons of Jacob" respond as one to Shechem with malicious intentions, then why don't these "sons of Jacob" participate in Dinah's rescue?[50]

An Unreasonable Condition

This brings us to an alternative reading – while it has its own issues, I believe that it ultimately lends cohesion to the entire narrative. This reading is accepted by medieval commentators; to quote Sforno as a representative example: "Deceptively – they asked that they perform circumcision, assuming that they would not agree, or that they would not be able to convince their town to do so" (similarly, see Ramban, R. Joseph Bekhor Shor, and Ḥizkuni). According to this reading, the brothers' "deception" is their hypocrisy: they act as if they will happily agree to the marriage, but only if Shechem accepts an impossible condition; thus, they believe, they will be able to take Dinah back and be on their way without further conflict. The brothers assume that there is no chance that the entire town will agree to circumcision just because their pampered prince has fallen in love with a pretty foreign girl.

Needless to say, this reading completely transforms our understanding of the plot. To the brothers' shock, Shechem and his town agree to this completely unreasonable condition and circumcise themselves. The plan has veered completely off course, and the brothers are paralyzed with indecision. What now?

50. Radak proposes that the other brothers are scared and back down from their original plan, but Simeon and Levi take charge.

Though it cannot be proven, according to this reading, it makes sense that Jacob has been present throughout the negotiations, and that he is even aware of his sons' bluff. Simeon and Levi's decision to massacre the town and bring Dinah back to her family is their own private decision, and for this reason Jacob is furious. If so, it emerges that Jacob is prepared to let Shechem marry Dinah – which was, after all, a common arrangement in the ancient world. Once Shechem and his people agree to circumcision, Jacob resigns himself to the marriage, and is even able to rationalize that his own culture has triumphed over Canaanite culture: the people of Shechem have accepted Israelite norms.

This reading also explains why Simeon and Levi act alone, without the rest of "Jacob's sons." It is likely that they kept their plan to themselves, afraid that their brothers – like Jacob – have accepted the outcome, and might even prevent them from its execution.[51]

In addition to the coherence this paradigm lends the plot, three literary elements also support it.

Firstly, Jacob's sons' response to Hamor and his son ends thus: "If you do not agree to be circumcised, we will take our daughter and go" (v. 17). In many such biblical speeches, it is the last line which holds the key to its true objective. One apt example is Judah's plea to the Egyptian ruler, who is about to enslave Benjamin for his "theft." After a long, compelling appeal (which some consider a paragon of ancient rhetoric), Judah reveals the heart of his speech: "So, please, let your servant stay as my lord's slave in place of the boy, and let the boy go back with his brothers. For how can I go back to my father if the boy is not with me? I could not bear to see the misery that would overwhelm my father!" (Gen. 44:33–34). The entire speech builds up to these last lines, the climax of his speech. In Jacob's sons' response to Hamor, their conclusion does not seem to be the obvious narrative climax – their focus is ostensibly on circumcision – but with Sforno's reading, its true meaning comes through. Their alleged terms of negotiation lead up to

51. As Bekhor Shor expresses: "Simeon and Levi, Dinah's brothers – they sacrificed themselves for her, but the others did not want to attack, saying that it was unethical because they fulfilled the agreement… but Simeon and Levi said even so, we will take revenge on them" (on 34:25).

their true objective: retrieving Dinah from Shechem's house and parting ways in peace.

Secondly, Simeon and Levi's attack takes place on third day following Shechem's circumcision: "On the third day, when the people were weak from pain" (34:25). Why do they wait until the third day? If their goal is to attack Shechem at their weakest, why not strike sooner, when their wounds are fresh and debilitating? One well-known excuse is that the pain of circumcision is worst on the third day (Radak); Ibn Ezra uses mathematical logic to explain that "the third day is always the most difficult because it is half of the monthly quarter"; R. Joseph Karo is cited by R. Joseph Bekhor Shor: "R. Joseph Karo says that it took three days to circumcise everyone, so they attacked when everyone was circumcised and in pain." These explanations are all feasible, but the most straightforward, perhaps, is that of Rashbam: "The plain meaning of the text is that they were still hurting after the first and second day." Rashbam explains that the verse means to say that on the third day – when their circumcision still hurt them – Simeon and Levi attacked. They suffered, of course, on the first and second days – perhaps even more – but they were still weak on the third day, as some modern translations have: "On the third day, when they were *still* in pain" (NAB; NIB; NIV; NJB).

Why do Simeon and Levi wait until the third day? This detail supports Sforno's reading. After Shechem and the town unexpectedly agree to their condition, the family have no idea what to do next. Their bluff has been called; is the game over? Jacob (as it later emerges) is opposed to any kind of violence, and for two days, the family bide their time. On the third day, Simeon and Levi finally decide to take action before it is too late, but this was not the original plan.

Thirdly, when Simeon and Levi take action to save Dinah, they are referred to as "Dinah's brothers," and several commentators explain that as sons of Leah, they have the strongest feelings toward their sister. If this had been the plan all along, this would not make sense; all of "Jacob's sons" took part in the negotiations with Shechem – her brothers and half-brothers alike. But if Jacob's family is torn about whether to leave Dinah behind with Shechem, it makes sense that some agree with Jacob, or at least hesitate whether to take action, while Simeon and Levi, fiercely protective of their younger sister, decide to take matters into their own hands. Perhaps they feel but dare not give voice to the painful question: "Would our father give up on her so if she was Rachel's daughter, not Leah's?"

CIRCUMCISION, MARRIAGE, AND ECONOMIC TIES

Hamor and Shechem go back to town, and to great surprise – more importantly, to Jacob's family's great surprise – the people of Shechem agree to their terms and circumcise themselves.

As Nechama Leibowitz shows, the subtle changes Shechem makes to the brothers' terms when appealing to his townsmen are rhetorical techniques he employs to persuade them.[52] Rather than mention his love for Jacob's daughter, he focuses on the potential benefits they will gain from a relationship with Jacob's family. In such cases, it is worth exploring whether the speaker intentionally makes these changes for rhetorical effect, or whether they are subconscious differences that illuminate the speaker's character.[53] I will now compare three stages of negotiation: Hamor's proposition to Jacob; Jacob's sons' response; and Hamor's appeal to his townsmen, with special focus on the relationship between marriage and economic ties:

Hamor's Proposal (vv. 8–10)	**Jacob's Sons' Response (vv. 13–17)**	**Hamor's Appeal to the Townsmen (vv. 20–23)**
Hamor spoke with them and said:	Jacob's sons responded to Shechem and his father Hamor, and they spoke deceptively: he had, after all, defiled their sister Dinah.	Hamor and his son Shechem came to the town gate and spoke to their fellow townsmen.
"My son Shechem has his heart set upon your daughter. Please give her to him as his wife.	They told them, "We cannot do this. To give our sister to an uncircumcised man would be a disgrace to us.	

52. Leibowitz, *Genesis*, 264–68.

53. See Grossman, "Joseph's Brothers."

Hamor's Proposal (vv. 8–10)	**Jacob's Sons' Response (vv. 13–17)**	**Hamor's Appeal to the Townsmen (vv. 20–23)**
	Only on one condition will we agree with you: If you become like us, circumcising all your males,	"These people are friendly toward us," they said. "*Let them live in the land and trade in it. We have space enough for them.*
Intermarry with us. Give us your daughters and take our daughters for yourselves.	then we will give you our daughters and take your daughters for ourselves.	We can marry their daughters and they can marry ours.
Settle with us. *The land is open to you. Live here, trade here, acquire property here."*	We will live with you and become one people.	But only on one condition will they agree to dwell with us as one people. Every male among us must be circumcised as they are.
	If you do not agree to be circumcised, we will take our daughter and go."	
		Will not their livestock, property, and all their animals be ours? Let us, then, agree to their terms and let them settle among us."
	Their words gratified Hamor and his son Shechem. The young man, the most honored of his father's family, lost no time in doing it, because he longed for Jacob's daughter.	All the people who went out by the town gate listened to Hamor and his son Shechem, and all the males who went out by the town gate were circumcised.

The slight differences between these stages are worthy of extensive analysis in themselves, but for the sake of the present discussion I wish to point out one motif that is salient in both of Hamor's speeches and absent in Jacob's sons' reply: the potential economic benefits of these ties. Note the different placement of this topic in Hamor's two speeches. When addressing Jacob's sons, he begins by expressing Shechem's desire to marry Dinah,[54] but he clearly views this marriage as a bridge to a broader alliance between the clans, especially from an economic perspective: "Settle with us. The land is open to you. Live here, trade here, acquire property here" (34:10). This conclusion ends his speech with a certain implication: if Jacob's sons give consent to their sister's marriage, then they are invited to settle, trade, and become part of society; but if not...

In his speech to the townsmen, Hamor begins with the potential economic benefits of ties with Jacob's clan: "These people are friendly toward us. Let them live in the land and trade in it. We have space enough for them" (34:21). Shechem implies that this new clan's presence is a factor they ought to take into consideration: they are here to stay, and it is in their interest to be on good terms and form economic ties with them. In a neat rhetorical move, he concludes his speech with the enormous benefits this union will bring, sandwiching the terms of this alliance between two descriptions of all they stand to gain: "Will not their livestock, property, and all their animals be ours? Let us, then, agree to their terms and let them settle among us" (34:23).

Hamor is presumably convinced that Jacob's sons will be swayed by the promise of economic growth, while his own townsmen are more likely to be convinced to agree to their terms if he presents Jacob's presence as an immutable fact. In any case, Hamor emphasizes the economic potential far more than the impending marriage. This is crucial in order to appreciate the sheer magnitude of Jacob's sons' total disregard for this aspect of the negotiations.[55] The disparity between Shechem and Jacob's sons' attitude is underscored through their discussion of the clans living together. Hamor proposes: "*Live with us*. The land is open to you. Live here, trade here, acquire property here" (v. 10), while Jacob's sons respond thus: "*We will live with you* and become one people"

54. "In his speech to Jacob he obviously mentions the family issue first, for he is interested in that" (Leibowitz, *Genesis*, 266).

55. Compare to Sternberg, "Delicate Balance," 206.

(v. 16). What are the implications of living together? Hamor is interested in potential economic benefits and growth, but Jacob's sons are focused on the question of marriage. Will they be one people, or two separate clans? It is interesting to note that Hamor echoes their words when he addresses his townsmen: "We can marry their daughters and they can marry ours. But only on one condition will they agree to *live with us as one people.* Every male among us must be circumcised as they are. *Will not their livestock, property, and all their animals be ours?* Let us, then, agree to their terms and let them live with us" (vv. 22–23).

Unlike the diplomatic Hamor, Shechem is focused on his marriage with Dinah. After Hamor's calculated speech, before the family responds, he blurts out: "Let me but find favor in your eyes and I will give whatever you ask. Set the bridal price and gifts as high as you like. I will give whatever you ask of me; only give me the young woman as my wife" (vv. 11–12). We can just picture his father, the seasoned politician, rolling his eyes and promising himself that this is the last time he lets his son tag along for negotiations. Not only is his position compromised by Shechem's desperate promise that he is willing to pay any price, but his son's fixation with this specific girl eclipses the "bigger picture" that Hamor is trying to paint. Hamor's vision of the two clans living side by side is ruined by mention of the daughter and sister his son has already violated, a violation that disgusts and angers her brothers: "They were shocked and furious, for Shechem had committed an outrage in Israel by sleeping with Jacob's daughter. Such a thing cannot be done!" (v. 7). Even though, as mentioned, Shechem's offer to marry Dinah characterizes him in a reasonable light, as a man who takes responsibility for his actions, the fact that they seek a marriage contract only after her violation reduces their agreement to a mere transaction. At the end of the story, Simeon and Levi accuse Shechem of this very crime: "Should our sister be treated like a whore?" (v. 31), and they may well be referring to these negotiations; from her brothers' perspective, Shechem is offering payment for sleeping with their unmarried sister.[56]

---

56. See further below, in my analysis of Simeon and Levi's dialogue with Jacob, regarding the brothers' disagreement with their father's readiness to accept Shechem's proposal.

THE BROTHERS' RESPONSE

The narrative's evaluation of Simeon and Levi's act is shrouded in mystery; the explicit argument between them and their father reflects the reader's own ambivalence. As is often the case, the text does not provide an explicit appraisal of the characters' actions, and it must be gleaned from hints and subtleties throughout the narrative.

Four separate hints imply that the text favors Simeon and Levi's action over Jacob's passivity; the first is hidden in the first scene; the second in the description of Shechem's death; the third is implied in the narrative's conclusion; the fourth is found beyond the boundaries of this narrative.

Response to the News

Upon hearing the news about Dinah and Shechem, Jacob's reaction is disturbing: "When Jacob heard that he had defiled his daughter Dinah, his sons were in the field with his livestock, and so he stayed silent until they came home" (34:5). Even if it makes sense to pause before taking action, especially if Jacob prefers to have his sons with him when dealing with Shechem, Jacob's lack of emotion is unsettling. A more appropriate reaction is presented in the very next verse: "Meanwhile, Jacob's sons, having heard what had happened, came back from the field. They were shocked and furious, for Shechem had committed an outrage in Israel by sleeping with Jacob's daughter. Such a thing cannot be done!" (34:7). As soon as her brothers hear the news, they rush back from the field,[57] furious. Moreover, how did they hear the news, if they were in "the field"? Presumably Jacob sent messengers to inform them, but why is this detail omitted? Instead of "staying silent," the text could have reported that "Jacob summoned his sons from the field" (cf. Gen. 31:4). This omission reinforces Jacob's passive characterization: perhaps Jacob's sons heard the news from a different source; perhaps Jacob did not even take care to inform them.[58]

57. Nonetheless, Sternberg claims that this is a case of intentional ambiguity (Sternberg, "Delicate Balance," 200).
58. Thus, even if Amnon Shapira is correct that Jacob's silence is a sign of discretion, the opposite of his sons' rashness (Shapira, "Response"), this still characterizes Jacob with passivity.

Moreover, their boiling rage is a poignant foil to Jacob's silence: "The men were shocked and furious." And lest the reader assume that their outrage is merely the anger of protective brothers, the narrator provides a more fundamental reason for their wrath – social and moral boundaries have been shattered: "For Shechem had committed an outrage in Israel by sleeping with Jacob's daughter. Such a thing cannot be done!" The fact that Dinah is presented here as "Jacob's daughter" only underscores her father's apparent apathy. By comparison, upon hearing of Tamar's rape, King David is "absolutely furious" (II Sam. 13:21). When Jacob hears about Dinah, he remains silent, but his sons are "absolutely furious" (v. 7).

A different portrait of Jacob's fatherhood can be found a few chapters later, when Joseph is sold. There, too, one of Jacob's children is captured and subjected to a foreign culture; Dinah could have theoretically become what Joseph becomes in Egypt: a noble of Shechem. Some point out linguistic connections between the two episodes: Jacob's sons come in from the field, "shocked (*vayitatzevu*) and furious (*vayiḥar*)" (34:7); later on, Joseph will reassure his brothers, "Now, do not be shocked or furious (*al te'atzevu ve'al yiḥar*) for having sold me" (45:5).[59] In both stories, Jacob is helpless and powerless, but his emotional reaction is completely different. He remains "silent" when he hears about Dinah, but upon hearing the news about Joseph, he "tore his clothes, put sackcloth on his loins, and mourned for his son for many days. All his sons and daughters tried to comfort him, but he refused to be comforted and said, 'I will go down to Sheol mourning for my son'" (37:34–35). Of course there is a substantial difference between the two stories: he believes that Joseph has been torn to pieces, while there is still hope for Dinah. Yet his response to Joseph's death shows that Jacob does express pain, and the lack of any emotional response in our story shifts the focus to his sons.

If so, then Meir Sternberg is correct in claiming that from the beginning, the narrative is subtly tilted in the sons' favor. They are appalled at their sister's distress and/or indignant at this insult to the

59. Mathews, *Genesis II*, 598.

family's honor, and this will move them to take action. Perhaps Jacob remains passive because he does not care enough.[60]

Massacre or Rescue Mission?

The next question is how the narrative relates to Simeon and Levi's deed. The narrative perspective and the way information is related are both crucial to determining the text's attitude toward them. How would the plot be related if the narrator wished to incriminate the brothers, and how would it unfold if they were considered its heroes? I believe that in this case, the narrator subtly favors these "weapons of violence" (Gen. 49:5): "On the third day, when the people were weak from pain, two of Jacob's sons, Simeon and Levi, Dinah's brothers, took their swords, entered the unsuspecting town, and killed every single male. They killed Hamor and his son Shechem by the sword, took Dinah from Shechem's house, and left" (25:26).

First, note their description: "Two of Jacob's sons, Simeon and Levi, Dinah's brothers." Their double family affiliation has deep significance in the narrative context. They act as "Jacob's sons" – as his emissaries, even if they do so against his will. The Midrash reads this description as subtle criticism: "Two of Jacob's sons – they were his sons, yet Simeon and Levi still acted as if they were not his sons, for they did not take counsel with him" (Rashi on 34:25). Yet it seems that this description has the opposite effect: it connects Simeon and Levi to their father, and they act as Jacob's sons – and even Jacob himself – are expected to act; they come to Shechem on his behalf – though they come without his knowledge or consent.

But they also act as "Dinah's brothers," and herein lies the difference between them and their father. As several commentators note, this epithet characterizes them as protective brothers who are willing to sacrifice themselves for her sake: "Because they risked their lives for her, they are called 'her brothers'" (Rashi), or "For they acted as her brothers should, risking their lives for her sake" (Bekhor Shor on 34:25).

---

60. Sternberg, "Delicate Balance." But note that Jacob is not simply silent, but silent "until their arrival" – this seems to indicate that Jacob waits for their return before responding.

This description may also hint to the reason why it is they, and not their father, who take action. We cannot fully imagine the atmosphere of a household with four mothers. From the episode of Laban and the teraphim, we learn that each mother sleeps in her own tent (together with her children); from the mandrakes incident, we learn that by default, Jacob sleeps in Rachel's tent.[61] That is, Leah's children grow up in their mother's tent, while their father lives together with Rachel – their mother's rival. This arrangement obviously invites tension; perhaps this tension is reflected here. Simeon and Levi are described as "Dinah's brothers" – that is, they are growing up in the same tent, part of the same group within Jacob's extended family. The narrative opening already emphasizes that Dinah is "Leah's daughter" (34:1), and now this epithet takes on its full significance.[62] It is her full brothers (rather than her half-brothers) who fight for her honor and risk their lives to save her from the house of Shechem. I have already hinted that Simeon and Levi may interpret their father's silence in light of the fact that he lives in Rachel's tent; they cannot help but wonder how he would act if the same were to happen to Rachel's child. Would he remain silent as he does now, or would he rent his clothes, don sackcloth, and mourn, refusing to be comforted?

These emotions burst out into the open at the end of the story. Note the barrier that Jacob builds between himself and these sons of Leah: "You have brought scourge upon *me* – you have made *me* odious to the inhabitants of the land, the Canaanites and Perizzites. *I* am few in number, and if they join forces and attack *me, I and my household* will be destroyed" (v. 30). Jacob berates Simeon and Levi (and not "his sons") and accuse them of endangering "him and his household" as if they are not part of this household; as if Simeon and Levi – and their sister Dinah – are not part of the family under his care and protection. Simeon and Levi's answer reflects his tension: "Should our sister be treated like a whore?" (v. 31). Jacob's family is divided into two "camps" – those that

---

61. According to the Sages, after Rachel's death Jacob moves to Bilhah's tent, presumably to help her raise Rachel's sons. See below in my discussion of Reuben's act.
62. See also Dishi, *Jacob*, 173–74, who argues that Jacob does not act because he believes that Leah is complicit in Laban's exchange between his daughters.

the father takes care of, and those – Leah's sons and "their sister" – who are forced to fend for themselves.

Even more crucial than the epithet "Dinah's brothers" is how their actions are described. The massacre of an entire town is a devastating act which could easily have been described in gruesome, elaborate detail. Yet the report is brief and economical: "Simeon and Levi, Dina's brothers, took their swords, entered the unsuspecting town, and killed every single male. They killed Hamor and his son Shechem by the sword, took Dinah from Shechem's house, and left" (vv. 25–26). This sequence presents their actions as an ad hoc rescue mission: they kill the men in order to be able to reach the royal house; they kill Hamor and Shechem; and, having reached Dinah, they take her and leave. The reader is free to express his or her opinion of the deed, but the narrator's succinct formulation gives the impression of a rescue mission rather than a gloating act of revenge.

Moreover, the description "They took Dinah from Shechem's house and left (*vayetze'u*)" forms an inclusio with the opening scene: "Dinah, Jacob's daughter, went out (*vatetzei*) to see the daughters of the land. When Shechem son of Hamor the Hivite, prince of the land, saw her, *he took her* (*vayikkaḥ*), lay with her, and violated her" (34:1–2).[63] The reverse order of the verbs reflects the plot's reversal. Dinah "goes out" and Shechem "takes her"; now the brothers "take her" back and "go out" from the city.

This is not merely a literary framework; it also serves as a justification. Dinah merely "goes out" and is taken by force; now Simeon and Levi must fight to take her out. All this time, throughout the negotiations, Dinah has been a captive in Shechem's house; now her brothers do what they must to take her out.

The Story's End

From a perspective of narrative sequence, the brothers maintain the upper hand: Simeon and Levi are given the final word. Jacob's deathbed legacy for each son is not an integral part of the story, and it does not

63. Sternberg, "Delicate Balance"; Sarna, *Genesis*, 238; Wenham, *Genesis II*, 307; Hamilton, *Genesis II*, 370; Vrolijk, *Jacob's Wealth*, 262, 276.

serve as an alternative ending. Moreover, although many read Jacob's final words to Simeon and Levi as a bitter moral condemnation of their deed, it is not at all clear that this is the case. He curses their "anger" and their "fury," their rash impulsiveness:

> Simeon and Levi are brothers; weapons of violence their wares.
> Let me never join their council, nor my honor be of their assembly.
> For in their anger they killed men; at their whim they hamstrung oxen.
> Cursed be their anger, for it is most fierce, and their fury, for it is most cruel.
> I will divide them up in Jacob, and scatter them in Israel. (49:5–7)

Jacob clearly refers to their deed against Shechem, but his criticism focuses on their hot-headed anger; on their acting from a place of wrath, rather than making a level-headed, more rational decision. Jacob does not curse the brothers themselves; he curses their "anger," which moved them to "kill men."[64]

Even if the reader disagrees with this reading of his deathbed speech, note that Jacob does not condemn his sons' deed from a moral perspective right after it takes place. Our scene ends with a rhetorical question (a rare occurrence in biblical narrative)[65] that serves as the narrative's moral backbone: the brothers will not accept Shechem's treatment of their sister or his sexual norms. Once again, it is important to note how the story does *not* end: Jacob is not given the final word. The scene could easily have ended with Jacob's reproach, or with Jacob's response to the brothers' accusation. Yet it does not, and the decision to end the narrative with the brothers' piercing question has crucial bearing on the reading experience and character assessment.

64. There is room to debate whether there is wordplay between Jacob's accusation that his sons "*ikkeru*" the oxen and his accusation: "*Akhartem oti*" (Hamilton, *Genesis II*, 651).
65. A striking example of such an ending is the book of Jonah. On possible connections between the story of Dinah and Jonah, see Ben Reuven, "The Story of Dinah's Rape."

Moreover, note the content of Jacob's reproach: "You have brought scourge upon me – you have made me odious to the inhabitants of the land, the Canaanites and Perizzites. I am few in number, and if they join forces and attack me, I and my household will be destroyed" (v. 30). He does not utter a word about the atrocity of slaying every male in town because of their ruler's offense; all that concerns him is the possible danger that Simeon and Levi have brought upon the family. While Jacob's concern certainly befits the head of a large clan, and his fears are rational in the narrative context, his words reveal that his conflict with Leah's sons is not moral but pragmatic. Does this imply that he does not disagree with his sons from a moral perspective, but rather takes issue with the possible political implications of their actions? The reader's appreciation for Simeon and Levi's attitude toward their sister gradually increases as the plot progresses, and Jacob's indignation does not undermine this appreciation.

The surprising lack of moral criticism in Jacob's reproach is underscored by the verb "you have brought scourge (*akhartem*)." This is a key verb in Joshua's conquest of Jericho, especially in regard to the spoil. Joshua warns the people against taking spoil from this first battle: "But beware of the ban lest you be subject to utter destruction; if you take anything banned, you will subject the camp of Israel to *scourge* (*vaakhartem*) and utter destruction" (Josh. 7:25); and after Achan takes the forbidden spoil, Joshua tells him: "A scourge have you been to us! Now, on this day, the Lord will bring scourge upon you" (7:25). The site in question is even named for Achan's "scourge": "To this day that place is called the Valley of the Scourge" (7:26).

There is certain dialogue between the narratives: in both, Israel wipe out the city and only some of them loot it; both refer to an "outrage" committed in Israel: "For he had committed an outrage in Israel by sleeping with Jacob's daughter. Such a thing cannot be done!" (Gen. 34:7)/"For he has committed an outrage in Israel" (Josh. 7:15).

This connection raises the reader's expectations that when Jacob begins with "You have brought scourge upon me – you have made me odious to the inhabitants of the land, the Canaanites and Perizzites," he will then criticize the brothers for looting the slaughtered city, just as Joshua berates Achan. Another expectation is that Jacob's use of the word "odious" will then unleash a barrage of reproach for their foul, noxious violence. Yet to great surprise, Jacob takes issue with a single aspect: the possible anger he might face from the neighbors. Even if Jacob disapproves of their actions (perhaps hinted in the phrase "You have brought scourge upon me"), he chooses to focus on pragmatic issues.[66]

What Happens Next?

The final indication that the text favors Simeon and Levi takes place beyond the boundaries of the narrative. The next scene sees Jacob's journey to Bethel to fulfill his vow. When the family leaves Shechem, "As they set out, the terror of God (*ḥittat Elohim*) fell on the surrounding towns so that no one pursued Jacob's sons" (35:5). Whether this verse is an expression of explicit divine intervention depends on the reading of "*ḥittat Elohim*": Does God actually strike the surrounding towns with paralyzing terror, or is the word "*Elohim*" an expression of the magnitude of their terror, i.e. "godly terror," "holy terror," "sheer terror," etc.? Either way, Jacob's fears are not realized. No one comes chasing after "Jacob's sons" for wiping out an old, distinguished local clan. Moreover, Jacob's pilgrimage to Bethel after leaving Shechem affects the tone of his departure: "Jacob does not flee Shechem as a refugee, but as a man preparing himself for the renewal of his covenant with God."[67] Referring to the family as "Jacob's sons" as they set out on their peaceful journey hints to the sons' victory over their father; Simeon and Levi emerge triumphant and doubly vindicated when no one comes chasing after them.

Once again, given that our question is the text's assessment, it is worth entertaining possible alternative formulations. The family's peaceful journey could have been reported without a word about the surrounding towns, but the fact that terror – from God, or simply "godly" – strikes their neighbors is a clear justification of Simeon and Levi's deed.

And Now, the Spoil

The latter analysis overlooks three verses that follow Dinah's rescue from the house of Shechem. These verses describe how Jacob's sons

66. See also Noble, "'Balanced' Reading," 184.
67. Ahuvia, "Genesis 35," 100.

loot the town, a description which invites further analysis of the characters' appraisal:

> Jacob's sons came upon the dead and plundered the town that had defiled their sister. They took their flocks, their cattle, their donkeys, and everything else of theirs in the town and out in the field. Their wealth, their children, and their women they took captive and looted, and all that was in the houses. (34:27–29)

The new opening ("Jacob's sons came") expresses that this is a new description, distinct from the previous verses. As mentioned, the previous verse sees an *inclusio* with the narrative opening ("they went out" + "they took"). This implies that the city's looting should be read separately from Dinah's rescue. Thus there is room to argue that even though the text approves of Simeon and Levi's mission, Jacob's sons are criticized for their ensuing actions. Simeon and Levi act as they do to save Dinah;[68] looting the city is an excessive, unwarranted act of vengeance.

The looting's differentiation from Dinah's rescue also raises the question of who is involved. Are Simeon and Levi included in "Jacob's sons," or does this expression refer to the other brothers, while Dinah's brothers are comforting their sister? Meir Sternberg favors the latter reading:

> Until this point, "Jacob's sons" have been presented as a unified body…from this verse and on, they are divided into two groups: on one side are "Jacob's two sons, Simeon and Levi," who executed the slaughter, and on the other side are "Jacob's sons," who pounce upon the spoil. The text signifies to the reader that just

68. Some believe that Dinah is brought back home against her will, and that she chooses to remain in Shechem's house, but the brothers force her to come back home (Fewell and Gunn, "Tipping the Balance"). There are similar hints in some midrashim. But even if so, it seems that the text favors the brothers' opinion that Dinah should not remain with Shechem, who violated her (while still uncircumcised) before marrying her.

> as the other brothers did not participate in the massacre, Simeon and Levi did not touch the spoil.[69]

According to this reading, after Simeon and Levi risk their lives to save their sister, the rest of the brothers join in and loot the now ownerless spoil. Jacob's sons march through Shechem in two camps: Simeon and Levi, who bring Dinah home, and the rest of the brothers, who loot the city. This dichotomy invites two separate appraisals: the text sides with Simeon and Levi, but disapproves of the other brothers.

But this conclusion is unconvincing. Firstly, the precise identity of the looters remains inconclusive. Three verses later, Jacob only criticizes Simeon and Levi; if the other brothers are responsible for looting the city, why doesn't Jacob reproach them as well? It would be somewhat farfetched to posit that the text favors Simeon and Levi and criticizes the other brothers while Jacob does the precise opposite.[70] It is also worth pointing out that in the previous verse, the narrative refers to Simeon and Levi as "Jacob's two sons" (v. 25); it thus could be that the description "Jacob's sons" refers to them as well.

Moreover, how does the text assess the looting of the city? Thus far, our assumption has been that the looting is perceived in a negative light. Dinah has already been freed, so this pillaging is not a rescue mission but a procession of greed and spiteful vengeance. But is this really the case?

Modern scholarship almost unanimously argues that the text perceives this looting as problematic. This is evident even among scholars who disagree about the main objective. Sternberg argues that the text favors Simeon and Levi,[71] while Fewell and Gunn contend that they are

69. Sternberg, "Delicate Balance," 212–13. A similar reading is proposed by Hamilton, *Genesis II*, 370.
70. See also Frankel, "Rape of Dinah." Hamilton proves from Jacob's reproach that he does not condemn Simeon and Levi on a moral level, just a pragmatic level. Because they are the ones who endanger the family, they are the ones chastised (Hamilton, *Genesis II*, 371).
71. Sternberg, "Delicate Balance."

criticized for the massacre.[72] Yet they are unanimous in their opinion that the text censures the act of looting. Sternberg, as mentioned, absolves Simeon and Levi by ascribing the deed to the other sons, while Fewell and Gunn perceive this offense as further proof that the text disapproves of the two brothers.

Yet a careful reading of these verses reveals that they contain no such criticism.

Firstly, certain justification for this looting is already mentioned: "Jacob's sons came upon the dead and plundered the town that had defiled their sister." Though it certainly presents the brothers' perspective, it is the narrator – not the characters themselves – who emphasizes that this town "had defiled their sister"; this illuminates the text's stance as well. Without this clause, the reader would presumably perceive the looting as a greedy exploitation of Simeon and Levi's deed; but when the text itself asserts that the entire town is complicit in Dinah's violation, it suggests that the brothers' motive is justified.

This statement functions similarly to the earlier description of Jacob's sons' initial conversation with Shechem: "Jacob's sons responded to Shechem and his father Hamor, and they spoke deceptively: *he had, after all, defiled their sister Dinah*" (34:13). Just as this clause justifies Jacob's sons' deception – he had, after all, defiled their sister Dinah – here, too, this clause serves the brothers' defense.

And yet again, we must ask ourselves how this could have been phrased differently, had the text wished to incriminate them for their looting. The clause "that had defiled their sister" would certainly have been omitted; use of the powerful word "defiled" – *tuma* – is no coincidence either. The word "defiled" or "impurity" has strong biblical connotations that transpose the event from its social-psychological context to a theological-spiritual one:

> There is a clear distinction between the term "*vaye'anneha*" and the term "*timmei*" in the affair of Dinah's rape. While the former

72. Fewell and Gunn, "Tipping the Balance." This dispute echoes a more ancient one between Rambam, who justifies Simeon and Levi's actions, and Ramban, who perceives Jacob's criticism as the voice of the text.

> expression is harsh, it is chiefly associated with suffering, subjection, force. In contrast, the expression "*timmei*" is first and foremost associated with sanctity; it is the opposite of "holiness" and "purity," and it signifies estrangement from purity; it leads not only to rape and adultery, but to murder and idolatry as well. This indicates that this expression is far more caustic than the expression "*vaye'anneha*"; its implied condemnation is even harsher.[73]

This incriminating language thus justifies the actions of Dinah's brothers;[74] as mentioned, the root T-M-A appears earlier in the narrative (34:5, 14) as well as in the context of looting the city (v. 27).[75]

More importantly, for the first time, the entire town of Shechem is implicated for Dinah's rape; plural form "the town that had defiled (*timme'u*)" replaces the singular form used in verse 13: "He had, after all, defiled (*timmei*) their sister Dinah." This has dramatic implications for whether looting the city is justified. Is Jacob's sons' vengeance warranted? Are the townspeople accountable for their leader's sin, or is he alone to blame? The use of plural form here suggests that guilt rests on the entire town, as Radak explains: "For many saw Shechem take her by force, but they did not protest" (on 34:27). Rambam also believes that the entire community bears responsibility for maintaining public order: "For this all the citizens of Shechem were sentenced to death: for they witnessed and were aware of Shechem's abduction, but they did not bring him to trial" (*Mishneh Torah*, Laws of Kings, 9:14).[76]

---

73. Polak, *Biblical Narrative*, 23.
74. For a different reading, see Frankel, "Rape of Dinah," 31. He believes that Simeon and Levi are criticized throughout the narrative.
75. Rofé shows that the expression "*tuma*" in a sexual context always refers to the violation of a betrothed or married woman. Thus he perceives the "*tuma*" in this narrative about an unmarried girl as related to her violation by a foreigner (Rofé, "Defilement of Virgins"). For objections to this reading, see Frankel, "Rape of Dinah," 32–33.
76. This is the plain meaning of Rambam's words. Noam Zohar offers an alternative reading that "all the citizens of Shechem" refers only to the city elders and judges, although he does add that this is not fully consistent with the Rambam's approach that all the males in the city should be killed (Zohar, "Boycott," 43, incl. n. 15). Yaakov Blidstein also favors this reading ("Shechem," 52–53). R. Rabinovitch also adopts this reading, and adds that the Rambam's words are supported in the text

Thus, the verse's formulation asserts that the entire city is accountable for Dinah's defilement. Though their responsibility is only indirect, it is no coincidence that the narrative's language is incriminating, and this hints that the looting of the city is justified. R. Medan makes a similar claim:

> In today's terms, the people of Shechem should be considered a non-combatant population who are aiding and abetting the enemy. The fighting force does not wish to kill them, but it will kill them in order to save its own people from clear danger. Had they not cooperated with the enemy, the fighting force would have refrained from killing them, even if this would mean risking their own lives.[77]

But another obstacle must be overcome before this looting can be justified. The list of spoil is unusually, unexpectedly long, and made even longer by various verbs that describe the looting:

> They took their flocks,
> their cattle,
> their donkeys,
> and everything else of theirs in the town
> and out in the field.
> Their wealth,
> their children,
> and their women they took captive and looted,
> and all that was in the houses. (34:28–29)

Some comment that this long list is calculated to make the reader feel uncomfortable, and hints to criticism at the brothers' greed. The narrative indeed lingers on the list longer than expected, but it is not at all

---

because the narrator only refers to those "at the city gate," which means the city's leaders and judges (Rabinovitch, *Mishneh Torah*, 733). This also implies that only the leaders circumcised themselves; this is possible but unlikely.

77. Medan, *Close to You*, 269.

clear that this implies criticism. Rather, the extent of detail serves as a foil to Shechem's economic goals. As mentioned, in both speeches Hamor focuses on the property he expects to gain from the agreement with Jacob's clan. Now, ironically, the narrative expresses how Shechem's property *is* transferred to Jacob's sons – but not at all how Hamor plans. Perhaps the text pokes even more fun at Hamor (which literally means "donkey") and his agenda by including "donkeys" (*ḥamoreihem*) in the list of spoil; such biblical lists do not usually mention "donkeys" after "flocks and cattle" (Gen. 46:32; 47:1; 50:8; Jer. 3:24; Hos. 5:6). This mocks the prince of the land – Hamor ("Donkey") plans to take Jacob's property, but instead his own donkeys are snatched away from him.[78]

From a literary perspective, too, the text seems to favor Jacob's sons. There is a striking linguistic connection between the looting of Shechem and the looting of Midian in the book of Numbers (with a chiastic reversal):[79]

The Looting of Shechem (Gen. 34:25–29)	**The Looting of Midian (Num. 31:7–10)**
On the third day, when the people were weak from pain, two of Jacob's sons, Simeon and Levi, Dinah's brothers, took their swords, entered the unsuspecting town, *and killed every single male.*	And they did battle against Midian as the Lord had commanded Moses, *and killed every single male.*
They killed Hamor and his son Shechem by the sword, took Dinah from Shechem's house and left.	And, among the slain, *they killed the kings of Midian*: Evi, Rekem, Zur, Hur, and Reba – all five kings of Midian. *At the sword's edge they also killed* Balaam son of Beor.
Jacob's sons came upon the dead and plundered the town that had defiled their sister.	

78. Mathews, *Genesis II*, 608.

79. Compare to Wenham, *Genesis II*, 316; see also Westermann, *Genesis II*, 543; Vrolijk, *Jacob's Wealth*, 276–77.

The Looting of Shechem (Gen. 34:25–29)	**The Looting of Midian (Num. 31:7–10)**
They took their flocks, their cattle, their donkeys, and everything else of theirs in the town and out in the field. Their wealth,	The Israelites took captive the Midianite women
their children,	and children,
and their women they took captive and looted,	and took as booty all their cattle, flocks, and wealth.
and all that was in the houses.	They burned all the towns where they lived and their encampments.

This analogy goes beyond the two episodes' similar language; their context is similar as well. The war against Midian is an act of divine revenge against the Midianites who defile the Israelites with ritual prostitutes, including the daughter of a local ruler, Cozbi daughter of Zur. The war against Shechem is Jacob's sons' revenge against Shechem, the son of a local ruler, for defiling their sister Dinah. Simeon and Levi are the heroes in the war against Shechem, and two of their descendants play a crucial role in the war against Midian: Phineas the Levite kills Zimri son of Salu, the leader of the tribe of Simeon.

A sneak peek at the next chapter – Jacob's departure from Shechem – raises a further connection between the narratives. Before Jacob leaves Shechem, he orders his family to change their clothes and purify themselves: "Jacob told his household and everyone with him, 'Be rid of the alien gods you have with you. Purify yourselves and change your clothes'" (35:2). The war against Midian ends similarly, when Elazar instructs the men returning from battle: "You shall wash your clothes on the seventh day and you will then be pure, and may enter the camp" (Num. 31:24).

This analogy implies that Jacob's sons' revenge on Hamor, his son, and his town is justified; after all, God commands the Israelites to attack Midian for defiling the camp. This theory is supported by their similar plots: Moses is angry at the soldiers who return from battle, just as Jacob is furious at Simeon and Levi when they return from the scene of revenge. But while Moses is angry at the soldiers for keeping the seductresses alive, Jacob is angry at his sons for making him seem odious in the eyes of his Canaanite neighbors. Careful attention to nuance gains further points for Simeon and Levi: they act as Moses expects his warriors to act in the war against Midian: they kill the perpetrators of sexual depravity, those who pervert and corrupt social norms.

A comparison between the two lists of spoil reveals that they are arranged in reverse order. The spoil taken from Midian is arranged in order of descending importance, from the inside out: the women of Midian / their children / their cattle, flocks, and wealth / they burned all the towns where they lived and their encampments. The spoil taken from Shechem is listed in the opposite order, from the outside in: They plundered the town / their flocks, cattle, donkeys, and all their wealth / their children / their women / and all that was in their houses.

Dinah's brothers come in from the outside, from the outskirts of Shechem, into the town, into the house where Dinah is being held captive. This inward movement reflects the true nature of their mission: it is not a barbaric conquest for the sake of gain, but a selfless rescue mission to save their sister and preserve the family honor. They do not plunder the city because they seek its wealth, but to avenge the sister from those who sought to justify her defilement with the promise of economic gain.

THE NARRATIVE OBJECTIVE

We can thus conclude that unlike Jacob, the narrative sympathizes with Simeon and Levi. How is this stance consistent with the narrative objective? I will now come back to two of the three themes I mentioned at the beginning of this chapter: the question of segregation or integration, and the intergenerational transition.

We Will Become One People

The question of Israel's separatism hovers over the entire narrative. From the beginning, Jacob forms a relationship with the people of Shechem, yet maintains a certain distance. Dinah's venture into the city – from the family sphere into a new social sphere – challenges this separatism. Should the people of the land be allowed to form marriage ties with Jacob's family? Not surprisingly, the answer is not clear.

When Hamor tells Jacob's family, "Settle with us. The land is open to you. Live here, trade here, take possession (*vehe'aḥazu*) here" (34:10), the text reverberates with God's promise to the forefathers. The term "take possession" echoes the promise Abraham hears during the Covenant of Circumcision: "I will give you and your descendants after you the land where you now live as strangers, the whole land of Canaan, an everlasting possession (*laaḥuzzat olam* – Gen. 17:8)." Hamor promises Jacob the fulfillment of God's promise: the land is open before them for their possession (and in return, Jacob demands their circumcision).[80] Is this how God's promise should be fulfilled – through ties with the people of the land?[81] In light of Israel's history, the answer is clear, but at that moment in time, Jacob's family cannot know for sure (see further below, in the discussion of Esau's history). On the one hand, Shechem is portrayed as a classic Canaanite (sexually corrupt), but on the other, he is genuinely smitten with Jacob's daughter, and genuinely interested in a marriage between the clans. Perhaps this is the path to settling the Promised Land – to develop diplomatic and economic ties with its people?

Jacob remains passive, and it seems that events that have been thrust upon him will lead to this path. Ultimately, however, Simeon and Levi make an active decision that God's promise cannot be fulfilled through their sister's defilement. From our more distant vantage point, we know that this is a broader biblical theme,[82] and the text is indeed disposed toward Simeon and Levi's position, rather than Jacob's.

The Rise of the New Generation

The story of Dinah is also the story of a generational transition. Jacob's passivity also serves to "make way" for the next generation. From this perspective, Jacob's silence until his sons come home is not merely a

---

80. The phrase "Settle with us, the land is open to you" especially recalls Abimelech's words to Abraham after Sarah is returned to him: "Here, my land is before you, live wherever you wish" (20:15). This, too, raises the question of the forefather's connection with the land.
81. Compare to Mann, *Torah*, 64; Vrolijk, *Jacob's Wealth*, 270.
82. This idea is especially salient in the final scenes of the Abraham cycle. See Grossman, *Abraham*, 338–97.

tactical decision, but a major theme: Jacob is silent and his sons are the ones who cry out; the ones who become furious; the ones who negotiate with Shechem; they are the ones who take action. Although Shechem initially appeals to Jacob (v. 6), he ends up negotiating with his sons (v. 8).

This literary model recalls how Phineas steps into Moses' shoes. There, too, foreigners defile Israel with sexual corruption, led by the daughter of the local ruler: "The name of the Midianite woman who was killed was Cozbi, daughter of Zur the tribal leader of a Midianite ancestral house" (Num. 25:15). It is not Moses who takes action against the guilty head of the tribe of Simeon, though the text explicitly notes his presence: "At that moment, an Israelite man brought a Midianite woman to his friends before the eyes of Moses and the entire Israelite community" (Num. 25:6). It is Phineas, his brother's grandson, who takes initiative: "When Phineas son of Elazar son of Aaron the priest saw this, he rose from the midst of the community, took a spear in his hand, went after the Israelite man into the tent, and stabbed both of them, the Israelite man and the woman, through the stomach – and the plague among the Israelites ended" (25:7–8). In this scene, it is Phineas, not Moses, who fulfills the divine will;[83] this marks a new phase of leadership, wherein Moses and Aaron are replaced by leaders from a younger generation.

The Motif of the Field

One significant motif in the story of Dinah is "the field." Throughout the Jacob cycle, the "field" (*sadeh*) is construed as the diametric opposite of the "home" (*bayit*). This story sees a subtle – but crucial – turning point in this motif.

Until Jacob leaves to Haran, the "field" is presented as Esau's domain: "Esau became a skilled hunter, a man of the field, while Jacob was an innocent man who stayed among the tents" (25:27). Esau is at home in the field, while Jacob remains indoors "among the tents." The next scene sees Esau coming in "from the field" while Jacob is inside, cooking a stew (25:29). The field also accompanies Esau in the theft of

83. See further in Grossman, "Divine Command," where I propose that the comparison between the act of Zimri and the sin of the golden calf raises expectations that Moses will take action, but Phineas does instead.

the blessings episode, where it emerges how central this motif is for characterization. Before he blesses him, Isaac tells Esau: "So now, take your weapons, your quiver and bow, and go out into the field and hunt me some game" (27:3); and Esau does so: "Esau went out into the field to hunt game" (27:5). The importance of this motif becomes apparent when Isaac kisses his son before blessing him: "So he came close and kissed him, and Isaac smelled the smell of his clothes and blessed him, saying: 'The smell of my son is the smell of a field the Lord has blessed'" (27:27). We will soon return to this crucial verse, which illuminates the symbolic meaning of the field in the Jacob cycle – the field the Lord has blessed.

Growing up in Canaan, Jacob is never in the "field." Upon his arrival in Haran, he finds himself in the field: "There he saw a well in a field" (29:2). During his exile in Haran he becomes well acquainted with "field" life, and in the mandrakes episode, the field becomes the narrative framework: "During the wheat harvest, Reuben went for a walk and found mandrakes in the field.... When Jacob came back from the field that evening, Leah went out to meet him" (30:14–16). Reuben goes for a walk in the field, but the fact that Jacob "came back from the field" depicts it as his permanent sphere. In his youth, it is Esau who "came back from the field"; now Jacob spends his days in the field.

When Jacob seeks to leave Haran, the "field" reverts to the symbolic opposite of the "home." Jacob and his wives plan their escape "in the field," away from home and Laban's ever-watchful eye: "So Jacob sent word to Rachel and Leah to come out to the field where his flock was" (31:4).

Jacob has evidently learned that the field is filled with God's blessing, because the first thing he does upon his return to Canaan is buy a field: "He bought the field where he pitched his tent from the sons of Hamor, father of Shechem, for one hundred *kesita* of silver" (33:19).[84]

84. It is not entirely clear how much a *kesita* is worth, which leads scholars to debate whether this is a large or modest sum. In any case, there is no focus on the transaction itself, as there is when Abraham purchases Machpelah (23:16). Some ancient translations interpret *kesita* as "lambs," such as Onkelos; the Septuagint (which also translates thus in Josh. 24:32; Job 42:11 – see Zipor, *Septuagint*, 419); the Vulgate and Peshitta (Maori, *Peshitta*, 123). This is also reflected in Genesis Rabba 79:7. See also Sperber, that the meaning of *kesita* is literally "sheep," and when sheep were worth the price of a certain coin, the name of that coin became *kesita* (Sperber, "Note").

Jacob's exile has transformed him. The quiet man who stayed among the tents, who dressed in his brother's clothing so that he would feel and smell like the field, has become a man of the field himself.

This is the final mention of this motif in relation to Jacob. What is the significance of the field in the Jacob cycle? As mentioned, the field becomes charged with meaning just before Isaac blesses Jacob (believing that he is Esau): the field is blessed by the Lord. The field is fertile earth that bears fruit and gives life, as Isaac explores in his blessing: "God endow you with dew of heaven, the cream of the land, much grain and wine" (27:28). In order for this blessing to be manifested through Jacob, he must become a man of the field like his brother Esau. Jacob must learn how to walk and work and flourish in the field in order to be a receptacle of God's blessing; he must feel at home in this place of earth and soil and life.

This story (and the story of Joseph, below) sees the next stage of this process. Having bought a field, it emerges that Jacob now stays home while his sons go out to work in the field in his stead: "When Jacob heard that he had defiled his daughter Dinah, his sons were in the field with his livestock, and so he stayed silent until they came home" (34:5); "Meanwhile, Jacob's sons, having heard what had happened, came back from the field" (v. 7). The fact that Jacob's sons have taken his place in the field is part of the generational transition in this narrative. The field, purchased just a few verses earlier, has already been passed on to Jacob's sons – who, after all, are to inherit God's blessing.[85] This is also reflected in the story of Joseph. In his dream, his brothers' sheaves bow down to his own – in the field: "We were binding sheaves in the field when my sheaf rose and stood upright and your sheaves gathered around mine and bowed down to it" (37:7); soon after, he goes to look for them in the field: "A man found him wandering lost among the fields and asked him, 'What are you looking for?'" (37:15).

In the story of Dinah, Jacob's sons have replaced their father as the protagonist. They, and not Jacob, spend their days in the field; they risk their lives to save their sister, while Jacob, silent, remains at home.

---

85. Perhaps this explains the emphasis of this motif when the brothers loot the city: "They took everything else in the town and the field" (34:28).

Coming Full Circle: An Altar, Benjamin, Reuben, and Isaac (Gen. 35)

Chapter 35 is a series of brief incidents that are not necessarily interrelated, although its narrative design is ultimately cohesive. The chapter comprises four distinct units:

1. The fulfillment of the vow in Bethel (and the death of Deborah) (vv. 1–8)
2. God's revelation to Jacob at Bethel (vv. 9–15)
3. Benjamin's birth and Rachel's death (vv. 16–20)
4. Reuben's deed at Migdal Eder and Jacob's reunion with his father Isaac (vv. 21–29)

From a perspective of narrative sequence, the first two scenes are obviously linked, but thereafter, there is no apparent relationship between the scenes that follow.

However, a careful reading of these units reveals linguistic and plot-related connections.[1] First and foremost, Jacob's journey weaves

1. Briend points out that Rachel's death and Reuben's act can be read as one sequence, but he exaggerates by claiming that this foreshadows the tribe of Benjamin's com-

these individual scenes into one story; each unit is a stop along the final leg of Jacob's journey back to his father. The first two units take place in Bethel; the third occurs "on the way," after they leave Bethel (curiously, Jacob's destination is not revealed at this point; the text merely reports "from Bethel they moved on"); one last stop before their final destination is Migdal Eder, where Reuben sleeps with his father's concubine, but most of this unit takes place in Hebron, where Jacob is reunited with his father.

Accordingly, the verb "*linso'a*" appears three times, weaving the chapter together as different parts of the same journey:

1. When Jacob leaves Shechem: "As they journeyed on, the terror of God fell on the surrounding towns so that no one pursued Jacob's sons" (v. 5).
2. Upon leaving Bethel: "From Bethel they journeyed on" (v. 16).
3. Upon leaving "the road to Efrat" where Rachel is buried: "Israel journeyed on, pitching his tent beyond Migdal Eder" (v. 21).

This verb does not appear at the end of the fourth unit, for Jacob's journey has at last come to an end. (The next time Jacob travels with his family is when they go down to Egypt: "So Israel set out with all he had, and arrived in Beersheba" – 46:1; this, of course, is entirely unrelated to the journey at hand.) This pattern already raises the question: Why do two separate units take place in Bethel, and what is the relationship between them? As we will see below, in Bethel Jacob comes full circle in two separate senses.

Aside from Jacob's journey functioning as a unifying theme in the chapter, two additional elements weave the units together: burial and naming.

The motifs of burial and naming accompany Jacob throughout the chapter. At the end of the first unit, the narrator reports that "Deborah, Rebecca's nurse, died and was buried under the oak outside Bethel. And so it was named Oak of Weeping" (v. 5). This burial separates the first two units in Bethel. At the end of the third unit, Rachel dies and is

plicated future, and that Reuben will rule over it (Briend, "Genèse 35").

buried "on the road to Efrat – that is, Bethlehem" (v. 19). At the end of the fourth unit, Isaac dies "aged, satisfied with his years. His sons Esau and Jacob buried him" (though for whatever reason, it is not mentioned that they bury him in the cave of Machpelah). If we include the "alien gods" that Jacob buries beneath the terebinth near Shechem (35:4), then this motif is dominant indeed.

Various kinds of naming also pervade the chapter. At the end of the first unit, Jacob names Deborah's burial site "Oak of Weeping" (35:8); at the end of the second unit, he names the place "El Bethel" – literally, "God, House of God" (35:15); the third unit sees a double naming: "With her last breath, she named him Ben Oni, but his father called him Benjamin" (v. 18). Instead of naming the site of Rachel's grave, he erects a monument: "To this day, that pillar marks Rachel's grave" (v. 20). There is no naming in the fourth unit, for Jacob returns to the home of his fathers before him.

Thus the four units of this chapter are all independent episodes with a unifying thread that binds them; they are all part of the same journey, with a covert dialogue between them. In the following analysis I will explore the significance of each unit and their interconnections.

THE WAY TO BETHEL AND THE VOW'S FULFILLMENT (VV. 1–8)

Divine Command

Jacob seems to procrastinate before fulfilling his vow, and he does not go up to Bethel of his own accord; God must command him: "Arise, go up to Bethel. Stay there, and there build an altar to God, who appeared to you as you fled your brother Esau" (35:1).[2] The Midrash expresses harsh criticism against Jacob for failing to fulfill his vow:

2. Gunkel is correct that the command to "go up" to Bethel is topographically appropriate because Bethel is 300m higher (Gunkel, *Genesis*, 367). But "to go up" is also used in the context of pilgrimage, regardless of the holy site's topography: one "goes up" to the place God chooses, wherever it may be (e.g., Deut. 17:8; see Merrill, "A-L-H," 403). Jacob purifies himself before the revelation, suggesting that he considers it a holy place regardless of its topography (compare to Judges 20:18).

"R. Abba said: In hard times, a person vows; in good times, the vow is washed away and forgotten."[3] Or in more caustic words:

> Note that it is written concerning the time that Jacob went to Aram-Naharaim: *"And Jacob vowed a vow, saying: 'If God be with me.'"* At first He granted his every request. He went there and became wealthy, but he returned without fulfilling his vow. He turned Esau against him, and Esau sought to kill him. And though Esau took the two hundred she-goats from him, Jacob did not fulfill his vow. Whereupon He turned the angel against him and they wrestled together, but still he did not take note ... then the tragedy of Dinah befell him ... then the tragedy of Rachel's death occurred, as it is said *"And Rachel died and was buried"* (ibid. 35:19) .... The Holy One, blessed be He, declared: How long shall this righteous man continue to be punished without comprehending the sin for which he is being afflicted? Indeed, I will inform him .... The Holy One, blessed be He, told him: These trials have befallen you only because you have not fulfilled your vow. If you do not wish to experience other afflictions, "Arise, go up to Bethel. Stay there, and there build an altar to God," at the very place at which you made your vow. (*Midrash Tanḥuma Vayishlaḥ* 8)[4]

Though the Midrash is typically hyperbolic, it draws upon the actual plot. Why does Jacob postpone the fulfillment of his vow? The argument that he is about to go to Bethel just as God commands him is unconvincing, for were he about to leave, there would be no need for any such divine revelation.

I will first rephrase the question. Jacob is clearly grateful to God for all the kindness bestowed upon him; Jacob expresses gratitude again and again. On the eve of his meeting with Esau, he prays: "I am unworthy

---

3. Genesis Rabba 81:2.
4. Compare to this harsh midrash: "R. Shmuel son of Naḥman said: Whoever delays the fulfillment of his vow will eventually come to idolatry, forbidden sexual relations, bloodshed, and slander. We learn all this from Jacob, who delayed the fulfillment of his vow and violated all this" (Leviticus Rabba 37:1).

of all the kindnesses and the faithfulness that You have bestowed upon Your servant" (32:11). As mentioned, his altar in Shechem alludes to his first revelation in Bethel, and to the beginning of the vow's fulfillment. Yet his vow will not be complete until he travels to Bethel, where he once anointed and sanctified his pillar.[5] The more precise question, therefore, is why does Jacob delay the fulfillment of his vow, even though he repeatedly expresses gratitude at various points in his journey?

The question also applies to God's perspective: Jacob's vow was made freely, out of his own initiative, and the same should be true of its fulfillment – it is up to Jacob to pay this vow when he feels that its conditions have been met. If God has not reminded him until now, then why does He intervene at this point, rather than let Jacob travel to Bethel of his own free will?

I believe that the answer lies in Jacob's vision of the ladder, and the disparity between God's promise to Jacob and the vow that Jacob himself makes. God's promise and Jacob's vow have two different time frames – God promises to bring Jacob back to his homeland: "I will protect you wherever you go, and I will bring you back *to this land*" (28:15), but Jacob conditions the fulfillment of his vow upon "if I return in peace *to my father's house*" (28:20–21). As discussed, this is one of several differences that reveal Jacob's tunnel vision and personal anguish. At this point, Jacob does not dream of the birth of nations or divine promises of the future; all he wants is to go back home and make amends with his family.

It is not that Jacob fails to fulfill his vow because he has forgotten (as the Midrash expresses), but because he has not yet returned to his father's house. In Mahanaim, Jacob leaves Haran; in Penuel, he reconciles with his brother and erects an altar; but he only plans to fulfill his vow after he reaches his father's house in Hebron and secures his forgiveness. Only upon seeing his father will Jacob truly feel that he has "returned in peace to his father's house."

This is a dramatic decision on Jacob's part; the way from Shechem to Hebron passes right next to Bethel, and should he walk past the pillar

5. As claimed by Micah Roi, "Conditional Vows." This clarifies why Absalom asks David for leave to go fulfill his vow in Hebron, for there he made his vow.

he set up years before, this will clearly express that Jacob will not fulfill his vow until he is reunited with his father.

God, however, has other plans: He intervenes and commands Jacob to proceed to Bethel *before* he reaches his father's house. After all, God has already kept His promise: Jacob has returned safely to "this land," and Jacob must fulfill his vow according to God's terms, not his own. Thus, just before Jacob clears the stage for his sons, he accepts the great future that has always accompanied God's promise; he rises above his own personal fears and accepts the greater destiny that awaits him. This is expressed through his acceptance of God's time frame rather than his own.

The Vow's Fulfillment

Though Jacob journeys to Bethel at God's command, he compensates for his lack of initiative by going above and beyond God's word in order to pay his vow. Though, as Westermann points out, Jacob fulfills both of God's commands in verses 6–7 by going to Bethel and building an altar,[6] there are slight discrepancies between the command and its execution – discrepancies which illuminate much about his character and mindset. Here, Jacob goes far beyond God's word, as is evident from a comparison between the divine command and its fulfillment:

The Command to Jacob (v. 1)	**Jacob to His Men (vv. 2–3)**	**Execution (vv. 4–7)**
	Jacob told his household and everyone with him, "Be rid of the alien gods you have with you. Purify yourselves and change your clothes.	They gave Jacob all the alien gods they had, and even the rings in their ears, and Jacob buried them under a terebinth near Shechem. As they set out, the terror of God fell on the surrounding towns so that no one pursued Jacob's sons.
God said to Jacob, "Arise, go up to Bethel. Stay there,	Then come, let us go up to Bethel,	Jacob and all the people with him came to Luz – that is, Bethel – in the land of Canaan.

6. Westermann, *Genesis II*, 552.

The Command to Jacob (v. 1)	**Jacob to His Men (vv. 2–3)**	**Execution (vv. 4–7)**
and there build an altar	and there I will make an altar	There he built an altar
to God, who appeared to you as you fled your brother Esau."	to God, who answered me in my time of trouble and who has been with me wherever I have gone."	and called the place El Bethel, because it was there that God had revealed Himself to him as he fled his brother.
		Deborah, Rebecca's nurse, died and was buried under the oak outside Bethel. And so it was named Oak of Weeping.

The divine command is directed at Jacob as an individual: "There build an altar to God, who appeared to you as you fled your brother Esau" (35:1). When Jacob flees to Haran, he is a frightened, lonely refugee, crossing the Jordan with nothing but his staff, with only God's promise of protection to sustain him. The command specifies that Jacob must build an altar to the "God who appeared to *you*," at the lowest point of his life.

Though the command is a personal one to Jacob, he turns to his family and "everyone with him" to include them in the preparations for the pilgrimage to Bethel. Jacob alone is told, "Arise, go up to Bethel," but he tells his entire household: "Come, let *us* go up to Bethel." The whole family participates in Jacob's fulfillment of his vow: "Jacob *and all the people with him* came to Luz – that is, Bethel – in the land of Canaan" (v. 6).

Jacob's expansion of the divine command is not merely "going above and beyond" God's word; it is far more significant. The divine command states that the altar must be built for "God, who appeared to you as you fled your brother Esau." Jacob indeed names the altar "El Bethel, because it was there that God had revealed Himself to him as he fled his brother" (v. 7). These two verses express how this act fulfills the vow that Jacob makes as he flees from Esau. But Jacob's instructions to his family imply that this altar will be an expression of greater, more general gratitude: "There I will make an altar to God, who answered me in my time of trouble and who has been with me wherever I have gone"

(v. 3). God has fulfilled Jacob's request: that God "be with me, protecting me on this journey I am taking" (28:20). Jacob acknowledges this to his whole family, who have shared God's protection throughout his long, difficult journey.

Jacob understands that he must give thanks to God together with his entire family. He does not stand alone before God as a frightened, lonely refugee; he includes his family in this celebration, and acknowledges God together with the clan that will become God's nation. Together, this nascent nation must rid themselves of all false gods and all impurities, and accept their true God together as one.

The magnitude of this occasion is also evident in the steps Jacob takes leading up to his pilgrimage. He gives his household three instructions:

1. Be rid of the alien gods you have with you.
2. Purify yourselves.
3. And change your clothes.

There is a clear connection between these three instructions. The alien gods are considered impure; thus the family must first be rid of them before purifying themselves and donning clean clothes which have not been tainted by impurity. These three elements recall another similar process in Israelite history: Israel's preparations before standing at Mount Sinai. There, God bids Moses: "Go to the people and consecrate them today and tomorrow; let them wash their clothes and be ready for the third day" (Ex. 19:10); at Sinai, too, Moses builds an altar (Ex. 24:4). Moreover, in both scenes, a stone pillar is erected: "Jacob set up a stone pillar at the place where God had talked with him" (35:14); and though such pillars are later banned in Israelite law, Moses erects twelve pillars at the foot of Mount Sinai: "Early the next morning he rose and built an altar at the base of the mountain, and also twelve pillars for the twelve tribes of Israel" (24:4).[7]

7. The Samarian version has "twelve stones." Rofé holds that "pillar" was replaced with "stones" because pillars were forbidden, and the translator felt uncomfortable describing the Sinai revelation with pillars (Rofé, *Faith*, 69–70).

This is not to say that the two narratives should be read against each other; rather, I wish to point out that these identical models both express acceptance of the Lord as the God of Israel. At Mount Sinai, Israel forges a covenant with God and becomes God's people; this, too, is how Jacob's actions at Bethel should be read: "Then the Lord will become my God" (28:21).

A further example is Joshua's covenant at Shechem. Jacob at Bethel and Moses at Sinai both follow a similar model, but our chapter's analogy with Joshua invites a closer look at the dialogue between them.

The final chapter of Joshua describes the leader's farewell address to his people: he gathers "all the tribes of Israel" to Shechem (Josh. 24:1). After a sweeping summary of Israelite history, Joshua urges the people to renew their covenant with God: "Now, purge the alien gods from your midst and direct your hearts toward the Lord, God of Israel!" (Josh. 24:23). This certainly reminds the reader of Jacob's request from the embryonic nation: "Remove the alien gods from your midst" (35:2).[8] The scenes are linked through their setting, Shechem, which is mentioned again at the end of his speech: "Joshua formed a covenant with the people on that day and instituted law and order *in Shechem*" (Josh. 24:25).[9] Of course this location has its own significance within the book of Joshua, given that the blessings and curses are pronounced in this region (Josh. 8:30–35), and there are further connections between the altar in Joshua 24 and the altar at Mount Ebal. But the fact that the name Shechem is missing in Joshua 8 serves to reinforce the connection between Shechem in Joshua 24 and the scene of Jacob's family's purification.

The third element of the three-stranded thread that binds the two narratives together is Joshua's placement of the stone "beneath the terebinth": "Joshua then inscribed these words in the book of God's Torah; he took a large stone and erected it there beneath the terebinth by the

8. Removing idols is already mentioned earlier, in Joshua's speech (24:14). Samuel's speech to the people also incorporates this phrase (I Sam. 7:3).
9. In this verse Joshua is characterized as similar to Moses, about whom it is also said: "There he was given decree and law" (Ex. 15:25). See further about Joshua's unique status in this chapter in Reiss, *Redaction*, 285. Another leader compared to Moses through this phrase is Ezra (Ezra 7:10); but whereas Moses and Joshua "establish" (*sam*) law and order, Ezra "learns and teaches" it.

Lord's Sanctuary" (24:26). Jacob also buries the alien gods "beneath the terebinth" at Shechem: "They gave Jacob all the alien gods they had, and even the rings in their ears, and Jacob buried them beneath a terebinth near Shechem" (Gen. 35:4).[10] Perhaps this is the very same tree; Jacob buries alien gods there, while Joshua builds a monument beneath it; both acts express Israel's acceptance of the Lord as their only God.[11] In fact, at the end of the book of Joshua, the reader is explicitly directed to the story of Jacob in Shechem: "As for Joseph's bones, which the Israelites brought up from Egypt, they were buried at Shechem in the field which Jacob had purchased from the sons of Hamor, the father of Shechem, for one hundred *kesita,* and they became the Josephites' heritage" (Josh. 24:32). Though this is mentioned in the context of Joseph's bones, its proximity to Joshua's speech in Shechem links the two narratives.

The connection between them is obvious: in both, Israel accepts the Lord as God and commits to worshiping Him alone. In the context of our discussion, however, this comparison makes a further contribution. The covenant in Joshua is largely based on Israel's gratitude toward God; Joshua asks them whether they wish to serve God or not (Josh. 24:14–15), and they declare that they will continue to be His people because the Lord has accompanied them throughout history: "For the Lord our God is the One who brought us and our ancestors up from the land of Egypt, from the house of slavery; who performed these great wonders before our eyes; *who watched over us wherever we went* and amidst all the peoples through whom we passed" (24:17). Israel, like Jacob, express gratitude to God at the end of their long journey. Jacob's fulfillment of his vow is not a mere technicality, but a celebration of reaching the end of a long, winding journey. Jacob offers thanksgiving for God's grace and protection by purging his clan of all alien gods and erecting an altar in Bethel.

10. Commentators debate whether the "rings" Jacob's family removes are from their own ears or from the idols' (as Bekhor Shor and Ḥizkuni explain). Modern scholars favor the latter opinion based on textual and archaeological evidence that such accessories for idols were prevalent in the Ancient Near East, including Israel (Hurowitz, "Who Lost an Earring?").
11. Zakovitch proposes that the burial of idols beneath the terebinth at Shechem is a polemic against the sanctity of that place (Zakovitch, "Burying Idols").

A final – perhaps more tentative – contribution can be garnered from this analogy. The scene in question marks the end of Joshua's leadership and the book of Joshua,[12] and in a certain sense, the same can be said of Jacob's fulfillment of his vow in the Jacob cycle. A few minor incidents occur before Jacob steps down from the stage and his sons – particularly Joseph – begin a new narrative cycle, but this scene, like the end of Joshua, sees Jacob come full circle, and ends his story on a note of gratitude and devotion to his God.

GOD'S REVELATION TO JACOB (VV. 9–15)

Immediately after the burial of Deborah, Rebecca's nurse, and the mourning expressed in the name "Oak of Weeping," a new unit begins; though it also takes place in Bethel, its tone is decidedly different. In a sublime revelation full of exalted promises, Jacob is given a new name as if he is born anew. Yet the fact that this unit consists of entirely repetitive material poses an exegetic challenge. Jacob's name has already been changed to Israel (32:28–29); Jacob has already erected a pillar in Bethel and poured oil over it (28:18); and the place has already been named "Bethel" (28:19). I believe that a single explanation clarifies all of this repetition.[13]

Jacob's second name change can be justified given that the first is bestowed hurriedly, suddenly, by a mysterious figure who has just spent the night wrestling against him. A new name deserves an "official" conferral by God Himself.[14] Moreover, as already discussed, the first naming uses unusual language: "Jacob will no longer be *said* as your name, but Israel" (32:29), hinting that his official naming is yet to come. Indeed, this scene employs classic naming language: "Your name is Jacob; no longer shall you be called Jacob; Israel shall be your name" (35:10). The "man's"

12. Joshua's farewell address is described in the previous chapter, Joshua 23, but the book ends with a renewal of the covenant.
13. Elie Assis believes that here, for the first time, it becomes clear that only Jacob will continue Abraham's line as the chosen son (*Identity in Conflict*, 84). If so, it is clear why previous motifs and content is repeated here.
14. For a different formulation, see Diebner, "Definition." He believes that the name change before meeting Esau reflects Israel's definition in relation to Edom, but here, at Bethel, it defines Israel in itself.

naming can be perceived as a harbinger of things to come, and even if his name was changed that dawn, there is value in announcing his name in a separate revelation, not at the end of a mysterious nocturnal attack. Another possibility of construing this scene is that Jacob's name change here is not a new event, but rather a divine confirmation of Jacob's new name for certain literary purposes in this context.[15]

Nonetheless, this repetition should be read as part of the recurring repetition in this unit. It is strange indeed that Jacob renames the place "Bethel" and sets up a pillar after having established the same name and pillar in the same place twenty years earlier. In order to understand this repetition, I will first contemplate the divine blessing that accompanies this name change.

At the Jabbok, Jacob's name is changed in the context of his struggle: "For you have struggled with God and with humans and have prevailed" (32:29). Naturally, when his name is given in a different context, the accompanying blessing will differ as well. This revelation – complete with blessing and name change – is fully parallel to God's revelation before Abraham's circumcision:

Abraham's Circumcision (Gen. 17)	**The Revelation at Bethel (Gen. 35)**
"No longer shall you be called Abram. Your name will be Abraham, for I have made you father to a multitude of nations." (v. 5)	"Your name is Jacob; no longer shall you be called Jacob; Israel shall be your name." Thus He named him Israel. (v. 10)
"I am El Shaddai." (v. 1)	God said to him: "I am El Shaddai." (v. 11)
"I will make you exceptionally fertile, I will turn you into nations; kings will come from you." (v. 6)	"Be fertile and multiply. A nation, a community of nations will come to be from you. Of your loins, kings shall come forth." (v. 11)

15. See further in Grossman, "Jacob's Struggle," 18–21.

Abraham's Circumcision (Gen. 17)	**The Revelation at Bethel (Gen. 35)**
"I will give you and your descendants after you the land where you now live as strangers, the whole land of Canaan, an everlasting possession." (v. 8)	"The land I gave to Abraham and Isaac I surely give to you; to your descendants after you I will give the land." (v. 12)
When He finished speaking with him, God went up from Abraham. (v. 22)	God went up from him at the place where He had spoken with him. (v. 13)

This leaves no room for doubt that this revelation sees the transferal of Abraham's blessing to his grandson Jacob.[16] It is worth pointing out that in the Covenant of Circumcision, God also blesses Abraham's wife: "As for Sarai your wife, you shall no longer call her Sarai. Her name will be Sarah. I will bless her and give you a son by her" (17:15–16), whereas God's revelation to Jacob is juxtaposed with the birth of his last son and the double naming by Rachel and Jacob.

In fact, instead of this full comparison, one keyword could have served as a code word for circumcision: the name "El Shaddai." From this name alone, it is clear that Jacob is about to receive Abraham's blessing. There are various explanations of its meaning; it is clearly related to fertility,[17] and is accordingly accompanied by a blessing to "be fertile and multiply."

The name "Israel" can also be explained in the context of fertility, the root S-R-R. I am not referring to its immediate etymological meaning, but as is often the case, biblical naming scenes employ wordplay that conforms to the narrative objective.[18] Just as Abram's name is changed to Abraham to represent this blessing of fertility, "*av hamon goyim* – father of many nations," here, too, the letters of Jacob's new name play on the blessing "of your loins, kings shall come forth." The wordplay is more striking in Sarah's name, of course – *sar* is a synonym for *melekh*, king.

16. Westermann, *Genesis II*, 552.
17. See the various opinions for this reading in Grossman, *Abraham*, 138–39.
18. On the various etymological understandings of "Israel," see Zobel, "*Yisrael*," 399–401.

This seems to be the meaning of Jacob's new name, Israel: God blesses him that he will be the father of kings and princes.[19]

This has immediate implications for the reading of this revelation. Jacob has already received the blessing associated with circumcision from his father on the eve of his departure to Haran: "May El Shaddai bless you, make you fertile, and multiply you so that you become a community of peoples. May He grant Abraham's blessing to you and your descendants, that you may possess the land where of your wayfaring you live as a stranger, which God gave to Abraham" (28:3–4). The striking similarity between Isaac's blessing and the blessing of circumcision leaves no room for doubt that this is what Isaac has in mind when he sends his son to find a wife.

This in turn reveals the covert dialogue between Isaac's blessing as he departs for Padan Aram (ch. 28) and the divine revelation at Bethel (ch. 35). I will mention just two of the many connections between them.

The language of the two blessings is similar: in parallel to Isaac's blessing, "May El Shaddai bless you, make you fertile, and multiply you so that you become a community of peoples" (28:3), God tells Jacob: "Be fertile and multiply. A nation, a community of nations will come to be from you" (35:11); in parallel to Isaac's portrayal of the land: "May He grant Abraham's blessing to you and your descendants, that you may possess the land where of your wayfaring you live as a stranger, which God gave to Abraham" (28:4), God promises Jacob: "The land I gave to Abraham and Isaac I surely give to you; to your descendants after you I will give the land" (35:12).

The connection between the scenes is further reinforced through the latter's introduction: "After Jacob had returned from *Padan Aram* God appeared to him again and blessed him" (35:9). As discussed at length, Jacob flees to a place with two names, Haran and Padan Aram, and each name reflects a different aspect of his journey. "Haran" is used by Rebecca in the context of Jacob's flight from his brother's wrath, while

19. Wächter perceives this as the same etymology hinted in Hosea, even though this passage clearly refers to the struggle at Jabbok (Hos. 12:4–5). Wächter, "Israel und Jeschurun," 62, n. 14. I find this doubtful – it cannot be that Hosea says that Jacob "rules" over God.

Isaac uses the name "Padan Aram" to refer to the place Jacob must seek a wife: "Go at once to Padan Aram, to the house of your mother's father Bethuel, and there marry a daughter of your mother's brother Laban" (28:2). Thus the surprising reference to Padan Aram expresses that Jacob has come full circle; his father blesses him as he leaves for "Padan Aram," and now, upon his return from "Padan Aram," he receives the same blessings from God Himself. Just before he returns to his father's house, the second revelation in Bethel – the name change, the erection of the pillar, and the re-naming of Bethel – reflects the successful completion of his father's mission, for Jacob stands by the altar with his wives and children, giving thanks to God for his safe return.

THE DOUBLE ARRIVAL IN BETHEL

Two distinct units take place in Bethel, closing two separate circles. The pilgrimage to pay his vow marks the end of his flight to Haran to escape his brother's wrath, while the scene of God's revelation marks the end of his journey to Padan Aram to find a wife.[20]

This is evident through a comparison between the two units. The first focuses on Jacob's flight from his brother: "As you fled from your brother Esau" (v. 1); "There he built an altar and called the place El Bethel, because it was there that God had revealed Himself to him as he fled his brother" (v. 7). Accordingly, this scene describes the fulfillment of the vow Jacob made in his fear and loneliness, and his second arrival in "Luz – that is, Bethel – in the land of Canaan" (35:6) recalls his earlier arrival and naming of that place: "He named the place Bethel; the town was originally called Luz" (28:19). This second naming is not repetition, but a development of the earlier scene: "There he built an altar and called the place El Bethel, because it was there that God had revealed Himself to him as he fled his brother" (35:7). Radak already points out that the entire region is called "Bethel," but given that the name's literal meaning is "the house of God," this is an appropriate name for the specific site of the altar:

20. For a different reading that the two episodes in Bethel are one sequence parallel to the vision of the ladder scene, see Assis, *Identity in Conflict*, 71–73.

> It says for the third time, "where God had spoken to him," to teach that he now names the specific site of the house of God, the altar and pillars "Bethel," whereas the first time he named the entire city "Bethel," and the entire city is named for the same place. (Radak on Gen. 35:15)

The fact that the word "El" is added to the name also supports Radak's reading: "There he built an altar and called the place El Bethel" – the name literally means "the God of Bethel." This is how the angel in Haran introduces itself: "I am the *God of Bethel,* where you anointed a pillar and made a vow to Me. Now – leave this land at once and return to the land where you were born'" (31:13). Jacob already names the site of his divine vision on the way to Haran; now he names the site of the new altar "El Bethel" as a sign that he has paid his vow.

This is a clear indication that this unit marks the end of Jacob's exile; in Bethel he pays his vow and gives thanks for God's protection throughout his long journey.

By contrast, the second unit hints to Isaac's mission: Jacob must travel to Padan Aram to find a wife. Even more indicative than the name "Padan Aram" is God's reiteration of Isaac's blessing to Jacob as he sets out: Isaac bestows a blessing of fertility upon his son as he leaves the land, and God echoes this blessing upon his return; thus Jacob's journey is enveloped with blessing from father and Father.[21] Within the plotline of Jacob-as-suitor, he names the site "Bethel" because of the revelation he is granted there; thus there is special emphasis on "the place" where this revelation took place: "God went up from him *at the place where He had spoken with him.* Jacob set up a stone pillar at the place where God had talked with him, and on it he offered a libation and poured oil. And Jacob named *the place where God had spoken to him* Bethel" (35:13–15).

This explains why two pillars are set up. On his journey to Haran, Jacob marks one stone as a pillar and anoints it with oil (28:18). This pillar is made from the stone(s) he places by his head the night he runs

21. Unlike Gunkel, who claims that the natural place of the divine revelation and name change is before he sets out on his journey, and the narrative is taken from there and inserted here, after the fulfillment of his vow (Gunkel, *Genesis,* 373).

away from his brother; as mentioned, Jacob has suddenly become a destitute, frightened refugee, with nothing but a stone to place by his head. This second pillar, however, has a completely different meaning: it is not the makeshift pillar of a runaway, but a symbol of a divine revelation, a pillar erected by the father of a nation that will produce princes and kings; a pillar that expresses joy and thanksgiving for Abraham's blessing.

Unlike the pillar in chapter 28, Jacob "offers a libation" upon the new pillar. Assuming this refers to a wine libation ("to be poured out in the Sanctuary as a libation of fermented drink to the Lord" – Num 28:7)[22] – then this is indeed an expression of joy. Wine is associated with joy throughout the Bible: "Their hearts will be glad like wine" (Zech. 10:7); "Wine to cheer people's hearts" (Ps. 104:15); "Wine fills life with joy" (Eccl. 10:19). The addition of wine is likely an expression of joy upon offering a sacrifice to God; appropriate for the erection of the pillar here, and obviously omitted in chapter 28, when Jacob's pillar is an expression of desperate prayer and hope for the future.

Thus, even if the reader adopts the reading that Jacob does not erect a second pillar but returns to the first (Radak and Ramban), from a literary view this pillar is now painted in entirely different colors, regardless of whether he actually builds a new one upon his return from Padan Aram.

THE DEATH OF DEBORAH, REBECCA'S NURSE

These two circles, perhaps, can also illuminate the sudden, surprising mention of the death of "Rebecca's nurse" in between the two units that take place in Bethel: "Deborah, Rebecca's nurse, died and was buried under the oak outside Bethel. And so it was named Oak of Weeping" (35:8).

At first reading, it is difficult to understand this unexpected piece of information's contribution: "There is not enough evidence to explain what this lonely obituary notice is doing here."[23] Plot-wise, it is not entirely clear why Rebecca's nurse is traveling with Jacob's clan; when

22. On the possibility that this verse hints to the wine libations in the Sanctuary, see Milgrom, *Leviticus 23–27*, 2093–94.

23. Alter, *Genesis*, 197.

did she join Jacob? Could it possibly be that Rebecca sent her along with Jacob when he fled to Haran? Did she join the household during Jacob's years in Haran (as Rashi explains)?[24] These questions remain unanswered; all we can do is explore the literary objective of their insertion at this point in the narrative.

The Sages, and some medieval commentators in their wake, associate Deborah's death with the death of Rebecca herself. Gary Rendsburg favors this direction, and proposes reading her death as an allusion to the death of Jacob's mother, which presumably occurs during Jacob's years in Haran; he sees Rebecca's death before her son's return as divine retribution for her role in Isaac's deception.[25]

Tying Rebecca's nurse to Rebecca herself makes sense, but it may be that this should be read in a more positive sense. Jacob's return to Bethel to pay his vow marks the successful end of his mother's mission: Rebecca sends him away to save his life, and now, the closing of this circle marks the closing of her own circle, too.

Rebecca's nurse is mentioned in a different narrative, albeit anonymously: "So they sent their sister Rebecca on her way, together with *her nurse* and Abraham's servant and his men. They blessed Rebecca and said to her, 'Our sister, may you grow into thousands of myriads, and may your descendants possess their enemies' gates.' Then Rebecca set off with her maids, riding on camels and following the man" (Gen. 24:59–61). Rebecca leaves her father's home accompanied by her nurse, presumably Deborah.[26]

As mentioned, Rebecca leaves Haran to build a family with Isaac in Canaan, and she is accompanied by her nurse and her family's blessing: "May you grow into thousands of myriads." When Jacob leaves Canaan and returns to Haran – the place of Rebecca's birth – her life's purpose is at risk: she sees Jacob as her successor, but now he is forced to go backwards, to the home she herself once left. Thus, with Jacob's

24. Keil and Delitzsch raise another interesting possibility: "Deborah was sent by Rebecca to care for her daughters-in-law and grandchildren, or she went herself after her mistress's death" (on 35:8).

25. Rendsburg, "Notes," 364–65. Similarly: Waltke, *Genesis*, 473; Zakovitch, *Jacob*, 149.

26. Rendsburg, "Notes," 365; Mathews, *Genesis II*, 621.

safe return to Bethel, Rebecca is also able to step down from the stage. The same nurse who once accompanied her on her journey to Canaan is buried "outside Bethel" right after Jacob's vow is paid.

Thus the two burials at the end of the first and last units bring the two circles of Jacob's journey to a close. The death of Deborah, Rebecca's nurse, symbolizes the successful end of Jacob's flight to Haran (and the continuation of Rebecca's own legacy); the burial of Isaac – as we will see below – marks the end of Jacob's journey to Padan Aram to raise a family. With four wives and twelve sons, Jacob succeeds beyond Isaac's wildest dreams.

BENJAMIN'S BIRTH AND RACHEL'S DEATH (VV. 16–20)

After two scenes that take place in Bethel, Jacob heads for Hebron. Yet before he can reach his father, two painful episodes tear his family apart. The first is the death of his beloved Rachel as she gives birth to his twelfth and final son.

Some claim that the Bible avoids portraying its characters' emotions and rarely offers a glimpse into their souls. This is not so; while the terse biblical style cannot be compared to that of modern literature, the Bible has other ways to reveal the inner workings of its characters.[27] There are, of course, narratives where the absence of a certain character's emotional reaction is surprising; the story of Rachel's death is one of them. Jacob only opens his mouth to (re)name the newborn child, and his only response to his beloved wife's death is: "Jacob erected a pillar at her grave. To this day, that pillar marks Rachel's grave" (35:20). In fact, not only is Jacob silent, but her death is mentioned almost incidentally, to explain the newborn's name: "With her last breath she named him Ben Oni" (v. 18).

The tragedy of Rachel's death is exacerbated by her death "on the way," before Jacob reaches the family burial plot in Hebron. In ancient times, burial in the family plot was perceived as being part of the family

27. See Bar Efrat, *Artistic Design*, 89–107; Polak, *Biblical Narrative*, 263–92. See also the psychological discussion of Kruger, "Emotions." Aharon Komem raises the intriguing idea that biblical narrative rarely penetrates its characters' hearts because only God can see into the human heart, and the narrative cannot cross these boundaries (Komem, "Limits").

legacy, and burial elsewhere was considered a tragedy in itself; this is evident, for example, in the punishment of the disobedient prophet who was sent to Bethel: "Your corpse shall not reach your ancestors' grave" (I Kings 13:22). Years later it will emerge that Jacob is haunted by the fact that he is forced to bury his beloved wife by the roadside: "For I – as I was returning from Padan, Rachel died beside me in Canaan while we were still on the way, a short distance from Efrat. And I buried her there beside the road to Efrat – that is, Bethlehem" (Gen. 48:7). It is only when Jacob adopts Ephraim and Menashe – the grandsons Rachel never got to meet – that he is able to come to terms with the site of her grave.[28]

Why, then, does the narrative withhold Jacob's response to this crushing tragedy? Perhaps the narrator's silence could be part of Michel de Montaigne's discussion of art's limited capacity to express sorrow:

> And, peradventure, something like this might be working in the fancy of the ancient painter, who having, in the sacrifice of Iphigenia, to represent the sorrow of the assistants proportionably to the several degrees of interest every one had in the death of this fair innocent virgin, and having, in the other figures, laid out the utmost power of his art, when he came to that of her father, he drew him with a veil over his face, meaning thereby that no kind of countenance was capable of expressing such a degree of sorrow.[29]

If visual art is thus limited in its power of expression, how much more so is verbal description. Yet this explanation is insufficient, given that when Joseph's death is reported a few chapters later, the reader *is* offered a glimpse into Jacob's tortured psyche.

---

28. I see no reason to adopt Ackerman and Cox's theory that Jacob does not bury Rachel in the family plot out of concern that the way she died will contaminate the family plot (Ackerman, "Rachel's Tomb"). The text itself hints to a much simpler explanation – she dies "on the way," and Jacob was unable to transport her body. Jacob and Joseph's corpses could be transported from Egypt because they were embalmed and placed in a suitable coffin.
29. De Montaigne, *Essays*, 34.

One possible explanation is that Jacob's silence reflects his complex emotional state: his beloved wife has just died, but she has given birth to his son; torn between intense grief and deep joy, Jacob remains silent.[30]

Indeed, Jacob's silence downplays his immense grief; no words hold space for the sorrow that crushes Jacob at the death of the wife whose tent he shares. Thus, to the reader, his pain is withheld. Does this silence invite room for joy at the birth of his son? Benjamin's birth, like Rachel's death, is not described with the usual emotion, or even the usual formula: "She conceived and gave birth to a son." In fact, there is no mention of her pregnancy, and the reader first learns of the impending birth when her labor begins: "While they were still some distance from Efrat, Rachel began to give birth; her labor pains were intense" (v. 16). For the first time in the Bible, the pain of birth effaces its outcome. Moreover, no explanation is given for the name of the son whose pregnancy is never announced, and the commentators are divided regarding its meaning.

The style of this brief, painful scene is unusual, and some scholars read it is as an "anecdote" rather than an actual "story."[31] Indeed, a string of opening expressions present the events as a series of anecdotes rather than as a developing plot:

> From Bethel they moved on.
> (*Vayehi*) When they were still some distance from Efrat Rachel began to give birth; her labor pains were intense.
> (*Vayehi*) When her labor was at its worst, the midwife said to her, "Don't be afraid. You have another son."
> (*Vayehi*) But she was dying. With her last breath, she named him Ben Oni; but his father called him Benjamin.
> So Rachel died and was buried on the road to Efrat – that is, Bethlehem.
> Jacob erected a pillar at her grave, and that pillar marks Rachel's grave to this day.

30. Samet, *Studies II*, 142–60.
31. Gunkel, *Genesis*, 369.

This language downplays the entire episode – the grief of Rachel's death, and the joy of Benjamin's birth. Why, then, is her death related with such casual brevity? It seems that the text seeks to suppress Jacob's bereavement following the celebratory revelation at Bethel. Just moments before, the reader hears about the divine blessings of fertility and greatness bestowed upon our hero; to focus on his grief as he kneels beside his dying wife would eclipse these promises of a future nation. Were the text to allow focus on the tragedy so soon after the family leaves Bethel, then for the reader, Amos' prophecy would come true: "Bethel would be as nothing" (Amos 5:5). By describing events thus, the narrator holds the stick at both ends: the reader learns of her death, but does not dwell upon Jacob's pain, and the glory of the revelation at Bethel does not fade away.

In fact, the scene's bleak tones are mitigated by the plot itself. How should the double naming of the newborn be understood? With her dying breath, Rachel names him "Ben Oni" (lit. "son of my affliction/sorrow"), a reflection of her tragedy. Rachel has always yearned for another son – her first son is even named for this hope – but just as her dream is about to come true, just as she is about to become "the happy mother of sons," she feels the life seeping out of her, and her dying words are a tribute to her shattered dreams. The immense dissonance between her deepest hopes and cruel reality is expressed in the name of the newborn son who will grow up without his mother: "Son of my sorrow."[32] Yet Jacob changes the baby's name (presumably after her death) to "Benjamin," thus denying his wife's final wish.

The rest of Jacob's sons are named by their mothers; why does Jacob change this name?

First of all, we must determine the meaning of the name "Benjamin" – *Binyamin*; that is, the component "*yamin*" (the first syllable, "Ben," means "son"). As mentioned, given the lack of any explicit

32. Because "*on*" is not only "sorrow" but also power, especially fertility (Gen. 49:3), there is room to debate whether the name Rachel gives her son is not an expression of her agony but of the fertility she is finally granted. Schäfer-Bossert favors this theory, and explains that Jacob does not change the meaning of the name, but only chooses a different synonym (Schäfer-Bossert, "Rahel"). Ramban also observes the word's ambiguity but sees it as a dispute between the parents, as above.

etymology in the narrative, there are various opinions regarding its meaning. The word "*yamin*" appears in the Bible in three senses:

1. The right side (especially in conjunction with the word "hand"), which is an expression of power and strength, as in: "Your right hand, Lord, majestic in power / Your right hand, Lord, shatters the enemy" (Ex. 15:6).
2. Given that the biblical map is orientated toward the east, "*yamin*" means "south."
3. (Possibly: joy and love).[33]

All three meanings are appropriate for a child's name. From an etymological perspective, Rashi's suggestion that Benjamin's name refers to the south is cogent: "It seems to me that because he alone is born in Canaan, which is in the south…'Benjamin' means 'son of the south'" (on 35:18). Benjamin is indeed born in the "south" compared to Jacob's other sons, who are born in north-eastern Haran; moreover, the tribe of Benjamin will one day reside in the "south" with Judah, as opposed to the kingdom of Ephraim, the northern kingdom.

In context, however, I believe that Radak and Ramban's wordplay is more convincing. Both read the name "Benjamin" in dialogue with the name Rachel gives her son, although they offer two different meanings of the component "*yamin*." Radak proposes that "*yamin*" should be read in the sense of "joy and love":

> As she was dying, close to death and devoid of hope, she named him "Son of my sorrow" before she died, for in great sorrow she bore him. "But his father named him Benjamin" – that is, the son of my affection, beloved to me, for he is born in my old age. As in "Let Your hand rest on the person at Your right hand"

33. As claimed by Soggin, "*Yamin*," 100–103. The first two meanings certainly appear in biblical Hebrew – and the connection between them is clear – whereas the third meaning is less established. In any case, the parallel word in Arabic is also ambiguous, meaning both "to go right" and "to be happy." If this is the meaning of Benjamin's name, this ambivalence Rachel seeks to express is clear (and see Radak's similar idea, above).

> (Ps. 80:18) – your favorite and most loved, as in "the son You nurtured as Your own." (Radak on 35:18)

According to Radak, the name his mother gives him expresses her suffering, while the name his father gives him expresses his special love for his youngest child. Ramban, by contrast, reads "Benjamin" as a new articulation of Rachel's name, "Ben Oni." He explains "*yamin*" as "strength," and proposes that while Rachel names him "*Ben Oni*" meaning "sorrow," Jacob reads "*Oni*" as a synonym for "strength" or "virility," thus deriving the name "Benjamin" from the name "Ben Oni."[34] R. Joseph Bekhor Shor favors this reading as well: "His father named him Benjamin – he did not wish to deprive him of his mother's name completely, so he emended it: 'Benjamin' is an expression of strength: '*yamin*' means strength" (on 35:18).[35] It is worth noting that Jacob makes use of the rare word "*on*" in this sense when he blesses Reuben on his deathbed: "Reuben, you are my firstborn, *my strength, first fruit of my manhood* (*atta koḥi vereshit oni*)" (Gen. 49:3). Rachel names Jacob's youngest son "*Ben Oni*," while Jacob refers to his firstborn as "*reshit oni*."

If so, then the rushed, brief form of the episode is consistent with its content: Jacob seeks to eclipse the pain and suffering of Rachel's death by giving their son a new name that expresses strength and power.

Perhaps this double name hints to the tribe of Benjamin's capacity for the depth of depravity (as seen in the Concubine at Gibeah episode) as well as the height of royalty and power (Saul). Whether so much can be loaded onto this character from the moment of his birth is difficult to say. But one thing is clear: despite the tragic loss of the child's mother, Jacob picks himself up and carries on.

Thus the glory of the Bethel revelation is not marred by the tragedy that follows; its powerful effect lingers. This anecdote's content and form are one and the same (or, in the words of Marshall McLuhan, "The medium is the message"). Rachel dies "on the way" and her death is told "by the way"; she is merely part of Jacob's journey, and she never comes

34. Ramban on 35:18.
35. See further in Zakovitch, *Riddles*, 129.

home with him. Her tragic death and lonely burial is consistent with her life's trajectory, as I will now explore.

By Whom Alone Actions Are Weighed

Why does Rachel have to die? Jacob has just paid his vow at Bethel, and God showers him with blessings. But just before he comes home to his father and introduces him to his wives and family, Rachel dies by the roadside.

Scholars point out two different scenes that foreshadow her early death.[36] Rachel mentions her own death when she demands of Jacob: "Give me children! If not, let me die" (30:1). R. Kasher cites a midrash that links this exclamation to her death: "'She said to Jacob, 'Give me children' – why was Rachel punished by death on the way? Because she equated the creation to her Creator."[37] He explains that Rachel's death is the result of her confusion between God, who grants fertility, and flesh and blood. Jacob's anger at her misguided demand is realized here, when she is punished with death.

Another scene that some associate with her death is her theft of the teraphim. When Jacob tells Laban to search for his stolen property, he adds: "But if you find your gods with anyone here, they shall not live" (31:32). The Midrash already reads her death as a fulfillment of Jacob's curse: "According to R. Yossi, she only died because of [Jacob]'s curse... like an error coming out of a ruler's mouth" (Genesis Rabba 74:4). The Midrash implies that the theft of the teraphim and Rachel's deception is what leads to her death, while Jacob inadvertently reveals the punishment awaiting the thief. When Laban enters Rachel's tent she tells him that "the way of women is with" her, and indeed, she dies as women often did – in childbirth.[38]

---

36. Ibid., 110.
37. Kasher, *Torah Shelema*, 1184 (on Gen. 30:7).
38. See further in Bazak, *Starting Point*, 84–85. Given the connection between "און" and teraphim (see I Sam. 15:23), R. Bazak proposes reading the name Rachel gives her son as confession, acceptance, and repentance. I find it difficult to accept that the two events are connected, for Jacob does not say "Whoever *stole* your gods shall not live," but "If you *find* your gods with anyone here, they shall not live," and the text emphasizes that Laban "found nothing... found nothing" (31:33–34).

Yet the scene of her death contains no hint that her death is a punishment, and one should be wary of baseless accusations. Rather than requital of earlier offenses, her death may be a necessary narrative recourse. As Ramban explains:

> And God, by whom alone actions are weighed, [caused] that Rachel died on the way when they started coming into the Land,. for on account of her own merit she did not die outside the Land, and for Jacob's merit, he could not dwell in the Land with two sisters, and she [Rachel] was the one by whose marriage the prohibition against marrying two sisters took effect [since Jacob was already married to Leah]. It seems that Rachel became pregnant with Benjamin before they came to Shechem, and while in the Land Jacob did not touch her at all, for the reason that we have mentioned. (Ramban on Lev. 18:25)

According to Ramban, "The entire Torah is fundamentally the Torah for the Land of Israel, and its laws are inherently the laws of God's land… this is not only true of the laws that only apply in the Land. It applies to every single one of the laws and to religious life in its fullest extent."[39] This approach is relevant to our scene: Ramban believes that so long as Jacob is outside of Canaan's borders, he can remain married to two sisters, but within the Land, it is inappropriate to disregard the law that prohibits this. Thus Rachel dies soon after Jacob enters the Land (for Leah is his first wife).

Ramban believes that this also explains why Jacob does not bury Rachel in the cave of Machpelah. Toward the end of his life, Jacob tells Joseph: "For I – as I was returning from Padan, Rachel died beside me in Canaan while we were still on the way, a short distance from Efrat. And I buried her there beside the road to Efrat – that is, Bethlehem" (Gen. 48:7). Jacob seems to be expressing regret that he could not bury his son's beloved mother in the family plot because she died "on the way," but Ramban suggests otherwise:

39. Ravitzky, "Road Markers," 8–9. See also Hanokh, "Ramban."

> I believe that these are words of apology, and Joseph, too, knows that she died on the way and was buried in the Land, and he honored her when she died, but the reason that Jacob did not bury her in the cave is so that two sisters would not be buried there, for he would be ashamed before his fathers, and Leah married him first, while he married Rachel because he had vowed to marry her in his love for her. (Ramban on Gen. 48:7)

Ramban's premise is that Jacob knows that marrying two sisters is prohibited in the Torah. This is not evident in the text, but I wish to adopt Ramban's fundamental direction, which dictates that Jacob cannot remain married to two sisters once he returns to the Land, or more precisely – to his father.

Jacob's marriage to Rachel and Leah remains an unresolved tension within Genesis. Abraham sends his servant to Padan Aram to bring back a wife for Isaac, and Jacob, too, is expected to marry one of his cousins. Yet Jacob somehow finds himself married to two sisters. Can this be resolved by defining one of his wives as his main wife, and the other the result of unforeseen circumstances? Jacob presumably considers Rachel his main wife, for he falls in love with her, and without Laban's manipulations, he would have never married Leah. Jacob indeed lives in Rachel's tent, and, as is evident from the story of Dinah, the whole family knows where Jacob's loyalties lie. One day, Jacob will even tell his sons the following poignant statement – as quoted by Judah, Leah's son (!): "You know that my wife bore me two sons" (Gen. 44:27).

But the reader, who knows of the complicated nature of Jacob's journey to Padam Aram, is able to see things in a different light.

Jacob meets Rachel as he runs away from his brother. As discussed in context, the scene of their encounter is framed as part of his escape narrative ("We are from Haran" – 29:4), not as a courting scene. His intended wife is waiting for him in Padan Aram. Having fallen in love with her sister before reaching Padan Aram, Jacob cannot discern this, but "God, by whom alone actions are weighed," orchestrates events so that Jacob marries Leah first.

When Jacob plans his escape from Haran – which maintains the thread of his flight narrative – Rachel is mentioned before Leah: "So

Jacob sent word to Rachel and Leah to come out to the field where his flock was" (31:4); "Rachel and Leah answered him" (31:14). In this context, Rashi is correct that "first Rachel [is mentioned] and then Leah, because she (Rachel) was the mainstay of the household, because, on her account, Jacob had joined Laban" (on 31:4).[40] Rachel is an active figure in this narrative; she steals the teraphim and deceives her father, while Leah plays no part at all. Yet Rachel is only a protagonist within this "refugee" thread; when Jacob returns to his father Isaac "from Padan Aram," the text lists Leah's sons first:

> Jacob had twelve sons.
>
> The sons of Leah were Reuben, Jacob's firstborn, Simeon, Levi, Judah, Issachar, and Zebulun.
> The sons of Rachel were Joseph and Benjamin.
> The sons of Rachel's maid Bilhah were Dan and Naphtali.
> The sons of Leah's maid Zilpah were Gad and Asher.
> These were the sons of Jacob, born to him in Padan Aram. (35:22–26)

Reuben is Jacob's firstborn and thus the list begins with Leah's sons, but this technicality shapes the narrative itself. The mother of Jacob's firstborn is Leah, and even though Reuben forfeits his primogeniture, it remains within Leah's sons, ultimately to settle upon Judah.

In the cave of Machpelah Jacob will be buried with a single wife, like his fathers before him. And God, by whom alone actions are weighed, ensures that this wife will be Leah, not Rachel.

REUBEN'S DEED (VV. 21–22A)

Just before Jacob reaches his father Isaac in Hebron, a brief episode takes place in "Migdal Eder" (35:21) – scholars identify this site as somewhere along Road 60, in between Neve Daniel and Efrat in Gush Etzion.[41] There

40. Also Abarbanel; Kiel, *Genesis II*, 366; Shemesh, "Rachel," 88–90.
41. According to Targum Pseudo-Jonathan, the Messiah will one day come from here. Ben-Zion Luria writes that Migdal Eder is "the highest hill in the Judean Hills" and

Jacob pitches his tent, and his firstborn Reuben sleeps with Bilhah: "While Israel was staying in that region, Reuben went and lay with his father's concubine Bilhah. And Israel heard" (35:22).

This terse description conceals more than it reveals. Sleeping with his father's concubine is a strange, problematic act, but there is no description of Reuben's motives. Even Jacob's response seems truncated: What is the meaning of "and Israel heard" and his ensuing silence? On his deathbed, Jacob will revoke primogeniture from Reuben for this act (Gen. 49:3–4), but no such response is recorded here; the reader only learns that "Israel heard."

There are various ways to fill in the gaps, but the most urgent question regarding this brief, shocking act is its objective. The Sages offer some much-needed context, and even if we choose to overlook some of its midrashic details, its premise is consistent with the overall plot.

> R. Shmuel son of Naḥmani said that R. Yonatan said: Whoever says that Reuben sinned is mistaken, as it says, "Now the sons of Jacob were twelve." This teaches that they were all equally [righteous]. How, then, should we understand "He lay with Bilhah, his father's concubine"? This teaches that he rearranged his father's bed, but the text incriminates him as if he had actually lain with her.
>
> It was taught in a *baraita* that R. Shimon son of Elazar says: This righteous person [Reuben] was saved from that sin [of adultery]. Otherwise, how could his descendants be destined to stand on Mount Ebal and say, "Cursed be he that lies with his father's wife," if he had committed this sin?! Rather, when it says "He lay with Bilhah his father's concubine," it means that he avenged his mother's shame, and said: "If my mother's sister was my mother's rival, why should the maid of my mother's sister be a rival for my mother?!" He rose at once to rearrange her bed. (Shabbat 55b)

---

suggests that the binding of Isaac took place there (Luria, "Holiness").

This reading is also embraced by Rashi:

> Because he rearranged his bed, the text accuses him as if he lay with her. Why did he rearrange and profane his bed? Because when Rachel died, Jacob moved his bed, which was usually in Rachel's tent rather than in the rest of the tents, to Bilhah's tent. Reuben came and avenged his mother's shame, saying: "If my mother's sister was my mother's rival, why should the maid of my mother's sister be a rival for my mother?!" For this reason, he rearranged them. (Rashi on 35:22)

This reading fills in the gaps by providing context: after Rachel's death, Jacob moves to the tent of Bilhah, Rachel's maid. More problematically, however, it contradicts the biblical text by claiming that Reuben does not actually sleep with Bilhah, but rather "rearranges her bed," so that when Jacob comes to Bilhah's tent, he finds Leah there. This attempt to reinterpret Reuben's act is understandable, for to sleep with his father's concubine is shocking indeed (to the extent that Reuben's own descendants, together with the rest of Israel, will one day pronounce: "Cursed be he that lies with his father's wife" – Deut. 27:20), but it is difficult to dismiss the narrator's explicit statement that "Reuben lay with his father's concubine."

This is compounded by the fact that on his deathbed, Jacob reiterates that Reuben actually lies with Bilhah: "Unstable as water, you shall not excel, for you went up onto your father's bed and defiled it – went up onto my couch" (Gen. 49:4). Jacob's words accuse Reuben of actual defilement, not of merely intervening in his father's marital preferences. This supports R. Eliezer and R. Yehoshua's stance in the Talmud: that Reuben is guilty of intercourse with Bilhah, as the biblical text describes.

Ibn Ezra seems to echo this process in his commentary on Reuben's deed: "Reuben went – our Sages of blessed memory provided a good interpretation – 'The wise one conceals disgrace'" (on Gen. 35:22). Ibn Ezra begins by stating that the Sages do well to explain that Reuben does not actually lie with Bilhah. Yet the verse from Proverbs he then adds, "The wise one *conceals* disgrace," implies that the Sages seek to conceal Reuben's disgrace; that is, the Sages' interpretation hides his shame, which should indeed be covered up.[42]

Nonetheless, even if Reuben is guilty of lying with Bilhah, it seems that the text downplays this offense – not because he does not lie with her, but because of her status. It is no coincidence that in this context, Bilhah is defined as "his father's *concubine*," whereas elsewhere, she is referred to as "Jacob's *wife*" (such as 37:2); her description here mitigates the gravity of his offense. From his perspective, he has not lain with his "father's wife" but with his "father's concubine"; this absolves him of the offense condemned in Deuteronomy, "Cursed be he that lies with his father's *wife*."

Why does Reuben act this way? Many argue that this is an attempt to assert his status as firstborn and Jacob's heir.[43] This reading is supported by Ahitophel's advice that Absalom sleep with his father's concubines in order to assert himself as the next king (II Sam. 16:21):[44] "Here, too, it seems that Reuben's deed is an expression of rebellion against his father's authority more than an act of forbidden sexuality."[45] I do not believe, however, that Reuben is driven by power lust; rather, his motive is closer to home.[46]

---

42. Ibn Ezra further develops this in his book *The Foundation of Reverence*: "Jacob never slept with a woman again, for Rachel had died, Bilhah had been violated, and because of this he rejected Reuben's mother and her handmaid" (Ibn Ezra, *Foundation*, 146).
43. See, for example, Mathews, *Genesis II*, 628. He links Reuben's motives to the Dinah affair, where Jacob remains silent and passive and Simeon and Levi are active; now Reuben attempts to assert his position.
44. This analogy will be further reinforced if we adopt Netziv's suggestion that at that time, Jacob was not with his family, but rather, broken by Rachel's death, he finds consolation in solitude (*Haamek Davar* on 35:21). Just as David flees to Mahanaim, leaving his concubines behind and Absalom lies with them, when Jacob leaves the family in his grief, Reuben steps up in his absence and asserts his position as Jacob's heir by lying with Bilhah.
45. Hoffmann, *Genesis II*, 537. He also mentions that the Sages' claim that Reuben does not actually lie with her "blatantly contradicts the plain meaning of the text" – ibid.).
46. I am not sure either that Absalom lies with his father's concubines to show that he is the heir; rather, in the words of Ahitophel: "You should go to bed with your father's concubines, the ones he left to mind the palace, and when all of Israel hears that you have become odious to your father, the hand of all your supporters will be strengthened" (II Sam. 16:21).

I wish to adopt the premise of the aforementioned midrash: that Reuben's response is driven by Jacob's move to Bilhah's tent after Rachel's death. Each of Jacob's wives has her own tent (as is evident from Laban's search for his teraphim – 31:33); from the mandrakes incident, it emerges that Jacob sleeps in Rachel's tent by default, and Leah must "hire" her husband from Rachel in order to spend the night with him.[47]

What happens after the death of Jacob's beloved? Even if the midrash's theory seems unfounded in the text, it is likely that Jacob does move in with Bilhah – not due to his love for her, but because, as Rachel's maid, she is presumably caring for the motherless newborn Benjamin and his older brother Joseph. Sure enough, we soon hear that Joseph is "an assistant to the sons of his father's wives Bilhah and Zilpah" (37:2) – for he lives together with the maids' sons. This transition has broad psychological effects on the family dynamics – to the extent that Ibn Ezra notes that Jacob's response to Joseph's dreams, "What kind of dream is this that you have had? Shall we really come, *I and your mother* and your brothers, to bow to the ground before you" (37:10), identifies Bilhah as Joseph's mother. Bilhah has become Joseph's mother; she cares for him and he grows up in her tent.

Given Jacob's infamous affection for Joseph and Benjamin, it is only logical that he moves in with Bilhah to help care for the living reminders of his beloved wife. Perhaps this can be traced in the verse before Reuben's deed: "Jacob pitched his tent beyond Migdal Eder" (35:21); the emphasis on "pitching his tent" perhaps represents a shift in the family order.

With this in mind, Reuben's motives are clear: all his life, he has watched his father enter his aunt's tent while his mother remains alone in hers, with only her children for company. And now, with his aunt's death, imagine his chagrin when instead of turning to his mother, his father moves into his aunt's maid's tent! As the Talmud expresses in his name: "If my mother's sister was my mother's rival, why should the maid of my mother's sister be a rival for my mother?!" His response is not baseless jealousy or uncontrollable rage; rather, his action is calculated to force his father into leaving Bilhah's tent. This, too, recalls Absalom's

47. Shemesh, "Rachel," 88–89.

rebellion: after Absalom sleeps with David's concubines, they become forbidden to the king: "David arrived at his palace in Jerusalem. The king took the ten concubine women he had left to mind the palace and placed them in a house under watch. He provided for them, but he did not come to bed with them, and until their dying day, they were shut up in living widowhood" (II Sam. 20:3). Sleeping with a "defiled" concubine is not only taboo in Jewish law (and to formulate it thus would be somewhat of an anachronism); a primal, innate aversion to incest or any similar practice has existed since ancient times, as discussed in Freud's classic work *Totem and Taboo*.[48] Israel's proclivity toward sexual purity is already clear from the story of Dinah. Reuben realizes that if he lies with Bilhah, Jacob will leave her tent.

Reuben's motives are similar to Homer's portrayal of Phoenix in *The Iliad*. Phoenix's father, King Amyntor, adores his "glistening haired" concubine, which moves his shunned wife to entreat her son to lie with her rival:

> How furious father was with me,
> over his mistress with her dark, glistening hair.
> How he would dote on *her* and spurn his wedded wife,
> my own mother! And time and again she begged me,
> hugging my knees, to bed my father's mistress down
> and kill the young girl's taste for an old man.
> Mother – I did your bidding, did my work...
> but father, suspecting at once, cursed me roundly,
> he screamed out to the cruel Furies – "Never,
> never let me bounce on my knees a son of his,
> sprung of his loins!" – and the gods drove home that curse.[49]

---

48. Freud, *Totem and Taboo*, mostly 19–40.
49. Homer, *The Iliad*, trans. Robert Fagles, 266–67. Zakovitch also notes this connection, *Jacob*, 142–43. Unlike Homer's hero, who seeks to kill his father after their quarrel, Reuben does not seem to resent his father, and even tries to save Joseph, Jacob's favorite son (although it is difficult to determine whether the sale of Joseph takes place before or after this incident).

Reuben will yet suffer his father's curse at the end of Genesis, but for now, this illuminates his motives in this scene. In *The Iliad*, too, sleeping with his father's concubine presumably does more than "kill a young girl's taste for an old man" – social conventions dictate that the concubine becomes off-limits for Amyntor.

Bekhor Shor points out this consequence of Reuben's deed: "And Israel heard – to find that he had lost two of his wives: Rachel, who died, and Bilhah, whom Reuben lay with and thus from that moment Jacob did not lie with her. As it is written of David's concubines after Absalom lay with them: 'He provided for them, but he did not come to bed with them, and until their dying day, they were shut up in living widowhood'" (on 35:22).[50]

Jacob did not necessarily move into Bilhah's tent because he loved her more than Leah; he presumably did so to care for Rachel's sons. But Reuben experiences this move through his mother's eyes, and senses her hurt and rejection: even after her sister's death, her husband does not move into her tent. We have already seen Reuben's sensitivity toward his mother in the mandrakes incident, and it is no coincidence that both scenes begin with the same phrase: "And Reuben went" (30:14/35:22). Reuben's "going" is an expression of initiative and action; in both scenes, he "goes" to ease his mother's pain.

I will tentatively add: not only should Reuben's act *not* be perceived as an assertion of his birthright as Jacob's eldest; but Reuben presumably understands that he is risking his primogeniture by forcing his father to leave Bilhah's tent. Yet he is willing to pay the price for his mother's sake. The embellished version of this scene in the book of Jubilees, in which Reuben sees Bilhah bathe "in a secret place" and falls in love with her (Jubilees 33:1–10), misconstrues the narrative and its objective.

Reuben indeed commits an unspeakable act, but nonetheless, in a certain sense, "whoever says that Reuben sinned is mistaken." He does not lie with Bilhah to serve his own interests or his lust; rather, he sacrifices his own honor for the sake of his mother's honor. Reuben is

50. Compare to Nicol, "Reuben's Reversal."

prepared to give up his birthright in order to bring his father into his mother's tent.

ISAAC'S DEATH (VV. 22B–29)

Jacob continues south and finally reaches Hebron. Just before he introduces his family to his father, the narrator provides a neat list for the reader:

> Jacob had twelve sons.
> The sons of Leah were Reuben, Jacob's firstborn, Simeon, Levi, Judah, Issachar, and Zebulun.
> The sons of Rachel were Joseph and Benjamin.
> The sons of Rachel's maid Bilhah were Dan and Naphtali.
> The sons of Leah's maid Zilpah were Gad and Asher.
> These were the sons of Jacob, born to him in Padan Aram. (35:22–26)

Jacob's sons are listed by mother. After Reuben's deed has brought the tense family dynamics to the surface, this is an appropriate place to set things straight. The narrator mentions that these sons are born to Jacob in Padam Aram (even though Benjamin is born in Canaan), and I will refer back to this emphasis in the context of Esau's genealogy. For now, I will point out that the name "Padan Aram" (as opposed to Haran) prepares the ground for Jacob's return to his father, who sends him to "Padam Aram" in the first place. Isaac sends him to find a wife, and now he comes back to him with twelve sons, born to him from four wives. Although Jacob's journey to Haran is beset with challenges and conflicts, Isaac's mission is a raging success.

And finally, after all this time, Jacob is reunited with his father:

> Jacob came home to his father Isaac at Mamre, near Kiryat Arba – that is, Hebron – where Abraham and Isaac had lived as strangers. Isaac lived one hundred and eighty years. Then he breathed his last, and died, and was gathered to his people, aged, satisfied with his years. His sons Esau and Jacob buried him. (35:27–29)

What happens during this reunion? Do father and son embrace, kiss, weep on each other's necks? Do they talk about Jacob's deception long ago? During the long years Jacob spends at his father's house, not a word is said of their relationship, and the narrative sequence implies that Isaac dies soon after Jacob returns home. Yet a simple calculation reveals that Jacob and his family go down to Egypt only ten years after Isaac's death – that is, Jacob and Isaac live together in Hebron for at least ten years (and possibly up to sixty!) after Jacob's return![51]

Various exegetes point out the disparity between this fabula and syuzhet (see, for example, Rashi or Ramban), and make various suggestions. In the end, this narrative ellipsis of Isaac's life reflects one of the most fundamental themes in the narrative: the *toledot* of Isaac.

As I have already pointed out in my discussion of the narrative cycle's introduction: "These are the *toledot* of Isaac, son of Abraham: Abraham was Isaac's father" (25:19) – this cycle focuses on Isaac's family line. One truly becomes the head of a clan only after grandchildren are born. Thus, when Jacob returns from Padan Aram and presents his twelve sons to his father, the "*toledot*" of Isaac are complete, and he steps down from the stage.

Intriguingly enough, the site of Isaac's burial is not mentioned. Abraham's burial is described thus:

> Abraham breathed his last and died in his ripe old age, aged and satisfied, and was gathered to his people.
> His sons, Isaac and Ishmael, buried him
> in the cave of Machpelah, near Mamre…
> There Abraham was buried with Sarah his wife. (25:8–9)

By contrast, even though he, too, is buried in Machpelah, only the first two components of Isaac's burial are mentioned:

51. Isaac was 60 when Jacob was born and died when he was 180 – that is, when Jacob was 120. When Jacob meets Pharaoh, he is 130 (Gen. 47:9).

> Isaac lived one hundred and eighty years. Then he breathed his last, and died, and was gathered to his people, aged, satisfied with his years.
> His sons Esau and Jacob buried him. (35:29)[52]

Why is the location of his burial omitted? Is it already implied in the description of Jacob's arrival: "Jacob came home to his father Isaac at Mamre, near Kiryat Arba – that is, Hebron" (35:27)? Even so, it is strange that there is no mention that Isaac is buried in the same place as his father. Perhaps the omission of the name "Machpelah" is in dialogue with Rachel's roadside burial: to emphasize Isaac's place in the family burial plot would underscore the great tragedy of her death – a mere day's walk away from where Jacob's father lived and where Jacob's father died. A mere day's walk from Hebron, yet she did not survive.

The fact that "his sons Esau and Jacob buried him" is also fascinating. To be buried by one's children is a sign of ripe old age, of a life lived to the full. What is more surprising is that Esau's name is listed before Jacob's. Abraham, too, is buried by his two sons, but the firstborn who moved away from his family and God's covenant is listed after his chosen younger brother: "His sons Isaac and Ishmael buried him" (25:9). Why is Esau's name mentioned first? Is it, perhaps, a nod to the special bond between Isaac and Esau?

Assis holds that this supports his theory that Isaac believes that both brothers will continue Abraham's covenant, rather than Jacob alone. Assis also points out that while Abraham sends his concubines' sons away with gifts before his death (25:6), Isaac does not send Esau away with gifts.[53]

I wish to follow in a similar direction, with different emphasis. Unlike Ishmael, Esau can choose whether or not he continues Abraham's covenant. If he remains in Canaan, under his brother's rule, then he, too, can be part of the covenant. But Esau chooses to move away and embrace

52. Compare also to Jacob's burial: "They carried him to Canaan and buried him in the cave of the field of Machpelah, near Mamre, which Abraham had bought as a burial site from Ephron the Hittite" (Gen. 50:13).
53. Assis, *Identity in Conflict*, 91–92.

the loophole Isaac opens up for him: "By your sword you will live, and your brother you will serve; *but when you move on, you will throw off his yoke from your neck*" (27:40). Isaac does not send Esau away with parting gifts; Esau and Jacob bury their father together, as equal heirs. Ishmael has no choice in the matter, but Esau can freely choose whether or not to participate in Abraham's covenant. This is the very heart of the next chapter – Esau's *toledot*.

The Genealogy of Esau (Gen. 36)

> The Egyptian, the Babylonian, and the Persian rose, filled the planet with sound and splendor, then faded to dream-stuff and passed away; the Greek and the Roman followed, and made a vast noise, and they are gone; other peoples have sprung up and held their torch high for a time, but it burned out, and they sit in twilight now, or have vanished. The Jew saw them all, beat them all, and is now what he always was, exhibiting no decadence, no infirmities of age, no weakening of his parts, no slowing of his energies, no dulling of his alert and aggressive mind. All things are mortal but the Jew; all other forces pass, but he remains. What is the secret of his immortality?
>
> – Mark Twain, "Concerning the Jews"

A friend of mine, who has the custom of standing during the weekly Torah reading, once sat down at the end of *Parashat Vayishlaḥ*. When I asked him if he was feeling well, he answered, "To stand for Esau? That's already going too far." Yet this chapter illuminates the process Jacob's family undergoes; moreover, it is no exaggeration to state that Esau's movement has profound implications for understanding the course of Israel's history.

Chapter 36 is entirely devoted to Esau's genealogy – in Canaan and especially in Mount Seir. The end of the previous chapter sees Esau and Jacob burying their father together, but their paths will never cross again. Yet even so, the figure of Jacob and his family hovers over the description of Esau's genealogy.

The main question raised by this chapter is its objective. There is certainly importance in tracing Esau's family line, just as the reader is informed of Ishmael's; the sons of ancestors who were not part of the chosen line are also blessed.[1] It is the comparison to Ishmael's line, however, that underscores the disparity between the two accounts. Ishmael's descendants are listed in just seven verses – their names together with a brief reference to their autonomy: "These were Ishmael's sons, and these are their names by their villages and encampments: twelve princes and their tribes" (25:16), and their territory: "The Ishmaelites dwelt from Havilah to Shur, up against Egypt, all the way to Assyria, settling up against all their brothers" (25:18).

By contrast, Esau's genealogy, territory, and structure is described in a full forty-three verses – in multiple sections whose contribution is not immediately apparent. The Talmud already questions the importance of this chapter through the skeptical voice of Manasseh son of Hezekiah:

> "But the person who acts high-handedly" – this is Manasseh son of Hezekiah, who would sit and teach flawed interpretations of biblical narrative. He said: "But why did Moses need to write only [trivial matters, such as] 'And Lotan's sister was Timna' or 'And Timna was the concubine of Eliphaz son of Esau'?" (Sanhedrin 99b)

These two verses are indeed surprising. Esau's genealogy includes an entire passage about the original inhabitants of Seir; Lotan is one Horite son. After his sons are listed, his sister is suddenly mentioned as well: "Lotan's sons were Hori and Hemam. Lotan's sister was Timna" (36:22). Similarly, in addition to the list of the sons of Eliphaz – Esau's firstborn – the narrator notes that Timna was his concubine: "Timna was the concubine of Eliphaz son of Esau" (36:12). These specific verses are only examples of the question that hovers over the entire chapter: Why is Esau's genealogy described in such detail?

1. For example, Keil and Delitzsch on 36:1.

Another element that invites special attention is the double heading: "These are the *toledot* of Esau" (36:1, 9). As mentioned, this heading plays a critical role in the structure of Genesis that holds the key to its inner structure and multiple layers. For some reason, Esau, who is ultimately excluded from Abraham's covenant, is awarded two separate headings in the same chapter.

One common medieval explanation of this chapter's objective is that it defines who the Edomites are for the purpose of understanding the prohibition, "You shall not detest the Edomite" (Deut. 23:8). (This is suggested by R. Abraham son of Rambam, and Radak, for example.) This moves Ramban to explain why the text emphasizes that Amalek is born to Eliphaz from his concubine rather than from his main wife:

> We are commanded not to hate the Edomites or take their land – this includes all of his sons who live in Seir, who are named Edom. But the concubine's son is not considered an Edomite and he does not dwell in their land, and concerning him, we are commanded the opposite: to despise him and wipe out his name. (Ramban on 36:12)

But there are two problems with this explanation. Firstly, it implies that the chapter's only significance can be found outside of its textual context; an explanation that illuminates the unit as the conclusion of the Jacob cycle is preferable. Secondly, as we will discuss below, besides Esau's genealogical lists, the chapter also includes lists of the Horites who lived in Seir before Esau's arrival; this, too, demands explanation.

In order to understand this chapter's significance, I will map out its structure, which comprises seven lists divided by headings and concluding formulae:

1. **1–5: "These are the *toledot* of Esau – that is, Edom":** This mentions Esau's three wives (Adah the Hittite; Oholibamah the Hivite; and Basemath daughter of Ishmael) and his five sons. This list ends with emphasis on the sons' birthplace: "These were the sons of Esau, born in the land of Canaan" (36:5). [6–8: the story of Esau's journey from Canaan to Edom]

2. **9–14: "These are the *toledot* of Esau, father of Edom, in the hill country of Seir":** This mentions Esau's ten grandchildren: six sons born to Eliphaz; four sons born to Reuel (for some reason, instead of grandchildren, the text relists Oholibamah's sons – v. 14). This list does not have a conclusion.
3. **15–19: "These were the tribal chiefs among Esau's descendants":** This mentions the fourteen "tribal chiefs" descended from Esau (his grandsons and three of his sons from Oholibamah, whose grandchildren are not mentioned in the previous list. The name "Korah" appears in this list twice – as the son of Eliphaz and the son of Oholibamah). This list ends with a double conclusion that also concludes the previous list: "These were the sons of Esau – that is, Edom – and these were their chiefs" (v. 19).
4. **20–28: "These are the sons of Seir the Horite, who were settled in the land":** This mentions the seven sons of Seir the Horite and his grandchildren, who lived in Edom before Esau's arrival. The sons are listed, followed by the grandsons, who are introduced with a separate subheading: "These were the chiefs of the Horites, descendants of Seir in the land of Edom" (v. 21). This list is not marked with a separate conclusion; once again, the conclusion of the next list will conclude this list as well.[2]
5. **29–30: "These were the tribal chiefs of the Horites":** This lists Seir's seven sons a second time,[3] this time with the title "chief," and the list ends thus: "These were the Horite chiefs by their divisions in the land of Seir" (v. 30). Once again, the emphasis on "the land of Seir" concludes this list together with the previous list.
6. **31–39: "These were the kings who reigned in the land of Edom":** This lists the eight kings who reigned in Edom, and it has no formal conclusion either.
7. **40–43: "These were the chiefs descended from Esau by their clans, localities, and names":** The Torah repeats the names of

2. As proposed by Bartel, "Lists," 364.
3. For this reason Gunkel perceived this list as part of the previous list (Gunkel, *Genesis*, 375), but the new heading shows that this is an independent list, even if it is connected to the previous one.

the chiefs descended from Esau, but unlike the third list, which focuses on their names, the heading emphasizes that they each rule over a separate geographic region. As Ibn Ezra explains: "This means that their territories are well-known [in Moses' time]. These are the words of Moses: those now mentioned are the offspring of the aforementioned chiefs [who rule over known regions in Moses' time]; only those who rule their own regions are mentioned" (on 36:40).

This final list ends thus: "These were the chiefs of Edom – of Esau, father of Edom – each with their own settlements in the land of their possession" (v. 43). This concludes all of Esau's genealogy in Seir (that is, from the second list to the seventh). The second begins thus: "These are the *toledot* of Esau, the father of Edom" (v. 9), and the chapter's conclusion reiterates that Esau is the father of Edom: "That is Esau, father of Edom."

Several details emerge from this summary. First and foremost, the first list is distinct from the rest of the chapter; as mentioned, this is established through the two separate "*toledot*" headings in verse 1 and verse 9. Both units have their own literary framework: the first unit opens and closes with "Esau – that is, Edom" (vv. 1, 8), whereas the second opens and closes with the statement that Esau is "the father of Edom" (vv. 9, 43). This chapter can thus be divided into two parts, based on the two "*toledot*" headings. The two parts are separated by the description of Esau's journey from Canaan to Edom (vv. 6–8).

Secondly, the six lists in the second part of the chapter are clearly divided into three pairs, each with its own subject. Although each list has its own heading, the conclusion of the second list in each pair serves as a conclusion for both lists:

1. **Esau's clan**
   Esau's sons and grandsons in Seir (vv. 9–14)
   The tribal chiefs of Esau (vv. 15–19)
   Conclusion: "These were the sons of Esau – that is, Edom – and these were their chiefs" (v. 19).

2. **Seir's clan**
   The Horite's sons and grandsons (vv. 20–28)
   The Horite tribal chiefs (vv. 29–30)
   Conclusion: "These were the Horite chiefs by their divisions in the land of Seir" (v. 30).
3. **Edom's government**
   The kings of Edom (vv. 31–39)
   The tribal chiefs of Edom (vv. 40–43)
   Conclusion: "These were the chiefs of Edom – of Esau, father of Edom – each with their own settlements in the land of their possession" (v. 43).

Let us now turn to the lists themselves, beginning with the first; the chapter's objective will emerge from a closer analysis.

THE FIRST LIST: "ESAU'S SONS, BORN IN THE LAND OF CANAAN"

Why does the key "*toledot*" heading appear twice in regard to Esau's genealogy? Although Esau's grandchildren are only mentioned under the second heading, this is strange in itself: they could have been included in the first list, after Esau's sons. The answer is geographical: the first list ends with the explicit statement that "these are the sons of Esau born in the land of *Canaan*" (v. 5). The text emphasizes that Esau's nuclear family is established in Canaan: "Esau took wives from among the daughters of Canaan" (v. 2).

The second "*toledot*" unit involves Esau's clan's establishment in the land of Seir: "These, then, are the *toledot* of Esau, father of Edom, in the hill country of Seir" (v. 9). The first list describes Esau, the individual living in Canaan: "Esau – that is, Edom." This can be understood similarly to the prevalent biblical formulation: "The Valley of Shiddim – *that is,* the Dead Sea" (Gen. 14:3) – "The Dead Sea" is another name for what was once called "The Valley of Shiddim";[4] "Edom" is an alternative name for the person who was once called Esau. In the second half, the name

4. On this unique biblical style, see Andersen, *Sentence,* 30.

"Edom" takes on a different meaning: "These, then, are the *toledot* of Esau, father of Edom" – "Edom" in the sense of a nation, the Edomites, who are descended from Esau (similar to "the father of Moab" or "the father of the Ammonites" in Gen. 19:37–38).[5] This difference is not merely technical; the subtle distinction serves to differentiate Esau the individual, whose children are born in Canaan, from Esau the father of the Edomite nation in "the hill country of Seir."

Appropriately enough, these two sections are separated by the description of Esau's move from Canaan to Seir:

> Esau took his wives, sons, and daughters, and all the members of his household, together with his livestock, his other animals, and all the possessions he had acquired in Canaan, and he moved to another region, away from his brother Jacob, for their possessions were too great for them to remain together; because of all their livestock, the land where they were living could not support them both. So Esau settled in the hill country of Seir. Esau is Edom. (36:6–8)

These verses hint to a reverse analogy between the twin brothers. The language describing Esau's journey to Seir recalls the description of Jacob's journey from Padan Aram to Canaan:

Jacob: from Padan Aram to Canaan (31:17–18)	**Esau: from Canaan to Seir (36:6–8)**
So Jacob put his children and wives on camels	Esau took his wives, sons, and daughters, and all the members of his household,
and drove all the livestock and wealth he had accumulated – the livestock he had acquired in Padan Aram –	together with his livestock, his other animals, and all the possessions he had acquired in Canaan,
heading for his father Isaac in the land of Canaan.	and he moved to another region, away from his brother Jacob.

5. Hoffmann, *Genesis II*, 544.

Perhaps this analogy would be insufficient in itself, built as it is on common biblical phrases,[6] but the comparison is reinforced through further analogies between the brothers:

Jacob	**Esau**
The sons of Leah were Reuben, Jacob's firstborn, Simeon, Levi, Judah, Issachar, and Zebulun. The sons of Rachel were Joseph and Benjamin. The sons of Rachel's maid Bilhah were Dan and Naphtali. The sons of Leah's maid Zilpah were Gad and Asher. These were the sons of Jacob, born to him in Padan Aram. (35:23–26)	Adah bore Eliphaz to Esau, and Basemath bore Reuel. Oholibamah bore Yeush, Yalam, and Korah. These were the sons of Esau, born in the land of Canaan. (vv. 4–5)
So Jacob put his children and wives on camels and drove all the livestock and wealth he had accumulated – the livestock he had acquired in Padan Aram – heading for his father Isaac in the land of Canaan. (31:17–18)	Esau took his wives, sons, and daughters, and all the members of his household, together with his livestock, his other animals, and all the possessions he had acquired in Canaan, and he moved to another region, away from his brother Jacob. (v. 6)
Jacob settled where his father had lived as a stranger, in the land of Canaan. (37:1)	So Esau settled in the hill country of Seir. (v. 8)
These are the *toledot* of Jacob. (37:1)	These are the *toledot* of Esau, father of Edom, in the hill country of Seir. (v. 9)
These are the names of the children of Israel – Jacob and his descendants – who came to Egypt. (46:8)	These were the chiefs descended from Esau, by their clans, localities, and names. (v. 40)

This comparison is fascinating given its repeated emphasis on geographic location. Jacob travels to Padan Aram to marry his maternal cousins,

6. See especially Avishur, "Literary Formulae."

while Esau marries his paternal cousin; Jacob's sons are born "in Padan Aram" but he moves the family to Canaan, while Esau's are born "in the land of Canaan" but he then moves eastward, to the hill country of Seir. Jacob eventually settles in Canaan "where his father lived," when Esau settles in "the hill country of Seir."

Perhaps this comparison also solves two difficulties in the second list – Esau's *toledot* in Seir, which lists his grandsons as well as his sons, implies that Esau is establishing a clan in his new home. For some reason, the narrator lists Esau's grandsons from his wives Adah and Basemath, but there is no mention of any grandsons from his wife Oholibamah, who bears him three sons (unlike his other wives, who have one each). The confusion is compounded by the fact that her sons are mentioned again in the same list as Esau's grandchildren, which creates strange asymmetry: the chiefs of Edom are Esau's *grandsons* from Adah and Basemath together with his *sons* from Oholibamah. R. David Zvi Hoffmann explains that "the text does not mention the sons of Oholibamah's sons because they were not chiefs,"[7] but this in itself demands explanation: Why are all of Esau's grandsons chiefs except for those of Oholibamah? Is this coincidental? I will soon propose that this reflects the complexity of Oholibamah's sons' status within Esau's dynasty, but for the sake of the present discussion, I wish to link this question to the analogy between the twin brothers – after I note a different question that arises from this list.

Esau's wives are mentioned repeatedly throughout the chapter, and his sons are grouped according to their mothers – just as Jacob's sons are. Typical of biblical genealogies, the sons' wives are not mentioned, with one surprising exception: "Timna, a concubine of Esau's son Eliphaz, bore him Amalek" (v. 12). What does this contribute to the understanding of Esau's genealogy? I will discuss this further below, but it may also be relevant to the analogy at hand.

It seems that these questions stem from a single root: from the text's desire to reach a total of twelve descendants. Together, Adah and Basemath have nine "official" grandsons (besides Amalek, who is born to his son's concubine). If we add the three sons of Oholibamah to the

7. Hoffmann, *Genesis II*, 545.

list, Esau's descendants number twelve. This excludes Amalek, who is not born to Eliphaz's "proper" wife, but to a mere concubine: "He is not counted among Esau's sons, and he does not dwell with them in Seir, for his name is borne by his wives' sons but not by the concubine's son, who will not inherit along with his sons, as per his [grand]father's custom" (Ramban on 36:12). Amalek is not included in the count because he is born to Esau's son's concubine, and without him, the total of Esau's descendants is twelve.[8]

If so, the comparison to Jacob is clear, Esau's twelve descendants are presented in parallel to Jacob's "twelve sons" (35:22).[9] The genealogy in chapter 36 is no random list; it hints that Esau's journey mirrors Jacob's. Esau starts a family in Canaan, but moves to Seir and grows into a nation; Jacob starts a family in Padan Aram, but travels back to his birthplace to raise his sons. Like Abraham, Jacob's sons are not born in Canaan, but Canaan is their destination and home, and this also reflects the nation's future path: Israel grow into a nation in Egypt, and they form a covenant with God at Sinai, but their destination and future lie in Canaan.

SEGREGATION OR ASSIMILATION?

The comparison between Jacob's journey to Canaan and Esau's journey to Seir takes on new significance in light of Esau's move to his new home. In a sense, Esau's second "*toledot*" heading is parallel to Jacob's "*toledot*" in the next chapter, which introduces the story of Joseph. Both "*toledot*" passages describe what happens after the brothers move to their new home. It goes without saying that the differences between the narratives far outweigh the similarities: whereas Esau settles down and

8. Although this is still doubtful, because Esau's sons are also mentioned in this list, and I propose that the count includes the grandsons from Adah and Basemath, and Oholibamah's sons. This is strange, but as mentioned, these are the descendants listed here.
9. Some scholars feel that it is appropriate for Esau to have twelve sons – like Nahor, Ishmael, and Jacob – and they therefore claim that in the original text, Esau has only twelve sons (Noth, *Zwölf Stämme*, 42–45). According to my proposal, the text – in its current form – does hint to this number, by omitting Oholibamah's grandsons, and emphasizing that Amalek is a mere concubine's son. For other ways to reach a total of twelve, see Hamilton, *Genesis II*, 394. In Chronicles, "*Timna*" also appears as a son of Eliphaz, so that he has six sons besides Amalek.

establishes an independent government, Jacob and his family eventually go down to Egypt.

The contrast between the brothers' path is not only present in the reader's consciousness; it is implied in the text itself. Beyond the various hints I will soon point out, I will first mention the most obvious difference, which is found in the sixth list in the chapter: the list of Edom's kings.

This list begins with the declaration that "these were the kings who reigned in Edom before any king reigned over the Israelites" (36:31). Commentators have long been troubled by this statement, which seems to have been written much later, presumably after Saul became the first king of Israel: only in retrospect can the narrator conclude that eight kings reigned in Edom before Israel ever crowned its own king.

The medieval commentators take various approaches.[10] I wish to focus on Ramban, who holds that the narrative is not presenting a broader historical perspective of Edom's monarchic period in relation to Israel's; rather, its emphasis is that Edom's monarchy rises and falls long before there is ever a king in Israel:

> The expression, "before there reigned any king," means "many years before." It does not mean that these kingdoms of Edom continued to exist until the kingdom of Israel. Instead, it means to say that at that time the Edomites will not have sovereignty, in order to fulfill Isaac's words, "And your brother you shall serve."[11]

To further clarify, R. D. Z. Hoffmann also favors this reading, and compares this to a verse about Moses' death: "And this is the blessing that Moses, man of God, blessed the Israelites before his death" (Deut. 33:1): it is not that the verse was necessarily written after Moses' death; rather, the verse means to say that Moses bestows these blessings before his death.

10. The two most prevalent are that Deuteronomy was written with prophetic foresight (as Bekhor Shor; this is also mentioned by Ibn Ezra), or that the king is Moses (Ibn Ezra prefers this reading).
11. Ramban on 36:31.

This helps illuminate the purpose that this list serves in the text, for beside the historical question of the list's dating, it contributes to its place within the broader narrative. The reader has already heard that Esau's sons become "chiefs," yet it is not at all clear that the kings mentioned in this list are descended from Esau. Ramban's reading reveals this list's objective: it emphasizes that Edom has established monarchy long before Israel even becomes a nation. Perhaps the reader expects to hear how Jacob and his family become a ruling power in Canaan, but this is not the case. While Esau settles the land successfully and establishes an organized government (if not a royal dynasty),[12] Jacob and his sons go down to Egypt and become enslaved to a foreign king.

R. D. Z. Hoffmann raises another important point to this end: this scene follows God's revelation to Jacob after he returns from Padan Aram. In Bethel, God promises Jacob: "A nation, a community of nations, will come to be from you. Of your loins, kings shall come forth. The land I gave to Abraham and Isaac I surely give to you; to your descendants after you I will give the land" (35:11–12). After this revelation, the reader expects to hear how Jacob-Israel settles in the land, rises to power, and sees his descendants growing into mighty "kings."[13] Yet the ensuing chapter does not tell how kings come forth from Jacob, but from neighboring Edom; and soon after that, instead of growing mighty in the land that God gave to Abraham and Isaac, Jacob and his family must leave the Promised Land for many years, and become slaves in Egypt.

If so, this reveals one of the chapter's objectives: Esau's journey to Seir and his rise to power is a foil to Jacob's journey to Canaan. Does this chapter also hint to the reason for this difference? Does it illuminate why Jacob goes down to Egypt, perhaps failing where his brother succeeds?

---

12. As rightly pointed out by Hamilton, *Genesis II*, 400. The kings in this list do not belong to a single dynasty; it is not written how each one comes to power. R. Itamar Eldar suggested to me that the Zohar's concept of "I will rule!" which leads to breakdown is derived from this list of seven kings due to their instability: this is not a stable dynasty, but a sequence of kings who each usurp their predecessor's throne. The royal line is constantly severed; the kings die and are not succeeded by their sons.
13. Hoffmann, *Genesis II*, 550–51. Similarly Assis, *Identity in Conflict*, 93.

The answer to this question is yes – and in this sense, this overlooked chapter serves as one of the most dramatic crossroads in biblical history.

This brings us to one of the other lists that describes Esau's settlement in "the hill country of Seir." The most convenient way to navigate these lists is by following the trail of Oholibamah, Esau's wife. As mentioned, the second list features Esau's grandchildren from his other two wives, but for some reason, only Oholibamah's sons are listed there.

Given that this list mentions her sons (rather than her grandchildren), the narrator repeats the verb "she bore": "The sons of Oholibamah, daughter of Anah and granddaughter of Esau's wife Tzivon, whom she bore to Esau, were Yeush, Yalam, and Korah" (36:14). This verb interrupts the flow of the verse because it opens with her sons and not with her; moreover, this verb does not feature here in relation to his two other wives. It is, in fact, a quote from the first list, which only serves to underscore that her sons are mentioned instead of her grandsons.

In fact, the first list already indicates that Oholibamah's status is complex. She is first introduced after Adah (v. 2), and is followed by Esau's third wife, "Basemath daughter of Ishmael," but when Esau's sons are listed, she is mentioned last, and this order is maintained throughout the chapter (36:5, 14, 18).[14] As Hamilton: writes: "In the references to these three women as wives the order is: Adah, Oholibamah, Basemath (vv. 2–3). In the references to these women as mothers the order is: Adah, Basemath, Oholibamah (vv. 4–5)."[15]

Oholibamah's special status is also evident in her genealogy throughout the chapter:

1. This is already salient in the introduction of Esau's wives: "Esau took wives from among the daughters of Canaan: *Adah daughter of Elon* the Hittite, and *Oholibamah daughter of Anah, granddaughter of Tzivon* the Hivite – and also *Basemath, daughter of Ishmael*

14. Rashbam assumes that Esau marries Oholibamah last and that is why she is mentioned last (on 36:2), but because there are further irregularities concerning her, her special status demands a different explanation.
15. Hamilton, *Genesis II*, 392.

and sister of Nevayot" (vv. 2–3). The other two wives are only introduced with their father's name (and their brother's name, in Basemath's case), while Oholibamah is presented as the daughter of Anah and the "*granddaughter* of Tzivon."

2. Her genealogy is also mentioned in the second list: "These are the names of Esau's sons: Eliphaz son of Esau's wife *Adah,* and Reuel, son of Esau's wife *Basemath* .... These are the descendants of Esau's wife *Adah* .... These were the descendants of Esau's wife *Basemath.* The sons of Esau's wife *Oholibamah, daughter of Anah and granddaughter of Tzivon* ..." (vv. 10–14).
3. In the third list – the tribal chiefs descended from Esau – only Oholibamah's father is mentioned, but given that the other two wives' fathers do not appear here, Oholibamah stands out once again: "They were the grandsons of *Adah*" (v. 16)/"They were the grandsons of Basemath" (v. 17)/"These are the chiefs descended from *Oholibamah daughter of Anah*" (v. 19).

Each list of Esau's descendants thus emphasizes Oholibamah's ancestry but omits her posterity.

The key to the mystery of Oholibamah lies in the third list: the list of Horite genealogy before Esau's arrival in Seir (vv. 20–28):

> These are the sons of Seir the Horite who were settled in the land: Lotan, Shoval, Tzivon, Anah, Dishon, Etzer, and Dishan.
> These were the chiefs of the Horites, descendants of Seir in the land of Edom.
>
> Lotan's sons were Hori and Hemam. *Timna was Lotan's sister.* Shoval's sons were Alvan, Manahat, Eival, Shefo, and Onam. Tzivon's sons were Ayah and Anah.[16] This is the Anah who discovered hot springs in the desert while pasturing the donkeys of his father Tzivon.

16. For the sake of the current discussion, I am overlooking the question of the brothers "Tzivon and Anah" at the beginning of the Seir genealogical list and this "Anah son of Tzivon." According to Rashi: "This shows that Tzivon lay with his mother and

> Anah's children were Dishon and *Oholibamah daughter of Anah.*
> Dishon's sons[17] were Hemdan, Eshban, Yitran, and Keran.
> Etzer's sons were Bilhan, Zaavan, and Akan.
> Dishan's sons were Utz and Aran.

Two women appear in this list, which is surprising, given that biblical dynasties generally focus on the male line. Why are Timna (Lotan's sister) and Oholibamah (Anah's daughter) mentioned?

Perhaps this anticipates the final list in the chapter, which lists various tribal chiefs who rule over specific regions. As I will discuss below, the list reflects that Esau does not rule over the entire land; the Horite maintains control over some regions, some of which are named for Horite women: "the chiefs *Timna,* Alva, Yetet, *Oholibamah...*" (vv. 40–41). But even if this refers to those same women, this answer is insufficient; it merely transfers the question to a different place in the text. Why are there regions under Esau's rule that are named for two Horite women who belong to the clan of Seir, who lived in the area before Esau's arrival?

The solution is that these two women are mentioned because they marry into Esau's clan: Oholibamah is Esau's wife (v. 2), while Timna is the concubine of Esau's son Eliphaz (v. 12).[18]

This sheds light on Esau's successful rise over the hill country of Seir, and also clarifies the surprising focus on Oholibamah. The usual assumption is that Esau conquers the Horites and takes over Seir; this is implied by Moses' description in Deuteronomy (2:12), and expressed by various commentators, such as Ramban: "He took his sons and all the members of his vast household, and went to Seir to settle there, and then fought against the Horites of Seir, who lived in the land" (on 36:6). Yet certain details in this chapter hint to a more complex picture.

---

fathered Anah" (on 36:24), while Radak claims: "This is a different Anah, not the one mentioned above, who was a Seirite; this is the son of Tzivon" (on 36:24).

17. A comparison of the sons of the first list and their grandsons suggests, perhaps, that the correct name is "Dishon" and not "Dishan."
18. Meyer, *Geschichte,* 343–44; Gunkel, *Genesis,* 378.

In addition to conquest, Esau also forms marriage ties with the local Horites: the Oholibamah mentioned in the third list is presumably the same Oholibamah daughter of Anah who marries Esau and bears him three sons. Ramban already points this out: "This is Anah son of Tzivon – that is, Esau's father-in-law" (on 36:24).

The name "Anah" appears twice in the third list (one is Tzivon's son, and the other is Tzivon's brother), and exegetes and scholars have long debated whether the two figures are one and the same. Some argue that Tzivon's son and brother are one person, born out of incest, while others propose that at one point, the son Anah is elevated to the rank of father (similar to "Menashe and Ephraim will be like Reuben and Simeon to me" – Gen. 48:6). This is a reasonable theory, given that Oholibamah is "the daughter of Anah the granddaughter of Tzivon."

In any case, there is no doubt that the text focuses on this clan, and even seeks to glorify it. Even without understanding the reference to "this is the Anah who discovered hot springs in the desert while pasturing the donkeys of his father Tzivon" (36:24), this is clearly a local legend of some kind: Anah the celebrated dowser. Esau seeks ties with this important clan and marries the daughter of the famous Anah.

The importance of this detail cannot easily be overstated. Esau assimilates with the people of Seir. It is not clear whether the two clans "become one people" (Gen. 34:16) or remain distinct with diplomatic marriage ties between them, but either way, Esau merges with the local culture.

I will support this reading further below, but a dramatically different portrait of Esau's history has already emerged. Esau marries Oholibamah before he settles in Seir (36:2), and she bears his sons while they still live in Canaan (36:5). His move to Seir can thus be read as a decision to join his wife's clan on the other side of the Jordan – including the famous Anah "who discovered hot springs in the desert." A powerful hunter, he rises within the ranks of the "family business," and quickly assimilates among the local people.

Perhaps this explains why his grandchildren from Oholibamah are not included in his genealogy along with his grandchildren from his other wives. His move to Seir is a move to the clan of his wife, Oholibamah daughter of Anah daughter of Tzivon. The sons born to him in Canaan are part of his patriarchal line, but the grandchildren born in his wife's homeland melt seamlessly into her clan; they are raised by Anah and Tzivon, ultimately indistinguishable from their Horite cousins. Only his grandsons from his other wives maintain their father's name and culture to a significant degree.

The fact that Esau's son Eliphaz takes another local girl – Timna – as a concubine further supports the reading that Esau's relationship with the local Horites is amiable, not hostile. Although some claim that Eliphaz takes a different Timna (Radak), while others suggest that he took her by force (Sforno), there is no basis for either claim. Rashi's reading is far more likely: Timna becomes his concubine through friendship and goodwill, and this offers a glimpse into the relationship between the two clans.

It is worth recalling that in Abraham's time, the Mesopotamian Empire – the "four kings" – conquer the Horites in Seir: "In the fourteenth year Chedorlaomer and his allied kings came and defeated the Rephaim in Ashterot Karnaim, the Zuzim in Ham, the Emim in Shaveh Kiryataim, *and the Horites in the hill country of Seir* as far as El Paran by the wilderness" (Gen. 14:5–6). Two generations later, the Horites Esau meets are still weakened from the empire's harsh campaign, and they cannot withstand Esau's force (which is at least four hundred strong); under such circumstances, it makes sense that they readily agree to a peaceful alliance, and Esau swiftly rises to power among them, his position bolstered by his marriage with a prominent local clan.

Besides the fact that the ancient Horite clan are important enough to be mentioned by name, and besides the diplomatic marriage ties hinted in the narrative, there are two further indications that Esau becomes fully assimilated with the local Horites

Tribal Chiefs

Firstly, the clans' convergence is hinted to through the rare word "*allufim*," which refers to the form of government established by Esau's line (36:15–19). The word's precise meaning is given to dispute; the most prevalent approach links the word to the root "A-L-P," "thousand" – one who rules over a thousand men, the tribal chief.[19] Others suggest that

19. For example, Cassuto, "*Alluf*."

the word is associated with the word trained (as in "trained lamb" – Jer. 11:19) – a trained animal that is placed at the head of the flock and thus helps guide them.[20] For our purposes, what matters is the fact that this unusual word seems to be borrowed from another language. As Keil and Delitzsch note: "*Allufim* was the distinguishing title of the Edomite and Horite phylarchs [=tribal heads]; and it is only incidentally that it is applied to Jewish heads of tribes in Zechariah 9:7, and Zechariah 12:5."[21]

In the Song of the Sea, too, the word "*allufim*" refers to Edom (and it is used in parallel to "gods"!): "The *chiefs of Edom* were dismayed, then / the gods of Moab were seized with trembling" (Ex. 15:15). It is no coincidence that the rulers descended from Esau are referred to with an Edomite title rather than an Israelite one (such as "*nasi*" or "*sar*"); this, too, reflects Esau's assimilation in Seir. Esau's descendants adopt the Horite political structure and government.

The Seventh and Final List

Secondly, the cooperation between Esau and the ancient Horites is evident in the final list – the "chiefs of Edom." This list reiterates the list of local tribal chiefs from a geographic perspective: "These were the chiefs of Edom, each with their own settlements in the land that they held" (v. 43). To the reader's surprise, this list merges chiefs descended from Esau with chiefs of Horite origin, and together, the two clans constitute "Edom":

> These were the chiefs descended from Esau, by their clans, localities, and names:

The chief Timna,	– a Horite (v. 22) who joined Esau's clan (v. 12).
The chief Alva,	– a Horite ("Alvan"? – v. 23).[22]
The chief Yetet,	– a Horite ("Yitran"? – v. 26).

20. Tur-Sinai, "*Alluf*."
21. Keil and Delitzsch on 36:15–19.
22. This son's name appears slightly differently in Chronicles, twice: "*Alyan*" (I Chr. 1:40); "the chief *Alya*" [*keri*: *Alva*] (51).

> The chief Oholibamah, – a Horite (v. 25) who joined Esau's clan (v. 2).
> The chief Ela,
> The chief Pinon,
> The chief Kenaz, – an Edomite (v. 15).
> The chief Teiman, – an Edomite (v. 15).
> The chief Mivtzar,
> The chief Magdiel,
> The chief Iram.
>
> These were the chiefs of Edom – of Esau, father of Edom – each with their own settlements in the land that they held.

Not all of the chiefs in this list can be identified as either Horite or Edomite, but the evident data is sufficiently surprising. Not only does Esau not conquer and drive out the land's previous population, but they share control of the land. Two chiefs can be identified as Horites, two as Esau's descendants, and two belong to both clans.

This surprising convergence can be explained as a historical process that developed over time. As Arieh Bartel proposes:

> We learn that over the course of time between the first list of chiefs and the last list, the ancient Horite contingency in Edom grew stronger. Therefore, the first four chiefs of the list are Horite. In the first lists, the Edomite chiefs and the Horite chiefs are listed separately, and from this we learn that at first, the population in the land of Edom was divided into two separate clans; this had changed by the time of the last list. In this list, we find representatives from all over the population: Edomites, Horites, and chiefs from different regions are represented in one supreme list. This fact testifies to socio-political integration in the land of Edom.[23]

It is certainly feasible that the final list is the product of a gradual historical process. Yet even so, the integration of the two clans is fundamental

23. Bartel, "Lists," 368–69.

to the chapter's main objective. Esau marries Oholibamah at the very beginning of the chapter, even before he moves to Seir – that is, he migrates with the intention of integrating with local society. The extent of force he uses to assert himself in his new environment is not entirely clear, but one thing is certain: the earlier lists in the chapter present the genealogy of two separate nations, but by the end of the chapter, through marriage and political cooperation, the two clans have largely converged.

This is even more salient in the first chapter of Chronicles, which presents the following lists:

- Esau's line (I Chr. 1:35–37)
- The Seirites (vv. 38–42)
- The kings of "Edom" (vv. 43–50)
- The chiefs of "Edom" (vv. 51–54)

These lists lead to the conclusion that whereas Esau's line can initially be distinguished from the people of "Seir," over time, the two clans merge and "become one people." Chapter 36 of Genesis follows the same path, although its focus on Esau means that the final list is presented as "The chiefs of Edom – of Esau, father of Edom" (v. 43), so that Esau's assimilation within Edom seems less absolute.

"I Granted Mount Seir as the Inheritance to Esau, While Jacob and His Sons Went down to Egypt" (Josh. 24:4)

The description of Esau's assimilation in Seir appears after Esau's second "*toledot*" heading. As mentioned, this is parallel to Jacob's "*toledot*" after his return to Canaan. After Esau's rise to power in his new home, the reader who is aware of this analogy might expect to hear how Jacob, too, rises to power in his alt-neu-home in Canaan. Esau travels east and produces chiefs in Seir; Jacob travels west and will now produce rulers in Canaan.

Needless to say, any such expectations are sorely dashed when just a few chapters later, Jacob and his family must go down to Egypt. Jacob's "*toledot*" – the story of his children and grandchildren – is told, but it is a tale of migration and uncertainty, not one of stability and establishment like Esau's.

The irony of Jacob's situation is underscored through the maintained analogy to his brother Esau's path. When Jacob goes down to Egypt, "They took their livestock and all the possessions they had acquired in Canaan. So Jacob and all his descendants came to Egypt. He brought with him to Egypt his sons and grandsons, daughters and granddaughters, and all his descendants" (46:6–7). Jacob's journey continues; the language recalls his travels from Padam Aram to Canaan, implying that this is simply the next leg of his never-ending journey.

The list of Jacob's descendants' names in this context once again mirrors Esau's move from Canaan to Seir: "Esau took his wives, sons and daughters, and all the members of his household, together with his livestock, his other animals, and all the possessions he had acquired in Canaan, and he moved to another region, away from his brother Jacob" (36:6). The list of "the names of the children of Israel – Jacob and his descendants who came to Egypt" (46:8) should be compared to the final list of Esau's descendants and their evident power in their land: "These were the chiefs descended from Esau, by their clans, localities, and names" (36:40). The rejected brother travels east, settles down, and rises to power in his new land, siring chiefs and kings, while the chosen brother returns to the Chosen Land, cannot thrive for long, does not sire the promised kings, and is forced to migrate once again, this time to Egypt.

Before the reader cynically questions, "This is Torah, and this is its reward?!" note that the key to this mystery is hidden in chapter 36. Esau's success is the result of his successful assimilation in his new home. He marries the Hivite-Horite Oholibamah, whose grandchildren, the narrative hints, are far more Horite than Edomite, despite their patrilineality – to the extent that they are not listed as part of Esau's line; his children adopt Horite forms of leadership and become *allufim*; eventually, his descendants rule over Seir together with the native Horites. Esau is granted full "possession" of the land,[24] but it comes at the price of full assimilation.

The analogy between Jacob and Esau hints that this could be Israel's future, should they assimilate with the people of the land. If they,

24. On the use of "*aḥuzza*" here (echoing the covenant of Abraham in Genesis 17), see Assis, *Identity in Conflict*, 93.

too, marry Canaanite women; if they, too, form ties with the "princes of the land," trade with them, and "become one people," then Esau's fate would be their own. Yet instead, they go down to Egypt, settle in "the region of Goshen" and keep to themselves, and are eventually oppressed and enslaved, unable to merge with the local culture:

> This is the meaning of "There I will make you into a great nation," for if your sons were to live here, they would marry the Canaanites and mix with them, but this will not happen in Egypt, where "the Egyptians would not break bread with the Hebrews." In the words of the Sages of blessed memory: "There they will become a nation – this teaches that they were singled out there." (Sforno on Gen. 46:3).[25]

Only after Israel is forged into a nation will Jacob's descendants return to Canaan and be able to conquer it, drive out its inhabitants, and settle there.

Reading Esau's *toledot* in chapter 36 – just a few chapters before Jacob's family goes down to Egypt – illuminates their unsettling story. Their exile to Egypt prevents them from assimilating in the land; by the time they return they will be a fully-fledged nation, a powerful entity in themselves. Note the emphasis on the fact that Jacob brings *all* of his family, every last descendant, with him to Egypt, so that none remain in Canaan: "So Jacob and *all his descendants* came to Egypt. He brought with him to Egypt his sons and grandsons, daughters and granddaughters, and *all his descendants*" (46:6–7). Not a single member of Jacob's family remains behind to assimilate in Canaan.[26] They all travel as one, settle in a specific region in Egypt, and are enslaved together, set apart from their foreign hosts. Unlike Esau, when they return to their land, they will drive out its inhabitants instead of living among them.

As Joshua expresses in his final speech at Shechem:

---

25. I am grateful to my friend Rami Yanai who drew my attention to this. Compare to *Meshekh Ḥokhma* on Leviticus 26:44.
26. Scholars debate whether any Israelites remained in the land while Jacob and his family went down to Egypt (see the discussion in Rowley, *Joseph to Joshua*, 122–24).

> To Isaac, I granted Jacob and Esau;
> I granted Mount Seir as the inheritance to Esau,
> while Jacob and his sons went down to Egypt. (Josh. 24:4)

Isaac has two sons: one inherits Seir, and the other…goes down to Egypt! This disturbing contrast reflects the reading experience of the end of the Jacob cycle. Perhaps the Sages had this in mind when they provide a surprising explanation for Esau's move to Edom: "He moved to another region, away from his brother Jacob – R. Eliezer said, because of the promissory note: 'Your descendants will become strangers'" (Genesis Rabba 82:13). According to this midrash, Esau moves to Seir in order to avoid the fate that awaits Israel; to remain in Canaan will not allow for tranquility or stability – like Israel, he would be subjected to further migration, enslavement, and volatility. For this reason, explains the midrash, Esau chooses to move to Seir.[27]

The challenge of maintaining one's identity as a nation in exile, of avoiding assimilation, is notorious;[28] but in biblical times, living as a distinct nation in Canaan posed no less of a challenge, and under certain circumstances, exile proved to be the solution – albeit a temporary one. Jacob's family is but a small clan, and the land is full of Canaanites – exogamy will inevitably lead to cultural assimilation as well. The forefathers' aversion to marriage with Canaanites should be understood in this context: bringing wives back from Haran detaches them from their culture and tucks them under Israel's wings, retaining Israel's identity; marriage with Canaanite women results in assimilation,

27. I am grateful to my uncle R. Shlomo Eytan for drawing my attention to this midrash and its possible connection to the above theory.
28. See Yehezkel Kaufmann's marvelous study *Exiled and Estranged.* It is worth noting that Kaufmann himself does not link the secret of Israel's endurance in exile to the nations' hatred, and he mentions the Return to Zion as an example: at that time, they were able to remain in Babylon and Persia without animosity. He believes that it is the Jewish religion – its monotheism and way of life – that preserves this tiny little people over the course of history. In this context, Zalman Shazar's comment is also intriguing: that "literary prophecy" is what preserves Israel during their exile in Babylon (Shazar, *Biblical Pardes*, 215–20).

in "becoming one people."[29] In Egypt, and throughout Israel's history, Israel remains in their ghetto in Goshen on the banks of the Nile, or in Worms and Mainz on the banks of the Rhine, or in Fez or Sijilmassa on the banks of the Ziz. This segregation sometimes allows for prosperity and harmony, more often leads to pain, oppression, and animosity, but it is the only way to maintain Israel's separate identity. When Israel returns to its land, they return as a people who have fought and sacrificed themselves to retain their identity, their truth, and their loyalty to God, and it is with this fervor and determination that they will settle the land, prosper within it, and appoint kings and leaders to establish a kingdom of Israel, descended from Jacob.

29. Thus the main reason Abraham sends his servant to Aram Naharaim is not to find a wife from his family, but from Aram Naharaim. His instructions focus on this geographic location, not on his family. See Grossman, *Abraham*, 358–60.

Few and Hard: A Summary of the Jacob Cycle

> Who can be wise, amazed, temp'rate, and furious, Loyal, and neutral, in a moment? No man.
>
> – Shakespeare, *Macbeth*, Act II, Scene III

Jacob's life is a series of challenges and conflicts. From the moment of his birth – or perhaps, even before – his relationship with his twin brother is a perpetual source of tension that defines them both. As soon as the brothers part ways, Jacob encounters his next adversary – his father-in-law Laban, who deceives him again and again. Soon after he leaves Laban, he is forced into a conflict with the men of Shechem; his beloved wife dies – and all this takes place before the greatest tragedy of his life: the loss of his favorite son, whom he believes dead.

Jacob himself summarizes his life similarly, when Pharaoh asks him his age: "Jacob said to Pharaoh, 'The years of my wandering are one hundred and thirty. Few and hard have been the years of my life, and I have not reached the age my fathers reached in their own wanderings'" (Gen. 47:9). The ambiguity of this response stems from the fact that Jacob cannot answer Pharaoh's straightforward question, "How old are you?" with an equally straightforward reply.

"The years of my wandering," Jacob explains, number one hundred and thirty, but I cannot honestly say that I have been "living" all this time. Such suffering cannot be called "living," and my years have been hard and few, even if I have technically been on this earth for one hundred and thirty years. There is no doubt that out of the three forefathers, Jacob suffers the most; through disasters, conflicts, and trials, and in this sense, he has "not reached the age my fathers reached in their own wanderings."

This brings us to a dramatic question that accompanies Jacob throughout his life: Is all his suffering the consequence of his theft of the blessings? As we have seen throughout the narrative cycle, so much of his conflict stems from this act of deceit. Perhaps there is room to argue that had Jacob refused to deceive his father, his life would have unfolded completely differently – along with the course of Israelite history.

I believe, however, that the answer is far more complex, and though there is room to make such a claim, Jacob's deed is but one facet of a restless, turbulent life. I will explore this complexity by going back to what I have already hinted to in the introduction: to the double causality that permeates the Jacob cycle.

"Better to Hold the One, Never Loosening Your Hand upon the Other" (Eccl. 7:18)

The Jacob cycle's plot is woven from two different threads that offer two separate perspectives. The most dramatic decision in Jacob's life – to leave his home in Canaan and travel to his uncle's house – is driven by two distinct motives. Rebecca urges him to flee to Haran to escape his brother's wrath; Isaac instructs him to travel to Padan Aram to marry one of his maternal cousins. This colors his journey in two completely different shades.

Two consecutive scenes offer different explanations of how Jacob becomes prosperous in Laban's house. The first describes how Jacob's diligence and manipulation earn him his fortune (30:25–43); the second depicts his success as the result of God's providence (31:4–13).

This dichotomy continues to accompany Jacob as he leaves Laban's house. On the one hand, he flees from Laban after he learns of his father-in-law's growing resentment; on the other, God explicitly orders him to return to Canaan: "Go back to the land of your fathers where you were born; I will be with you" (31:3). Once again, these motives are not incongruous, but they each paint the scene in different colors.

Bethel also sees the closure of two separate circles: Jacob pays his vow and thus ends the story of his flight to Haran (35:1–8), while his name change and God's blessing of fertility marks the end of his journey to find a wife (35:9–15).

The entire Jacob cycle, it thus emerges, is built on two parallel narrative axes; even if they cannot be unraveled into two separate threads, the plot can still be deciphered in two different ways. Our question, therefore, can be understood from two distinct theological perspectives, and it is up to us to define how these two perspectives mesh into a single narrative.

According to the story of his flight to Haran at his mother's insistence, it indeed seems that Jacob's life unfolds as it does due to his theft of the blessings. Were it not for his actions, he would not need to leave the land; perhaps a servant would be sent to fetch him a wife from Padan Aram. We can even entertain the notion that Laban would have sent Leah as his wife, sparing them both a life of heartbreak, rivalry, and tension, for when Jacob is forced to travel to Haran himself, he meets Rachel at the well and falls in love with her before he ever meets the elder sister Laban deceives him into marrying.

It is the rivalry between the sisters that leads to bitter conflict when Dinah is captured; as we saw, Simeon and Levi, "Dinah's brothers," must fight for their sister, and their conflict with Jacob reveals the different factions within Jacob's family. Given that the sale of Joseph is also the result of this rivalry within the family, then this tragedy can indeed be traced back to Jacob's theft of the blessings.[1] According to this interpretation of events, the Jacob cycle is governed by the fundamental principle of free choice. It is difficult to overstate the Bible's adherence to the law that the choices characters make govern their reality. God appears to Cain before and after he murders his brother, but at the moment of his actual murder, God is absent from the scene, leaving Cain to act out of free will.[2] The story of Jacob is consistent with this fundamental theme; in fact, it becomes its paradigm: the process

---

1. I do not mean to say that Jacob should not have received these blessings. As we saw in context, the text is ambivalent on this issue. But even if Jacob should have received them instead of Esau, Jacob certainly pays for this decision for the rest of his life.
2. See further: Grossman, *Beginnings*, 126–27.

of Abraham's selection and the establishment of the Israelite nation is dramatically shaped by Rebecca and Jacob's decision to deceive Isaac and steal Esau's blessing, and then by Esau's ensuing decision to leave Canaan and Abraham's covenant.

Yet according to the narrative thread of Jacob's journey to Padan Aram at his father's bidding, a different story unfolds. Jacob makes his way to Padan Aram as a suitor, and Laban's deception (assuming that this scene is part of this axis, of which I am not quite convinced) should not be strictly read as a deception, but rather as an expression of divine will that he marry Leah, the elder sister. Though Laban attempts to swindle Jacob out of his fair wages, God ensures that Jacob's flock grows. In other words, this thread describes how Jacob marries his maternal cousins, starts a family, and fulfills his father's command. When Jacob returns to Canaan, El Shaddai confirms the blessings that Isaac bestows upon his son on the eve of his departure, and Jacob presents his wife Leah and his children to his father. According to this reading, it is not Jacob's theft of the blessings that governs the plot, but his father's mission, which begins with Abraham's blessing of fertility and inheritance of the land. God supports Isaac's decision and grants the ancestral blessing to Jacob, and though this character encounters obstacles along the way, they should not be perceived as the consequences of his actions, but rather as a necessary process of trials and tribulations that all of Israel's ancestors must endure as part of the establishment of their nation. "*Maaseh avot siman labanim* – "The ancestors' deeds are a sign for their children"; Israel's exile echoes their ancestors' trials and tribulations.

Two parallel axes, then, present Jacob's story, and address to what extent the protagonist's decisions shape the course of his life. This should be contemplated within the broader context of Genesis, given that this doubleness appears elsewhere; the Abraham cycle also contains several double narratives, and there, too, I conclude:

> These pairs – and others throughout Genesis – present a fundamental doubleness that reflects a broader biblical doctrine. The characters' lives unfold along two axes, neither of which can be omitted. The patriarchs were chosen to establish a nation, and they fulfill the divine plan (the revised plan, of a postdiluvian

> world), but they are also portrayed in light of their moral decisions. God responds to their actions and treats them as is their due.[3]

However, whereas this doubleness takes place in several dramatic junctions within the Abraham cycle,[4] in the Jacob cycle, it permeates the entire plot. How do we explain this?

I have already mentioned in the introduction that within the broader process of Genesis, the Jacob cycle is in between: between the Abraham cycle and its extensive, sweeping divine intervention and the Joseph cycle, where God's hand is hidden, and Joseph is not granted a single divine revelation, only dreams.

The Jacob cycle plays a decisive role within Genesis – it is inherently transitional. The character's double motives reflect certain theological ambivalence in which God intervenes in reality and orchestrates the characters as He sees fit, while at the same time, reality is also shaped by the characters' own decisions. The two axes could have been fully converged into one narrative with double causality (similar to the Joseph cycle), yet the Jacob cycle maintains this doubleness, so that the two perspectives remain dovetailed side by side, inviting this lenticular portrait of Jacob-Israel, the character who retains both names.

DOES THE JACOB CYCLE SHOW CHARACTER DEVELOPMENT?

Does biblical narrative show character development? This is a broad debate in research. In general literature, character development is a marker of complexity. Since Forster's definition in *Aspects of the Novel*, characters are generally defined as either "flat" – constructed around a single idea or quality – or "round" – a complex character of various qualities, one who generally develops over the course of the narrative.[5]

3. Grossman, *Abraham*, 419.
4. This happens at three important junctions: the birth of Ishmael; the birth of Isaac; Lot's rescue from Sodom (see Grossman, *Abraham*, 164–70; 281–89; 208–17).
5. Later literary scholars question this dichotomy, and propose different definitions along a continuous scale. See especially Even, *Fictional Characters*, 33–44; Rimmon-Kenan, *Poetics*, 44–46.

It is generally agreed that some biblical characters are "round" to the extent that they have multiple characteristics, but do they also develop over the course of the narrative?

I believe, without question, that this is so: some characters certainly show development. This cannot be said of all characters in biblical narrative, but certain protagonists – such as Joseph, Saul, and David – definitely undergo certain processes over the course of their story, in various ways.

Can the same be said of Jacob? I do not refer to the character's psyche – the terse biblical text rarely offers a glimpse into the character's emotional life – but at least in the sense of what befalls him and how he reacts to these events.

One of the lone scholars who argues for Jacob's development is Fokkelman, who rightly argues that when considering Jacob's character development, the Joseph cycle should also be taken into account, given that it is a "prolongation" of the Jacob cycle. He claims that reading the second half of Genesis reveals a "reversal of a reversal": in the first half of Jacob's life, he causes suffering to his brother and father by deceiving them; his twenty years of exile arouse his conscience and his personal growth; and in the second half of his life, as the father, he suffers from his own family: his sons deceive him and do not reveal what happened to their brother. Eventually, their conscience, too, is stirred, and they too change following Joseph's attitude toward them.[6]

This is an interesting theory that certainly exposes fundamental themes of the plot and of Jacob's characterization. At the same time, however, it is not entirely supported by the text: it is difficult to say that Jacob causes his family pain in the first half – this is only true of his theft of the blessings. As soon as he reaches Haran, it is Laban who deceives Jacob, and this already marks the reversal of Jacob's relationship with those around him. Moreover, there is no evidence that Jacob's conscience stirs during his exile; although, as I have argued, he returns the blessings to Esau, his treatment of his sons remains complex.

Instead, I wish to trace the central motif of deception in the Jacob cycle, and define his journey through this lens. I have already mentioned,

6. Fokkelman, "Jacob as a Character."

in context, that Jacob's confrontation with Laban marks a turning point in his characterization. After this aggressive speech, Jacob forms a covenant with Laban as his equal; he is his servant no longer. In a certain sense, one might claim that his theft of the blessings (ch. 27) mirrors what can be considered his brother's compensation (chs. 32–33). Jacob takes the blessings from Esau at his mother's bidding; he can hardly be considered active in this scene, even though he is the one who executes her instructions. As we saw, the verses that describe how Jacob prepares for the deception minimize his culpability: "*Then Rebecca took* her elder son Esau's best clothes, which were with her in the house, and *put them on Jacob*, her younger son. *She put the goatskins on his hands* and the smooth part of his neck. *She then handed her son Jacob* the delicious food and bread that she had prepared" (27:15–17). By contrast, while Jacob bows before Esau as if accepting his authority, Jacob is essentially active and decisive. Although he is tempted to flee his brother once again to avoid confrontation, his struggle with the angel keeps him in the area, and he reconciles with his brother.

It is inaccurate to state that Jacob is passive in the first half of the cycle and active in the second; the picture is far more complex. I am not sure that it is correct to define him as a developing character; but he is certainly far from "flat." But even if the plot does not follow a clear linear sequence when focalized through Jacob, we can organize the narrative through key motifs that appear again and again.

"YOU DWELL IN THE MIDST OF DECEIT" (JER. 9:5)

The motif of deceit is salient throughout the Jacob cycle, and it proves to be a cornerstone. Ironically, Jacob is described in his youth as an "*ish tam yoshev ohalim*" (25:27) – perhaps best translated as "innocent," "simple," or "straightforward," many question why it is innocent Jacob who is dragged into a lifetime of deception. Why is he portrayed as "*ish tam*"?

This initial description is calculated to provide a certain mindset for the reader before he or she sets out on Jacob's long and winding journey; beneath the deceptions, schemes, and manipulations, Jacob is essentially an "innocent man." I will now explore how this motif unfolds over the course of the narrative – along with Jacob's relationship with deceit.

Firstly, it is worth noting that although Jacob gets caught up in various schemes, the narrator never states that Jacob "deceived" or "cheated." This is expressed by various characters, but never through the narrator's "objective" view; on the contrary, in scenes where Jacob is potentially subject to criticism, the text itself mitigates such criticism by presenting a complex picture. When Jacob exploits Esau's weakness in order to secure the birthright, the scene ends with criticism that "Esau disdained the birthright" (25:24). The text emphasizes Rebecca's hand in the theft of Esau's blessings (27:8–18). Moreover, the prophecy Rebecca receives during her pregnancy serves as a divine justification for her actions, whether or not this was the motive behind her actions. Laban is a devious cheater who exploits Jacob, and thus Jacob is only able to survive and prosper in his home through manipulation (29:25–26):[7] "If you lie – you get to the truth! I tell lies; therefore, I'm human. Not one truth has ever been reached without first lying fourteen times or so."[8]

Against this complex background, I wish to explore the recurring acts of deceit and the pattern they form across the Jacob cycle:

1. **In Canaan: The birthright and blessings**
   25:19–34: Jacob and Esau struggle over the birthright (in childhood and adulthood).
   27: *Jacob and Rebecca obtain the blessings through deceit ("Your brother came in deceit").*[9]
   28: The blessing "May El Shaddai bless you and make you fertile" (from Isaac), and God's blessing in Jacob's dream (and the naming of the place).
2. **In Haran I: Jacob's wives**
   29:1–12: Jacob meets Rachel at the well; draws water for her flock, and kisses her.

7. Evans, "The Patriarch Jacob." He reaches the conclusion that Jacob maintains his integrity throughout the cycle.
8. Dostoevsky, *Crime and Punishment*, trans. Michael R. Katz, 223.
9. As we saw, the narrative emphasizes how Jacob is executing his mother's instructions.

29:13–30: *Laban's deceit – Jacob's marriage to Leah and then Rachel ("I served you for Rachel, did I not? Why have you deceived me?").*
29:31–30:24: Jacob's wives give birth to his sons (and name them).

3. **In Haran II: Jacob's flock**
   30:25–34: Jacob and Laban's agreement about the flock.
   30:35–31:2: *Jacob's "manipulation" to increase his flock.*[10]
   [31:10–13: Jacob's revelation in a dream: "I have seen all that Laban is doing to you."][11]
4. **Leaving Haran**
   31:1–16: The reason for departure: tension with Laban's family, God's revelation, Rachel and Leah's consent.
   31:17–43: *Escape and the theft of the teraphim: "Rachel stole the teraphim that belonged to her father. Jacob deceived Laban (lit. "stole Laban's heart").*
   31:43–32:2: The covenant with Laban and the angels' revelation to Jacob (and naming of that place).
5. **In Canaan**
   32:3–33:17: Jacob and Esau: Jacob "returns" the stolen blessings (Jacob is active).
   33:18–34:31: *Jacob's sons deceive the men of Shechem ("Jacob's sons answered Shechem and Hamor with deceit").*
   35:1–15: The vow is paid at Bethel and revelation: "Be fruitful and multiply" (and naming of the place).
6. **Coming full circle in Canaan: Jacob's sons**
   35:16–20: Rachel's death and Benjamin's birth.
   35:21–22: *Reuben lies with his father's concubine (an act of deceit?)*
   35:23–29: The list of Jacob's twelve sons, and reunion with Isaac.

---

10. In this case, it is not clear to what extent Jacob is actually deceiving Laban by using these shoots. As seen in context, it may be a common shepherd's trick that Laban expects him to use. At the same time, the text implies that this is a trick Jacob does behind Laban's back, perhaps in violation of their agreement.
11. This dream is not described by the narrator – only through Jacob's report to his wives. Yet because Jacob tells them of a dream that he has already had, one that describes how Jacob's flock has already increased, it can be read as the aftermath of his deception. We have already discussed the relationship between his actions and the dream in context.

Each of these six units comprise three scenes; to reassure those disappointed that the number falls short of a symbolic seven, an additional unit within the Jacob cycle – the story of Isaac in Gerar, which I will discuss below – also comprises three scenes.

At the heart of each of these units – which follow a clear geographic pattern as well as a thematic pattern – is an act of deceit. Various characters are responsible for these deceptions; some, like Jacob and Laban, are sometimes the deceivers and sometimes deceived. The deceptions are sometimes described as such with the root "*mirma*" (deceit) or a similar word, such as "stole." Reuben's deed is not explicitly described as a deception, but as he goes behind his father's back to manipulate the family dynamics, it certainly falls under this category.

This repetition raises several questions: In each scene, is the deception successful? Does the deceiver achieve what he or she sought? Secondly, how does the text perceive each of these deceptions? Is there an overall pattern in this respect? And above all – why is this motif so central in the Jacob cycle?

The answer to the first question is disturbing. With the exception of one, all these deceptions achieve their goal: Jacob obtains the blessings that are intended for his brother; Laban successfully tricks Jacob into marrying Leah; Jacob's flock increases; Simeon and Levi rescue Dinah and avenge her honor; Reuben (presumably) prevents Jacob from living with Bilhah after Rachel's death.

In only one scene, the deception fails: Jacob flees from Laban's house, but Laban catches up with him. Were it not for God's warning, Laban would have harmed Jacob and his family, or at least forced them back to Haran.

The Jacob cycle, therefore, progresses through acts of deceit – by Jacob or against Jacob. In each of the six units, the act of deceit is the central unit: the first scene anticipates the deception; the third scene describes God's response to it in some form of blessing (revelation, the birth of children). But in this respect the fourth unit, Jacob's flight from Haran, is also anomalous: it is the only unit which also *begins* with divine revelation. Moreover, the revelation at the end of this unit only takes place after Jacob's covenant with Laban, and its form is unusual: Jacob encounters angels, but they do not utter a word.

We can connect these two phenomena through the following formulation: each successful deception is succeeded by revelation, but Jacob's flight from Laban is *preceded* by a revelation that commands Jacob to return to Canaan, and in this context, Jacob's attempt at deceit emerges as superfluous. In fact, this is obvious from the outset: when God commands Jacob to return, He also promises: "I will be with you" (31:3). Thus there is no need to "steal Laban's heart" or the teraphim that would make it difficult for him to find them – for God has promised to protect Jacob on his way home.

It is tempting to adopt the other side of the coin – that is, to perceive the revelation that follows this failed deception as validation that Jacob's attempt was justified. Simeon and Levi's scheme – a deception of the highest order! – is validated not only by the lack of divine criticism, but through the "godly terror" that strikes the entire region when Jacob and his family pass through. In many senses, Jacob's theft of the blessings is validated by his father's blessings and God's promise of protection as he leaves for Haran. Nor is Jacob criticized for his attempt to increase his flock at Laban's expense; God's revelation and the dream he describes to his wives support his course of action.

Yet two issues pose a challenge to this theory. Firstly, this would assume that Laban's deception is also a positive act that propels the plot in the desired direction. Although this goes against Jacob's interests, his marriage to Leah reveals that Jacob is supposed to marry the firstborn daughter, and Laban's deception fulfills this. I have already discussed this reading in context, and if the reader is willing to adopt it, then Laban's deception is consistent with the broader pattern of this motif in the cycle (see further below).

Secondly, because this concerns an entire narrative cycle, we have to take the broader conclusions into account, rather than the individual evaluation of each narrative. While the initial impression might be that Jacob has triumphed by taking his brother's blessings, his "return" of these blessings later on sheds new light on the earlier scene: "In biblical narrative, which maintains certain moral standards, the disguised [Jacob] will eventually pay for this deceit, and indeed, later events that befall Jacob and his mother testify that there is a Judge and there is justice."[12]

With this in mind, I wish to rephrase the question: What does this theme serve in the Jacob cycle? Whether or not individual acts of deceit can be justified, it cannot be that so many scenes hinge on this motif unless there is a higher literary purpose. This certainly demands explanation given that Jacob is initially characterized as an "*ish tam*."

In this context, it seems that deceit serves as a foil to divine revelation or blessing: in each unit, the second scene is an act of deceit, whereas the third scene is an act of God. As I discuss in the introduction, in the Jacob cycle, human initiative and divine intervention are in constant negotiation. Unlike the Abraham cycle, where the protagonist rarely acts without divine accompaniment,[13] in Jacob's cycle, the characters constantly act, take initiative, and make decisions without God's input or command. This is true throughout the cycle: there is no mention of God at all in the birthright scene; nor, of course, is there any divine intervention when Jacob steals the blessings; God does not intervene in Jacob's meeting with Rachel at the well, nor in his marriage with Leah (in stark contrast to the story of Isaac's betrothal!); God's attitude toward Jacob and Esau's reunion is not clear (though certain hints can be garnered from the struggle with the angel). The same model also applies to Jacob's sons' deeds: Simeon and Levi rescue Dinah without any divine help – unlike the story of Sarai and Pharaoh, where God intervenes directly.

The motif of deception – both justified and unjustified – is an expression of human initiative; of the need for manipulation and guile to achieve one's ends. In order to navigate a world full of conflicting interests, the hero must resort to manipulation – to donning his brother's

12. Zakovitch, *Jacob*, 37.

13. The story of Abraham and the four kings is an exception that proves the rule. In my analysis of Genesis 14, I argue that God's absence from the story of Lot's rescue characterizes Abraham as a key political figure on the global map (Grossman, *Abraham*, 90–94).

hunting clothes; to peeled shoots propped up by a trough of water. Were God to interfere – as the reader expects, after the Abraham cycle – there would be no need for any deceit, but now it is the characters who control the narrative arena, and the plot is propelled by their decisions.

At the same time, however, God accompanies Jacob wherever he goes. His recurring revelations encourage him and promise him protection. Jacob acts as he does, while God travels along with him, occasionally guiding him when necessary (as when he is bid to go to Bethel to pay his vow). The revelation that follows validates his situation – these revelations generally encourage Jacob on his way more than actively instruct him how to act.

This explains why the attempt to deceive Laban deviates from the usual pattern. In this unit, God intervenes from the outset, demanding that Jacob return home. Under these circumstances, Jacob and Rachel's attempted deceit does not change the plot; on the contrary, it almost brings disaster upon the family.

The Story of Isaac (Chapter 26)

In light of this discussion, I wish to return to the seventh literary unit I omitted from the general structure – the story of Isaac and Rebecca in Gerar. This unit also comprises three-four scenes, and its pattern is consistent with the aforementioned structure:

> 1–5: God's revelation to Isaac, instructing him to move to Gerar.
> 6–11: Deceit – Isaac pretends that Rebecca is his sister.
> 12–22: The quarrel over the wells and Isaac is driven out.
> 23–33: A second revelation, followed by his covenant with Abimelech in Beersheba.

Given that the covenant with Abimelech is the aftermath of Isaac's quarrel over the wells, these two scenes can arguably be combined into one. If so, then this unit can also be considered a story in three acts, with deceit at its center, just like the rest of the Jacob cycle. Isaac claims that Rebecca is his sister, which is liable to lead to a Philistine sleeping with his wife (26:10). In context, we already explored how this chapter is in profound dialogue with the story of Jacob's exile. Now, within this pattern of deceit coupled with revelation, it emerges that the story of Isaac follows the same pattern as the rest of the Jacob cycle.

In this respect, Isaac has a unique status within Genesis. As mentioned, God does not appear to the Philistine king Abimelech – in contrast to the parallel incident with Abraham (Gen. 20), and thus Isaac's act of deceit is a reflection of his own initiative, similar to Jacob and his sons. And similarly to Jacob, the revelation in Beersheba encourages Isaac after he leaves Gerar: "I am the God of your father Abraham. Do not be afraid, for I am with you. I will bless you and multiply your descendants for the sake of Abraham My servant" (26:24). God does not make any demands of Isaac in this revelation, but merely encourages him and validates his decisions.

Yet Isaac's story also begins with revelation; one that points him in a different direction than his original plan. While Isaac intends to go down to Egypt because of the famine, God stops him and demands that he travel to nearby Gerar instead. This recalls the explicit intervention in the Abraham cycle, when God visits Abraham in his own tent, bringing tidings for his wife; engages in a fierce debate about the fate of Sodom; and changes Abraham's mind about his son Ishmael. Thus, at the beginning of his brief stint in the spotlight, Isaac is portrayed as Abraham's son, but by its end he is characterized as Jacob's father.

It is thus no surprise that the Joseph cycle is one long ruse from beginning to end. The brothers sell Joseph and dip his coat in blood to deceive their father about his beloved son's fate; Judah tricks Tamar (38:11) and Tamar tricks him back (38:14–18); Potiphar's wife deceives her household and her husband; and finally, Joseph hides his true identity from his brothers and deceives them when they go down to Egypt to seek relief from the famine. Throughout this cycle, God waits in the wings, behind the scenes. There is no revelation, and it is up to the human actors to doom or redeem themselves.

OUR FATHER JACOB DID NOT DIE

The Jacob cycle has come to an end, but Jacob's story is not over. The Joseph cycle, which concludes the book of Genesis, constantly echoes the Jacob cycle – sometimes explicitly, as when Reuben loses the birthright because he "went up onto [his] father's bed and defiled it" (49:3–4), and sometimes in covert but unmistakable dialogue (such as the birth of twins to Judah – 38:27–30). Unlike the Abraham cycle, which ends with his death and burial, Jacob does not die at the end of his narrative cycle; he only dies toward the end of the Joseph cycle. Although he plays a minor role, his presence in the Joseph cycle makes it difficult to summarize his character at the end of his own narrative cycle.

In a certain sense, the Jacob cycle's meta-objective still remains a mystery even after close analysis, and perhaps this is no coincidence. As noted in the introduction, unlike Abraham, who is granted God's constant presence and revelation after revelation, Jacob receives the promise of divine protection, but its fulfillment is often hidden from the reader. Hidden providence is vital to the story of a protagonist who must navigate a world of conflicting interests. God's hand is not fully hidden as it is in the Joseph cycle, but the arena is still kept clear to allow for human action. Jacob must act in parallel to God, and when he does not step up to the task, his sons take his place.

The Talmud describes a meal shared by R. Naḥman – among the greatest of Babylonian Amora'im, the head of the Yeshiva in Pumbedita – and R. Yitzḥak – among the greatest of Amora'im in Israel. R. Naḥman asks R. Yitzḥak to share some words of Torah. R. Yitzḥak quotes R. Yoḥanan: "One may not speak during a meal, lest the esophagus precede the trachea, and lead to choking." The Talmud then continues and adds that after the meal, R. Yitzḥak quotes R. Yoḥanan again: "Our father Jacob did not die" (Taanit 5b).

This is a surprising statement, and R. Naḥman justifiably points out that Jacob's death, mourning, embalming, and burial is explicitly described in Genesis (49:33–50:13). R. Yitzḥak responds:

> I am interpreting a verse, as it is stated: "Therefore do not fear, Jacob My servant, says the Lord, neither be dismayed, Israel, for I will save you from afar, and your seed from the land of their captivity" (Jer. 30:10). This verse juxtaposes Jacob to his seed: Just as his seed is alive [when redeemed], so too [Jacob himself] is alive.

Just as Israel seem to die away in exile and captivity, but will one day return to live in their homeland, Jacob, too, seems to die, but he truly lives on forever through his descendants (see Rashi, ibid.). Abraham and Isaac serve their purpose in Genesis and die, but Jacob, who founds the people of Israel, continues to live on through them. Jeremiah's prophecy, quoted by R. Yitzḥak, refers to the entire nation as "My servant Jacob" – he is his people, and they are him.

For the sake of our discussion, I wish to explore the relationship between R. Yoḥanan's two quotations – that which R. Yitzḥak mentions during their meal, and that which he quotes after it. Ostensibly, the first is a brief excuse explaining why he cannot talk during their meal – "lest the esophagus precede the trachea" – while the second is a more leisurely tribute to his esteemed teacher, R. Yoḥanan.

Despite the difference in tone, both of R. Yoḥanan's statements discuss life and death, although the first can hardly be classified as "Torah." It is simply common sense; a practical tip that touches upon the dangers of everyday life and the frailty of the human body. When eating, it is best to refrain from speech – even meaningful speech.

By contrast, R. Yoḥanan's second statement is practically antithetical: far removed from reality, it denies the essence of life itself – the inevitability of death. Even after R. Naḥman reminds R. Yitzḥak that Jacob was mourned, embalmed, and buried, he adheres to his stance and insists that he has "textual proof" – in this way these verses transcend reality and thus triumph over death.

This juxtaposition is an apt reflection of Jacob the biblical protagonist. On the one hand, Jacob's life is a series of obstacles, and he must fight to survive the human jungle of conflicting interests, deception, and manipulation. From the womb he grasps at his brother's heel; he wheedles his brother out of his birthright, and he snatches away his blessings. He flees to Haran and manipulates the flock under his devious father-in-law's jealous eye. His wife steals the teraphim in order to outwit Laban. His sons deceive the people of Shechem to rescue and avenge their sister. Alone on the road, Jacob is intent on survival. He overlooks exalted blessings of divine promise and fixes his gaze on the way ahead: on "food to eat and clothes to wear." Jacob cannot be enticed into philosophical discussion or Torah study when he is eating: he remains silent, "lest the esophagus precede the trachea."

But on the other hand, Jacob sees a divine ladder stretching from heaven to earth; he builds pillars, makes vows, and encounters angels. He struggles with God and with men and prevails; he is the heir and receiver of God's eternal promise. His name will live on through his descendants, far transcending the banalities of day-to-day life. Jacob will never die.

Out of the forefathers, it is Jacob who serves as the archetype for Israel in exile; as Ramban hints, Jacob's exile in Haran is an omen of the long exile his descendants, too, will experience. But Jacob is "juxtaposed to his seed" – just as Jacob eventually returns to Bethel, pays his vow, and receives a new name, so too will Israel eventually emerge from exile, return to the land of their ancestors, and spread out to the west and the east, to the north and the south.

List of Abbreviations

Abbreviations used in footnotes and bibliography:
AB – Anchor Bible
ABD – Anchor Bible Dictionary
ACEBT – Amsterdamse Cahiers voor Exegese en Bijbelse Theologie
ANET – Ancient Near Eastern Texts
BA – The Biblical Archaeologist
BASOR – Bulletin of the American Schools of Oriental Research
BDB – Brown-Driver-Briggs (Hebrew and English Lexicon)
BDD – Bekhol Derakheikha Da'ehu
BZ – Biblische Zeitschrift
BZAW – Beihefte zur Zeitschrift für die alttestamentliche Wissenschaft
CAD – Chicago Assyrian Dictionary
CBC – Cambridge Bible Commentary
CBQ – Catholic Bible Quarterly
EvQ – Evangelical Quarterly
FOTL – Forms of Old Testament Literature Series
HAT – Handbuch zum Alten Testament
ICC – International Critical Commentary
JANES – Journal of Ancient Near Eastern Studies
JAOS – Journal of the American Oriental Society
JBL – Journal of Biblical Literature
JBQ – Jewish Bible Quarterly
JCS – Journal of Cuneiform Studies
JETS – Journal of the Evangelical Theological Society
JHS – Journal of Hellenic Studies
JJS – Journal of Jewish Studies

JSOT – *Journal for the Study of the Old Testament*
JSOTSup – *Journal for the Study of the Old Testament, Supplement*
JSS – *Journal of Semitic Studies*
JTS – *Journal of Theological Studies*
NAB – New American Bible
NAC – New American Commentay
NCB – New Century Bible
NEB – New English Bible
NIB – New Interpreter's Bible
NICOT – New International Commentary on the Old Testament
NIDOTTE – *New International Dictionary of Old Testament Theology and Exegesis*
NIV – New International Version
OTL – Old Testament Library Commentary Series
OTS – *Oudtestamentische Studiën*
RB – *Révue Biblique*
SJOT – *Scandinavian Journal of the Old Testament*
TDOT – *Theological Dictionary of the Old Testament*
VT – *Vetus Testamentum*
VTSup – Vetus Testamentum, Supplements
WBC – Word Biblical Commentary
WTJ – *Westminster Theological Journal*
ZAW – *Zeitschrift für die alttestamentliche Wissenschaft*

Bibliography

Abramsky, S. "The Woman Looking Out the Window." *Beit Mikra* 28 (1994): 124–14 [Hebrew].

Ackerman, J. S. "The Literary Context of the Moses Birth Story." In K. R. R. Gros Louis, ed. *Literary Interpretation of Biblical Narratives*. Vol. 1. Nashville, 1974, 74–119.

Ackerman, S. and B. D. Cox. "Rachel's Tomb." *JBL* 128 (2009): 135–48.

Ackroyd, P. R. "Hosea and Jacob." *VT* 13 (1963): 245–59.

Adar, Z. *The Book of Genesis – Introduction to the Biblical World*. Tel Aviv, 2007 [Hebrew].

Agyenta, A. "The Jacob Cycle Narratively Speaking: The Question of the Extent of the Jacob Cycle in the Book of Genesis." *Journal of Northwest Semitic Languages* 31 (2005): 59–74.

Aharoni, R. "Jacob and Esau – A Play in Three Acts." *Beit Mikra* 23 (1966): 327–40 [Hebrew].

Aharoni, R. "On Three Similar Stories in the Book of Genesis (Genesis 12, 20, 26)." *Beit Mikra* 24 (1979): 223–13 [Hebrew].

Aharoni, Y. "*Gerar*." *Encyclopedia Biblica*. Vol. 2. 561–64.

Ahituv, Y. "Father Jacob: Father of the Hebrew Slaves." *Megadim* 48 (2006): 9–22 [Hebrew].

Ahuvia, A. "And God Appeared to Jacob Again (Genesis 35:1–15)." *Beit Mikra* (1958): 99–101 [Hebrew].

Albertz, R. "Die soziale und rituelle Bedeutung von Essen und Trinken in der Jakoberzählung." In M. Geiger, C. M. Maier, and U. Schmidt, eds. *Essen und Trinken in der Bibel: Ein literarisches Festmahl für Rainer Kessler zum 65*. Gütersloher Verlagshaus, 2009, 131–46.

Albright, W. F. "The Names 'Israel' and 'Judah' with an Excursus on the Etymology of *Tôdâh* and *Tôrâh*." *JBL* 46 (1927): 151–85.

Alden, R. L. "A-T-F." *NIDOTTE* 3: 381–82.

Alexander, P. S. "Early Jewish Geography." *ABD* 2: 977–88.

Alexander, T. D. "Are the Wife/Sister Incidents of Genesis Literary Compositional Variants?" VT 42 (1992): 145–53.

Allen, C. G. "On Me Be the Curse, My Son: Who was Rebecca?." In R. M. Gross, ed. *Beyond Androcentrism: New Essays on Women and Religion*. Missoula, 1977, 183–216.

Alter, R. *Genesis*. New York, 1996.

Alter, R. *The Art of Biblical Narrative*. New York, 1981.

Alter, R. *The Five Books of Moses*. New York and London, 2004.

Alterman, N. *City of the Dove*. Tel Aviv, 1978 [Hebrew].

Amit, Y. *Hidden and Revealed in the Bible: Overt, Indirect and Mostly Covert Polemics*. Tel Aviv, 2003 [Hebrew].

Andersen F. I. and D. N. Freedman. *Hosea*. AB. New York, 1983.

Andersen, F. I. *The Sentence in Biblical Hebrew*. Berlin, 1980.

Anderson, J. E. *Jacob and the Divine Trickster: A Theology of Deception and YHWH's Fidelity to the Ancestral Promise in the Jacob Cycle*. Diss., Baylor University, 2010.

Angel, H. "'Heeling' in the Torah: A Psychological-Spiritual Reading of the Snake and Jacob's Wrestling Match." *JBQ* 42 (2014): 178–84.

Ararat, N. "Two Encounters by the Well in Aram Naharaim: An Intertextual Analysis of Two Narratives." *Shaanan* 12 (2007): 15–23 [Hebrew].

Ararat, N. *Truth and Grace in the Bible*. Jerusalem, 1993 [Hebrew].

Arzi, A. "The Priestly Blessing, A Model of the Jewish People's Needs." *BDD* 20 (2008): 85–99 [Hebrew].

Assis, E. *From Moses to Joshua, from Miracles to Nature: A Literary Analysis of the Chapters of Conquest in the Book of Joshua*. Jerusalem, 2015 [Hebrew].

Assis, E. *For His People and His Country: Three Leaders in the Book of Judges*. Tel Aviv, 2006 [Hebrew].

Assis, E. *Identity in Conflict: The Struggle Between Jacob and Esau, Israel and Edom*. Alon Shvut, 2009 [Hebrew].

Astour, M. C. "Political and Cosmic Symbolism in Genesis 14 and Its Babylonian Sources." In A. Altmann, ed. *Biblical Motifs: Origins and Transformations*. Cambridge, 1966, 65–112.

Avishur, Y. "Literary Formulae for the Description of Journeys in the Bible and Ugaritic Literature." *Beit Mikra* 30 (1985): 133–41.

Avishur, Y. *Genesis*. World Bible Series. Tel Aviv, 1993.

Baden, J. S. "A Narrative Pattern and Its Role in Source Criticism." Hebrew Studies 49 (2008): 41–54.

Bar Efrat, S. *The Artistic Design of Biblical Narrative*. 2004 (2nd ed. – Hebrew).

Bartel, A. "A Study of the Lists of Genesis 36." *Beit Mikra* 32 (1987): 364–72 [Hebrew].

Bauer, H. "Die hebräischen Eigennamen als sprachliche Erkenntnisquelle." *ZAW* 48 (1930): 73–80.

Bazak, A. "Each Month and Each Shabbat." In Rabbi E. Bick and Y. Feintuch, eds. *Torat Etzion – Bamidbar*. Alon Shvut, 2006, 401–6 [Hebrew].

Bazak, A. *Starting Point: Anecdotes for the Weekly Parasha*. Rishon Lezion. 2009 (2nd ed. – Hebrew).

Bechtel, L. M. "What If Dinah Is Not Raped? (Genesis 34)." *JSOT* 62 (1994): 19–36.

Ben Reuven, S. "The Mandrakes Transaction as Retribution for the Birthright Transaction." *Beit Mikra* 28 (1983): 230–31 [Hebrew].

Ben Reuven, S. "The Story of Dinah's Rape and Its Approaches." *Beit Mikra* 43 (1998): 319–22 [Hebrew].

Ben Yehuda, A. *Dictionary of the Old and New Hebrew Language*. Jerusalem and Tel Aviv, 1909–1999 [Hebrew].

Benor, Y. L. "Blood Groom and Jacob-Israel." *Beit Mikra* 19 (1934): 435–40. [Hebrew].

Berlin, A. "Literary Approaches to Biblical Literature: General Observations and a Case Study of Genesis 34." In F. E. Greenspahn, ed. *The Hebrew Bible: New Insights and Scholarship*. New York, 2008, 45–75.

Berlin, A. *Poetics and the Interpretation of Biblical Narrative*. Sheffield, 1983.

Berman, Y. "Jacob's Four Pillars of a Single Foundation." *Megadim* 13 (2011): 9–23 [Hebrew].

Bin-Nun, Y. *Chapters of the Fathers: Studies of the Patriarch Cycles in Genesis*. Alon Shvut, 2003 [Hebrew].

Bledstein, A. J. "Binder, Trickster, Heel and Hairy-Man: Rereading Genesis 27 as a Trickster Tale Told by a Woman." In A. Brenner, ed. *Feminist Companion to Genesis*. Sheffield, 1993, 282–95.

Blidstein, Y. "The Deed of Shechem: Collective Punishment and Contemporary Halachic Thought." *Et HaDaat* 1 (2017): 48–55 [Hebrew].

Blum, E. "Die Komplexität der Überlieferung: zur diachronen und synchronen Auslegung von Gen. 32,23–33." In W. Oswald, ed. *Textgestalt und Komposition: Exegetische Beiträge zu Tora und Vordere Propheten*. Tübingen, 2010, 43–84.

Boase, E. "Life in the Shadows: The Role and Function of Isaac in Genesis: Synchronic and Diachronic Readings." VT 51 (2001): 312–55.

Boling, R. G. *Judges*. AB. New York, 1981.

Bompiani, B. "Style Switching in the Jacob and Laban Narratives." *Hebrew Studies* 55 (2014): 43–57.

Brenner, A. "My Beloved Is Bright and Glowing." *Beit Mikra* 27 (1982): 166–73 [Hebrew].

Brenner, A. "*Atufim U'Keshurim*: Genesis 30:41–42." *Beit Mikra* 24 (1979): 77–80 [Hebrew].

Breuer, M. *Chapters of Genesis* (two parts). Alon Shvut, 2009 [Hebrew].

Briend, J. "Genèse 35, 16–22A." In J-D. Macchi and T. Römer, eds. *Jacob: commentaire à plusieurs voix de Gen 25–36. Mélanges offerts à Albert de Pury* (2001). Genève, 1989, 267–75.

Brin, J. *Studies of the Bible and Megillot*. Tel Aviv, 1994 [Hebrew].

Brooke, G. J. "D-B-K." *NIDOTTE*. Vol. 1. 910–12.

Buber, M. *Ways of the Bible*. Jerusalem, 2004 [Hebrew].

Burrows, M. "The Complaint of Laban's Daughters." *JAOS* 57 (1937): 259–76.

Burton, S. Z. *Orot Yaakov: Selected Sermons About the Deeds of the Forefathers*. 2017 [Hebrew].

Cassuto, M. D. "*Alluf*." *Encyclopedia Biblica*. Vol. 1. 332 [Hebrew].

Cassuto, M. D. *From Noah to Abraham*. Jerusalem, 2009 (5th ed. – Hebrew).

Cassuto, M. D. *Genesis and Its Structure*. Translated by E. Hartum. Jerusalem, 1957 [Hebrew].

Clifford, R. G. "Genesis 25:19–34." Interpretation 45 (1991): 397–401.

Coats, G. W. "Moses in Midian." *JBL* 92 (1973): 3–10.

Coats, G. W. *Genesis*. FOTL. Michigan, 1983.

Cogan, M. "'The City I Chose' – Jerusalem in Light of Deuteronomistic Literature." *Tarbiz* 55 (1956): 301–9 [Hebrew].

Cohen, J. M. "Patriarchal History: Action and Reaction." *JBQ* 35 (2007): 161–65.

Cohn, H. "Shalem: City or Safely?" *JBQ* 36 (2008): 121–23.

Conrad, J. "K-SH-R." *TDOT* 13: 196–201.

Cotter, D. W. *Genesis*. Berit Olam. Collegeville, 2003.

Couffignal, R. "Le Songe de Jacob: Approches nouvelles de Gn 28, 10–22." *Biblica* 58 (1977): 342–60.

Craigie, P. C. *The Book of Deuteronomy*. NICOT. Grand Rapids, 1976.

Cross, F. M. *Canaanite Myth and Hebrew Epic: Essays in the History of the Religion of Israel*. Cambridge, MA, 1971.

Culley, R. C. *Studies in the Structure of Hebrew Narrative*. Philadelphia, 1976.

Curtis, E. M. "Structure, Style and Context as a Key to Interpreting Jacob's Encounter at Peniel." *JETS* 30 (1987): 129–37.

Daube, D. *Studies in Biblical Law*. London, 1947.

Daube D. and R. Yaron. "Jacob's Reception by Laban." *JSS* 1 (1956): 60–62.

Davidson, R. *Genesis 1–11*. CBC. Cambridge, 1973.

Davidson, R. *Genesis 12–50*. CBC. Cambridge, 1979.

De Montaigne, M. *Essays*. Translated by Charles Cotton. www.gutenberg.org.

De Vaux, R. *Daily Life in Israel in Biblical Times*. Translated by A. Amir. Two Volumes. Tel Aviv, 1969 [Hebrew].

DeWitt, D. S. "The Generations of Genesis." *EvQ* 48 (1976): 196–211.

Diebner, B. J. "Eine 'enge Definition' von 'Israel': Genesis 35, 6–15." In J-D. Macchi and Römer T., eds. *Jacob: commentaire à plusieurs voix de Gen 25–36. Mélanges offerts à Albert de Pury* (2001), Genève, 1989, 257–66.

Dieckmann, D. "Gen. 26 als Segenerzählung." *Biblische Zeitschrift* 49 (2005): 264–74.

Dieckmann, D. *Segen für Isaak: Eine rezeptionsästhetische Auslegung von Gen 26 und Kotexten*. Berlin and New York, 2003.

Dillmann, A. *Genesis: Critical and Exegetically Expounded*. Translated by B. Stevenson. 2 vols. Edinburgh, 1897.

Dishi, G. *Jacob's Family Dynamics: Climbing the Rungs of the Ladder*. New York, 2010.

Drews, R. "Canaanites and Philistines." *JSOT* 81 (1998): 39–61.

Driver, G. R. "Studies in the Vocabulary of the Old Testament." *JTS* 31 (1930): 250–57.

Dvir, Y. *Destiny and Purpose of the Biblical Name.* Tel Aviv, 2009 [Hebrew].

Ehrlich, A. *The Bible Literally* – Torah. Berlin, 1890 [Hebrew].

Ehrlich, E. L. *Der Traum im Alten Testament* (BZAW 73). Berlin, 1953.

Eising, H. *Formgeschichtliche Untersuchung zur Jakobserzählung der Genesis.* Diss. Miinster, 1940.

Eldar, A. "The Story of the Servant and Rebecca." *Alon Shvut* 153 (2009): 137–49 [Hebrew].

Elitzur, Y. "*Tzafon.*" In *Places in the Parsha: Geography and Meaning in the Bible.* Tel Aviv, 2015 [Hebrew].

Elitzur, Y. *Israel and the Bible: Geographical, Historical, and Philosophical Studies.* Ramat Gan, 2005 [Hebrew].

Emanueli, Y. M. *Genesis – Explanations and Illuminations.* Tel Aviv, 1978 [Hebrew].

Emerton, J. A. *Studies in the Pentateuch* (VTSup 41). Leiden, 1990.

Emmerson, G. I. *Hosea: An Israelite Prophet in Judean Perspective* (JSOTSup 28). Sheffield, 1984.

Eshbal, D. "*Akuddim, Nekuddim U'Veruddim.*" *Beit Mikra* 10 (1966): 48–52 [Hebrew].

Evan Shoshan, A. *New Concordance.* Revised ed. Jerusalem, 1988 [Hebrew].

Evans, C. D. "The Patriarch Jacob: An Innocent Man." *Bible Review* 2 (1986): 32–37.

Even, Y. *Fictional Characters.* Tel Aviv, 1980.

Fabry, H. "Y-KH-Ḥ." *TDOT* 6: 64–71

Feinstein, E. L. *Sexual Pollution in the Hebrew Bible.* Oxford, 2014.

Feintuch, Y. "The Ladder and the Well – A Study of the Jacob Stories." *Megadim* 39 (2004): 9–32 [Hebrew].

Felix, Y. "Inheritance in the Case of Jacob and the Sheep." *Tehumin* 3 (1982): 461–72 [Hebrew].

Fewell D. N. and D. Gunn. "Tipping the Balance: Sternberg's Reader and the Rape of Dinah." *JBL* 110 (1991): 193–211.

Fidler, R. "Genesis XV: Sequence and Unity." VT 57 (2007): 162–80.

Fidler, R. *"Shall False Dreams Speak?" Dreams of Revelation in the Bible and Their Place in the History of Faith and Tradition in Ancient Israel.* Jerusalem, 1995 [Hebrew].

Finkelstein, J. J. "An Old Babylonian Herding Contract and Genesis 31:38f." *JAOS* 88 (1968): 30–36.

Fishbane, M. A. "Composition and Structure in the Jacob Cycle." *JJS* 26 (1975): 15–38.

Fishbane, M. A. *Biblical Text and Texture*. Oxford, 1979.

Fleischman, J. "Social and Legal Aspects of the Shechem and Dinah Affair (Genesis 34)." *Annual of Bible and Ancient Near Eastern Studies* 13 (2002): 141–55 [Hebrew].

Fleming, E. E. "'She Went to Inquire of the Lord': Independent Divination in Genesis 25:22." *Union Seminary Quarterly Review* 60 (2007): 1–10.

Flynn, S. W. "The Teraphim in Light of Mesopotamian and Egyptian Evidence." *CBQ* 74 (2012): 694–711.

Fokkelman, J. P. "Jacob as a Character." In C. Focant and A. Wénin, eds. *Analyse narrative et Bible*. Leuven, 2005, 3–17.

Fokkelman, J. P. "Jakob en de geheimen van de nacht." *ACEBT* 27 (2012): 97–106.

Fokkelman, J. P. *Narrative Art in Genesis: Specimens of Stylistic and Structural Analysis*. 2nd ed.. Sheffield, 1991.

Fokkelman, J. P. *Narrative Art and Poetry in the Books of Samuel*, IV. Assen, 1993.

Frank, A. S. "The 'Face of God': Esau in Canonical Context." In C. A. Evans and S. Talmon, eds. *The Quest for Context and Meaning*. New York, 1997, 3–25.

Frankel, D. "The Final Form of the Rape of Dinah Narrative in Light of Text Criticism and Redaction." *Annual of Bible and Ancient Near Eastern Studies* 25 (2017): 13–57 [Hebrew].

Frankel, L. *Biblical Chapters: New Methods of Interpretation*. Jerusalem, 1981 [Hebrew].

Frankena, R. "Some Remarks on the Semitic Background of Chapters XXIX–XXXI of the Book of Genesis." *OTS* 17 (1972): 53–64.

Fretheim, T. E. "Which Blessing Does Isaac Give Jacob?." In A. O. Bellis and J.S. Kaminsky, eds. *Jews, Christians, and the Theology of the Hebrew Scripture*. Atlanta, 2000, 279–91.

Freud, S. *Culture, Religion and Judaism* (Selected Works, vol. 5). Tel Aviv, 2008.

Freud, S. *Totem and Taboo* (Selected Works, vol. 9, translated by R. Ginzburg). Tel Aviv, 2013 [Hebrew].

Frisch, A. "'Your Brother Came with Guile': Responses to an Explicit Moral Evaluation in Biblical Narrative." *Prooftexts* 23 (2003): 271–96.

Frisch, A. *The Great Schism: The Story of the Division of the Kingdom in the Book of Kings*. Be'er Sheva, 2004 [Hebrew].

Frolov, S. "Sarah, Rebecca, and the Unchangeable Ruble: Unrecognized Folkloric Background of the 'Wife-Sister' Stories in Genesis." Biblische Notizen 150 (2011): 3–7.

Fuchs, E. *Sexual Politics in the Biblical Narrative: Reading the Hebrew Bible as a Woman*. Sheffield, 2000.

Galender, S. *Genesis*. 2 vols. The Open University, Ra'anana, 2011 [Hebrew].

Galpaz-Feller, P. "The Stela of King Piye: A Brief Consideration of 'Clean' and 'Unclean' in Ancient Egypt and the Bible." *Revue biblique* 102 (1995): 506–21.

Gamberoni. "B-L-H." *TDOT* 2: 128–31.

Garsiel, M. "The Literary Structure and Message of the Jacob and Esau Narratives." *Biblical Thought* 4 (2004): 63–81 [Hebrew].

Garsiel, M. *I Samuel: A Literary Study of Systematic Comparisons, Analogies, and Parallels*. Ramat Gan, 1973 [Hebrew].

Garsiel, M. *Midrashic Name Derivations in the Bible*. Ramat Gan, 1948 [Hebrew].

Geoghegan, J. C. "The 'Biblical' Origins of Passover." In *Sacred History*. Winona Lake, IN, 2008, 147–62.

Gesenius, W. *Hebrew Grammar*. Translated by A. E. Cowley. 2nd ed. Oxford, 1910.

Gibran, K. *Sand and Foam*. Delhi, 2012.

Gilad, H. "Encounters by the Well." *Beit Mikra* 22 (1977): 220–23 [Hebrew].

Ginat, L. "'*VeHaya Kaasher Tarid*': A Study of Isaac's Blessing of Esau (Genesis 27:31–40)." *Beit Mikra* 36 (1991): 84–90 [Hebrew].

Good, E. M. *Irony in the Old Testament*. Philadelphia, 1965.

Gordon, C. "The Story of Jacob and Laban in the Light of the Nuzi Texts." *BASOR* 66 (1937): 25–27.

Gordon, C. H. "Biblical Customs and the Nuzi Tablets." *BA* 3 (1940): 1–12.

Greenberg, M. "Another Look at Rachel's Theft of the Teraphim." *JBL* 81 (1962): 239–48.

Greenberg, U. Z. *Complete Works*. Edited by Dan Miron. Jerusalem, 1996 [Hebrew].

Greenstein, E. "On Some Metaphors in the Book of Job." *Biblical Studies and Interpretation* 9 (2006): 231–41 [Hebrew].

Griffiths, J. G. "The Celestial Ladder and the Gate of Heaven (Gen 28:12 and 17)." *Expository Times* 76 (1964–5): 229–30.

Grintz, Y. M. *The Origin of Generations*. Tel Aviv, 2009 [Hebrew].

Grisanti, M. A. "P-G-A." *NIDOTTE*. Vol. 3. 575–76.

Grossfeld, B. ed. *The Targum Onqelos to Genesis*. Wilmington, 1988.

Grossman, A. *Pious and Rebellious: Jewish Women in Europe in the Middle Ages*. Jerusalem, 2001 [Hebrew].

Grossman, J. *Abram to Abraham: A Literary Analysis of the Abraham Narrative* (Das Alte Testament im Dialog, 11). Bern, 2016.

Grossman, J. *Ambiguity in the Biblical Narrative and Its Contribution to the Literary Formation*. PhD diss., Bar-Ilan University, 2006.

Grossman, J. "Associative Meanings in the Character Evaluation of Lot's Daughters." *CBQ* 76 (2014): 40–57.

Grossman, J. *Creation: The Story of Beginnings*. Jerusalem and New York, 2019.

Grossman, J. "Different Dreams: Two Models of Interpretation for Three Pairs of Dreams (Genesis 37–50)." *JBL* 135 (2016): 717–32.

Grossman, J. "Divine Command and Human Initiative: A Literary View on Numbers 25–31." *Biblical Interpretation* 15 (2007): 54–79.

Grossman, J. "'Dynamic Analogies' in the Book of Esther." *VT* 59 (2009): 394–414.

Grossman, J. "Jacob's Struggle at Jabbok – A New Reading." *SJOT* 34 (2020): 134–56

Grossman, J. "More on the Literary Structure of the Paradise Narrative (Gen 2:4–3:24)." *Beit-Mikra* 56 (2011): 5–39 [Hebrew].

Grossman, J. *Ruth: Bridges and Boundaries* (Das Alte Testament im Dialog, 9). Bern, 2015.

Grossman, J. "Stability and Surprise in the Book of Ruth's Exposition." *Beit Mikra* 60 (2015): 202–37 [Hebrew].

Grossman, J. "The Stories about Abraham and Jacob – A Comparison." *Megadim* 27 (1997): 9–27.

Grossman, J. "The Story of Joseph's Brothers in Light of the 'Therapeutic Narrative' Theory." *Biblical Interpretation* 21 (2013): 171–95.

Grossman, J. *Text and Subtext: On Exploring Biblical Narrative Design*. Tel Aviv, 2015 [Hebrew].

Grossman, J. *The Sacrificial Service: Gestures of Flesh and Spirit*. Jerusalem, 2021 [Hebrew].

Grossman, J. "The Double Etymology of Babel in Genesis 11." *ZAW* 129 (2017): 1–13.

Grossman, J. "The Expulsion of Ishmael Narrative – Boundaries, Structure, and Meaning." In E. R. Hayes and K. Vermeulen, eds. *Doubling and Duplicating in the Book of Genesis: Literary and Stylistic Approaches to the Text*. Winona Lake, 2016, 27–37.

Grossman, J. "The Structural Paradigm of the Ten Plagues Narrative and the Hardening of Pharaoh's Heart." *VT* 64 (2014): 588–610.

Grossman, J. "'Structural Ambiguity' in Ezekiel 33–48." *Beit Mikra* 49 (2004): 194–224 [Hebrew].

Gruber, M. "Accusations Against Shechem Son of Hamor – A Recurring Discussion." *Beit Mikra* 44 (1997): 119–27 [Hebrew].

Grüneberg, K. N. *Abraham, Blessing and the Nations: A Philological and Exegetical Study of Genesis 12:3 in Its Narrative Context*. Diss., Durham University, 2001.

Gunkel, H. *Genesis – Translated and Interpreted*. Translated by M. E. Biddle. Macon, 1997.

Günther Plaut, W. *The Torah: A Modern Commentary, Genesis*. New York, 1981.

Gutman, N. "The Voice Is Jacob's Voice, the Hands Are Esau's Hands." *Megadim* 21 (1994): 17–22 [Hebrew].

Hadad, E. "And the Crooked Shall Be Made Straight – from Jacob to Israel." *Megadim* 38 (2003): 9–15 [Hebrew].

Hakham, A. *Isaiah 1–35, Daat Mikra*. Jerusalem, 1994 [Hebrew].

Hamilton, V. P. *The Book of Genesis, vol. I, Chapters 1–17*. NICOT. Michigan, 1990.

Hamilton, V. P. *The Book of Genesis, vol. II, Chapters 18–50*. NICOT. Michigan, 1995.

Hamori, E. J. "Echoes of Gilgamesh in the Jacob Story." JBL 130 (2011): 625–42.

Hamori, E. J. *Women's Divination in Biblical Literature: Prophecy, Necromancy, and Other Arts of Knowledge*. New Haven and London, 2015.

Hanokh, H. "Clarifications of the Ramban's Mishnat Eretz Yisrael." *Or HaMizrah* 29 (1981): 31–42 [Hebrew].

Haran, M. "*Neder*." *Encyclopedia Biblica*. Vol. 5. 786–90 [Hebrew].

Heintz, J. G. "B-A-R." *TDOT* 1: 463–66.

Helfmeyer. "Ḥ-N-H." *TDOT* 5: 4–19

Hendel, R. S. *The Epic of the Patriarch: The Jacob Cycle and the Narrative Traditions of Canaan and Israel*. Atlanta, 1987.

Hendricks, W. O. "The Structural Study of Narration: Sample Analyses." *Poetics* 3 (1972): 100–123.

Hepner, G. *Legal Friction: Law, Narrative, and Identity Politics in Biblical Israel* (Studies in Biblical Literature 78). New York, 2010.

Herion, G. A. "Succoth-Benoth." *ABD*. Vol. 6. 218.

Hertz, J. H. *The Pentateuch and Haftarot: Hebrew Text, English Translation and Commentary*. London, 1956.

Heschel, A. J. *Between God and Man: An Interpretation of Judaism*. New York, 1997.

Hidary, V. "A Journey to Succoth." *JBQ* 43 (2015): 185–90.

Hoffmann, D. Z. *Genesis*. 2 vols. Bnei Brak, 1969 [Hebrew].

Hoffmeier, L. K. "The Wives' Tales of Genesis 12, 20 and 26 and the Covenants at Beer-Sheba." Tyndale Bulletin 43 (1992): 81–99.

Holladay, W. L. *Jeremiah 1*. Hermeneia. Minneapolis, 1986.

Holmgren, F. C. "Holding Your Own Against God!: Genesis 32:22–32 (In the Context of Genesis 31–33)." *Interpretation* 44 (1990): 5–17.

Horowitz, T. "Mother Rachel, Israel's Redemption, and Her Legacy in Poetry." *Kivunim* (eJournal, 2010) [Hebrew].

Houtman, C. "Jacob at Mahanaim: Some Remarks on Genesis xxxii 2–3." *VT* 28 (1978): 37–44.

Houtman, C. "What Did Jacob See in His Dream at Bethel?." *VT* 27 (1977): 337–51.

Hubbard, D. A. *Hosea*. TOTC. Downers Grove, 1989.

Huehnergard, J. "Biblical Notes on Some New Akkadian Texts from Emar (Syria)." *CBQ* 47 (1985): 428–34.

Humphreys, W. L. *Character of God in the Book of Genesis: A Narrative Appraisal*. Leiden, 2001.

Hurley, D. "Trait vs. Fate." *Discover* 34 (2013): 48–55.

Hurowitz, A. "Who Lost an Earring?: Genesis 35:4 Reconsidered." *CBQ* 62 (2000): 28–32.

Husser, J. M. "Les Métamorphoses d'un Songe: Critque Litteraire de Genese 28,10–22." *RB* 98 (1991): 321–42.

Ilan, T. "Review on *The Empowerment of Women in the Book of Jubilees*, by Betsy Halpern-Amar." *Journal of Jewish Studies* 52 (2001): 161–64.

Jackson, B. S. *Theft in Early Jewish Law*. Oxford, 1972.

Jacob, B. *Das erste Buch der Tora: Genesis*, Berlin 1934.

Jacobs, J. "The Principle of Foreshadowing in Rashbam's Commentary on the Torah." *Biblical Studies and Interpretation* 8 (2008): 451–79 [Hebrew].

Jacobs, J. *Measure for Measure in Biblical Narrative*. Alon Shvut, 2006 [Hebrew].

Janzen, J. G. *Genesis 12–50: Abraham and All the Families of the Earth*. Grand Rapids, 1993.

Jarrell, R. H. "The Birth Narrative as Female Counterpart to Covenant." *JSOT* 97 (2002): 3–18.

Jones III, E. A. "'Who Are You, My Daughter?' A Reassessment of Ruth and Naomi in Ruth 3." *CBQ* 76 (2014): 653–64.

Kahn, P. "Balaam Is Laban." *JBQ* 35 (2007): 222–30.

Kasher, M. M. *Ḥumash Torah Shelema*. Vol. 4. Jerusalem, 1992 [Hebrew].

Kasher, R. *Yeḥezkel 1–24*. Mikra LeYisrael Series. Jerusalem and Tel Aviv, 2004 [Hebrew].

Kaufmann, Y. *Exile and Foreigner: A Historical-Sociological Research on the Question of Jewish People's Fate from Ancient Times to the Present*. Two volumes. Tel Aviv, 1930 [Hebrew].

Kaufmann, Y. *The Religion of Israel*. Four volumes. Jerusalem and Tel Aviv, 1954 [Hebrew].

Kautzsch, E. *Die Heilige Schrift des Alten Testament*. Vol. 1. 3rd ed. Tübingen, 1909.

Keil C. F. and F. Delitzsch. *Biblical Commentary on the Old Testament, Vol. I: The Pentateuch*. Translated by J. Martin. Reprint. Grand Rapids, 1980.

Kellenberger, E. K. "Wie sind Geburtsorakel und Betrugserzählung aufeinander bezogen? Auslegungsgeschichtliche und narratologische Überlegungen zu Gen 25,23 und 27, 1ff." *Communio Viatorum* 58 (2016): 241–55.

Kiel, Y. *Genesis II: Parashat Vayera-Vayishlaḥ*. Daat Mikra. Jerusalem, 2004 [Hebrew].

Koch, K. "*Pahad jishaq*: eine Gottesbezeichnung?" In R. Albertz et al., eds. *Werden und Wirken des Allen Testaments: Festschrift für Claus Westermann*. Göttingen, 1980, 107–15.

Köckert, M. "War Jakobs Gegner in Gen 32, 23–33 ein Dämon?" In A. Lange; H. Lichtenberger, and D. Römheld, eds. *Die Dämonen: die Dämonologie der israelitisch-jüdischen und frühchristlichen Literatur im Kontext ihrer Umwelt* (Tübingen, 2003): 160–81.

Kodell, J. "Jacob Wrestles with Esau (Gen 32:23–32)." *Biblical Theology Bulletin* 10 (1980): 65–70.

Komem, A. "'Let's Play God': On the Limits of Omniscience in Fiction." *Jerusalem Studies in Hebrew Literature* 17 (1969): 121–44 [Hebrew].

Kruger, P. A. "Emotions in the Hebrew Bible: A Few Observations on Prospects and Challenges." *Old Testament Essays* 28 (2015): 395–420.

Kugel, J. L. *The Ladder of Jacob: Ancient Interpretation of the Biblical Story of Jacob and His Children*. Princeton, 2006.

Kuperman, Y. *Rabbi Ovadia Sforno's Commentary on the Torah.* Two volumes. Jerusalem, 1992 [Hebrew].

Lambert, W. G. *Babylonian Creation Myths.* Winona Lake, IN, 2013.

Landsberger, B. "Assyrische Königsliste und dunkles Zeitalter." *JCS* 8 (1954): 31–73.

Leibowitz, N. *Studies in the Book of Genesis.* Jerusalem, 2009 (2nd ed. – Hebrew).

Limburg, J. "The Root ריב and the Prophetic Lawsuit Speeches." *JBL* 88 (1969): 291–304.

Lincoln, L. "Translating Hebrew and Greek Terms for Sheep and Goats." *The Bible Translator* 47 (1996): 322–35.

Lipiński, E. "M-H-R." *TDOT* 8: 142–49.

Lipton, D. *Revisions of the Night: Politics and Promise in the Patriarchal Dreams of Genesis* (JSOTSup 288). Sheffield, 1999.

Lisowsky, G. *Konkordanz zum hebräischen Alten Testament.* Stuttgart, 1958.

Loewenstamm, S. A. "*Beer Sheva.*" *Encyclopedia Biblica.* Vol. 2. 6–8 [Hebrew].

Loza Vera, J. "La berît entre Laban et Jacob (Gn. 31.43–54)." In P. Daviau et al., eds. *The World of the Aramaeans.* Vol 1. Sheffield, 2001, 57–69.

Lundbom, J. R. *Jeremiah 1–20.* AB. New York, 1999.

Luria, B. C. "The Holiness of Migdal Eder." *Beit Mikra* 34 (1989): 198–202 [Hebrew].

Luzzatto, S. D. *Commentary on the Five Books of the Torah.* Tel Aviv, 2006 [Hebrew].

Macchi, J. D. "Genèse 31, 24–42. La dernière rencontre de Jacob et de Laban." In J. D. Macchi and T. Römer, eds. *Jacob: Un commentaire à plusieurs voix de Gen 25–36. Ein mehrstimmiger Kommentar zu Gen 25–36. A plural Commentary of Gen 25–36.* Genève, 2001, 144–62.

Malul, M. "Jacob's Heel and His Act of Deceit: Inheritance in the Bible." In *Society, Law and Customs in Israel in Biblical Times and Ancient Near Eastern Cultures.* Ramat Gan, 2006, 133–50 [Hebrew].

Mandelkorn, S. *Biblical Concordance.* 3rd ed., revised. Jerusalem and Tel Aviv, 1995 [Hebrew].

Mann, *The Book of the Torah: The Narrative Integrity of the Pentateuch.* Atlanta, 1988.

Maori, Y. *The Peshitta Translation of the Torah and Early Jewish Exegesis.* Jerusalem, 1995 [Hebrew].

Mariottini, C. F. "Laban." *ABD.* Vol. 4. 113–14.

Martin, M. W. "Betrothal Journey Narratives." *CBQ* 70 (2008): 505–23.
Maslow, A. "A Theory of Human Motivation." In M. Gardner, ed. *Motivation and Personality*. Ch. 2. New York, 1987
Mathews, Kenneth A. *Genesis*. 2 vols. NAC. Nashville, 2005.
Mazar, B. "*Kaftor*." *Encyclopedia Biblica*. Vol. 4. 236–38 [Hebrew].
Medan, Y. *Close to You: The Language of the Bible and the Language of the Sages – Genesis*. Tel Aviv, 2014 [Hebrew].
Meir, E. I. *Shabbat Revived Him: A Psychological Perspective of the Weekly Parasha – Genesis*. Othniel, 2008 [Hebrew].
Meitlis, Y. *Crossroads: Archaeological and Geographical Perspective of the Weekly Parasha*. Jerusalem, 2014 [Hebrew].
Melamed, A. Z. *The Biblical Commentators*. Jerusalem, 2008 (2nd ed. – Hebrew).
Mendelson, I. "On the Preferential Status of the Eldest Son." *BASOR* 156 (1959): 38–40.
Merrill, E. H. *Deuteronomy*, NAC, Nashville, 1994.
Merrill, E. H. "A-L-H." *NIDOTTE*. Vol. 3. 402–404.
Meyer, E. *Die Israeliten und ihre Nachbarstämme alttestamentliche Untersuchungen*. Halle, 1906.
Meyer, E. *Geschichte des Altertums*. Vol. 1. Stuttgart and Berlin, 1909.
Milgrom, J. *Leviticus 23–27*. AB. New Haven and London, 2001.
Millard, A. R. "The Celestial Ladder and the Gate of Heaven (Gen 28:12–17)." *Expository Times* 78 (1966): 86–87.
Miller, J. E. "Dreams and Prophetic Visions." *Biblica* 71 (1990): 401–4.
Miller Jr., P. D. "Eridu, Dunnu, and Babel: A Study in Comparative Mythology." *Hebrew Annual Review* 9 (1985): 227–51.
Mitchell, C. W. *The Meaning of BRK in the Old Testament*. Diss. Madison, 1983
Moberly, R. W. L. "The Earliest Commentary on the Akedah." *VT* 38 (1988): 302–23.
Moore, G. F. *Judges*. ICC. Edinburgh, 1895.
Morrison, M. A. "The Jacob and Laban Narrative in Light of Near Eastern Sources." *Biblical Archeologist* 46 (1983): 155–64.
Nakarai, T. W. "LMH and MDU in the TANAK." *Hebrew Studies* 23 (1982): 45–50.
Ne'eman, N. "Beit-El and Beit-On: The Problem with Ancient Worship Sites in Israel." *Zion* 50 (1985): 15–25 [Hebrew].
Neufeld, E. *Ancient Hebrew Marriage Laws*. London, 1944.

Nicol, G. G. "Genesis xxix.32 and xxv.22a: Reuben's Reversal." *JTS* 31 (1980): 536–39.

Nicol, G. G. *Studies in the Interpretation of Gen 26:1–33*. Diss. Oxford, 1987.

Niditch, S. *Underdogs and Tricksters: A Prelude to Biblical Folklore*. San Francisco, 1987.

Niehoff, M. R. "The Buber-Rosenzweig Translation of the Bible within Jewish-German Tradition." *JJS* 44 (1993): 258–79.

Noble, P. "A 'Balanced' Reading of the Rape of Dinah: Some Exegetical and Methodological Observations." *Biblical Interpretation* 4 (1996): 173–203.

Noegel, S. B. "Drinking Feasts and Deceptive Feats: Jacob and Laban's Double Talk." In S. B. Noegel, ed. *Puns and Pundits: Wordplay in the Hebrew Bible and Ancient Near Eastern Literature*. Bethesda, MD, 2000, 163–80.

Noegel, S. B. "Sex, Sticks, and the Trickster in Gen 30:31–43." *JANES* 25 (1997): 7–17.

Nõmmik, U. "Inclusio in Genesis 28 and 32: Synchronically and Diachronically." In E. R. Hayes and K. Vermeulen, eds. *Doubling and Duplicating in the Book of Genesis: Literary and Stylistic Approaches to the Text*. Winona Lake, 2016, 183–97.

Noth, M. *A History of Pentateuchal Traditions*. Translated by B. Anderon. Chico, 1981.

Noth, M. *Das System der zwölf Stämme Israels*. Darmstadt, 1966.

Oblath, M. "'To Sleep, Perchance to Dream': What Jacob Saw at Bethel (Genesis 28:10–22)." *JSOT* 95 (2001): 117–26.

Olrik, A. "Epic Laws of Folk Narrative." In A. Dundes, ed. *The Study of Folklore*. Englewood, 1965, 129–41.

Oppenheim, A. L. "The Interpretation of Dreams in the Ancient Near East, with a Translation of an Assyrian Dream-Book." *Transactions of the American Philosophical Society* 46 (1956): 179–373.

Paradise, J. "What Did Laban Demand of Jacob?: A New Reading of Genesis 31:50 and Exodus 21:10." In M. Cogan et al., eds. *Tehillah le-Moshe*. Winona Lake, 1997, 91–98.

Parker, S. B. "The Vow in Ugaritic and Israelite Narrative Literature." *Ugarit Forschungen* 11 (1979): 693–700.

Patai, R and M. Zohary, "*Dudaim*." *Encyclopedia Biblica*. Vol. 2. 645–46 [Hebrew].

Peleg, Y. "What is the '*Sulam*' that Jacob saw in his dream?" *Annual of Bible and Ancient Near Eastern Studies* 14 (2004): 7–26 [Hebrew].

Perry, M. "The Dynamics of the Literary Text: How the Order of the Text Determines Its Meaning." *HaSifrut* 28 (1979): 6–46 [Hebrew].

Phillips, A. *Ancient Israel's Criminal Law*. New York, 1970.

Polak, F. *Biblical Narrative*. Jerusalem, 2009 (2nd ed. – Hebrew).

Polzin, R. "'The Ancestress of Israel in Danger' in Danger." *Semeia* 3–4 (1975): 81–97.

Posen, R. B. *Parshagan: Annotations and Sources for the Onkelus Translation (Genesis)*. Jerusalem, 2013 [Hebrew].

Pratt, R. "Pictures, Windows, and Mirrors in Old Testament Exegesis." *WTJ* 45 (1983): 156–67.

Prignaud, J. "Caftorim et Keretim." *RB* 71 (1964): 215–29.

Quack, J. F. "Zur Beschneidung im Alten Ägypten." In A. Berlejung, J. Dietrich, and J. F. Quack, eds. *Menschenbilder und Körperkonzepte im Alten Israel in Ägypten und im Alten Orient* (ORA 9). Tübingen, 2012, 561–629.

Rabinovitch, N. E. *Yad HaPeshuta on Mishneh Torah – Judges*. Jerusalem, 2011 [Hebrew].

Rackman, J. "Was Isaac Deceived?" *Judaism* 43 (1994): 37–45.

Ramon, L. *Through the Window: Reflection of this Motif in the Bible and in Post-Biblical Literature*. Tel Aviv, [Hebrew].

Ratzabi, Y. "Fear – A Euphemism for *Gid HaNasheh*." *Beit Mikra* 49 (2004): 235–36 [Hebrew].

Ravid, L. *The Bible Really Happened*. Tel Aviv, 2009 [Hebrew].

Ravitzky, A. "Set Yourself Road Markers for Zion: The Metamorphosis of an Idea." In M. Halamish and A. Ravitzky, eds. *Eretz Yisrael in Medieval Jewish Thought*. Jerusalem, 2011, 1–39 [Hebrew].

Reich, R. *The Woman You Put Here With Me: Women as the Basis of Conflict and War in the Bible*. Tel Aviv, 2006 [Hebrew].

Reiss, Y. *The Art of Redaction in the Book of Joshua* – Structure, Ideology, and Historiography. PhD diss., Bar-Ilan University, 2008 [Hebrew].

Rendsburg, G. A. "Confused Language as a Literary Technique in Biblical Narrative." *Biblical Studies and Interpretation* 9 (2009): 27–43 [Hebrew].

Rendsburg, G. A. "Notes on Genesis xxxv." *VT* 34 (1984): 361–66.

Rendsburg, G. A. *The Redaction of Genesis*. Winona Lake, 1986.

Rendtroff, R. "Jakob in Bethel: Beobachtungen zum Aufbau und zur Quellenfrage in Gen 28:10–22." *ZAW* 94 (1982): 511–23.

Richter, W. "Traum und Traumdeutung im Alten Testament: Ihre Form und Verwendung." *BZ* 7 (1963): 202–20.

Rimmon-Kenan, S. *The Poetics of Contemporary Fiction*. Translated by H. Herzig. Tel Aviv, 1989 [Hebrew].

Ringgren, H. "*Bavel*." *TDOT* 1: 466–67.

Ringgren, H. "R-Y-B." *TDOT* 13: 473–79.

Rofé, A. "Defilement of Virgins in Biblical Law and the Case of Dinah (Genesis 34)." *Biblica* 86 (2005): 369–75.

Rofé, A. *Angels in the Bible: Israelite Belief in Angels as Evidenced by Biblical Traditions*. 2nd ed. Jerusalem, 2012.

Rofé, A. *The Faith of Israel and the Text of the Bible*. Jerusalem, 2009 [Hebrew].

Roi, M. "Conditional Vows – Where They Are Made and Paid." *Biblische Notizen* 167 (2015): 3–24.

Ronning, J. "The Naming of Isaac: The Role of the Wife/Sister Episodes in the Redaction of Genesis." *WTJ* 53 (1991): 1–27.

Rosenzweig, F. *Naharaim – Selected Writings*. Jerusalem, 1958 (2nd ed. – Hebrew).

Rotenberg, M. "The Meaning of the Word *Kayom* in Its Eight Appearances in the Bible." *Leshonenu* 48–49 (2004): 60–62 [Hebrew].

Roubach, S. "'Two Are Covered in the Veil': The Image of Twins in the Bible." *Beit Mikra* 50 (2005): 366–90 [Hebrew].

Rouillard H. and J. Tropper, "Trpym, rituels de guérison et culte des ancêtres d'après 1 Samuel xix 11–17 et les textes parallèles d'Assur et de Nuzi." *VT* 37 (1987): 340–61.

Rowley, H. H. *From Joseph to Joshua*. London, 1950.

Rowley, H. H. *The Servant of the Lord and Other Essays on the Old Testament*. London, 1952.

Rudolph, W. *Jeremia*. HAT. 3rd ed. Tübingen, 1968.

Rundgren, F. "Zum Lexikon des Alten Testaments." *Acta Orientalia* 21 (1953): 301–45.

Runge, S. E. "Paradigmatic Effects of Semantically Redundant Anchoring Expressions in Biblical Hebrew Narrative." *Journal of Northwest Semitic Languages* 32 (2006): 87–104.

Rüterswörden. "A-B-D." *TDOT* 10: 376–92.

Sabato, M. "The Meeting of Jacob and Esau." *HaMaayan* 20 (2004): 1–8 [Hebrew].

Salman E. and A. Wénin. "Un rêve qui tombe à pic: La rhétorique de Jacob en Gn 31:4–13." *VT* 63 (2013): 440–52.

Samet, E. *Studies in the Weekly Parasha*. First series. Jerusalem, 2002.

Samet, E. *Studies in the Weekly Parasha*. Second series. Jerusalem, 2004.

Samet, E. *Studies in the Weekly Parasha*. Third series. Jerusalem, 2013.

Samet, O. "'For Blessing and Not for Cursing': The Theft of the Blessings Narrative." *Kinusim* 1 (2017): 66–75 [Hebrew].

Sarna N. *Genesis*. JPS, Philadelphia, New York, and Jerusalem, 1989.

Sarna, N. *Understanding Genesis*. The Heritage of Biblical Israel Series 1. New York, 1966.

Sasson, J. and J. Grossman. "On Hidden Biblical Analogies in Midrash." *Megadim* 46 (2007): 17–42 [Hebrew].

Sasson, J. M. "Love's Roots: On the Redaction of Genesis 30:14–24." In *Love and Death in the Ancient Near East: Essays in Honor of Marvin H. Pope*. Guilford, CT, 1987, 205–9.

Saviv, A. "Seeking the Lord in the Bible." *Beit Mikra* 32 (1987): 33–34 [Hebrew].

Schäfer-Bossert, S. "Den Männern die Macht und der Frau die Trauer?: Ein kritischer Blick auf die Deutung von און–oder: Wie nennt Rahel ihren Sohn?" In U. Bail, et al., eds. *Feministische Hermeneutik und Erstes Testament: Analysen und Interpretationen*. Stuttgart, 1994, 106–25.

Scheinhorst, L. "N-G-A." *TDOT* 9: 203–9.

Schwantes, M. "Abrao sabe o que importa: Gênesis 21, 22–34." *Revista de Cultura Teológica* 14 (2006): 61–72.

Schwartz, S. "Narrative Toledot Formulae in Genesis: The Case of Heaven and Earth, Noah, and Isaac." JHS (2016): 1–37.

Schwartz, S. *The Isaac Narrative: A Literary Analysis of Genesis 25:19–28:9*. PhD diss., Bar-Ilan University [Hebrew].

Seeligmann, I. L. "A Psalm from Pre-Regal Times." *VT* 14 (1964): 75–92.

Seely, J. A. H. "Succoth." *ABD*. Vol. 6. 217–18.

Seeman, D. "The Watcher at the Window: Cultural Poetics of a Biblical Motif." *Prooftexts* 24 (2004): 1–50.

Segal, B. "Double Meanings in the Song of Songs." *Dor le Dor* 16 (1987–88): 249–55.

Segal, M. Z. "The Names Jacob and Israel in the Book of Genesis." *Tarbiz* 9 (1908): 243–56 [Hebrew].

Seidel, M. "Parallels Between the Book of Isaiah and the Book of Psalms." *Biblical Studies*. Jerusalem, 2008, 1–97 [Hebrew].

Seligmann, I. L. "Hebräische Erzählung und biblische Geschichtsschreibung." *Theologische Zeitschrift* 18 (1962): 305–25.

Shalem, N. "On the Names of Colors in Hebrew." *Leshonenu* 4 (1932): 61–69 [Hebrew].

Shapira, A. "Accusations Against a Ben-Hamor Neighbor – Rediscussion: A Response to Meir Gruber's Article." *Beit Mikra* 44 (1999): 281–82 [Hebrew].

Shapira, A. "Jacob and Esau: A Multivalent Reading." *Biblical Studies and Interpretation* 4 (2017): 249–82 [Hebrew].

Shapira, Y. *A Postmodernist Reading of the Biblical Book of Esther: From Cultural Disintegration to Carnivalesque Text*. PhD diss. Ann Arbor 1996.

Shaviv, Y. "*Zot HaPaam*." *Beit Mikra* 33 (1988): 129–30 [Hebrew].

Schweid, E. *Biblical Philosophy as the Foundation of Israeli Culture*. Tel Aviv, 2004 [Hebrew].

Shazar, Z. *The Biblical Pardes: Studies in the Bible and the History of Biblical Criticism*. Jerusalem, 1979 [Hebrew].

Shemesh, A. O. "Water Sources in Biblical Lands: Ownership and Struggles for Control, Rights of Use, and Budgeting and Pumping Arrangements" (two parts). *Beit Mikra* 50 (2005): 55–73, 99–108 [Hebrew].

Shemesh, Y. "The Character of Rachel: Beloved Wife, Mother of the Nation." *Biblical Studies and Interpretation* 9 (2009): 81–110 [Hebrew].

Shemesh, Y. "Rape Is Rape Is Rape: The Story of Dinah and Shechem (Genesis 34)." *ZAW* 119 (2007): 2–21.

Sherwood, S. K. *"Had God Not Been on My Side": An Examination of the Narrative Technique of the Story of Jacob and Laban: Gen. 29.1–32.2*. Frankfurt am Main, 1990.

Shifra S. and J. Klein. *In Those Distant Days: Anthology of Mesopotamian Literature in Hebrew*. Tel Aviv, 1996 [Hebrew].

Shiloah, M. "And He Said...and He Said." In A. Weiser and B. C. Luria, eds. *The Book of Korengreen*. Tel Aviv, 2004, 251–67 [Hebrew].

Simon, U. "An Ironic View of a Biblical Narrative – Interpreting the Story of David and Batsheva." *HaSifrut* 2 (1970): 598–607 [Hebrew].

Simon, U. "The Birth Story of Samuel." *Biblical Studies and Interpretation* 2 (2006): 57–110 [Hebrew].

Simon, U. *Literary Reading in the Bible: Stories of the Prophets*. Jerusalem and Ramat Gan, 2017 [Hebrew].

Ska, J. L. *Introduction to Reading the Pentateuch*. Translated by P. Dominique. Winona Lake, 2006.

Ska, J. L. "Sommaires proleptiques en Gen 27 et dans l'histoire de Joseph." *Biblica* 73 (1992): 518–27.

Ska, J. L. "The Limits of Interpretation." In T. B. Dozeman, K. Schmid, and B. Schwartz, eds. The Pentateuch: International Perspectives on Current Research. Tübingen, 2011, 109–22.

Skinner, J. *Genesis*. ICC. Edinburgh, 1930.

Smith, C. "Reinstating Isaac: The Centrality of Abraham's Son in the 'Jacob-Esau' Narrative of Genesis 27." *Biblical Theology Bulletin* 31 (2001): 130–34.

Snaith, N. H. *Leviticus and Numbers*. NCB, London, 1967.

Soggin, J. A. "*Yamin*." *TDOT* 6: 99–104.

Spanier, K. "Rachel's Theft of the Teraphim: Her Struggle for Family Primacy." *VT* 42 (1992): 404–12.

Speiser, E. A. "Word Plays on the Creation Epic's Version of the Founding of Babylon." *Orientalia* 25 (1956): 317–23.

Speiser, E. A. *Genesis*. AB. New York, 1962.

Sperber, D. "A Note on the word *Kesita*." *Acta Antique Academiae Scientiarum Hungarica* 19 (1971): 37–39.

Spero, S. "Jacob's Growing Understanding of His Experience at Beth-El." *JBQ* 26 (1998): 211–15.

Stendebach, F. J. "R-G-L." *TDOT* 13: 309–24.

Sternberg, M. "A Delicate Balance in the Story of Dinah's Rape." *HaSifrut* 4 (1973): 193–231 [Hebrew].

Sternberg, M. *The Poetics of Biblical Narrative: Ideological, Literature and the Drama of Reading*. Bloomington, 1985.

Sylva, D. "The Blessing of a Wounded Patriarch: Genesis 27.1–40." *JSOT* 32 (2008): 267–86.

Taschner, J. *Verheissung und Erfüllung in der Jakoberzählung (Gen 25,19–33,17): Eine Analyse ihres Spannungsbogens*. Freiburg, 2000.

Terino, J. "A Text Linguistic Study of the Jacob Narrative." *Vox Evangelica* 18 (1988): 45–62.

Tor-Sinai, N. H. "*Alluf*." *Encyclopedia Biblica*. Vol. 1. 332–33 [Hebrew].

Tzohar, Y. *Barrenness in the Bible – A Literary Analysis.* Master's thesis, Bar-Ilan University [Hebrew].

Van Seters, J. "Jacob's Marriages and Ancient Near East Custom." *HTR* 62 (1969): 377–95.

Van Seters, J. *Abraham in History and Tradition.* New Haven, 1975.

Van Wolde, E. "Does *innâ* Denote Rape?: A Semantic Analysis of a Controversial Word." *VT* 52 (2002): 528–44.

Vaughn, A. G. "'And Lot Went With Him': Abraham's Disobedience in Genesis 12:1–4a." In B. F. Batto and K. L. Roberts, eds. *David and Zion: Biblical Studies in Honor of J. J. M. Roberts.* Winona Lake, 2004, 111–23.

Volz P. and W. Rudolph. *Der Elohist als Erzähler ein Irrweg der Pentateuchkritik? An der Genesis erläutert* (BZAW 63). Giessen, 1933.

Von Rad, G. *Genesis.* OTL. Translated by J. H. Marks. 2nd ed. London, 1963.

Von Soden, W. *The Akkadisches Handwörterbuch.* 3 vols. Wiesbaden, 1959–1981.

Vrolijk, P. D. *Jacob's Wealth: An Examination into the Nature and Role of Material Possessions in the Jacob-Cycle (Gen 25:19–35:29).* Leiden and Boston, 2011.

Wächter, L. "Israel und Jeschurun." In K. H. Bernhardt, ed. *Schalom: Studien zu Glaube und Geschichte Israels* (ArbT 1/46). Stuttgart, 1971, 58–64.

Wallis, H. "D-B-K." *TDOT* 3: 79–84.

Walsh, J. T. *Style and Structure in Biblical Hebrew Narrative.* Collegeville, 2001.

Waltke, B. K. and C. J. Fredricks. *Genesis: A Commentary.* Grand Rapids, 2001.

Waltke, B. K. *Genesis: A Commentary.* Grand Rapids, 2001.

Walton, K. *Thou Traveller Unknown: The Presence and Absence of God in the Jacob Narrative.* Cumbria, 2003.

Waxman, Ch. "And Jacob Was Left Alone." In Rabbi E. Bick and Y. Feintuch, eds. *Torat Etzion – Bamidbar.* Alon Shvut, 2014, 331–36 [Hebrew].

Webb, B. G. *The Book of Judges,* NICOT. Grand Rapids, 2012.

Weimar, P. "Beobachtungen zur Analyse von Gen 32,23–33." *Biblische Notizen* 50 (1989): 58–94.

Weinfeld, M. "Jeremiah and the Spiritual Metamorphosis of Israel." *ZAW* 88 (1976): 17–56.

Weinfeld, M. *Genesis.* World Bible Series. Tel Aviv, 1993 [Hebrew].

Weiss, A. "Jacob's struggle: A Psycho-Existential Exegesis." *Journal of Psychology and Judaism* 18 (1994): 19–31.

Weissman, Z. and D. Levinstein. *Minor Prophets I – Hosea*. World Bible Series. Tel Aviv, 2002 [Hebrew].

Weissman, Z. *From Jacob to Israel: The Jacob Narrative Cycle*. Jerusalem, 1956 [Hebrew].

Wellhausen, J. *Die composition des Hexateuchs und der historischen bücher des Alten Testaments*. Berlin, 1899.

Wellhausen, J. *Prolegomena to the History of Ancient Israel*. Vol. 2. Translated by Y. Yevrachihu. Jerusalem, 2008 [Hebrew].

Wenham, G. J. *Genesis*. WBC. 2 vols. Waco, TX, 1987–1994.

Westermann, C. *Genesis: A Continental Commentary*. 3 vols. Translated by J. J. Scullion. Minneapolis, 1986–1995.

Wilson, R. R. "An Interpretation of Ezekiel's Dumbness." *VT* 22 (1972): 99–104.

Wiseman, P. J. *New Discoveries in Babylonia about Genesis*. London, 1936.

Wolff, H. W. *Anthropology of the Old Testament*. Translated by M. Kohl. Philadelphia, 1974.

Wolff, H. W. *Hosea*. Hermeneia. Philadelphia, 1974.

Yeivin, S. "The Conquest of the Land." *Maarakhot* 24–25 (1995): 61–74 [Hebrew].

Yee, G. A. "Leah." *ABD* 4, 268.

Zakovitch, Y. "Foreshadowing in Biblical Narrative." *Be'er Sheva* 2 (1985): 85–105 [Hebrew].

Zakovitch, Y. *I Will Utter Riddles from Ancient Times*. Am Oved, 2005 [Hebrew].

Zakovitch, Y. "Jabok, Penuel, Mahanim, Bethel: Biblical Name Explanations as a Mirror of Ideological Struggles." *Ariel* 100–101 (1994): 191–204 [Hebrew].

Zakovitch, Y. "Jacob, Deceit." In B. C. Luria, ed. *The Book of Baruch Ben Yehuda*. Tel Aviv, 1981, 121–44 [Hebrew].

Zakovitch, Y. *"On Three...and on Four": The Literary Model Three-Four in the Bible*. Jerusalem, 1979 [Hebrew].

Zakovitch, Y. "The Meaning of Burying Idols in Shechem (Genesis 35:2–4)." *Beit Mikra* 25 (1985): 30–37 [Hebrew].

Zakovitch, Y. *Jacob – the Surprising Story of the National Patriarch*. Or Yehuda, 2012 [Hebrew].

Zakovitch, Y. *Texts in the Land of Mirrors*. Tel Aviv, 1995 [Hebrew].

Zakovitch, Y. *The Life of Samson – A Literary-Critical Analysis*. Jerusalem, 1982 [Hebrew].

Zetterholm, K. H. *Portrait of a Villain: Laban the Aramean in Rabbinic Literature.* Leuven, 2002.

Zimran, Y. *Conflicts between Brothers and Sisters in the Bible.* Jerusalem, 2023 [Hebrew].

Zipor, M. *The Septuagint Translation of Genesis.* Ramat Gan, 2006 [Hebrew].

Zobel, H. "*Yisrael.*" *TDOT* 6: 397–420.

Zobel, H. "*Yaakov.*" *TDOT* 6: 185–208.

Zohar, N. J. "Boycott, Crime, and Sin: Ethical and Talmudic Responses to Injustice Abroad." *Ethics and International Affairs* 7 (1993): 39–53.

Zucker, D. "The Deceiver Deceived: Rereading Genesis 27." *JBQ* 39 (2011): 46–58.

Maggid Books
The best of contemporary Jewish thought from
Koren Publishers Jerusalem